GUINNESS WORLD RECORDS 2005

Dedicated to Norris McWhirter MBE
1925–2004

ISBN 1 892051 22 2

MANAGING EDITOR
Claire Folkard

SENIOR EDITOR
Jackie Freshfield

EDITORS
Robert Dimery
Carla Masson

DESIGN CONCEPT & CREATION
55 DESIGN
Matt Purkiss-Webb
Paul Deacon
Mel Fisher

COVER DESIGN
Ron Callow at Design 23

HEAD OF PICTURE/MEDIA DESK
Betty Halvagi

PICTURE RESEARCH
Maureen Kane
Caroline Thomas
Louise Thomas

**KEEPER OF
THE RECORDS**
Stewart Newport

RESEARCH TEAM
Stuart Claxton
Jerramy Fine
David Hawksett
Keely Hopkins
Kim Lacey
Hein Le Roux
Chris Marais
Susan Morrison
Della Torra Howes

PROOFREADING
Craig Glenday
Ben Way

INDEX
Susan Bosanko

**PRODUCTION
DIRECTOR**
Patricia Langton

**PRODUCTION
CO-ORDINATOR**
Colette Concannon

**PRINTING
AND BINDING**
Printer Industria Grafica, SA,
Barcelona, Spain

**TECHNICAL CONSULTANT
(COVER)**
Esteve Font Canadell

COLOUR ORIGINATION
Resmiye Kahraman
Colour Systems,
London, UK

ACCREDITATION Guinness World Records Limited has a very thorough accreditation system for records verification. However, whilst every effort is made to ensure accuracy, Guinness World Records Limited cannot be held responsible for any errors contained in this work. Feedback from our readers on any point of accuracy is always welcomed.

ABBREVIATIONS AND MEASUREMENTS Guinness World Records Limited uses both metric and US imperial measurements. The only exception is for some scientific data, where metric measurements only are universally accepted, and for some sports data. Where a specific date is given the exchange rate is calculated according to the currency values that were in operation at the time. Where only a year date is given the exchange rate is calculated from December of that year. 'One billion' is taken to mean one thousand million. 'GDR' (the German Democratic Republic) refers to the East German state which unified with West Germany in 1990. The abbreviation is used for sports records broken before 1990. The Union of Soviet Socialist Republics split into a number of parts in 1991, the largest of these being Russia. The Commonwealth of Independent States replaced it and the abbreviation 'CIS' is used mainly for sporting records broken at the 1992 Olympic Games.

Guinness World Records Limited does not claim to own any right, title or interest in the trademarks of others reproduced in this book.

GENERAL WARNING Attempting to break records or set new records can be dangerous. Appropriate advice should be taken first and all record attempts are undertaken entirely at the participant's risk. In no circumstances will Guinness World Records Limited have any liability for death or injury suffered in any record attempts. Guinness World Records Limited has complete discretion over whether or not to include any particular records in the book.

GUINNESS WORLD RECORDS 2005

Contents

Introduction

This year marks the 50th anniversary of the first edition of what is now known as *Guinness World Records*.

In 2003, the 100-millionth copy of the book was published – a staggering achievement in publishing history, making *Guinness World Records* the biggest selling copyright book ever. From its relatively humble beginnings, today the book is sold in 100 countries around the world and translated into 23 languages.

The origins of the book date back to a shooting party in County Wexford,

Ireland, in 1951, when Sir Hugh Beaver (above), Managing Director of Guinness Brewery, was involved in a dispute as to whether or not the golden plover was Europe's fastest game

bird. To his frustration, he was unable find a book that could give him an accurate answer.

It occurred to Sir Hugh that disputes such as this must happen often, especially in social gatherings, and so a book that could provide all the answers would be in great demand. At the time, the record-breaking athlete Chris Chataway was working as an underbrewer at Guinness's Park Royal Brewery in London and he recommended Norris and Ross McWhirter (both left), whom he had met at athletic events, to Sir Hugh as the ideal people to compile such a book. At the time, the McWhirters were running a fact-finding agency and publishing company in London, specializing in athletics records. Indeed, when Roger Bannister (above right) broke the four-minute-mile barrier on May 6 1954, with a time of 3 min 59.4 sec, it was Norris McWhirter who announced the

record-breaking time at that historic event. This was one of the 'new' athletics records to make it into the first edition. Sir Hugh liked the idea of a book of superlatives and commissioned the twins to create what was to become the first edition of *The Guinness Book of Records*.

After a busy year of research into the fastest and the slowest, the biggest and the smallest, the heaviest and the lightest, and the longest and the shortest of everything, the first copy was printed and bound on August 27 1955. An instant success, the book was quickly recognized as the authoritative source of records in Britain and around the world.

Although the death of Norris McWhirter (pictured below right with the first edition of *The Guinness Book of Records*) in April 2004 in some ways marked the end of an era, the legacy of the iconic book he and his brother Ross created all those years ago lives on. Over the years, Norris inspired generations of children, delighting them with his encyclopedic knowledge and remarkable ability to recall records in a moment – as regularly demonstrated on the long-running BBC TV children's program, *Record Breakers*.

As well as his famous television partnership with the late Roy Castle, he also worked with Sir David Frost (above right) on Sir David's American Guinness Specials from 1973 to 1988. Sir David remembers Norris as 'a man with a passion for facts and the accuracy of them, but also a man who had a heart-warming appreciation of man's ingenuity and determination to succeed. He loved

to recount anecdotes about the remarkable individuals he had met over the years, whether they were Olympic record holders or people who had established records in fields that nobody else might have ever wished to attempt – like Mark Gottlieb, the underwater violinist, or Frank Freer, the man who peeled the world's longest unbroken apple peel. In their different ways, in Norris's eyes they were all superlatives.'

Today around 3.5 million copies of *Guinness World Records* are sold annually, demonstrating that humankind's desire for knowledge combined with a passion to be a Guinness World Record

holder is undiminished. Now a household name around the world, no other enterprise collects, confirms, accredits and presents world record data with the same investment in comprehensiveness and authenticity.

Although no longer part of or associated with the Guinness Brewery, *Guinness World Records* remains the global authority on world records. This year's edition offers some unique features: we tell the story behind some of the most famous world records, and also hear from a selection of record breakers themselves in a number of fascinating and exclusive interviews.

As ever, remember that you don't have to be a movie star or world-class athlete to have a Guinness World Record. You just need to have the determination and dedication to succeed!

If you want to approach us with an idea for a record, turn to the back page to find out how.

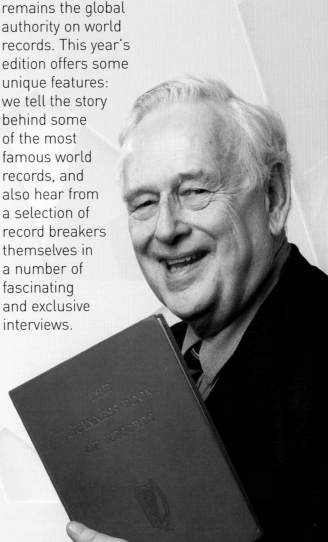

Fifty years of change
1955–2005

The world's population has more than doubled since the first edition of *Guinness World Records* (formerly *The Guinness Book of Records*) went on sale in 1955. Here we chart some other key changes that have taken place over the past 50 years.

1955: the first edition

The Guinness Book of Records was launched in the same year that a truck driver from Mississippi named Elvis Presley (USA) signed for RCA Victor. Fast-food entrepreneur Ray Kroc (USA, left) opened his first McDonald's restaurant in April of that year, and Walt Disney (USA) opened a theme park in Anaheim, California, USA.

Other firsts

Competing with Guinness for bookshelf space in 1955 were J.R.R. Tolkien's (UK) *The Lord of the Rings: The Return of the King* and Ian Fleming's (UK) third James Bond novel *Moonraker*.

Playing on the jukebox was Bill Haley and His Comets' (USA, below right) 'Rock Around the Clock' (which is still the biggest selling single by a band), and the rights to the design of the 'Pluto Platter' – the toy that would be better known as the 'Frisbee' – were sold by the inventor Walter Morrison (USA) to the Wham-O toy company.

Births and deaths

In 1955, three giants of modern communications were born: Bill Gates (USA), Tim Berners-Lee (UK) – the inventor of the World Wide Web – and Apple Macintosh cofounder Stephen Jobs (USA). The year also saw the deaths of Sir Alexander Fleming (UK) – the bacteriologist who discovered the effects of penicillin – and the physicist Albert Einstein (USA, b. Germany, below left).

The world today is a very different place, of course. Over the past five decades we've seen the advent of space travel and satellite communication, the creation of a global marketplace, the seemingly limitless expansion of the Internet coupled with an equally astonishing miniaturization of technology, and a worldwide population explosion (about 1,000 more people will be born in the time it takes you to read this page).

Charting the change

Here's a selection of Guinness World Records – past and present – that illustrate some important changes that have taken place over the last 50 years. Figures from 1955 are taken from the first edition of *The Guinness Book of Records* and are quoted verbatim.

★ **World population (2005): 6.31 billion**

★ **Remotest known body**
Using the Hubble Space Telescope and the Keck Observatory, astronomers from the California Institute of Technology (USA) have discovered a small and compact system of stars about 2,000 light-years across, with a redshift of 7.0. This corresponds to a distance of about 13 billion light-years away.

★ **Highest soccer transfer fee**
The highest club-to-club payment quoted for a player is a reported 13 billion Spanish pesetas ($66 million) for Zinedine Zidane (France) from Juventus to Real Madrid on July 9 2001.

2005
1955

★ **World population (1955): 2.56 billion**

★ **Remotest known body**
The first record published in the first edition of GWR!
The universe is the entirety of space and matter. The remotest known heavenly bodies are extra-galactic nebulae at a distance of some 1,000 million light-years or 6,000,000,000,000,000,000,000,000 miles. There is reason to believe that even remoter nebulae exist but, since it is possible that they are receding faster than the speed of light (670,455,000 mph) (1,078,992,730 km/h), they would be beyond man's 'observable horizon.'

★ **Highest football transfer fee**
The world record transfer fee is the 105,000,000 lire (£60,375) ($167,000) paid in May 1952 by Napol to Genoese Atlanta for the former Swedish International Hans Jeppson, 27.

Did you know... not all the records have been broken?

Here are some records that haven't been broken in 50 years!

Tallest man
The tallest man in medical history for whom there is irrefutable evidence is Robert Pershing Wadlow (USA), who when last measured on June 27 1940 was 8 ft 11.1 in (2.72 m) tall.

Longest solar eclipse
A total eclipse of the Sun that took place on June 20 1955 west of the Philippines lasted for 7 min 8 sec. The maximum possible duration of an eclipse of the Sun is 7 min 31 sec.

Longest reign as world heavyweight boxing champion
Joe Louis (USA) was champion for 11 years 252 days, from June 22 1937 – when he knocked out James Joseph Braddock (USA) in the eighth round in Chicago, Illinois, USA – until announcing his retirement on March 1 1949. During his reign, Louis made a record 25 defenses of his title.

Largest concrete dam
The Grand Coulee dam on the Columbia River, Washington, USA, has a concrete volume of 285,766,282 ft^3 (8,092,000 m^3) to a weight of 43,199,528,900 lb (19,595,000 tonnes). It was finally completed in 1942 at a cost of $56 million. It has a crest length of 4,173 ft (1,272 m) and is 550 ft (168 m) high.

Best selling record
In 1955, Irving Berlin's (USA) 'White Christmas' had sold 18 million copies. By 2005, sales exceeded 100 million copies. Bing Crosby's (USA) recording of this song accounts for more than 50 million copies.

Largest office building
The Pentagon, in Arlington, Virginia, USA, built to house the US Defense Department's offices and completed in January 1943, is the world's largest office building. Each of the outermost sides is 921 ft (281 m) long and the perimeter of the building measures about 4,610 ft (1,405 m). Its five stories enclose a floor area of 149.2 acres (604,000 m^2), the corridors total 17.5 miles (28 km) in length, and there are 7,754 windows to be cleaned. There are over 26,000 military and civilian employees working in the building.

Largest stadium
The Maracanã Municipal Stadium (below) in Rio de Janeiro, Brazil, has a standard capacity of 205,000 spectators, 155,000 of whom can be seated. It was built for the 1950 soccer World Cup and housed a crowd of 199,854 for the final match of the tournament, Brazil v. Uruguay, on July 16 1950 – the greatest ever attendance for a sporting event.

★ Most expensive bottle of wine
The most expensive commercially available bottle of wine is the Chateau d'Yquem Sauternes (1787), priced between $56,000 and $64,000 depending on the retailer.

★ Highest paid TV performer
The world's highest paid TV actor per episode is Ray Romano (USA), who earned $1.8 million per episode of *Everybody Loves Raymond* (CBS, USA) for the eighth series in 2004/05.

★ Largest passenger liner
The Cunard Line's *Queen Mary 2*, which made its maiden voyage in January 2004, is 1,132 ft (345 m) long and has a beam (width) of 135 ft (41 m). At approximately 150,000 gross registered tonnes (grt), *Queen Mary 2* is nearly three times larger than *Titanic* (46,000 grt), and has space for 2,620 passengers and 1,253 crew.

★ Most expensive bottle of wine
The most expensive bottle of wine obtainable would be a bottle of Feinste Trockenbeeran Auslese of 1949 or any other good vintage. This is a white wine made in the Rhine Valley in very small quantities from specially selected grapes and retails at £8 [$22] or more.

★ Highest paid TV performer
The biggest contract ever signed for television appearances was between Jackie Gleason, the American comedian, and the Columbia Broadcasting System on behalf of the Buick Division of General Motors, in December 1954. Under this contract, Jackie Gleason will receive £2.5 million [$7 million] over the next two years for a once-weekly half-hour programme.

★ Largest passenger liner
The *Queen Elizabeth*, of the Cunard fleet, is the largest passenger vessel in the world and also has the largest displacement of any ship in the world, with a gross tonnage of 83,673. She has an overall length of 1,031 feet (314.2 m), and is 118 feet 7 inches (387.17 m) in breadth. She is powered by steam turbines which develop about 200,000 hp (149,140 kw).

GWR on TV

From BBC TV's *Record Breakers* to FOX's *Guinness World Records: Primetime*, Guinness World Records on television has always been loved for the programs' celebration of amazing achievements. Today, Guinness World Records appears on TV in about 85 countries!

GWR comes to TV

Guinness World Records' most famous television past is, of course, BBC TV's *Record Breakers*, which appeared on UK TV screens for over 30 years. Fronted by the energetic and enthusiastic Roy Castle (below, right, with Norris McWhirter and a model of Robert Wadlow), the show featured a weekly array of record attempts, along with the chance to put Norris McWhirter 'on the spot' and test his encyclopedic record knowledge – a test that he famously only failed once!

In the 1980s, Sir David Frost fronted *The Spectacular World of Guinness Records* – a show featuring many more weird and wonderful human achievements – which ran successfully for six years.

Guinness World Records: Primetime

The end of the 1990s saw the arrival of a spectacular new show launched in the USA on the FOX network. *Guinness World Records: Primetime* was a dramatic, exciting show that has since gone on to be shown around the world in over 75 countries, including Canada, Brazil, the Seychelles, the Philippines, and the Czech Republic.

L'Été de Tous les Records

After a hugely successful initial run in 2003, 2004 saw the return of *L'Été de Tous les Records* – a fun summertime road show that traveled each week to a different location in France. An entertaining mixture of record attempts by local people combined with some impressive feats by established record holders, the show was a huge hit. Fronted by well-known TV sports host Pierre Sled, the show also featured Barry White as the Guinness World Records official judge, who, with his catchphrase 'Are you ready?,' proved immensely popular.

Guinness World Records: Die Grössten Weltrekorde

An exciting new show was launched in Germany in 2004 – a two-hour special hosted by Oliver Welke, with celebrated professional boxer Henry Maske as the Guinness World Records judge. Four new records were set on the show, including Wim Hof's famous ice endurance record (opposite, bottom right) – he managed to stay in the ice box for an incredible 1 hr 7 min. Broadcast live from the studio, the show was a huge success, and is to be followed by a second one in fall 2004.

Guinness World Records: Fifty Years, Fifty Records

In celebration of the 50th anniversary, this year sees the long-awaited return of Guinness World Records to the UK TV screens in the form of a two-hour live extravaganza broadcast from a massive soundstage in London on September 11 – almost 50 years to the day since the historic first meeting between Sir Hugh Beaver and the McWhirter twins. Over the duration of the show, an attempt will be made to break 50 records – an impressive record in itself!

Opposite, clockwise from top: Oliver Welke, host of *Guinness World Records: Die Grössten Weltrekorde*; the 2003 *L'Été de Tous les Records* team; Wim Hof (Netherlands) on *Guinness World Records: Die Grössten Weltrekorde*; Georges Christen (Luxembourg), holder of the record for most telephone directories torn in two minutes, on *L'Été de Tous les Records*; Shridhar Chillal (India), owner of the world's longest nails on a single hand, on *Guinness World Records: Primetime*.

GWR TV

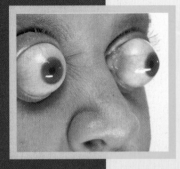

Human beings

Contents

Extreme bodies
Human beings

« Longest tongue

Stephen Taylor's (UK, left) tongue measures 3.7 in (9.4 cm) from the tip to the center of his closed top lip. It was measured at Westwood Medical Centre, Coventry, Warwickshire, UK, on May 29 2002.

Shortest man ⌃

The shortest mature human of whom there is independent evidence was Gul Mohammed (India, above).

On July 19 1990, he was examined at Ram Manohar Hospital, New Delhi, India, and found to measure a height of 22.5 in (57 cm).

★ Tallest living man
After seven measurements taken over the course of April 22–23 1999 in Tunis, Tunisia, Radhouane Charbib's (Tunisia) height was confirmed as 7 ft 8.9 in (2.35 m).

★ Tallest woman
Zeng Jinlian (China) measured 8 ft 1.75 in (2.48 m) when she died on February 13 1982.

★ Tallest living woman
When last measured, Sandy Allen (USA) was 7 ft 7.25 in (2.31 m) tall. Her birth weight was a normal 6 lb 7 oz (2.95 kg) but her abnormal growth began almost immediately. She stood 6 ft 3 in (1.9 m) by the age of 10 and was 7 ft 1 in (2.16 m) at the age of 16.

★ Shortest woman
Pauline Musters (Netherlands, b. February 26 1876), measured 12 in (30 cm) at birth, and at nine years of age she was 21.5 in (55 cm) tall and weighed 3 lb 5 oz (1.5 kg). When she died of pneumonia with meningitis on March 1 1895 in New York City, USA, aged 19, a postmortem examination showed her to be exactly 24 in (61 cm). Her 'vital statistics' were 18.5–19–17 in (47–48–43 cm).

★ Shortest living woman
Madge Bester (South Africa) is only 25.5 in (65 cm) tall. She suffers from osteogenesis imperfecta (characterized by brittle bones and other deformities of the skeleton) and is confined to a wheelchair.

★ Heaviest man
The heaviest person in medical history was Jon Brower Minnoch (USA), who had suffered from obesity since childhood. He was 6 ft 1 in (1.85 m) tall and weighed 392 lb (178 kg) in 1963, 698 lb (317 kg) in 1966 and 974 lb (442 kg) in September 1976. In March 1978, Minnoch was admitted to University Hospital, Seattle, USA, where consultant endocrinologist Dr. Robert Schwartz calculated that Minnoch must have weighed more than 1,399 lb (635 kg), much of which was water accumulation due to his congestive heart failure.

★ Heaviest woman
Rosalie Bradford (USA) is claimed to have registered a peak weight of 1,199 lb (544 kg) in January 1987.

★ Living person with the largest hands
Hussain Bisad (Somalia), who resides in the UK, has hands measuring 10.59 in (26.9 cm) from the wrist to the tip of his middle finger.

★ Longest ear hair
Radhakant Bajpai (India) has hair sprouting from the center of his outer ears (middle of the pinna) that measures 5.19 in (13.2 cm) at its longest point.

★ Longest hair
The longest documented hair belonged to Hoo Sateow (Thailand), a tribal medicine man from Muang Nga, Chang Mai, Thailand. On November 21 1997, his hair was unraveled and officially measured at 16 ft 11 in (5.15 m) long. He stopped cutting his hair in 1929 at the age of 18.

★ Longest fingernails on a single hand
The aggregate measurement of the five nails on the left hand of Shridhar Chillal (India) was 23 ft 1.5 in (7.05 m) on February 4 2004. His thumbnail measured 62.2 in (158 cm), his index fingernail 51.5 in (131 cm), his middle fingernail 54.3 in (138 cm), his ring fingernail 140 cm (55.1 in), and his little fingernail 138 cm (54.3 in). Chillal last cut his nails in 1952.

★ Largest chest measurement
Robert Earl Hughes (USA) had a chest measurement of 124 in (315 cm).

Heaviest twins »

Twins Billy Leon
(1946–79) and Benny Lloyd
(1946–2001) McCrary, alias
McGuire (both USA,
right), were normal in
size until the age of six.
By November 1978,
Billy and Benny weighed

742 lb (337 kg) and 723 lb
(328 kg) respectively, and
each had a waist measuring
84 in (2.13 m). Both died
from heart failure.

★ GWR TALKS TO
Lee Redmond

Lee Redmond (USA, right)
holds the record for the longest
fingernails. She hasn't cut her
nails since 1979, and has grown
and manicured them to a total
length of 24 ft 7.8 in (7.51 m).

Why did you grow your nails?
I didn't want to – they were
really healthy and I decided to
grow them to see how long
they'd get before they twisted
out of shape. But they never
did twist so I just grew them!

Would you ever cut them?
I trim them back once in a while,
but cut them clear off? No way!
Psychologists have said my nails
were a shield I'd put up to stop
men getting near me. And you
know what? All my fans are male!

Have you ever bitten your nails?
Oh, I just couldn't imagine it!
People chew their nails because
they're lacking a certain mineral
in their body. They tell me that

if a bomb was to go off, I could
go into a shelter and live off
my fingernails!

**Is it true that some people
want to buy your nails?**
Yeah – I turned down $10,000
when they were just nine inches
(22.8 cm)! It was for a TV show –
I was asked along with the lady
with the longest hair. I didn't
accept, but she had over
7 feet (2.13 m) of hair cut off!
My nails are priceless!

**What kind of reaction do
your nails usually get?**
It used to be negative. Now, so
many people have seen me in
the *Guinness World Records*
books and on TV shows, they're
more amazed by them. People
see the difference between my
nails and those on the man from
India [Shridhar Chillal, see p.14]:
they want to know how I keep
my nails looking so much
better than he does.

So, what's your secret?
You are what you eat, for one
thing – the nail is nothing but
protein – so I eat high protein.
But they get dry and brittle so I
soak them in warm olive oil.

**Do you worry about damaging
them in your sleep?**
No – they just hang off the side of
the bed! I don't even think about it.

How do you get dressed?
My nails are like an extension of
my fingers, so I just slide them
down the sleeves as usual. Now
that gravity has pulled my nails
straighter they're much easier
to slip through. I just can't put
on anything that goes over
my head because I can't
coordinate putting my hands
up and feeding the nails
through, so everything has
to come up over my bottom!

**How does it feel to be
in the book?**
It's an honor. I get asked to
sign a lot of books! I use them
to teach self-esteem classes.
I really think it helps kids:

meeting me and seeing me in
the books gets their minds going,
knowing they can do anything.

**One more question! How do
you go to the bathroom?**
That's usually the first question
people ask! I usually say, 'Very
carefully... and I don't have
hemorrhoids!'

Tallest man

Human beings

The record for the tallest man ever was held by Robert Pershing Wadlow (USA, below), who stood at 8 ft 11.1 in (2.72 m). His record is one of the most popular Guinness World Records and is recognized as a true classic.

Early days

Robert Pershing Wadlow (USA) was born at 6:30 am in Alton, Illinois, USA, on February 22 1918 to Addie and Harold Wadlow (both USA). Robert was the eldest of five children. He had two sisters and two brothers, all of whom were of normal height and weight. His birth weight of 8 lb 8 oz (3.85 kg) gave no indication of the amazing growth that was to come. In fact, Robert grew at a normal rate until the age of two, when he underwent a double hernia operation. From then on, he grew at an astonishing speed, so that by the age of five he stood 5 ft 4 in (1.63 m) tall and weighed 105 lb (48 kg). By the age of nine, he was able to carry his 5-ft 11-in (1.8-m), 169-lb (77-kg) father up the stairs of the family home. With a peak daily food consumption of 8,000 calories, his greatest recorded weight was 491 lb (223 kg) on his 21st birthday.

Robert's Guinness World Records

As well as being the tallest man in medical history for whom there is irrefutable evidence, he also holds Guinness World Records for the largest hands and feet. His hands measured 12.75 in (32.3 cm) from the wrist to the tip of his middle finger, and his feet were 18.5 in (47 cm) long – his shoes were size 37AA. When he was 12 years old, doctors found that he had an overactive pituitary gland, the source of the human growth hormone somatotropin. Corrective surgery was dangerous and not guaranteed to work, so his parents let nature take its course.

Robert's everyday life

Robert tried to lead as normal a life as possible. He enjoyed photography and collecting stamps, and at 13 years old he became the world's tallest Boy Scout when he measured 7 ft 4 in (2.23 m). By the time he reached 18, he was 8 ft 3.5 in (2.53 m) tall – his clothing required three times as much cloth as normal-sized clothes and his massive size 37 shoes cost $100 a pair. Robert's younger brother Harold once recalled on Guinness World Records: Primetime how his brother went about his day-to-day living: 'He had to duck to go through all doorways. No room on a bus, no room on a train, no seats, no airplane – everything was made for a person six feet tall or under. He probably wished that he wasn't as tall as he was and wanted a normal life, which he couldn't possibly live.'

Incredible feet!

Robert had his shoes custom made by the International Shoe Company, and when he was aged 20 he was invited to become a goodwill ambassador for the firm. Robert and his father made an extensive tour around the western USA, promoting the company who made his shoes free of charge. His brother Harold commented:

'He couldn't go anywhere without being stared at and drawing a crowd. Some people would bother him, you know, because of his height. They might come up behind him and pinch his leg or something else, you know, or even maybe try to kick him in the shins, make sure he wasn't on stilts.'

How big is your hand compared with Robert's?

Robert Wadlow pictured above with his family (from left to right): brother Eugene, mother Addie with brother Harold Jr., sister Betty, father Harold, and sister Helen.

Robert Wadlow height chart

Age	Height	Weight
5	5 ft 4 in (1.63 m)	105 lb (48 kg)
8	6 ft (1.83 m)	169 lb (77 kg)
9	6 ft 2.25 in (1.89 m)	180 lb (82 kg)
10	6 ft 5 in (1.99 m)	210 lb (95.6 kg)
11	6 ft 7 in (2.00 m)	-
12	6 ft 10.5 in (2.10 m)	-
14	7 ft 5 in (2.26 m)	301 lb (137 kg)
15	7 ft 8 in (2.34 m)	355 lb (161 kg)
16	7 ft 10.24 in (2.40 m)	374 lb (170 kg)
17	8 ft 0.38 in (2.45 m)	315 lb (143 kg)
18	8 ft 3.5 in (2.53 m)	-
19	8 ft 5.5 in (2.58 m)	480 lb (218 kg)
20	8 ft 6.75 in (2.61 m)	-
21	8 ft 8.25 in (2.65 m)	491 lb (223 kg)
22.4	8 ft 11.1 in (2.72 m)	439 lb (199 kg)

When did he break the record?

Robert gained a place in the history books when he exceeded 8 ft 3.5 in (2.53 m) in 1936, beating the record held by Irishman Patrick Cotter O'Brien who measured 8 ft 1 in (2.46 m) before he died in 1806.

Why did he die so young?

Apart from the difficulties associated with his abnormal height, Robert was very healthy, but for many years he was troubled by medical problems with his huge feet. He had poor circulation in his long legs as well as limited sensation in his feet and did not feel any rubbing or chafing until blisters had formed.

In July 1940, when aged 22, Robert was provided with a brace designed to strengthen his ankles. However, the brace was poorly fitted and a septic blister formed on his right ankle. His poor circulation and lack of sensation meant that the blister went unnoticed for some days and by the time he arrived in Manistee, Michigan, a week later to make a guest appearance, a fatal infection had set in.

Robert passed away in his sleep at 1:30 am on July 15 1940. He was buried in Oakwood Cemetery in his hometown of Alton, Illinois. The 10-ft 9-in-long (3.28-m) coffin was carried by 12 men. Out of respect, the town of Alton closed for the day and over 40,000 people signed the register at his funeral. After Robert's death, his family destroyed most of his belongings as they did not want collectors to put his personal items on display.

Robert Wadlow is remembered by his family as a 'quiet young man who overcame a unique handicap, and who was an inspiration to all of those that knew him.' His record remains one of the most popular and memorable in the 50-year history of *Guinness World Records*.

Amazing anatomy
Human beings

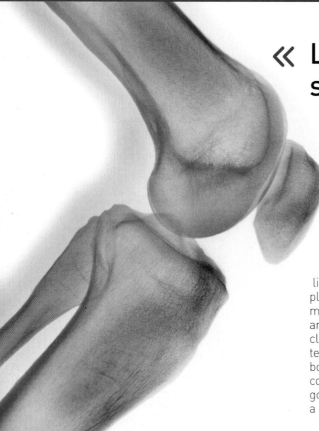

❮❮ Largest sesamoid bone

The patella or kneecap (left) is the largest sesamoid bone in the human body. Sesamoids are ovoid like the seeds of the sesame plant and most are only a few millimeters in diameter. They are usually embedded tendons close to joints or where the tendons angle sharply around bone. Their function is to take compression when a tendon is going around a joint, as when a person is kneeling.

Smallest joint ❮❮

The smallest joint is in the ear, between the smallest bone, the stapes or stirrup bone (above, bottom), and the incus or anvil bone (above, middle). The stapes measures a mere 0.1–0.13 in (2.6–3.4 mm) in length and weighs 0.03–0.066 grains (2–4.3 mg).

★ Largest muscle
Muscles normally account for 40% of human body weight in men and 35% in women. The bulkiest of the 639 named muscles in the human body is usually the gluteus maximus or buttock muscle, which extends the thigh. However, in pregnancy the uterus or womb can increase from about 1 oz (30 g) to over 2 lb 3 oz (1 kg) in weight.

★ Smallest muscle
The smallest muscle in the human body is the stapedius, which controls the stapes in the ear. The muscle is less than 0.05 in (0.127 cm) long.

★ Most active muscle
It has been estimated that the eye muscles move more than 100,000 times a day. It is believed that many of these rapid eye movements take place during the dreaming phase of sleep.

★ Longest muscle
The longest muscle in the human body is the sartorius, which is a narrow, ribbonlike muscle running from the pelvis and across the front of the thigh to the top of the tibia below the knee. Its action is to draw the lower limb into the cross-legged position.

★ Longest bone
Excluding a variable number of sesamoids (small, rounded bones), there are 206 bones in the adult human body, compared with about 300 for children (as they grow, some bones fuse together). The thighbone, or femur, is the longest. It constitutes 27.5% of a person's stature normally, and may be expected to be 19.75 in (50 cm) long in a man measuring 6 ft (1.8 m) tall. The longest recorded bone was a femur measuring 29.9 in (76 cm), which belonged to Constantine, a German giant.

★ Largest internal organ
The largest organ in the human body, the adult liver can weigh between 2 lb 10 oz and 3 lb 4 oz (1.2 and 1.5 kg) – about one thirty-sixth of the total body weight. Located behind the lower ribs and below the diaphragm, it performs over 100 separate bodily functions and can measure up to 8.6 in (22 cm) long and 3.9 in (10 cm) wide.

★ Largest gallbladder
On March 15 1989, at the National Naval Medical Center in Bethesda, Maryland, USA, Prof. Bimal C. Ghosh (USA) removed a gallbladder weighing 23 lb (10.4 kg) from a 69-year-old woman.

★ Largest gallstone
The largest gallstone reported in medical literature was one of 13 lb 14 oz (6.29 kg) removed from an 80-year-old woman by Dr. Humphrey Arthure (UK) at Charing Cross Hospital, London, UK, on December 29 1952.

★ Largest bladder stone
Dr. Kadri Al-Ban removed from one of his patients, Mohammed Ali A. Al-Muleiki (both Yemen), a vesical (bladder) stone weighing 9.17 oz (260 g) and with a diameter of about 2.75 in (7 cm) at the Al-Kadri Clinic, Ibb, Yemen, on October 25 1998.

★ Rarest blood group
A type of Bombay blood (subtype h-h) has so far been found only in a Czechoslovak nurse in 1961 and in a brother (Rhesus positive) and sister (Rhesus negative) named Jalbert in Massachusetts, USA, reported in February 1968. Using the ABO system, one of 14 systems, group AB occurs in less than 3% of persons in the UK and 1% in the USA.

★ Most common blood group
On a world basis, group O is the most common blood group (46%), but in some countries, for example Norway, Group A predominates.

★ Largest artery
The aorta is 1.18 in (3 cm) in diameter where it leaves the heart and by the time it ends at the level of the fourth lumbar vertebra, it is about 0.68 in (1.75 cm) in diameter.

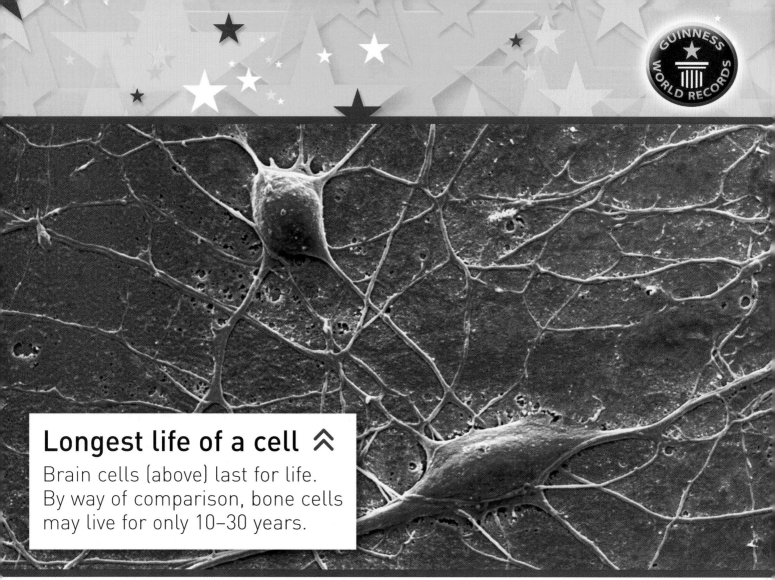

Longest life of a cell ⌃

Brain cells (above) last for life. By way of comparison, bone cells may live for only 10–30 years.

★ **Largest vein**
The inferior vena cava, which returns the blood from the lower half of the body to the heart and is slightly larger than the aorta, is the largest vein in the body.

★ **Largest cell**
The megakaryocyte, a blood cell, measures 0.007 in (0.2 mm). It is found in the bone marrow and produces the 'stickiest' particles in the body – the platelets – which play an important role in blood clotting.

★ **Smallest cell**
The brain cells in the cerebellum measure about 0.0001968 in (0.005 mm) or 5 microns.

★ **Longest cell**
Motor neurons are some 4 ft 3.12 in (1.3 m) long; they have cell bodies (gray matter) in the lower spinal cord with axons (white matter) that carry nerve impulses from the spinal cord down to the big toe. The cell systems that carry certain sensations

(vibration and positional sense) back from the big toe to the brain are even longer. Their uninterrupted length, from the toe and up the posterior part of the spinal cord to the medulla of the brain, is about equal to the height of the body.

★ **Most abundant cell**
The body contains in the region of 30 billion red blood cells (erythrocytes), approximately 8.75×10^{12} in every pint of blood (5×10^{12} in every liter). The function of these cells is to carry oxygen around the body.

★ **Longest-lived human cells**
The cells of Henrietta Lacks (USA) are still alive and being grown in laboratories worldwide decades after her death from cancer on October 4 1951 when she was 31. A single cell was removed and was subsequently found to lack chromosome 11, which is now known as the 'tumor suppressor.' As a result of this biological error, the cell is immortal and is one of the most helpful tools in biomedical research.

★ **Fastest turnover of body cells**
The body cells with the shortest life are in the lining of the alimentary tract, where the cells are shed every three to four days.

★ **Longest memory of a cell**
A lymphocyte is a type of white blood cell that is part of the body's immune defense system. As successive generations of lymphocytes are produced during one's life, they never forget an enemy.

★ **Heaviest brain**
In December 1992, Dr. George T. Mandybur (USA), at the University of Cincinnati, Ohio, USA, reported the weight of a 30-year-old male's brain as being 5 lb 1.1 oz (2.3 kg).

★ **Lightest brain**
The lightest 'normal' or non-atrophied brain on record was one weighing 1 lb 8 oz (680 g). It belonged to Daniel Lyon (Ireland), who died aged 46 in New York, USA, in 1907. He was

just over 5 ft (1.5 m) in height and weighed 145 lb (66 kg). A normal adult brain weighs in the region of 3 lb (1.4 kg).

★ **Highest hyperacuity**
The human eye is capable of judging relative position with remarkable accuracy, reaching limits of from 3 to 5 seconds of arc. In April 1984, Dr. Dennis M. Levi (USA) of the College of Optometry, University of Houston, Texas, USA, repeatedly identified the relative position of a thin, bright green line within 0.85 seconds of arc. This is equivalent to a displacement of some 0.25 in (6 mm) at a distance of 1 mile (1.6 km).

★ **Strongest joint**
The hip joint is the strongest and one of the most stable joints as the head of the femur fits almost perfectly into the socket of the pelvis.

★ **Most mobile joint**
The shoulder joint is the most mobile and as a result is the joint that is easiest to dislocate.

Medical phenomena
Human beings

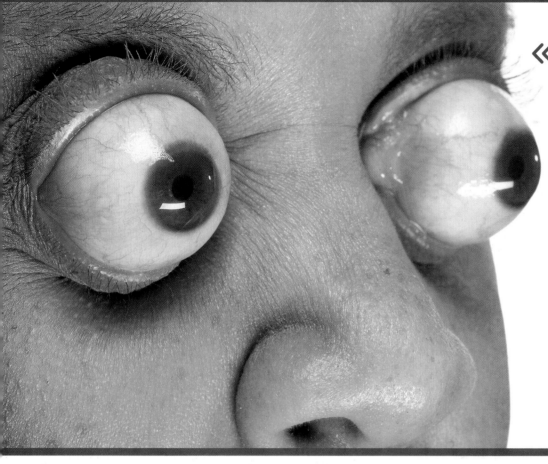

≪ Farthest eyeball popper

Kim Goodman (USA, left) can pop her eyeballs to a distance of 0.43 in (11 mm) beyond her eye sockets. Her eyes were measured on the set of the television show *Guinness World Records: Primetime* in Los Angeles, California, USA, on June 13 1998. Kim first discovered her unique and somewhat startling talent when she was accidentally hit on the head with a hockey mask and one of her eyeballs popped out much further than normal. Ever since that day, Kim's eyes would protrude out of her head every time she yawned, and she has now taught herself to pop her eyes out on cue.

★ Earliest successful artificial eye

On January 17 2000, it was announced that Jeremiah Teehan (USA), who lost his sight after a blow to his head 36 years before, could see again thanks to an artificial eye developed by William Dobelle (USA). Jeremiah became the second person to receive surgery of this kind, and the first to have had successful results.

★ Largest plate inserted in human skull

Tom Thompson (USA) had a titanium plate measuring 5.9 x 4.33 in (15 x 11 cm) inserted into the left side of his head by neurosurgeons at DeKalb General Hospital, Decatur, Georgia, USA, on April 30 1971. The surgery took place after he had been struck by a car and was pronounced dead on arrival at the local hospital.

★ Strangest diet

Michel Lotito (France), known as Monsieur Henri Mangetout, has been eating metal and glass since 1959. Gastroenterologists have X-rayed his stomach and have described his ability to consume 2 lb (900 g) of metal per day as unique.

★ Heaviest object removed from stomach

The heaviest object extracted from a human stomach was a ball of hair weighing 5 lb 3 oz (2.53 kg) from a 20-year-old female compulsive swallower in the South Devon and East Cornwall Hospital, UK, on March 30 1895.

★ Oldest patient to undergo surgery

The greatest recorded age at which anyone has undergone an operation is 111 years 105 days for a hip operation on James Henry Brett Jr. (USA) on November 7 1960.

★ Farthest distance traveled by a human voice

The normal intelligible outdoor range of the male human voice in still air is 590 ft (180 m). Silbo, the whistled language of the Spanish-speaking inhabitants of the Canary Island of La Gomera, is intelligible under ideal conditions at 5 miles (8 km).

There is a recorded case, under optimal acoustic conditions, of a Silbo speaker being heard at a distance of 10.5 miles (17 km) across still water at night.

★ Highest G force endured nonvoluntarily

Racing driver David Purley (UK) survived a deceleration from 108 mph (173 km/h) to zero in 26 in (66 cm) in a crash at Silverstone, Northamptonshire, UK, on July 13 1977. He endured 179.8 G and suffered 29 fractures, three dislocations, and six heart stoppages.

★ Highest blood sugar level

Two-year-old Alexa Painter (USA) survived a blood sugar level 20.7 times above average at 2,495 mg/dekaliter (139 mmol/liter) when she was admitted to the Community Hospital of Roanoke, Virginia, USA, to be treated for severe diabetic ketoacidosis on December 30 1991. The normal blood sugar range is between 80 and 120 mg/dekaliter (4.4–6.6 mmol/liter).

★ Longest medical operation

The most protracted operation reported lasted for 96 hours and was performed in Chicago, Illinois, USA, on February 4–8 1951 when an ovarian cyst was removed from Gertrude Levandowski (USA). During the operation her weight fell 616 lb (280 kg) to 308 lb (140 kg).

★ Earliest heart transplant patient

The first heart transplant was performed on Louis Washkansky (South Africa), aged 55, at the Groote Schuur Hospital, Cape Town, South Africa, between 1 am and 6 am on December 3 1967, by a team of 30 headed by Prof. Christiaan Barnard (South Africa). The donor was Denise Ann Darvall (South Africa), aged 25. Washkansky lived for 18 days.

First hand ⌃⌃ transplant

During a 14-hour operation in Lyon, France, in 1998, an international team of eight surgeons attached the hand of a dead man to the wrist of 48-year-old Clint Hallam (Australia, above).

Furthest traced descendant by DNA »

Adrian Targett (UK) has been linked through some 300 generations and shown to be a direct descendant, on his mother's side, of Cheddar Man, a 9,000-year-old skeleton (right), one of the oldest complete skeletons, found in Great Britain in 1903.

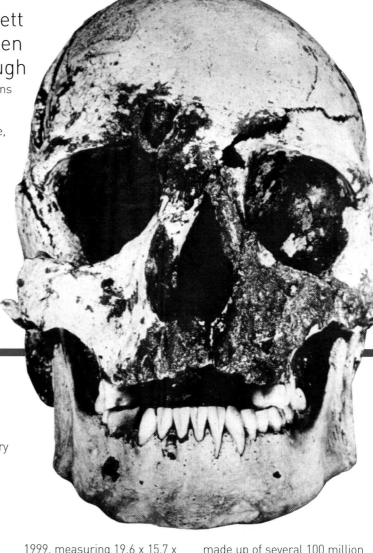

★ **Longest heart transplant survival**
Sammy Katy King (USA) survived 24 years 142 days after having received a 24-year-old male's heart at Stanford University, Palo Alto, California, USA, on April 4 1975.

★ **Earliest recipient of an artificial heart**
On December 1–2 1982, at the Utah Medical Center, Salt Lake City, Utah, USA, 61-year-old Barney Clark (USA) became the first recipient of an artificial heart, a Jarvik 7. The patient died on March 23 1983, 112 days later.

★ **Longest artificial heart transplant survival**
After his heart transplant on November 25 1984, William J. Schroeder (USA) survived 620 days.

★ **Longest cardiac arrest**
The longest cardiac arrest is four hours in the case of fisherman Jan Egil Refsdahl (Norway), who fell overboard into the icy waters off Bergen, Norway, on December 7 1987. He was rushed to nearby Haukeland Hospital after his body temperature fell to 75°F (24°C) and his heart stopped beating. He made a full recovery once he was connected to a heart-lung machine.

★ **Earliest successful kidney transplant**
The first successful kidney transplant in a human was performed by R.H. Lawler (USA) at Little Company of Mary Hospital, Chicago, Illinois, USA, on June 17 1950.

★ **Most fluid removed after hydronephrosis**
A 35-year-old Egyptian patient suffering from hydronephrosis – an enlargement of the kidney caused by a blockage of normal urine flow – had 46.49 pints (22 liters) of urine removed from his kidney on June 16 1999, at the Bugshan Hospital, Jeddah, Saudi Arabia. (The kidney's normal urine capacity is 0.105–0.175 fl oz or 3–5 ml.) The kidney was eventually removed on July 6 1999, measuring 19.6 x 15.7 x 9.8 in (50 x 40 x 25 cm) and weighing 24.6 oz (700 g).

★ **Most sets of teeth**
Cases of the growth of a third set of teeth in late life have been recorded several times. A reference to a case in France of a fourth dentition, known as Lison's case, was published in 1896.

★ **Most lightning strikes survived**
The only man in the world to be struck by lightning seven times was ex–park ranger Roy C. Sullivan (USA), the 'human lightning conductor' of Virginia, USA. A single lightning strike is made up of several 100 million volts (with peak current in the order of 20,000 amps).

★ **Longest survivor of a porcine aortic valve replacement**
Harry Driver (UK) received a porcine (pig's) aortic valve replacement on April 12 1978 under surgeon Dr. John Keats (UK). It functioned for 25 years 238 days until it was replaced by another on March 16 2004 by Dr. Philip Kay (UK).

★ **Fastest sneeze**
The highest speed at which expelled particles from a sneeze have been measured to travel is 103.6 mph (167 km/h).

Rarest « form of Siamese twins

The most extreme form of Siamese twins is known as *dicephales tetrabrachius dipus* (two heads, four arms, and two legs). The only fully reported example of this is Masha and Dasha Krivoshlyapovy (USSR, left), who were born on January 3 1950 and died within 17 hours of each other on April 17 2003, aged 53 years 104 days.

Most children delivered ⌃ at a single birth to survive

Bobbie McCaughey (USA) gave birth to a set of septuplets (above) on November 19 1997 at the University Hospital, Iowa, USA. Conceived by in-vitro fertilization, the four boys and three girls were delivered after 31 weeks by cesarean section, and weighed between 2 lb 5 oz and 3 lb 4 oz (1,048 g and 1,474.3 g). Another set of surviving septuplets was born eight weeks prematurely on January 14 1998 to Hasna Mohammed Humair (Saudi Arabia). The four boys and three girls were born at the Abha Obstetric Hospital, Aseer, Saudi Arabia.

★ Lightest birth
A premature baby girl weighing 9.87 oz (280 g) was reported to have been born on June 27 1989 at the Loyola University Medical Center, Illinois, USA. The lowest birth weight recorded for a surviving infant, of which there is definite evidence, is 10 oz (283 g) in the case of Marian Taggart (UK), who was born six weeks premature in 1938 in South Shields, Tyne & Wear, UK.

★ Heaviest birth
Anna Bates (Canada), who measured 7 ft 5.5 in (2.27 m), gave birth to a boy weighing 23 lb 12.8 oz (10.8 kg) and who measured 30 in (76 cm) in length at her home in Seville, Ohio, USA, on January 19 1879, but the baby died 11 hours later.

★ Most premature baby
James Elgin Gill was born to Brenda Gill (Canada) on May 20 1987 in Ottawa, Ontario, Canada, 128 days (18 weeks) premature and weighing 1 lb 6 oz (624 g). The normal human gestation period is 280 days (40 weeks).

★ First 'Siamese' twins
The term 'Siamese' was first applied to congenitally united twins in connection with the celebrated Chang and Eng Bunker, born at Meklong, Siam (now Thailand), on May 11 1811. They were joined by a cartilaginous band at the chest. In April 1843, the twins married sisters Sarah and Adelaide Yates (USA) and fathered 10 and 12 children respectively. The twins died within three hours of each other on January 17 1874 aged 62 years 251 days.

★ Oldest mother
It was reported that Rosanna dalla Corte (Italy, b. February 1931) gave birth to a baby boy on July 18 1994 when she was 63 years old.

★ Most albino siblings
Of the eight children born to George and Minnie Sesler (both USA), four of their five sons were born with the rare genetic condition albinism. John, George, Kermit, and Kenneth were born with translucent skin, pinkish blue eyes, and white hair.

★ Most generations born on leap day
The only verified example of a family producing three consecutive generations born on February 29 is that of the Keoghs. Peter Anthony (Ireland, b. 1940), his son Peter Eric (UK, b. 1964), and his granddaughter Bethany Wealth (UK, b. 1996) all celebrate their birthdays every four years.

★ Most generations born on the same day
Four families hold this record. Ralph Betram Williams (USA) was born on July 4 1982 in Wilmington, North Carolina, USA. His father, grandfather, and, in 1876, his great-grandfather were also born on July 4.
Veera Tuulia Tuijantyär Kivistö (Finland), born in 1997, shares her birthday of March 21 with her mother (b. 1967), her grandfather (b. 1940), and great-grandfather (b. 1903).
Maureen Werner (USA) was born on October 13 1998 and shares her birthday with her mother (b. 1970), her

grandfather (b. 1938), and great-grandmother (b. 1912).
Jacob Camren Hildebrandt (USA) was born in 2001 and shares his birthday of August 23 with his father (b. 1966), his grandmother (b. 1944), and great-grandmother (b. 1919).

★ Most children delivered at a single birth
The highest recorded number of children born at a single birth is nine to Geraldine Brodrick (Australia) at the Royal Hospital for Women, Sydney, Australia, on June 13 1971. None of the children (five boys and four girls) lived for more than six days.

★ Most consecutive generations of twins
Three consecutive generations of the Roy family (Canada) have given birth to twins: Joyce Roy, a twin born May 22 1951, gave birth to Diane and Carole on January 17 1973. Diane gave birth to twin boys Derek and Ricky (b. December 16 1999) and Carole had twin girls Kelly and Ashley (b. May 12 2001).

Oldest »
woman ever

The greatest fully authenticated age to which any human has ever lived is 122 years 164 days by Jeanne Louise Calment (France, right). Born on February 21 1875, she died at a nursing home in Arles, southern France, on August 4 1997.

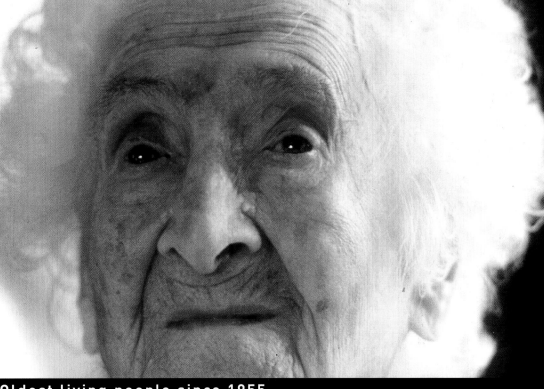

Centenarians surviving beyond their 113th year are extremely rare: the present absolute proven limit of human longevity is just over 122 years. Data on centenarians has shown that only one 115-year life can be expected in 2.1 billion lives.

★ **Oldest living woman**
Hendrikje Van Andel-Schipper (Netherlands, b. June 29 1890) took the title of the world's oldest living woman at the age of 113 years 335 days on May 29 2004.

★ **Oldest living man**
American Fred Hale (b. December 1 1890) became the world's oldest living man on March 5 2004 at the age of 113 years 95 days.

★ **Oldest man ever**
Born on June 29 1865, the oldest man ever recorded was Shigechiyo Izumi (Japan), who was listed as a six-year-old in Japan's first census of 1871. He died on February 21 1986 aged 120 years 237 days.

Oldest living people since 1955

Name	Country born	Born	Died	Country died	Age
1. Betsy Baker	UK	August 20 1842	October 24 1955	USA	113 years 65 days
2. Martha Graham	USA	December 1844	June 25 1959	USA	114 years ca.180 days
3. James Henry Brett Jr.	USA	July 25 1849	February 10 1961	USA	111 years 200 days
4. James Hull	UK	April 23 1852	September 9 1961	Australia	109 years 139 days
5. Lovisa Svensson	Sweden	November 20 1853	February 17 1963	Sweden	109 years 89 days
6. Kiet Portier-Tan	Netherlands	May 13 1855	April 21 1963	Netherlands	107 years 343 days
7. John Mosely Turner	UK	June 15 1856	March 21 1968	UK	111 years 280 days
8. Johanna Booyston	South Africa	January 17 1857	June 16 1968	South Africa	111 years 151 days
9. Marie Bernatkova	Czech Republic	October 22 1857	alive October 1968		111 years +days
10. Ada Roe	UK	February 6 1858	January 11 1970	UK	111 years 339 days
11. Josefa Salas Mateo	Spain	July 14 1860	February 27 1973	Spain	112 years 228 days
12. Alice Stevenson	UK	July 10 1861	August 18 1973	UK	112 years 39 days
13. Elizabeth Watkins	UK	March 10 1863	October 31 1973	UK	110 years 235 days
14. Mito Umeta	Japan	March 27 1863	May 31 1975	Japan	112 years 65 days
15. Niwa Kawamoto	Japan	August 5 1863	November 16 1976	Japan	113 years 103 days
16. Shigechiyo Izumi	Japan	June 29 1865	February 21 1986	Japan	120 years 237 days
17. Mamie Eva Keith	USA	March 22 1873	September 20 1986	USA	113 years 182 days
18. Mary McKinney	USA	May 30 1873	February 2 1987	USA	113 years 248 days
19. Anna Williams	UK	June 2 1873	December 27 1987	UK	114 years 208 days
20. Florence Knapp	USA	October 10 1873	January 11 1988	USA	114 years 93 days
21. Carrie White [1]	USA	November 18 1874	February 14 1991	USA	116 years 88 days
22. Jeanne Calment	France	February 21 1875	August 4 1997	France	122 years 164 days
23. Marie-Louise Meilleur	Canada	August 29 1880	April 16 1998	Canada	117 years 230 days
24. Sarah Knauss	USA	September 24 1880	December 30 1999	USA	119 years 97 days
25. Eva Morris	UK	November 8 1885	November 2 2000	UK	114 years 360 days
26. Marie Bremont	France	April 25 1886	June 6 2001	France	115 years 42 days
27. Maud Farris Luse	USA	January 21 1887	March 18 2002	USA	115 years 56 days
28. Kamato Hongo	Japan	September 16 1887	October 31 2003	Japan	116 years 45 days
29. Mitoyo Kawate	Japan	May 15 1889	November 13 2003	Japan	114 years 182 days
30. Ramona Trinidad Iglesias-Jordan [2]	Puerto Rico	August 31 1889	May 29 2004	Puerto Rico	114 years 272 days
31. Hendrikje Van Andel-Schipper	The Netherlands	June 29 1890			113 years 335 days*

[1] Authentication called into question by census data

*still living as of May 29 2004

[2] Title given to Charlotte Benkner (USA, b. November 16 1889, d. May 14 2004 aged 114 years 181 days) on November 13 2003 aged 113 years 362 days and withdrawn on March 29 2004 following receipt of documentation supporting Ramona Trinidad Iglesias-Jordan's claim.

Young talent

Human beings

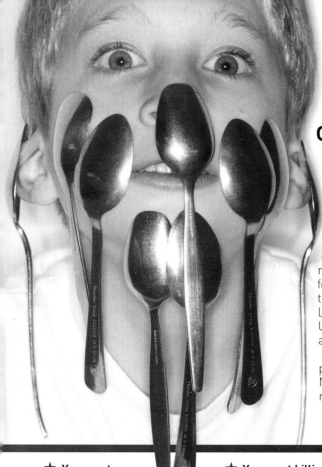

Most » spoons balanced on the face

Jonathan Friedman (USA) was able to balance 13 stainless-steel spoons on his face (one on each ear, two on each cheek, two on his chin, one on his lips, one on his nose, and three on his forehead). He balanced them for 2 minutes at Lake Oswego, Oregon, USA, on March 30 2004, aged 12.

Guinness World Records photographed Jonathan in November 2003 balancing nine spoons (left).

Youngest solo « circumnavigation

The youngest person to sail solo around the world is David Griffiths Dicks (Australia, above), who was 18 years 41 days old when he completed his circumnavigation back to Freemantle, Western Australia, in a time of 264 days 16 hr 49 min on November 16 1996.

★ **Youngest physician**
Balamurali Ambati (USA, b. July 29 1977) became the world's youngest doctor when he graduated from the Mount Sinai School of Medicine in New York City, USA, on May 19 1995 at the age of 17.

★ **Youngest actor to receive star billing**
Leroy Overacker (USA, b. May 12 1932), known on screen as 'Baby Leroy,' was chosen at the age of six months to play opposite Maurice Chevalier in *A Bedtime Story* (USA, 1933).

★ **Youngest consultant**
On April 15 2000, supermarket chain Tesco announced that it had procured the services of seven-year-old Laurie Sleator (UK) to advise senior executives on the Pokémon craze that was sweeping the globe. His advice contributed to Tesco selling over £1 million ($1.55 million) worth of Pokémon goods over the Easter weekend. Laurie was remunerated in the form of Pokémon products.

★ **Youngest billionaire**
The world's youngest billionaire is His Serene Highness 12th Prince Albert von Thurn und Taxis (Germany, b. June 24 1983) with an estimated net worth of $2.1 billion according to the *Forbes* Rich List 2004. On his 18th birthday, he became the sole heir of a royal family fortune that includes extensive landholdings, real estate, castles, works of art, and businesses.

★ **Youngest person to visit both poles**
The youngest person to have visited both geographical poles is Jonathan Silverman (USA, b. June 13 1990), who reached the North Pole on July 25 1999 and the South Pole on January 10 2002, aged 11 years 211 days.

★ **Youngest person to visit the North Pole**
Alicia Hempleman-Adams (UK, b. November 8 1989) stood at the geographic North Pole at the age of 8 years 173 days on May 1 1998, the youngest person ever to have done so.

She flew to the pole to meet her father, the well-known adventurer David Hempleman-Adams (UK), at the end of his successful trek to the pole.

★ **Youngest person to walk to the South Pole**
Andrew Cooney (UK, b. April 9 1979) became the youngest person to walk from the edge of the Antarctic continent to the South Pole, when he arrived there at the age of 23 years 268 days on January 2 2003, 54 days after setting out.

★ **Youngest person to travel to all seven continents**
The youngest person to have traveled to all seven continents is Tanya Daniella Donkin (South Africa), who visited her seventh continent on November 16 2000 at the age of 3 years 319 days. All her travels were with her parents, Dave and Irene Donkin (both South Africa). Tanya was born in South Africa (Africa) on January 2 1997; landed in Zurich, Switzerland (Europe) on February 20 1997; in Buenos

Aires, Argentina (South America) on December 14 1997; on Deception Island (Antarctica) on December 28 1997; in Miami, USA (North America) on December 17 1998; in Sydney, Australia (Australasia) on December 17 1999; and in Dubai, United Arab Emirates (Asia) on November 16 2000.

★ **Youngest published male author**
At the age of six, Dennis Vollmer (USA, b. July 21 1980) wrote and illustrated *Joshua Disobeys* and had it commercially published by Landmark Editions, Inc., of Kansas City, Missouri, USA, after his story won a national student writing contest in 1987.

★ **Youngest published female author**
The youngest commercially published female author is Dorothy Straight (USA, b. May 25 1958), who wrote *How the World Began* in 1962, aged only four. It was published by Pantheon Books in August 1964.

Youngest ⌃ published cook

Justin Miller (USA, b. January 10 1990; above) was seven years old when *Cooking with Justin: Recipes for Kids (And Parents)* was published in 1997. Apart from writing, he also advises the Marriott Hotel chain on its children's menus.

Youngest ⌄ radio host

On January 16 1999, Cody Morton (Canada, b. June 12 1988; below) hosted a show on CHOO FM in Tofino, British Columbia, Canada, aged 10 years 218 days.

★ **Youngest figure skating world champion**
The youngest female winner of a world title is Tara Lipinski (USA, b. June 10 1982), who won the individual title on March 22 1997 aged just 14 years 286 days.

★ **Youngest Wimbledon competitor**
The youngest Wimbledon competitor was Mita Klima (Austria) who was just 13 years old in the 1907 singles competition.

★ **Youngest person to win a match at Wimbledon**
The youngest person to win a match at Wimbledon is Jennifer Capriati (USA, b. March 29 1976), who was aged 14 years 89 days when she competed in her first Wimbledon tennis match on June 26 1990.

★ **Youngest soccer World Cup player**
The youngest player to play in football's premier tournament is Souleymane Mamam (Togo) who played for Togo against Zambia aged 13 years 310 days in a preliminary qualifying game on May 6 2001.

★ **Youngest professional artist**
Dante Lamb (USA, b. November 16 1999) is the youngest artist to have his work purchased and displayed. Dante's abstract paintings hang in the Monkey Love Dessert Bar & Gallery, St. Simons Island, Georgia, USA, and his first piece sold on October 6 2003 for $85 when he was only three years old.

★ **Most consecutive pea shooting world championships**
The most consecutive pea shooting world championships won is three by Mike Fordham (UK) in 1983–85 and David Hollis (UK) in 1999–2001. Hollis was also the youngest world champion, aged just 13 when he scooped the title in 1999. The championships are held every year in Witcham, Cambridgeshire, UK.

★ **Youngest international gymnast**
Pasakevi Voula Kouna (Greece, b. December 6 1971) was aged 9 years 299 days at the start of the Balkan Games in Serres, Greece, on October 1 1981, when she represented Greece.

★ **Youngest world line dance champion**
Siobhan Dunn (UK, b. June 30 1991) won the Junior World Line Dance Championship in Nashville, Tennessee, USA, on January 10 1998 aged just 6 years 194 days.

★ **Youngest TV host**
The world's youngest host of a regular television program is Sheridan Jobbins (Australia) who, at the age of nine, began hosting *Cooking With Sheri* (Channel 7, Australia) in April 1969. The five-minute weekly (and then daily) show continued to air nationally for three consecutive years, ending when she was 11 years old. In total, 26 episodes were filmed.

★ **Youngest solo rap artist**
Jordy Lemoine (France, b. January 14 1988) was at No.1 in the French charts with techno/house rap 'Dur dur d'être Bébé' ('It's Hard to Be a Baby') at the age of four and a half in September 1993. The song later entered the US *Billboard* chart.

★ **Youngest DJ**
Llewellyn Owen aka 'DJ Welly' (UK, b. February 21 1992) headlined at London's Warp Club on May 1 2000 aged 8 years 70 days. Welly was paid the standard rate for headlining DJs, $190 an hour. Since his professional debut, he has headlined at famous clubs such as Ministry of Sound (UK).

★ **Youngest film director-writer-producer**
Lex the Wonderdog (Netherlands, 1973), a thriller of canine detection, was written, produced, and directed by Sydney Ling (Netherlands, b. November 20 1959) when he was 13 years old. He was the youngest ever director of a professionally made feature-length film.

Most balloon »
sculptures
created in one hour

John Cassidy (USA, right)
made 529 balloon sculptures
in one hour in New York City, USA, on October 14
2003. He made one sculpture every 6.8 seconds.

★ Most body skips
in a minute
Ved Prakash Sharma (India)
was able to 'skip' with his arms
while handcuffed, by stepping
through his arms and bringing
them up and over his head, a
total of 27 times in a minute at
Bhim Stadium, Bhiwani, India,
on August 15 2003.

★ Furthest basketball slam
dunk from a trampoline
Jonathon Thibout (France)
managed to slam-dunk a
basketball from a trampoline
placed 19 ft (5.8 m) from
the backboard of the net on
the set of *L'Eté de tous les
Records*, Port Leucate,
France, on August 29 2003.

★ Greatest
distance zorbing
The greatest distance
traveled by a zorb ball in a
single roll is 1,059 ft 8.5 in
(323 m) by Rich Eley (UK) near
Glynde, East Sussex, UK, on
May 10 1999. During the
attempt, the zorb reached a
record speed of 31 mph
(49.8 km/h). The zorb

originated in New Zealand and
is a large, round, bouncy ball
that can accommodate one
person. As it rolls, the person
strapped inside rolls too. A
zorb ball weighs approximately
198 lb (89 kg), and keeps the
'zorbonaut' in an air cushion
about 2 ft (60 cm) off the ground.

★ Most divisions
of a human hair
Alfred West (UK) succeeded
in splitting a human hair
17 times into 18 parts on eight
occasions. All the divisions
were made from the same point.

★ Tallest coin column
The tallest single column
of coins ever stacked on the
edge of a coin was built by
Dipak Syal (India) on May 3
1991 and was made up of 253
Indian one-rupee pieces on
top of a vertical five-rupee coin.

★ Greatest number of
skips on a tightrope
Walfer Guerrero (Colombia)
achieved 1,250 consecutive
turns skipping with a rope on
a high wire at the Wereldcircus

Carré, Haarlem, The
Netherlands, on June 1
1995. The tightrope was
31 ft 5 in (9.6 m) high.

★ Most 'ducks and drakes'
The record for the most
consecutive skips of a stone
on water is 40, held by Kurt
Steiner (USA). The cast was
achieved at the Pennsylvania
Qualifying Stone Skipping
Tournament held at Riverfront
Park, Franklin, Pennsylvania,
USA, on September 14 2002.

★ Most tennis balls
held in the hand
Francisco Peinado Toledo
(Spain) placed 18 tennis balls in
his left hand and held them for
10 seconds at Valencia, Spain,
on September 18 2003.

★ Furthest toss
of a cowpat
The record distances in the
country sport of throwing dried
cowpats, or 'chips,' depend
on whether or not the projectile
may be 'molded into a
spherical shape.' The greatest
distance achieved under the

'non-sphericalization and
100 per cent organic' rule
(established in 1970) is 266 ft
(81.1 m), by Steve Urner (USA)
at the Mountain Festival,
Tehachapi, California, USA,
on August 14 1981.

★ Most teacups
caught on the head
while unicycling
In 1952, unicyclist Rudy Horn
(Germany) became the first
person to throw six cups and
saucers with his feet and
balance them on his head,
while mounted on a unicycle.
He rounded off this feat by
adding a teaspoon and a lump
of sugar. At the time, he was
performing with the Bertram
Mills Circus at Olympia,
London, UK.

★ Most powerful lungs
The inflation of a standard
35-oz (1,000-g) meteorological
balloon to a diameter of 8 ft
(2.44 m) against set times was
achieved by Manjit Singh (UK)
in 42 minutes at Rushley
Pavilion Centre, Leicester,
UK, on September 16 1998.

Most basketballs ⌃ spun simultaneously

Michael Kettman (USA) spun 28 basketballs simultaneously on May 25 1999 at Guinness World Records, London, UK. He is pictured above, setting his previous record of 25 in 1998.

Most rattlesnakes held in the mouth

Jackie Bibby (USA, right) held eight live rattlesnakes in his mouth by their tails for 12.5 seconds without any assistance at the Guinness World Records Experience, Orlando, Florida, USA, on May 19 2001.

≫

★ GWR TALKS TO
Ashrita Furman

Ashrita Furman (USA, below) holds an amazing total of 19 Guinness World Records, including the fastest mile traveled on a pogostick – 12 min 16 sec – set at Iffley Field, Oxford, UK, on July 24 2001. His latest record successes include balancing 23 milk crates with a total weight of 88.01 lb (39.92 kg) on his chin for 11.23 seconds on June 17 2002 in Jamaica, New York, USA, and the record for the running a mile while balancing a full milk bottle on his head, which he achieved in a record time of 8 min 27 sec at the TSV 1880 Sports Association Track, Starnberg, Germany, on November 9 2003.

You set your first record in 1979. Why did you choose the jumping jacks record?
Well, I knew how to do it! At first I tried juggling – 100,000 throws and it took all night – but there was no category! So I trained for the jumping jacks record.

How do you get the inspiration for your records?
I take inspiration from all sorts of different places. Most records are already in the book, but I'm more open-minded now; anything is possible. I like the idea of people competing for the same record. It just comes down to 'Can I do better?' It's fun to create your own category but it's also a challenge to break an existing record – you have a certain standard to reach.

What do you think about your versatility record?
I'm really chuffed. A lot of it is just down to having an active imagination. The fastest milk bottle mile, the hula-hooping record – they were just off the top of my head.

What's the attraction of breaking records all over the world?
I travel a lot anyway, so while I'm away I try to break records. I really wanted to go to Antarctica because I wanted to have set records on all seven continents. Someone I know in the Argentinian Navy got me a flight over to the Antarctic where I was able to set my 'fastest mile on a pogostick' record.

How do you train for pogo-sticking in Antarctica?
It's difficult! It was certainly not the best place to set a pogo-stick record but it was a fantastic adventure! I almost got blown off the pogo by a helicopter leaving the base and at about the 0.75-mile point the spring of the pogostick got more and more

sluggish until it froze and I fell off! Fortunately we had a spare.

What's your next record attempt going to be?
I'll try skipping again, then glass balancing, then something in China. Maybe a somersault record. My current record is 8,341 forward rolls in 10 hr 30 min over 12 miles (19.67 km). I set it in 1986, but now I think I'm fitter.

What do you do to keep fit?
I go to the gym and I run a couple of times a week. Skipping keeps you in great shape. And I juggle shotputs!

What would you say to young people wanting to break records?
I became interested in breaking records as a kid and I still feel like a big kid! My dream was to get in the book and I didn't think I could, and now I have 19 records. Everyone has a special talent. I really believe there is something that everyone can do that will get you into *Guinness World Records*.

Lifelong achievements
Human beings

Oldest barefoot ⌃ waterskier

George Blair, aka Banana George, (USA, above, b. January 22 1915) successfully waterskied barefoot on Lake Florence, Winter Haven, Florida, USA, at the age of 87 years 18 days on February 10 2002.

★ Longest working career as a barber
Peter J. Vita (USA, b. April 30 1910) has been cutting hair professionally since 1922. Mr Vita started his career in his father's barbershop when he was 12 years old. He opened his own barbershop in 1930 where he worked until 1988, before moving his business to Port Chester, New York, USA, where he continues today.

★ Longest working career in the merchant navy
From May 2 1953 until June 23 1969, Robert Morris (UK, b. September 16 1928) served as cook on a total of 50 ships.

★ Longest working career as a bartender
Angelo Cammarata (USA) started his career as a bartender on April 7 1933 when Prohibition was repealed. He served beer at his family's grocery store on the stroke of midnight and was still working in his own bar Cammarata Days in July 1998 – 69 years later.

★ Longest working career as a radio DJ
Ray Cordeiro, aka 'Uncle Ray', (UK, b. December 12 1924) has been a regular disc jockey since 1949, first working for the station Rediffusion Ltd. (Hong Kong) and then moving to (the now) Radio Television Hong Kong on September 15 1960. He still hosts a regular four-hour nightly show called All the Way with Ray transmitted 10 pm until 2 am Monday to Friday.

★ Oldest working mime artist
American mime artist Arnold Jones (USA, b. January 13 1914) is still working six hours a day, five days a week entertaining crowds in Hollywood, California, USA. He has been a professional mime artist for over 70 years, starting at the age of 14 as 'The Mechanical Man' at fairs across America's Midwest.

★ Longest working career as a circus bandmaster
Merle Evans (USA) was bandmaster with Ringling Brothers–Barnum & Bailey Circus for 50 years. From 1919 to 1969 he led the band for about 30,000 performances, never missing a show.

★ Longest career as a radio actor in the same role
Norman Painting (UK) took part in the first broadcast of BBC Radio 4's The Archers on January 1 1951 and is still in the series as Philip Archer.

★ Oldest chorus line member
The oldest 'showgirl' who is still regularly performing in a chorus line is Beverly Allen (USA, b. November 4 1917). A member of The Fabulous Palm Springs Follies, her jitterbug routine – in which her partner lifts her over his head to spin her 'head-over-heels' – has become an audience favorite.

★ Longest working career as a stadium announcer
Walter Miceli (Brazil) has been the stadium announcer at the Estádio de São Januário, Rio de Janeiro, Brazil, home of Club de Regatas Vasco da Gama, since February 12 1947.

★ Oldest BASE jumper
James Talbot Guyer (USA, b. June 16 1928) parachuted off the 486-ft-high (148-m) Perrine Bridge, Idaho, USA, on August 2 2002 aged 74 years 47 days.

★ Longest distance covered over a working career
Stanley E. Rychlicki (USA) walked for 37 years of his 40-year career as a 'pipeline inspector' and covered a distance of 136,880 miles (220,288 km), sometimes walking in excess of 20 miles (32 km) daily in Pennsylvania and New York, USA.

Fastest time to 〈 type one to one million

Les Stewart (Australia, above) has typed the numbers one to one million manually in words on 19,990 quarto sheets. Starting in 1982, his target to become a 'millionaire' became a reality on December 7 1998.

Longest 〉〉 working career as a salsa artist

Celia Cruz (Cuba, right) was a leading salsa artist for 50 years and recorded over 50 albums. She began her career singing with Cuba's then-leading band Sonora Matancera in 1950, before leaving Cuba permanently to pursue a career in the USA in 1960. She recorded some 20 gold LPs and received more than 100 awards.

★ **Oldest dance instructor**
Gisel Weser (Germany, b. February 1 1921) is the oldest dancing teacher, having worked at Triebel-Hölzer (founded 1883) in Lutherstadt Eisleben, Saxony-Anhalt, Germany, since 1949. She became head of the school in 1968 and continues to teach.

★ **Oldest bell ringer**
Reginald Bray (UK, b. October 28 1902) is an active member of the bell-ringing team of St. Cyr and St. Julitta, Newton St. Cyres, Devon, UK. He rang bells on October 30 2003, two days after his 101st birthday, and continues bell-ringing today.

★ **Oldest authors**
The oldest male author is Constantine Kallias (Greece, b. June 26 1901), who published a 169-page paperback entitled *A Glance of My Life* in February 2003 at the age of 101.
Sisters and coauthors A Elizabeth Delany and Sarah Louise Delany (both USA) published *The Delany Sisters'*

Book of Everyday Wisdom in October 1994, when Sarah Louise was 105 years old and Elizabeth was 103.

★ **Oldest competitive billiards player**
Jim Turton (UK, b. January 2 1909) has been playing competitive billiards since 1924.

★ **Oldest competitive pool player**
Wesley Walker (USA, b. April 24 1916) plays for Southern Vending in the Valley National 8-Ball Association league in Oklahoma, USA.

★ **Longest working career as a builder**
Edward William Beard (UK, 1878–1982) retired in October 1981 after 85 years with the firm he founded in 1896.

★ **Oldest drivers**
Two male drivers were issued with new driver's licenses at the advanced age of 104: Fred Hale Sr (USA, b. December 1 1890 – currently the oldest living man) was issued with his

license in February 1995, and drove until it expired on his 108th birthday in 1998. Layne Hall (USA), whose date of birth is uncertain (b. December 24/25 1884 or March 15 1880), was issued with a license on June 15 1989 when he was either 104 (according to his death certificate) or 109 (according to his driver's license). It was valid until his birthday in 1993, but he died on November 20 1990.
The oldest female driver was Maude Tull (USA), who took to driving aged 91 after her husband died. She was issued a renewal on February 5 1976 when aged 104.

★ **Oldest competing aerobatic pilot**
Ian Metcher (Australia) was 85 years old when he won the basic aerobatics section of the Western Australia Light Aircraft Championships at Jandakot Airport near Fremantle, Australia, on February 24 2001.

★ **Oldest person to rappel**
Mary Maughan (UK, b. October 3 1908) rappelled

down a 124-ft (38-m) cliff in Parrock Quarry, Ambleside, Cumbria, UK, on June 30 2000 when aged 91 years 8 months and 27 days.

★ **Oldest person to 'loop the loop'**
On May 21 1998, 95-year-old Adeline Ablitt (UK, b. 1903) flew in a glider as it performed a loop over the Soaring Centre, Leicestershire, UK.

★ **Most blood donated**
Maurice Creswick (South Africa) has donated blood for a record 59 consecutive years since 1944, giving his record 336th unit of blood on July 9 2003. Having given blood since turning 18, he has donated a total of 50 gal (188.9 liters).

★ **Oldest working general practitioner**
Dr. Kauromal M. Chandiramani (India, b. May 9 1899) practiced as a general practitioner in Mumbai (Bombay), India, for 75 years 198 days from September 22 1923 to May 9 1999 – his 100th birthday.

Mass participation
Human beings

Longest human domino line ⌃⌃

On September 30 2000, 9,234 students aged 18–21 from NYAA Poly Connects formed a human domino chain (above) stretching 2.6 miles (4.2 km) across Siloso Beach, Sentosa Island, Singapore.

★ **Largest human chain**
On August 23 1989 up to 2 million people joined hands to form a human chain 370 miles (595 km) long across Estonia, Latvia, and Lithuania, commemorating the 50th anniversary of the nonaggression treaty between the USSR and Nazi Germany.

★ **Largest human rainbow**
The world's largest human rainbow was made up of 11,273 staff, students, alumni, and families from Hong Kong Polytechnic University, and was formed at Hong Kong Stadium, Hong Kong, China, on October 6 2002.

★ **Largest human national flag**
A total of 10,371 spectators at the Scotland v. Germany soccer match on September 10 2003 in Westfalenstadion, Dortmund, Germany, formed the shape and colors of the German flag in the south grandstand. Participants wore colored T-shirts and caps to form the black, red, and gold flag.

★ **Largest walking bus**
On October 8 2003, the Royal Borough of Kingston-upon-Thames and Transport for London (both UK) organized a 'walking bus' of 1,109 people to the schools of Fern Hill Primary, St. Agatha's Catholic Primary, and Latchmere Infants and Junior Schools (all UK).

★ **Largest human logo**
On July 24 1999, 34,309 people organized by Realizar Eventos Especias gathered at the national stadium of Jamor, Lisbon, Portugal, to create the Portuguese logo for Euro2004, as part of the successful Portuguese bid to UEFA to hold the European Football Championships in 2004.

★ **Longest human conveyor belt**
A conveyor belt consisting of 1,000 students from the University of Guelph, Canada, was formed on September 7 1998. A surfboard was transported along its length.

★ **Largest group hug**
A total of 5,117 students, staff, and friends from St. Matthew's Secondary School in Orleans, Ontario, Canada, hugged each other for 10 seconds on April 23 2004 in support of The Force, a local cancer charity.

★ **Largest circle dance**
The greatest number of participants in a circle formation dance were the 6,748 people who performed the hokey pokey at Bangor, County Down, UK, as part of the VE Day anniversary celebrations on May 6 1995.

★ **Largest locomotion dance**
A total of 669 people danced the locomotion for seven minutes in the grounds of Haydon Bridge High School, Hexham, Northumberland, UK, on October 19 2001.

★ **Largest game of musical chairs**
On August 5 1989, the largest game of musical chairs began with 8,238 participants at the Anglo-Chinese School in Singapore. Three and a half hours later, the game ended with the lucky 15-year-old winner Xu Chong Wei on the last chair.

★ **Largest simultaneous yodel**
The world's largest simultaneous yodel involved 937 people all yodeling the popular Swiss song 'Von Luzern uf Wäggis zue' for more than one minute. The event was staged at the Ravensburger Spieleland, Meckenbeuren, Germany, on October 5 2002.

« Largest yoga class

Manoj Gupota (India) led a yoga class of 6,315 people (left) at Pandit Ravishankar Shukla (Wright Town) Stadium, Jabalpur, India, on February 13 2003.

Most people brushing their » teeth in the same venue

A total of 10,240 students brushed their teeth simultaneously for at least 60 seconds at Ai Guo Road, Luohu District, Shenshen City, China, on September 20 2003. The event was organized by the Health Bureau of Luohu District, the Education Bureau of Luohu District, and the Chamber of Commerce of Luohu District and sponsored by Colgate-Palmolive (Guangzhou) Co. Ltd.

★ Most people on unicycles

On May 18 2003, 100 students from the circus school Circus Jopie traveled on unicycles for a distance of 1,150 ft (350 m) at Utrecht, The Netherlands. Their first attempt was in a single line wearing a 1,475-ft-long (450-m) dragon costume. Unfortunately, the costume separated into two halves during the journey.

★ Most people sitting on one chair

On September 20 2002, 407 pupils from Otto-Hahn-Gymnasium (high school) in Springe, Germany, sat on one chair at the same time. The unbroken line of pupils, each seated on the knees of the person behind, measured 199 ft 1.2 in (60.7 m) long.

★ Largest unsupported circle

The largest number of people in an unsupported circle (where you sit on the lap of the person behind you) is 10,323, achieved by employees of the Nissan Motor Company at Komazawa Stadium, Tokyo, Japan, on October 23 1982.

★ Most people skipping rope simultaneously

On April 2 2003, a total of 1,356 schoolchildren skipped ropes simultaneously at Bishopston School, Swansea, UK.

★ Largest snowball fight

The world's largest snowball fight involved 2,473 participants (1,162 against 1,311) and took place at Triel in the ski resort of Obersaxen-Mundaun in Graubunden, Switzerland, on January 18 2003.

★ Largest dog walk

A total of 4,372 dogs took part in the Catherine Cookson Great North Dog Walk, organized by Anthony Carlisle (UK). The walk was held on June 22 2003 and started from Gypsies Green Stadium, South Shields, UK.

★ Largest simultaneous 'dog stay'

Dogs for the Disabled and Pets at Home organized a 'dog stay' involving a record 514 dogs on August 16 2003 at The Wag and Bone Show, Ascot, Berkshire, UK.

★ Largest cookery lesson

Princess Household Appliances BV (Netherlands) organized a cookery lesson involving 357 students who were taught how to make paella by Cas Spijkers (Netherlands) on June 15 2003 at Estepona, Marbella, Spain.

★ Largest water balloon fight

On September 13 2003, the University at Buffalo, New York City, USA, played host to a water balloon fight involving 422 students throwing 5,214 water balloons.

★ Largest simultaneous whoopee cushion sit

The UK's CBBC Xchange TV show organized a simultaneous whoopee cushion sit involving 1,504 participants at Tottenham Hotspur Football Club's stadium, White Hart Lane, London, UK, on January 13 2004.

★ Most people simultaneously slimed

On October 27 2003, during Nickelodeon's Slimetime Live show at Universal Studios in Orlando, Florida, USA, 762 people were simultaneously slimed by around 150 gal (568 liters) of green slime.

★ Most people to pop balloons simultaneously

On January 22 2004, 1,603 basketball fans popped balloons simultaneously during halftime of the Metro State against Fort Hays State University men's basketball game at Gross Memorial Coliseum at Hays, Kansas, USA.

★ Most couples kissing simultaneously

A total of 5,327 couples kissed simultaneously for 10 seconds on February 14 2004 as part of the Close-up Lovapalooza festival in Manila, Philippines.

★ Largest sleepover/ pajama party

On February 1 2003, McLean Bible Church and Dulles Town Center, Virginia, USA, hosted a sleepover party for 1,045 students. All participants wore pajamas and slept on the floor in sleeping bags.

Team efforts
Human beings

Fastest 4-x-100-m ⌃ sack relay race

The 4-x-100-m sack relay race, held on June 17 2003 at Ivanhoe Grammar School, Mernda, Victoria, Australia, was won in 2 min 29.09 sec. The members of the winning team were Patrick Holcolmbe (above, second from left), James Osbourne (fifth from left), Luke MacFarlane (sixth from left), and Andrew Rodaughan (second from right, all Australia).

★ Fastest men's mobile garbage-bin race
On February 21 1999, at Westfield Devils Junior Soccer Club, Launceston, Tasmania, Australia, Shaun Viney and Aaron Viney (both Australia) completed a 360-ft 9.6-in (110-m) mobile garbage-bin race in 31.1 seconds.

★ Fastest women's woolsack race
The 'Mega Movers' team of four ladies completed the woolsack World Championships in Tetbury, Gloucestershire, UK, in 3 min 52.01 sec on May 25 1989. The event involves competitors racing up and down a steep hill while carrying a 60-lb (27.21-kg) bag of wool on their shoulders.

★ Fastest 31-legged race over 50 m
Students from the Sugikami Elementary school in the Kumamoto Prefecture, Japan, ran a 31-legged race covering a total of 164 ft (50 m) in 8.94 seconds at Yokohama Arena, Japan, on November 23 2002.

★ Farthest distance covered in a lawn mower race
Ian Dobson, Robert Jones, and Steve Williams (all UK) of the team 'Extreme Headless Chickens' covered 313.6 miles (504.7 km) in the annual 12-hour lawn mower race at Wisborough Green, UK, on August 29–30 1998, organized by the British Lawn Mower Racing Association.

★ Longest supermarket cart push
A team of 801 staff from Woolworths, BCC, and Jack-the-Slasher supermarkets took turns to push a supermarket shopping cart from Cairns to Brisbane, Queensland, Australia, covering 1,098 miles (1,767 km) in 36 days, from June 20 to July 26 1987.

★ Farthest distance to push a bed
A team of nine employees from Bruntsfield Bedding Centre, Edinburgh, UK, pushed a wheeled hospital bed 3,233.65 miles (5,204 km) from June 21 to July 26 1979.

★ Fastest time to dismantle a car
A team from Espoon Ammattioppilaitos technical school (Finland) consisting of Tapio Heino, Panu Natunen, Aaro-Pekka Nousiainen, Sami Rissanen, Sampo Vuolteenaho, Ahmed Abdirizag, Mikael Gorski, Janne Spanow, and Juha Määttä (all Finland) dismantled a five-door sedan in 35 minutes on November 28 2001. All parts were removed except for the bodywork, chassis, and axles.

★ Fastest time to swap an engine
A team of four mechanics – Stefan Klotz, Markus Jung, Ralf Kaelche, and Stefan Worner (all Germany) – took the engine from one Volkswagen Beetle and installed it in another, then drove the car 16 ft 5 in (5 m) in a time of 1 min 37 sec on the set of *Guinness – Die Show der Rekorde*, Munich, Germany, on January 17 1999.

★ Most people on a motorcycle wheelie
On June 12 1998, a total of nine people, led by Todd Colbert (USA), did a motorcycle wheelie in Lake Whales, Florida, USA.

★ Most people crammed into a Smart car
A total of 13 girls from Team IGA-Optic (Germany) crammed into a Smart car on the set of *Guinness – Die Show der Rekorde*, Munich, Germany, on April 2 1999.

Farthest wheelchair ⌃⌃ push over 24 hours

A team of 75 volunteers pushed
a wheelchair a distance of
240 miles (386.2 km) in 24 hours
at Copeland Stadium, Whitehaven, Cumbria, UK, on
September 8–9 2000 (above). The event was organized by
the Maryport branch of the Cumbria Cerebral Palsy Society.

Fastest Boeing 737 ⌃⌃ 100-m pull by a team

On January 27 2001, a team of 10
Royal Marine reserves (UK, above)
pulled a Boeing 737-300, weighing 81,500 lb (37 tonnes),
over a distance of 328 ft (100 m) in 43.2 seconds at
Manchester Airport, UK.

★ **Most plaster casts applied
in an hour by a team**
A team of 10 people applied
forearm plaster casts (one per
person) to 825 volunteers in
an hour at the main square of
Herentals, Belgium, on July 5
2003. The event was organized
to celebrate the 750th year of
Herentals Hospital.

★ **Most faces painted
in an hour by a team**
At an attempt organized
by Face2Face International
(UK), a team of five people
consisting of Susan Howard,
Rosemary Jones, Emma
Edworthy, Ann Ardern, and
Andrew Griffiths (all UK)
painted a total of 239 faces
in an hour, using a minimum
of three colors per face at
Crealy Park, Exeter, Devon,
UK, on August 1 2003.

★ **Longest daisy chain**
The longest daisy chain
measured 1.31 miles (2.12 km)
and was made in seven hours
by a team of 16 villagers from
Good Easter, Chelmsford,
Essex, UK, on May 27 1985.

★ **Fastest loaf
from field to oven**
On August 21 1999, a team led
by baker John Haynes and
farmer Peter Rix (both UK) at
Alpheton, Suffolk, UK, took
18 min 11.4 sec to produce 13
loaves from growing wheat.

★ **Most trees
planted in an hour**
A team of 96 people, including
schoolchildren from
St. Therese's School and other
volunteers (all UK) from Neath
Port Talbot, planted 4,100 trees
in one hour on April 8 2003.
The event was organized by
Neath Port Talbot County
Borough Council (UK) and was
held at Margam Country Park,
West Glamorgan, UK.

★ **Largest human mobile**
The largest human mobile
was made up of 24 people
from the Height Rescue Fire
Department Team, at Fire
station 33, Veddel, Hamburg,
Germany, on June 14 2003.
Suspended from a crane, the
lowest point of the mobile was
164 ft (50 m) off the ground.

★ **Most heads shaved
in an hour by a team**
A team of 10 hairdressers
shaved a total of 56 heads in
one hour at the Victoria Oval,
Dubbo, New South Wales,
Australia, in aid of the Cancer
Council's Relay for Life on
September 28 2002.

★ **Fastest time to pop
1,000 balloons**
A team of 37 participants (all
UK) popped 1,000 balloons
in 1 min 44 sec on the set
of *Blue Peter* at BBC Television
Centre, London, UK, on
November 7 2003.

★ **Largest can pyramid
built in 30 minutes**
On September 23 2000, the
Malaysia can team, consisting
of students from the INTI
College Subang Jaya, built a
pyramid created from 9,455
empty aluminum drink cans
in 24 minutes at the Midvalley
Mega Mall in Kuala Lumpur,

Malaysia. It had a square base
of 30 x 30 cans, measuring 6 ft
6 in x 6 ft 6 in (1.98 x 1.98 m).

★ **Farthest distance
traveled by a team on a
water slide in 24 hours**
Harald Bachmann, Markus
Ullmann, Jörg Hofmann,
Robert Bachmann, Franz
Walter, Werner Müller, Aaron-
Pfeffer, Dominik Radler, and
Stefan Wolf (all Germany) slid a
total distance of 420.652 miles
(676.974 km) together on a
334-ft (102-m) water slide in
24 hours in Kempten, Germany,
on July 12 and 13 2002.

★ **Longest reading-aloud
marathon by a team**
Phillipp Haag, Eduard Maier,
Martina Holdermann, Sabrina
Holzäpfel, Simone Jordan, and
Franziska Sobe (all Germany)
from Calmbach Secondary
School, Bad Wildbad, Germany,
read aloud for a record 75 hours
from July 16 to 19 2003.

« Heaviest aircraft pulled by an individual

David Huxley (Australia, left) pulled a Boeing 747-400 weighing 412,264 lb (187 tonnes) a distance of 298 ft 6 in (91 m) in 1 min 27.7 sec on October 15 1997 in Sydney, Australia.

Bed of nails concrete block break ∧

Chad Netherland (USA, above) had 21 concrete blocks weighing a total of 692 lb 10.8 oz (314.21 kg) placed on his chest and then broken with a 16-lb (7.25-kg) sledgehammer while he lay on a bed of nails at The Great Lakes Aquarium, Duluth, Minnesota, USA, on November 9 2003.

★ Heaviest aircraft pull by wheelchairs

A team of eight members of the Suffolk Braves Wheelchair Basketball Club (UK) pulled a Cessna 421 Eagle executive aircraft weighing 8,818 lb (4 tonnes) a distance of 1,640 ft (500 m) in 16 min 20 sec on December 9 1998 at Marshall Airport, Cambridge, UK.

★ Longest duration aircraft restraint

Using ropes looped around his arms, Ilkka Nummisto Finland) prevented the takeoff of two Cessna airplanes pulling in opposite directions for 54 seconds at Räyskälä Airport, Finland, on August 1 2001.

★ Fastest 50-m trailer pull

Juan Antonio Valdecantos Mayor (Spain) pulled a trailer weighing 1,554 lb (705 kg) a distance of 164 ft (50 m) in a time of 17.95 seconds at the studios of *El Show de los Récords*, Madrid, Spain, on November 22 2001.

★ Heaviest vehicle pulled by hair

The heaviest vehicle to have been pulled by the hair alone over a distance of 98 ft (30 m) is a double-deck bus weighing 17,359 lb (7,874 kg), by Letchemanah Ramasamy (Malaysia) at Bruntingthorpe Proving Ground, Leicestershire, UK, on May 1 1999.

★ Heaviest vehicle pulled by teeth

Walter Arfeuille (Belgium) used his teeth to pull eight railway passenger coaches with a total weight of 493,570 lb (223.8 tonnes) over a distance of 10 ft 5 in (3.2 m) along rails at Diksmuide, Belgium, on June 9 1996.

★ Heaviest train pulled by beard

Ismael Rivas Falcon (Spain) pulled a train weighing 6,069 lb (2,753.1 kg) over a distance of 32 ft 9.6 in (10 m) using only his beard at the studios of *El Show de los Récords*, Madrid, Spain, on November 15 2001.

★ Heaviest vehicle pulled over 100 ft

Kevin Fast (Canada) pulled a truck weighing 55,512 lb (25,180 kg) over a distance of 100 ft (30.48 m) along Queen Street, Cobourg, Ontario, Canada, on June 7 2003.

★ Heaviest ship pulled by teeth

Omar Hanapiev (Russia) pulled the 1,269,861-lb (576-tonne) tanker *Gunib* a distance of 49 ft 2.4 in (15 m) using a rope connected only to his teeth, on November 9 2001 at Makhachkala, Russia.

★ Heaviest boat pulled

David Huxley (Australia) pulled the *Delphin*, weighing in at 2,217,847 lb (1,006 tonnes), with a cargo of 175 cars plus passengers over a distance of 23 ft (7 m) on 19 November 1998 in Rostock, Germany.

★ Heaviest truck pulled by arm

The heaviest truck pulled with an arm-wrestling move weighed 7,185 lb 7 oz (3,259.3 kg). Oscar Olaria Paris and Mariano Macor Stopello (both Spain) set the record on *El Show de los Récords* in Madrid, Spain, on October 4 2001.

★ Heaviest human pyramid

Tahar Douis (Morocco) supported 12 members of the Hassani Troupe (three levels in height) with a total weight of 1,700 lb (771 kg) at the BBC television studios, Birmingham, UK, on December 7 1979.

★ Heaviest dead lift with the little finger

The heaviest dead lift with the little finger is 197 lb 8 oz (89.6 kg) by Barry Anderson (UK) on October 14 2000 at the Bass Museum, Burton-upon-Trent, Staffordshire, UK.

Greatest weight « balanced on teeth

Frank Simon (Hungary, left) lifted a 136-lb (61.8-kg) motorcycle above his head and balanced it on his teeth for 10 seconds on the set of *El Show de los Récords* in Madrid, Spain, on October 4 2001. He is pictured here demonstrating his skills with another bike at Red Rock Canyon, Nevada, USA.

★ **Greatest weight lifted by nipples**
Sage Werbock (USA) lifted a total weight of 48 lb 4.2 oz (21.9 kg) suspended from his pierced nipples for five seconds at the Tritone Bar in Philadelphia, Pennsylvania, USA, on May 20 2003.

★ **Greatest weight lifted by teeth**
Walter Arfeuille (Belgium) lifted weights totaling 620 lb 10 oz (281.5 kg) a distance of 6.75 in (17 cm) off the ground using only his teeth in Paris, France, on March 31 1990.

★ **Greatest weight balanced on the head**
The greatest weight ever balanced on the head and held for 10 seconds is 416 lb (188.7 kg), by John Evans (UK) who lifted 101 bricks at BBC Television Centre, London, UK, on December 24 1997.

★ **Most boat lifts**
Sami Heinonen and Juha Räsänen (both Sweden) continuously lifted a boat and 10 crew with a combined weight of 1,440 lb (653.2 kg) 4 in (10 cm) off the ground a total of 24 times on October 9 2000 on the set of *Guinness World Records*, at Studio Werne, Helsinki, Finland.

★ **Greatest weight of bricks lifted**
Fred Burton (UK) lifted a horizontal row of 20 bricks, weighing a total of 226 lb 7 oz (102.73 kg), and held them at chest height for two seconds on June 5 1998 at Cheadle, Staffordshire, UK.

★ **Most weight sustained on the body**
Eduardo Armallo Lasaga (Spain) lay beneath 3,086 lb (1,399.8 kg) of concrete blocks on the set of *El Show de los Récords*, Madrid, Spain, on October 18 2001.

★ **Greatest weight lifted by beard**
The heaviest weight lifted with a human beard is 135 lb (61.3 kg) when Antanas Kontrimas lifted Ruta Cekyte (both Lithuania) off the ground for 15 seconds on August 18 2001 at the VIII International Country Festival 2001, Visaginas, Lithuania.

★ **Longest four-finger hang**
Daniel Dulac (France) was hoisted up to a bar housing two fingerholds (as used in artificial climbing walls). Using just two fingers of each hand, he was suspended for 2 min 18.1 sec on the set of *L'Émission des Records*, Paris, France, on May 14 2002.

★ **Fastest time to bend an iron bar and fit it into a suitcase**
Firas Kichi (Spain) bent an iron bar 19 ft 7.2 in (6 m) long and with a diameter of 0.47 in (12 mm) a total of 16 times to fit it into a suitcase measuring 19.6 x 27.5 x 7.87 in (50 x 70 x 20 cm), all within 38.61 seconds on the set of *El Show de los Récords*, Madrid, Spain, on December 14 2001.

★ **Most telephone directories torn in three minutes**
Mike West (USA) ripped 30 telephone books, each containing 1,052 pages, from top to bottom, at Eclectics Training Center, New Albany, Indiana, USA, on December 14 2002.

★ **Longest duration lance lifting**
Raymond Janin (France) held a lance measuring 9 ft 2.16 in (2.8 m) long and weighing 6 lb 8.53 oz (3 kg) horizontally at shoulder height for 26 seconds on the set of *L'Été de Tous les Records*, Sete, France, on August 21 2003.

★ **Most flips of a 25-kg weight in a minute**
Johnny Lindström (Sweden) flipped over a 55-lb 1.54-oz (25-kg) weight with one hand a total of 24 times in a minute on the set of *Guinness World Rekords*, Stockholm, Sweden, on November 24 2001.

Staying power
Human beings

Longest guitar marathon by ⯆ an individual

Sanjeev Babu (India, below center) played a guitar for 24 hr 30 min from August 14 to 15 2003 at the YMCA Ground, Trivandrum, Kerala, India.

★ **Longest banjo marathon**
Doug Young (USA) played a banjo for 24 hr 57 sec at the Good/Bad Art Collective, Brooklyn, New York City, USA, on May 12–13 2001.

★ **Longest church organ marathon**
On June 20–21 2003, Roelof Hamberg (Netherlands) played a church organ for 32 hours at the Joris Church, St. Jorissant, Venlo, The Netherlands.

★ **Longest drumming marathon**
Allister Brown (UK) played the drums for 58 hr 17 min on September 8–10 2003 at the Lisburn School of Music, Lisburn, County Antrim, Northern Ireland.

★ **Longest percussion marathon**
Hermes Arango Saenz (Colombia) played nine different percussion instruments for 40 hours in Medellín, Colombia. The instruments played were: drum kit, kettledrums, congas,

bongos, guiro, dominican guiro, cumbiemberan maracas, salsa maracas, and bell. The marathon started at 6 am on August 2 2001 and finished at 10 pm on August 3 2001.

★ **Longest tuba marathon**
The longest tuba marathon by an individual lasted for 24 hr 8 min and was achieved by Rodney Kenny (UK), on August 16–17 2002 at The Salvation Army, Gosport, Hampshire, UK.

★ **Longest karaoke marathon featuring multiple participants**
Organized by Mark Pearson (UK), the karaoke marathon at the Keighley Festival, Keighley, West Yorkshire, UK, featured 85 different acts and continued for 80 hours from June 14 to 18 2003.

★ **Longest singing marathon by an individual**
A.C.E. Anderson (USA) sang continuously for 49 hr 30 min at Washington County Regional Park, Hurricane, Utah, USA, on June 27–29 2003.

★ **Longest club DJ marathon**
Club DJ Martin Boss (USA) performed a mixing session that lasted 74 hours at Vinyl Frontier in Orlando, Florida, USA, from February 1 to 4 2002.

★ **Longest radio DJ marathon**
DJ Christoph Stöckli's (Switzerland) broadcast on Radio Extra Bern, Bern, Switzerland, lasted for 105 hours. He began his marathon attempt at 6 am on July 24 and finally closed his program at 3 pm on July 28 2002.

★ **Longest joke-telling marathon**
Working on the basis that a joke must have a beginning, a middle, and an end, Mike Hessman (USA) told 12,682 jokes in 24 hours on November 16–17 1992.

★ **Longest dance party**
The 'Heart Health Hop,' a dance party marathon organized by St. Joseph® Aspirin, held at the Rock and Roll Hall of Fame

and Museum, Cleveland, Ohio, USA, began on July 29 2003 with 42 dancers, 41 of whom completed the marathon after 52 hr 3 min on July 31 2003.

★ **Longest ironing marathon**
Eufemia Stadler (Switzerland) ironed continuously for 40 hours while standing at an ironing board on September 16–18 1999. She ironed a total of 228 shirts.

★ **Longest rocking chair marathon**
Garry Hamilton (UK) rocked on a rocking chair continuously from August 24 to 26 1999 for 21 hours at the Hilton Hotel, Glasgow, UK.

★ **Longest card-playing marathon**
Gareth Birdsall, Simon MacBeth, Finn Clark, Gad Chadha, Sonia Zakrezewski, Tim West-Meads, Sebastian Kristensen, and David Gold played bridge for 72 hr 9 min at St. John's Wood Bridge Club, London, UK, from October 31 to November 3 2003.

Longest TV-watching ⌃ marathon

Nick Tungatt, Adam King, Steven Hayes (all UK, above from left to right), and Sam Beatson (UK) continually watched television screens for 47 hr 16 sec from December 4 to 6 2002, in an event sponsored by CNX at Covent Garden, London, and at The Printworks, Manchester, UK.

Most consecutive ⌃ Texas skips

Andrew Rotz (USA, above) achieved 11,123 consecutive Texas skips at the National Convention of the Wild West Arts Club in Las Vegas, Nevada, USA, on March 11 2003, smashing the previous record set at 4,011. The attempt took 3 hr 10 min to complete. A Texas skip is a vertical loop that is repeatedly pulled from one side of the body to the other. With each pass, the roper jumps through the center of the loop.

★ **Longest time spent on a bed of nails by a woman**
Geraldine Williams (UK, aka Miranda, Queen of the Fakirs) lay on a bed of sharp nails 6 in (15.2 cm) tall and 2 in (5 cm) apart for 30 hours on May 18–19 1977.

★ **Longest lecture marathon**
Errol E.T. Muzawazi (Zimbabwe) talked on the subject of democracy for 62 hr 30 min from December 12 to 15 2003 at a student residence at Politechnika Wroclawska, Wroclaw, Poland.

★ **Longest quizmaster marathon**
Quizmaster Gavin Dare (UK) asked a total of 3,668 questions continuously in 32 hr 15 min at The Goff's Oak Public House, Hertfordshire, UK, from October 25 to 26 2003.

★ **Farthest pool-rescue marathon**
The farthest pool-rescue distance is 63,320 ft (19,300 m) and was completed by the Wong Tai Sin District Life Saving Society at Morse Park Swimming Pool, Kowloon, Hong Kong, China, on August 31 2002. A total of 386 trained lifesavers towed a mannequin for a distance of 164 ft (50 m) each for 8 hr 27 min.

★ **Fastest backward-run marathon**
Timothy Bud Badyna (USA) ran a marathon backward in 3 hr 53 min 17 sec in Toledo, Ohio, USA, on April 24 1994.

★ **Longest parasailing marathon**
Berne Persoon (Sweden) parasailed for 24 hr 10 min on Lake Graningesjön, Sweden, on July 19–20 2002.

★ **Longest sustained ball control by a female**
Cláudia Martini (Brazil) juggled a regulation soccer ball for 7 hr 5 min 25 sec nonstop using her feet, legs, and head without the ball ever touching the ground in Caxias do Sul, Brazil, on July 12 1996.

★ **Longest skiing marathon**
Christian Flühr (Germany) skied nonstop for 168 hours at Tyrol, Westendorf, Austria, on March 8–15 2003. During that time he skied a combined distance of 4,101.06 miles (6,600.03 km) and a combined altitude of 2,972,559 ft (906,036 m).

★ **Longest duration for underwater kissing**
Antonio de la Rosa Suarez (Spain) was able to stay underwater at the bottom of a water-filled tank for 6 min 13.49 sec by being given air through kisses from Nerea Martinez Urruzola and Vanesa de la Rosa Suarez (both Spain), who took it in turns to swim down to him. The attempt was made at the studios of El Show de los Récords, Madrid, Spain, on November 22 2001.

★ **Longest spinning marathon**
The record for the longest spinning (static bicycling) marathon belongs to Jennifer Johnston (USA) who bicycled for 73 hr 13 min continuously at the National Fitness and Racquet Club, Klamath Falls, Oregon, USA, from November 8 to 11 2003.

Pushing the limits
Human beings

Greatest altitude ⌃ reached by helium- filled toy balloons

Ian Ashpole (UK, above) achieved the highest flight powered by toy helium balloons, reaching 11,000 ft (3,350 m) on October 28 2001 over Chatteris, Cambridgeshire, UK. Owing to the low air pressure at this altitude, some of the 600 balloons (each with a diameter of 3 ft or 90 cm) burst, forcing him to parachute to safety. Ian is shown here during a non-record-related stunt: he lies in a hammock suspended between hot-air balloons, then free-falls out of the hammock and parachutes to the ground.

★ Highest dry-air temperature endured
During US Air Force experiments held in 1960, the highest dry-air temperature endured by heavily clothed volunteers was measured at 500°F (260°C).

During the same tests, the highest dry-air temperature endured by naked volunteers was measured at 400°F (205°C).

Temperatures of 284°F (140°C) in saunas have been found quite bearable.

★ Longest time to remain standing motionless
Om Prakash Singh (India) stood motionless, except for involuntary blinking, for 20 hr 10 min 6 sec on August 13–14 1997. Om Prakash Singh started his attempt on the eve of the golden jubilee of India's independence as an homage to unknown martyrs.

★ Longest time spent balancing on one foot
Arulanantham Suresh Joachim (Sri Lanka) balanced on one foot for 76 hr 40 min at Uihara Maha Devi Park Open Air Stadium, Sri Lanka, from May 22 to 25 1997.

★ Longest time spent balancing on a tightrope
Jorge Ojeda-Guzman (USA) spent 205 days, from January 1 to July 25 1993, on a wire 36 ft (11 m) long and 35 ft (10.7 m) above ground.

During his time on the tightrope, he entertained crowds by walking, dancing, and balancing on a chair.

★ Farthest distance walked backward
The greatest exponent of reverse pedestrianism was Plennie L. Wingo (USA), who completed his 8,000-mile (12,875-km) transcontinental walk from Santa Monica, California, USA, to Istanbul, Turkey, from April 15 1931 to October 24 1932.

★ Longest fire walk
Gérard Moccetti (Switzerland) walked 165 ft 8 in (50.5 m) over embers with an average temperature of 1,230°F (665°C) at Scairedo, Barbengo, Ticino, Switzerland, on January 19 2003.

★ Longest time to endure full-body ice contact
Wearing only a pair of swimming trunks, Wim Hof (Netherlands) was able to stand in a tube filled with ice cubes for 1 hr 7 min, beating his previous record by 56 seconds at the studios of Guinness World Records: Die Grössten Weltrekorde on January 23 2004.

★ Longest time spent in a balloon
The Fédération Aéronautique Internationale (FAI) endurance record for a gas and hot-air balloon is 19 days 21 hr 47 min. It was set by Brian Jones (UK) and Bertrand Piccard (Switzerland) from March 1 to 21 1999, when they flew from Chateau d'Oex, Switzerland, and landed 300 miles (500 km) from Cairo, Egypt.

★ Greatest height to jump onto an air bag
On August 7 1997, Stig Günther (Denmark) jumped from a height of 342 ft (104.5 m) off a crane on to an air bag measuring 39 x 49 x 15 ft (12 x 15 x 4.5 m). His impact speed was about 90 mph (145 km/h).

★ Longest full-body burn (without oxygen)
Stig Günther (Denmark) endured a full-body burn without oxygen supplies for 2 min 6 sec in Copenhagen, Denmark, on March 13 1999.

Highest bungee ⌃ jump from a building

A.J. Hackett (New Zealand, above) leaped off the Sky Tower Casino, the highest building in Auckland, New Zealand, plunging 590 ft 10 in (180.1 m) on October 5 1998. His fall ended just 40 ft (12 m) above the concrete sidewalk before he rebounded.

Blindfold motorcycle speed record ⌄

Billy Baxter (UK, below left) reached a speed of 164.87 mph (265.33 km/h) while riding a 1200-cc Kawasaki Ninja motorcycle blindfolded at RAF Boscombe Down, Wiltshire, UK, on August 2 2003.

★ **Highest bungee jump by altitude**
Curtis Rivers (UK) performed a bungee jump from a hot-air balloon at 15,200 ft (4,632 m) over Puertollano, Spain, on May 5 2002.

★ **Highest bungee jump from a structure**
Chris Allum (New Zealand) jumped 823 ft 6 in (251 m) from the New River Gorge Bridge, West Virginia, USA, in 1992.

★ **Deepest freshwater cave scuba dive**
On August 23 1996, Nuno Gomes (South Africa) scuba-dived to a depth of 927 ft 2 in (282.6 m) at the Boesmansgat Cave in the Northern Cape province of South Africa. Essentially a very deep sinkhole, the cave at the surface resembles a small lake with vertical sides.

★ **Deepest seawater scuba dive**
The deepest scuba dive was one of 1,010 ft (307.8 m) made by John Bennett (UK)

on November 6 2001 off Escarcia Point, Puerto Galera, The Philippines. The descent, aided by a weighted sled, took just over 12 minutes, while the ascent took 9 hr 36 min to allow for decompression.

★ **Highest shallow dive**
Danny Higginbottom (USA) dived from 29 ft 2 in (8.9 m) into 12 in (30 cm) of water at the studios of *Guinness World Records: Die Grössten Weltrekorde* on January 23 2004.

★ **Longest scuba dive in open freshwater**
Jerry Hall (USA) spent 71 hr 39 min 40 sec underwater in South Holston Lake, Bristol, Tennessee, USA, using scuba gear from 6 to 9 August 2002.

★ **Longest scuba submergence using one air tank**
Mick Brown (UK) remained underwater for 7 hr 15 min 44 sec, breathing off a single standard 12-liter scuba tank, in a swimming pool at

Walton-on-the-Naze, Essex, UK, on 1 February 2003.

★ **Blindfold car speed record**
Mike Newman (UK) reached 144.755 mph (232.960 km/h) in a Jaguar XJR at Elvington Airfield, North Yorkshire, UK, on August 13 2003.

★ **Highest speed on a quad bike (ATV)**
Graham 'G-Force' Hicks, a deaf-blind daredevil from Peterborough, Cambridgeshire, UK, reached 104.02 mph (167.4 km/h) on a quad bike, or ATV (all-terrain vehicle), at Bruntingthorpe Proving Ground, Leicestershire, UK, on June 22 2002. He received instructions from his passenger Rob Hall, who told him where to steer via a system of touch-based commands.

★ **Longest time spent on 'Wall of Death'**
Martin Blume (Germany) spent 7 hr 13 sec on a 'Wall of Death' in Berlin, Germany, on April 16 1983. He rode a Yamaha XS 400

over 12,000 laps on a wall with a diameter of 33 ft (10 m), averaging 30 mph (48 km/h) over 181.5 miles (292 km).

★ **Longest time to keep an aircraft airborne**
Robert Timm and John Cooke (both USA) kept their Cessna 172 Hacienda aloft for 64 days 22 hr 19 min 5 sec, from December 4 1958 to February 7 1959. They took off from McCarran Airfield, Las Vegas, Nevada, USA, and landed at the same place after covering a distance equivalent to six times around the world, with refueling taking place in the air.

★ **Greatest distance flown in a wing suit**
Sky diver Adrian Nicholas (UK) flew 10 miles (16 km) in a wing suit over Yolo County, California, USA, on March 12 1999. He exited the plane at 33,850 ft (10,317 m) and reached speeds of approximately 150 mph (241 km/h). He 'flew' for 4 min 55 sec and only opened his parachute 500 ft (152 m) from the ground.

Against the odds
Human beings

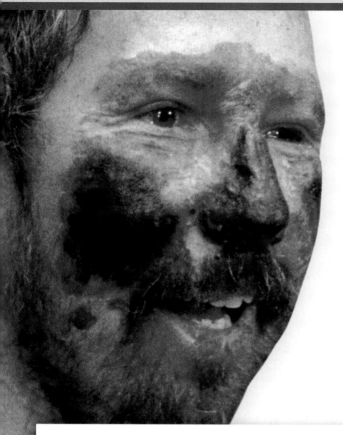

Highest fall survived ⌃ without a parachute

Vesna Vulovic (Yugoslavia, above) was 23 and working as a Jugoslavenski

Aerotransport hostess when the DC-9 she was working aboard blew up on January 26 1972. Vulovic survived a fall inside a section of tail unit from 33,333 ft (10,160 m) over Srbsk, Kamenice, Czechoslovakia (now Czech Republic), despite breaking many bones. She was in a coma for 27 days and remained in the hospital for 16 months. On the left is one of her rescuers, Zdenko Kubik.

Most deaths on ⌃ Mount Everest in one day

On May 10 1996, a blizzard with winds of up to 90 mph (145 km/h) and temperatures of -40°F (-40°C) claimed the lives of eight climbers on Mount Everest – the most in one day. Dr. Seaborn 'Beck' Weathers (USA, above) was trapped on the South Col of Mount Everest for 16 hours. He lost his right hand, part of his left hand, and his nose owing to frostbite.

★ Lowest body temperature survived
The lowest authenticated body temperature is 57.5°F (14.2°C), the rectal temperature for Karlee Kosolofski (Canada), then aged two, on February 23 1994. She had accidentally been locked outside her home for six hours in a temperature of -8°F (-22°C). Despite severe frostbite, which meant the amputation of her left leg above the knee, she made a full recovery.

★ Most operations endured
From July 22 1954 to the end of 1994, Charles Jensen (USA) had 970 operations to remove tumors associated with basal cell nevus syndrome.

★ Longest underwater submergence survival
In 1986, two-year-old Michelle Funk (USA) made a full recovery after spending 66 minutes underwater in a swollen creek.

★ Deepest underwater escape with no equipment
The greatest depth from which an underwater escape has been made without any equipment is 225 ft (68.6 m) by Richard A. Slater from the rammed submersible Nekton Beta off Catalina Island, California, USA, on September 28 1970.

★ Longest time trapped in an elevator
At the age of 76, Kively Papajohn (Cyprus) was trapped in her apartment block elevator for six days from December 28 1987 to January 2 1988. She survived the cold and beat dehydration by rationing out some fruit, vegetables, and bread that she had in her shopping bag.

★ Longest fall survived in an elevator
Betty Lou Oliver (USA) survived a plunge of 75 stories (over 1,000 ft or 300 m) in an elevator in the Empire State Building in New York City, USA, on July 28 1945, after an American B-25 bomber crashed into the building in thick fog, severing all the elevator's cables.

★ Highest fall survived down an elevator shaft
Stuart Jones (New Zealand) fell 23 stories (229 ft 7 in or 70 m) down an elevator shaft while carrying out structural work on the roof of a temporary elevator compartment at the Midland Park Building, Wellington, New Zealand, in May 1998. He suffered multiple injuries, including a broken hip, broken left kneecap, open fracture in his left lower leg, and broken rib.

★ Longest time adrift at sea
The longest known time that anyone has survived adrift at sea is approximately 484 days, by the Japanese Captain Oguri Jukichi and one of his sailors, Otokichi. Their ship was damaged in a storm off the Japanese coast in October 1813 and they drifted in the Pacific before being rescued by an American ship off California, USA, on March 24 1815.

★ Longest time adrift at sea alone
The longest recorded survival alone on a raft is 133 days by Second Steward Poon Lim (Hong Kong) of the UK Merchant Navy, whose ship, the SS Ben Lomond, was torpedoed in the Atlantic 565 miles (910 km) west of St. Paul's Rocks at 11:45 am on November 23 1942.

He was finally picked up by a Brazilian fishing boat off Salinópolis, Brazil, on April 5 1943 and was able to walk ashore.

Longest post-earthquake survival by a cat

On September 21 1999, an earthquake struck Taiwan, killing an estimated 2,400 people. Eighty days later in December 1999, a cat (right) was discovered alive in Taichung after being trapped by a message board that had fallen during the quake, pinning it to the ground in the rubble of a collapsed building. The cat, dehydrated and barely breathing, weighed less than half the weight of a healthy cat of its size. It was rushed to a veterinary hospital where it made a full recovery.

★ **Longest survival without food and water**
The longest recorded case of survival without food and water is 18 days by Andreas Mihavecz (Austria), then aged 18. He was put into a holding cell on April 1 1979 in a local government building in Höchst, Austria, but totally forgotten by the police. On April 18 1979, he was discovered close to death.

★ **Longest survival with heart outside body**
Christopher Wall (USA, b. August 19 1975) is the longest known survivor of the condition ectopia cordis, in which the heart lies outside the body at birth. The mortality rate is high, with most patients not living beyond 48 hours, but Wall still lives with the condition.

★ **Longest time survived without a pulse**
The longest time a human has survived without a pulse in their vascular system is three days. Julie Mills (UK) was at the point of death from severe heart failure and viral myocarditis when, on August 14 1998, cardiac surgeons at the John Radcliffe Hospital, Oxford, UK, used a nonpulsatile blood pump (AB180) to support her for one week. Her heart recovered in this time and the pump was removed.

★ **Greatest ever lifesaving operation at sea**
The greatest ever rescue at sea was that of 2,735 people from the American aircraft carrier *CV-2 USS Lexington* on May 8 1942 after it had been sunk between Australia and New Caledonia in the Battle of the Coral Sea.

★ **Greatest rescue at sea without loss of life**
All 2,689 people on board the American vessel *Susan B. Anthony* survived when it was sunk off Normandy, France, on June 7 1944.

★ **Largest object removed from human skull**
The largest object removed from a human skull is a 8-in (20-cm) survival knife with a serrated blade, which was plunged into the head of 41-year-old Michael Hill (USA) on April 25 1998. Michael survived the operation and the next day astonished doctors by being able to speak and function normally, although the years to come proved that the knife had permanently damaged his memory and paralyzed his left hand.

★ **Most hangings survived**
There is a tie for this record. The survivor of the most legal hanging attempts is Joseph Samuel (Australia), a 22-year-old who was sentenced to death for murder in Sydney, Australia. On September 26 1803, the first attempt at execution failed when the rope broke. The second attempt failed when the rope stretched so much that the victim's feet touched the ground. At the third attempt, the second replacement rope broke, after which Samuel was reprieved.

In Exeter, Devon, UK, in 1885, John Lee (UK) also survived three attempted hangings. On each occasion that his hanging was due to take place, the trapdoor failed to open.

★ **Longest surviving headless chicken**
On September 10 1945, a Wyandotte chicken named Mike had its head chopped off but went on to survive for 18 months. Mike's owner, Lloyd Olsen (USA), fed and watered the headless chicken directly into his gullet with an eyedropper. Mike eventually choked to death on a corn kernel in an Arizona motel.

★ **Longest survival of a sheep in a snowdrift**
On March 24 1978, Alex Maclennan (UK) found one ewe still alive after he had dug out 16 dead sheep buried in a snowdrift for 50 days near the River Skinsdale on Mrs. Tyser's Gordonbush Estate in Sutherland, Highland, UK, after the great January blizzard in that year. The sheep's hot breath had created airholes in the snow, and the animal had gnawed its own wool for protein.

Longest motorcycle ⌄ ride by a team

Chris and Erin Ratay (both USA, below) covered 101,322 miles (163,061 km) on separate motorcycles on a journey that covered 50 countries on six continents. They departed from Morocco on May 21 1999 and returned home to New York City, USA, on August 6 2003.

Fastest circumnavigation by male sailing solo ⌃

Francis Joyon (France, above) carried out a solo nonstop circumnavigation in the 88-ft 6-in (27-m) trimaran *IDEC* in a time of 72 days 22 hr 54 min 22 sec, from November 22 2003 to February 3 2004.

★ GWR TALKS TO
Sir Ranulph Fiennes

Explorer Sir Ranulph Fiennes (UK, above) currently holds four Guinness World Records: the first pole-to-pole circumnavigation, the longest self-supporting trek (1,350 miles or 2,170 km during a 94-day trek with fellow Briton Michael Stroud), which was also the longest unsupported Antarctic trek, and the fastest Antarctic crossing. The last record comprised the 2,600-mile (4,185-km) transantarctic leg of the 1980–82 Trans-Globe Expedition from Sanae to Scott Base, and was achieved in 55 days, from October 28 1980 to January 11 1981. The expedition reached the South Pole on December 15 1980. For this record-breaking attempt, Sir Ranulph was accompanied by Oliver Shepard and Charles Burton (both UK).

How did you come to be an explorer?
I spent eight years in the army and led a number of adventure training journeys. When I left the army in 1970 I extended these activities to make a career out of expedition organizing and leading: the expeditions became a way of life.

What drives you to take on these great challenges?
To keep at 'the top of the tree' internationally in expedition work it was, through the 70s, 80s and 90s, necessary to attempt the biggest available geographical challenges and succeed, where possible, before my rivals.

What do you consider to be your greatest achievement to date?
If pressed to name which of the expeditions over a 32-year period I am most proud of, I would find it very difficult to be specific. I'd say it was the discovery of the lost city of Ubar. It took me a period of 26 years on and off, and some seven separate expeditions between 1968 and 1991, before I finally discovered the site in the oasis of Shis'r in Dhofar, Oman.

What other challenges do you wish to take on in the future?
There are various challenges in the pipeline but the rule of our expedition group is to discuss them as little as possible to avoid others getting there first.

How do you prepare for some of these expeditions/challenges?
Our group has usually prepared for expeditions with meticulous care and by choosing the best available team, equipment, and advisors. This includes physical fitness and nutrition experts. Fitness regimes and special diets alter according to the nature of each challenge.

What does it mean to you to have a Guinness World Record?
Many sponsors, without whom our projects would be impossible, respect the internationally accepted judgment of Guinness World Records as to what does or does not constitute a world record. Also the ability to cite Guinness World Records we've previously achieved always helps when requesting sponsorship.

What advice would you offer anyone seeking a similar career?
I usually recommend joining the Royal Geographical Society and taking advantage of its unique Expedition Advisory Centre, the nerve centre of 90% of all ongoing UK expedition work.

Who inspired you as a child?
As a child in South Africa, I was inspired by stories about my father (killed in World War II, four months before I was born) and about his father, both of whom led adventurous lives in often remote regions. Later on I was inspired by the desert travels of Wilfred Thesiger and the polar travels of Wally Herbert.

Fastest time to visit ⌃ all NFL stadiums

Peter Baroody (USA, above) watched a complete National Football League (NFL) game at all 31 NFL stadiums in the USA in just 107 days, from September 5 to December 22 2002. He began in New York City and finished in Kansas City.

32 Games
31 Stadiums
17 Weeks
30,000 Miles

★ **Longest lifeboat journey**
When his ship, the *Endurance*, became trapped in Antarctic sea-ice, Sir Ernest Shackleton (UK) and his 28-strong crew had to abandon her. Their three lifeboats set course for Elephant Island, 100 miles (161 km) to the north. Once there, and knowing that rescue was unlikely, Shackleton selected five of his best men to sail the largest lifeboat, the 22-ft 6-in-long (6.85-m) *James Caird*, towards a whaling station in South Georgia, 800 miles (1,287 km) away. In a journey that is still regarded as one of the greatest rescue journeys of all time, Sir Ernest and his men reached the island after 17 days, on May 19 1916.

★ **Longest nonstop ocean voyage by raft**
During the Raft Transpacific Expedition, the raft *Nord*, captained by Andrew Urbanczyk (USA), sailed from Half Moon Bay, California, USA, to the US-owned Pacific island of Guam, a straight-line distance of 5,110 nautical miles (5,880 miles or 9,463 km), in 136 days from August 26 2002 to January 28 2003.

★ **Fastest circumnavigation by a crewed sailing vessel**
Millionaire adventurer Steve Fossett (USA) and a crew of 13 sailed around the world nonstop in 58 days 9 hr 32 min aboard the 125-ft (38-m) catamaran *Cheyenne*, from February 7 to April 5 2004. The voyage started and finished at Le Stiff Lighthouse, Ushant, France.

★ **Longest motorcycle ride**
Emilio Scotto (Argentina) covered over 457,000 miles (735,000 km) through 214 countries and territories on a motorcycle from January 17 1985 to April 2 1995.

★ **Fastest solo unsupported trek to the South Pole**
Fiona Thornewill (UK) walked and skied her way to the South Pole from Hercules Inlet at the edge of the Antarctic continent in 42 days from November 30 2003 to January 10 2004. She was pulling a 285-lb (130-kg) sled containing all her supplies and equipment, yet still managed to cover up to 22 miles (35 km) per day.

★ **Most sovereign countries visited in six months**
John Bougen and James Irving (both New Zealand) visited 191 of the world's 193 sovereign countries in 167 days 15 hr 39 min from August 28 2002 to February 12 2003. Their journey, called the All Nations Quest, was in support of the Save the Children charity.

★ **Fastest time to travel the Pan-American Highway by bicycle**
Giampietro Marion (Italy) bicycled the Pan-American Highway, from Prudhoe Bay, Alaska, to Ushuaia, Argentina, in 140 days 6 hr, from June 28 2000 to November 15 2000.

★ **Fastest circumnavigation by car**
The record for the fastest circumnavigation by car (under the rules applicable in 1989 and 1991) embracing more than an equator's length of driving (24,901 road miles or 40,750 km) was by Mohammed and Neena Choudhury (India). The journey took 69 days 19 hr 5 min from September 9 to November 17 1989.

★ **Greatest distance covered in 24 hours by wheelchair**
Rafael Emilio de León Lebrón (Dominican Republic) wheeled himself over 112.5 miles (181.147 km) in 24 hours on December 13–14 2001 at the Juan Pablo Duarte Centro Olímpico, Santo Domingo de Guzmán, Dominican Republic.

★ **Longest journey by wheelchair**
Rick Hansen, paralyzed from the waist down in 1973 as a result of a motor accident, wheeled his wheelchair 24,901.55 miles (40,075.16 km) through four continents and 34 countries. He started his journey from Vancouver, British Columbia, Canada, on March 21 1985 and arrived back there on May 22 1987.

Natural world

Contents

The universe
The natural world

Nearest « extrasolar planet

On August 7 2000, a team led by Dr. William Cochran (USA) of the University of Texas McDonald Observatory announced its discovery of the nearest planet outside the Solar System. The planet, which is probably slightly larger than Jupiter, orbits the star Epsilon Eridani (an artist's impression of the planet is shown left). This star, only 10.5 light-years away, is one of the closest stars to the Sun.

★ Brightest nebula
The Orion Nebula (M42 or Messier 42 – i.e. number 42 in Charles Messier's 1781 catalog of nebulous objects) is the brightest nebula in the sky with an apparent magnitude of 4. Located in the 'sword' of the constellation Orion, only the brightest central part of this vast, diffuse cloud of gas and dust is easily visible to the naked eye.

★ Brightest supernova remnant
The Crab Nebula (M1) in the constellation of Taurus is the brightest supernova remnant in the sky, with a magnitude of 8.4. It is around 6,300 light-years distant. One light-year is the distance light travels in a year, about 6 trillion miles (9.5 trillion km).

★ Deepest note in the universe
The deepest note in the universe is caused by acoustic waves generated by a supermassive black hole in the center of the Perseus cluster of galaxies, 250 million light-years away. The sound, which propagates through the extremely thin gas surrounding the black hole, is a B-flat, 57 octaves below middle C. This is more than a million billion times lower than a human ear can detect. The sound waves are estimated to have been consistently produced by the black hole for around 2.5 billion years. They were discovered using observations by the Chandra X-Ray Observatory, by astronomers led by Professor Andrew Fabian, Cambridge University, Cambridge, UK.

★ Biggest globular cluster in the Milky Way
Omega Centauri, in the constellation of Centaurus, is the most massive of the roughly 140 globular clusters surrounding our galaxy. Consisting of several million stars whose combined mass equates to five million Suns, it is just visible to the naked eye. It is about 10 times more massive than the other large globular clusters and some astronomers have suggested that it is the remnants of the nucleus of another galaxy which merged with ours billions of years ago.

★ Coldest place in the Milky Way
The Boomerang Nebula, a cloud of dust and gases 5,000 light-years from Earth, has a temperature of -457.6°F (-272°C). It is formed by the rapid expansion of gas and dust flowing from its central star.

★ Nearest globular cluster
The nearest globular cluster to the Earth is M4. It is located in the constellation of Scorpius at a distance of around 5,600 light-years and is visible through binoculars and small telescopes as a fuzzy smudge.

★ Most distant object in the universe
Astronomers from Caltech (USA), using the Hubble Space Telescope and the Keck Observatory, have discovered a small and compact system of stars about 2,000 light-years across, with a redshift of 7. This corresponds to a distance of about 13 billion light-years away. These results were announced in February 2004.

★ Most distant planet with an atmosphere
On November 27 2001, astronomers using the Hubble Space Telescope announced the discovery of an atmosphere on a planet orbiting another star. This unnamed planet orbits the star HD209458, 150 light-years away. It was discovered in 1999 thanks to the wobble its gravity inflicts upon HD209458 as it orbits it.

★ Most massive extrasolar planet
Announced in January 2001, the discovery of the planet HD168443 orbiting a star 123 light-years away challenges conventional definitions of planets. Jupiter, the largest planet in our Solar System, weighs more than all the other planets and moons combined. But HD168443 is 17 times more massive even than Jupiter.

Flattest star »

The least spherical star in our galaxy studied to date is the southern star Achenar (Alpha Eridani, right).

Observations made from September 11 to November 12 2002 using the Very Large Telescope (VLT) Interferometer at the European Southern Observatory's Paranal Observatory, in Atacama, Chile, have revealed that Achenar is spinning so rapidly that its equatorial diameter is more than 50% greater than its polar diameter. The results were released on June 11 2003.

« Greatest explosion ever

Most astronomers now believe that the universe began around 13.7 billion years ago in a cataclysmic explosion called the Big Bang (shown left in an artist's impression). All the matter and energy in the universe had its origins in this event, along with time itself. One second after the Big Bang, the temperature was around ten billion degrees, or about six hundred times hotter than the interior of the Sun.

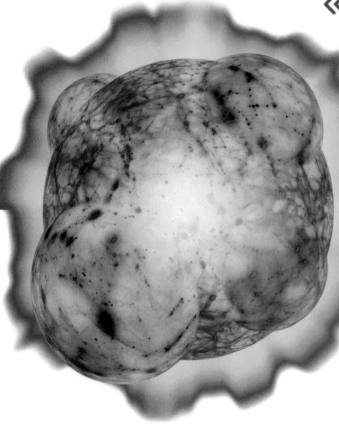

★ Most massive star visible to the naked eye

Eta Carinae is a rare supergiant some 9,000 light-years from Earth. With a mass estimated at between 100 and 200 times that of the Sun, it is one of the most massive stars in the galaxy. It is just visible to the naked eye with a magnitude of 6.21.

★ Oldest planet in the Milky Way

The oldest planet discovered so far in our galaxy is an extrasolar planet in the globular cluster M4, some 5,600 light-years from Earth.

With an estimated age of at least 10 billion years, this distant planet is more than twice as old as our Solar System. Its discovery was announced in July 2003.

★ Oldest star in the Milky Way

The oldest star identified to date in the Milky Way galaxy is HE0107-5240, a giant star around 36,000 light-years from Earth. Its age is measured by its composition: when the universe formed, it consisted of hydrogen with some helium. As it evolved, the rest of the chemical elements appeared, formed by nuclear synthesis in stars. HE0107-5240 has almost no metal content in it, meaning it must have formed from clouds of gas consisting of almost pure hydrogen and helium when the universe was young. It could date back to the very beginning of the universe.

★ Most luminous star in the galaxy

The latest observations of LBV1806-20, a star 45,000 light-years from Earth, indicate it is between five and 40 million times more luminous than the Sun. It has a mass of at least 150 times that of the Sun and has a diameter at least 200 times greater.

★ Farthest object visible to the naked eye

The most remote heavenly body visible to the naked eye is the Andromeda Galaxy in the constellation of Andromeda (M31, magnitude 3.47), a spiral galaxy 2.2 million light-years away. Under good observation conditions the spiral galaxy in Triangulum, (M33, magnitude 5.79) can be seen by the naked eye at a distance of 2.53 million light-years.

★ Largest galaxy

The central galaxy of the Abell 2029 galaxy cluster, 1.070 billion light-years distant in Virgo, has a major diameter of 5.6 million light-years – 80 times the diameter of our own Milky Way galaxy – and a light output equivalent to two trillion (2×10^{12}) Suns.

★ Closest planet to a star

A Jupiter-sized gas giant orbits the star OGLE-TR-3. This 'hot Jupiter' orbits just 2.1 million miles (3.5 million km) from its parent star and has an orbital period of just 28 hr 33 min. OGLE-TR-3 is a G-type star (similar to the Sun) some 4,900 light-years away. The planet was discovered using the Optical Gravitational Lensing Experiment, and announced in April 2003.

The Solar System
The natural world

Largest recorded ⌄ solar flare

On November 4 2003, the Sun unleashed a solar flare rated as an X28 event by the Space Environment Center of the National Oceanic and Atmospheric Administration (NOAA) in Boulder, Colorado, USA. Considered a major event, X-class flares are the most powerful and can cause planet-wide radio disruption. Images of solar flares (left) and other phenomena are captured daily by the Extreme ultraviolet Imaging Telescope (EIT) on board the SOHO spacecraft.

Largest cyclone ⌃ in the Solar System

The Great Red Spot (above) on the planet Jupiter is the largest cyclone in the Solar System. It varies in size but can be up to 24,800 miles (40,000 km) long and 8,700 miles (14,000 km) wide.

★ Fastest winds in the Solar System
The planet Neptune has the fastest winds anywhere in the Solar System. Measured by NASA's *Voyager 2* probe in 1989, they blow at around 1,500 mph (2,400 km/h).

★ Most distant object in the Solar System
The minor planet 1999DG8 was discovered by a team of astronomers led by Brett Gladman (Canada) from the Canadian Institute of Theoretical Physics, using the 11.81-ft (3.6-m) Canada-France-Hawaii Telescope (USA) in February 1999. With a diameter of around 62 miles (100 km), this icy body was around 5.6 billion miles (9 billion km) from the Sun when it was observed on two different nights. Because its orbit has yet to be properly calculated, 1999DG8 could follow a path which takes it closer to or further from the Sun.

★ Hottest place in the Solar System
Although never visited by man, the very center of the Sun is the hottest place in the Solar System. The latest estimates of the temperature are 15.6 billion°C (60 billion°F). The pressure in the core is also immense, around 250 billion times the pressure at sea level on Earth. It is here that around 600 million tonnes of hydrogen are fused into helium every second. This ongoing nuclear reaction is what makes the Sun shine.

★ Closest moon to a planet
Of all the moons in the Solar System, the one that orbits closest to its planet is the tiny Martian satellite Phobos. Phobos is 5,827 miles (9,378 km) from the center of Mars, which is 3,716 miles (5,981 km) above the Martian surface. Using the surface-to-surface measurement, Phobos is roughly 60 times closer to Mars than the Moon is to Earth.

★ Largest corona
Coronae (roughly circular features surrounded by multiple concentric ridges) are so far unique to the planet Venus. They were discovered by the US *Magellan* spacecraft, which orbited the planet for just over four years from August 10 1990 to October 11 1994. The largest is Artemis Corona, which has a diameter of 1,300 miles (2,100 km). Planetary scientists are in disagreement as to the origin of coronae, but it seems likely that they are the result of hot magma welling up from the Venusian mantle.

★ Largest canyon in the Solar System
The Valles Marineris canyon on the planet Mars has an overall length of around 4,500 km (2,800 miles). At its widest it is 600 km (370 miles) across and is also up to 7 km (4.3 miles) deep. It is named after the *Mariner 9* spacecraft, which discovered it in 1971.

★ Satellite with the thickest atmosphere
Saturn's large moon Titan has the thickest atmosphere of any moon in the Solar System, and exerts a surface pressure of 1.44 bar. Consisting mainly of nitrogen gas, Titan's atmosphere is the most similar to our own in the Solar System.

Most volcanically >> active body

Photographs of Jupiter's moon Io (right), taken from the *Galileo* spacecraft, revealed enormous volcanic eruption plumes reaching hundreds of miles into space. Io's activity is driven by tidal energy – the result of gravitational interactions between Jupiter, Io and one of the other moons, Europa. Io is so active that it has turned itself inside out during its lifetime.

⌃ Highest mountain in the Solar System

The peak of Olympus Mons (above) on Mars rises 15 miles (25 km) above
its base – nearly three times the height of Mt. Everest. Despite its great height, Olympus Mons has a very gentle slope and is therefore designated a shield volcano: it is over 20 times wider than it is high.

★ **Largest observed coma**
The coma (the cloud around the nucleus in the head of a comet) on a comet seen in 1811 was thought to be around 1.2 million miles (2 million km) in diameter.

★ **Highest volcanic eruption**
On August 6 2001, NASA's *Galileo* spacecraft performed a close flyby of Jupiter's volcanically active satellite, Io. Over the following months, as the data was transmitted back to Earth, scientists realised that the spacecraft had passed through the top of a 310-mile (500-km) high volcanic plume. This is the highest volcanic eruption plume ever witnessed in the Solar System.

★ **Most distant moon from a planet**
Announced by the International Astronomical Union on September 3 2003, S/2003 N1 orbits Neptune at an average distance of approximately 31 million miles (49.5 million km). It has an orbital period of approximately 26 years and measures around 24 miles (38 km) across.

★ **Fastest planet**
Mercury, which orbits the Sun at an average distance of 35.9 million miles (57.9 million km), has an orbital period of 87.9686 days, thus giving the highest average speed in orbit of 107,030 mph (172,248 km/h). This is almost twice as fast as the Earth.

★ **Largest planet**
Jupiter has an equatorial diameter of 89,405 miles (143,884 km) and a polar diameter of 83,082 miles (133,708 km). It has a mass 317.828 times – and a volume 1,323.3 times – that of the Earth.

★ **Smallest planet**
The discovery of Pluto by Clyde William Tombaugh (USA) of the Lowell Observatory, Flagstaff, Arizona, USA, was announced on March 13 1930. The planet has a diameter of 1,444 miles (2,324 km) and a mass 0.0022 that of the Earth.

★ **Largest moon compared to its planet**
Charon, the only known satellite of Pluto, has a diameter of 790 miles (1,270 km). Pluto itself is only 1,444 miles (2,324 km) across. The Pluto-Charon System is regarded by some as a 'double planet'.

★ **Hottest planet**
Venus has an average temperature of around 896°F (480°C). This scorching heat is hot enough to melt lead and, coupled with the atrocious atmosphere, makes exploration of the surface by probes very difficult. If you were to step onto the surface of Venus you would be simultaneously crushed by the pressure, incinerated by the heat, dissolved by the sulfuric acid, and suffocated by the carbon dioxide.

★ **Planet with the longest day**
While the Earth takes 23 hr 56 min 4 sec to complete one rotation, Venus takes 243.16 'Earth days' to spin once through 360°. As Venus is closer to the Sun, its year is shorter than Earth's, lasting only 224.7 days, so a day on Venus is actually longer than its year. Another Venusian curiosity is that it rotates backwards compared with all of the other major planets (apart from Uranus, which spins on its side).

★ **Planet with the shortest day**
Jupiter spins around on its axis once every 9 hr 55 min 29.69 sec.

★ **Most powerful aurorae in the Solar System**
The aurorae on Jupiter are around 1,000 times more powerful than the aurorae seen on Earth. Jupiter's aurorae are caused by energetic particles from the Sun being channeled onto the planet's poles by Jupiter's magnetic field and causing atoms in its upper atmosphere to glow like the gas in a neon tube. This process produces around a million megawatts of energy, enough to power 100 major cities on Earth.

Greatest snowfall in 12 months

Over a 12-month period from February 19 1971 to February 18 1972, 102 ft 0.5 in (31,102 mm) of snow fell at Paradise, Mt. Rainier, Washington, USA. ⌄

⌃ Most powerful short-term natural climate change

The El Niño Southern Oscillation occurs as a result of cyclic warming of the eastern and central Pacific Ocean. Apart from the seasonal effects of the Earth moving around the Sun, it is the most powerful short-term natural climate change on Earth. The entire cycle of El Niño and La Niña (its cooler counterpart and opposite) lasts between three and seven years. It causes unusual weather conditions all around the world, particularly notable in the 1982/83 and 1997/98 events.

★ GWR TALKS TO
Professor Joshua Wurman

Professor Joshua Wurman (USA, above), a professional 'storm chaser', runs the Center for Severe Weather Research in Boulder, Colorado, USA. He operated the University of Oklahoma's 'Doppler on Wheels' mobile weather observatory when it measured the highest winds ever, during theBridgecreek/Moore/Oklahoma City tornado that caused F5 damage and nearly 40 deaths. The wind speed on this occasion was between 281 and 321 mph (452–516 km/h).

How long have you been a storm chaser?
Professionally, since 1995; for recreation, since 1992.

What was it that inspired you to do this as a career?
Interest in nature combined with the excitement of a young science that had big questions to be answered.

How close do you get to tornadoes?
We have been hit by weak tornadoes, but we usually stay 1–3 miles (1.6–4.4 km) away from the centers.

What is your favorite part of the job?
Discovering new things. Observational scientists like myself are the inheritors of the tradition of exploration. In the future we may explore space further. But for now, the reachable unknowns are inside tornadoes

and hurricanes, and in deep sea trenches, et cetera.

What has been the scariest moment in your career?
It sounds boring, but we actually are very, very safe. We are constantly tracking the course of the tornado and plotting escape routes if necessary.

What does it mean to you to have a Guinness World Record?
Since I was a very small child, I read the Guinness book every year and memorized a lot of it. As an adult, to finally have a record in the book is great.

What advice would you give to anyone following in your footsteps?
Stay curious... and be very determined.

★ Greatest depth of snow
In March 1911, the snow on the ground at Tamarac, California, USA, was recorded as 37 ft 7 in (11.46 m) deep.

★ Most destructive geomagnetic storm
The most destructive geomagnetic storm ever recorded was the 'Great Geomagnetic Storm' of March 13 1989, which was classified G5 (the most severe) on the space weather scale. The result of an abnormally strong solar wind, it caused major disruption to the power grid all over North America and changed the orbit of a satellite. The solar wind is a stream of particles radiating from the Sun into the Solar System, and it is this phenomenon that is responsible for the northern and southern lights (aurora borealis, aurora australis).

Most tornadoes ⌃ in 24 hours

The record number of tornadoes in a 24-hour period is 148. They swept through the southern and mid-western states of the USA on April 3–4 1974. This region of America is often referred to as 'Tornado Alley'.

★ Lowest temperature in an inhabited area

The coldest permanently inhabited place in the world is the Siberian village of Oymyakon (pop. 4,000), 63°16'N, 143°15'E (2,300 ft), in Russia, where the temperature reached -68°C (-90°F) in 1933. An unofficial -72°C (-98°F) has been published more recently.

★ Lowest temperature on Earth

A low of -128.6°F (-89.2°C) was registered at Vostok, Antarctica (altitude 11,220 ft), on July 21 1983.

★ Clouds with the greatest vertical range

The cloud form with the greatest vertical range is cumulonimbus, which has been observed to reach a height of nearly 65,600 ft (20,000 m) in the tropics – that's nearly three times the height of Mt. Everest.

★ Longest lightning flash

At any time, around 100 lightning bolts per second hit the Earth. Typically, the actual length of these bolts can be around 5.5 miles (9 km). In 1956 meteorologist Myron Ligda (USA) observed and recorded a lightning flash, using radar, that covered a horizontal distance of 93 miles (149 km) inside clouds.

★ Greatest pressure drop measured in a tornado

The greatest pressure drop ever measured inside a tornado was 100 millibars. It was recorded by severe storms researcher Tim Samaras (USA), who was able to successfully place an instrument probe in the path of an F4 tornado, near Manchester, South Dakota, USA, on June 24 2003.

★ Driest place

For the period between 1964 and 2001, the average annual rainfall for the meteorological station in Quillagua, located in the Atacama Desert, Chile, was just 0.02 in (0.5 mm). This fascinating discovery was made during the making of the documentary series *Going to Extremes*, by Keo Films in 2001.

★ Largest hole in the ozone layer

Scientists at NASA's Goddard Space Flight Center, Maryland, USA, detected the largest hole so far seen in the ozone layer in September 2000. With an area of around 11 million miles^2 (28.3 million km^2), this hole above Antarctica is roughly three times the area of the USA. The ozone layer in the stratosphere (about 7–28 miles above the ground) shields the Earth's surface from the Sun's damaging ultraviolet (UV-B) rays.

★ Greatest display of solar halos

On January 11 1999, at least 24 types of solar halo were witnessed by scientists at the geographic South Pole. Solar halos are formed by sunlight being reflected and refracted by ice crystals in the atmosphere, causing rings around the Sun. Atmospheric conditions at the South Pole are conducive to this type of phenomenon.

★ Oldest fossilized raindrops

On December 15 2001, Indian geologist Chirananda De announced his discovery of the fossilized imprints of raindrops in ancient rocks in the lower Vindhya Range, Madhya Pradesh, India. These fossils prove that rain fell on Earth at least 1.6 billion years ago.

★ Greatest annual rainfall

By average annual rainfall, the world's wettest place is Mawsynram, Meghalaya, India, with 4,678 in (11,873 mm) of rain per annum.

The Earth
Natural world

Largest land gorge ⌃⌃

The largest land gorge in the world is the Grand Canyon (above) on the Colorado River in north-central Arizona, USA. It extends from Marble Gorge to the Grand Wash Cliffs, over a distance of 277 miles (446 km). It averages 10 miles (16 km) in width and 1 mile (1.6 km) in depth.

Highest natural arch ⌃⌃

The red sandstone Rainbow Bridge (above) on Lake Powell National Monument, Utah, USA, is the highest natural arch in the world. It is only 270 ft (82.3 m) long, but is a massive feature, rising to a height of 290 ft (88.4 m). The Rainbow Bridge was formed when an ancient stream eroded away some of the weaker sedimentary rock in the area, leaving the natural bridge behind.

★ **Coolest erupting lava**
The natrocarbonatite lava of the volcano Oldoinyo Lengai, Tanzania, erupts at temperatures of 930–1,110°F (500–600°C). Common basaltic lavas erupt at temperatures between 2,010 and 2,190°F (1,100 and 1,200°C).

★ **Tallest sea stack**
Ball's Pyramid near Lord Howe Island (Australia) in the Pacific Ocean is 1,843 ft (561 m) high but has a base axis of only 660 ft (200 m).

★ **Largest active volcano**
Mauna Loa, Hawaii, USA, is the largest active volcano. It has the shape of a broad gentle dome 75 miles (120 km) long and 31 miles (50 km) wide (above sea level), with lava flows that occupy more than 1,980 miles^2 (5,125 km^2) of the island. It has a total volume of 10,200 miles^3 (42,500 km^3), of which 84.2% is below sea level.

★ **Largest geode**
A geode is a rock cavity filled with minerals – most are small enough to fit in the palm of a human hand. The largest geode discovered to date is near Almería, Spain. It forms a mineral-lined cave 26 ft (8 m) long, 6 ft (2 m) wide and 6 ft (2 m) high, and is around six million years old.

★ **Deepest valley**
The Yarlung Zangbo valley, in Tibet, has an average depth of 16,400 ft (5,000 m). In 1994 explorers discovered that its deepest point was 17,657 ft (5,382 m). The peaks either side of the valley – Namche Barwa (25,436 ft) and Jala Peri (23,891 ft) – are just 13 miles (21 km) apart with the Yarlung Zangbo river flowing between them at an elevation of 8,000 ft (2,440 m).

★ **Deepest canyon**
The Vikos Gorge in the Pindus mountains of northwest Greece is 2,950 ft (900 m) deep with only 3,600 ft (1,100 m) between its rims. Gorges in many countries have a higher depth/width ratio, but none are as deep.

★ **Oldest confirmed impact on Earth**
On August 23 2002, a team of US scientists led by Gary Byerly and Donald Lowe (both USA) announced their discovery of a 3.47-billion-year-old asteroid impact on Earth. They had studied ancient rock samples from Australia and South Africa and analyzed the spherules contained within. These tiny particles are a common by-product of meteoritic strikes and, along with local zircon crystals, were used to date the impact. The spherule beds in the rock indicate that the impacting body had a rough diameter of around 12 miles (20 km). No crater has been found, as the Earth's geological processes have erased it.

★ **Highest continent**
Excluding its ice shelves, Antarctica has an average elevation of 7,198 ft (2,194 m) above the OSU91A Geoid (similar to, but more accurate than, sea level).

★ **Largest geological feature discovered from space**
The Richat Structure in the Sahara Desert of Mauritania is an almost circular, multi-ringed sedimentary basin with a diameter of around 30 miles (50 km). Originally thought to be an impact crater, it is now believed to be the eroded remains of an uplifted sedimentary dome. The distinctive 'bull's-eye' shape was discovered from orbit by US astronauts Jim McDivitt and Ed White during the Gemini IV mission in June 1965.

Largest modern-day landslide ⌃

The landslide on Mt. St. Helens, Washington, USA (above), was the largest ever observed by a survivor. On May 18 1980, about 96,000 million ft³ (2,800 million m³) of rock slipped off the mountain immediately prior to the volcanic eruption. This is equivalent to a block of earth nearly 0.8 miles (1.2 km) high, wide, and long.

★ **Largest liquid body on Earth**
The largest liquid body on Earth is its outer core. The inner core is solid iron/nickel and measures around 758 miles (1,221 km) across. This is surrounded by the liquid outer core, with a thickness of 1,403 miles (2,259 km). The outer core has a total volume of around 1.719×10^{20} m³. It represents around 29.3% of Earth's mass and 16% of Earth's volume, or 100 times the volume of water in Earth's oceans.

★ **Largest doline**
Xio Zhai Tien ('The Great Doline'), situated in the Sichuan region of central southern China, measures 1,600 ft (500 m) across and 2,100 ft (660 m) deep. Dolines are basins formed when limestone caves subside.

★ **Largest sandstone monolith**
Uluru, also known as Ayers Rock, is a huge exposed sandstone monolith that rises 1,143 ft (348 m) above the surrounding desert plain in Northern Territory, Australia. It is 1.5 miles (2.5 km) long and 1 mile (1.6 km) wide.

★ **Fastest land mass on Earth**
Owing to convection currents in the Earth's mantle, all the continental plates slowly move relative to each other. The greatest movement occurs at the Tonga microplate, near Samoa, which is moving further into the Pacific at a rate of 9.4 in (24 cm) per year.

★ **Deepest permafrost**
Permafrost more than 4,500 ft (1,370 m) deep was reported from the upper reaches of the Viluy River, Siberia, Russia, in February 1982.

★ **Largest steam rings**
The active volcano Mount Etna in Sicily, Italy, is the tallest and most active volcano in Europe. A complex physical process is causing it to emit huge steam rings, similar to more familiar smoke rings. Etna's steam rings are around 650 ft (200 m) across and can last for around 10 minutes, as they slowly drift upward to a height of about 3,300 ft (1,000 m) above the volcanic vent.

★ **Weakest region in the Earth's magnetic field**
The Southern Magnetic Anomaly, found off the coast of Brazil, is a region in the Earth's magnetic field that is some 30% weaker than the average for the whole planet. This 'dip' is due to eccentricities in the Earth's core, and causes increased doses of radiation in satellites passing over this region.

★ **Longest day on Earth**
The tidal bulges in the Earth's oceans caused by the gravitational effect of the Moon are gradually transferring momentum from the Earth's rotation to the Moon's orbit. As a result, the Earth's rotation is slowing at a rate of around 0.02 seconds per century, and each day is a little longer than the day before. Therefore, the longest day is always today.

★ **Oldest volcanic rocks on Earth**
Volcanic rocks dated at 3.825 billion years have been discovered in the Inukjuak area in the northern reaches of the province of Québec, Canada. The precise dating of the rocks was performed by the University of Québec, Montréal, and the Simon Fraser University in British Columbia (both Canada).

Highest mountain
Natural world

The highest mountain in the world is Mount Everest. Its peak rises to 29,028 ft 9 in (8,848 m) – the highest point in the world.

Mount Everest is situated in the eastern Himalayas – its summit ridge separates Nepal and Tibet. It was discovered to be the world's highest mountain in 1856 by the Survey Department of the Government of India. Measurements from theodolite readings taken in 1849 and 1850 gave the first accurate measurement and revealed the peak to be the world's highest.

Naming Everest
The mountain was named after Col. Sir George Everest (UK), who was Surveyor-General of India from 1830 to 1843, and who, in fact, pronounced his name 'Eve-rest' as opposed to 'Ever-est.' Mount Everest is also known by the Tibetan name Chomolungma (Goddess Mother of the World) and by the Nepali name Sagarmatha (Forehead in the Sky).

Climbing Everest
Many human triumphs and tragedies have been played out on Everest's slopes. George Mallory (UK) was one of the first to lead an expedition to climb the peak, in 1921. He perished not far from the summit on his 1924 expedition and his body was discovered in 1999. The challenge to climb the highest mountain has not waned since the peak was first conquered in 1953 by Sherpa Tenzing Norgay (Nepal) and Sir Edmund Hillary (New Zealand).

A record-breaking mountain
Mount Everest has been the inspiration for many Guinness World Records: from the simple fact of being the world's highest peak, to being the site for the world's highest-altitude concert. Many of the records achieved on Everest are broken regularly – and some of the current record holders are featured on these pages. As the world's highest peak, Everest will always attract adventurous climbers and records will continue to be broken on its slopes.

★ **Fastest ascent of Everest**
Lakpa Gelu Sherpa (Nepal) made a successful ascent of Mount Everest in 10 hr 56 min 46 sec on May 26 2003, the fastest ever climb from Base Camp to the summit.

★ **Longest stay on the summit**
Babu Chhiri Sherpa (Nepal) stayed at the summit of Mount Everest for 21 hours without using bottled oxygen in May 1999. Most climbers stay less than an hour. He climbed Mount Everest again just weeks later, becoming the first person to climb the mountain twice in the same season.

★ **Most conquests**
Apa Sherpa (Nepal) completed his 13th successful climb of Mount Everest when he reached the summit on May 26 2003. The dates of his climbs are: 1990, 1991, 1992 (spring and fall), 1993, 1994, 1995, 1997, 1998, 1999, 2000, 2002, and 2003.

★ **Oldest man to reach the summit**
Yuichiro Miura (Japan) reached Mount Everest's summit aged 70 years 222 days on May 22 2003, becoming the oldest person ever to have done so. Miura, a professional skier, formerly achieved fame by skiing down Everest from 26,246 ft (8,000 m) in 1970.

★ GWR TALKS TO
Sir Edmund Hillary

Mount Everest was first conquered at 11:30 am on May 29 1953, when the summit was reached by Edmund Percival Hillary (New Zealand, far left) and Sherpa Tenzing Norgay (Nepal, left). The successful expedition was led by Col. (later Hon. Brigadier) Henry Cecil John Hunt (UK).

How did you become involved in mountaineering?

When I was 16 years old I traveled with a school party 200 miles (320 km) south to the Tongariro National Park, and that was the first time I saw snow, really heavy winter snow, and for ten days I skied and scrambled around the snowy mountainside. I was by now pretty big and strong, and I reveled in this new experience. There was no doubt that it changed my life. I'd found something that I could enjoy and do well and it became an important part of my existence.

How did you come to be involved in the 1953 Everest Expedition?

I did a great deal of mountaineering in New Zealand and Europe, so I'd become a pretty competent climber. Then four of us decided to go to the Himalayas and we climbed a number of peaks well over 20,000 ft (6,090 m). Eric Shipton – the famous explorer/ mountaineer – invited two of us to join him. He'd just got permission to approach Everest from the south side, which nobody had done before. So I sort of got swept in.

During the ascent did you experience doubts that you'd reach the summit?

I was never completely confident at any stage that I was going to get to the top. My whole attitude was that I would tackle any problems that I happened to meet, hopefully overcome them, and then if all went well I'd get up to the south summit and finally to the top. And that's the way it worked out. I've always felt that if there's a big challenge ahead of you, and you're absolutely confident that you can do it, why bother starting – it's not worth the effort to give it a crack. But that wasn't the case with Everest – I didn't really know whether or not I would be successful, so I was determined to give it everything I had.

What was for you the single biggest challenge?

Probably the most demanding bit was on the summit ridge, this rock step around 40 ft (12 m) high, which nowadays they call the Hillary Step. I had to find a way up this so I wiggled and jammed between the rock and the ice cornice, never knowing if the ice would break off, but I did it. That was the first time I was confident that I was going to be successful.

What are your thoughts on how Everest is tackled today?

I don't like the increasing commercialization of Himalayan mountaineering. If you have $60,000 you can more or less buy your way into an expedition and be conducted up the mountain. We were in Kathmandu recently and there were 15 expeditions located at Base Camp on the south side of Everest, and another 15 on the north side – literally hundreds of people trying to climb the mountain, many with little or no experience, being conducted by more experienced leaders. I strongly believe that the number of expeditions on the mountain at any one time should be reasonably limited. To have 30 expeditions on the mountain at any one time is absolutely ridiculous. There's no challenge to it, and that's the whole point.

Why was climbing Everest an important thing to have done?

It was the biggest and the best, so it was the major challenge. And of course I'd read so much about George Mallory and Andrew Irvine and the enthusiastic climbers in the 1920s and 1930s, which had built up a feeling that it would be great to have a chance to have a crack at the mountain, to see if we could get up it too.

Could you tell us a bit about your work with the Sherpas?

As I got older I became more interested in the welfare of the Sherpa people and have worked with charitable institutions for 40 years building schools, hospitals, and many other projects for the Sherpas. We've also helped train their teachers. We love doing it – it's no sacrifice as far as we're concerned. We're very fond of our Sherpa friends and they work hard on these projects too, so it's been a very satisfying experience.

Is there somebody that you particularly admire?

To me Ernest Shackleton epitomized the great explorer, the man who could deal with great problems when they arose, the man who kept his team alive, kept their spirit up.

Do you have any unfulfilled ambitions?

Well I'm pretty ancient, you know, I'm fast approaching 85, but I'm still very energetic about raising funds for Sherpa projects and I'm still very enthusiastic on environmental matters as well, and with the reestablishing of the forests in the Mount Everest area. So, the environment and the welfare of the mountain people, I would say, are now my main motivations in life.

★ Oldest woman to reach the summit
Tamae Watanabe (Japan) reached the summit of Mount Everest at the age of 63 years 177 days at 9:55 am on May 16 2002, becoming the oldest woman ever to do so. More than 50 people reached the summit on the same day.

★ Earliest solo summit
Reinhold Messner (Italy) was the first to successfully climb Mount Everest solo, reaching the summit on August 20 1980. It took him three days to make the ascent from his base camp at 21,325 ft (6,500 m), and the climb was made all the more difficult by the fact that he did not use bottled oxygen.

Lakes, rivers & oceans
Natural world

«

Largest iceberg

The largest tabular iceberg measured over 12,000 miles² (31,000 km²).

The flat-topped, blocky iceberg was 208 miles (335 km) long and 60 miles (97 km) wide – that's larger than Belgium – and was sighted 150 miles (240 km) west of Scott Island in the Southern Ocean, Antarctica, by the USS *Glacier* on November 12 1956.

★ Deepest point in the ocean
The deepest part of the ocean is 'Challenger Deep', which lies at a depth of 35,797 ft (10,911 m) in the Marianas Trench in the Pacific Ocean. Named after HM Survey Ship *Challenger II* (UK), which discovered it in 1951, it was first reached in 1960 by the manned US Navy bathyscaphe *Trieste*. The record depth – almost 7 miles (11 km) – was confirmed in March 1995 by the unmanned Japanese probe *Kaiko*.

★ Largest continuous ocean current system
The Thermohaline Conveyor is a vast global system of ocean circulation driven by differences in sea water density and salinity. It transports cold and salty deep water from the North Atlantic down to the Southern Ocean where it then travels east and north to the Indian and Pacific Oceans. Here it rises and becomes warm, traveling back westward where it sinks again in the North Atlantic. The entire cycle can last for a thousand years.

★ Greatest submarine mountain range
The submarine Mid-Ocean Ridge extends 40,000 miles (65,000 km) from the Arctic Ocean to the Atlantic Ocean, around Africa, Asia, and Australia, and under the Pacific Ocean to the West Coast of North America. Its greatest height is 13,800 ft (4,200 m) above the base ocean depth.

★ Fastest ocean current
During the monsoon, the Somali current in the northern Indian Ocean flows at 9 mph (12.8 km/h).

★ Highest ocean temperature
The highest temperature recorded in the ocean is 759°F (404°C) for a hydrothermal vent measured by an American research submarine some 300 miles (480 km) off the American West Coast in 1985.

★ Largest ocean
Excluding adjacent seas, the Pacific Ocean represents 45.9% of the world's oceans and covers 64,186,000 miles² (166,241,700 km²) in area. The average depth is 12,925 ft (3,940 m).

★ Largest area of calm water
An area known as the Sargasso Sea in the north Atlantic Ocean covers about 2.4 million miles² (6.2 million km²) of relatively still water. Its surface is largely covered by sargassum seaweed.

★ Longest river
From its farthest stream in Burundi, the Nile extends 4,160 miles (6,695 km) in length. Credited as the longest river, the Nile's main source is Lake Victoria in East Africa.

★ Greatest river flow
The Amazon discharges an average of 7.1 million ft³/sec (200,000 m³/sec) into the Atlantic Ocean, increasing to more than 12 million ft³/sec (340,000 m³/sec) in full flood. The lower 900 miles (1,450 km) average 55 ft (17 m) in depth, but the river has a maximum depth of 407 ft (124 m). The flow of the Amazon is 60 times greater than that of the Nile.

★ Largest basin
The vast Amazon river basin covers around 2,720,000 miles² (7,045,000 km²). It has countless tributaries, including the Madeira, which at 2,100 miles (3,380 km) is the longest tributary in the world, being surpassed in length by only 17 rivers.

★ Deepest brine pool
The Orca Basin in the Gulf of Mexico lies 7,200 ft (2,200 m) below sea level. This 4 x 13-mile (7 x 21-km) depression is filled with water that has a salt content of around 48 oz/gal (300 g/liter) – around eight times saltier than the Gulf itself. Effectively a hypersaline lake at the bottom of the sea, the salinity is caused by salt leaching out of the salt deposits under the sediment on the sea floor.

★ Largest inland island
The largest inland island (i.e. land surrounded by rivers) is Ilha do Bananal, Brazil, at 7,700 miles² (20,000 km²).

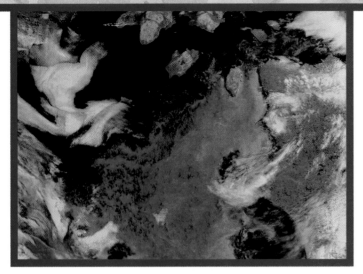

Highest waterfall

The Salto Angel (below) on a branch of the Carrao River, Venezuela, is the highest waterfall (as opposed to vaporized 'Bridal Veil') in the world.

It has a total drop of 3,212 ft (979 m) – the longest single drop being 2,648 ft (807 m). The Angel Falls were named after the American pilot Jimmie Angel, who recorded them in his logbook on November 16 1933. The falls, known by the native Venezuelans as Churun-Meru, had been reported by the Spanish explorer Ernesto Sánchez la Cruz in 1910.

Largest lagoon ⌃

Lagoa dos Patos ('Lagoon of Ducks', above), located near the seashore in Rio Grande do Sul, southern-most

Brazil, is 174 miles (280 km) long and extends over 3,803 miles² (9,850 km²). It has a maximum width of 44 miles (70 km), and is separated from the Atlantic Ocean by long sand strips.

★ **Largest freshwater island**
The largest island surrounded mostly by freshwater is the Ilha de Maraj in the mouth of the Amazon River, Brazil, which measures 18,500 miles² (48,000 km²).

★ **Largest lake island**
The largest island in a lake is Manitoulin Island, which covers an area of 1,068 miles² (2,766 km²) in the Canadian section of Lake Huron.

★ **Saltiest lake**
Don Juan Pond in Wright Valley, Antarctica, is so salty that it remains liquid even at temperatures as low as -63.4°F (-53°C). The percentage of salt by weight is 40.2%, compared with 23.1% and 3.38% for the Dead Sea and the world's oceans respectively.

★ **Greatest waterfall annual flow**
On the basis of the average annual flow, the greatest waterfall in the world is the Boyoma Falls in the Congo (former Zaïre), with a flow of

600,000 ft³/sec (17,000 m³/sec). The flow of the Guaíra (Cascade of the Seven Waterfalls) on the Paraná River between Brazil and Paraguay attained a rate of 1,750,000 ft³/sec (50,000 m³/sec), although the closing of the Itaipú Dam gates in 1982 ended this claim to fame. However, it now holds the record for the greatest waterfall submerged by a reservoir.

★ **Highest tides**
The greatest tides occur in the Bay of Fundy, which divides the peninsula of Nova Scotia, Canada, from the USA's North-eastern-most state of Maine and the Canadian province of New Brunswick. Burncoat Head in the Minas Basin, Nova Scotia, Canada, has the greatest mean spring range, with 47 ft 6 in (14.5 m). A tide range of 54 ft 6 in (16.6 m) was recorded at springs in Leaf Basin in Ungava Bay, Québec, Canada, in 1953.

★ **Largest polynya**
The largest area of open sea surrounded by sea ice ever recorded, measured around

106,000 miles² (275,000 km²). It occurred in the Weddell Sea, off Antarctica, during the winter months of 1974, 1975, and 1976. This spectacularly large polynya was discovered using satellite imagery.

★ **Largest atoll**
The slender 176-mile (283-km) coral reef of Kwajalein, in the Marshall Islands in the central Pacific Ocean, encloses a lagoon of 1,100 miles² (2,850 km²).

★ **Largest atoll land area**
Christmas Atoll in the Line Islands in the central Pacific Ocean has an area of 251 miles² (649 km²), of which 124 miles² (321 km²) is land.

★ **Most southerly ocean**
The most southerly part of any ocean is located at 87°S, 151°W, at the snout of the Scott Glacier, 200 miles (320 km) from the South Pole.

Prehistoric life
Natural world

Largest « crocodile ever

Sarchosuchus imperator (left) was a prehistoric crocodile species that lived around 110 million years ago. Fossilized remains found in the Sahara Desert suggest that this creature took around 50–60 years to grow to its full length of 37–40 ft (11–12 m).

★ **Largest dinosaur skull**
Torosaurus ('piercing lizard'), a ceratopsid, had the largest skull of all known land animals. A herbivore, *Torosaurus* measured around 25 ft (7.6 m) in length and weighed up to 17,600 lb (8 tonnes). Its skull measured up to 9 ft 10 in (3 m) in length and weighed up to 4,400 lb (2 tonnes).

The largest single dinosaur skull ever found measures 10 ft 6 in (3.2 m) in height and belonged to a *Pentaceratops* ('five-horn lizard') skeleton.

★ **Dinosaur with the longest tail**
The diplodocid *Diplodocus* ('double beamed') was a long-necked sauropod dinosaur from the late Jurassic period (145 to 155 million years ago). It had a tail length of up to 43–45 ft (13–14 m).

★ **Oldest fossilized animal food store**
In November 2003, a team of scientists from the University of Bonn (Germany) announced their discovery of a 17-million-year-old fossilized rodent burrow – probably for a hamster or a squirrel – containing more than 1,200 fossilized nuts.

★ **Oldest known marsupial**
The *Deltatheridium* ('little delta (tooth) beast') found in Mongolia's Gobi Desert in November 1988 has been estimated by scientists to be 80 million years old. This means it lived among dinosaurs and that marsupials possibly originated here.

★ **Oldest fossilized embryos**
Around 100 embryos of *Markuelia hunanensis* – an extinct species of worm – were discovered in Hunan, southern China, by a team from Bristol University (UK) and Beijing University (China). They date back around 500 million years. The discovery was announced in January 2004.

★ **Largest carnivore ever**
A skeleton of *Giganotosaurus carolinii*, the largest predatory dinosaur, was discovered in Neuquen, Patagonia, Argentina,

in 1995. It was 41 ft (12.5 m) long, and weighed 17,600 lb (8 tonnes). The bones suggest that it is taller than *Tyrannosaurus rex*. It lived about 110 million years ago – 30 million years before *T. rex*.

★ **Longest prehistoric tusks**
The average length for the tusks of the straight-tusked elephant *Hesperoloxodon antiques germanicus*, which lived about two million years ago in what is now Germany, was 16 ft 4.75 in (5 m).

★ **Largest duck-billed dinosaur**
The duck-billed *Lambeosaurus* ('Lambes lizard') grew to 30–50 ft (9–15 m) long and weighed roughly 12,000 lb (5.6 tonnes). A herbivore that lived during the Cretaceous period, it roamed the Earth in herds 65–83 million years ago.

★ **Longest dinosaur**
The longest vertebrate on record was a diplodocid excavated in 1980 from New Mexico, USA. It was named

Seismosaurus halli ('earth-shaking lizard') and estimated to be 128–170 ft (39–52 m) long based on comparisons of individual bones. In 1999, the bones were reconstructed at the Wyoming Dinosaur Center and measured 134 ft (41 m).

★ **Largest herbivorous dinosaur**
Sauropod dinosaurs, a group of long-necked, long-tailed, four-legged plant-eaters, lumbered around most of the world during the Jurassic and Cretaceous periods 65–208 million years ago. The largest measured 131 ft (40 m) and weighed up to 220,000 lb (100 tonnes).

★ **Oldest spider in amber**
A spider trapped in amber has been dated at 125–135 million years old. From the family Linyphiidae, it was found in Lebanon and analyzed by David Penney and Paul Selden (both UK) and announced on December 26 2002.

Largest and most complete *Tyrannosaurus rex* skeleton »

The largest, best preserved, and most complete skeleton of a *Tyrannosaurus rex* that has ever been found is 'Sue' (right). It measures 13 ft (4 m) tall and 41 ft (12.5 m) long, and is approximately 90% complete.

It was found in South Dakota, USA, on August 12 1990 by explorer Sue Hendrickson (USA), after whom the dinosaur has been named. The skeleton is currently displayed at The Field Museum, Chicago, Illinois, USA.

★ Oldest spider silk

The oldest spider silk in the world dates from the early Cretaceous period, more than 120 million years ago, and was described in the journal *Nature* by Swiss researcher Dr. Samuel Zschokke from the University of Basel. The strand is 0.1 in (4 mm) long and has tiny glue droplets which, in modern-day spiders, are used to catch insects. The specimen was recovered in 1969 from amber beds located near Jezzine, Lebanon, but it was only in 2003 that its importance was recognized.

★ Largest prehistoric mammal

The largest prehistoric mammal was *Indricotherium* (also *Baluchitherium* or *Paraceratherium*) of the family Hyrachyidae, a long-necked, hornless rhinocerotid that roamed across western Asia and Europe roughly 35 million years ago. It was first known from bones discovered in the Bugti Hills of Baluchistan, Pakistan, in 1907–8. A restoration in the American Museum of Natural History, New York City, USA, measures 17 ft 9 in (5.4 m) to the top of the shoulder hump and 37 ft (11.2 m) in total length.

★ Earliest prehistoric salamanders

The earliest salamanders date back 165 million years and thousands of fossilized remains have been discovered in volcanic ash beds in China and Mongolia. These animals are related to the salamanders that now inhabit North America and Asia.

★ Longest prehistoric snake

The longest prehistoric snake was the python-like *Gigantophis garstini*, which inhabited what is now Egypt around 38 million years ago. Parts of a spinal column and a small piece of jaw discovered at Fayum in the Western Desert indicate a length of roughly 36 ft (11 m). This is 3 ft 3 in (1 m) longer than the present-day longest snake.

★ Most dinosaur footprints discovered in one place

About ten different dinosaurs are thought to have made the 100 or more impressions in China's northwest Gansu Province. The prints date from around the junction of the late Jurassic and early Cretaceous periods, 140 million years ago. One of the footprints was approximately 5 ft (1.5 m) long and 4 ft (1.2 m) wide.

★ Largest prehistoric insect

The dragonfly *Meganeura monyi* lived around 280 million years ago. Fossil remains (i.e. impressions of wings) discovered at Commentry, France, indicate a wing expanse of up to 27.5 in (70 cm). This compares with the largest dragonfly living today (*Megaloprepus caeruleata*) from Central and South America, which has been measured up to 4.72 in (120 mm) in length with a wingspan of up to 7.52 in (191 mm).

★ Largest prehistoric bird

The largest prehistoric bird was the flightless *Dromornis stirtoni*, a huge emu-like creature that lived in central Australia between 25 thousand and 15 million years ago. Fossil leg bones found near Alice Springs, Northern Territory, Australia, in 1974 indicate that the bird must have stood around 10 ft (3 m) tall and weighed about 1,100 lb (500 kg).

★ Largest armored dinosaur

Ankylosaurus ('armored lizard'), a herbivore protected with thick plates covering the skin, also had a double row of spikes running down from the back of its head to its club tail. Measuring 24 ft 7 in–35 ft (7.5–10.7 m) long, 6 ft (1.8 m) wide, and 4 ft (1.2 m) tall, it had plates to protect its eyes and only its belly was left unprotected. The last, and at 8,800 lb (4 tonnes), by far the largest of all the ankylosaurids, it lived in the late Cretaceous period, about 65–70 million years ago.

« Largest eyes on a mammal

The Philippine tarsier (*Tarsius syrichta*, left) is one of the world's smallest primates. They have a tail measuring 5.3–10.8 in (135–275 mm), a head and body length of 3.3–6.3 in (85–160 mm), and their large forward-pointing eyes have a diameter of 0.6 in (16 mm). Their eyes are so enormous that they would be equivalent to grapefruit-sized eyes in a human being. They are the only primates, along with animals from the Galago genus, able to turn their heads through 180° in each direction. Tarsiers live in the forests of Borneo, Sumatra, and the Philippines.

★ Largest land mammal
The adult male African elephant (*Loxodonta africana*) stands 9 ft 10 in–12 ft 1 in (3–3.7 m) at the shoulder and weighs 8,800–15,400 lb (4–7 tonnes). The largest specimen ever recorded measured 13 ft 7 in (4.16 m) in a projected line from the highest point of the shoulder to the base of the forefoot, indicating a standing height of about 12 ft 11 in (3.96 m).

★ Smallest elephant species
The world's smallest elephant is the Borneo pygmy, which is 30% smaller than the Asian elephant (*Elephas maximus*). Adult males are 5 ft 6 in–8 ft 6 in (1.7–2.6 m) tall, whereas female are slighlty smaller at 4 ft 11 in–7 ft 2 in (1.5–2.2 m). The average estimated weight is 5,500 lb (2,500 kg). The current population is under 2,000, all living in Borneo, Malaysia, where they were confirmed as being a separate subspecies in September 2003, following DNA research funded by the World Wildlife Fund.

★ Longest gestation period for a mammal
The Asian elephant (*Elephas maximus*) has an average gestation period of 650 days (over 21 months) and a maximum of 760 days (over two years) – more than twice that of humans.

The shortest mammalian gestation period is 12–13 days and is common in a number of species, including the Virginia opossum (*Didelphis virginiana*) of North America, and the rare water opossum or yapok (*Chironectes minimus*) of central and northern South America.

★ Fastest mammal on land over short distances
Repeated modern scientific studies have shown that over a short distance on level ground, the cheetah (*Acinonyx jubatus*) can maintain a steady maximum speed of approximately 62 mph (100 km/h). However, research completed by Professor Craig Sharp (UK) of Brunel University, London, UK, back in 1965 recorded accurate speeds of 64.3 mph (104.4 km/h) for a 77-lb (35-kg) adult female over a distance of 660 ft (201.2 m).

★ Fastest mammal on land over long distances
The pronghorn (*Antilocapra americana*) is the fastest land animal when measured steadily over a long distance. These antelope have been observed to travel continuously at 35 mph (56 km/h) for as far as 4 miles (6 km). The pronghorn is found in western USA, southwestern Canada and parts of northern Mexico.

★ Largest litter for a wild mammal
The greatest number of young born to a wild mammal at a single birth is 31 (30 of which survived) in the case of a tail-less tenrec (*Tenrec ecaudatus*), a hedgehog-like insectivore found in Madagascar.

★ Largest mouth for a land animal
The hippopotamus (*Hippopotamus amphibious*) of Africa can open its jaws to almost 180°. In a fully grown male hippo, this equates to an average gape of 4 ft (1.2 m). Although they are herbivores, hippos have canine teeth that typically measure 28 in (71 cm) and which continually grow. The largest canine recorded for a hippo is 48 in (122 cm).

★ Fastest heartbeat in a mammal
The shrew (family Soricidae) has the fastest heartbeat of any mammal, with a rate of 1,200 beats per minute, which is similar to that of a hummingbird when hovering. Shrews are roughly the size of a thumb and weigh a tiny 0.15 oz (4.5 g).

★ Largest structure built by a land animal
Beavers (*Candor canadensis*) of North America use mud, wood, vegetation, and stones to dam up water and form a pond, then build a lodge for winter refuge. The largest lodge ever recorded was 40 ft (12.1 m) across and 16 ft (4.8 m) high, and the longest beaver dam measured 0.9 miles (1.5 km) long.

Largest mammal to build a nest

The largest mammal to construct a nest is the gorilla (*Gorilla gorilla*, left) of Africa, where adult males measure 5 ft 6 in–5 ft 9 in (1.7–1.8 m) tall and weigh 300-500 lb (136-227 kg). Every day, the gorillas each create a new ground nest from the surrounding vegetation. The nests are circular and typically measure 3 ft 3 in (1 m) in diameter.

Tallest mammal

The giraffe (*Giraffa camelopardalis*, below), found in the dry savannah and open woodland areas of sub-Saharan Africa, is the tallest mammal. An adult male giraffe typically measures 15–18 ft (4.6–5.5 m) tall.

★ Mammal with the most names

In the English language alone, the puma (*Puma concolor*) has over 40 names, including cougar, mountain lion, red tiger, and Florida panther.

★ Highest living mammal

The large-eared pika (*Ochotona macrotis*) has been recorded at a height of 20,100 ft (6,130 m) in Asian mountain ranges.

The yak (*Bos mutus*) found in Tibet and China climbs to an altitude of 20,000 ft (6,100 m) when foraging.

★ Largest colony of mammals

The black-tailed prairie dog (*Cynomys ludovicianus*), a rodent of the family Sciuridae found in the western USA and in northern Mexico, builds large colonies. One single 'town' discovered in 1901 contained about 400 million individuals and was estimated to cover 23,706 miles^2 (61,400 km^2) – the size of the Republic of Ireland.

★ GWR TALKS TO
Sir David Attenborough

Sir David Attenborough (UK, above) has had the longest working career as a writer and presenter of TV nature programs. His first series, *Zoo Quest* (BBC, UK), was broadcast in 1954 and his most recent, the BBC's *Life of Mammals*, was broadcast in the UK in 2002.

What has been the most enjoyable TV series to put together?
Life on Earth. At the time it was the most ambitious series ever produced by the BBC Natural History Unit. It was seen by an estimated 500 million viewers and people still comment on the impact that the series had.

Have you ever been attacked by any animals?
No, never. Usually the only scary moments are when human beings are involved. But having said that, I was once filming in Kenya with Iain Douglas Hamilton, the elephant expert, and we were on the receiving end of a nasty rhino charge which wrecked our Land Rover.

Is there any particular creature that fascinates you over and above all others?
I have a private passion about birds of paradise which are found only in New Guinea and its offshore islands. Their courtship displays are simply ravishing and many have never been filmed. Once when we were trying to film Wilson's Bird of Paradise, we'd been waiting in the bird hide since before dawn and the sound recordist waiting some distance away told me that he knew when the bird arrived as he heard my heartbeat double!

If you could bring back any extinct species of plant or animal what would it be?
A giant plant-eating dinosaur.

Do you intend to keep on making television wildlife programs?
I'm doing what I want to do and as long as people want me to go on doing it, I'll continue. I don't know what I'd do otherwise!

What advice would you give any budding naturalist?
Learn all you can about animals.

What does it mean to you to have a Guinness World Record?
It's something with which to surprise my friends!

« Longest bills

The longest bill belongs to the Australian pelican (*Pelecanus conspicillatus*, left), and measures 13–18.5 in (34–47 cm) long.

The longest beak in relation to overall body length is that of the sword-billed hummingbird (*Ensifera ensifera*) found in the Andes from Venezuela to Bolivia. The beak measures 4 in (10.2 cm) making it longer than the bird's actual body (excluding the tail).

Highest density ⌄ of feathers

The penguin (below) has the highest density of feathers. In his book, *The General Biology and Thermal Balance of Penguins* (1967), Dr. Bernard Stonehouse (UK) counted 70 feathers per in² (11–12 per cm²) in emperor, Adélie, yellow-eyed and little (blue) penguins. Each feather has its own small muscles associated with it to allow control. On land the feathers stay erect to trap air, insulating them; in the water they flatten to form a watertight barrier.

★ Largest bird
The largest living bird is the North African ostrich (*Struthio camelus camelus*). Male examples of this ratite (flightless) subspecies have been recorded up to 9 ft (2.75 m) tall and weighing 345 lb (156.5 kg).

★ Smallest bird
The smallest bird is the bee hummingbird (*Mellisuga helenae*) of Cuba and the Isle of Youth. Males measure 2.25 in (57 mm) in total length, half of which is taken up by the bill and tail, and weigh only 0.05 oz (1.6 g). Females are slightly larger. This is believed to be the lowest weight limit for any warm-blooded animal.

★ Most abundant bird
The red-billed quelea (*Quelea quelea*), a seed-eating weaver of the drier parts of sub-Saharan Africa, has an estimated adult breeding population of 1.5 billion. At least 200 million of these 'feathered locusts' are slaughtered annually without reducing this overall number.

★ Highest G force experienced by a bird
American experiments have shown that the beak of the red-headed woodpecker (*Melanerpes erythrocephalus*) hits the bark of a tree with an impact velocity of 13 mph (20.9 km/h), subjecting the brain to a deceleration of about 10 G when the head snaps back.

★ Longest feathers
The longest feathers grown by any bird were recorded in 1972 on a phoenix fowl or Yokohama chicken (a strain of red jungle fowl, *Gallus gallus*) whose tail covert measured 34 ft 9.5 in (10.6 m). It was owned by Masasha Kubota (Japan). The longest feathers on a bird found in the wild (i.e. not bred for ornamental purposes) are those of the male crested Argus pheasant (*Rheinhartia ocellata*), whose feathers reach 5 ft 8 in (1.73 m).

★ Fastest bird swimmer
The gentoo penguin (*Pygoscelis papua*) has a maximum speed of about 17 mph (27 km/h).

★ Shortest bills
The shortest bills in relation to body length belong to the smaller swifts (the Apodidae family), and in particular to the glossy swiftlet (*Collocalia esculenta*), whose bill is almost nonexistent.

★ Fastest wing beat of a bird
During courtship, the ruby-throated hummingbird (*Archilochus colubris*) can produce a wing beat rate of 200 beats/sec as opposed to the normal 90 beats/sec of all other hummingbirds.

★ Highest flying birds
The highest altitude recorded for a bird is 37,000 ft (11,300 m) for a Ruppell's vulture (*Gyps rueppellii*) that collided with an airplane over Abidjan, Ivory Coast, on November 29 1973. The impact damaged one of the aircraft's engines, but the plane landed safely.

★ Largest bird's nest
A pair of bald eagles (*Haliaeetus leucocephalus*), and possibly their successors, built a nest near St. Petersburg, Florida, USA, that measured an incredible 9 ft 6 in (2.9 m) wide and 20 ft (6 m) deep. When it was examined in 1963 it was estimated to weigh more than 4,400 lb (2 tonnes).

★ Smallest bird's nest
Hummingbirds build the smallest nests. That of the vervain hummingbird (*Mellisuga minima*) is about half the size of a walnut shell, while the deeper but narrower nest of the bee hummingbird (*M. helenae*) is thimble-sized.

★ Smallest bird egg
The smallest egg laid by any bird is that of the vervain hummingbird (*Mellisuga minima*) of Jamaica and two nearby islets. Two specimens measuring less than 0.39 in (10 mm) in length weighed a minute 0.0128 oz (0.365 g) and 0.0132 oz (0.375 g).

Keenest » vision of all birds

Large birds of prey have the keenest vision as they can detect a target object at a distance three or more times greater than that achieved by humans. A peregrine falcon (*Falco peregrinus*, right) can spot a pigeon at a range of over 5 miles (8 km) under ideal conditions.

★ **Most airborne land bird**
The common swift (*Apus apus*) remains airborne for two to four years, during which time it sleeps, drinks, eats, and even mates on the wing. It has been calculated that a young swift completes a nonstop flight of 310,000 miles (500,000 km) between fledging and its first landing at a potential nesting site some two years later.

★ **Most airborne bird**
The most airborne of all birds is the sooty tern (*Sterna fuscata*) which, after leaving the nesting grounds as a youngster, remains aloft for three to 10 years while maturing, settling on water occasionally, before returning to land to breed as an adult.

★ **Fastest land bird**
The world's fastest bird on land is the ostrich (*Struthio camelus*), which can reach speeds of up to 30 mph (50 km/h) when running. Unlike most birds, the ostrich cannot fly, and therefore uses its powerful legs to sprint at such speeds. The

ostrich has one of the largest strides of any animal – it can exceed 23 ft (7 m) at full pace.

★ **Fastest bird in level flight**
The fastest fliers in level flight are found among the ducks and geese (Anatidae). Some powerful species such as the red-breasted merganser (*Mergus serrator*), the eider (*Somateria mollissima*), the canvasback (*Aythya valisineria*), and the spur-winged goose (*Plectropterus gambensis*) can sometimes reach 56–62 mph (90–100 km/h).

★ **Slowest-flying bird**
The slowest-flying birds are the American woodcock (*Scolopax minor*) and the Eurasian wood-cock (*S. rusticola*), which have been timed during courtship displays at only 5 mph (8 km/h) without stalling.

★ **Largest penguin colony**
The largest penguin colony is on Zavodovski Island in the South Sandwich Islands. Approximately two million chinstrap penguins

(*Pygoscelis antarctica*) breed on the slopes of the island, which is an active volcano. Chinstraps get their name from a thin line of black feathers that runs under their chin. They are also considered the most common penguins in the world with a population of around 12 million, mainly found in the Antarctic.

★ **Smallest bird of prey**
The smallest bird of prey in the world is a title held jointly by the black-legged falconet (*Microhierax fringillarius*) of Southeast Asia and the white-fronted or Bornean falconet (*Microhierax latifrons*) of northwestern Borneo. Both species have an average length of 5.5–6 in (14–15 cm), including a 2-in (5-cm) tail, and a weight of about 1.25 oz (35 g).

★ **Longest migration by a bird**
The Arctic tern (*Sterna parasidaea*) migrates the greatest distance of any bird species. It breeds north of the Arctic Circle and then flies south to the Antarctic for the

northern winter and then back again, a round-trip of about 21,750 miles (35,000 km).

★ **Longest incubation**
An egg of the mallee fowl (*Leipoa ocellata*) of Australia, took 90 days to hatch, compared with its normal 62 days.

★ **Lowest temperature endured by a bird**
The lowest temperature endured by any bird is an average of -4°F (-20°C) by the breeding emperor penguin (*Aptenodytes forsteri*) on the Antarctic sea ice where wind speeds can vary between 16 and 47 mph (25 and 75 km/h).

★ **Largest wingspan of any living species of bird**
A male wandering albatross (*Diomedea exulans*) of the southern oceans holds the record with a wingspan of 11 ft 11 in (3.63 m). The bird was caught by members of the Antarctic research ship USNS *Eltanin* in the Tasman Sea on September 18 1965.

⌃ Highest jump by a dolphin

Some bottlenose dolphins (*Tursiops truncatus*, above) have been trained to jump as high as 26 ft (7.92 m) from the surface of the water.

Fastest marine mammal ⌃

On October 12 1958, a bull killer whale (*Orcinus orca*, above) an estimated 20–25 ft (6.1–7.6 m) long, was timed at 34.5 mph (55.5 km/h) in the northeastern Pacific.

Similar speeds have also been reported for Dall's porpoise (*Phocoenoides dalli*) in short bursts.

★ Smallest whale

There are two contenders for the smallest cetacean: Hector's dolphin (*Cephalorhynchus hectori*) and vaquita (*Phocoena sinus*), which grow to only 3 ft 11 in (1.2 m) long.

★ Largest animal brain

The brain of the sperm whale or cachalot (*Physeter macrocephalus*) weighs approximately 19 lb 13 oz (9 kg). In comparison the weight of a bull African elephant's brain reaches 11 lb 14 oz (5.4 kg) and a human brain is, on average, 3 lb (1.4 kg). Sperm whales are found in all waters except the polar regions. Their name comes from the waxy oil, which is produced by the spermaceti organ on their heads.

★ Largest offspring

In the two months before it is born, a blue whale (*Balaenoptera musculus*) increases in weight by as much as 4,400 lb (2 tonnes) – it grows about 1,000 times faster than a human baby in the womb. The newborn calf is 19–26 ft (6–8 m) long and weighs 4,400–6,600 lb (2–3 tonnes). Everyday, the baby drinks about 350 pints (200 liters) of its mother's milk and gains as much as 198 lb (90 kg) in weight – the same as the weight of an adult human being. By the time it is weaned at seven months old it has roughly doubled in length and weighs an amazing 44,000 lb (20 tonnes). The blue whale is the world's largest mammal.

★ Greatest weight loss

During her seven-month lactation period, a 264,000-lb (120-tonne) female blue whale (*Balaenoptera musculus*) can lose up to 25% of her body weight nursing her calf.

★ Slowest heartbeat in a mammal

The mammal that is presumed to have the slowest heartbeat of any warm-blooded animal is the blue whale (*Balaenoptera musculus*), with between four and eight beats per minute – dependent upon whether or not the whale is diving. By comparison, the average adult human heart beats at 70 beats per minute. Blue whales also have the largest heart of any animal and their heartbeat can be heard up to 20 miles (32 km) away underwater.

★ Largest jaw for a mammal

The largest jaw ever recorded on a mammal measured 5 m (16 ft 5 in) and belonged to a male sperm whale (*Physeter macrocephalus*) nearly 25.6 m (84 ft) in length. The massive lower jaw is now exhibited in the Museum of Natural History, London, UK. Sperm whales are also the largest-toothed whales.

★ Densest fur

The sea otter (*Enhydra lutris*) has over 650,000 hairs per in^2 (100,000 per cm^2) that insulate its skin. Most of the world's sea otters are found off the coast of Alaska, USA.

★ Oldest pinniped

A pinniped is a carnivorous aquatic mammal with flipper-like limbs (such as a seal). The greatest proven age for a pinniped was estimated by the Limnological Institute in Irkutsk, former USSR, to be 56 years for the female Baikal seal (*Phoca sibirica*) and 52 years for the male.

Largest pinniped ⌄

The largest of the 34 known species of pinniped is the southern elephant seal (*Mirounga leonina*, below) of the sub-Antarctic islands. Bulls average 16 ft 6 in (5 m) in length from the tip of the inflated snout to the tips of the outstretched tail flippers, have a maximum girth of 12 ft (3.7 m), and weigh about 4,400–7,720 lb (2,000–3,500 kg).

The largest accurately measured specimen of the elephant seal was a bull, killed at Possession Bay, South Georgia, on February 28 1913, that weighed at least 8,800 lb (4 tons) and measured 21 ft 4 in (6.5 m) after flensing (stripping of the blubber or skin).

★ Smallest pinniped
The smallest pinniped, by a small margin, is the Galapagos fur seal (*Arctocephalus galapagoensis*). Adult females average 3 ft 11 in (1.2 m) in length and weigh about 60 lb (27 kg). Males are usually considerably larger, averaging 4 ft 11 in (1.5 m) in length and weighing around 141 lb (64 kg).

★ Rarest seal
With fewer than 400 remaining, the rarest seal species is the Mediterranean monk seal (*Monachus monachus*), found in remote and undisturbed areas of the Mediterranean Sea and northwest African coast. Its closest relative, the Caribbean monk seal (*M. tropicalis*), is already extinct.

★ Largest gray seal colony
Over 100,000 gray seals (*Halichoerus grypus*) arrive at Sable Island off Nova Scotia, Canada, every winter to breed. After 18 days the resulting pups are then left to fend for themselves. The gray seal's name *Halichoerus grypus* comes from the Greek, meaning 'hook-nosed sea pig'.

★ Largest amphibian
The largest of the amphibians are the giant salamanders (family Cryptobranchidae) of which there are three species. The record holder is the Chinese giant salamander (*Andrias davidianus*), which lives in mountain streams in north-eastern, central, and southern China. One record-breaking specimen collected in Hunan Province measured 5 ft 11 in (1.8 m) in length and weighed a massive 143 lb (65 kg).

★ Smallest newt
The smallest newt or salamander is the Mexican lungless salamander (*Bolitoglossa mexicana*), which only grows to about 1 in (2.54 cm), including the tail.

★ Largest frog
A specimen of the African goliath frog (*Conraua goliath*) captured in April 1889 on the Sanaga River, Cameroon, by Andy Koffman (USA) had a snout-to-vent length of 14.5 in (36.8 cm) and an overall length of 34.5 in (87.6 cm) with its legs extended.

★ Smallest toad
The smallest toad is the subspecies *Bufo taitanus beiranus* of Africa, the largest specimen of which measured only 0.94 in (24 mm) long.

★ Most paternal amphibian
The West European midwife toad (*Alytes obstetricans*) takes its name from the behavior of the male. When the female lays its eggs, the male fertilizes them and then winds the string of eggs (which can be 3–4 ft or 0.9–1.2 m long) around his thighs. The male, who is only 3 in (7.6 cm) long, carries the eggs in this manner for up to four weeks. When the eggs are ready to hatch, the toad swims into suitable water for the tadpoles to be released.

« Most ferocious freshwater fish

Attracted to blood and frantic splashing, a school of piranhas (left) can completely strip an animal as large as a horse of its flesh within minutes, leaving only its skeleton.

The most ferocious piranhas are those of the genera *Serrasalmus* and *Pygocentrus*, found in the large rivers of South America.

⌃ Slowest fish

The swimming ability of sea horses (family Syngnathidae, above) is severely limited by a rigid body structure – only their pectoral and dorsal fins can move rapidly. Sea horses propel themselves along in an erect posture, never attaining speeds of more than 0.001 mph (0.016 km/h). Incapable of swimming against the current, they hang on to coral and marine plants with their prehensile tails to avoid being swept away.

★ Largest fish
The largest fish is the rare plankton-feeding whale shark (*Rhincodon typus*), which is found in the warmer areas of the Atlantic, Pacific, and Indian Oceans. The largest scientifically recorded example of one of these creatures was 41 ft 6 in (12.65 m) long, 23 ft (7 m) around the thickest part of the body and weighed an estimated 33,000–46,200 lb (15–21 tonnes). It was captured off Baba Island, near Karachi, Pakistan, on November 11 1949.

★ Largest predatory fish
The largest predatory fish is the rare great white shark (*Carcharodon carcharias*). Adult specimens average 14–15 ft (4.3–4.6 m) in length, and weigh between 1,150 lb and 1,700 lb (520–770 kg). There are many claims of huge specimens up to 33 ft (10 m) in length and, although few have been authenticated, there is plenty of circumstantial evidence to suggest that great whites can grow to over 20 ft (6 m) in length.

★ Largest freshwater fish
The largest fish to spend their whole life in fresh or brackish water are the rare Mekong giant catfish (*Pangasius gigas*), principally of the Mekong River basin in Southeast Asia, and *Pangasius sanitwongsei*, principally of the Chao Phraya River basin, Thailand, both of which are reputed to attain a length of 10 ft (3 m) and weigh 660 lb (300 kg). However, *Arapaima giga* of South America is reported to attain a length of 14 ft 9 in (4.5 m), but weighs only 440 lb (200 kg).

★ Heaviest bony fish
The heaviest bony fish in the ocean is the sunfish (*Mola mola*), which has been recorded weighing 4,400 lb (2 tonnes) and measuring 10 ft (3 m) from fin tip to fin tip.

★ Deepest fish
The fish that lives at the greatest recorded depth is a species of cusk-eel (family Ophidiidae) called *Abyssobrotula galatheae*. The 8-in (20-cm-long) fish has been collected from the Puerto Rico Trench in the Atlantic Ocean at a depth of 27,460 ft (8,370 m).

★ Longest fish migration
Many fish species undertake long annual migrations between their feeding grounds. The longest straight line distance known to have been covered by a marine fish is 5,800 miles (9,335 km) for a bluefin tuna (*Thunnus thynnus*) that was dart tagged off Baja California, Mexico, in 1958 and caught 300 miles (483 km) south of Tokyo, Japan, in April 1963. During its journey, its weight increased from 35 lb (16 kg) to 267 lb (121 kg).

For freshwater fish, the European eel (*Anguilla anguilla*) holds the record. It spends between seven and 15 years in freshwater in Europe then suddenly changes into breeding condition and begins a marathon journey that may take it from landlocked waters to the Atlantic, where it heads for the species' spawning grounds in the Sargasso Sea. The entire journey – between 3,000 and 4,000 miles (4,800 and 6,400 km) – takes about six months.

★ Highest living fish
The highest living fish is the Tibetan loach (Cobitidae), found at an altitude of 17,000 ft (5,200 m) in the Himalayas.

★ Fastest fish
The cosmopolitan sailfish (*Istiophorus platypterus*) is considered to be the fastest species of fish over short distances, although practical problems make it difficult to establish precise measurements of its speed. In a series of trials carried out at the Long Key Fishing Camp, Florida, USA, one sailfish took out 300 ft (91 m) of line in three seconds, which is equivalent to a velocity of 68 mph (109 km/h), compared with 60 mph (96 km/h) for the cheetah at high speed.

Most poisonous edible fish ⌃

The most poisonous fish are the puffer fish (*Tetraodon*, above) of the Red Sea and Indo-Pacific region that deliver a fatal toxin called tetrodotoxin, one of the most powerful nonproteinous poisons. Less than 0.004 oz (0.1 g) is enough to kill an adult person in as little as 20 minutes. In Japan, the puffer fish is served as a delicacy known as fugu-sashi. Improper preparation of this dish can cause fatal poisoning, so only specially licensed cooks are allowed to prepare it.

Most venomous mollusk ⟪

The two closely related species of blue-ringed octopus *Hapalochlaena maculosa* and *H. lunulata* (left) – found around the coasts of Australia and parts of Southeast Asia – carry a neurotoxic venom so potent that their relatively painless bite can kill a human in a matter of minutes. It has been estimated that each individual, which measures just 4 in (10 cm) in length, carries sufficient venom to cause the paralysis (or even death) of 10 adult people.

★ **Lightest fish**
The lightest of all vertebrates is the dwarf goby (*Schindleria praematurus*), which weighs only 2 mg (equivalent to 14,184 to the ounce) and is 0.47–0.74 in (12–19 mm) long. It is found throughout the Indo-Pacific.

★ **Largest eye**
The Atlantic giant squid (*Architeuthis dux*) has the largest eye of any animal – living or extinct. It has been estimated that the record example from Thimble Tickle Bay, Newfoundland, Canada, found in 1878 had eyes measuring 15.75 in (40 cm) in diameter – almost the width of an open *Guinness World Records* book.

★ **Largest squid**
The largest intact specimen of a squid ever found was an immature female of the species *Mesonychoteuthis hamiltoni* that was caught in March 2003 in the Ross Sea, Antarctica. It had a total length of 16 ft (5 m), a mantle length of 8 ft (2.5 m), and weighed

330 lb (150 kg). This species swims to a depth of 6,500 ft (2,000 m) and is an aggressive killer, eating large prey like Patagonian toothfish, *Dissostichus eleginoides*, which can grow to more than 6 ft (1.8 m) long. Mantle length (not total length) is the standard measure in cephalopods.

★ **Animal with the most chromosomes**
The king crab has 208 pairs of chromosomes per cell. By comparison, humans have 23 pairs of chromosomes in each cell.

★ **Most heat-tolerant water-based organism**
The most heat-resistant organism discovered to date is strain 121, a microbe belonging to the ancient group of bacteria-like organisms called archae. Strain 121 was discovered in superheated water from hydrothermal vents at the bottom of the Pacific Ocean. This organism can survive temperatures of 249.8°F (121°C).

★ **Most dangerous sea urchin**
The most dangerous sea urchin is the flower sea urchin (*Toxopneustes pileolus*). Toxin from the spines and pedicellaria (small pincer-like organs) causes severe pain, respiratory problems, and paralysis in humans.

★ **Deepest starfish**
The greatest depth from which a starfish has been recovered is 24,881 ft (7,584 m) for a specimen of *Porcellanaster ivanovi* collected by the Soviet research ship *Vityaz* in the Marianas Trench in the Pacific Ocean ca. 1962.

★ **Smallest starfish**
The asterinid sea star (*Patiriella parvivipara*) discovered on the west coast of Eyre Peninsula, South Australia, in 1975 has a maximum radius of only 0.18 in (4.7 mm) and a diameter of less than 0.35 in (9 mm).

★ **Largest concentration of crustaceans**
The largest single concentration of crustaceans ever recorded was a swarm of krill (*Euphausia superba*), estimated to weigh 10 million tonnes, tracked by US scientists off Antarctica in March 1981.

★ **Largest crustacean**
The largest of all marine crustaceans is the giant spider crab (*Macrocheira kaempferi*). A specimen with a claw span of 12 ft 1.5 in (3.7 m) weighed 41 lb (18.6 kg).
The largest freshwater crustacean is the crayfish or crawfish (*Astacopsis gouldi*), found in the streams of Tasmania, Australia. It has been measured up to 2 ft (61 cm) in length and may weigh as much as 9 lb (4.1 kg).

★ **Largest oyster**
In 1999, a common oyster (*Ostrea edulis*) taken from Chesapeake Bay, Virginia, USA, weighed in at 8 lb (3.7 kg) and measured 12 in (30.5 cm) long and 5 in (14 cm) wide.

Fastest-flying « insect

Acceptable modern experiments have established that the highest maintainable airspeed of any insect, including the deer bot fly (*Cephenemyia pratti*), hawk moths (Sphingidae, left), horseflies (*Tabanus bovinus*), and some tropical butterflies (Hesperiidae), is 24 mph (39 km/h), rising to a maximum of 36 mph (58 km/h) for the Australian dragonfly (*Austrophlebia costalis*) for short bursts.

★ **Fastest wing beat of an insect**
The fastest wing beat of any insect under natural conditions is 62,760 per minute by a tiny midge of the genus *Forcipomyia*. The muscular contraction-expansion cycle of 0.00045 seconds, necessary for such rapid wing beats, moreover represents the fastest muscle movement ever measured.

★ **Heaviest insect**
The heaviest insects are the goliath beetles (family Scarabaeidae) of equatorial Africa. *Goliathus regius*, *G. meleagris*, *G. goliathus* (=*G. giganteus*), and *G. druryi* are the largest. In measurements of one series of males (females are smaller), the lengths from the tips of the small frontal horns to the end of the abdomen were up to 4.3 in (11 cm), with weights of 2.5–3.5 oz (70–100 g).

★ **Largest colony of ants**
The largest recorded colony of ants stretches 3,700 miles (6,000 km) from northern Italy, through France to the Atlantic coast of Spain, and is made up of a species of Argentine ant (*Linepithema humile*) introduced into Europe around 80 years ago. The ants have shown an amazing ability to recognize each other even though they may come from opposite ends of the colony.

★ **Largest dragonfly**
Megaloprepus caeruleata of Central and South America has been measured up to 4.7 in (120 mm) in length with a wing span up to 7.5 in (190 mm).

★ **Largest butterfly**
The huge and poisonous Queen Alexandra's birdwing (*Ornithoptera alexandrae*) of Papua New Guinea may have a wingspan that exceeds 11 in (280 mm) and weigh over 0.9 oz (25 g).

★ **Largest millipede**
The largest millipede is a full-grown African giant black millipede (*Archispirostreptus gigas*) owned by Jim Klinger (USA). It measures 15.2 in (38.7 cm) in length, 2.6 in (6.7 cm) in circumference, and has 256 legs. The average length for this type of millipede is between 6.5 and 11 in (16 and 28 cm).

★ **Largest grasshopper**
An unidentified species of grasshopper from the border of Malaysia and Thailand measures 10 in (25.4 cm) in length and is capable of leaping 15 ft (4.6 m).

★ **Highest jump by an insect**
The best jumping performance by an insect is the froghopper (spittlebug, *Philaenus spumarius*), which can reach heights of 28 in (70 cm) or more than 115 times its body length.

★ **Longest insect**
The longest known specimen of *Pharnacia kirbyi*, a stick insect from the rainforests of Borneo, is in the Natural History Museum in London, UK. It has a body length of 12.9 in (328 mm) and a total length, including the legs, of 21.5 in (546 mm). In the wild this species is often found with some legs missing because they are so long and easily trapped when the insect sheds its skin.

★ **Largest scorpion**
One of the *Heterometrus swannerdami* species, found during World War II in the village of Krishnarajapuram, India, measured 11.5 in (29.2 cm) in overall length from the tips of the pedipalps or 'pincers' to the end of the sting.

★ **Most venomous scorpion**
The Tunisian fat-tailed scorpion (*Androctonus australis*) is responsible for 80% of stings and 90% of deaths from scorpion stings in North Africa.

★ **Heaviest scorpion**
The large, black West African species *Pandinus imperator* can weigh up to 2 oz (60 g). It can also measure between 5 and 7 in (13 and 18 cm) in length, the same average length as the hand of an adult human being.

Largest « wasp nest

A wasp nest found by Yoichiro Kawamura (Japan, left) on May 18 1999 at Yonegaoka, Japan, had a circumference of 8 ft (2.45 m) and weighed 17 lb 8 oz (8 kg).

Oldest insect ⌃

The longest-lived insects are the splendor beetles (Buprestidae, above). On May 27 1983, a specimen of *Buprestis aurulenta* appeared from the timber staircase in a house in Essex, UK, after at least 47 years as a larva.

Fastest-moving insect »

Periplaneta americana, a large tropical cockroach of the family Dictyoptera (right), clocked a record speed of 3.36 mph (5.4 km/h), or 50 body lengths per second, at the University of California at Berkeley, USA, in 1991. There are about 4,000 species of cockroaches, known mainly from the tropics, as they prefer warm, humid climates.

★ Smallest spider

The smallest known spider is *Patu marplesi* (family Symphytognathidae) of Western Samoa. A specimen (male) found in moss at an altitude of 2,000 ft (600 m) in Madolelei, Upolu, inJanuary 1965 measured 0.017 in (0.43 mm) overall – about the size of a period on this page.

★ Largest spider

The largest known spider is a male goliath bird-eating spider (*Theraphosa blondi*) collected by members of the Pablo San Martin Expedition at Rio Cavro, Venezuela, in April 1965. It had a record leg span of 11 in (28 cm) – sufficient to cover a dinner plate. This species is found in the coastal rainforests of Surinam, Guyana and French Guiana, but isolated specimens have also been reported from Venezuela and Brazil.

★ Heaviest spider

Female bird-eating spiders (family Theraphosidae) are more heavily built than males,

and in February 1985 Charles J. Seiderman (USA) captured a female example near Paramaribo, Surinam, that weighed a record 4.3 oz (122.2 g) before its death from molting problems in January 1986. Other measurements included a maximum leg-span of 10.5 in (267 mm), a total body length of 4 in (102 mm), and 1-in (25-mm-long) fangs.

★ Most venomous spider

The Brazilian wandering spiders of the genus *Phoneutria*, and particularly the Brazilian huntsman (*P. fera*), has the most active neurotoxic venom of any living spider. Its venom is so potent that only 0.00000021 oz (0.006 mg) is sufficient to kill a mouse. *Phoneutria* are usually dark in color and have a body-and-leg spread of approximately 6.75 in (17 cm). These large and highly aggressive creatures often enter human dwellings and hide in clothing or shoes. When disturbed, they bite

furiously several times, and hundreds of accidents involving these species are reported annually.

★ Strongest spider

The strongest spider is the Californian trapdoor spider (*Bothriocyrtum californicum*), which is able to resist a force 38 times its own weight attempting to open its trapdoor: a silken structure covering the entrance to its underground burrow. If the average adult male human being weighs 180 lb (82 kg), it would be similar to a man trying to hold a door closed while it was being pulled on the other side by the weight of a small jet.

★ Largest continuous area of spiderwebs

The largest continuous areas of spiderwebs are created by members of the Indian genus *Stegodyphus*. They build huge three-dimensional

interwoven and overlapping webs that have been known to cover vegetation in a continuous silken mass for several miles.

★ Simplest spiderweb

The simplest web is that of the species of the genus *Miagrammopes*, found in Africa, Australia, and North America. They have reduced their web to a single strand averaging 3 ft (1 m) long. This is woven between two small branches.

★ Strongest spider's web

The American house spider (*Achaearenea tepidariorum*) spins an irregular cobweb strong enough to ensnare and hold small mice.

★ Oldest spider

The oldest spider recorded lived for an estimated 26–28 years. It was a female of the tropical bird-eaters (family Theraphosidae) that was collected in Mexico in 1935.

Oldest chelonian ⌄

The greatest authenticated age recorded for a chelonian is at least 188 years,

achieved by a Madagascar radiated tortoise (*Astrochelys radiata*, below) that was presented to the Tonga royal family by Captain Cook (UK) in either 1773 or 1777. The animal was called Tui Malila and remained in their care until its death in 1965.

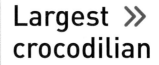

Largest ≫ crocodilian

The largest reptile in the world is the estuarine or saltwater crocodile (*Crocodylus porosus*, above), which ranges throughout the tropical regions of Asia and the Pacific. The Bhitarkanika Wildlife Sanctuary in Orissa State, India, houses four protected estuarine crocodiles measuring more than 20 ft (6 m) in length, the largest being over 23 ft (7 m) long. There are several unauthenticated reports of specimens up to 33 ft (10 m) in length.

★ **Oldest living chelonian**
Harriet, one of three giant tortoises (*Geochelone nigra porteri*) collected by Charles Darwin (UK) from the Galapagos Islands in 1835, is thought to be the world's oldest resident at 173 years old. Born in November 1830, she currently resides at the Australia Zoo, near Brisbane, Queensland, Australia.

★ **Deepest dive by a chelonian**
In May 1987, Dr. Scott Eckert (USA) reported that a leatherback turtle (*Dermochelys coriacea*) fitted with a pressure-sensitive recording device had reached a depth of 3,937 ft (1,200 m) off the Virgin Islands in the West Indies.

★ **Largest chelonian**
The leatherback turtle (*Dermochelys coriacea*) averages 6–7 ft (1.8–2.1 m) from the tip of the beak to the end of the tail (with a carapace of 5–5 ft 6 in or 1.52–1.67 m). They measure about 7 ft (2.1 m) across the front flippers and can weigh up to 1,000 lb (450 kg).

★ **Fastest chelonian**
The highest speed claimed for any reptile in water is 22 mph (35 km/h) by a frightened Pacific leatherback turtle (*Dermochelys coriacea*).

★ **Largest tortoise**
The largest specimen was a Galapagos tortoise (*Chelonoidis nigra*) named Goliath, who resided at the Life Fellowship Bird Sanctuary in Seffner, Florida, USA, from 1960 to 2002. He was 4 ft 5 in (135.8 cm) long, 3 ft 4 in (102 cm) wide and 2 ft 3 in (68.5 cm) high, and weighed 920 lb (417 kg).

★ **Oldest crocodilian**
The greatest authenticated age for a crocodilian is 66 years – achieved by a female American alligator (*Alligator mississippiensis*) that arrived at Adelaide Zoo, South Australia, on June 5 1914 when she was two years old. She died on September 26 1978.

★ **Most dangerous lizard**
With a length of up to 24 in (60 cm), the Gila monster (*Heloderma suspectum*) is a large, heavily built, brightly colored lizard that lives in the arid parts of Mexico and southwestern USA. They have eight well-developed venom glands in their lower jaws and carry enough venom to kill two adult humans. The venom is not injected but seeps into the wound inflicted when the Gila monster bites its victim with its sharp, fragile teeth. Because of this, a lizard may continue to hang on after

it has bitten and actively chew for several minutes. In one study of 34 people bitten by these animals, there were eight fatalities. The lizard only attacks when provoked.

★ **Largest lizard**
The largest lizard is the Komodo dragon (*Varanus komodoensis*), otherwise known as the Komodo monitor or ora, found on the Indonesian islands of Komodo, Rintja, Padar, and Flores. Males average 7 ft 5 in (2.25 m) in length and weigh about 130 lb (59 kg). The largest accurately measured specimen was a male presented to an American zoologist in 1928 by the Sultan of Bima. For a short period in 1937 it was put on display in St. Louis Zoological Gardens, Missouri, USA, by which time it was 10 ft 2 in (3.10 m) long and weighed 365 lb (166 kg).

Oldest snake ⌃

The greatest reliable age recorded for a snake is 40 years 3 months and 14 days for a male common boa (*Boa constrictor*, above) named Popeye, who died at Philadelphia Zoo, Pennsylvania, USA, on April 15 1977.

★ Longest lizard
The slender Salvadori or Papuan monitor (*Varanus salvadorii*) of Papua New Guinea has been reliably measured at up to 15 ft 7 in (4.75 m) in length. Nearly 70% of its total length is taken up by the tail.

★ Fastest lizard
The highest burst of speed recorded for any reptile on land is 21.7 mph (34.9 km/h), achieved by *Ctenosaura*, a spiny-tailed iguana from Central America.

★ Fastest land snake
The fastest land snake is the aggressive black mamba (*Dendroaspis polylepis*) of southeastern, tropical Africa. The snake can reach speeds of 10–12 mph (16–19 km/h) in short bursts over level ground.

★ Heaviest living snake
The heaviest living snake is a Burmese python (*Python molurus bivittatus*) that weighed 403 lb (182.5 kg) on November 20 1998. She is 25 years old, 27 ft (8.22 m) long, and has a girth of 28 in (71.1 cm). Known as 'Baby', she lives at the Serpent Safari Park in Gurnee, Illinois, USA, and is owned by Lou Daddano (USA). Snakes continue to grow throughout their lives, so Baby is still growing.

★ Longest snake
The reticulated python (*Python reticulatus*) of Southeast Asia, Indonesia, and the Philippines regularly exceeds 20 ft 6 in (6.25 m), and the record length is 32 ft 9.5 in (10 m) for a specimen shot in Celebes, Indonesia, in 1912.

★ Longest venomous snake
The longest venomous snake is the king cobra (*Ophiophagus hannah*), also called the hamadryad, which measures 12–15 ft (3.65–4.5 m) in length and is found in Southeast Asia and India. The king cobra can stand tall enough to look an adult human in the eye and its head is as big as a man's hand. Its venom can stun the nervous system and cause asphyxiation while other toxins start digesting the paralyzed victim. The venom in a single bite from a king cobra is enough to kill an elephant or 20 people.

★ Most venomous land snake
The small-scaled fierce snake or taipan (*Oxyuranus microlepidotus*) measures up to 5 ft 7 in (1.7 m) and is found mainly in the Diamantina River and Cooper Creek drainage basins in Queensland and western New South Wales, Australia. In a single strike, a taipan can inject 0.002 oz (60 mg) of venom, sufficient to quickly paralyze a small marsupial, but also more than enough to kill several human adults. The average venom yield after milking is 0.00155 oz (44 mg) but one male specimen yielded 0.00385 oz (110 mg) – enough to kill 250,000 mice. Fortunately this species only lives in the arid deserts of central eastern Australia and no human death has been reported from its bite.

★ Heaviest venomous snake
The heaviest venomous snake is probably the eastern diamondback rattlesnake (*Crotalus adamanteus*) of the southeastern USA, which weighs 12–15 lb (5.5–6.8 kg) and is 5–6 ft (1.52–1.83 m) in length. The heaviest on record weighed 33 lb (15 kg) and was 7 ft 9 in (2.36 m) long.

Smallest living dog ⌃

The smallest living dog in terms of length is Tiny Pinocchio (above),

who measured 8 in (20.3 cm) long on May 23 2003. Tiny Pinocchio is owned by Linda Skeels-Hopson (USA). The smallest dog in terms of height is Whitney, a Yorkshire terrier who measured 3 in (7.6 cm) to the shoulder on November 26 2002. Whitney is owned by Christopher and Patricia Sheridan (both UK).

Tallest and longest dog ⌃

Harvey, a Great Dane owned by Charles Dodman (UK, both above), stands at 41.5 in (105.41 cm) tall

and measures 91 in (231.14 cm) from nose to tip. Great Danes are one of the tallest dog breeds, with an average height from the ground to the top of the shoulder of around 29.5 in (75 cm).

★ **Fastest car window opening by a dog**
The world record for the fastest time a dog has unwound a non-electric car window is 13 seconds and belongs to Striker, a border collie owned and trained by Francis Gadassi (Hungary). The record was set on August 14 2003 in Québec City, Canada. Striker used his paw and nose to perform the record attempt.

★ **Longest dog tongue**
Brandy, a boxer owned by John Scheid (USA), had a tongue that measured 17 in (43 cm).

★ **Smallest dog ever**
The smallest dog was a fist-sized dwarf Yorkshire terrier owned by Arthur Marples (UK). Fully grown, this tiny dog stood 2.8 in (7.11 cm) at the shoulder and measured 3.75 in (9.5 cm) from its nose to the tip of its tail.

★ **Highest jump by a dog**
The world record for the highest jump cleared by a dog is 66 in (167.6 cm), achieved by Cinderella May A Holly Grey, a greyhound owned by Kathleen Conroy and Kate Long (both USA), at the Purina Dog Chow Incredible Dog Challenge show, Gray Summit, Missouri, USA, on October 3 2003.

★ **Largest dog litter**
Three dogs are on record as having given birth to 23 puppies. An American foxhound belonging to W. Ely (USA) is the first dog to have recorded this feat, on June 19 1944. Between February 6 and 7 1975 a St Bernard belonging to R. and A. Rodden (USA) had 14 of its puppies survive. A Great Dane belonging to M. Harris (UK) had 16 of its litter survive in June 1987.

★ **Longest ears on a dog**
The longest ears on a dog each measured 13 in (33.2 cm) in length when they were measured on December 11 2003. They belong to a basset hound named Jack vom Forster Wald, who lives with his owners, Claudia and Carsten Baus, in Fulda, Germany.

★ **Most tennis balls held in the mouth by a dog**
Augie, a golden retriever owned by the Miller family (USA), successfully gathered and held five regulation-sized tennis balls in his mouth on July 6 2003.

★ **Oldest horse ever**
The greatest age reliably recorded for a horse is 62 years for Old Billy (foaled 1760), bred by Edward Robinson, Woolston, Lancashire, UK. Old Billy died on November 27 1822.

★ **Oldest donkey ever**
The donkey with the oldest documented age is Suzy, who reached the age of 54 in 2002. Suzy was owned by Beth Augusta Menczer (USA). The average life span of a donkey is 25–30 years.

« Tallest living horse

Goliath (left) measured 19 hands 1 in (195.58 cm or 77 in) on July 24 2003.

Goliath is owned by Priefert Manufacturing, Inc. (USA) and is a male black Percheron draft horse, whose pedigree name is Prince Jordan of Lakeview. On average, he eats 50 lb (22.6 kg) of hay and drinks 30 gallons (113.5 liters) of water per day.

Largest horn circumference

Lurch (below), an African watusi steer owned by Janice Wolf (USA), had a horn circumference of 37.5 in (95.25 cm) when measured on May 6 2003. Although they are not the longest horns on record, Lurch's horns are each approximately 7 ft (2.1 m). ⌄

★ **Oldest pony ever**
The world's oldest pony was Sancho, a Welsh/Arab cross who reached the age of 54 years in 2003. Sancho was owned by Elizabeth Saunders (UK) and was discovered by the Veteran Horse Society, North Pembrokeshire, UK. The pony died in August 2003.

★ **Oldest living rabbit**
The world's oldest living rabbit is Baby, a Holland Lop born in August 1990 and owned by Kayla and Sue Bulos (both USA). House rabbits usually live for around 7–10 years.

★ **Oldest rabbit ever**
A wild rabbit named Flopsy was caught on August 6 1964 and died 18 years and 10 months later at the home of L.B. Walker (Australia).

★ **Longest rabbit ears**
The longest rabbit ears measured 31.1 in (79 cm) in a complete span on November 1 2003 at the American Rabbit Breeders Association National Show in Wichita, Kansas, USA. The ears belong to an English Lop called Nipper's Geronimo, who is owned by Waymon and Margaret Nipper (USA).

★ **Highest rabbit high jump**
The highest rabbit high jump is 18 in (46 cm), achieved by Golden Flame, a castor satin rabbit belonging to Sam Lawrie (UK), on August 29 2002.

★ **Largest mouse litter**
A mouse belonging to M. Ogilvie (UK) gave birth to a litter of 34 on February 12 1982, 33 of which survived.

★ **Smallest breed of domestic hamster**
The Roborovski hamster (*Phodopus roborovskii*) typically grows to a length

of 1.5–2 in (4–5 cm). These hamsters originate from Mongolia and northern China.

★ **Largest hamster litter**
On February 28 1974, a hamster belonging to the Miller family (USA) gave birth to a litter of 26. The average is eight babies per litter.

★ **Largest cat litter**
On August 7 1970 a Burmese/ Siamese cross cat owned by V. Gane (UK) gave birth to 19 kittens, four of which were stillborn.

★ **Oldest kinkajou in captivity**
The oldest living kinkajou (*Potos flavus*) in captivity is Huggy Bear, who turned 27 years 6 months old in January 2004 and belongs to Sonja Pedersen (USA). A kinkajou is a member of the raccoon family.

★ **Oldest goat ever**
The world's oldest goat was McGinty, who lived to the age of 22 years 5 months. Until her death in November 2003, she was owned by Doris C. Long (UK).

★ **Oldest caged parrot**
The longest lived caged parrot was Prudle, owned by Iris Frost (UK). Prudle was captured in 1958 and lived to the age of 35. Before dying in 1994, Prudle had learned over 800 words and could even conduct polite conversation.

★ **Cat with the most toes**
Jake, a male ginger tabby cat, has 28 toes, with seven on each paw, as counted by a veterinarian on September 24 2002. Jake lives in Bonfield, Ontario, Canada, with his owners Michelle and Paul Contant (Canada).

Largest flower

The mottled orange-brown and white parasite *Rafflesia arnoldii* (right) has the largest of all blooms. These attach themselves to the cissus vines in the jungles of Southeast Asia. They measure up to 3 ft (91 cm) across, weigh up to 24 lb (11 kg) and their petals are 0.75 in (1.9 cm) thick.

»

Smallest seed ⪢

Epiphytic orchids (orange epiphytic orchid, below) produce 28,130 million seeds per oz (992.25 million per gram). The largest seed is that of the giant fan palm or double coconut (*Lodoicea maldivica*). The single-seeded fruit weighs up to 44 lb (20 kg) and can take 10 years to develop.

★ GWR TALKS TO
Ron Hildebrant

Ron Hildebrant (USA) has spent much of his life tracking down the record-breakers of the tree world. He helped to measure the tallest living tree, the 396-ft 4.8-in (112.6-m) Stratosphere Giant (see right) in August 2000, and he's more than happy to share his enthusiasm for trees with *Guinness World Records* readers!

What exactly is a tree hunter?
A tree hunter is someone who looks for the biggest, tallest, and oldest trees. Sometimes unusual ones are sought, such as rare specimens or those with unusually shaped trunks or strange branching, but most of the time tree hunters are searching for trees with measurable parameters – such as height, diameter, or age.

Redwoods are the tallest trees in the world. What is the most amazing one you have seen?
I'd say the late great Dyerville Giant, which fell after a storm in March 1991. It was, until then, the world's tallest tree, being 113.4 m (372 feet) high, and indeed the tallest tree of modern times. It was 16.6 ft (5.06 m) in diameter and perhaps up to 2,500 years old – I haven't yet determined its exact age – and had a trunk volume of 28,500 ft³ (807 m³), making it one of the largest redwoods of modern times. After its fall I discovered it had at one time been even taller – 390 to 400 ft (119 to 122 m) high a couple of centuries ago.

You've seen the world's tallest tree. How old is it?
Yes, I have; this is the well-named Stratosphere Giant, which towers very, very high, at 369 ft 4.8 in (112.6 m) as of 2002 – and is still growing. I recently did an accurate age estimate of the tree after having greatly improved my methods for coast redwoods, and it's about 1,600 years old, plus or minus about a hundred years.

How do you measure a tree?
In the pre-laser days it was a lot of grunt work – we'd lay out tape lines, plumbing treetops from three places and using a good surveyor's transit. It required taking slope angles into account, but the hardest part was adjusting for leaning or off-centered treetops. In the mid-1990s, the laser came out. These revolutionary devices have greatly reduced the time, labor, and effort involved, and are extremely accurate. With the laser, leaning tops are no longer an issue, for a direct measurement is determined by the laser itself. We can point and shoot at a tree and get a reading accurate to within a few feet in just seconds.

How do you become a tree hunter?
If you're willing to invest in some good tools and you have some good math skills in algebra and trigonometry and keep yourself in good physical shape, that's a good start. It's helpful to know how a particular tree species behaves in certain environments, making it easier to find particular types of trees. A background in botany, geology, meteorology, soils, and ecology are all a big plus. Expect to do plenty of hiking: in some of my hikes I do 10 miles (16 km) or more in a day, or hike up to 11,000 ft (3,350 m) or more in elevation. Finally, expect to fail in your quests now and then, but never give up!

Oldest living individual tree ⌃

The oldest living individual tree is the ancient bristlecone pine (*Pinus longaeva*) called Methuselah (above), which is 4,733 years old. It was found by Dr. Edmund Schulman (USA) in the White Mountains, California, USA, and dated in 1957.

★ Tallest living tree
The world's tallest living tree is the Stratosphere Giant, which measured 369 ft 4.8 in (112.6 m) as of 2002. This coast redwood (*Sequoia sempervirens*) was discovered by Chris Atkins (USA) in August 2000 in the Rockefeller Forest of the Humboldt Redwoods State Park, California, USA.

★ Fastest growing tree
The fastest recorded rate of growth for any tree (discounting bamboo, which is classified as a woody grass) is 35 ft 2.8 in (10.74 m) in 13 months, or approximately 1.1 in (2.8 cm) per day by an *Albizzia falcata* planted on June 17 1974 in Sabah, Malaysia.

★ Earliest tree
The earliest surviving species of tree is the maidenhair (*Ginkgo biloba*) of Zhejiang, China, which first appeared about 160 million years ago during the Jurassic era. It was rediscovered by Engelbert Kaempfer (Germany) in 1690. It has been grown in Japan since c. 1100, where it was known as ginkyou (silver apricot) and is now known as ichou.

★ Oldest tree ever documented
The oldest age for a tree ever recorded is for a bristlecone pine (*Pinus longaeva*) known as Prometheus, which was cut down from Mt. Wheeler in Nevada, USA, in 1963 and dated at approximately 5,200 years old. Although 4,867 rings were counted – the most ever – the tree was growing in a harsh environment which slowed its development, and so its actual age has been adjusted to approximately 5,200 years old.

★ Largest prey for carnivorous plants
Of all the carnivorous plants or pitcher plants, the ones that digest the largest prey belong to the Nepenthaceae family (genus *Nepenthes*). Both the *Nepenthes rajah* and *N. rafflesiana* have been known to consume frogs, birds, and even rats, digesting their prey using enzymes. These species are commonly found in the rainforests of Asia, notably Borneo and Indonesia.

★ Most dangerous stinger
New Zealand's tree nettle (*Urtica ferox*) has been known to kill dogs and horses. Its stinging hairs inject potent toxins into the skin. The tree nettle can grow up to 10 ft (3 m) in height. Fine white stinging hairs line its green leaves and contain many toxins, the main ones being histamine, 5-hydroxytryptamine, acetylcholine, and formic acid.

★ Smelliest flower
Also known as the corpse flower, the *Amorphophallus titanum* is the smelliest flower on Earth. When it blooms, it releases an extremely foul odor – comparable to that of rotten flesh – that can be smelled half a mile away. This plant is native to the Sumatran rainforests and very few have flowered in Europe or the USA since first discovered in 1878.

★ Tallest wild cactus
The tallest cacti ever recorded is a cardon (*Pachycereus pringlei*) found in the Sonoran Desert, Baja California, Mexico. It measures 63 ft (19.2 m) and was discovered by Marc Salak and Jeff Brown (both USA) in April 1995. Its incredible height is about the same as the combined height of four giraffes.

Heaviest lemon

The heaviest lemon (below) weighed 11 lb 9.7 oz (5.26 kg) on January 8 2003 and was grown by Aharon Shemoel (Israel) on his farm in Kefar Zeitim, Israel. Its circumference was 29 in (74 cm), it was 13.7 in (35 cm) high, and it grew alongside another large lemon.

★ Longest zucchini
A zucchini measuring 76 in (1.93 m) on September 22 2003 was grown by Sher Singh Kanwal (USA) in his garden in Niagara Falls, New York, USA.

★ Longest beetroot
A beetroot grown by Richard Hope (UK) measured 20 ft 2 in (6.146 m) on September 27 2003 at the Llanharry Giant Vegetable Championships, Rhondda Cynon Taff, UK.

★ Most heads on one sunflower
A sunflower plant with 837 heads was grown by Melvin Hemker (USA). The heads were counted on September 18 2001.

★ Largest rosebush
A specimen of the rosebush Lady Banks (*Rosa banksiae*), known as Banks at Tombstone, Arizona, USA, has a trunk circumference of 13 ft 5 in (4.09 m), stands 9 ft (2.75 m) high, and covers an area of 8,000 ft² (743 m²). The bush is supported by 77 posts, and 250 people can sit under the arbor.

★ Largest homegrown lily bloom
A lily bloom measuring 23.2 in (59 cm) long on March 21 2002 was grown by Natividad Rico Pérez (Spain) at her home in Monóvar, Alicante, Spain.

★ Largest gourd circumference
Robert Weber (Australia) grew a gourd with a circumference of 69.6 in (1.77 m) and presented it at the Australasian Giant Pumpkin and Vegetable Competition in Victoria, Australia, on April 7 2001.

★ Largest tomato truss
A record 185 tomatoes were counted on a tomato plant grown by Joe Hallam (UK) on August 19 2003.

★ Tree with most different fruit
The record for the most fruits produced from the same tree is five: apricot, cherry, nectarine, plum, and peach. The fruit species were grafted on to a prune tree in 2000 by Luis H. Carrasco E (Chile).

Heaviest Fruit and Vegetables

Fruit/Vegetable	Weight	Name & Venue	Date
Apple	3 lb 11 oz (1.67 kg)	Alan Smith (UK), Linton, Kent, UK	1997
Beetroot	51 lb 9 oz (23.4 kg)	Ian Neale (UK), Shepton Mallet, Somerset, UK	2001
Brussels sprout	18 lb 3 oz (8.3 kg)	Bernard Lavery (UK), Llanharry, Rhondda Cynon Taff, UK	1992
Cabbage	124 lb (56.24 kg)	Bernard Lavery (UK), Llanharry, Rhondda Cynon Taff, UK	1989
Cantaloupe	63 lb 8 oz (28.8 kg)	Bill Rogerson (USA), Robersonville, North Carolina, USA	1997
Carrot	18 lb 13 oz (8.61 kg)	John Evans (USA), Palmer, Alaska, USA	1998
Cauliflower	54 lb 3 oz (24.6 kg)	Alan Hattersley (UK), Sheffield, UK	1999
Celery	63 lb 4.8 oz (28.7 kg)	Scott and Mardie Robb (both USA), Palmer, USA	2003
Cherry	0.76 oz (21.69 g)	Gerado Maggipinto (Italy), Sammichele di Bari, Italy	2003
Courgette	64 lb 8 oz (29.25 kg)	Bernard Lavery (UK), Llanharry, Rhondda Cynon Taff, UK	1990
Cucumber	27 lb 3 oz 12.4 kg)	Alfred J. Cobb (UK), Shepton Mallet, Somerset, UK	2003
Garlic head	2 lb 10 oz (1.19 kg)	Robert Kirkpatrick (USA), Eureka, California, USA	1985
Gooseberry	2.15 oz (61.04 g)	K Archer (UK), Scholar Green, Cheshire, UK	1993
Gourd	94 lb 5 oz (42.8 kg)	Robert Weber (Australia), Victoria, Australia	2001
Grapefruit	6 lb 12 oz (3.065 kg)	Debbie Hazelton (Australia), Queensland, Australia	1995
Leek	17 lb 13 oz (8.1 kg)	Fred Charlton (UK), Somerset, UK	2002
Lemon	11 lb 9.7 oz (5.26 kg)	Aharon Shemoel (Israel) Kefar Zeitim, Israel	2003
Mango	4 lb 4 oz (1.94 kg)	John Painter (USA), Bokeelia, Florida, USA,	1999
Marrow	135 lb (61.23 kg)	John Handbury (UK), Temple Normanton, Chesterfield, UK	1998
Onion	15 lb 15.5 oz (7.24 kg)	Mel Ednie (UK), Anstruther, Fife, UK	1994
Parsnip	8 lb 6 oz (3.8 kg)	Norman Lee Craven (Canada), Toronto, Ontario, Canada.	2003
Peach	25.6 oz (725 g)	Paul Friday (USA), Coloma, Michigan, USA	2002
Pear	4 lb 8 oz (2.1 kg)	Warren Yeoman (Australia), Arding, New South Wales, Australia	1999
Pineapple	17 lb 12 oz (8.06 kg)	E. Kamuk (Papua New Guinea), Ais Village, West New Britain Province, Papau New Guinea	1994
Potato	7 lb 11 oz (3.5 kg)	K. Sloane (UK), Patrick, Isle of Man, UK	1994
Pumpkin	1,337 lb 9 oz (606.7 kg)	Charles Houghton (USA), Massachusetts, USA	2002
Quince	5 lb 2 oz (2.34 kg)	Edward Harold McKinney (USA), Citronelle, Alabama, USA	2002
Radish	68 lb 9 oz (31.1 kg)	Manubu Oono (Japan), Kagoshima, Japan	2003
Squash	962 lb (436 kg)	Steve Hoult (Canada), Toronto, Ontario, Canada	1997
Strawberry	8.14 oz (231 g)	G. Andersen (UK), Folkstone, Kent, UK	1983
Swede (rutabaga)	75 lb 12 oz (34.35 kg)	Scott Robb (USA), Palmer, Alaska, USA	1999
Sweet potato	49 lb 9oz (22.5 kg)	Belinda Love (Australia), Gingin, Western Australia	1998
Tomato	7 lb 12 oz (3.51 kg)	G. Graham (USA), Edmond, Oklahoma, USA	1986

Heaviest cucumber

Alfred J. Cobb (UK) grew a cucumber (held above by Mr. Atherton) weighing 27 lb 5.3 oz (12.4 kg). It was presented at the National Amateur Gardening Show's UK National Giant Vegetables Championship at Shepton Mallet, Somerset, UK, on September 5 2003.

Tallest Plants

Plant	Height	Name & Venue	Date
Bean	46 ft 3 in (14.1 m)	Staton Rorie (USA), Rienzi, Mississippi, USA	2003
Celery	9 ft (2.74 m)	Joan Priednieks (UK), Westonzoyland, Somerset, UK	1998
Cactus (homegrown)	70 ft (21.3 m)	Pandit S. Munji (India), Dharwad, Karnataka, India	2004
Chrysanthemum	14 ft 3 in (4.34 m)	Bernard Lavery (UK), Spalding, Lincolnshire, UK	1995
Dandelion	39.3 in (100 cm)	Ragnar Gille and Marcus Hamring (both Sweden), Uppsala, Sweden	2003
Fuchsia	21 ft 7 in (6.58 m)	The Growing Place (UK), Spalding, Lincolnshire, UK,	2003
Papaya tree	44 ft (13.4 m)	Prasanta Mal (India), Arambagh, Hooghly, India	2003
Parsley	55 in (1.39 m)	Danielle, Gabrielle, and Michelle Kassatly, (all USA), San Jose, California, USA	2003
Pepper	16 ft (4.87 m)	Laura Liang (USA), Irvine, California	1999
Periwinkle	7 ft 2 in (2.19 m)	Arvind, Rekha, Ashish and Rashmi Nema (all India), Indrapuri, Bhopal, India	2003
Petunia	19 ft 1 in (5.8 m)	Bernard Lavery (UK), Llanharry, Rhondda Cynon Taff, UK	1994
Potato or brinjal	18 ft 0.5 in (5.5 m)	Abdul Masfoor (India), Karnataka State, India	1998
Rosebush	11 ft 1 in (3.38 m)	Kathleen Mielke-Villalobos (USA), San Diego, California, USA	2003
Sunflower	25 ft 5.5 in (7.76 m)	M. Heijms (Netherlands), Oirschot, Netherlands	1986
Tomato	65 ft (19.8 m)	Nutriculture Ltd. (UK), Mawdesley, Lancashire, UK	2000

★ GWR TALKS TO
Bernard Lavery

From monster corncobs to fantastic fuchsias, Bernard Lavery's (UK, below right) records for giant fruit, vegetables, and plants are some of the best loved Guinness World Records. He currently holds 12 records, including the longest gourd, which grew to 41 ft 4 in (12.6 m) in 1992, and the longest corncob, which grew to a length of 36.25 in (92 cm) in 1994.

How did you get involved in growing giants?
I first caught the 'growing' bug over 20 years ago while growing my first pumpkin (right). Although this didn't break any records, the pleasures I got from the experience were immense and soon multiplied when I directed my efforts to a whole range of different vegetable subjects. In 1985, I organized the first UK Giant Vegetable Championships in Cardiff.

How do you grow giant vegetables?
The most important factor is to use the varieties of seeds that have the genetic capabilities to produce larger than average specimens. It's then advisable to obtain some advice from books or other giant growers. If these options are unavailable then you must just have a go yourself. You must remember that when you make a mistake another year will have to pass before you can try again. The second most important thing you must have is the presence of 'Lady Luck'. If she's sitting on your shoulder then you're halfway there.

What would you like to grow that you haven't tried?
The aubergine (eggplant) would be my choice for a new challenge. I've grown some large ones already, but nowhere near a world record weight.

Can you eat these giants after they have been shown?
Giant vegetables are much the same as ordinary size ones. When they're young and freshly harvested they are superb, but when they're grown on to well past their best, then like ordinary ones, they become tough and tasteless.

What is the record you are most proud of?
I am most proud of the record I set in 1991 for the longest carrot that measured 16 ft 10.5 in (5.14 m).

What's your best advice for growing giant plants?
Just try to enjoy it. It's a real challenge to stretch Mother Nature to her limits and beyond, but if at first you don't succeed then try, try again. It's magical when you succeed.

Modern world

Contents

« Highest life expectancy

Japan had the highest life expectancy at birth in 2002 with a total population average of 81.1 years (77.5 years for men and 84.7 years for women).

˅ Lowest life expectancy

According to 2001 data, life expectancy at birth in the Republic of Botswana in Africa is only 37.1 years (36.8 years for men and 37.5 years for women).

★ Largest country
Russia's total area covers 11.5% of the world's total land area – 6,592,848 miles² (17,075,400 km²). It is 70 times larger than the UK, with a population of 144,417,000 in 2001.

★ Most maritime boundaries
The country with the largest number of maritime boundaries is Indonesia, with 19 (including boundaries with disputed territorial claims).

★ Most land boundaries
The countries with the most land boundaries are China and Russia, both with 14. China's are: Mongolia, Russia, North Korea, Vietnam, Laos, Burma (Myanmar), India, Bhutan, Nepal, Pakistan, Afghanistan, Tajikistan, Kyrgyzstan, and Kazakhstan. These extend for 14,900 miles (24,000 km). Russia has boundaries with Norway, Finland, Estonia, Latvia, Lithuania, Poland, Belarus, Ukraine, Georgia, Azerbaijan, Kazakhstan, China, Mongolia, and North Korea. These boundaries extend for 12,365 miles (19,900 km).

★ Country of origin for most refugees
The country from which most people seek asylum is Iraq. According to the 2002 figures from the United Nations High Commission for Refugees (UNHCR), 51,000 Iraqis applied for political asylum to one of 37 industrialized nations. The total number of applications made in 2002 was 587,400.

★ Country receiving most applications for political asylum
According to figures from UNHCR, of the 587,400 applications for political asylum that were submitted in 2002, the country that received the highest number was the UK with 111,606 (19%).

★ Country with most administrative divisions
The UK has a record 235 administrative divisions.

★ Country from which the most countries have gained independence
A total of 62 countries have gained independence from the UK.

★ Country with the most official languages
The Republic of South Africa has 11 official languages: English, Afrikaans, isiZulu, isiXhosa, Sesotho, Setswana, Sepedi, Xitsonga, siSwati, isiNdebele, and Tshivenda.

★ Highest and lowest inflation
Zimbabwe has the highest inflation according to the Economist Intelligence Unit 2003 forecast, with consumer prices rising at over 300%. Hong Kong currently has the lowest inflation at -2.5 %.

★ Highest and lowest cost of living
According to the Economist Intelligence Unit's Worldwide Cost of Living Survey of January 2003 (for December 2002 results), Japan's capital city, Tokyo, is the most expensive city in the world. Harare, the capital of Zimbabwe, is the world's cheapest.

★ Most and least taxed country
In Denmark the highest rate of personal income tax is 62.9%, with the basic rate of income tax starting at 43.7% (June 2003). Bahrain and Qatar are the lowest taxed countries, where the rate, regardless of income, is zero. For both nations, oil provides over half of government revenues.

Highest and lowest ⌃⌃ government revenues

The country that produced the highest government revenues

from taxation per km² of physical land is the Vatican City (above) with $476,363,636 (£302,031,217) as of 2001. The lowest is the Democratic Republic of the Congo with only $115 (£72) per km² of land.

★ **Highest and lowest GNI per capita**

According to the World Bank Atlas, the country with the highest Gross National Income (GNI) for 2002 was Bermuda, which overtook Luxembourg with $38,830 (£25,627). The Democratic Republic of Congo had the lowest GNI per capita with $90 (£59). GNI is the total value of goods and services produced by a country in one year, divided by its population. GNI per capita shows what part of a country's GNI each person would have if it was divided equally.

★ **Country with the largest energy consumption**

The USA is the world's largest consumer of both fossil fuels (coal, oil, and natural gas) and commercial energy (fossil fuels plus nuclear and hydro power). In 1998, it consumed a total of 1,937 million tons of oil equivalent (Mtoe) of fossil fuels and 2,147 Mtoe of commercial energy. The total world energy consumption of fossil fuels was 7,624 Mtoe and the world

total energy consumption of commercial fuel was 8,477 Mtoe.

★ **Most densely populated country**

Monaco has a population density of 42,840 per mile² (16,476 per km²) in 2003. Its population that year was 32,130 with a total area of 0.75 miles² (1.95 km²). This equates to each person having 652 ft² (60.6 m²) of land.

★ **Most sparsely populated country**

In 2001, Mongolia had a population of 2,435,000 in an area of 603,930 miles² (1,564,160 km²), giving a density of 4 people to every 1 mile² (1.6 people to every 1 km²).

★ **Most populous country**

In 2003, China had an estimated population of 1,286,975,468 – higher than that for the whole world 150 years ago, when the world population stood at 1,260,000,000. The UN's predicted population for China in 2025 is 1.48 billion.

★ **Least populous country**

The Vatican City, or Holy See, had approximately 911 inhabitants in 2003. The Vatican is the world's smallest country.

★ **Largest population of children**

In the Marshall Islands, in the north of the Pacific Ocean, 39.1% of the population were under the age of 15 in 2003. Out of an estimated total population of 56,429, approximately 22,063 individuals were aged between 0 and 14 years.

★ **Most bombed country**

The most heavily bombed country has been Laos. It has been estimated that between May 1964 and February 26 1973 some 5 billion lb

(2.26 million tonnes) of bombs were dropped along the North to South Ho Chi Minh Trail supply route to South Vietnam.

★ **Country with highest military expenditure per capita**

Israel has the highest military expenditure per capita, with $1,487.68 (£819.07) spent per person as of 2003. Israel had a population of 6,258,000 in 2001.

★ **Country with lowest military expenditure per capita**

From available figures, the country that spends the least money on military expenditure is Swaziland, with $17.80 (£9.80) per person as of 2003. Swaziland had a population of 1,104,000 in 2001.

Longest reigning queen ⌄

The longest reigning queen is Victoria (below), Queen of Great Britain and, from 1876, Empress of India. She ruled for 63 years 216 days, from 1837 to 1901.

« Youngest reigning monarch

Swaziland's King Mswati III (left) was crowned on April 25 1986 when aged 18 years 6 days. He was born Makhosetive, the 67th son of King Sobhuza II.

★ Longest lived prime minister

The longest lived prime minister of any country was Antoine Pinay (France), who was born on December 30 1891 and died on December 13 1994 aged 102 years 348 days. He was his country's prime minister from March to December 1952.

★ Most reelected prime minister

Lebanese prime minister Rashid Karami was first elected in 1955 and then officially reelected seven additional times between 1958 and 1976. His final term of office was in 1984, when most people hoped he would end the country's civil war, but he was assassinated

in 1987 by a bomb thrown at his helicopter. Karami served in 1955–56; 1958–60; 1961–64; 1965–66; 1966–68; 1969–70; 1975–76; and 1984–87.

★ Longest ruling party

The party with the longest uninterrupted spell in government is the PRI (Partido Revolucionario Institucional) of Mexico, which won every Mexican presidential election from 1929 to 2000, when it lost to the PAN (Partido de Accion Nacional).

★ Youngest president

Jean-Claude Duvalier (Haiti, b. July 3 1951) succeeded his father, François Duvalier, as Haitian president for life on April 22 1971, becoming the

world's youngest president at the age of 19 years 293 days. He served as president of Haiti until 1986.

★ Longest serving living president

General Gnassingbe Eyadema (Togo) became president of the Togolese Republic on April 14 1967 after leading a coup to oust President Nicolas Grunitzky.

★ Oldest president

Joaquin Balaguer was president of the Dominican Republic in 1960–62, 1966–78, and 1986–96. He ultimately left office at the age of 89, having held the presidency for no fewer than 22 years.

★ Youngest UN ambassador

Laura Sweeting (UK, b. June 1 1984) became the United Nations' youngest Goodwill Ambassador on June 9 2000. The 16-year-old schoolgirl's role in the Water4Life Appeal/ Children Helping Children

campaign raised awareness of the fact that over 5,000 people die each day because of the lack of clean water.

★ Youngest current head of state

Yahya Jammeh (b. May 25 1965) became president of the Provisional Council and Gambian head of state following a military coup on July 26 1994. On September 27 1996, he was elected president following a return to civilian government.

★ Longest serving mayor

The longest recorded mayoralty was that of Edmond Mathis (France), who served as mayor of Ehuns, Haute-Sàne, France, for 75 years (1878–1953).

★ Youngest mayor

The youngest mayor on record is Shane Mack (USA), born on November 15 1969. Shane was elected Mayor of Castlewood, South Dakota, USA, at the age of 18 years 169 days on May 3 1988 and held office for eight years.

Largest parliament ⌃

The largest legislative assembly in the world is the National People's Congress (NPC, above) of the People's Republic of China.

The 10th National People's Congress, elected at the beginning of 2003, is composed of 2,985 deputies legally elected by 35 electoral units nationwide. It is comprised of 31 provinces, autonomous regions, and municipalities, Hong Kong and Macao special administrative regions, and the Chinese People's Liberation Army. Every minority ethnic group has an appropriate number of representatives in the NPC.

★ **Wealthiest queen**
Owing to rising UK property values, the net worth of Queen Elizabeth II (UK) has increased nearly 60% in the last year. *Forbes World's Richest People 2004* estimates her wealth at £358.8 million ($660 million).

★ **Largest political constituency**
The Kalgoorlie Australian federal parliamentary constituency in Western Australia covers more than 1,000,000 miles² (2,600,000 km²), an area greater than the whole of western Europe. The constituency measures 1,400 miles (2,250 km) from north to south and 1,000 miles (1,600 km) from east to west, and covers the whole state of Western Australia except for Perth in the southwest.

★ **Most votes for a chimp in a political campaign**
In the 1988 mayoral elections campaign in Rio de Janeiro, Brazil, the antiestablishment 'Brazilian Banana Party' presented a chimpanzee named Tião as their candidate. The chimp came third out of 12 candidates, taking just over 400,000 votes. Known for his moody temper, the chimp's campaign slogan was 'Vote monkey – get monkey'. Tião died in 1996 aged 33. Tião means 'Big Uncle' in Portuguese.

★ **Heaviest monarch**
In September 1976, King Taufa'ahau Tupou IV of Tonga recorded a weight of 462 lb (209.5 kg). He is 6 ft 3 in (1.9 m) tall. By 1985, he was reported to have slimmed down to 307 lb (139.7 kg); in early 1993, he was 279 lb (127.0 kg); and by 1998 he had lost further weight as a result of a fitness program.

★ **Oldest ruling house**
The Emperor of Japan, Akihito (b. December 23 1933), is the 125th in line from the first Emperor, Jimmu Tenno, whose reign was traditionally from 660 BC to 581 BC but more probably dates from c. 40 BC to c.10 BC.

★ **Largest royal family**
There are more than 4,200 royal princes and more than 40,000 other relatives in the Saudi royal family.

★ **Longest reigning living queen**
Born on April 21 1926, Queen Elizabeth II (UK) is currently the longest reigning living queen.

She succeeded to the throne on February 6 1952 on the death of her father, King George VI. She is Queen of the United Kingdom and Head of the Commonwealth. The year 2002 saw the Queen's Golden Jubilee, marking 50 years since her accession.

★ **Longest reigns ever**
Minhti, King of Arakan (now part of Burma [Myanmar]), is reputed to have reigned for 95 years between 1279 and 1374, but the longest well-documented reign of any monarch was that of Phiops II (also known as Pepi II), or Neferkare, a Sixth-Dynasty pharaoh of ancient Egypt. His reign began c. 2281 BC, when he was six years old, and is believed to have lasted around 94 years.

Musoma Kanijo, although not a monarch, was chief of the Nzega district of Tanganyika (now part of Tanzania) and reputedly reigned for more than 98 years from 1864, when he was eight years old, until his death on February 2 1963.

The environment
Modern world

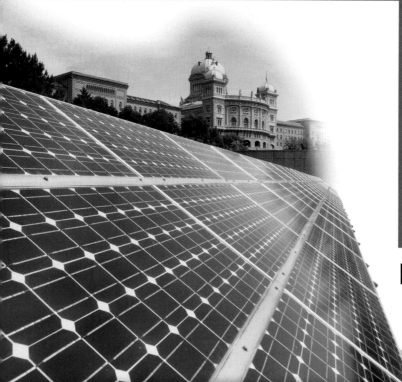

Largest olive cultivator ⌃

Spain is the world's leading cultivator of olives, producing 2.1 billion lb (970,000 tons) of olives annually.

The principal olive-producing regions are Catalonia and Andalusia. Spain and Italy together account for 54% of the total amount of olive oil produced worldwide.

Highest solar energy ⌃ use per capita

At 1.82 W per capita, Switzerland has the highest solar energy usage in the world.

The picture above shows a photovoltaic generating plant installed at a government office building in Berne, Switzerland.

★ Largest solar power facility

In terms of nominal capacity, the largest solar electric power facility in the world is the Harper Lake Site (LSP VIII & IX) in the Mojave Desert, California, USA, operated by UC Operating Services (USA). The two solar electric generating stations (SEGS) at Harper Lake have a nominal capacity of 160 MW (80 MW each). The site covers 1,280 acres (518 hectares) and houses 400,000 solar collectors – mirrors that concentrate solar energy – over a 1,000-acre](400-hectare) area.

★ Largest solar-slate roof

In 1999, a former grain storage facility in Berne, Switzerland, was fitted with a 22,000-ft^2 (2,050-m^2) solar-slate roof comprising 16,650 photovoltaic cell-embedded slates known as Sunslates. The project was planned and engineered by Atlantis Energy Ltd., and generates 167,000 kWh (kilowatt-hours) of electrical energy, which is fed into the city's electricity grid. The total investment in the project was 2.6 million Swiss francs ($1.7 million or £1.1 million).

★ Most environmentally friendly country

The country regarded as the most environmentally sustainable is Finland, which heads the Environmental Sustainability Index (ESI) compiled in 2002 by the World Economic Forum.

Based on 20 core indicators covering five broad areas – environmental systems (e.g. air and water quality); reducing environmental stress (e.g. pollution levels) reducing human vulnerability to environmental degradation, social and institutional capacity to respond to environmental threats and contribution to global stewardship – Finland scored 73.9 out of 100. The lowest was Kuwait with 23.9.

★ Largest producer of energy

In 2001, the USA produced 75,295 petajoules of commercial energy, including solid, liquid and gaseous fuels as well as primary electricity. A petajoule is 1,000,000,000,000,000 joules.

★ Fastest forest depletion

Burundi, Central Africa, suffers the fastest decrease in forested area with an average loss of 9% every year between 1990 and 2000. If this rate was permanently sustained, Burundi's forested areas would be completely cleared in just over 11 years.

★ Largest deforestation

The greatest deforestation rate is in Brazil where, between 1990 and 2000, an average of 8,596 miles^2 (22,264 km^2) of forest was cleared every year. This is equivalent to a country the size of Wales.

★ Largest reforestation

The greatest reforestation rate is in China where, between 1990 and 2000, enough trees were replanted every year to cover an average area of 6,974 miles^2 (18,063 km^2). This is equivalent to a country the size of Kuwait.

★ Highest carbon dioxide emissions

The USA has the highest emissions of CO_2, one of the key gases responsible for the 'greenhouse effect'. The USA emitted 11,578 billion lb (5,789 million tonnes) of CO_2 in 2001, a 1.1% decrease on the previous year. The decrease in CO_2 emissions in 2001 was reportedly due to a reduction in US economic growth from 3.8% in 2000 to 0.3% in 2001.

Largest » turkey farm

The world's largest turkey farm belongs to Bernard Matthews plc (UK). The farm is situated in North Pickenham, Norfolk, UK, and processes 1 million turkeys per year.

★ **Highest carbon dioxide emissions per capita**
The United Arab Emirates (UAE) has the highest carbon dioxide (CO_2) emissions per capita. In 1999, the emissions level reached 68,750 lb (31.25 tons) of CO_2 per capita. The total amount of CO_2 emissions for the UAE in 1999 was 190 billion lb (88 million tonnes).

★ **Greatest shrinkage of a lake**
The Aral Sea, on the border between Uzbekistan and Kazakhstan, has lost more than 60% of its area and approximately 80% of its volume since 1960. From 1960 to 1998, the lake decreased in area from 26,300 miles² (68,000 km²) to 11,000 miles² (28,700 km²) and in volume from approximately 250 miles³ (1,040 km³) to 43 miles³ (180 km³). The water level has dropped about 60 ft (18 m) in the same time period. This dramatic shrinkage is almost entirely due to the large amounts of water being extracted from the major rivers that feed it. This water is diverted for irrigation purposes.

★ **Greatest modern loss of agricultural land to aridity**
The greatest rate at which land has become arid in modern times has been experienced in Portugal where, since 1970, over 51% of agricultural land has become unable to support agriculture at former levels.

★ **Highest glass recycling rate**
Switzerland leads the world in recycling glass. An estimated 91% of glass products sold in Switzerland are recycled.

★ **Highest paper recycling rate**
Germany recycles between 70% and 80% of its consumption of paper and cardboard per year.

★ **Waste generation**
The USA produces the most municipal waste per capita according to figures issued by the Organization for Economic Cooperation and Development in 2001. The estimated figure stands at 1,675 lb (760 kg) per capita.

★ **Highest proportion of organic farming**
In Austria, an estimated 10% of agricultural land is farmed organically. Austria has more than 20,000 organic farms. Although Italy is believed to have around 40,000 organic farms, they represent a lower proportion of the total land organically farmed.

★ **Most polluted major city**
Mexico City is the world's most polluted major city and the most polluted capital city. The city is classified as having serious problems associated with sulfur dioxide, suspended particulate matter, carbon monoxide, and ozone (in all of which World Health Organization guidelines are exceeded by more than a factor of two), plus moderate to heavy pollution from lead and nitrogen dioxide. Factors contributing to the high pollution levels include the high altitude and geographical location, as high emissions from industry and vehicles are trapped by surrounding mountains.

★ **Most acidic acid rain**
A pH reading of 1.87 was recorded at Inverpolly Forest in the Scottish Highlands, UK, in 1983, and a reading of 2.83 was recorded over the Great Lakes, USA/Canada, in 1982. These are the lowest pH levels ever recorded in acid precipitation, making it the most acidic acid rain; pH values range from 0 to 14, with 7 being neutral.

★ **Worst oil spill disaster**
The worst oil spill occurred as a result of a marine blowout beneath the drilling rig *Ixtoc I* in the Gulf of Campeche, Gulf of Mexico, on June 3 1979. The oil slick had reached 400 miles (640 km) by August 5 1979. The spill was capped on March 24 1980, following a loss of up to 140 million gallons (500,000 tonnes or 636 million liters) of oil.

War & peace
Modern world

Largest anti-war rally ⌃

On February 15 2003, anti-war rallies took place across the globe – the largest occurring in Rome, Italy (above), where a crowd of three million gathered to protest the USA's threat to invade Iraq. Police figures report that millions more demonstrated in nearly 600 cities worldwide.

★ Largest tank battle

The largest tank battle ever is generally acknowledged to be the Battle of Kursk during World War II. On July 12 1943, in the Prokhorovka region near the Russian town of Kursk, a total of 1,500 German and Russian tanks amassed for close-range fighting. By the end of the day both sides had lost over 300 tanks.

★ Costliest civil war

The costliest civil war, in terms of the number of lives lost during combat and in events directly relating to the war, is the Russian Civil War of 1917–22. It is estimated that the former Soviet Union lost 939,755 soldiers, and over eight million civilians died following armed attacks, famine and disease.

★ Longest continuous period of civil war

The longest period of continuous civil warfare lasted for 254 years from 475 to 221 BC in China, and is known as the Warring States Period. Feudal lords in seven major state kingdoms sought dominance over each other in numerous intensive battles. King Ying Zheng of the Qin state was eventually victorious, becoming the first emperor (Qin Shihuang) of a unified China.

★ Most nationalities in one military force

As of January 2004 the French Foreign Legion had 7,622 men serving in its ranks, with a diverse range of nationalities from 136 countries. Legionnaires serve in France and around the world.

★ Youngest modern conscripts

In March 1976 President Francisco Macías Nguema of Equatorial Guinea (deposed in August 1979) decreed compulsory military service for all boys aged between seven and 14 years old. The edict stated that any parent that refused to hand over his or her son 'will be imprisoned or shot'.

★ Longest-serving military mule

The unit mascot for the 853 AT Coy ASC (MA Mules) was a Spanish mule called Pedongi, who was on active service with the Indian Army from May 4 1965 until her death on March 25 1998 aged 37. Her name was derived from the first battle area she was sent to at Pedong, northeast India.

★ Largest contributors to peacekeeping

Canada and Fiji have been part of almost all 55 United Nations (UN) peacekeeping operations.

★ Longest-running peacekeeping operation

The UN Truce Supervision Organization (UNTSO) has been in place since June 1948. UNTSO is based in Jerusalem but maintains military posts throughout the Middle East.

★ Largest current peacekeeping force

The largest current peacekeeping force is the UN Mission in Liberia (UNMIL). On September 19 2003 the UN Security Council agreed to the deployment of a 15,000-strong force on October 1 2003 for a 12-month stay. Following the civil war, a cease-fire was signed in June 2003, but the UNMIL mandate is there to ensure that peace is maintained and that humanitarian relief is supplied, as well as to support the establishment of democratic elections.

★ Largest peacekeeping deployment ever

The United Nations Protection Force (UNPROFOR), which was deployed in the former Yugoslavia from February 1992 to March 1995, reached a maximum strength of 39,922 military personnel in September 1994. Serious fighting in Croatia began in June 1991 when that Republic and its northern neighbour, Slovenia, declared themselves independent from Yugoslavia, and Serbs living in Croatia, supported by the Yugoslav People's Army, opposed this move.

Earliest use of marine mammals in defense

In 1970–71 during the Vietnam War, five US Navy bottlenose dolphins (*Tursiops truncatus*, left) were sent to Cam Ranh Bay, Vietnam, to defend US military boats from enemy swimmers. The most recent deployment of dolphins in active duty was during the Umm Qasr mission in the waters off Iraq in March 2003. Dolphins were trained by the US to detect underwater mines in the Gulf, so that military boats and ships loaded with humanitarian aid could pass safely. The dolphins did not touch the mines, but released a balloon showing their location.

Highest percentage of military personnel

In North Korea (above) in 1999, 5.05% of the total population of 21,386,000 (or one for every 19 people) was a member of the armed forces.

★ Most expensive peacekeeping operation
UNPROFOR cost $4.6 billion (£2.96 billion) from February 1992 to March 1995. This cost covers all missions deployed during this period, and equates to just under $3 million (£1.93 million) per day.

★ Bloodiest UN peacekeeping operation
The conflict in the Balkans led to more fatalities than any other UN peacekeeping mission. The total number of fatalities for all missions in the region was 268, including 210 fatalities in UNPROFOR alone.

★ Peacekeeping mission with most contributing nations
The United Nations Mission in Bosnia and Herzegovina (UNMIBH) drew troops from 44 different nations until the end of its mandate on December 31 2002. UNMIBH was an umbrella organization overseeing the activities of the International Police Task Force (IPTF) that was set up in Bosnia and Herzegovina after the United Nations Protection Force (UNPROFOR) mission came to an end in 1995.

★ Largest humanitarian agency
The UN World Food Program (WFP) is the largest humanitarian agency in the world. The organization was established in 1963 and to date has delivered a staggering 151 billion lb (68.7 million tonnes) of food to over 1.2 billion people in 100 countries, with a total cost of $32 billion (£19.1 billion).

★ Largest single humanitarian operation
The largest and most expensive humanitarian operation ever undertaken was feeding the 27.1 million people of Iraq following the 2003 war. The food-aid operation, organized by the WFP, began on April 1 2003 and finished in October 2003 with 4.8 billion lb (2.2 million tonnes) of food commodities being delivered under a budget of $1.5 billion (£927 million).

★ Largest and longest-running humanitarian airdrop
The World Food Program has been in southern Sudan since 1992. Drought, civil war, flooding, and remote locations mean that an average of 2.5 million people suffer from food shortages annually. At its peak, the WFP operated 14 aircraft per day, each making three trips and delivering an average of 352,000 lb (16 tonnes) of food per drop.

★ Most Nobel Peace Prizes
The International Committee of the Red Cross, founded in Geneva, Switzerland, in 1893, has received three awards for Peace: 1917, 1944, and 1963. The latter award was shared with the League of the Red Cross Societies.

★ Largest demonstration
A figure of 2.7 million demonstrators was reported from China for a demonstration against the USSR in Shanghai on March 3–4 1969 following border clashes.

★ Largest landlocked navy
Paraguay, a totally landlocked South American state, has a navy with 3,595 personnel (in 2000). The navy operates on the nation's major rivers, the Paraguay and Paraná. Military service in Paraguay is compulsory; for those opting for naval service the period in uniform is two years.

★ Oldest air force
The earliest autonomous air force is the Royal Air Force (UK), the origins of which can be traced back to 1878, when the War Office commissioned the building of a military balloon. The Royal Air Force itself came into existence on April 1 1918. The British were not the first to utilize balloons, however. The French used them for military observations at the Battle of Fleurus in June 1794 during the French Revolutionary Wars.

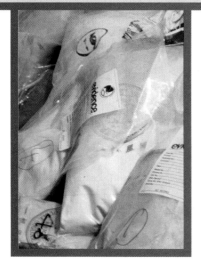

« Largest heroin seizure

According to the Drug Enforcement Administration (DEA), the largest heroin seizure (left) took place in Bangkok, Thailand, on February 11 1988 when 2,816 lb (1,277 kg) was seized. It had an estimated street value of $75 million (£45.5 million).

Highest-ranking camel «

The world's highest-ranking law-enforcement camel is BERT (USA, left), who was accepted as Reserve Deputy Sheriff for the Los Angeles County Sheriff's Department in San Dimas, California, USA, on April 5 2003 and who regularly goes on patrol with his handler Nance Fite (USA). Born on March 3 1997, BERT, which stands for 'Be Enthusiastic Responsible and True', is a dromedary (one hump). He weighed 1,770 lb (802 kg) on May 27 2003 and stands at a height of 82 in (208 cm) to the top of his hump, although he will not be considered fully grown until he is eight years old.

★ Highest murder rate per capita
According to the seventh UN Survey of Crime Trends and Operations of Criminal Justice Systems, covering the period 1998–2000, Colombia has the most recorded intentional homicides per capita, with 65 murders per 100,000 people.

★ Most murders by a doctor
Family doctor Harold Shipman (UK) murdered 215 of his patients between 1975 and 1998. Shipman killed his elderly victims, most of whom were women, with high doses of diamorphine injections. In January 2000, he was sentenced to a life term in prison for the 15 murders of which he was found guilty. Shipman hanged himself in his prison cell on January 13 2004.

★ Greatest mass arrest
The greatest mass arrest reported in a democratic country was that of 15,617 demonstrators rounded up on July 11 1988 by South Korean police to ensure security in advance of the 1988 Olympic Games in Seoul.

★ Largest white-collar crime
In February 1997, copper trader Yasuo Hamanaka (Japan) pleaded guilty to fraud and forgery in connection with illicit trading that cost the Japanese company Sumitomo an estimated $2.6 billion (£1.37 billion) accumulated over a 10-year period of unauthorized transactions.

★ Highest rate of gun ownership
Among countries not at war or suffering civil unrest, the USA has the highest rate of civilian gun ownership. Surveys in 1999 found that around 40% of US households have at least one firearm. The USA has over 200 million guns – more than the number of adults in the country.

★ Largest reward for counter-terrorism
In July 2003, the US government approved the payment of a $30-million (£16.4-million) reward to the informant who led US forces to Saddam Hussein's (Iraq) two eldest sons, Uday and Qusay (both Iraq), in Mosul, Iraq. The $15 million (£8.2 million) for each is the largest ever paid by the USA under its Rewards for Justice program.

★ Fastest recorded speed on public roads
Andrew Osborne (UK) was sentenced to 28 days in prison at Aylesbury Magistrates Court on July 16 2003 after being clocked in March 2003 travelling at 252 km/h (158 mph) on his 1200-cc Kawasaki motorcycle at Tingewick bypass, Bucks, UK.

★ Longest serving judge
The oldest recorded active judge was Judge Albert R. Alexander (USA). He was enrolled as a member of the Clinton County Bar, Missouri, USA, in 1926 and was later the magistrate and probate judge of Clinton County until his retirement aged 105 years 8 months on July 9 1965.

★ Most viewed trial
A daily average of 5.5 million Americans watched live coverage of the O.J. Simpson (USA) trial on three major cable television networks between January 24 and October 3 1995. Simpson, an American football player and actor, was on trial for the June 12 1994 murder of his ex-wife, Nicole, and a waiter, Ronald Goldman (both USA). He was acquitted of the charges when the jury reached a verdict of not guilty on October 3 1995.

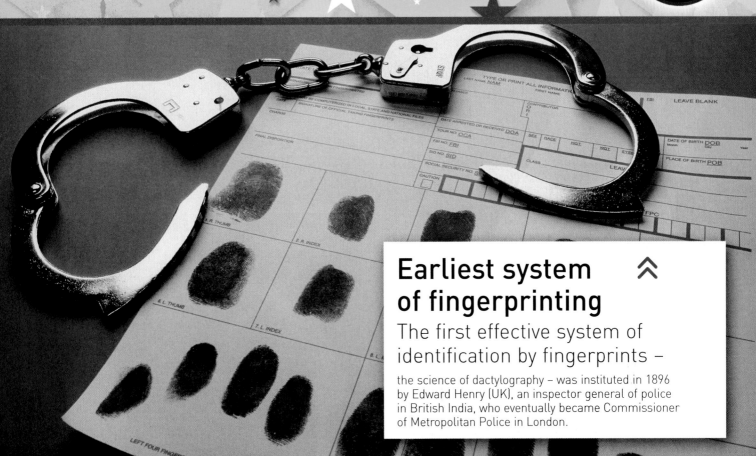

Earliest system of fingerprinting ⌃

The first effective system of identification by fingerprints –

the science of dactylography – was instituted in 1896 by Edward Henry (UK), an inspector general of police in British India, who eventually became Commissioner of Metropolitan Police in London.

★ GWR TALKS TO
Lois Gibson

Since 1982, over 150 criminals have been identified and brought to justice in Texas, USA, thanks to the detailed composites drawn by forensic artist Lois Gibson (USA, above). This figure represents the record for most criminals positively identified from one artist's composites.

How did you become a forensic artist?
I became a forensic artist because someone tried to kill me for fun when I was 21. My attacker got into my apartment

and choked me for about half an hour straight. I couldn't bring myself to tell the authorities, but about six weeks later I got lost in Los Angeles and was driving by a house just as my attacker was being arrested. This changed my life. I want my witnesses to have that wonderful feeling when they know their attacker is caught.

What did you do next?
After the attack, I got a Bachelor of Fine Arts with honors from the University of Texas in Austin, and went on to produce about 3,000 fine-art portraits for tourists. Then I moved to Houston, and was amazed to discover that they had had over 700 murders there that year. One day it just hit me: I could draw attackers' faces from witnesses' descriptions. I approached the Houston Police Department, who had no one doing that at the time. Every third sketch I did helped solve a crime, but it took them seven years to give me that job!

Four years later, I went to the FBI Academy in Quantico, Virginia, and completed the Forensic Art course there. Now I teach this profession at Northwestern University in Evanston, Illinois.

Do you work for different police forces across the USA or is it always the same one?
I work at the Houston Police Department, but cities and counties near and far bring witnesses to me.

How long have you been doing it? Do you get better with practice?
I've been a forensic artist for 21 years. One definitely gets better with practice, way better.

How long does it take to do each drawing?
Now my drawings take one hour. In the beginning it took almost three hours. If I have a reclusive witness who definitely doesn't want to talk, I can do the sketch in 25 minutes. If the witness needs to talk a lot, it can take two hours.

Talk us through your procedure.
I start at the top and go down. So, hair, forehead, eyebrows, eyes, nose, lips, chin, throw on the ears if they are seen, then neck and shoulders, in that order.

Do you do drawings digitally?
No, I draw everything by hand. It is much faster to draw by hand than with a computer... and way more accurate.

What does it mean to you to have a Guinness World Record?
It makes all that brutal, heart-wrenching work seem worthwhile. Since I deal with armed officers, I never say my sketch actually solved a case – indeed, the sketch can only help the officers make an arrest. But my fellow and future forensic artists need to know that forensic art can help solve cases.

Guinness World Records has given me a forum to spread compositry to other countries in the world besides the USA and Canada. All those countries need forensic artists too!

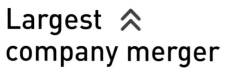

Largest global brand ⌄

According to a study released by ACNielsen, the largest global brand in the world based on sales is Coca-Cola, which in 2002 had sales of $19 billion (£13 billion). The brand is present in over 200 countries.

Largest ⌃ company merger

America Online (AOL), the largest Internet company, announced a $350 billion (£213 billion) merger with media corporate Time Warner on January 10 2000. The completed merger created AOL Time Warner, the world's largest media company. The brands owned by the new company include AOL, Time, CNN, Warner Bros., Netscape, Sports Illustrated, TNT, and Cartoon Network.

★ Largest corporate bankruptcy
In terms of assets, the largest corporate bankruptcy amounted to $103.9 billion (£65.8 billion) filed by the telecommunications company WorldCom, Inc. on July 21 2002.

★ Largest corporation
Based on revenues, the largest corporation as of 2003 was integrated oil company ExxonMobil (USA), which had revenues of $246.738 billion (£138.781 billion).

★ Highest share value
On March 27, 2000 the share price of Yahoo! Japan stood at JPY120.4 million ($1.12 million). Yahoo! Japan is the nation's dominant information portal, and the scarcity of the stock contributed to the dramatic rise in price. Japanese company Softbank owns 41.93% of the company, with US-based Yahoo! owning 33.49%. Yahoo! Japan's share price has increased 4,700% since December 1998.

★ Largest publishing company
With 80,632 employees, the world's largest printing and publishing company is Bertelsmann AG (Germany). In 2002, the company had revenues of $19,192 million (£11,965 million) with profits of $972 million (£606 million).

★ Greatest annual profit
In 2001, integrated oil company ExxonMobil (USA) announced profits of $15.320 billion (£10.932 billion), which represented a 13.5% growth in net income in 12 months. Exxon's refineries can handle over 6 million barrels daily.

★ Largest music company
Universal Music Group (USA) is the largest music company with revenues of $6.276 billion (£3.455 billion) as of December 2002. Based in New York, USA, the Universal Music Group has more than 12,000 employees, operates in 71 countries, and had an estimated worldwide market share in 2002 of 24.4%.

★ Largest retail company by number of outlets
By the end of January 2003, Wal-Mart (USA) operated 4,688 retail stores worldwide.

★ Largest cell phone telecommunications company
Vodafone Group plc (UK) is the world's largest cell phone telecommunications group, with revenues of $48.005 billion (£30.333 billion) in the fiscal year ending March 2003. The company reported more than 119.7 million subscribers worldwide as of March 2003. It operates in 28 countries on five continents.

★ Oldest stock exchange
The Stock Exchange in Amsterdam, The Netherlands, was founded in 1602. It dealt in printed shares of the United East India Company of The Netherlands in the Oude Zijds Kapel.

★ Largest lottery
By the end of January 2004, ticket sales for the UK's National Lottery (launched in November 1994) had reached £45 billion ($81 billion).

★ Richest woman
Alice Walton (USA), daughter of Sam Walton, founder of the world's largest retailer Wal-Mart, and Helen, his widow, each have an estimated net worth of $20 billion (£11 billion) according to the Forbes 2004 Rich List.

Largest company by assets

American multinational motor manufacturer Ford Motor Company (USA, left) is the largest company in the world in terms of assets (excluding banks and financial institutions). At June 2003, its assets were worth a total of $311.791 billion (£189.113 billion).

«

★ GWR TALKS TO
Bill Gates

Bill Gates (USA, above) is Chairman and Chief Software Architect of Microsoft Corporation. As well as being the world's richest living person, worth $46.6 billion (£25.4 billion) in March 2004 according to *Forbes* magazine, Bill and his wife Melinda hold the record for the largest single private charitable donation ($6 billion or £4.2 billion), which they made to their own Bill & Melinda Gates Foundation. The foundation itself holds the record for the largest single

donation to AIDS research ($25 million or £15.08 million) and is also the world's largest charitable foundation. Its largest donation was $1 billion (£700 million) over 20 years for minority student scholarships, via the Gates Millennium Scholars Program.

How and when did you first become interested in technology and computers?
When I was 13, my school installed a teletype machine that connected to a mainframe computer in downtown Seattle. From that point on, my friends and I spent most of our free time writing programs and figuring out how to make the computer do interesting things.

What are you working on for Microsoft now?
My job is to figure out new ways to make computers more useful, and work with our software developers

and product groups to set the technical direction for the company. Right now I'm working on a number of projects, including the next major release of our Windows operating system.

What do you think will be the interesting developments in technology in the near future?
Everything from the TV to the refrigerator is taking on the intelligence and connectivity of the PC, and this opens up some amazing new possibilities. I think computers will change our lives more in the next ten years than they have in the past 20.

What personal achievement are you most proud of?
Although it's great that I get to do the work I love and have been very successful at it, I'm proudest of my three children.

What does your charity do and what is the most satisfying part of running it?
The Bill & Melinda Gates Foundation focuses most of its efforts on long-term global

health issues. We have a tremendous opportunity to improve the quality of life for billions of people by treating and preventing disease, improving child and reproductive health, and slowing the spread of HIV and other global health threats. My wife and I are privileged to work with some of the world's smartest people to develop sustainable solutions to problems that affect a large percentage of the world's population.

What does it mean to have a Guinness World Record?
It's a great honor, but I'm just happy that I've been able to use what I have to help improve people's lives.

What advice would you give to any young people who would like to follow in your footsteps?
Most important of all is to choose work that you are truly passionate about. If you really love what you do, you'll barely notice how hard you work at it.

≪ Highest and lowest health budget

The USA has the largest health expenditure at $3,724 (£2,359) per capita according to the World Health Organization's World Health Report 2000. Somalia has a health budget of only $11 (£6.80) per capita.

★ Most and least hospital beds
According to 2002 data, Switzerland has one bed per 155 people. Niger has only one hospital bed per 2,000 people.

★ Most and least physicians
In Monaco, there is one physician for every 170 people. The country with the highest number of people per physician is Malawi with 49,118 people for every one doctor.

★ Most prevalent allergic disease
Bronchial asthma affects up to 150 million people worldwide, with deaths from the condition reaching 180,000 each year. Globally, it is estimated that the economic costs associated with this disease exceed those of tuberculosis and HIV/AIDS combined.

★ Most common infectious disease
The common cold is almost universal, afflicting everyone but those living in isolated communities or in Antarctica (no virus will survive the extreme cold). There are at least 40 cold viruses that are airborne or transmitted by direct contact.

★ Highest number of people with HIV/AIDS
In the Republic of South Africa, one in nine people are affected by HIV/AIDS. In 2001, out of a total population of 43.5 million, 4.7 million people carried the virus.

★ Highest death rate from infectious disease
The west African island-republic of São Tomé and Princípe has 241 deaths from infectious diseases per 100,000 annually.

★ Leading cause of death
In industrialized countries, diseases of the heart and of blood vessels (cardiovascular disease) account for more than 50% of deaths. The most common are heart attacks and strokes, generally due to atheroma (degeneration of the arterial walls) obstructing the flow of blood.

Most and least ⋀ expensive office location

Based on March 2003 prices, London (UK, above) has the most expensive office space in the world. Cost per m² including rent, taxes, and service charges is £1,014 ($1,596). Where country-comparable data is available, Sandton, in Johannesburg, South Africa, is the least expensive location for office space. Cost per m², allowing for similar expenses, is $125 (£79).

Lowest and highest »
spending on education

Somalia allocates just 0.4% of its Gross National Income (GNI) to primary, secondary, and tertiary education. The USA spent 5.4% of its GNI on education in 1997.

★ **Largest school by pupils**
The largest school in terms of pupils is the City Montessori School in Lucknow, India, which had a record enrollment for the 2003/04 academic year of 27,911 pupils on September 24 2003.

★ **Oldest university**
The oldest existing and continually operating educational institution is the University of Karueein, founded in AD 859 in Fez, Morocco.

★ **Longest lesson**
Murry Burrows (Australia) taught biology to his class of 26 students at Laidley State High School, Queensland, Australia, for 54 hours on April 15–17 2003.

★ **Most expensive course**
The Ivor Spencer International Finishing School for Young Ladies and Gentlemen, London, UK, began a one-month £77,500 ($126,000) 'finishing' course in 1998. Students stayed at a top London hotel, went to the ballet and opera, and took lessons in protocol, etiquette, food, wine, cooking, and style.

★ **Oldest doctorate**
On May 12 2000, Elizabeth Eichelbaum (USA) received her doctorate in Education from the University of Tennessee, USA, at the age of 90 years 58 days.

★ **Longest time to complete a degree**
Robert F.P. Cronin (UK) began his biology degree on February 9 1948 at Princeton University, New Jersey, USA, and graduated on May 30 2000, 52 years 111 days later at the age of 73 years 272 days. He is the world's oldest graduate.

★ **Longest elapsed time before a class reunion**
The 1929 class of Miss Blanche Miller's kindergarten and continuation school, Bluefield, West Virginia, USA, had their first reunion after 70 years. Ten members of the class had died but of the remaining group, 55% were in attendance.

★ **Largest school reunion**
A total of 2,521 former pupils of Pestalozzi School, Guben, Germany, attended the school's 100th anniversary celebrations on June 29 2002.

★ **Longest annual class reunion**
The Cherokee County Community High School's class of 1929 held its 74th class reunion in Columbus, Kansas, USA, on June 7 2003. Of the original class of 110, 30 graduates remain, but only nine could make the reunion.

★ **Largest employer**
Indian Railways had 1,583,614 regular employees when it was last assessed in March 1997. The Indian Railways' wage bill for the period 1996–97 worked out at a massive 105,145,000,000 rupees ($2.1 billion or £1.5 billion).

★ **Longest working career**
The longest working life has been the 98 years worked by Shigechiyo Izumi (Japan), who began work goading draft animals at a sugar mill at Isen, Tokunoshima, Japan, in 1872. He retired as a sugarcane farmer in 1970 aged 105. He attributed his long life to 'God, Buddha, and the Sun'.

★ **Highest and lowest rates of unemployment**
According to information available in 2002, the country with the highest rate of unemployment is Liberia with 70% of its labor force not in paid employment. Andorra and the South Pacific island of Nauru had the lowest rate of unemployment for any country with 0%.

★ **Longest working career in a single company**
Thomas Stoddard (USA) started working at Speakman Company, Delaware, USA, on February 16 1928 as a 16-year-old mail boy. He remained an employee of the plumbing and pipe-fitting company until his retirement (as a member of the board of directors) 75 years later on February 16 2003, when he was 91 years old.

« Highest apple consumption

In 1998, China consumed the greatest amount of apples in the world overall with a total of 32.3 billion lb (14.694 million tonnes) or 25 lb 9 oz (11.6 kg) per capita. Assuming an apple weighs 5.2 oz (150 g), this is equivalent to 77 apples per person. Moldova consumes the most apples per person, with 156 lb 4.9 oz (70.9 kg) consumed per person in 1998. The country got through 682 million lb (310,000 tonnes) of apples in that year – equivalent to 472 per person.

Highest vodka consumption ⌃

Russia is the leading vodka consumer with 25.5 pints (14.5 liters) per capita consumed in 1999. Considering that there is a proportion of Russians who do not drink, it is estimated that 80% of adult men consume, on average, 0.87 pints (220 half-liter) bottles of vodka per year.

★ **Highest bread consumption**
As of 2000, the country with the largest per capita consumption of bread was Turkey with 440 lb (199.6 kg) per person. Turkish people eat more than three times their own body weight in bread annually.

★ **Highest baked bean consumption**
The country with the largest annual consumption of baked beans per capita is the UK with 11 lb 10 oz (5.3 kg) per person according to surveys in 1999.

★ **Highest chocolate consumption**
In Switzerland, the average person consumed 25 lb 6 oz of chocolate (11.5 kg) during 2000. This is equivalent to 230 1.76-oz (50-g) bars a year.

★ **Largest consumption of cigarettes**
The world's largest consumer of cigarettes, in terms of volume purchased, is China with 1.69 trillion sold in 2002. With a global consumption in 2000 of 5.5 trillion, this means that approximately one in every three cigarettes smoked today is smoked in China.

★ **Highest wine consumption**
Luxembourg consumes an average of 111.3 pints (63.3 liters) of wine annually per person. The smallest measurable wine consumer is Egypt, where the average yearly wine consumption is about two tablespoons per person.

★ **Highest alcohol consumption**
The alcohol consumption rate is highest in Ireland where 21.6 pints (12.3 liters) of pure alcohol per person is consumed annually according to surveys done in 2000. This intake is based on the amount of pure alcohol consumed within wine, beer, and spirits.

★ **Highest beer consumption**
The Czech Republic consumes 281 pints (160 liters) of beer annually per person as of 2000. The country that consumed the greatest volume of beer in the same year was the USA with 42.895 billion pints (24.376 billion liters). This is equivalent to a per capita consumption of 156 pints (89 liters).

★ **Highest tea consumption**
In Ireland, the average annual consumption of tea is 5 lb 14 oz (2.69 kg) per capita, the equivalent of 1,184 cups per person each year.

★ **Highest organic produce sales**
Denmark has annual organic retail sales of $349.2 million (£220 million) in a population of 5.3 million, averaging sales of $65.88 (£41.51) per capita.

★ **Greatest fast-food expenditure**
In 2000, Americans spent over $110 billion (£166 billion) on fast-food – more than on higher education, personal computers, or new cars. On any one day, approximately 25% of adults in the USA visit a fast-food outlet. The typical American eats roughly three hamburgers and four orders of french fries a week. The USA has more than 300,000 fast food restaurants.

★ **Most meat waste**
The country that wastes the most bovine meat (beef and veal) per year is Argentina, where 730 million lb (332,000 tonnes) was thrown away in 1998.

★ **Most and least telephones**
Monaco has the most telephones per 1,000 people with 1,000 receivers as of 1998. Nauru in the South Pacific has the least with 0.2 per 1,000 people in 1998.

★ **Country with most cell phones**
There were 69,209,000 cell phones in the USA in 1998. By contrast, only 35 million people in the USA were cell phone subscribers in 1996.

★ **Most Internet users**
As of the end of 2001, Sweden had 554.18 Internet users per 1,000 people.

Fastest growing »
tourism region

According to the World Tourism Organization (WTO), the region showing the greatest annual growth in the number of tourists in 2002 was the Middle East (Egypt's Sphinx shown right), where the 26.7 million international travelers reflected a 16.7% increase over the previous year. Saudi Arabia, the United Arab Emirates, Lebanon, Egypt, and Bahrain all showed double-digit growth during the year.

★ **Most TV sets**
The country with the most televisions is China, which had 400 million TV sets in 1997.

★ **City to hold the most wedding ceremonies**
Las Vegas, Nevada, USA, has over 100 chapels performing approximately 8,400 marriage ceremonies per month – that's about 280 per day or one wedding every 5 min 17 sec.

★ **Highest divorce rate**
As of September 2002, the country with the highest divorce rate was the Maldives, with 10.97 divorces per 1,000 inhabitants each year.

★ **Longest marriage**
Wesley and Stella McGowen (both USA) have been married since February 6 1920 – over 84 years.

★ **Biggest tourist spenders**
The biggest overseas travel spenders are US citizens, who in 2002 spent $58 billion (£36.8 billion) while on holiday in foreign countries (excluding airfares) according to the World Tourism Organization.

★ **Highest earnings from tourism**
Despite a fall of 7.4% in 2002, the USA remains the world leader in terms of earnings from international tourism, taking $66.5 billion (£44.3 billion) in that year. This is equivalent to a world market share of 14%.

★ **Most popular tourist destination**
According to the WTO, in 2002 France attracted 77 million international visitors, single-handedly accounting for 11% of all international travellers in that year.

★ **Most visited theme park**
An estimated 16.5 million people passed through the gates of Tokyo Disneyland in 2000. During the 1990s, the park had an estimated 179,112,000 visitors, making it the most visited park of the decade. This is well above the total population of the country (about 126 million).

★ **Most popular form of international travel**
According to the WTO, 43.7% of tourists visiting foreign countries in 1998 arrived by air, compared with 41.4% who traveled by road.

★ **Busiest airport for international passengers**
According to the Airports Council International, London's Heathrow Airport handled 53.79 million passengers arriving from, or departing to, destinations outside the UK during 2001.

★ **Busiest airport by number of aircraft**
A total of 909,535 aircraft takeoffs and landings were made during 2001 at O'Hare International Airport, Chicago, Illinois, USA. In terms of the number of passengers served, O'Hare is in second place behind Atlanta's Hartsfield International.

★ **Highest and lowest rate of car ownership**
The wealthy European state of Luxembourg has 576 cars per 1,000 people, or one for every 1.7 people. By contrast, Somalia and the former Soviet republic of Tajikistan jointly have the world's lowest rate of car ownership, with 0.1 cars per 1,000 people, or one car per 10,000 people.

★ **Longest traffic jam**
The longest traffic jam ever stretched 109 miles (176 km) northward from Lyon towards Paris, France, on February 16 1980. The biggest jam in terms of the number of cars was estimated to involve 18 million cars crawling bumper-to-bumper on the East-West German border on April 12 1990.

★ **Best-selling car**
The Ford Focus was the world's best-selling car in 2000 (the latest year for which statistics are available), with global sales of 941,938. This means that one in every 40 cars sold worldwide was a Focus.

Religion & beliefs
Modern world

Highest pilgrimage ⌄

A route (below) on Mount Kailash (or Khang Rimpoche) in western Tibet, which measures 33 miles (53 km), reaches an altitude of 22,028 ft (6,714 m). The mountain is sacred to followers of Buddhism, Jainism, Hinduism, and Bonpo, a pre-Buddhist religion.

Largest church ⌃

The largest church in the world is the Basilica of Our Lady of Peace

(Notre Dame de la Paix, above) at Yamoussoukro, the legal and administrative capital of Ivory Coast/Côte d'Ivoire. It was completed in 1989 at a cost of $164 million (£100 million) and has a total area of 322,917 ft² (30,000 m²) with seating for 7,000 people. Including its golden cross, it is 518 ft (158 m) high.

★ **Largest religious structure**
The largest religious structure ever built is Angkor Wat (City Temple), enclosing 401 acres (162.6 hectares) in Cambodia. It was built to honour the Hindu god Vishnu by the Khmer King Suryavarman II in the period 1113–50. Its curtain wall measures 4,200 ft (1,280 m), and its population, before it was abandoned in 1432, was 80,000. The whole complex of 72 major monuments, begun c. AD 900, extends over 15.4 miles (24.8 km).

★ **Largest Buddhist temple**
The largest Buddhist temple in the world is Borobudur, near Yogyakarta, central Java, Indonesia, built between AD 750 and 842. The 2,118,880-ft³ (60,000-m³) stone structure is 113 ft (34.5 m) tall and its base measures 403 x 403 ft (123 x 123 m).

★ **Largest cathedral**
The world's largest cathedral is the Gothic church of the diocese of New York, USA, St. John the Divine, which has a floor area

of 120,986 ft² (11,240 m²), equivalent to 43 tennis courts. The nave is the longest in the world at 601 ft (183.2 m). (In comparison, Notre Dame de Paris is 427 ft (130 m) long.) The vaulted roof reaches a height of 124 ft (37.8 m), around 10 stories above floor level. The cornerstone was laid on December 27 1892 but, incredibly, the building is only two-thirds complete.

★ **Largest Hindu temple in use**
Srirangam Temple, at Tiruchirappalli, Tamil Nadu, India, is the world's largest Hindu temple. Dedicated to the Hindu god Vishnu, the temple complex covers an area of 156 acres (63.1 hectares) with a perimeter of 32,592 ft (9,934 m).

★ **Largest monolithic church**
The largest monolithic (or rock-hewn) church is Bet Medhane Alem in Lalibela, Ethiopia. The structure measures 110 ft (33.5 m) long, 78 ft (23.5 m) wide, and 36 ft (11 m) high.

It was carved from volcanic rock in the 12th or 13th century AD by King Lalibela.

★ **Largest mosque**
The largest mosque is Shah Faisal Mosque, near Islamabad, Pakistan. The total area of the complex is 46.87 acres (18.97 hectares), with the covered area of the prayer hall being 51,666 ft² (4,800 m²). The mosque can accommodate 100,000 worshipers in the prayer hall and the courtyard plus a further 200,000 people in the adjacent grounds.

★ **Largest synagogue**
The largest synagogue in the world is Temple Emanu-El on Fifth Avenue at 65th Street, New York City, USA, which has a total area of 37,922 ft² (3,523 m²). The synagogue's main sanctuary is able to accommodate 2,500 people, while the adjoining Beth-El Chapel seats 350. When these and the temple's other three sanctuaries are in use, a combined total of 5,500 people can be accommodated.

★ **Temple at highest altitude**
The Rongbuk temple, between Tingri and Shigatse in Tibet, China, is situated at an altitude of approximately 16,700 ft (5,100 m). It is just 25 miles (40 km) from Mount Everest.

★ **Most valuable sacred object**
The 15th-century gold Buddha in Wat Trimitr Temple in Bangkok, Thailand, has the highest intrinsic value of any sacred object. It is 10 ft (3 m) tall and weighs an estimated 12,125 lb (5.5 tonnes). As of January 2004's price of gold ($415 or £226 per fine ounce), it is now worth $78 million (£39.8 million). The gold under the plaster exterior was found only in 1954.

★ **Largest statue of the Virgin Mary**
The largest statue of the Virgin Mary with Jesus measures 46 ft (14 m) high and stands on a 55-ft 9-in (17-m-tall) base. It was unveiled on September 8 2003 and stands overlooking the city of Haskovo, Bulgaria.

Most Muslim pilgrims ⌃

The annual pilgrimage (Hajj) to Mecca, Saudi Arabia (above), attracts greater numbers than any other Islamic mission – an average of two million people a year from 140 countries.

★ Largest single tomb
The Mount Li tomb – the burial place of Qin Shihuang, the first emperor of a unified China – was constructed during his reign, from 221 to 210 BC, and is situated 25 miles (40 km) east of Xian, China. The two walls around the grave measure 7,129 x 3,195 ft (2,173 x 974 m) and 2,247 x 1,896 ft (685 x 578 m).

★ Most Christian pilgrims
The House of the Virgin Mary at Loretto, Italy, receives a total of 3.5 million pilgrims (as opposed to tourists) a year, over three times the number visiting the more famous shrine at Lourdes, France. The basilica of St. Antony at Padua, Italy, receives a similar number of pilgrims a year.

★ Largest religious crowd
The greatest recorded number of people assembled with a common purpose was an estimated 20 million who gathered at the Hindu festival of Kumbh Mela, held at the confluence of the Jumna, the Ganges, and the mythical 'Saraswati' rivers at Allahabad (Prayag), Uttar Pradesh, India, on January 30 2001.

★ Tallest cemetery
The permanently illuminated Memorial Necrópole Ecumônica, in Santos, near São Paulo, Brazil, is 10 stories high and occupies an area of 4.4 acres (1.8 hectares). Construction on the cemetery began in March 1983 and the first burial was on July 28 1984.

★ Longest papal reign
The longest papal reign was that of Pius IX (Giovanni Maria Mastai-Ferretti, Italy), who was pope for 31 years 236 days between 1846 and 1878. St. Peter (c. AD 33–67), the first pope, is said to have been head of the Church for 34 years, although his papacy cannot be dated accurately.

★ Fastest growing religion
Islam is the fastest growing religion in the world. In 1990, 935 million of the world's population were Muslims; however, the estimate for January 2004 is 1.4 billion, or 23% of the world's population. Although the religion originated in Arabia, in 2002 around 80% of all believers lived outside the Arab world.

★ Longest pole-sitting by an individual
The monk St. Simeon the Stylite (c. AD 386–459) spent about 39 years on a stone pillar on the Hill of Wonders, near Aleppo, Syria – the longest time someone has remained on top of a pole. He did so as an act of self-persecution for people's sins, and in order to be nearer to God. The Church of St. Simeon or Qalaat Samaan was built in honour of the monk and houses the ruins of the column. St Simeon's pole-sitting feat is the longest-standing record to be chronicled in the book of Guinness World Records.

★ Oldest Koran
The Holy Koran Mushaf of Othman, owned by the Muslim Board of Uzbekistan, once belonged to Caliph Othman (c. AD 588–656), third successor to the Prophet Mohammed. Only about half of the original 706 pages survive. The parchment-made Mushaf Koran was compiled between AD 646 and 656.

Most pumpkins carved in one hour

School teacher and sports coach Steven Clarke (USA, above) set a new world record when he carved 42 pumpkins in one hour for the Halloween celebrations of CBS TV's *The Early Show* on October 31 2002 in New York, USA. He also holds the record for fastest pumpkin carver, having sculpted a single jack-o'-lantern in just 54.72 seconds.

★ **Most participants in a ribbon-cutting ceremony**
There were 3,238 participants in the ribbon-cutting ceremony at the official launch of Raffles The Plaza and Swissotel The Stamford hotels in Singapore on January 6 2002. The ribbon was 13,789 ft (4,203 m) long.

★ **Fastest youth team in a woolsack race**
In May 1997, the Raggy Dolls team from Sir William Romney School (UK) completed the World Woolsack Championship race in a record time of 3 min 20.01 sec. The Annual Woolsack Champion Races, held in Tetbury, Gloucestershire, UK, involve relay teams of four that run up and down a steep hill while carrying a 60-lb (27.2-kg) bag of wool on their shoulders.

★ **Tallest erected maypole**
A maypole 127 ft 7 in (38.89 m) tall was erected in New Westminster, British Columbia, Canada, on May 20 1995. A maypole dance was performed around it on May 27 1995.

★ **Most participants in a ground-breaking ceremony**
On September 27 2003, 2,453 people dug with shovels simultaneously to break the ground for the new Providence Newberg Medical Center in Newberg, Oregon, USA.

★ **Largest bonfire**
The largest bonfire measured 123 ft (37.5 m) high, and had a base of 86 ft² (8 m²) and an overall volume of 28,251 ft³ (800 m³). The event was organized by Kure Commemorative Centennial Events Committee and lit on February 9 2003 at Gohara-cho, Hiroshima, Japan, as part of a traditional ceremony to encourage good health and a generous harvest.

★ **Thickest makeup**
The thickest three-dimensional makeup is Chutti, unique to the southwest Indian Kathakali dance-theatre tradition. The villainous Redbeard characters have mask-like attachments that are built up using rice paste and paper and which extend 6 in (15 cm) from the face. The makeup takes hours to apply and the colors used, together with the styles of the costumes, denote the different nature of each of the characters.

★ **Largest annual gathering of women**
In February or March each year, over 1 million women gather at the Attukal Bhagavathy Temple, Thiruvananthapuram, Kerala, India, for the 'Pongala' offering. The women, who come from all religions and communities in Kerala, gather with their cooking pots to perform a ritual for the health and prosperity of their families. The highest ever attendance was 1.5 million women at the festival on February 23 1997. The ceremony, which involves cooking rice as an offering to the deity, lasts six hours.

★ **Largest gathering of giant papier-mâché models**
A total of 215 papier-mâché giants, made by 88 organizations, were gathered at Solsona, Catalonia, Spain, on July 6 2003 to celebrate the third annual Colla Gegantera del Carnaval de Solsona. The origins of this tradition are unknown, although many European countries have adopted the practice of having these giants dance down the streets as part of their festival celebrations. In Catalonia, the earliest known records are from the 14th century when models of the biblical characters David and Goliath were created for the procession of the feast of Corpus Christi in Barcelona, Spain.

Fastest snail ⌄

The annual World Snail Racing Championships held every July at Congham, Norfolk, UK,
is conducted on a 13-in (33-cm) circular course outside St. Andrews Church. The 'runners' (below) race from the center to the perimeter. Some race several times as they are divided into heats to cater for the 150 snail competitors who enter every year. The all-time record holder is a snail named Archie, trained by Carl Bramham (UK), who sprinted to the finish line in 2 min 20 sec in 1995.

Largest ⌃ annual food fight

On the last Wednesday in August, the town of Buñol near Valencia, Spain, holds its annual tomato festival, the Tomatina (above).

In 1999, 25,000 people spent one hour at this giant food fight throwing about 275,500 lb (125 tonnes) of tomatoes at each other. From the backs of trucks, attendants dump the red fruit onto the streets for people to scoop up and throw. By the time the food fight is over, the streets and everyone in them is saturated with sloppy tomato paste. Rivers of tomato juice, as much as 12 in (30 cm) deep, run through the town until area fire engines come in to hose down the streets and the people in them. The Tomatina was first held in 1944.

★ **Longest firework waterfall**
The 'Niagara Falls' measured 10,255 ft 2.5 in (3,125.79 m) when ignited on August 24 2003 at the Ariake Seas Fireworks Festival, Fukuoka, Japan.

★ **Largest jazz festival**
The Festival International de Jazz de Montreal in Québec, Canada, lasts 11 days over June and July each year and attracts more than 1.5 million people who watch around 400 concerts.

★ **Largest beer festival**
Oktoberfest '99 (Munich, Germany), held September 18–October 5, was visited by

7 million people who consumed a record 1.53 million gal (5.8 million liters) of beer in 11 beer tents covering an area as large as 50 football fields.

★ **Largest maple syrup festival**
The 36th annual Elmira Maple Syrup Festival held in Elmira, Ontario, Canada, attracted 66,529 people on April 1 2000.

★ **Largest frogs' leg festival**
The Fellsmere Frogs' Leg Festival held in Fellsmere, Florida, USA, annually attracts 75,000 visitors. Between January 18 and 21 2001, more

than 6,600 lb (3,000 kg) of battered fried frogs' legs were served during the free four-day festival to 13,200 diners.

★ **Largest garlic festival**
The three-day Gilroy Garlic Festival, held each summer in Gilroy, California, USA, attracts 130,000 people, who can sample garlic-flavored food ranging from meat to ice cream. The event begins with the lighting of a 25-ft (7.6-m-high) garlic bulb effigy.

★ **Longest festival snake**
On August 27 2000, 500 people were required to carry a monstrous 271-ft 7-in-long (82.8-m), 4,400-lb (2-tonne) serpent made of bamboo and rice straw through the village of Sekikawa, Japan, in honor of the 12th annual Taishita Monja Festival.

★ **Largest audience at a camel wrestling festival**
At the 1994 Camel Wrestling Festival in Selçuk, Turkey, 20,000 people gathered to watch 120 dromedaries wrestle in a

2,000-year-old stadium in Ephesus. There are around 1,200 specially bred wrestling camels in Turkey – known as tulu camels – and the sport extends over the Marmara, Aegean, and Mediterranean coasts of western Turkey.

★ **Largest monkey buffet**
The Kala Temple (also known as Monkey Temple) in Lopburi province, north of Bangkok, Thailand, provides an annual spread of tropical fruit and vegetables weighing 6,600 lb (3,000 kg) for the population of about 2,000 monkeys to enjoy.

★ **Largest origami paper crane**
On January 20–21 2001, an origami paper crane with a wingspan of 256 ft 6 in (78.19 m) was folded by 1,000 people at the Odate Jukai Dome in Odate City, Japan. The participants, mostly residents of Odate, spent eight hours on the first day sticking 80 pieces of paper together, creating a sheet of 861 ft^2 (80 m^2). It took another 8 hr 40 min to fold the crane.

Material world

Contents

Spending power
Material world

Most expensive mass-produced yo-yo

Cold Fusion and Cold Fusion GT yo-yos, manufactured by Playmaxx, Inc. (USA) retail between $150 and $250. There is also a special version called Gold Fusion (below), which is plated with 24 karat gold and sells for between $200 and $300. In 1998, Playmaxx, Inc. generated approximately $96 million (£57.9 million) in retail sales and was given the Craze of the Year Award by the British Toy Association.

Most valuable grass

On May 17 2000, Ken Bates (UK), then chairman of Chelsea Football Club, paid £20,000 ($29,884) for a piece of turf from London's Wembley Stadium. The area of grass is fondly remembered by English soccer fans as the spot on the goal line where, during the 1966 World Cup final against Germany, the ball landed for the controversial goal scored by Geoff Hurst (above right, with German goalkeeper Hans Tilkowski). At this rate, the entire field would have cost around £800 million ($1.2 billion).

The cage-cup is so called because the body and base of the vessel are completely surrounded by a delicate network or 'cage' of glass. Cage-cups were owned by the very wealthiest of Roman society, and this is the only remaining example known to be in private hands.

★ Most valuable bicycle
An 1891 diamond-frame safety bicycle was sold at Phillips, London, UK, in August 1999 for £105,000 ($170,310), breaking the previous record for a bicycle sold at auction by over 200%.

★ Most valuable glass
A record £520,000 ($1,078,480) was paid at auction for a Roman glass cage-cup of ca. AD 300 known as the 'Constable-Maxwell cage-cup'. It measures 7 in (17 cm) in diameter and 4 in (10 cm) in height, and sold at Sotheby's, London, UK, on June 4 1979 to Robin Symes (UK) on behalf of the British Rail Pension Fund.

★ Most valuable single-page music manuscript
The greatest amount a single-page music manuscript has raised at auction is £1,326,650 ($1,932,398), paid for the earliest draft of Ludwig van Beethoven's (Germany) Ninth Symphony at Sotheby's, London, UK, on May 17 2002. The buyer was an anonymous telephone bidder.

★ Most valuable music manuscripts
The auction record for a musical manuscript is £2,585,000 ($4,340,215), paid by UK dealer James Kirkman at Sotheby's, London, UK, on May 22 1987

for a 508-page, 8.5 x 6.5-in (21.6 x 16.5-cm) bound volume of nine complete symphonies written in Wolfgang Amadeus Mozart's (Austria) hand.

★ Most valuable coin collection
The highest price ever paid for a coin collection is $44.9 million (£31.8 million) for the Eliasberg Collection, which was sold over three auctions in 1982, 1996, and 1997 at Bowers and Merena Galleries, New Hampshire, USA. From the 1930s until 1950, Louis E. Eliasberg Sr. (USA), a leading Baltimore financier, attempted and accomplished what had never been tried before – to collect an example of every major US coin variety from the 1793 half cent to the 1933 double eagle.

★ Most valuable clock
The world record for a clock sold at auction is £1,926,500 ($3,001,294), paid for a Louis XVI

ormulu-mounted ebony grande sonnerie astronomical perpetual calendar regulateur de parquet at Christie's, London, UK, on July 8 1999.

★ Most valuable carpet
A Louis XV Savonnerie carpet measuring 18 x 19 ft (5.4 x 5.8 m), which was probably made for Louis XV's Château de la Mouette, ca. 1740–50, realized $4,406,000 (£2,993,512) at Christie's, New York, USA, in November 2000.

★ Most valuable philatelic item
A letter to wine merchants in Bordeaux, France, dated 1847 and franked with 1d (one penny) and 2d (two penny) first-issue stamps from Mauritius was bought anonymously in under a minute for CHF6,123,750 ($4,075,165) in a sale that was conducted by David Feldman (Ireland) at the Hotel International in Zürich, Switzerland, on November 3 1993.

Most valuable edible fungus

A white truffle (*tuber magnatum pico*) ⌄
weighing 2 lb 3 oz (1 kg) was sold

in November 2002 for a record $35,000 at the annual charity truffle auction held simultaneously in Los Angeles, New York, USA, and Alba in northern Italy, where the giant fungus was unearthed. It was bought by Joe Pytka (USA), owner of the Bastide restaurant in Los Angeles, California, USA, and prepared by head chef Alain Giraud (France, right, with the truffle).

★ **Most valuable kaleidoscope**
A fine English kaleidoscope in a mahogany case (ca.1830) sold at Christie's, London, UK, in November 1999 for £45,500 ($74,934).

★ **Most valuable comic**
The world's most valuable comic is the 1939 'Pay Copy' of *Marvel Comics* No. 1, which was sold to Jay Parrino's The Mint (USA) for $350,000 in November 2001. It is called the Pay Copy because some of its pages have notations relating to the payments to the creators of each piece.

★ **Most valuable horse**
Cash Run, a six-year-old broodmare, was purchased on behalf of the Coolmore Stud for $7,100,000 by John Magnier (Ireland) in Lexington, Kentucky, USA, on November 3 2003.

★ **Most valuable letter**
The highest price ever paid on the open market for a single signed letter was $748,000. This was paid on December 5

1991 at Christie's, New York, USA, for a letter written by Abraham Lincoln (USA) on January 8 1863 defending the Emancipation Proclamation. It was sold to Profiles in History of Beverly Hills, California, USA.

★ **Most valuable jewel**
A 'D' color internally flawless pear-shaped diamond weighing 100.1 carats was sold for CHF19,858,500 ($16,561,171) at Sotheby's, Geneva, Switzerland, on May 17 1995. 'D' is the highest grade that can be given to a diamond and indicates that the diamond is the finest white in color.

★ **Most valuable jewelry collection**
The world's largest jewelry collection, which included a Van Cleef and Arpels 1939 ruby and diamond necklace, belonged to Wallis Simpson, the Duchess of Windsor (USA). It realized £31,380,197 ($50,427,977) when sold at Sotheby's, Geneva, Switzerland, on April 3 1987.

★ **Most valuable telephone number**
The most valuable telephone number is 8888-8888. It was bought by a bidder representing Sichuan Airlines Co. Ltd. (China) on August 19 2003 for 2.33 million yuan ($280,723) during an auction in Chengdu, China, of more than 100 telephone numbers. Eight is considered lucky in China as it is similar to the Cantonese word for 'getting rich'.

★ **Most valuable Old Master painting**
The Massacre of the Innocents by Peter Paul Rubens Netherlands) was sold at Sotheby's, London, UK, for a record £49.5 million ($76.7 million) on July 10 2002 to David Thomson (Canada), chairman of the Thomson Newspapers empire.

★ **Most valuable Old Master drawing**
The record for most valuable Old Master drawing is held jointly between *The Risen Christ* by Michelangelo Buonarroti

(Italy) sold in July 2000 and *Horse and Rider* by Leonardo da Vinci (Italy) sold in July 2001. Both raised £8,143,750 ($12,212,449 [2000] and $11,440,340 [2001]) at Christie's, London, UK.

★ **Most valuable photograph**
Athènes, 1842, a photograph taken of the Athenian Temple of Olympian Zeus on the Acropolis in Athens, Greece, sold at Christie's, London, UK, for £565,250 ($922,488) on May 20 2003. It was taken in 1842 by the 19th-century French artist and historian Joseph Philibert Girault de Prangey.

★ **Most valuable illuminated manuscript**
The Rothschild Prayerbook (c.1505), an illuminated manuscript, sold for £8,580,000 ($13,400,000) at Christie's, London, UK, on July 8 1999. For the four-hour-long sale, 380 seats had been prebooked and 70 phones were in use. The entire sale made nearly three times its high presale estimate.

Largest bobblehead «

Standing 11 ft (3.35 m) tall and in the likeness of game show host Chuck Woolery (left), the world's largest bobblehead weighs 900 lb (408 kg). It was created by the Game Show Network (USA) and displayed at McCormick Place, Chicago, Illinois, USA, on June 8 2003. The head on this oversized novelty item really bobbles.

Largest rubber ∧ band ball

John J. Bain (USA, above) constructed a rubber band ball with a circumference of 15 ft 1 in (4.59 m) that weighed 3,120 lb (1,415.2 kg) when measured on October 22 2003 at the Port Contractors in Wilmington, Delaware, USA.

★ **Largest condom**
A 72-ft-tall (21.94-m) condom was fitted over the obelisk in the Place de la Concorde, Paris, France, on December 1 1993 to mark World AIDS Day. The condom was funded by Italian clothes firm Benetton.

★ **Largest beer bottle**
A beer bottle measuring 8 ft 4 in (2.54 m) tall and 7 ft 1.5 in (2.17 m) in circumference was unveiled at the Shepherd Neame Brewery in Faversham, Kent, UK, on January 27 1993. It took 13 minutes to fill the bottle with 164.6 gal (625.5 liters) of Kingfisher beer.

★ **Largest beach towel**
A beach towel depicting the Walt Disney character Mickey Mouse measures 30 ft 10 in x 47 ft 5 in (9.4 x 14.46 m). It was manufactured by Maiden Sunshine (Spain) and displayed at the textile fair 'Textile Hogar' held in Valencia, Spain, on January 25 2000.

★ **Largest continental broom**
On January 3 2002, a continental (witch's) broom constructed by Comitato Festeggiamenti Campagnari (Italy) measured 72 ft 9.5 in (22.19 m). The handle alone measured 39 ft 8.75 in (12.11 m).

★ **Largest boomerang**
A boomerang made from wood, plywood, and steel and measuring 5 ft 11.25 in (1.81 m) from tip to tip was successfully thrown by Heikki Niskanen (Finland) at Kuopio, Finland, on June 5 2000. The boomerang traveled past the qualifying 65-ft (20-m) mark and returned into the accuracy circle from where it was thrown.

★ **Largest ceramic plate**
A plate created by the Inatsu Town Planning Association (Japan) on August 14 1996 measured 9 ft 2 in (2.8 m) in diameter. Made from 2,690 lb (1,220 kg) of clay, it was left to dry out for five months before being painted and finally baked in a kiln for seven days.

★ **Largest flag draped**
The American 'Superflag' owned by 'Ski' Demski (USA) measures 154 x 78 m (505 x 255 ft) and weighs 3,000 lb (1.36 tonnes). It was made by Humphrey's Flag Co. (USA), delivered to Demski on June 14 1992, and unfurled in 1996 at Hoover Dam on the Colorado River, Arizona/Nevada, USA, to mark the passing of the Olympic Torch.

★ **Largest disco ball**
Derek Dyer (USA) has built a disco ball 10 ft (3 m) in diameter that weighs 1,000 lb (453.5 kg). It was unveiled at the Salt Palace in Salt Lake City, Utah, USA, on December 31 2002.

★ **Largest drum**
A drum made from Japanese cedar and cowhide measuring 15 ft 9 in (4.80 m) in diameter, 16 ft 3 in (4.95 m) deep, and weighing 4,400 lb (2,000 kg) was built by the Asano Taiko Company Ltd. (Japan). The final section of the drum was completed just a few hours before its first performance, on January 1 2001.

★ **Largest kettle**
A copper kettle that stood 3 ft (0.9 m) high, with a 6-ft (1.8-m) girth and a 23.6-gal (90-liter) capacity, was built in Taunton, Somerset, UK, ca. 1800, for the hardware merchants Fisher and Son.

Largest dental caps

Dental caps approximately 19 in (50 cm) long, 5 in (13 cm) in diameter, and weighing 28 lb (13 kg) each were fixed onto a pair of cracked tusks belonging to Spike (below), a resident Asian elephant at the Calgary Zoo, Alberta, Canada, during a 3 hr 30 min operation on July 4 2002. The stainless steel caps were designed and manufactured by the Southern Alberta Institute of Technology with metal donated by Corus Steel and adhesive by 3M (all Canada).

Largest accordion ⤊

The largest playable accordion in the world (above) is 8 ft 3.5 in (2.53 m) tall, 6 ft 2.75 in (1.9 m) wide,

2 ft 9.5 in (85 cm) deep, and weighs approximately 440 lb (200 kg). The instrument, built by Giancarlo Francenella (Italy), was begun in 2000 and finished in 2001. The giant accordion took over 1,000 hours to create and features 45 treble piano keys, 120 bass buttons, and 240 reeds. Built on a 5:1 ratio from the original, the instrument is made of wood (fir, cedar, mahogany, and walnut), metals (aluminum and steel), cardboard, cloth, and special varnishes.

★ Largest flute
The largest playable flute is 5 ft (1.52 m) long and 3.5 in (8.89 cm) in diameter and was made out of PVC by Dinesh Shandilya (India) in 1996.

★ Largest fountain pen
A pen made by Zbigniew Rozanek (Poland) in 1991 measured 2.22 m (7 ft) long and 4 in (11 cm) in diameter and had a 18-in (48-cm) nib. The weight of the pen, including ink, was 20 lb (9.5 kg). Without ink it weighed 7 lb (3.3 kg).

★ Largest jukebox
A jukebox named 'The Wall', which stood 41 ft 4 in (12.6 m) high and 63 ft (19.2 m) wide, was built by Namco Ltd (Japan) and unveiled in Sunshine Namjatown, Tokyo, Japan, in July 1996. Various features on the jukebox come to life when the music begins.

★ Largest hourglass
The largest hourglass stands 42 in (1.06 m) tall with a diameter of 15 in (38 cm). Built by Bob Ciscell (USA), the hourglass contains 65 lb (29.4 kg) of sand, which takes eight hours to run through.

★ Largest carpet of flowers
A carpet of flowers measuring 21,958 ft² (2,040 m²) was created by the Dubai Municipality at the Dubai Shopping Festival, Dubai, UAE, on February 12 2003.

★ Largest set of wind chimes
A 16-ft 8-in-tall (5.1-m) set of wind chimes built by Steve Kubler (USA) in May 2002 stands in front of the West Point Town Hall, Alabama, USA.

★ Largest piggy bank
A piggy bank called Pink Pig measured 10 ft 9 in tall, 16 ft 8 in long and 26 ft 2 in in circumference (3.28 m x 5 m x 7.9 m) on November 8 2002. Pink Pig is owned by C. Michael Davenport (USA).

★ Largest wreath
An Advent wreath measuring 164 ft (50 m) in diameter was made from fir by Otter-Zentrum Hankensbüttel and Landfrauen Isenhagener (both Germany) on November 25 2002.

★ Longest paper-clip chain made by an individual
Between February 13 and 14 2004, Dan Meyer (USA) created a paper-clip chain 5,340 ft (1,627.6 m) long, consisting of 54,030 1.2-in-long (3-cm) clips. The chain is nearly three times longer than the height of the CN Tower in Toronto, Canada.

★ Largest garland
A 14,550-ft (4,434-m) paper flower garland (or lei) was made by local citizens at the Hyatt Regency Waikiki, Honolulu, Hawaii, USA, on December 19 1992.

★ Largest ball of string
From 1989 to 1992, J.C. Payne (USA) amassed enough string to create a ball 13 ft 2.5 in (4.03 m) in diameter and 41 ft 6 in (12.65 m) in circumference.

Largest autographed ⌄ drumstick collection

Since 1980, Peter Lavinger (USA, below) has accumulated over 1,300 drumsticks,

all of which have been played and handed to him by drummers from various popular bands, including Ringo Starr of The Beatles. He caught his first drumstick from the front row of a Good Rats concert in 1980.

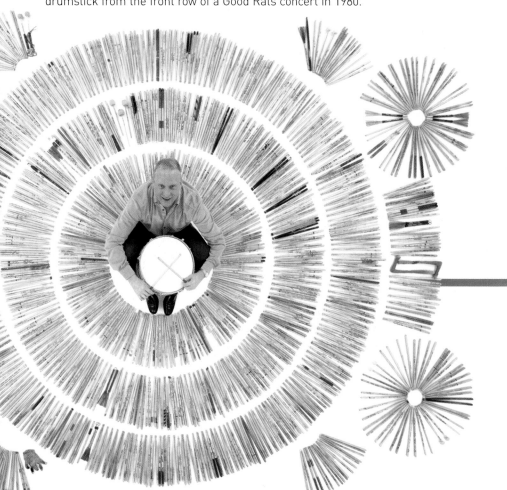

Largest ⌃ collection of yo-yos

John 'Lucky' Meisenheimer (USA, above) has a collection of 4,251 yo-yos, which he has amassed since 1971. His current collection is housed in 23 custom-made cases and is estimated to be worth around $100,000.

He also has a photo of himself with his all-time football hero Paul Merson.

★ Largest collection of uncut bank notes

Leigh Follestad (Canada) has 123 sheets of uncut bank notes from 33 countries, representing 73 denominations, which he has been collecting since 1982.

★ Largest jet-fighter collection

The world's biggest private collection of jet fighters numbers 110 and belongs to French winemaker Michel Pont. he started his collection in 1985, and it includes Russian MiGs, British Jaguars, and French Mirages. Michel buys the jets from governments, but is not permitted to fly the aircraft over French airspace. He also has a collection of 500 motorbikes, and 24 Fiat Abarth racing cars.

★ Largest beer bottle collection

The largest collection of beer bottles in the world is owned by Peter Broeker (Germany), who has amassed 12,548 bottles since 1980. The collection derives from 2,440 different breweries within 153 countries. Peter estimates that if all of his beer bottles were piled one on top of each other they would reach to a height of 9,983 ft (3,043 m), which is almost eight times the height of the Empire State Building in New York, USA.

★ Largest passport collection

Guy Van Keer (Belgium) owns 7,637 passports and documents used in lieu of passports. They represent 130 countries and passport-issuing authorities, including many countries that no longer exist. The passports date from 1615 to the present day. The collection's most expensive item is a rare Chinese passport from 1898 valued at $52,830.

★ Largest collection of colored vinyl records

Alessandro Benedetti (Italy) has collected 1,180 music records made of colored vinyl. His collection includes 866 LPs (792 colored, 74 with pictures), 291 singles (277 colored, 14 with pictures), and 23 in unusual shapes.

★ Largest collection of photographs of professional sporting personalities

Since 2000, Thomas Gill (UK) has built up a collection of 510 photographs taken of himself with professional soccer players. Thomas has photographs of himself with well-known British soccer players such as David Beckham, Sir Geoff Hurst, and Ryan Giggs.

Largest » banana collection

Ken Bannister (USA, right), owner of the International Banana Club Museum in Altadena, California, USA, has 17,000 different banana-related objects that he has amassed since 1972. All are on display in the museum.

⭐ **Largest collection of royal memorabilia**
Ronny Bragança (Portugal) has a collection of 2,950 pieces of memorabilia relating to Diana, Princess of Wales, which he has accumulated since 1991. He has items from many countries, including Japan, Mexico and Australia. In 1999, he was fortunate enough to purchase a Christmas card signed by Charles and Diana in 1989.

⭐ **Largest chamber pot collection**
Manfred Klauda (Germany) has amassed 9,400 chamber pots, the earliest dating from the 16th century. Currently his collection can be seen at the Zentrum für Aussergewöhnliche Museen, Munich, Germany.

⭐ **Largest valid credit card collection**
Walter Cavanagh (USA) has accumulated 1,397 individual valid credit cards. The cost of acquisition to 'Mr. Plastic Fantastic' was nothing, but they are worth more than $1.65 million in credit. They are kept in a 250-ft-long (76.2-m) wallet – the world's longest.

⭐ **Largest collection of soft drink cans from the same brand**
Christian Cavaletti (Italy) has a collection of 3,284 different Pepsi cans from 71 different countries. Christian, who has been collecting since 1989, belongs to the two largest soft drink can collectors' clubs: the National Pop Can Collectors (NPCC) and the Pepsi-Cola Collectors Club (PCCC).

⭐ **Largest Popsicle stick collection**
Since 1988, Poul Lykke Jepsen (Denmark) has collected 449 different Popsicle sticks. Poul started collecting the sticks after he had eaten two Popsicles and noticed that they had different sticks. His collection grew after he got a job as a storage worker in 2001 – his new employers manufactured Popsicle sticks.

Collections

Collection	Quantity	Holder
airsickness bags	3,307 from 755 airlines	Niek Vermeulen (Netherlands)
airline tags	469 from 115 airlines	Raghav Somani (India)
badges	13,516	Daniel Hedges (UK)
ballpoint pens	285,150 . from 148 countries	Angelika Unverhau (Germany)
Band-Aids (unused)	4,500	Brian Viner (UK)
Barbie dolls	1,125	Tony Mattia (UK)
beer cans	75,000 from 125 countries	William B. Christensen (USA)
bottle openers	20,884 from 136 countries	Dale Deckert (USA)
bottled water labels	5,115	Lorenzo Pescini (Italy)
bus tickets (used)	14,000	Yacov Yosipow (Israel)
car bumper stickers	3,230	Bill Heermann (USA)
clothing tags	2,180	Angela Bettelli (Italy)
condoms	1,947	Amatore Bolzoni (Italy)
decorative pins	1,457	Gerhard Kühler (Germany)
five-leaf clovers	31,336	George Kaminski (USA)
fruit stickers	34,500	Antoine Secco (France)
hats	25,777	Tustumena Lodge (USA)
hotel baggage labels	2,016	Robert Henin (USA)
key chains	24,810	Kurt Meadows (USA)
mouse mats	1,947	Daniel Evans (UK)
mugs	4,567	Harold Swauger (USA)
pencils	6,885	Emilio Arenas (Uruguay)
pencil sharpeners	8,514	Demetra Koutsouridou (Greece)
phonecards	4,531 from 239 countries and territories	Harvinder Chohan (Canada)
piggy banks	5,750	Ove Nordström (Sweden)
rubber ducks	1,439	Charlotte Lee (USA)
rubber stamps	1,251	James Burton (UK)
shoehorns	1,594	Martien Tuithof (Netherlands)
shot glasses	8,411	Brad Rodgers (USA)
tea bag labels	8,661 from 88 countries	Felix Rotter (Germany)
thermometers	4,580	Richard T. Porter (USA)
traffic cones	137	David Morgan (UK)

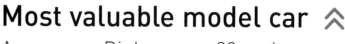

Most valuable model car ⟰

A very rare Dinky green 28 series 2nd Type Bentalls Department Store Promotional Delivery Van

with yellow upper side panels and a white roof (above) was sold for £12,650 ($20,147) at Christie's, London, UK, on October 14 1994. This example is believed to be one of only three known by Christie's experts to have survived.

Most valuable teddy bear ⟰

A Steiff bear named Teddy Girl (above) was sold for £110,000 ($171,600),

more than 18 times the estimate and twice the previous world record, by Christie's, London, UK, on December 5 1994. The buyer was Japanese businessman Yoshihiro Sekiguchi.

★ Largest stitched teddy bear

The bear measuring 38 ft 8.2 in (11.79 m) in length was designed and made by Dana Warren (USA) over a period of six months.

★ Largest model railway engine

A model of *Thomas the Tank Engine* character James, measuring 104 in high, 59 in wide, 256 in long (264 x 150 x 652 cm) and weighing nearly 3,351 lb (1.52 tonnes) was built by BBC Visual Effects (UK) for a Thomas the Tank Engine tour in 2003. Models of Thomas, Percy, and Gordon were also part of the tour.

★ Largest kite flown

The largest kite ever flown has a total lifting area of 7,319.4 ft² (680 m²). When laid flat, it has a total area of 10,042.7 ft² (933 m²). The 'Megabite', designed by Peter Lynn (New Zealand), measured 210 ft (64 m) long and 72 ft (22 m) wide. The kite was officially measured on September 7 1997.

★ Longest kite flown

'The Cracken', created by Michel Trouillet (France), measures 3,394 ft (1,034.45 m) in length, with a total mass of 233 lb (106 kg). It was flown by Trouillet and his team on November 18 1990 in Nîmes, France.

★ Largest spinning top

A team of 25 workers from the Mizushima Plant of Kawasaki Steel Works in Okayama, Japan, created a spinning top measuring 6 ft 6.75 in (2 m) tall and 8 ft 6.25 in (2.6 m) in diameter and weighing 793 lb (360 kg). They spun it for 1 hr 21 min 35 sec on November 3 1986.

★ Tallest LEGO structure

A LEGO tower built in Tallinn, Estonia, on August 18–21 1998 reached a height of 81 ft 8.7 in (24.91 m). It consisted of 391,478 plastic, eight-stud toy bricks. Over 6,000 children helped in the construction, which was organized by A.S. Rekato Ltd (Estonia), to beat the previous record set in Moscow, Russia, in July 1998 by 9 in (25 cm).

★ Longest LEGO structure

A LEGO structure in the shape of a millipede measuring 3,451 ft (1,052 m) and consisting of 2,477,140 bricks, was built by 20,000 children in Bangkok, Thailand, on April 27 2003.

★ Largest hula hoop spun

The largest hula hoop successfully rotated at least three times around a person's waist had a diameter of 13 ft 4 in (4.08 m). Nozomi Tsuju and Ai Kago (both Japan) rotated the hoop for 30 seconds each at the studios of Nippon Television Network, Tokyo, Japan, on January 1 2004.

★ Longest Hot Wheels track

The longest Hot Wheels track measured 1,650 ft (502.92 m) and consisted of 2,100 pieces of track, held together by 2,150 connectors. The attempt was organized by Mattel Canada, Inc., for Big Brothers Big Sisters of Canada and was completed on July 7 2002 at Thunder Alley, Toronto, Ontario, Canada.

★ Largest chess piece

Mats Allanson (Sweden) has made a scaled-up king measuring 13 ft (4 m) high and 4 ft 6 in (1.4 m) in diameter at the base.

Most valuable >> Mickey Mouse toy

A rare clockwork Mickey Mouse motorcycle (ca. 1939, right) in its original box sold at Christie's, London, UK, on June 16 1997 for £51,000 ($83,466).

★ **Earliest chess pieces**
Chessmen found at Nashipur, modern-day Bangladesh, have been dated to ca. AD 900 and are the oldest known in existence.

★ **Largest commercially available board game**
Galaxion, manufactured by Cerebe Design International (Hong Kong), is played on a board measuring 33 x 33 in (83.8 x 83.8 cm).

★ **Largest commercially available jigsaw puzzle**
The largest commercially available jigsaw puzzle is made by Ravensburger of Ravensburg, Germany, and measures 9 ft 0.5 in x 6 ft 3.5 in (2.76 x 1.92 m). It has 18,000 pieces – another record for a commercially available jigsaw.

★ **Smallest commercially available jigsaw puzzle**
A 1,000-piece jigsaw puzzle manufactured by Educa Sallent (Spain) measures 18 x 12 in (46 x 30 cm). The miniature puzzles made by Educa Sallent are all made from recycled materials and depict a variety of images, ranging from European landmarks to Disney and Sesame Street characters.

★ **Largest jigsaw puzzle**
A puzzle devised by Great East Asia Surveyors & Consultants Co. Ltd measured 58,435.1 ft² (5,428.8 m²) and consisted of 21,600 pieces in total. It was assembled by 777 people at the former Kai Tak Airport, Hong Kong, China, on November 3 2002.

★ **Largest set of Russian nesting dolls (matrioshka)**
A 51-piece set of nesting dolls was hand painted by Youlia Bereznitskaia (Russia). The largest doll is 1 ft 9.25 in (54 cm) in height, while the smallest measures 0.125 in (0.31 cm) in height. The set was completed on April 25 2003.

★ **Largest ball bath**
The bath had a surface area of 2,722.2 ft² (252.9 m²) with an average depth of 1 ft 4 in (0.4 m) and contained about 130,000 balls. It was made on December 30 1999 in Plantagebaan, Wouwse Plantage, The Netherlands, by the Stichting Carnaval Wouwse Plantage as part of the festivities for a millennium carnival.

★ **Largest yo-yo**
A yo-yo measuring 10 ft 4 in (3.17 m) in diameter and weighing 897 lb (407 kg) was devised by J.N. Nichols (Vimto) Ltd. (UK) and constructed by engineering students at Stockport College. It was launched by crane from a height of 188 ft 6 in (57.5 m) at Wythenshawe, Greater Manchester, UK, on August 1 1993 and subsequently yo-yoed about four times.

★ **Largest permanent Monopoly board**
A Monopoly board made of granite and located in San Jose, California, USA, measures 31 x 31 ft (9.44 x 9.44 m). All the playing pieces are proportionally scaled up. The board was opened to the public on July 26 2002.

Most stories in a house of cards «

The tallest freestanding house of cards was 131 stories high. The 25-ft 3.48-in-tall (7.71-m) structure was built by Bryan Berg (USA, left) on November 6 1999. The house was created using 91,800 cards in the lobby of the casino at Potsdamer Platz, Berlin, Germany, and recorded for the *Guinness die Show der Rekord*. The total weight of the 1,765 packs of cards used was 242 lb 8 oz (110 kg).

Highest single ⋀ game score when bowling backwards

Del Lawson (USA, above) registered a score of 139 in a single game of backwards bowling at Cypress Lanes, Winter Haven, Florida, USA, on April 21 2002. He bowled a series of three games with a total score of 376.

★ Most darts bull's-eyes in 10 hours
Perry Prine (USA) hit 1,432 bull's-eyes in 10 hours at the Lake Erie Classic Dart Tournament in Mentor, Ohio, USA, on March 27 1998.

★ Largest game of Poohsticks
On July 22 2000, the largest ever game of Poohsticks was played on the River Tweed from the Chain Bridge, Horncliffe, in the Scottish Borders, UK. A total of 2,313 Poohsticks were launched from the bridge to sail downriver to the finish line at Paxton House Boathouse. A stick stamped 8702 won. Poohsticks is a game invented by A.A. Milne (UK) of *Winnie the Pooh* fame – Christopher Robin and Pooh threw sticks in the water from one side of a bridge, then ran over to see which stick floated out first on the other side.

★ Farthest wink shot in tiddlywinks
At the Queen's College Tournament, Cambridge, UK, Ben Soares (UK) of the St. Andrews Tiddlywinks Society made a wink shot measuring 31 ft 3 in (9.52 m), on January 14 1995.

★ Most opponents in consecutive chess games
On February 27 and 28 2001, Anna-Maria Botsari (Greece) played 1,102 consecutive games of chess against different opponents, with just seven draws and the rest wins, at Kalavryta, Greece.

★ Most simultaneous checkers opponents
Ronald Suki King (Barbados) played 385 games of checkers simultaneously at the Houston International Festival, Texas, USA, on April 26 1998. King donned roller skates to move between the 385 games.

★ Largest game of pass the parcel
On February 28 1998, 3,918 students removed 2,200 wrappers from a parcel measuring 4 ft 11 in x 4 ft 11 in x 1 ft 7 in (1.5 x 1.5 x 0.5 m) in two and a half hours at Nanyang Technological University, Singapore. Owing to the numbers involved, the parcel went round on a cart and took an hour to complete one circuit.

★ Fastest Jenga tower built to 30 levels
The fastest time to build a stable Jenga tower 30 levels high, within the rules of the game, is 11 min 55 sec by Sabrina Ibrahim, John Chua, and Alex Agboola (all UK) on the BBC's *Big Toe Radio Show*, London, UK, on January 28 2003.

★ Most dominoes set up and toppled single-handedly
Ma Li Hua (China) single-handedly set up and toppled 303,621 dominoes out of a total of 303,628 at Singapore Expo Hall, Singapore, on August 18 2003. The event was organized by LG Electronics, Inc.

★ Most dominoes set up and toppled by a group
The record for most dominoes toppled is 3,847,295 (from a possible 4 million). The attempt was organized by Endemol Netherlands and took place at FEC EXPO, Leeuwarden, The Netherlands, on November 15 2002. The 4 million dominoes were divided into 51 interconnected projects, all of which related to one central theme.

Largest game of pick-up sticks

Newmarket Recreation have made a game of pick-up sticks that was 36 times larger than the commercially available item (below). It consisted of 30 plastic sticks (7 gold, 7 red, 7 blue, 8 green, and 1 black), each measuring 19 ft 10.5 in (6.05 m) in length and 4.5 in (11.4 cm) in width. A full game was played by four teams of 75 children at Newmarket, New Hampshire, USA, on July 21 2003.

★ **Most dominoes stacked on a single domino**
Matthias Aisch (Germany) stacked 726 dominoes on a single vertically standing supporting domino on December 28 2003 in Radeburg, Germany. The stack remained standing for an hour.

★ **Largest quiz**
A record 888 participants took part in a quiz at the Radisson SAS Hotel, Galway, Ireland, on October 14 2003. Teams of four answered 10 rounds of 12 questions.

★ **Fastest time to solve a Rubik's cube**
The fastest time to solve a Rubik's cube in an official championship is 16.53 sec by Jess Bonde (Denmark) at the 2003 World Championships in Toronto, Ontario, Canada.

★ **Fastest time to solve a Rubik's cube blindfolded**
The fastest time to solve a Rubik's cube in an official championship while blindfolded is 3 min 56 sec by Dror Vomberg (Israel) at the 2003 World Championships in Toronto, Ontario, Canada.

★ **Highest overall Scrabble score**
Phil Appleby (UK) achieved a Scrabble score of 1,049 on June 25 1989 at Wormley, Herts, UK. His opponent scored 253 and the margin of victory, 796 points, is also a record.

★ **Largest sack race competition**
A total of 2,095 Dutch students – from Agnieton College and elementary schools in Zwolle, Wezep and Hattem, The Netherlands, took part in a sack race on October 11 2002 in Zwolle, The Netherlands.

★ **Most participants in a wheelbarrow race**
The largest wheelbarrow race involved 318 people (159 pairs) and took place at Alexandra Park, London, UK, on August 31 2002 in an attempt organized by Starwood Hotels & Resorts, London, UK.

★ **Largest game of leapfrog**
A total of 849 people took part in a game of leapfrog at Brookfield Community School, Chesterfield, Derbyshire, UK, on September 26 2003.

★ **Highest altitude by a single kite**
Richard P. Synergy (Canada) flew a kite to an altitude of approximately 14,509 ft (4,422 m) above the point of takeoff on August 12 2000 near Kincardine, Ontario, Canada. The kite, a high-tech delta, had an area of 270 ft^2 (25 m^2) and was designed and built by Synergy himself. At its maximum altitude, the kite had 4.5 miles (7.31 km) of woven kevlar line connecting it to a winch on the ground. The record-breaking flight lasted 8 hr 35 min.

★ **Most powerful games console**
Microsoft's Xbox is powered by a 733-MHz Intel CPU, the fastest of any current games console. Its graphics processor, a custom-designed chip that runs at 250 MHz, is also the field leader. The Xbox's main rivals, the Sony Playstation 2 and Nintendo GameCube, have CPU clock speeds of 300 and 405 MHz respectively, and graphics chips running at 150 and 202.5 MHz respectively.

★ **Best-selling Xbox game**
According to *Screen Digest*, the best-selling Xbox game is 'Halo', which had sold 4 million units as of December 2003.

★ **Best-selling Playstation 2 game**
According to *Screen Digest*, the best-selling Playstation 2 game is 'Grand Theft Auto Vice City', which had sold 9 million units as of December 2003.

★ **Best-selling GameCube game**
The best-selling GameCube game is 'Mario Sunshine', which had sold 3.5 million units as of December 2003 according to *Screen Digest*.

« Largest popcorn sculpture

The world's largest popcorn sculpture (left) is 13 ft (4 m) tall and 8 ft 9 in (2.67 m) wide, and is made in the likeness of King Kong. The giant popcorn ape was displayed in front of Leicester Square's Odeon cinema, London, UK, on July 24 2003 to celebrate the 70th anniversary of the original *King Kong* film (USA, 1933).

Largest gingerbread man «

Chefs at the Hyatt Regency Hotel, Vancouver, Canada, made a gingerbread man (above) that measured 13 ft 11 in (4.23 m) high, 5 ft 8 in (1.72 m) wide and 2 in (5.08 cm) deep, on November 19 2003. The gingerbread figure weighed 372 lb 1.82 oz (168.8 kg).

★ Curly Wurly stretching
Craig Glenday (UK) stretched a Curly Wurly chocolate bar a total distance of 3 ft (0.91 m) in three minutes at the offices of Guinness World Records, London, UK, on June 27 2003.

★ Fastest sandwich made using only feet
Using just his feet, Rob Williams (USA) made a bologna cheese and lettuce sandwich, complete with sliced tomatoes, mustard, mayonnaise, sliced pickles, and olives on cocktail sticks, in 1 min 57 sec on the set of *Guinness World Records: Primetime*, Los Angeles, California, USA, on November 10 2000.

★ Fastest time to husk a coconut using only teeth
In 28.06 seconds, Sidaraju S. Raju (India) husked a coconut measuring 30.7 in (78 cm) in circumference and weighing 10 lb 6.4 oz (4.74 kg) using only his teeth at the Ravindra Kalashetra, Bangalore, India, on March 30 2003.

★ Fastest time to drink two pints of stout
Scott Williams (Canada) drank two pints of Guinness in 6.3 seconds on May 23 2003.

★ Most brussels sprouts eaten in one minute
Dave Mynard (UK) consumed 43 cooked brussels sprouts in 1 minute on December 10 2003.

★ Most ice cream eaten in 30 seconds
Diego Siu (USA) ate 9.3 oz (264 g) of ice cream in 30 seconds at the Central Florida Fair, Orlando, USA, on March 2 2003.

★ Fastest time to eat raw onion
In only 2 min 40 sec, Danny Healy (UK) ate a raw onion weighing 7.47 oz (212 g) at the BBC Television Centre, London, UK, on November 15 2003.

★ Greatest egg-dropping height
The greatest height from which fresh eggs have been dropped to the ground and remained intact is 700 ft (213 m) by David Donoghue (UK), who dropped a number of eggs from a helicopter onto a golf course in Blackpool, Lancs, UK, on August 22 1994.

★ Most eggs crushed with wrist
K.S. Raghavendra (India) crushed 13 eggs with the back of his wrist in 30 seconds at the Sree Rama Vidyalaya School, Bangalore, India, on September 9 2003.

★ Farthest marshmallow nose-blow
Scott Jeckel (USA) blew a marshmallow out of one nostril a distance of 16 ft 3.5 in (4.96 m), caught in the mouth of Ray Perisin (USA), on the set of *Guinness World Records: Primetime*, Los Angeles, California, USA, on August 13 1999.

★ Most baked beans eaten in five minutes
Andy Szerbini (UK) ate a total of 226 baked beans in 5 minutes using a cocktail stick at London Zoo, UK, on November 18 1996.

Most Smarties eaten in three minutes

The record for the most Smarties eaten in three minutes using chopsticks is held by Kathryn Ratcliffe (UK, below), who ate 138 Smarties at the Metro Centre, Gateshead, Tyne and Wear, UK, on October 25 2003, breaking her own record of 112.

Most expensive burger ⌃

The DB Burger Royale (above), created by chef Daniel Boulud

(France), is available on the menu of DB Bistro Moderne, New York, USA, for $59. The original DB burger was created to mark DB Bistro Moderne's opening in 2001, and the restaurant added the DB Royale burger to the menu in January 2003. It is served exclusively during the black truffle season.

★ **Most baked beans flicked**
The largest quantity of baked beans flicked from a bathtub into a bucket is 34.63 oz (982 g) by Jamie Rickers (UK) on GMTV's program *Up On The Roof*, London, UK, on October 30 2002.

★ **Most expensive cocktail commercially available**
The Ritz Side Car, costing €400 ($496), features on the cocktail menu at Bar Hemingway, in the Hotel Ritz, Paris, France. The cocktail was invented by head bartender Frank Meier in 1923 and contains Ritz Fine Champagne, 1865 (pre-phylloxéra) cognac, Cointreau, and lemon juice. The cocktail could be bought for just $5 in 1923. (In terms of purchase power, the current-day equivalent of this is $67.)

★ **Longest champagne-cork flight**
Heinrich Medicus (USA) ejected a cork from an untreated and unheated champagne bottle standing 4 ft (1.22 m) from level ground to a distance of 177 ft 9 in (54.18 m) at the Woodbury Vineyards Winery, New York, USA, on June 5 1988.

★ **Most grapes stuffed in the mouth**
Michael Levinson (Canada) stuffed 54 seedless grapes, weighing 4 oz (113 g) into his mouth on the set of *Guinness World Records: Primetime*, Los Angeles, California, USA, on September 27 1999.

★ **Most candles on a cake**
The St. Ignatius Cub Scouts (USA) lit 12,432 candles on an iced cake measuring 75 x 25 in (190.5 x 63.5 cm) as part of Ohio's bicentennial celebrations on May 9 2003.

★ **Most champagne bottles sabered in one minute**
Using a saber, Dean Opsal (USA) cut off the upper portion of the neck from each of 20 champagne bottles at the Coeur d'Alene Resort Hotel, Coeur d'Alene, Idaho, USA, on October 31 2001. He achieved this in one minute and without shattering the glass, leaving the contents safe to drink.

★ **Most cherry stems knotted in three minutes**
Al Gliniecki (USA) tied 39 cherry stems into knots with his tongue in three minutes at the Guinness World of Records Experience, Orlando, Florida, USA, on January 26 1999.

★ **Oldest restaurant**
Restaurante Botín in Calle de Cuchilleros, Madrid, Spain, was opened in 1725 by a French cook named Jean Botín and his Asturian wife. Today the restaurant is run by the third generation of the Gonzalez family, Antonio and José Gonzalez (all Spain). Located in the heart of Madrid near the Plaza Mayor, it now has four floors which retain the original 18th-century interiors as well as the original firewood oven.

Largest » pumpkin pie

The largest pumpkin pie (below) weighed 418 lb (189.6 kg).

It was made by the Windsor Certified Farmers Market and the Windsor High School Culinary Arts Program (both USA) and served at the Farmers Market, Windsor, California, USA, on October 26 2003. The pie was 6 ft 4 in (1.936 m) in diameter and 3 in (7.62 cm) deep.

★ Longest sesame twist
The longest sesame twist measured 4 ft 10.8 in (1.5 m) and was made by chefs at Guifa Xiang, Tianjin, China, on December 1 1999. A sesame twist is a traditional Chinese delicacy made from fried dough with a crispy stuffing.

★ Largest bag of cookies
The largest bag of cookies was made by Loblaws Supermarkets Ltd. and was 10 ft 8 in (3.29 m) high, 7 ft (2.13 m) deep and 45 in (1.14 m) wide. It contained 3,852 trays, each with 26 cookies, making a total of 100,152. It went on display at Loblaws Wonderland Market, London, Ontario, Canada, on September 6 and 7 2001.

★ Largest lollipop
The largest lollipop weighed 4,759 lb 1.6 oz (2,158.7 kg) and was made by Franssons (Sweden) for a festival in Gränna, Sweden, on July 27 2003. The lollipop was 6 ft 6 in (1.98 m) wide, 9 ft 10 in (3 m)

long, and 9.5 in (24 cm) thick and was peppermint-striped like traditional Gränna rock candy.

★ Largest marzipan confection
The world's largest pistachio marzipan confection weighed 9,255 lb (4.2 tons) and was made by 225 chefs in an event organized by Spacetel Syria at Hamadanya Stadium, Aleppo, Syria, on July 1 2003.

★ Largest bowl of pasta
The largest ever bowl of pasta weighed 3,265 lb (1,480 kg), excluding the weight of the bowl. It was created by Nintendo of America, Inc., in conjunction with Buca Di Beppo restaurants (USA) on August 22 2002 in Washington Square, San Francisco, USA. The fiberglass bowl measured 3 ft (0.91 m) high and 10 ft (3.048 m) wide.

★ Longest salami
A salami measuring 498 ft 3.6 in (151.89 m) was made by the Association of Friulian Butchers and the Udine Chamber of Commerce (both Italy) and was displayed at the Piazza San Giacomo, Udine, Italy, on October 13 2002. The average circumference of the salami was 5.5 in (14 cm) and the entire salami weighed 590.8 lb (269 kg).

★ Largest serving of fish-and-chips
The largest serving of fish-and-chips had a combined weight of 72 lb (32.66 kg) and was made by Fedics Food Services, Port Elizabeth, Eastern Cape, South Africa, on November 22 2003. Individually, the fish weighed 31 lb 8 oz (14.30 kg) and the french fries weighed 40 lb 8 oz (18.36 kg).

★ Largest pizza commercially available
Paul Revere's Pizza (USA) will bake and deliver a pizza with a 4-ft (1.21-m) diameter and an area of 12.59 ft² (1.17 m²). The pizza, named the 'Ultimate Party Pizza', is sold at $99.99. It is made up of 170 oz (4.81 kg) of dough, 48 fl oz (1.36 liters) of sauce, various meats and vegetables, and about 5 lb (2.25 kg) of cheese.

★ Largest box of chocolates
Marshall Field's, Chicago, Illinois, USA, created a box of Frango mint chocolates weighing 3,226 lb (1,463 kg) on November 14 2002.

★ Largest cup of coffee
On January 29 2002, Ettore Diana and Luca Braguti (both Italy) made a 394.7-gal (1,500-liter) cappuccino at the Hotel Leon d'Oro, Verona, Italy.

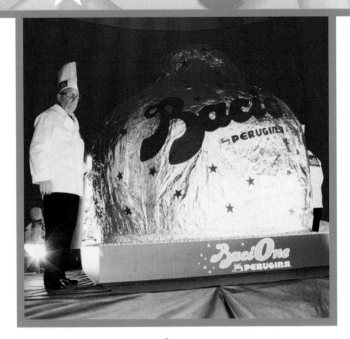

Largest ⋀ individual chocolate

The largest single chocolate is a 13,183-lb (5,980-kg) BaciOne (above). Made by Nestlé (Italy), it was displayed at the Perugina factory, San Sisto, Italy, on October 26 2003.

Largest wedding cake ⋙

The largest wedding cake ever (below) weighed 6,818.40 kg (15,032 lb) and was made by chefs at the Mohegan Sun Hotel and Casino, Uncasville, Connecticut, USA, and displayed at their New England bridal showcase on February 8 2004.

★ **Largest cocktail**
The world's largest cocktail was a 7,012-gal (26,645-liter) margarita made on May 17 2001 by staff at Jimmy Buffett's Margaritaville and Mott's, Inc., Universal City Walk, Orlando, Florida, USA.

★ **Largest milkshake**
The Comfort Diners, Parmalat USA, and the American Dairy Association (all USA) made the world's largest milkshake, with a volume of 5,977 gal (22,712.47 liters) in New York, USA, on August 1 2000.

★ **Largest tea bag**
The world's largest tea bag was made by Lipton Yellow Label of Lever Brothers Pakistan Ltd. on June 22 2002. The tea bag weighed 19 lb 10 oz (8.9 kg) and was displayed at the Avari Towers Hotel, Karachi, Pakistan. The giant tea bag measured 10 ft (3.18 m) long and 7 ft 3 in (2.21 m) wide, and attached to the tea bag was a string measuring 14 ft (4.26 m) long. The bag was made from

original filter paper and contained 15 lb 7 oz (7 kg) of black tea. It is estimated that 3,500 cups of tea could be made from the tea bag.

★ **Largest pizza**
On December 8 1990, the largest pizza ever was baked at the Norwood Hypermarket, Johannesburg, South Africa. It was 122 ft 8 in (37.4 m) in diameter and took about 39 hours to prepare and cook.

★ **Longest hot dog**
The world's longest hot dog measured 34 ft 5.25 in (10.5 m). It was made by students from the University of Pretoria and displayed at the Sonop Hostel, Pretoria, South Africa, on October 18 2003.

★ **Largest box of popcorn**
On September 11 2003, BR Turbo (Brazil) filled a huge box with popcorn, 880 ft³ (24.92 m³) in volume, at the Mercado Público, Porto Alegre, Rio Grande do Sul, Brazil. It took them 5 hr 59 min to fill the box.

★ **Largest candy cane**
Employees of Fabiano's Chocolates and Ice Cream (USA) made a candy cane measuring 36 ft 7 in (11.14 m) long and 4 in (10.1 cm) in diameter at Lansing City Market, Michigan, USA, on December 5 1998.

★ **Largest bubble-gum bubble blown from the mouth**
The greatest reported diameter for a bubble-gum bubble blown from the mouth under the strict rules of this highly competitive activity is 23 in (58.4 cm), and was achieved by Susan Montgomery Williams (USA) at the ABC-TV studios in New York City, USA, on July 19 1994.

★ **Largest bubble-gum bubble blown through the nose**
After pre-chewing for at least an hour, Joyce Samuels (USA) blew, from her nose, a bubblegum bubble with a diameter of 11 in (28 cm) on *Guinness World Records: Primetime*, Los Angeles, USA, on November 10 2000.

★ **Fastest jellybean sorting using a straw**
The fastest time in which 30 Jelly Belly jellybeans have been sorted into five flavors using a drinking straw is 1 min 3.58 sec by Euan Hamilton (UK) in a competition organized by the *Beano* comic (UK) in May 2004.

Feats of engineering

Contents

Big buildings
Feats of engineering

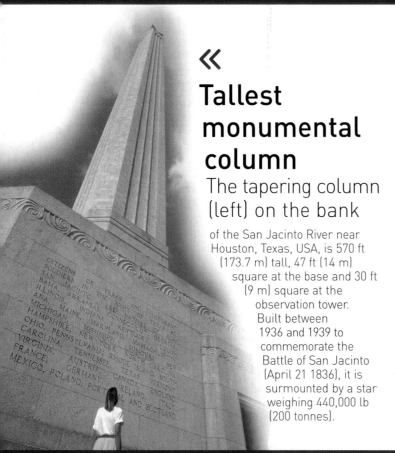

«
Tallest monumental column

The tapering column (left) on the bank

of the San Jacinto River near Houston, Texas, USA, is 570 ft (173.7 m) tall, 47 ft (14 m) square at the base and 30 ft (9 m) square at the observation tower. Built between 1936 and 1939 to commemorate the Battle of San Jacinto (April 21 1836), it is surmounted by a star weighing 440,000 lb (200 tonnes).

Largest stadium roof ⌃

The transparent acrylic glass 'tent' roof over the Munich Olympic Stadium, Germany (above) measures 915,000 ft^2 (85,000 m^2) in area. It rests on a steel net supported by masts.

★ Largest ice village
A village of 140 'igloos' – huts constructed solely of ice – was built near the famous Icehotel at Jukkasjärvi, Sweden, to accommodate 700 employees of Tetra Pak International during a conference at the hotel in December 2002. Each hut had a diameter of 14 ft (4.3 m) and was 7 ft (2.1 m) tall. The igloos slept up to five people each and were constructed of around 1,765 ft^3 (50 m^3) of ice.

★ Largest wooden building
Built in 1912, the Woolloomooloo Bay Wharf, Sydney, Australia, is 1,312 ft (400 m) long, 206 ft (63 m) wide, and stands on 3,600 piles. The building on the wharf is five stories high, 1,150 ft (350.5 m) long, and 141 ft (43 m) wide with a floor area of 688,890 ft^2 (64,000 m^2), and has been converted into a marina complex and hotel apartments.

★ Tallest residential-only building
The tallest purely residential building in the world is the 21st Century Tower in Dubai,

UAE, which has 54 floors and tops out at 882 ft (269 m). Its main roof is at 622 ft (189.7 m). However, the roof of the 866-ft (264-m) Tower Palace 3 Tower G, in Seoul, South Korea, is also its highest point, meaning that it can accommodate 69 floors of living space. Both towers were completed in 2003.

★ Tallest obelisk
The world's tallest obelisk is the Washington Monument in Washington D.C., USA. It stands 555 ft (169 m) tall and was completed in 1884 to honor George Washington. An obelisk is specifically classified as a tapered four-sided column, usually with a pointed top.

★ Tallest freestanding structure
The tallest freestanding structure on Earth is the Petronius oil and gas drilling platform, which stands 1,870 ft (570 m) above the ocean floor in the Gulf of Mexico. Operated by Texaco, the platform began commercial production on

July 21 2000. The highest point on the platform, the vent boom, stands in excess of 2,000 ft (610 m) above the ocean floor. The tallest freestanding structure on land is the 1,815-ft 5-in (553.34-m) CN Tower in Toronto, Canada.

★ Largest airport roof
The Hajj Terminal at the $5.3-billion King Abdul-Aziz Airport near Jeddah, Saudi Arabia, which was designed to cater for the annual influx of pilgrims, is the world's largest roofed structure, covering a total area of 370 acres (150 hectares).

★ Largest airport terminal
The Hong Kong International Airport passenger terminal building is 0.8 miles (1.3 km) long and covers 5.92 million ft^2 (550,000 m^2). The baggage hall of this gargantuan structure is as big as the Yankee Stadium in New York, USA, and could hold five Boeing 747s parked wing tip to wing tip. The terminal is designed to accommodate 45 million

passengers a year and handles 460 flights a day. It contains 3 km (1.8 miles) of moving walkways, 592,000 ft^2 (55,000 m^2) of glass cladding, and around 1.25 million ft^2 (117,000 m^2) of carpeting.

★ Largest soccer stadium
The Maracanã Municipal Stadium in Rio de Janeiro, Brazil, has a standard capacity of 205,000 spectators, 155,000 of whom can be seated. It was built for the 1950 Football World Cup and housed a crowd of 199,854 for the final match of the tournament, Brazil v. Uruguay, on July 16 1950 – the greatest ever attendance for a sporting event. The oval stadium is 105 ft (32 m) high and the distance between the middle of the field and the furthest spectator is 413 ft (126 m).

★ Longest stadium roof span
The longest roof span is 787 ft 4 in (240 m) for the major axis of the elliptical Texas Stadium, completed in 1971 at Irving, Texas, USA.

Largest palace »

The Imperial Palace in the centre of Beijing, China (above), covers an area measuring 3,150 x 2,460 ft (960 x 750 m) over an area of 178 acres (72 hectares). The outline survives from the construction of the third Ming emperor, Yongle (1402–24), but owing to constant reconstruction work, most of the intramural buildings (five halls and 17 palaces) are from the 18th century.

★ Largest retractable roof

The world's largest retractable roof covers the SkyDome, home of the Toronto Blue Jays baseball team, near the CN Tower in Toronto, Canada. Completed in June 1989, the roof covers 8 acres (3.2 hectares), spans 685 ft (209 m) at its widest, and rises to 282 ft (86 m). It weighs 24.6 million lb (11,000 tons) and takes 20 minutes to open fully. When retracted, the entire field and 91% of the seats are uncovered. The stadium has a capacity of 67,000 for concerts, 55,000 for Canadian football, and 50,600 for baseball.

★ Largest stadium with air-supported roof

The Pontiac Silverdome Stadium in Detroit, Michigan, USA, has a capacity of 80,311. The 10-acre (4-hectare) translucent roof covering the 770 x 600-ft (235 x 183-m) octagonal stadium is held up by pressurized air provided by 25 large fans. Made from flexible Teflon-coated fiber-glass, the roof is 202 ft (62 m) high. The air pressure in the stadium causes no discomfort and is within the limits of natural atmospheric pressure variations. The building is equipped with revolving doors to ensure that the air doesn't leak out as people enter.

★ Largest residential palace

The Istana Nurul Iman – the palace of the Sultan of Brunei in the capital Bandar Seri Begawan – was completed in January 1984 at a reported cost of $422 million. It is the largest residence in the world, with a floor space of 2,152,780 ft² (200,000 m²), 1,788 rooms, and 257 lavatories.

★ Largest pyramid

The largest pyramid, and the largest monument ever built, is the Quetzalcóatl Pyramid at Cholula de Rivadavia, 63 miles (101 km) southeast of Mexico City. It is 177 ft (54 m) tall, and its base covers nearly 45 acres (18.2 hectares). Its volume is estimated at 116.5 million ft³ (3.3 million m³), compared with a volume of 84.8 million ft³ (2.4 million m³) for the Pyramid of Khufu, or Cheops, at Giza.

★ Largest hotel

The MGM Grand Hotel and Casino, Las Vegas, Nevada, USA, consists of four 30-story towers on a 112-acre (45.3-hectare) site. The hotel has 5,005 rooms, with suites of up to 6,000 ft² (560 m²), a 15,200-seat arena, and a 33-acre (13.3-hectare) theme park.

★ Tallest door

Each of the four doors in the NASA Vehicle Assembly Building near Cape Canaveral, Florida, USA, is 460 ft (140 m) high, as tall as a 35-story building. They were originally designed to allow fully assembled Saturn and Apollo rockets to pass through them.

★ Highest clock

The world's highest two-sided clock is 580 ft (177 m) above street level on top of the Morton International building, Chicago, Illinois, USA.

★ Largest shopping centre

West Edmonton Mall in Edmonton, Alberta, Canada, covers an area of 5.3 million ft² (492,386 m²). The mall cost a staggering CAN$1.2 billion ($927 million) to build and features over 800 stores and services, as well as 11 major department stores.

★ Tallest air-traffic control tower

The 425-ft (130-m) tower at Kuala Lumpur International Airport, Malaysia, is the world's tallest air-traffic control tower. Its design imitates an Olympic torch.

Tallest structures
Feats of engineering

From earliest times, humans has aimed for the sky, originally to glorify a secular ruler or religious deity, but now mainly to gain international prestige.

Foundations

Built as a tomb for a god-king, Egypt's Great Pyramid at Giza was probably the world's tallest building for 3,500 years, from 2500 BC until the construction of the great European cathedrals in the Middle Ages. The modern era of tall buildings was heralded by the completion in 1889 of the 1,023-ft-high (312-m) Eiffel Tower in Paris, France. And from La Tour Eiffel onward, it has been big business, rather than religion, that has driven the construction of ever taller buildings. There is enormous prestige attached to being the home of the world's tallest structure – and some recent record holders are featured here (to scale).

The advent of skyscrapers

During the early 20th century, the USA dominated the race to be the home of the world's tallest building. New York is still the most famous home of the 'skyscraper', as these giants became known. New York's tallest ever buildings were the Twin Towers of the World Trade Center, dedicated in 1973 but destroyed in the terrorist atrocity of September 11 2001. The north tower was the taller of the two and stood an amazing 1,368 ft (417 m) high. The World Trade Center was the tallest building for a relatively short time, as in 1974, Chicago's Sears Tower was completed and took the title. Sears held on to that record for over 20 years.

Competition from Asia

From the 1990s, the USA has had some stiff competition from Asia, and in 1996 the title of world's tallest building passed to the 88-story, 1,483-ft (452-m) Petronas Twin Towers in Kuala Lumpur, Malaysia. The completion of the 1,667-ft (508-m) Taipei 101 in Taipei, Taiwan, in 2004 means that the title remains in Asia for now, but several new proposed buildings, including the new Freedom Tower on the site of the World Trade Center in New York City, USA, and the Burj Dubai in the United Arab Emirates – whose final height will not be made public until it is completed – means that the crown is likely to change hands several times in the near future.

1931 Empire State Building
New York City, New York, USA
Height to tip of antenna: **1,472 ft (449 m)**
Height to roof: **1,250 ft (381 m)**

1974 Sears Tower
Chicago, Illinois, USA
Height to tip of antenna: **1,728 ft (527 m)**
Height to roof: **1,450 ft (442 m)**

1996 Petronas Twin Towers
Kuala Lumpur, Malaysia
Height to tip of spire: **1,483 ft (452 m)**
Height to roof: **1,242 ft (378.6 m)**

Tallest freestanding structure

But no building standing today is as tall as the world's tallest structure on land – the CN Tower in Toronto, Ontario, Canada. This communications tower is entirely freestanding and has no residential or office space. 'Topped out' in April 1975, it measures a staggering 1,815 ft 5 in (553.33 m).

The future ...

Skyscraper buffs will continue to argue as to which of the world's architectural gems constitute the world's tallest building. There are plans being drawn up all over the world for new high-rise buildings so perhaps when Guinness World Records celebrates its centennial in 2055, there will be a building in existence that's twice the height of the current record holder!

2004 Taipei 101
Taipei, Taiwan
Height to tip of spire:
1,666 ft (508 m)
Height to roof: **1,470 ft (448 m)**

1975 CN Tower
Toronto, Ontario, Canada
Height to tip of spire/
antenna: **1,815 ft 5 in
(553.33 m)**

★ GWR TALKS TO
Ron Klemenic

Chairman, Council on Tall Buildings & Urban Habitat (CTBUH), the body that decides which building is the world's tallest.

Who makes the decision on the tallest building for the CTBUH?
There's a committee of about a dozen people, and it's made up of architects and engineers from around the world.

How does the CTBUH define the height of a building?
Our definition was put together by Fazlur Khan, the structural engineer on the Sears Tower in Chicago, who said that the height of the building should be measured from the elevation of the main entrance of the building to the top of the architecture. So you then have to interpret what the 'top of the architecture' is. For the Sears Tower it's pretty clear – it's to the elevation of the main flat roof. Here, for instance, the antennae don't count, because if you remove them the fundamental appearance of the building doesn't change, it's still the same from an architectural point of view. Whereas if you removed the spire from the Chrysler building in New York it doesn't look like the Chrysler building any longer. That's really how the Petronas Towers captured the title, because if you were to remove the the architectural spires, somehow the buildings wouldn't look the same.

Why is the CN Tower not considered to be the tallest building in the world?
The CN Tower is the tallest free-standing structure in the world, but we don't consider it to be a building; it's a tower. The reason we look at it that way is because the lion's share of the tower is not occupiable space, it's simply a tower or a shaft.

Would you agree that since 9/11 the days of the skyscraper are numbered?
It certainly doesn't appear to be the case. In North America, there aren't really any proposals for anything that would surpass the Sears Tower, aside from the proposed Freedom Tower in New York. It's mostly driven by economics – once buildings get above 80 stories or so, they start to lose their economic viability.

However, when we look at Asia and the Middle East, there's still great interest in designing the tallest building in the world, and in Dubai there's a building being planned right now [the Burj Dubai] that would surpass everything that I'm aware of in terms of height.

So having the tallest building is all about prestige?
For sure. For instance, the Petronas Towers remain only partially occupied, because the economy of Malaysia really can't support those buildings as economic entities. But they were symbolic for the Malaysian economy and people.

Is there a theoretical upper limit to tall buildings?
From a structural point of view, there really is not; the limitations are primarily economic. I doubt that the new building in Dubai makes any sound financial sense. However, there's an individual behind that project who has the financial fortitude to fund it, despite the fact that it might never make him any money from leasing space. However, it may pay for itself in other ways, such as notoriety.

What are the biggest challenges facing anyone planning to build the tallest building in the world?
Certainly if you want it to be a revenue-producing, profitable enterprise, one of the greatest challenges is moving people around. In other words, the amount of space the elevators consume as a ratio of the floor that's remaining to be leased. As you go taller and taller, you need more and more elevators to get the people up and down, and at some point – roughly around 80 stories – the floor area consumed by the elevators is so great that the area remaining to lease is too small to make the building economically viable. So one of the technical challenges is advances in elevator technology.

[At the time of going to press, the CTBUH had not yet officially confirmed Taipei 101 as the tallest building, because it had not yet been opened for business.]

Constructions
Feats of engineering

Longest wall ⌃

The Great Wall of China (above) has a main-line length of 2,150 miles (3,460 km) – nearly three times the length of the UK – plus 2,195 miles (3,530 km) of branches and spurs. Construction of the wall began during the reign of Qin Shi Huangdi (221–210 BC). The height of the Great Wall varies from 15 to 39 ft (4.5 to 12 m) and it is up to 32 ft (9.8 m) thick. It stretches from Shanhaiguan, on the Gulf of Bohai, to Yumenguan and Yangguan.

★ Largest solar energy roof
A huge solar energy roof was installed to cover the exposition hall at the Floriade 2002 flower festival, Haarlemmermeer, The Netherlands. The area of the roof is 281,045 ft² (26,110 m²) and it has a generating capacity of 2.3 MW. It was created by Nuon Renewables. The festival opened on April 6 2002 and ran until October 20 2002.

★ Furthest distance to move a bridge
London Bridge proved unable to handle increasing volumes of traffic in the 20th century. It was auctioned in 1962 to Robert McCulloch (USA) for $2,460,000 (then £876,068). The bridge was dismantled and moved brick by brick to Lake Havasu City, Arizona, USA, where it was reassembled and opened in 1971. It had been moved a total of 5,300 miles (8,530 km). Legend has it that McCulloch had bought the wrong bridge – he had presumed he was buying the more decorative Tower Bridge.

★ Highest causeway
In the mid-1990s, a causeway was constructed to replace a Bailey bridge that spanned Khardungla Pass, Ladakh, India. (A Bailey bridge is made out of prefabricated sections and is named after its inventor, Sir Donald Bailey.) At one time, this Bailey bridge had the highest altitude of any road bridge in the world: 18,380 ft (5,602 m). However, because of constant damage from avalanches it was replaced by the causeway.

★ Longest cable suspension bridge
The main span of the Akashi-Kaikyo road bridge, which links the Japanese islands of Honshu and Shikoku, is 1.24 miles (1,990.8 m) long. The overall suspended length, with side spans, is 2.43 miles (3,911.1 m). Two towers rise 974 ft 5 in (297 m) above water level and the two main supporting cables are 44 in (1.12 m) in diameter, making both the tower height and the cable diameter world

records. Work on the bridge began in 1988, and it was opened to traffic on April 5 1998.

★ Longest bridge-tunnel
The Chesapeake Bay bridge-tunnel, which opened to traffic on April 15 1964, extends 17.65 miles (28.4 km) from the Eastern Shore region of the Virginia Peninsula to Virginia Beach, USA. The longest bridged section is Trestle C, at 4.56 miles (7.34 km), and the longest tunnel is the Thimble Shoal Channel Tunnel, at 1.09 miles (1.75 km).

★ Longest cantilever bridge
The Québec Bridge (Pont de Québec) over the St. Lawrence River, Canada, has the longest cantilever truss span of any bridge in the world, measuring 1,800 ft (549 m) between the piers and 3,239 ft (987 m) overall. It carries a railroad track and two highways.

Work started in 1899, and the bridge was finally opened to traffic on December 3 1917, having cost a staggering CAN$22.5 million ($22.5 million) and, sadly, 87 lives.

★ Longest Tibetan bridge
The longest Tibetan bridge (a bridge made entirely from rope) has a span of 1,187 ft (362 m). It connects the islands of Procida and Vivara, Italy, and was constructed by the Sportchallengers (Italy) organization. The bridge was completed on July 15 2001.

★ Highest bridge
The world's highest bridge spans the Royal Gorge of the Arkansas River in Colorado, USA, at 1,053 ft (321 m) above the water. It is a suspension bridge with a main span of 880 ft (268 m). The bridge took six months to construct and was completed on December 6 1929.

Longest steel arch bridge ⌄

The Lupu Bridge (below), Shanghai, China, which stretches across the Huangpu River, has a span of 1,804 ft (550 m). The bridge took three years to construct and opened on 28 June 2003. It is 104.9 ft (32 m) longer than the previous record holder, the New River Gorge Bridge, near Fayetteville, West Virginia, USA.

Longest bridge ⌃

In 1969, the Second Lake Pontchartrain Causeway, which joins Mandeville and Metairie, Louisiana, USA, and is 38.42 km (23.87 miles) long, was completed. It is shown above with the First Causeway, built in 1956.

★ Deepest road tunnel

The Hitra Tunnel in Norway, linking the mainland to the island of Hitra, reaches a depth of 866 ft (264 m) below sea level. It is 3.47 miles (5.6 km) long, with three lanes, and was opened in December 1994. The tunnel was built to provide an all-weather link to Hitra island across the turbulent waters of the Norwegian Sea.

★ Longest big-ship canal

The Suez Canal links the Mediterranean Sea and the Red Sea. It took ten years to construct, employing a workforce of 1.5 million people – 120,000 of whom perished during the construction – and finally opened on November 17 1869. The canal runs from Port Said lighthouse to Suez Roads. It is 100.8 miles (162.2 km) long in total, with a minimum width of 984 ft (300 m) and a maximum width of 1,198 ft (365 m).

★ Longest bikeway bridge

A bikeway bridge 779 ft 6 in (237.6 m) in length spans the 17 tracks at Cambridge Railway Station, UK.

★ Longest floating bridge

The Second Lake Washington Bridge, Seattle, Washington State, USA, has a total length of 2.39 miles (3.839 km), with a floating section measuring 1.42 miles (2.291 km). The bridge was built at a total cost of $15 million and was finally completed in August 1963.

★ Longest wooden bridge

The Lake Pontchartrain Railroad Trestle, Louisiana, USA, which connects the cities of New Orleans and Kenner, is 5.82 miles (9.369 km) long. Construction began on the bridge in February 1882 and was completed in September

of that year. When it opened in 1883, the bridge originally stretched for 21.49 miles (34.6 km). It is made from reinforced creosoted yellow-pine timber.

★ Longest plastic bridge

The longest reinforced-plastic span bridge is at the Aberfeldy Golf Club at Aberfeldy, Perth and Kinross, UK. The main span is 206 ft 8 in (63 m) and the overall bridge is 370 ft 9 in (113 m) long.

★ Longest sewage tunnel

When it is complete, the Chicago TARP (Tunnels and Reservoir Plan) in Illinois, USA, will involve 131 miles (211 km) of machine-bored sewer tunnels 9 to 33 ft (2.7 to 10 m) in diameter. The system helps to control pollution and flooding and will service 3.9 million people in 52 communities over an area of 375 miles^2 (971 km^2).

★ Longest road- and rail-bridge system

Japan's Seto Ohashi Bridge consists of six bridge sections stretching a distance of 5.8 miles (9.4 km). The bridge, which opened on April 10 1988 (100 years after it was first proposed by the Japanese authorities), joins the city of Kurashiki on the island of Honshu with Sakaide City on the island of Shikoku.

★ Tallest structure

The KVLY-TV tower, a stayed television transmitting mast between Fargo and Blanchard, North Dakota, USA, is 2,063 ft (629 m) tall. The tower and its anchors cover 160 acres (64 hectares), an area that is equivalent to 130 American football fields. The total weight of steel in the tower is 864,500 lb (392 tons), and the total length of the guylines is 7.6 miles (12.2 km).

Most visited garden ⌄ with paying visitors

The most visited garden for which an admission charge applies is the Royal Botanic Gardens, Kew, Surrey, UK (below), which has an average of one million paying visitors per year. The 326-acre (132-hectare) site has 40 historically important buildings and collections of more than 40,000 species of plants. Kew Gardens became a United Nations World Heritage site on July 3 2003.

Largest temporary ⌃ corn maze and pathway

Stewarts GardenLands Maize Maze (above) covered an area of 16.9 acres (68,271 m^2) when it opened on July 10 2003 in Christchurch, Dorset, UK. The maze, which has a central lobster shape, was designed by Adrian Fisher (UK) and created by Martin and Susie Stewart (both UK). A 8.83-mile-long (14.22-km) pathway in the maze holds the record for the longest path in a temporary maze.

★ **Largest garden**
In the late 17th century, André Le Nôtre (France) created a magnificent garden for King Louis XIV at Versailles, France. The gardens and parkland were created out of what had once been marshland. They cover more than 15,000 acres (6,070 hectares), of which the famous formal garden covers 247 acres (100 hectares).

★ **Oldest botanical gardens**
The Orto Botanico in Padua, Italy, was created in 1545. The original design of a circular central plot (which symbolizes the world) surrounded by a ring of water, remains, as does the gardens' original purpose – to serve as a place for scientific research.

★ **Largest rose garden**
The Roseto di Cavriglia in Cavriglia, Italy, has more than 7,500 varieties of rose.

★ **Largest scented garden**
The largest scented garden is at the Kirstenbosch National Botanical Gardens on the slopes of Table Mountain, Cape Town, South Africa. The Fragrance Garden includes a Braille Trail and many aromatic plants offering the opportunity for blind and visually impaired visitors to enjoy the plants.

★ **Smallest park**
Circular in shape, Mill Ends Park, located on a safety island on SW Front Avenue, Portland, Oregon, USA, measures a tiny 24 in (60.96 cm) diameter and 452.16 in^2 (2,917.15 cm^2) in area. On March 17 1948, it was designated as a city park, for snail races and as a colony for leprechauns, at the behest of the city journalist Dick Fagan (USA).

★ **Largest saltwater garden park**
The largest gardens irrigated by saltwater are those that form the Zayed Project for Seawater Irrigation, on the coast of the Arabian Gulf in Abu Dhabi, United Arab Emirates. The gardens measure 215,278 ft^2 (20,000 m^2) and contain 22,000 specimens from 40 types of plants, all of which tolerate pure saltwater or a saltwater/freshwater mixture, either naturally or by genetic modification.

★ **Largest permanent hedge maze and pathway**
The largest permanent hedge maze is the Peace Maze at Castlewellan Forest Park, County Down, Northern Ireland, UK, which has a total area of 2.77 acres (11,215 m^2) and a total path length of 2.18 miles (3.51 km). The maze opened on September 12 2001 and was designed by Beverley Lear (UK) and created by the Forest Service, Northern Ireland, UK, assisted by members of the public. The 2.18-mile-long (3.51-km) pathway holds the record for the longest pathway in a permanent hedge maze.

Oldest topiary garden «

Topiary (left) is the art of clipping bushes and shrubs into

ornamental shapes. The topiary garden at Levens Hall, Cumbria, UK, features designs that are more than 300 years old and were initially planted and trained during the 1690s. The topiary shapes in the garden include a judge's wig and umbrellas.

★ **Oldest cultivated decorative plant**
The oldest species of plant cultivated and used for decoration is the rose (*Rosa*). Documents dating back to AD 50 suggest that ancient Romans grew the flowers in plantations and local hothouses to ensure a year-round supply of medicinal extracts, cooking ingredients, and ornamentation.

★ **Largest plant conservatory**
The Eden Project, near St. Austell, Cornwall, UK, consists of two giant transparent domes, or 'biomes'. The largest of these, the humid tropics biome, stands 180 ft (55 m) tall, covers 273,295 ft² (25,390 m²), and has a total volume of 14.681 million ft³ (415,730 m³). The smaller warm temperate biome has 70,395 ft² (6,540 m²) of floor space and a volume of 3.02 million ft³ (85,620 m³).

★ **Largest seed collection**
The Millennium Seed Bank Project at Wakehurst Place Garden, West Sussex, UK, had 6,655 identified species preserved in its cold store as of July 4 2003. In total, there are three million individual seeds preserved in the underground frozen vault. This amounts to 15,613 collections and represents approximately 2.8% of the world's flora.

★ **Largest herbarium**
The largest herbarium contains 8,880,000 species of preserved plants and is in the Muséum National d'Histoire Naturelle, Paris, France.

★ **Oldest vine**
Scientific measurement of the 'Old Vine' in Maribor, Slovenia, carried out in 1972, established that it was then at least 350 years old and may have been up to 400 years old.

★ **Largest vineyard**
A vineyard in the Languedoc region of France extends over the Mediterranean slopes between the Pyrénées and the Rhône in the départements Gard, Hérault, Aude, and Pyrénées-Orientales. It covers an area of 2,075,685 acres (840,000 hectare), 52.3% of which is 'monoculture viticole', i.e. consisting only of wine crops.

★ **Tallest and longest hedge**
The Meikleour beech hedge in Perthshire, UK, was planted in 1746 by Jean Mercer and Robert Murray Nairne (both UK) to define the eastern border of their land. The hedge is 1,771 ft (540 m) long and averages 98 ft (30 m) in height.

★ **Largest permanent tree maze**
Designed by Erik and Karen Poulsen (both Denmark), the Samso Labyrinten on the Island of Samso in Denmark has an area of 645,835 ft² (60,000 m²) and its path measures 16,830 ft (5,130 m). It was created in September 1999 and opened to the public on May 6 2000.

★ **Oldest hedge maze**
The maze in the gardens of Hampton Court Palace, Surrey, UK, was built for King William III of England. Designed by royal gardeners George London and Henry Wise (both UK), it was planted between 1689 and 1695 using hornbeam *Carpinus*. The maze covers an area of 0.5 acres (0.2 hectares), with a total path length of 0.5 miles (800 m).

★ **Longest running horticultural show**
The Shropshire Horticultural Society's 'Shrewsbury Flower Show' celebrated its 116th event on August 15–16 2003. The annual show has been held since 1875 at the Quarry Showground, Shrewsbury, UK, but stopped during the war years 1914–18 and 1940–45.
The earliest documented horticultural show, a 'carnation and gooseberry' display held in July 1836, was organized by the Salop Horticultural Society in Shropshire, UK.

★ **Largest horticultural library**
The Royal Horticultural Society's Lindley Library in London, UK, has more than 50,000 books. The library was established in 1861 and is named after the botanist John Lindley (UK).

Theme parks & rides
Feats of engineering

Roller coaster with ≫ the most inversions

'Colossus', which opened in March 2002 at Thorpe Park, Surrey, UK, turns riders upside down ten times during each 2,789-ft (850-m) run. It reaches a maximum height of 98 ft (30 m) and a top speed of 40 mph (65 km/h).

★ **Oldest operating amusement park**
Bakken, located in Klampenborg, Denmark, opened in 1583. It features over 150 attractions, including a wooden roller coaster dating from 1932.

★ **Greatest number of roller coasters in an amusement park**
In 2003, both Six Flags Magic Mountain in Valencia, California, USA, and Cedar Point near Sandusky, Ohio, USA, opened their 16th roller coaster to the public.

★ **Largest amusement resort**
Walt Disney World in Orlando, Florida, USA, is set in 30,000 acres (12,140 hectares) – twice the size of Manhattan. It opened on October 1 1971 and cost $400 million.

★ **Amusement park with the most rides**
Six Flags Great Adventure in Jackson, New Jersey, USA, has a total of 71 different mechanical rides. The park,

which now boasts 12 roller coasters, opened its doors on July 4 1974 and covers a total area of 140 acres (56.6 hectares).

★ **Largest indoor amusement park**
The world's largest shopping mall, West Edmonton Mall, Alberta, Canada, is home to Galaxyland, which covers 400,000 ft² (37,160 m²). It holds 30 skill games and 27 rides and attractions, including 'Mindbender' – a 14-story, triple-loop roller coaster – and 'Drop of Doom', a 13-story free-fall ride.

★ **Largest wave pool**
According to the World Waterpark Association, the largest wave pool covers around 4 acres (1.6 hectares) and can be found at Siam Park City, Bangkok, Thailand.

★ **Longest full-circuit roller coaster**
'Steel Dragon', which opened on August 1 2000 at Nagashima Spaland, Mie, Japan, is the longest

full-circuit roller coaster at 8,133 ft (2,479 m). It is a non-inversion steel-track giga-coaster that lifts riders a terrifying 311 ft 8 in (95 m) before dropping them 306 ft 9 in (93.5 m).

★ **Tallest amusement park big wheel**
The 'Dai-Kanransha' big wheel, at Pallet Town grounds, Tokyo, Japan, stands 377 ft (115 m) from the base of its pedestal to the top of the wheel. It has a revolution velocity of 0.06 rpm, a wheel diameter of 328 ft (100 m), and can carry up to 384 passengers.

★ **Largest observation wheel**
The British Airways London Eye, designed by London architects David Marks and Julia Barfield (both UK), has a diameter of 443 ft (135 m). Constructed on London's South Bank, it made its first 'flight' on February 1 2000, with regular service commencing the following month. The wheel continuously turns during

normal operation. Each of the 32 fully enclosed capsules, carrying up to 25 passengers, completes a full 360° rotation every 30 minutes.

★ **Greatest capacity observation wheel**
Walter Bassett (UK) constructed his first and largest observation wheel for the Oriental Exhibition at Earls Court, London, UK, in 1895. It had ten first-class and 30 second-class cars, each carrying 30 people. The wheel could carry a maximum of 1,200 passengers to a height of 276 ft (84 m), before it was scrapped in 1906.

★ **Longest walk-through horror house**
'Labyrinth of Terror' at Fujikyu Highland Amusement Park, Yamanashi Prefecture, Japan, is a hospital-themed house of horrors that opened on July 19 2003. It has a 2,021-ft (616-m) walk-through course, which takes visitors between 30 and 40 minutes to complete.

Largest indoor ⌃⌃ water park

The Ocean Dome (above) at Sheraton Resort Phoenix Sengaia near Miyazaki, Japan, is 984 ft (300 m) long, 328 ft (100 m) wide, and 125 ft (38 m) high, and contains a beach 459 ft (140 m) long.

Fastest full-circuit roller coaster »

The world's fastest and tallest roller coaster is 'Top Thrill Dragster' (right), a hydraulically launched 'strata-coaster' at Cedar Point, near Sandusky, Ohio, USA, which reaches its maximum speed of 120 mph (193 km/h) just four seconds after launch. The ride, which opened in May 2003, is 420 ft (128 m) tall, 2,800 ft (853 m) long, and cost $25 million to build.

★ Tallest and fastest wooden roller coaster

The first hill of 'Son of Beast' at Paramount King's Island in Kings Mills, Ohio, USA, is 218 ft (66.4 m) high, making it the tallest wooden roller coaster in the world. The ride, which is roughly as high as a 16-story building, opened in April 2000. It was built by the Roller Coaster Corporation of America, and is also the world's fastest wooden coaster at 78.3 mph (126 km/h).

★ Steepest wooden roller coaster

'Colossos' at Heide-Park near Soltau, Germany, has the steepest drop of any wooden roller coaster, with an angle of 61°. The 4,921-ft (1,500-m) ride lasts for 2 min 25 sec, during which it can reach speeds of up to 74.6 mph (120 km/h).

★ Oldest continually operating roller coaster

'The Scenic Railway' at Luna Park, St. Kilda, Victoria, Australia, opened to the public on December 13 1912 and has remained in operation ever since. This traditional wooden coaster was designed by La Marcus Adna Thompson (USA), who is regarded as the father of the modern roller coaster.

★ Highest average age for a roller-coaster ride

The highest average age of roller coaster passengers is 75.25 years, set by a group of 32 riders on the 'Big Dipper' at Blackpool Pleasure Beach, Lancashire, UK, on September 24 2003.

★ Longest roller-coaster marathon

Richard Rodriguez (USA) rode the Expedition GeForce and Superwirbel roller coasters at Holiday Park, Hassloch, Germany, for 192 hours (8 days) nonstop, from August 20 to 28 2003.

★ Most roller coasters ridden in 24 hours

The greatest number of different roller coasters ridden in a 24-hour period is 74, a feat achieved by Philip A Guarno, Adam Spivak, John R Kirkwood and Aaron Monroe Rye (all USA) on August 9 2001. The four rode coasters in ten parks in four US states, using helicopters to travel between each park.

★ Longest inner-tube water slide

The 874-ft 4-in-long (266.5-m) 'Triple Saurus' slide at Shibamasa World Water Amusement Park in Fukui, Japan, opened on July 7 2001. The longest of three similar slides attached to the same tower, it stands 86 ft 11 in (26.5 m) high.

★ Tallest vertical-drop amusement ride

The 'Giant Drop' at Dreamworld, near Coomera, Queensland, Australia, drops from a height of 390 ft (119 m), giving riders a terrifying five seconds of free-fall time before being brought to a halt by electromagnetic brakes.

★ Oldest operating merry-go-round

The Vermolen Boden-Karussel at Efteling Theme Park in Kaatsheuvel, The Netherlands, was built in 1865. Originally powered by horses, it was converted to electric power during restoration.

Longest small-scale ⌃ model railway track

The Great American Railway (above) has a total track length of more than 50,000 ft (15,250 m) of H0 scale (1:87.1) track and is the star exhibit at the Northlandz attraction in Flemington, New Jersey, USA. The model railway and its miniature world covers an area of 50,000 ft^2 (4,645 m^2), including 4,000 buildings and over half a million lichen trees, and is the culmination of 25 years of single-handed work for Bruce Williams Zaccagnino (USA, pictured above).

★ **Earliest railway**
As early as 1550, wagons running on wooden rails were used for mining at Leberthal, Alsace, France.

★ **Earliest public electric railway**
On May 12 1881, a public electric railway opened at Lichtervelde near Berlin, Germany. It was 1.5 miles (2.5 km) long, ran on 100 V current, and carried 26 passengers at up to 30 mph (48 km/h).

★ **Longest train**
The longest freight train was 4.57 miles (7.35 km) long and consisted of 682 ore cars pushed by eight powerful diesel-electric locomotives. Assembled by BHP Iron Ore (Australia), it traveled 171 miles (275 km) from the company's Newman and Yandi mines to Port Hedland, Western Australia, on June 21 2001.

★ **Longest model train**
The longest model train was 230 ft 3 in (70.2 m) in length and consisted of 650 wagons hauled by four locomotives. It was run by the Arid Australia model railway group in Perth, Western Australia, on June 3 1996. The train was built in the H0 scale of 1:87.1, meaning it was the equivalent length of a full-scale train measuring 3.8 miles (6.11 km).

★ **Heaviest train pulled by single locomotive**
The heaviest train ever hauled by a single engine is believed to be one of 34.2 million lb (15,545 tonnes) made up of 250 freight cars stretching 1.6 miles (2.5 km) and pulled by the *Matt H. Shay* (No. 5014), a steam engine that ran on the Erie Railroad in the USA from 1914 until 1929.

★ **Largest steam locomotive**
The largest steam locomotives are generally considered to be the 4-8-8-4 'Big Boys', which were built by the American Locomotive Company from 1941 to 1944. They are 130 ft 9 in (39.85 m) long and weigh 1.12 million lb (508.02 tonnes), including their tenders.

★ **Largest railroad station by number of platforms**
In terms of the number of platforms, the world's largest railroad station is Grand Central Terminal, Park Avenue and 42nd Street, New York City, USA. It was built from 1903 to 1913 and has 44 platforms situated on two underground levels, with 41 tracks on the upper level and 26 on the lower. The station covers 19 hectares (47 acres), and about 550 trains and 200,000 commuters use it daily.

★ **Fastest speed on a national rail system**
Atlantique, a French SNCF high-speed TGV train, achieved a speed of 320.2 mph (515.3 km/h) between Courtalain and Tours, France, on May 18 1990.

★ **Highest sustained average train speed**
The highest average speed by a train over a distance in excess of 621 miles (1,000 km) is 190.37 mph (306.37 km/h) by a French Societé Nationale des Chemins de fer Français (SNCF) Train à Grande Vitesse (TGV) traveling between Calais and Marseille on May 26 2001. The unmodified train covered the 663 miles (1,067 km) between the cities in 3 hr 29 min, reaching a top speed of 227 mph (366 km/h).

Fastest steam locomotive

The London North Eastern Railway 'Class A4' (4-6-2) No. 4468 *Mallard* (below, later numbered 60022) recorded a speed of 125 mph (201 km/h) over a distance of 1,319 ft (402 m) while hauling seven coaches weighing 535,722 lb (243 tons) gross down Stoke Bank, near Essendine, (now) Rutland, UK, on July 3 1938.

Fastest average speed for a scheduled train journey ⌄

The West Japan Railway Company operates its 500-Series Nozomi bullet trains (above), or 'shinkansen', at an average speed of 162.7 mph (261.8 km/h) on the 119-mile (192-km) line between Hiroshima and Kokura on the island of Honshu, Japan.

★ Fastest railed vehicle

A four-stage rocket-sled system accelerated an 192-lb (87-kg) payload to a speed of 9,468 ft/s (2,886 m/s) in 6.031 seconds at Holloman High Speed Test Track, Holloman Air Force Base, New Mexico, USA, on 30 April 30 2003. This is equivalent to a speed of 6,453 mph (10,385 km/h).

★ Fastest diesel train

The former British Rail (UK) inaugurated its HST (High Speed Train) daily service between London, Bristol, and South Wales on October 4 1976 using InterCity 125 trains. One of these holds the world speed record for diesel trains, at 148 mph (238 km/h), set on a test run between Darlington, York, and Durham, North Yorks, UK, on November 1 1987.

★ Fastest train in regular public service

The magnetically levitated (maglev) train linking China's Shanghai International Airport to the city's financial district reaches a top speed of 267.8 mph (431 km/h) on each 18-mile (30-km) run. The train, which was built by Transrapid International (Germany), had its maiden run on December 31 2002.

★ Fastest maglev train

The MLX01, a manned superconducting magnetically levitated (maglev) train operated by the Central Japan Railway Company and Railway Technical Research Institute, reached a speed of 361 mph (581 km/h) on the Yamanashi Maglev Test Line, Yamanashi Prefecture, Japan, on December 2 2003.

★ Highest railroad line

At La Cima, Peru, the standard-gauge (1,435-mm or 56.5-in) track on the main line between Lima and La Oroya reaches 15,806 ft (4,818 m) above sea level as it crosses the Andes. There are 67 tunnels and 59 bridges on the line. However, in 2001, China began building the Qinghai–Tibet railroad, which is planned to reach a height of 16,640 ft (5,072 m).

★ Highest railway station

Cóndor Station on the meter-gauge (39-in) Río Mulatos–Potosí line in Bolivia lies at an altitude of 15,702 ft (4,786 m).

★ Longest railroad platform

The platform at Kharagpur Station, West Bengal, India, is 2,733 ft (833 m) in length.

★ Least extensive subway

The Carmelit underground system in Haifa, Israel, is just 5,905 ft (1,800 m) long. The Carmelit, which opened in 1959, is a funicular railroad running at a gradient of 12 degrees and is the only subway in Israel. The line, which starts at Paris Square and finishes at Carmel Central, has six stations.

★ Longest monorail

The Osaka Monorail in Osaka, Japan, has a total length of 13.8 miles (22.2 km). Fully operational since August 1997, the monorail runs between Osaka International Airport and Hankyu Railway Minami Ibaraki Station, with a second stage running between Hankyu and Keihan Railway Kadomashi Station.

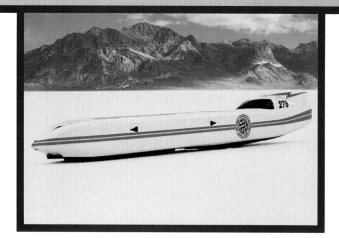

Fastest electric car ⌃

On October 22 1999, the *White Lightning* electric streamliner (above), driven by Patrick Rummerfield (USA), achieved a speed of 245.951 mph (395.821 km/h) at the Bonneville Salt Flats, Utah, USA. With its slender, aerodynamic carbon-fiber body, the 25-ft (7.62-m) *White Lightning* looks more like a rocket than a car and can reach a speed of 100 mph (161 km/h) in eight seconds.

Earliest internal-combustion car ⌄

The first successful gasoline-driven car, the Motorwagen (below), built by Karl Friedrich Benz (Germany), ran at Mannheim in late 1885. The three-wheeler weighed 560 lb (254 kg) and could reach 8–10 mph (13–16 km/h). Its single-cylinder engine delivered 0.85 hp (0.63 kW) at 400 rpm. It was patented on January 29 1886.

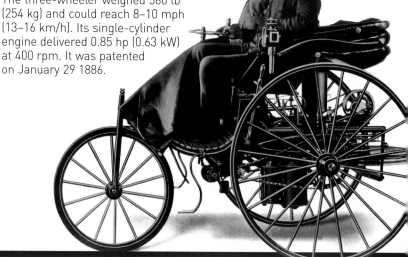

★ Earliest full-scale automobile
Nicolas-Joseph Cugnot (France) made a military steam tractor for the Paris Arsenal in October 1769 with a top speed of 2.5 mph (4 km/h). Cugnot's second, larger tractor, completed in May 1771, survives in the Conservatoire Nationale des Arts et Métiers in Paris, France.

★ Fastest production car
On March 31 1998, Andy Wallace (UK) drove a standard McLaren F1 production car at 240.14 mph (386.46 km/h) at the Volkswagen Proving Ground, Wolfsburg, Germany. Various de-tuned track cars have been licensed for road use but are not normal production models.

★ Fastest steam car
On August 19 1985, Robert E. Barber (USA) broke the 79-year-old speed record for a steam car when *Steamin' Demon*, built by Barber-Nichols Engineering Co. (USA), reached 145.607 mph (234.331 km/h) at Bonneville Salt Flats, Utah, USA.

★ Fastest wheel-driven vehicle
The highest speed achieved by a wheel-driven car is 409.986 mph (659.808 km/h), with a peak speed of 432.692 mph (696.331 km/h), by Al Teague (USA) in *Spirit of '76* at Bonneville Salt Flats, Utah, USA, on August 21 1991.

★ Fastest diesel-engined car
Virgil W. Snyder (USA) drove a diesel-powered streamliner called *Thermo King-Wynns* at 235.756 mph (379.413 km/h) at Bonneville Salt Flats, Utah, USA, on August 25 1973.

★ Fastest open-road race
The fastest road race in the world is the Silver State Classic on Route 318, Nevada, USA, in which drivers maintain average speeds in excess of 190 mph (305 km/h) over the 90-mile (145-km) course. The highest ever average speed attained was 207.78 mph (334.38 km/h), set by Chuck Shafer and Gary Brockman (both USA) in May 2000.

★ Most valuable car
The greatest confirmed price paid for a car is £8.45 million ($15 million) for the 1931 Bugatti Type 41 'Royale' Sports Coupé by Kellner. It was sold by Nicholas Harley (UK) to the Meitec Corporation of Japan on April 12 1990.

★ Most expensive production car
The Mercedes-Benz CLK/LM cost $1,547,620 when launched in 1997. It can travel from 0 to 62 mph (100 km/h) in 3.8 seconds and has a top speed of 200 mph (320 km/h).

★ Most valuable pop memorabilia
John Lennon's 1965 Phantom V Rolls-Royce was bought for $2,229,000 by Jim Pattison, chairman of the Expo 86 World Fair in Vancouver, Canada, at Sotheby's, New York, USA, on June 29 1985.

★ Longest car
Jay Ohrberg (USA) created a 100-ft-long (30.5-m) 26-wheeled limousine. Its many features include a king-sized water bed and a swimming pool with diving board. It can be driven as a rigid vehicle or adapted to bend in the middle, and was designed for use in films and displays.

★ Largest production car
The largest car produced for private use was the Bugatti Type 41 'Royale', known in the UK as the 'Golden Bugatti', which was assembled at Molsheim, France, by the Italian Ettore Bugatti. First built in 1927, it measures over 22 ft (6.7 m) in length with a hood more than 7 ft (2.13 m) long.

★ Most powerful production car
The 5,998-cc V12 engine of the Ferrari Enzo is claimed by its makers to generate 660 hp (492 kW) of power, making it the most powerful car ever to enter series production. Ferrari claims that the Enzo reaches 62 mph (100 km/h) in 3.65 seconds and has a top speed of 217 mph (349 km/h).

Fastest production pickup truck »

A standard 2004 Dodge Ram SRT-10 pickup truck (right), driven by National Association for Stock Car Auto Racing (NASCAR) driver Brendan Gaughan (USA), reached a speed of 248.783 km/h (154.587 mph) at the DaimlerChrysler Proving Grounds, Chelsea, Michigan, USA, on February 2 2004.

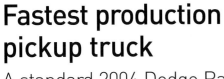

★ Best-selling two-seater sports car
Mazda (Japan) has sold in excess of 677,000 units of its MX-5 Miata sports car. Production began in April 1989.

★ Highest car mileage
A 1966 Volvo P-1800S owned by Irvin Gordon (USA) had covered in excess of 2,219,751 miles (3,572,342 km) by March 2004. The car is still driven on a daily basis and covers more than 100,000 miles (160,000 km) per year, thanks in part to being driven to numerous events in Europe and the USA.

★ Longest journey by solar electric vehicle
The *Radiance*, a sleek solar car built by the Queen's University Solar Vehicle Team (Canada), traveled 4,376 miles (7,043 km) across Canada from Halifax, Nova Scotia, to Vancouver, British Columbia, from July 1 to 29 2000. *Radiance* was built for the annual World Solar Challenge between Darwin and Adelaide in Australia, and achieved second place in 1999.

★ Longest lawn mower ride
Gary Hatter (USA) traveled 14,594 miles (23,487 km) in 260 consecutive days from May 31 2000 to February 14 2001 on his Kubota BX2200-60 mower. Starting in Portland, Maine, he passed through all contiguous US states, as well as Canada and Mexico, ending his trip in Daytona Beach, Florida.

★ Longest-manufactured production car
The Morgan 4/4 has been in production since December 1935. Produced by the Morgan Motor Car Company (UK), all Morgans are hand built and take an average of 23 days to make. The company's total production for all four of its models is around 540 per year.

★ Longest single-model vehicle parade
A total of 2,728 VW Beetles took part in a parade organized by the Volkswagen Aficionado Club of Brazil on a racetrack near São Paulo, Brazil, on May 1 1995.

★ Most 360-degree spins ('doughnuts') in a production car in one minute
Alistair Weaver (UK) performed 22 doughnuts in one minute in a 1.8-liter Caterham Superlight at Elvington Airfield, North Yorkshire, UK, on April 8 2002.

★ Longest ramp jump by car
The longest ramp jump, with the vehicle landing on its wheels and driving on, is 237 ft (72.23 m) by Ray Baumann (Australia) in a Chrysler VH Valiant at Ravenswood International Raceway, Perth, Western Australia, on August 23 1998.

★ Longest ramp jump in a limousine
Michael Hughes (USA) jumped a distance of 103 ft (31.4 m) in a 6,600-lb (3-tonne) Lincoln Town Car stretched limousine at Perris Auto Speedway, Perris, California, USA, on September 28 2002.

★ Largest parking lot
West Edmonton Mall in Edmonton, Alberta, Canada, is the world's largest shopping and entertainment center and also houses the largest parking lot. The parking area can hold 20,000 vehicles, with overflow facilities on an adjoining lot for an additional 10,000 cars.

★ Largest automobile producer by country
In 2002, the USA manufactured around 12.27 million vehicles, according to the Organization Internationale des Constructeurs d'Automobiles (OICA).

★ Largest car engine
The production cars with the largest engines were the US Pierce-Arrow 6-66 Raceabout of 1912–18, the US Peerless 6-60 of 1912–14, and the Fageol of 1918. Each had an engine of 823.8 in³ (13.5 liters).

Land speed record
Feats of engineering

Man has always been obsessed with speed. But it was the invention and refinement of the automobile that heralded a new century of land speed record breaking. Here are some highlights.

How it all began
In the first edition of *Guinness World Records* (formerly *The Guinness Book of Records*) back in 1955, the land speed record was held by John Cobb (UK) and stood at 394.19 mph (634.39 km/h). But this was by no means the first record set. Land speed record attempts as we know them date back to **1898** when Count Gaston de Chasseloup-Laubat (France) did a single run through a measured kilometre, and registered an average speed of 39.24 mph (63.13 km/h). In **1904**, Henry Ford (USA) sought to prove the speed of his new automobiles and duly set a new record in the Ford *Arrow* on the frozen Lake St. Clair in Michigan, USA. He reached an average speed of 91.37 mph (147.04 km/h), but said that it scared him so much he never wanted to race again.

Breaking the 100-mph barrier
The 100-mph (161-km/h) barrier was broken later in **1904** when Louis Emile Rigolly (France) drove through the kilometre at 103.55 mph (166.64 km/h) and the land speed record went back to France. **1904** also marks the birth of the Fédération Internationale de l'Automobile (FIA), the governing body of motor sport worldwide, who officiate at devery attempt on the land speed record. The rules have changed little over the years: the challenging car has to make two timed runs in opposite directions over a measured mile (or kilometre) within one hour.

Early triumphs
Perhaps the most famous attempts on the record were by Malcolm Campbell and later his son Donald (both UK). On February 4 **1927** Campbell Snr. drove the Napier-Campbell *Bluebird* to 174.88 mph (281.45 km/h) on the beach at Pendine, Carmarthenshire, UK. Rivalry between Campbell Snr. and Major Henry Seagrave (UK) drove the record through the 300-mph (482.8-km/h) barrier on September 3 **1935** when Campbell achieved an average speed of 301.13 mph (484.62 km/h) on the Bonneville Salt Flats, Utah, USA.

UK/US rivalry
John Cobb's (UK) record speed of 394.19 mph (634.39 km/h), set in his *Railton Mobil Special* in **1947**, stood for nearly 16 years. The 400-mph (643.7-km/h) barrier was eventually breached by Craig Breedlove (USA) in **1963**, driving the *Spirit of America*. Breedlove reached an average speed of 407.45 mph (655.72 km/h), although the record was disallowed at the time as the FIA did not recognize the use of jet power for land speed attempts.

Donald Campbell claimed the land speed record for Britain again on July 17 **1964** at Lake Eyre, Australia, in *Bluebird*, powered by a gas turbine engine. His 403.10-mph (648.73-km/h) record was the only one not set in the USA during that period of record attempts.

The second half of the **1960s** saw a battle for the record between two Americans: Art Arfons and Craig Breedlove. Arfons triumphed, achieving a speed of 576.55 mph (927.87 km/h) in *Green Monster* on the Bonneville Salt Flats on November 7 **1965**.

Through the sound barrier
Advances in technology meant that breaking the sound barrier was becoming an increasingly real prospect. In **1970** Gary Gabelich (USA) drove through the 1,000-km/h (621.3-mph) barrier in *Blue Flame*, reaching a speed of 622.40 mph (1,001.66 km/h), and on October 4 **1983**, Richard Noble (UK) set a record of 633.47 mph (1,019.46 km/h) in *Thrust 2* in the Black Rock Desert, Nevada, USA.

The next challenge was to build and drive a land speed vehicle that would break the sound barrier. This was achieved in October **1997**, when RAF fighter pilot Andy Green (UK), driving in the 10-tonne, twin-jet-engine *Thrust SSC* (below and right), did the unimaginable by achieving a speed of 763.03 mph (1,227.98 km/h), or Mach 1.02. Green made the two runs through the measured mile, each time generating a shockwave in front of the car and a massive sonic boom. This record, which still stands, came almost 100 years after the first record was set in 1898.

1904
Henry Ford: Ford *Arrow*
91.37 mph (147.04 km/h)

1935
Malcolm Campbell: *Bluebird*
301.13 mph (484.62 km/h)

1947
John Cobb: *Railton Mobil Special*
394.19 mph (634.39 km/h)

1963
Craig Breedlove: *Spirit of America*
407.45 mph (655.72 km/h)

★ GWR TALKS TO
Richard Noble OBE

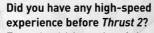

Richard Noble (UK, right) set a land speed record of 633.47 mph (1,019.46 km/h) in *Thrust 2* in 1983 and was Project Director for the successful *Thrust SSC* (supersonic car) land speed record attempt in 1997.

Did you have any high-speed experience before *Thrust 2*?
From the driving point of view, no, I had no experience when I started off. As the *Thrust 2* project developed I learnt to fly, and the discipline of flying is much more akin to record breaking than driving a race car.

Why didn't you drive *Thrust SSC* yourself?
I wanted to, but I realized that combining the jobs of driving the car and raising the money was absolutely hopeless. I decided that because I already held the land speed record I would raise the money and run the project.

Why go after the record again?
We actually saw *Thrust SSC* as the third car in a range of three. *Thrust 1* was a very simple, elementary jet-powered vehicle to introduce the project. *Thrust 2* was the record breaker, and *Thrust 3* we saw as being the supersonic car.

What was the biggest challenge?
One was the culture challenge, because we were up against a mass of companies that said it couldn't be done. The second was that the funding was so difficult.

Are you planning to break the record again?
We're very proud of what we've actually achieved, but nobody wants to go back again! The reality was that when we started going supersonic, I think it frightened a lot of us. I was watching this car coming up at supersonic speeds, and I realized what an enormous risk was being run by Andy [Green, the driver]. Andy's comment was that he'd driven the car twice too often, so that was it really.

Is there a limit to this record?
Yes, although it's a long way off. It's all about the human body's ability to withstand acceleration. If you think that 9 G is the upper limit of acceleration at which a human can usefully work, with acceleration of 9 G, speeds of twice or three times the speed of sound are possible. In terms of the car, the forces it experiences are absolutely enormous, so you need something that's as tough as a locomotive or a submarine. To give you an idea, the wheels on *SSC* were turning at 8,000 RPM, which means that you're running 35,000 radial G at the edge of the wheels. You're right at the limits of what materials will do.

Why is this record important?
I think it's very, very important because it's a measure of a man's or a nation's ability to take on a challenge. It's very important because it inspires the next generation to do something similar.

1997
Andy Green: *Thrust SSC*
763.03 mph (1,227.98 km/h) or Mach 1.02

1970
Gary Gabelich: *Blue Flame*
622.40 mph (1,001.66 km/h)

1983
Richard Noble: *Thrust 2*
633.47 mph (1,019.46 km/h)

Land speed records since 1947

Year	Date	Car and driver	mph	km/h
1947	Sept 16	*Railton Mobil Special*: John Cobb	394.19	634.39
1963⁺	Aug 5	*Spirit of America*: Craig Breedlove	407.45	655.72
1964	July 17	*Bluebird*: Donald Campbell	403.10	648.73
1964	Oct 2	*Wingfoot Express*: Tom Green	413.20	664.98
1964	Oct 5	*Green Monster*: Art Arfons	434.02	698.49
1964	Oct 13	*Spirit of America*: Craig Breedlove	468.72	754.33
1964	Oct 15	*Spirit of America*: Craig Breedlove	526.28	846.97
1964	Oct 27	*Green Monster*: Art Arfons	536.71	863.75
1965	Nov 2	*Spirit of America*: Craig Breedlove – Sonic I	555.48	893.96
1965	Nov 7	*Green Monster*: Art Arfons	576.55	927.87
1965	Nov 15	*Spirit of America*: Craig Breedlove – Sonic I	600.60	966.57
1970	Oct 23	*Blue Flame*: Gary Gabelich	622.40	1,001.66
1983	Oct 4	*Thrust 2*: Richard Noble	633.47	1,019.46
1997	Sept 25	*Thrust SSC*: Andy Green	714.10	1,149.29
1997	Oct 15	*Thrust SSC*: Andy Green	763.03	1,227.98

⁺ not recognized by FIA

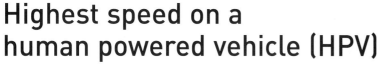
Highest speed on a human powered vehicle (HPV)

⌄

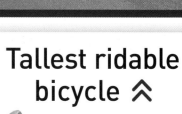

Sam Whittingham (Canada, below) reached a speed of 81 mph (130.36 km/h) on a flat road surface in his streamlined recumbent bicycle *Varna Diablo* (left) at the World Human Powered Speed Challenge near Battle Mountain, Nevada, USA, on October 5 2002.

Tallest ridable bicycle ⌃

Brad Graham (Canada, above) successfully rode his SkyCycle, which measures 14 ft 3 in (4.34 m) to the handlebars, on July 1 2003 at Thunder Bay, Ontario, Canada. The bicycle has only two wheels and no stabilizers of any kind.

★ **Most stairs climbed on a bicycle**
On October 16 2003, Javier Zapata (Colombia) climbed 1,318 steps on a bicycle in the Torre Major skyscraper, Mexico City, Mexico, without his feet touching the ground. The building is approximately 738 ft (225 m) high and has 55 stories. The climb lasted 1 hr 38 min.

★ **Longest signposted bicycle route**
The North Sea Cycle Route is a signposted route that follows the coastline of the North Sea through The Netherlands, Germany, Denmark, Sweden, and Norway. It continues through Scotland and England, covering a distance of about 3,700 miles (6,000 km).

★ **Furthest distance bicycled backward in one hour**
Markus Riese (Germany) bicycled 18 miles (29.1 km) backward in one hour at the Velocipedclubs Darmstadt 1899 eV bicycling club, Darmstadt, Germany, on May 24 2003.

★ **Longest snowmobile ramp jump on water**
Vance Irwin (Canada) performed a 48-ft (14.6-m) ramp jump on water riding his unmodified Polaris 600 snowmobile at Fox Lake Municipal Park, Hanna, Alberta, Canada, on July 1 2002.

★ **Earliest motorcycle**
Gottlieb Daimler built the *Einspur*, a motorized bicycle with an internal combustion engine, in October and November 1885 at Bad Cannstatt, Germany. The wooden-framed machine was first ridden by Wilhelm Maybach. It had a top speed of 12 mph (19 km/h) and developed 0.5 hp (0.37 kW) from its single-cylinder 264-cc four-stroke engine at 700 rpm. It was lost in a fire in 1903.

★ **Earliest mass-production motorcycle**
In 1894, Heinrich and Wilhelm Hildebrand and Alois Wolfmüller (all Germany) opened a motorcycle factory at Munich, Germany. In its first two years, this factory produced over 1,000 machines, each having a water-cooled 1,488-cc twin-cylinder four-stroke engine developing about 2.5 hp (1.9 kW) at 600 rpm.

★ **Longest motorcycle ramp jump with passenger**
Jason Rennie (UK) jumped his Yamaha YZ250 motorcycle a distance of 96 ft (29.2 m) with his girlfriend Sian Phillips on the back on November 12 2000, at the Rednall airfield near Oswestry, Shropshire, UK.

★ **Longest distance jumped on a trial motorcycle**
Joachim Hindren (Finland) jumped a distance of 13 ft (4 m) on a trial motorcycle without the use of a ramp at Sipoo, Finland, on October 13 2001.

★ **Tallest ridable motorcycle**
Bigtoe, built by Tom Wiberg (Sweden), is 7 ft 6 in (2.3 m) tall at its highest point. The motorcycle has a top speed of 62 mph (100 km/h) and is powered by a Jaguar V12 engine.

★ **Longest motorcycle**
Rick Dozer, Bill Decker, Rob Moore, and William Longest (all USA) built a ridable motorcycle measuring 29 ft 3 in (8.9 m) wheel to wheel. The chopper-style Harley-Davidson monster has forks 15 ft (4.6 m) long and is 6 ft (1.72 m) tall at its highest point. William Longest rode it on a public road near Georgetown, Kentucky, USA, on June 15 2003.

★ **Fastest motorcycle speed**
Riding a 23-ft-long (7-m) streamliner named *Easyriders*, powered by two 1,500-cc Ruxton Harley-Davidson engines, Dave Campos (USA) set AMA and FIM absolute speed records with an average of 322.101 mph (518.522 km/h) over two 1-km runs in opposite directions at Bonneville Salt Flats, Utah, USA, on July 14 1990.

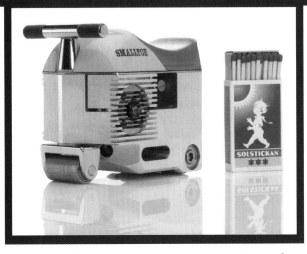

Largest engine capacity for a production model motorcycle

The Triumph Rocket III (below) is powered by a three-cylinder 2,294-cc engine, the largest ever fitted to a production motorcycle. The 705-lb (320-kg) machine produces 140 hp (104 kW) of power and 147 lbf/ft (200 Nm) of torque, making it more powerful than most sedans.

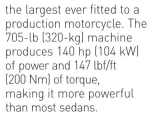

Smallest motorcycle ⌃

Tom Wiberg (Sweden) built a motorcycle (above) with a front wheel diameter of 0.62 in (16 mm) and a rear wheel diameter of 0.86 in (22 mm), and rode it for over 33 ft (10 m) in Hökerum, Sweden, in 2003. The micro machine, called *Smalltoe*, has a seat height of 2.55 in (65 mm), weighs 2.4 lb (1.1 kg), and is powered to a top speed of 1.24 mph (2 km/h) by its 0.3-hp (0.22-kW) engine.

★ Fastest motorcycle and trailer
On February 28 2002, Kevin Smith (UK) reached 139.5 mph (224.5 km/h) on a Kawasaki ZZR1100 while towing a standard Squire D21 trailer at Millbrook Proving Ground, Bedfordshire, UK.

★ Fastest production motorcycle
The Suzuki GSX-1300R Hayabusa is reported to reach speeds of 194 mph (312 km/h), making it the fastest production bike in the world.

★ Highest speed traveled seated backward on a motorcycle
Szabolcs Borsay (Hungary) reached a speed of 124.725 mph (200.726 km/h) sitting backwards on his Suzuki GSX-R1000 at Balaton Airport, Sármellék, Hungary, on July 2 2002.

★ Longest solo motorcycle ride by a woman
Benka Pulko (Slovenia) traveled 111,856 miles (180,016 km) on a solo motorcycle journey that took her through 69 countries and seven continents. Her journey started in Ptuj, Slovenia, on June 19 1997 and ended at the same location precisely 2,000 days later on December 10 2002.

★ Longest continuous ride while standing on a motorcycle
On December 13 2002 in Beijing, China, Liu Jichun (China) rode 3.30 miles (5.32 km) while standing on the seat of a motorcycle and without touching the handlebars.

★ Longest motorcycle wheelie
Yasuyuki Kudo (Japan) covered 205.7 miles (331 km) nonstop on the rear wheel of his Honda TLM220R motorcycle at the Japan Automobile Research Institute Proving Ground, at Tsukuba, near Tsuchiura, Japan, on May 5 1991.

★ Fastest motorcycle wheelie over one kilometer
Christopher McInnes (UK) reached a speed of 126.4 mph (203.4 km/h) while performing a motorcycle wheelie over a kilometer at Elvington airfield, North Yorkshire, UK, on November 18 2001. He was riding a Suzuki GSX-R750.

★ Longest stoppie (front-wheel wheelie) on a motorcycle
Craig Jones (UK) covered 873 ft (266 m) on the front wheel of his Buell XB12R motorcycle at the Florida Evaluation Center, Naples, USA, on August 15 2003.

★ Largest motor scooter by engine capacity
The Suzuki Burgman 650 motor scooter has a 638-cc four-stroke, two-cylinder engine, the largest available on any standard production model today. The 524-lb (238-kg) Burgman went on sale in 2003, with a manufacturer's suggested retail price of $7,699.

★ Largest motorcycle manufacturer
The Honda Motor Company of Japan is the world's largest manufacturer of motorcycles, having sold 8.08 million vehicles globally during the 2002/03 fiscal year. This figure includes quad motorcycles, or all-terrain vehicles (ATVs), and aquabikes, or personal watercraft (PWCs).

Largest propeller ⌄

A six-bladed propeller (below)
weighing 206,100 lb (93.5 tonnes)
and measuring 29 ft 6 in (9 m) in diameter was designed and
manufactured by Stone Manganese Marine Ltd. (UK) for a
PO NedLloyd container ship. The six-bladed propeller was cast
on January 30 1997 with 284,400 lb (129 tonnes) of liquid metal.

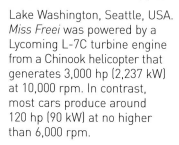

Earliest hovercraft flight

The first public flight by a full-sized
hovercraft was made by the 8,800-lb
(4-tonne) Saunders-Roe Nautical
One (SR.N1, above) at Cowes,
Isle of Wight, UK, on June 11 1959. With a 1,500-lb-thrust
(680-kg) Viper turbojet engine, this craft reached 68 knots
(78 mph or 126 km/h) in June 1961. The hovercraft
was the brainchild of Sir Christopher Cockerell (UK). ⌃

★ Oldest active sailing ship
The oldest square-rigged
sailing vessel that is still
seagoing is thought to be the
2.64 million-lb (1,200-tonne)
iron bark *Star of India*, built at
Ramsey, Isle of Man, UK, in
1863 as the full-rigged ship
Euterpe. She has been restored
and is now preserved as a
museum ship in San Diego,
California, USA. The *Star of
India* still makes occasional
day trips under sail.

★ Highest speed on water
Ken Warby (Australia) recorded
a speed of 275.97 knots
(317.58 mph or 511.11km/h) in
the unlimited-class jet-powered
hydroplane *Spirit of Australia*
on Blowering Dam Lake, New
South Wales, Australia, on
October 8 1978. A hydroplane
is a lightweight flat-bottomed
boat designed to 'plane' (or
skim) just above the surface
with only its propellers and
rudders in the water.

★ Fastest human powered speed on water
Mark Drela (USA) pedaled the
hydrofoil *Decavitator* at a speed
of 18.5 knots (21.28 mph or
34.26 km/h) over a 328-ft
(100-m) course on the Charles
River, Boston, Massachusetts,
USA, on October 27 1991.
Hydrofoils are light vessels, the
hulls of which are lifted out of
the water when in motion by
winglike 'foils' under them.

★ Fastest sailing vessel
On October 26 1993, the trifoiler
Yellow Pages Endeavour reached
a speed of 46.52 knots
(53.53 mph or 86.15 km/h)
while on a timed run of 1,640 ft
(500 m) at Sandy Point near
Melbourne, Victoria, Australia.

★ Fastest propeller-driven boat
Russ Wicks (USA) achieved
a speed of 178.61 knots
(205.54 mph or 330.79 km/h)
in his hydroplane *Miss Freei*
on June 15 2000 at

Lake Washington, Seattle, USA.
Miss Freei was powered by a
Lycoming L-7C turbine engine
from a Chinook helicopter that
generates 3,000 hp (2,237 kW)
at 10,000 rpm. In contrast,
most cars produce around
120 hp (90 kW) at no higher
than 6,000 rpm.

★ Largest passenger liner
The Cunard Line's *Queen Mary 2*,
which made its maiden voyage
in January 2004, is 1,132 ft
(345 m) long, has a beam (width)
of 135 ft (41 m), and space for
2,620 passengers and 1,253
crew. At approximately 150,000
gross registered tons (grt), the
Queen Mary 2 is nearly three
times larger than *Titanic*, which
had a tonnage of 46,000 grt.

★ Largest container ship
The 1,059.61-ft-long (322.97-m)
Orient Overseas Container Line
(OOCL) SX-class vessels have a

registered capacity of 8,063
Twenty-foot Equivalent Units
(TEU) of standard containers.
The first, OOCL *Shenzhen*, was
launched on April 30 2003. It
was built by Samsung Heavy
Industries Co., Ltd. (South
Korea), and is owned and
operated by OOCL (China).
Capable of carrying
253.5 million lb (115,000 tonnes)
of cargo, ships of this size
will coast for 5 miles (8 km)
when the engine is cut.

★ Largest sailing ship by weight
The *France 2* was a steel-
hulled, five-masted bark
launched at Bordeaux, France,
in 1911. Her hull measured
418 ft (127.4 m) overall and
she had a deadweight
tonnage (cargo-carrying
capacity) of 17.6 million lb
(8,000 tonnes). She was
wrecked off New Caledonia
on July 12 1922.

Largest steamboat ⌄

The *American Queen* (below), a luxurious traditional steamboat (paddle-wheeled riverboat) launched in 1995, is 418 ft (127.4 m) long and has a displacement of 10.78 million lb (4,891 tonnes). Built at a cost of $65 million by the Delta Queen Steamboat Company (USA), it has six passenger decks and can accommodate around 450 people.

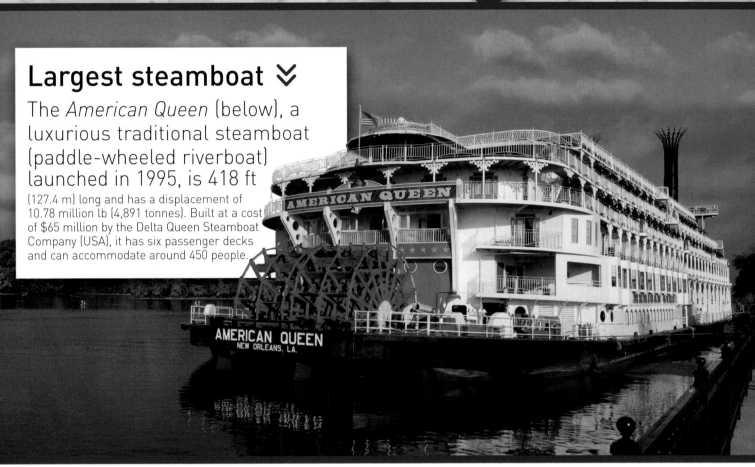

★ **Largest ship**
The world's largest ship of any kind is the oil tanker *Jahre Viking* (formerly the *Happy Giant* and *Seawise Giant*), which has a deadweight tonnage of 1.24 billion lb (564,763 tonnes). The tanker is 1,504 ft (458.45 m) long, has a beam of 226 ft (68.8 m), and a draft of 80 ft 9 in (24.6 m).

★ **Longest sailing ship**
The French-owned sister ships *Club Med I* and *Club Med II* are each 187 m (613 ft) long. They have five aluminum masts and 30,100 ft² (2,800 m²) of computer-controlled polyester sails. Each ship caters for around 400 passengers, with roughly half as many crew members. With their relatively small sail area and powerful engines, they are strictly motor-sailers.

★ **Tallest sailing-ship mast**
The 246.7-ft-long (75.2-m) luxury yacht *Mirabella V*, launched in November 2003, has a single carbon-fiber mast 295 ft (90 m) tall. The largest ever single-masted yacht,

Mirabella V was built by Vosper Thornycroft in Southampton, UK, and is available for rent at a rate of £200,000 ($250,000) per week.

★ **Largest ship ever scrapped**
The 555,051-deadweight-tonne (dwt) ultra-large crude carrier (ULCC) *Sea Giant* was bought by Wirana Shipping Corp. of Singapore in August 2003 for $17.6 million to be broken up for scrap metal. The second largest ship ever constructed, the giant tanker was 1,391 ft (424 m) long and 206 ft (63 m) wide.

★ **Fastest hovercraft**
At the 1995 World Hovercraft Championships, Bob Windt (USA) recorded a speed of 85.38 mph (137.4 km/h) on the Rio Douro River, Peso de Regua, Portugal. Windt was driving a streamlined 19-ft (5.8-m) Universal UH19P hovercraft called *Jenny 2* that had a 110-hp (82-kW) V6 car engine driving its two fans

(one at the rear to provide propulsion, and one underneath to provide lift). The speed of the craft was measured over a flying kilometer.

★ **Largest car ferryboat**
Irish Ferries' *Ulysses*, launched on September 1 2000, can carry 1,342 cars. The ship is 685 ft (209 m) long and 104 ft 6 in (31 m) wide and has a capacity of 50,938 grt.

★ **Deepest-diving submersible currently in service**
The Japanese research submarine *Shinkai 6500* is a three-person submersible 31 ft (9.5 m) long, 8 ft 10 in (2.7 m) wide, and 10 ft 6 in (3.2 m) high. It reached a depth of 21,414 ft (6,526 m) in the Japan Trench off Sanriku, Japan, on August 11 1989.

★ **Largest shipwreck**
On December 12 1979, the 708 million-lb (321,186-deadweight-tonne) Very Large Crude Carrier

(VLCC) *Energy Determination* blew up and broke in two in the Strait of Hormuz, in the Persian Gulf. Although the ship was not actually carrying any cargo at the time, the value of the hull alone was estimated at $58 million.

★ **Greatest distance sailed in 24 hours**
On June 12 and 13 2002, the 110-ft (33.5-m) maxi catamaran *Maiden 2* covered 694.78 nautical miles (800.04 miles or 1,287.55 km) under sail in the North Atlantic. The average speed was 28.95 knots (33.31 mph or 53.61 km/h).

★ **Fastest Atlantic crossing in a monohull yacht**
The monohull yacht *Mari-Cha IV*, captained by Robert Miller (UK), took 6 days 17 hr 52 min 39 sec to cross the Atlantic. It set off from Ambrose Light Tower, New York, USA, on October 2 2003 and arrived at Lizard Point, Cornwall, UK, on October 9 2003. A crew of 24 sailed the yacht.

First power-driven flight ⌃

At 10:35 am on December 17 1903 near Kitty Hawk, North Carolina, USA,

Orville Wright (USA) flew the 12-hp (9-kW) chain-driven *Flyer I* (above) for 120 ft (36.5 m). He traveled for 12 seconds at a speed of 6.8 mph (10.9 km/h) and an altitude of 8–12 ft (2.5–3.5 m).

★ Earliest manned flight
Frenchman François Pilâtre de Rozier is widely regarded as the first person to have flown. On October 15 1783 he rose 84 ft (26 m) into the air in a tethered hot-air balloon built by the inventors Joseph and Jacques-Etienne Montgolfier (France).

★ Earliest balloon flight
A model hot-air balloon invented by Father Bartolomeu de Gusmão (*né* Lourenço) was flown indoors at the Casa da India, Terreiro do Paço, Portugal, on August 8 1709.

★ Fastest circumnavigation by balloon
Steve Fossett (USA) flew around the world alone in 13 days 8 hr 33 min in *Bud Light Spirit of Freedom* from June 19 to July 2 2002. He took off from Northam, Western Australia, and landed at Eromanga, Queensland, Australia.

★ Highest altitude attained by a hot-air balloon
Per Lindstrand (UK) achieved an altitude of 64,997 ft (19,811 m) in a Colt 600 hot-air balloon over Laredo, Texas, USA, on June 6 1988.

★ Largest working airship
The largest working airship is the WDL 1B, three of which have been built at Mulheim, Germany. Each WDL 1B is 197 ft (60 m) in length and has a volume of 7,200 m³ (254,300 ft³).

★ First jet-engined flight
Flugkapitän Erich Warsitz (Germany) flew a Heinkel He 178 at Marienehe, Germany, on August 27 1939. It was powered by a Heinkel He S3b turbojet engine weighing 834 lb (378 kg) designed by Dr Hans Pabst von Ohain (Germany).

★ Fastest biplane
The Italian Fiat CR42B, which had a 1,010-hp (753-kW) Daimler-Benz DB601A engine, attained a speed of 323 mph (520 km/h) in 1941.

★ Fastest ever transatlantic flight
Flying a Lockheed SR-71A 'Blackbird' eastwards, Majors James V Sullivan and Noel F Widdifield (both USA) crossed the Atlantic in a time of 1 hr 54 min 56.4 sec on September 1 1974. The average speed for the New York–London stage of 3,461.53 miles (5,570.8 km) was 1,806.96 mph (2,908.02 km/h). This figure was reduced because of a period spent refuelling from a Boeing KC-135 tanker aircraft.

★ First circumnavigation by an aircraft without refuelling
Richard 'Dick' Rutan and Jeana Yeager (both USA) circumnavigated the world in a westward direction from Edwards Air Force Base, California, USA, from December 14 to 23 1986. Their aircraft *Voyager* was specially designed by Dick's brother Burt.

★ Fastest air speed
The fastest recorded speed in an aircraft capable of taking off and landing under its own power is 2,193.17 mph (3,529.56 km/h), by Captain Eldon W Joersz and Major George T Morgan Jr (both USA) in a Lockheed SR-71A 'Blackbird' near Beale Air Force Base, California, USA, on a 15.5-mile (25-km) course on July 28 1976.

★ Fastest air-launched aircraft
The experimental X-15A-2 aircraft flown by USAF test pilot Pete Knight (USA) reached a speed of 4,520 mph (7,274 km/h) over California, USA, on October 3 1967.

Largest airship »

The world's largest airships were
the 471,568-lb (213.9-tonne) German
Hindenburg (LZ 129, right) and *Graf Zeppelin II* (LZ 130), each of
which had a length of 804 ft (245 m) and a hydrogen gas capacity
of 7,062,000 ft³ (200,000 m³). The *Hindenburg* first flew in 1936,
exploding and crashing on May 6 1937; the *Graf Zeppelin II* first
flew in 1938, although it was decommissioned within a year,
broken up for scrap and melted down to build fighter planes.

Largest flying boats
« in passenger service

The Boeing Model 314 'Clipper'
aircraft (left) had a wingspan of
152 ft (46.3 m), a length of 106 ft (32.3 m) and a maximum
take-off weight of 84,000 lb (38.1 tons). Clippers were operated by
Pan American Airlines during the 'golden age' of flying boats
in the late 1930s.

★ Fastest piston-engined aircraft

On August 21 1989, in Las Vegas, Nevada, USA, the *Rare Bear*, a modified Grumman F8F 'Bearcat' piloted by Lyle Shelton (USA), set the world record of 528.31 mph (850.24 km/h) for a 1.8-mile (3-km) course, as officially approved by the Fédération Aéronautique Internationale (FAI).

★ Fastest propeller-driven aircraft

The Russian Tupolev Tu-95/142 (NATO code-name 'Bear') long-range bomber is the fastest propeller-driven aircraft in standard production form, with a maximum level speed of 575 mph (925 km/h). First produced in the 1950s, it is still in service with several air forces.

★ Fastest airliner

The Tupolev Tu-144, first flown on December 31 1968 in the former USSR, was reported to have reached approximately 1,600 mph (2,500 km/h). The aircraft was taken out of service in 1978. The BAC/Aerospatiale Concorde, first flown on March 2 1969, cruised at up to 1,450 mph (2,330 km/h) and on January 21 1976 became the first supersonic airliner to be used on passenger services. The Concorde was finally taken out of service by British Airways on October 24 2003 because it was no longer profitable to run.

★ Largest amphibious aircraft currently in operation

The Russian Beriev A-40 'Albatross' aircraft, which is capable of taking off and landing on both land and water, has a maximum take-off weight of 189,600 lb (86 tonnes), a wingspan of 139 ft (42.5 m) and is 150 ft (45.7 m) long. The 'Albatross' is powered by two turbojet engines with 33,000 lb (15,000 kg) of thrust each. The multi-purpose aircraft can be used for search and rescue, cargo and passenger transport, maritime patrol, and military applications.

★ Largest wingspan

The Hughes H4 Hercules flying boat, commonly known as the *Spruce Goose*, has a wingspan of 319 ft 11 in (97.51 m) and a length of 218 ft 8 in (66.65 m). The eight-engined 425,500-lb (193-tonne) aircraft was raised 70 ft (21 m) into the air in a test run of 3,000 ft (914 m), piloted by Howard Hughes (USA) off Long Beach Harbor, California, USA, on November 2 1947, but never flew again.

★ Largest wingspan of an aircraft currently flying

A modified six-engine version of the Antonov An-124 'Ruslan', known as An-225 'Mriya' ('Dream'), which was built to carry the former Soviet Union space shuttle *Buran*, has a wingspan of 290 ft (88.4 m).

★ Longest flight by an unmanned aircraft

A USAF Northrop Grumman Global Hawk *Southern Cross II* completed a flight of 8,600 miles (13,840 km) on April 22 2001. The *Southern Cross II*, a full-scale unmanned conventional aircraft, took off from Edwards Air Force Base, California, USA, and landed at RAAF Base Edinburgh, South Australia, 23 hr 23 min later. Global Hawks can stay aloft for over 30 hours at altitudes of 65,000 ft (20,000 m).

★ Highest altitude attained by a propeller-driven aircraft

The unmanned, solar-powered *Helios* prototype flying wing achieved a height of 96,863 ft (29,524 m) over the Hawaiian island of Kauai on August 13 2001. Commissioned by NASA and developed by AeroVironment, Inc., of Monrovia, California, USA, *Helios* is one of a new breed of slow-flying, high-altitude aircraft that its makers believe will present a viable alternative to communications satellites.

★ Greatest passenger load

On May 24 1991 an El Al Boeing 747 commercial airliner transported 1,088 passengers as part of Operation Solomon, which involved the evacuation of Ethiopian Jews from Addis Ababa, Ethiopia.

Largest objects transported by air ⨠

Though not the heaviest, the largest single objects to be transported by air are the 122.17-ft-long (37.23-m) reusable NASA space shuttles,

which are 'piggy-backed' on top of modified Boeing 747 jets from various landing strips back to Florida's Cape Canaveral. The shuttles – *Discovery*, *Atlantis*, and *Endeavour* (right) – weigh around 220,500 lb (100 tonnes) each when being transported.

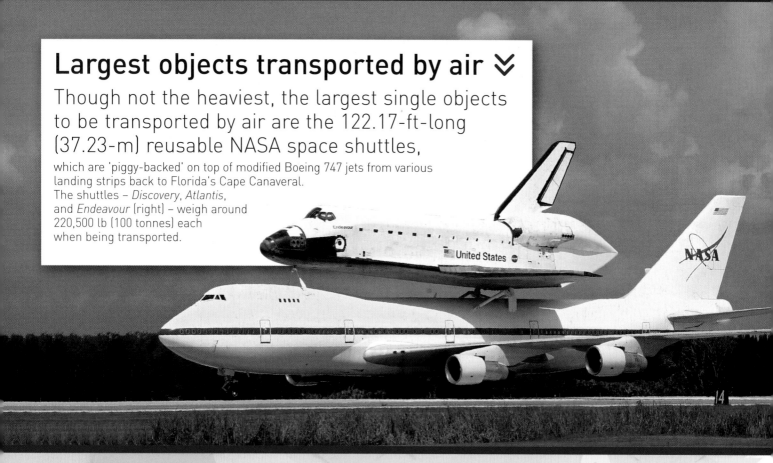

★ GWR TALKS TO
Mike Bannister

For many people, a flight on Concorde was a once-in-a-lifetime taste of real luxury. The aircraft held several Guinness World Records, including those for the fastest transatlantic flight by a commercial aircraft and the fastest aerial circumnavigation. Mike Bannister (UK, above right) piloted Concorde for a record 22 years, and though the aircraft was taken out of service last year, he cherishes very fond memories of it.

When did you first decide to become a pilot?
When I was a little boy my family used to take holidays on the English south coast and the journey would take us five and a half hours by coach. One day I saw an airplane fly overhead while we were on the beach. I worked out the same journey would only take 20 minutes by air and immediately decided I wanted to learn to fly!

How long have you been flying?
I went to pilot training school in 1967, and in 1969 I saw the first flight of Concorde and decided that was what I wanted to fly. I first flew Concorde on August 18 1977 and worked as a copilot and instructor until 1989. I flew other aircraft for a few years and then, in 1995, I was offered the chance to go back to Concorde as Chief Pilot. I flew her 'til her retirement on November 25 2003.

Is flying Concorde different to flying other aircraft?
Yes, it's a completely different experience. Concorde flew at both supersonic and subsonic speeds, and cruised at twice the altitude of normal aircraft. She was a delight to fly – you could control her using only your fingertips! Because she had a very tough fuselage, the cabin only needed to be pressurized at 5,000 feet; most aircraft are pressurized at 8,000 feet. Flying at the edge of space, you could see the Earth's curvature! Also, the aircraft traveled faster than the Earth rotates, so the sun was in effect going backward and your bodyclock would reset. This is why you'd feel less jetlagged flying by Concorde.

Did you have many memorable passengers?
There was a subdued elegance about Concorde, and there were always a lot of business passengers on board. There were also always people taking the trip of a lifetime, and we had a number of celebrities too. After its retirement was announced, the atmosphere on board became more like a party!

What other aircraft have you flown?
I've flown over 100 different types of aircraft over the years but most recently flew a Tiger Moth for the first time.

Finally, what tips would you give to any aspiring pilots?
Whatever you dream of, live your dream – chase it! If you find something you want to do as a child and you do it in your adult life it's very satisfying and leads to a very happy life!

Heaviest production aircraft ⌄

The Ukrainian Antonov An-124 'Ruslan' cargo aircraft (below) has a maximum take-off weight of 892,000 lb (405 tonnes). It has a cargo hold with a usable volume of 35,800 ft^3 (1,014 m^3).

Largest helicopter ⌃ currently in production

The five-person Russian Mil Mi-26 (above) has a maximum take-off weight of 123,500 lb (56,000 kg). Unladen it weighs 62,200 lb (28,200 kg) and its overall length is 131 ft (40 m). The eight-bladed main rotor has a diameter of 105 ft (32 m) and it is powered by two 11,400-hp (8,500-kW) turbine engines.

★ **Fastest aerial circumnavigation**
The fastest flight under the Fédération Aéronautique Internationale (FAI) rules, which permit flights that exceed the length of the Tropic of Cancer or Capricorn (36,787.6 km or 22,858.8 miles), was one of 31 hr 27 min 49 sec by an Air France Concorde (Capts Michel Dupont and Claude Hetru, both France) from JFK airport in New York, USA, eastbound via Toulouse, Dubai, Bangkok, Guam, Honolulu and Acapulco on August 15 and 16 1995. There were 80 passengers and 18 crew on board flight AF1995.

★ **Fastest transatlantic flight by a commercial aircraft**
A British Airways Concorde took 2 hr 52 min 59 sec to travel the 8,750 miles (6,035 km) between New York (JFK airport) and London (Luton) on February 7 1996, breaking its own record set in April 1990 by one and a half minutes. The plane, piloted by Captain Leslie Scott (UK), averaged more than 1,250 mph (2,011 km/h).

★ **Largest helicopter ever**
The Russian Mil Mi-12 was powered by four 6,500-hp (4,850-kw) turboshaft engines and had a rotor diameter of 219 ft 10 in (67 m). It was 121 ft 5 in (37 m) long and had a maximum take-off weight of 227,000 lb (103 tonnes). Only one was ever produced.

★ **Longest helicopter flight**
Robert Ferry (USA) piloted his Hughes YOH-6A helicopter 2,213.1 miles (3,561.6 km) from Culver City, California, USA, to Ormond Beach, Florida, USA, without landing. He completed his FAI-approved flight on April 6 1966.

★ **Fastest circumnavigation by helicopter**
John Williams and Ron Bower (both USA) flew around the world in a Bell 430 helicopter in 17 days 6 hr 14 min 25 sec (average speed of 57.02 mph or 91.76 km/h). They left Fair Oaks, London, UK, on August 17 1996 and flew west, against prevailing winds, arriving back at Fair Oaks on September 3 1996.

★ **Greatest altitude reached in an autogyro**
On April 17 1998 William B Clem III (USA) flew his home-built Dominator autogyro 24,462 ft (7,456 m) above Wauchula, Florida, USA. It was powered by an 115-hp (85-kW) Rotax 914 engine.

★ **Fastest speed in an autogyro**
On September 18 1986, Wing Cdr Kenneth H Wallis (UK) flew his WA-116/F/S autogyro, with a 60-hp (45-kW) Franklin aero-engine, at 120.3 mph (193.6 km/h) over a 1.8-mile (3-km) straight course at Marham, Norfolk, UK.

★ **Most powerful jet engine**
A General Electric GE90-115B turbofan engine achieved steady state thrust of 127,900 lb (568,927 N) during final certification testing at Peebles, Ohio, USA, in December 2002.

★ **Largest ever airline**
In the last complete year of the former USSR's existence (1990), the official state airline Aeroflot employed 600,000 people – more than the top 18 US airlines put together at that time. Aeroflot flew 139 million passengers annually with 20,000 pilots along 620,000 miles (1,000,000 km) of domestic routes across 11 time zones.

★ **Longest duration flight in a human-powered vehicle**
Kanellos Kanellopoulos (Greece) kept his *Daedalus 88* aircraft aloft for 3 hr 54 min 59 sec on April 23 1988 while pedaling the 71.53 miles (115.11 km) between Heraklion, Crete, and the Greek island of Santorini. His flight ended prematurely when an offshore gust of wind broke off the plane's tail and it crashed into the sea a few metres from shore.

★ **Largest parafoil**
The largest parafoil parachute has a span of 143 ft (43.6 m) and a surface area of 7,500 ft^2 (700 m^2), nearly one and a half times the size of the wings of a Boeing 747. It was developed by NASA to bring its X-38 craft back to the Earth's surface after re-entering the atmosphere.

Large vehicles
Feats of engineering

Largest land ≪ transport vehicle

The two 6 million-lb (2,721-tonne) crawler-transporters (left) that carry space shuttles to their launchpad at Kennedy Space Center, Florida, USA, are the largest vehicles used for moving objects between two points (though they are not the largest mobile machines). Each one is 131 ft (40 m) wide, 114 ft (35 m) long, and runs on eight giant tank-style tracks.

★ **Largest land vehicle**
The largest machine capable of moving under its own power is the 31.3 million-lb (14,196-tonne) RB293 bucket wheel excavator, an earthmoving machine manufactured by MAN TAKRAF of Leipzig, Germany. Employed in an opencast coal mine in the German state of North Rhine-Westphalia, it is 722 ft (220 m) long, 310 ft (94.5 m) tall at its highest point, and is capable of shifting 8.475 million ft^3 (240,000 m^3) of earth daily.

★ **Longest vehicle**
The longest land vehicles ever made were the overland supply trains built by RG Le Tourneau, Inc. of Longview, Texas, USA, for the US Army. One example: the Arctic Snow Train, owned by the famous wire-walker Steve McPeak (USA), had 54 wheels, was 572 ft (174.3 m) long, and had a gross weight of about 880,000 lb (400 tonnes). The Snow Train had a top speed of 20 mph (32 km/h), and it was driven by a crew of six when used as an overland train for the military.

★ **Longest road train**
A road train 4,052 ft (1,235 m) long and comprising 87 trailers and a single prime mover was assembled near Mungindi, New South Wales, Australia, on March 29 2003 at the Mighty Mungindi Truck and Trailer Pull.

★ **Largest fork-lift truck**
In 1991, Kalmar LMV of Lidhult, Sweden, manufactured three counterbalanced fork-lift trucks capable of lifting loads up to 198,500 lb (90 tonnes) at a load center of 7.87 ft (2.4 m). They were built for a great man-made river project in Libya comprising two separate pipelines, one 620 miles (998 km) long, running from Sarir to the Gulf of Sirte, and the other 557 miles (897 km) long, running from Tazirbu to Benghazi.

★ **Largest bulldozer**
The Komatsu D575A Super Dozer is the world's largest bulldozer, weighing in at 336,425 lb (152.6 tonnes). Its 24.27 x 10.66-ft (7.4 x 3.2-m) blade has a capacity of 2,437 ft^3 (69 m^3). The 38-ft 5-in-long (11.72-m) pusher moves on tank-style tracks and is powered by a 1,150-hp (858-kW) turbocharged diesel engine.

★ **Largest two-axle dump truck**
The T-282, manufactured by the Liebherr Mining Equipment Co. (USA), is the world's largest two-axle dump truck, with a payload capacity of about 720,900 lb (327 tonnes). The diesel-electric-powered vehicle is 47 ft 6 in (14.47 m) long, 28 ft 7 in (8.7 m) wide, 24 ft (7.3 m) high, and weighs around 443,100 lb (201 tonnes).

★ **Largest front-end loader**
The largest wheel-driven front-end loader is the LeTourneau L-2350, which weighs 578,000 lb (262 tonnes) and can lift up to 160,000 lb (72.5 tonnes) in its 1,430-ft^3-capacity (40.5-m^3) bucket. This massive earth-mover is powered by a giant diesel engine that develops 2,300 hp (1,715 kW).

★ **Largest dragline excavator**
Big Muskie, a walking earth-moving machine weighing 29.1 million lb (13,200 tonnes), was the largest ever dragline excavator, weighing as much as nearly 10,000 sedans. It stood at the Central Ohio Coal Co.'s Muskingham opencast coal mine in Ohio, USA, but was dismantled in 1999.

Tallest limousine

The world's tallest limousine (below) measures 10 ft 11 in (3.33 m) from the ground to the roof.

Built by Gary and Shirley Duval (both Australia), it has an eight-wheel independent suspension system and sits on eight monster-truck tires. It has two separate engines and took a little over 4,000 hours to build.

Largest monster truck

Bigfoot 5 (above) is 15 ft 4 in (4.7 m) tall with 10-ft-tall (3-m) tires and weighs 38,000 lb (17,200 kg). It was built in the summer of 1986 and is one of a fleet of 17 *Bigfoot* trucks created by Bob Chandler (USA). Now permanently parked in St. Louis, Missouri, USA, it makes occasional exhibition appearances at local shows.

★ **Largest operating dragline excavator**
The largest operating dragline excavator is the Bucyrus 2570WS, which is based at Peak Downs mine in Queensland, Australia, and weighs 16 million lb (7,271 tonnes). It has a boom length of 360 ft (109.7 m) to carry its giant 4,238-ft³ (120-m³) bucket, which is in turn suspended from 5.62-in-thick (14.3-cm) cables.

★ **Largest shovel**
The largest mechanical shovel ever built was the Marion 6360 stripping shovel, which had an operating weight of around 28.6 million lb (13,000 tonnes) and a bucket capacity of 4,860 ft³ (137 m³). It had a 236-ft (72-m) reach, a dumping height of 153 ft (46.6 m), and was in service at an opencast coal mine near Percy, Illinois, USA, until 1991, when it was taken out of service after a fire.

★ **Largest operating shovel**
The largest mechanical shovel currently in use is the Bucyrus 1950B stripping shovel – known

as 'The Silver Spade' – which weighs in at approximately 14 million lb (6,350 tonnes). It operates at an opencast coal mine near New Athens, Ohio, USA.

★ **Largest hydraulic shovel excavator**
The RH 400-2000 hydraulic shovel excavator manufactured by O&K Mining (Germany) is the largest of its kind in the world. The giant crawler, which is capable of filling the world's largest dump truck in just six passes, weighs 1,985,000 lb (900 tonnes) and has a shovel capacity of 1,825.7 ft³ (51.7 m³). The top of the driver's cab is 33 ft 6 in (10.2 m), or about three stories, above the ground, and the machine is powered by a 4,400-hp (3,280-kW) Cummins diesel engine, which is fed by a 4,210-gal (16,000-liter) fuel tank.

★ **Tallest mobile crane**
The Demag CC 12600, made by Mannesmann Dematic, is 650 ft (198 m) high in

its tallest configuration, which comprises a 394-ft (120-m) 'fixed jib' attached to a 374-ft (114-m) near-vertical boom. It has a maximum lifting capacity of 3.5 million lb (1,600 tonnes) at a 72-ft (22-m) radius and is so large that it requires 100 trucks to transport all of its different parts to a site.

★ **Largest tire**
Standing 13 ft 1 in (4 m) tall and weighing more than 8,800 lb (4 tonnes), the world's largest tires are built by Michelin to fit onto the world's biggest dump trucks.

★ **Longest ramp jump in a monster truck**
Bigfoot 14, driven by Dan Runte (USA), jumped 202 ft (61.5 m) over a Boeing 727 passenger jet on September 11 1999 at Smyrna Airport, Nashville, Tennessee, USA. He was the first person to achieve this feat.

★ **Fastest speed in a monster truck**
Dan Runte (USA) reached a speed of 69.3 mph (111.5 km/h) in *Bigfoot 14* on September 11 1999, at Symrna Airport, Nashville, Tennessee, USA, the highest speed ever recorded in a monster truck. The speed was recorded during the run-up to the longest ever monster truck jump of 202 ft (61.5 m).

★ **Longest bus**
The articulated DAF Super CityTrain buses of the Democratic Republic of Congo are 105 ft (32.2 m) long and can carry 350 passengers comfortably. Each bus weighs 61,700 lb (28 tonnes) unladen.

★ **Largest bus fleet**
The Andhra Pradesh State Road Transport Corporation (India) operates around 18,900 buses on 8,678 routes, carrying an estimated 13 million passengers every day.

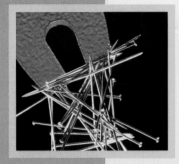

Science & technology

Contents

Least « dense solid

Lawrence Livermore National Laboratory (USA) has produced an aerogel (left) with a density of just 0.47 grains/in^3 (1.9 mg/cm^3).

Aerogels are nanoporous, lightweight solids that physically resemble 'solid smoke'. Aerogels also have the lowest refractive index and the highest thermal insulation of any solid material.

★ Most accurate kilogram

The kilogram is the only Système International (SI) base unit of measurement whose definition is still based on a physical prototype. The world's most accurate kilogram is a cylinder of platinum and iridium that was made in 1889. It is maintained at the Bureau International des Poids et Mesures (BIPM) at Sèvres near Paris, France.

★ Smallest microchain drive

The links on a microchain drive created by Sandia National Laboratories in Albuquerque, New Mexico, USA, and announced in January 2002, are only 50 micrometers apart. The microchain is constructed of silicon and is designed to transmit power in micro-electromechanical devices.

★ Darkest man-made substance

A black coating composed of a nickel-phosphorus alloy, first developed by researchers in the USA and India in 1980, reflects just 0.16% of visible light, making it about 25 times less reflective than conventional black paint. In 1990, the Anritsu Corporation (Japan) refined this coating to produce the darkest version so far. In 2002, the National Physical Laboratory, UK, developed a new method for the commercial manufacturing of this coating.

★ Lowest man-made temperature

Scientists at the Massachusetts Institute of Technology, Cambridge, USA, led by Aaron Leanhardt (USA), announced in September 2003 that they had achieved a temperature of 450 picokelvin above absolute zero (0.00000000045° above absolute zero).

★ Most powerful pulsed neutron spallation source

ISIS, at the Rutherford Appleton Laboratory, Chilton, Oxfordshire, UK, is the world's most powerful pulsed neutron source. Covering the size of a soccer field, it produces 4 x 10^{16} fast neutrons per second. These are focused into beams in a neutron microscope, which allows scientists to study, at a microscopic scale, the atomic and molecular arrangements that give materials their unique properties.

★ Longest continuous observational science data

Astronomers have access to a continuous set of observational data on the sunspot number (number of sunspots on the Sun) dating back to 1750.

★ Quietest place on Earth

Ultrasensitive tests carried out on January 21 2004 at the Anechoic Test Chamber, Orfield Laboratories, Minneapolis, Minnesota, USA, gave a background noise reading of -9.4 decibels A-weighted (dBA).

★ Longest-running laboratory experiment

The Pitch Drop Experiment has been running since 1930 at the University of Queensland, Australia. It consists of black pitch contained in a glass funnel, with the entire apparatus enclosed in a container. It demonstrates that pitch is actually an extremely viscous liquid. Once the stem of the funnel was cut, the pitch slowly began to drip. In late 2000, the eighth drop fell. From this experiment, it has been possible to show that the viscosity of pitch is about 100 billion times that of water. There is enough pitch left for this experiment to run for another hundred years.

★ Smallest abacus

In November 1996, scientists at the IBM Research Division's Zurich laboratory built an abacus with individual molecules as beads, each with a diameter of less than one nanometer (one millionth of a millimeter). The IBM scientists succeeded in forming stable rows of 10 molecules along steps just one atom high on a copper surface. The steps acted as rails, similar to the earliest form of the abacus, which had grooves instead of rods to keep the beads in line.

Most sensitive ⌃ gamma ray detector

Gammasphere (above) at the
Argonne National Laboratory, Illinois, USA, is a gamma ray 'microscope' used in nuclear physics research. It is a cylinder measuring 10 ft (3 m) high, pierced with 110 gamma ray detectors. These focus inward to a central target area that is bombarded with ions from a particle accelerator.

Highest-intensity ⌄ focused laser

The Vulcan laser (right) at the Rutherford Appleton Laboratory, Chilton, Oxfordshire, UK, is the highest-intensity focused laser in the world. Following its upgrade, which was completed in 2002, it is now capable of producing a laser beam with an irradiance (focused intensity) of 10^{21} W/cm^2.

★ **Discoverer of greatest number of elements**
Albert Ghiorso (USA) has discovered or codiscovered 12 chemical elements since he began his scientific career in 1942. The first was element 95, americium, in 1944. Albert is still at the Lawrence Berkeley Laboratory, California, USA, where he has worked since 1946.

★ **Shortest flash of light**
In February 2004, a team of physicists led by Dr. Ferenc Krausz (Austria) of Vienna University of Technology, Vienna, Austria, announced that they had created pulses of ultraviolet laser light lasting just 250 attoseconds (250 x 10^{-16} seconds). Using these attosecond light pulses, they were able to observe electrons in neon atoms and distinguish between events just 100 attoseconds apart.

★ **Largest telescope**
The twin Keck telescopes, on the summit of Hawaii's dormant Mauna Kea volcano, are the largest optical and infrared telescopes. Each of them is eight stories tall and weighs 661,000 lb (300 tonnes). Both Kecks have a 32-ft 9.6-in (10-m) mirror composed of 36 hexagonal segments that act together to create a single reflective surface. Keck I began scientific observations in May 1993 and Keck II began in October 1996.

★ **Largest robotic telescope**
The Liverpool Telescope, owned by the Astrophysics Research Institute (ARI) of Liverpool John Moores University, UK, has a main mirror with a diameter of 6.56 ft (2 m). Located on La Palma, Canary Islands, Spain, it was designed for observing invisible and near-infrared wavelengths and achieved first light on July 27 2003.

★ **Highest-resolution optical image**
The highest-resolution image ever taken shows details smaller than 20 billionths of a meter across. Using a technique called 'near-field Raman scattering', a team at the University of Rochester, New York, USA, led by Professor Lukas Novotny (USA), was able to image individual carbon nanotubes with visible light. The research was announced in March 2003.

★ **Most powerful X-ray generator**
The Z Machine at the Sandia National Laboratories in Albuquerque, New Mexico, USA, can, very briefly, generate X rays with a power output roughly the equivalent to 80 times that of all the world's electrical generators.

★ **Largest Van de Graaff generator**
In 1931 Dr. Robert J. Van de Graaff built the largest Van de Graaff generator at the Massachusetts Institute of Technology, USA. It was originally used to help with research into high-energy X rays and atom smashing, and is now on permanent display at the Thomson Theater of Electricity at the Boston Museum of Science, USA. It consists of two columns each with a 15-ft-wide (4.57-m) hollow aluminum sphere at the top. Originally, the two spheres were oppositely charged, which resulted in lightning-like discharges of 5 million volts. Today, both spheres are joined together and discharge to props and grounded probes, rather than discharging to each other.

★ **Greatest altitude achieved by a laser-powered craft**
On October 2 2000, Lightcraft Technologies (USA) successfully flew a 4.8-in-diameter (12.2-cm) craft to a height of 233 ft (71 m), powered only by light. They used a US Army 13.4-hp (10-kW) pulsed carbon dioxide laser on the ground, fired upward at the 1.8-oz (51-g) craft, which reflects the light backward to a point just beneath it. The resulting expansion of the superheated air provides the craft with thrust. These test flights took place at the White Sands Missile Range, New Mexico, USA.

Amazing science
Science & technology

Hardest element ⌄

Carbon (C) has three different allotropes (different configurations of atoms),

but the diamond allotrope, which has an extremely strong lattice structure, has the maximum value of 10 on Mohs' relative scale of hardness. Diamonds (below) are formed at least 93 miles (150 km) beneath the Earth's surface, where the pressures and temperatures are great enough to force the carbon atoms to adopt this structure.

Weakest force ⌃

Four fundamental forces in the universe account for all interactions

between matter and energy. They are the strong nuclear, weak nuclear, electromagnetic, and gravitational forces. The weakest of these is gravity. A good example of how much weaker gravity is compared to, say, electromagnetism, is that it is easy for a toy magnet to pick up a handful of nails while the whole of Earth's gravity is trying to pull them back down. The strongest force is the strong nuclear.

★ **Heaviest and lightest quarks**
Of the six 'flavors' of quarks (subatomic particles) – known as 'up', 'down', 'top', 'bottom', 'strange', and 'charmed' – the heaviest is the 'top' quark, which has a mass of 170 giga-electron-volts (GeV). It was discovered in February 1995 at Fermilab, Batavia, Illinois, USA. The lightest are the 'up' and 'down' quarks, both at 0.15 GeV.

★ **Fastest speed possible**
The speed of light is achieved only by light and other forms of electromagnetic radiation, e.g. radio waves, infrared radiation and X rays. The speed of light varies depending on what it is traveling through. Light travels fastest through a vacuum, where its velocity is 299,792,458 m/s (about 300,000 km/s or 186,000 miles per second). This means that when you look at the Moon, you see it as it was about 1.3 seconds ago, and the Sun as it was around 8.3 minutes ago.

★ **Most common element**
Hydrogen (H) represents over 90% of all matter in the universe and 70.68% of all matter in the Solar System. Iron (Fe) is the most common element on Earth, making up 36% of its mass, and molecular nitrogen (N_2) is the most common element in the atmosphere at 75.52% by mass or 78.08% by volume.

★ **Rarest element on Earth**
Only around 0.9 oz (25 g) of the element astatine (At) occurs naturally in the Earth's crust. Astatine was discovered in 1931 by Fred Allison and E.J. Murphy (both USA).

★ **Element with the highest melting and boiling point**
Of all the metals, tungsten (W) has the highest melting point at 6,177°F (3,414°C) and the highest boiling point at 10,557°F (5,847°C). The graphite form of carbon (C) sublimes directly to vapor at 6,699°F (3,704°C) and can be obtained as a liquid only from above a temperature of 8,546°F (4,730°C) and a pressure of 10 megapascals (100 atmospheres).

★ **Most ductile element**
One gram of gold (Au) can be drawn to 1.5 miles (2.4 km), or 1 oz to 43 miles (69 km).

★ **Oldest biological molecules**
Biological molecules extracted from the rib of an iguanodon – a huge herbivorous dinosaur – found in a quarry in Surrey, UK, have been dated at about 125 million years old. The research was carried out by Liverpool University, the University of Wales, and the Natural History Museum (all UK), and the results were announced in September 2003.

★ **Oldest living bacteria**
Bacteria trapped in suspended animation inside salt crystals for 250 million years have been revived and cultured by US scientists. Designated *Bacillus 2-9-3*, this species is 10 times older than the previous oldest revived bacteria.

Element with the ⌄ lowest melting and boiling point

For metallic elements, mercury (Hg, below) has the lowest melting and

boiling points at -37.892°F (-38.829°C) and 673.92°F (356.62°C) respectively. Helium (He) cannot be obtained as a solid at atmospheric pressure, the minimum pressure required being 2.532 megapascals (24.985 atmospheres) at a temperature of -458.275°F (-272.375°C). Helium also has the lowest boiling point at -452.070°F (-268.928°C).

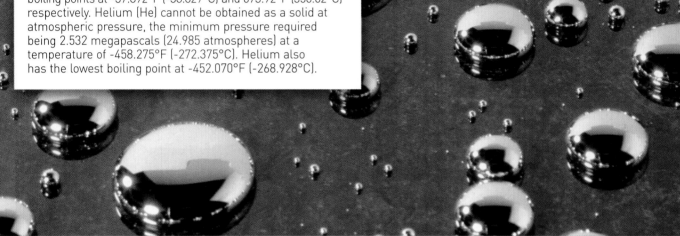

★ Most radiation-resistant microbe

The bacterium *Deinococcus radiodurans* (formerly *Micrococcus radiodurans*) can withstand atomic radiation of 6.5 million röntgens, or 10,000 times the level that would be fatal to the average human.

★ Highest microbe

In April 1967, NASA reported that bacteria had been discovered at an altitude of 25.56 miles (41.13 km).

★ Smelliest molecules

Ethyl mercaptan (C_2H_5SH) and butyl seleno-mercaptan (C_4H_9SeH) have an odor reminiscent of a combination of rotting cabbage, garlic, onions, burnt toast, and sewer gas. Ethyl mercaptan is added to odorless gas to act as a warning agent.

★ Smelliest substances

The smelliest substances are the man-made 'Who-Me?' and 'US Government Standard Bathroom Malodor', which have five and eight chemical ingredients respectively. 'Who-Me?' was developed by the US military during World War II and was intended to be sprayed on German troops, then occupying France, to humiliate them. Bathroom Malodor smells primarily of human feces and becomes incredibly repellent to people at just two parts per million. The substance was originally created to test the power of deodorizing products.

★ Lightest known particle

Neutrinos are the lightest known particles in the universe, with a maximum mass of 0.000000000000000 00000000000000000000018 kg. Neutrinos come in three varieties – electron, muon, and tau neutrinos. The mass is an average of the three types.

★ Oldest irrational number

An irrational number is a number that cannot be expressed as a fraction or an integer. The first irrational number discovered was the square root of 2, by Hippasus of Metapontum (then part of Magna Graecia, southern Italy) in about 500 BC.

★ Lowest temperature possible

Temperature is a direct result of the vibrations of the atoms or molecules that make up matter. The coldest that any substance can be is when there is no vibration in its atoms or molecules. This is referred to as absolute zero, and is at 0 K (zero Kelvin) or -459.67°F (-273.15°C). Absolute zero has never been achieved in an Earth laboratory, and even in the coldest parts of deep space, the temperature is slightly above absolute zero. There is no upper limit to how hot something can be.

★ Largest known prime number

A prime number is a number that is only divisible by 1 and itself. The largest known prime number is $2^{20,996,011}-1$, which contains 6,320,430 digits. It was discovered by Michael Shafer (USA), a chemical engineering student, on November 17 2003. Shafer was running software on his computer as part of the Great Internet Mersenne Prime Search, or GIMPS.

★ Greatest time dilation

The most time dilation experienced by an individual is around 1/50th of a second, for Russian cosmonaut Sergei Avdeyev. This is a consequence of the 747 days 14 hr 22 min he has spent in low Earth orbit, traveling at about 17,000 mph (27,000 km/h). Relative to people on Earth, Avdeyev has 'time traveled' 1/50th of a second into the future, a phenomenon consistent with Albert Einstein's theory of relativity.

★ Longest time survived in space by bacteria

From April 7 1984 to January 11 1990, *E. Coli* bacteria cells survived unshielded on board NASA's Long Duration Exposure Facility satellite in low Earth orbit. The satellite and its 57 experiments were retrieved by the space shuttle *Challenger*.

Archaeology
Science & technology

Largest ancient stone circle

The 28.4-acre (11.5-hectare) earthworks and stone circles of Avebury, Wiltshire, UK (above), which were 'rediscovered' in 1646, represent the UK's largest prehistoric monument and largest henge (a circular area, often containing a circle of stones or wooden posts). The earliest calibrated date in the area of this Neolithic site is ca. 4200 BC. The work is 1,200 ft (365 m) in diameter with a ditch 40 ft (12 m) wide around the perimeter.

★ **Largest prehistoric building**
Archaeological tests reveal that a 5,000-year-old structure, probably a temple, discovered at a sacred Stone Age site at Stanton Drew, Somerset, UK, had a diameter of 295 ft (90 m) and was at least six times the size of Stonehenge. The building is estimated to have been 33 ft (10 m) high, possibly with a thatched roof supported by more than 400 wooden columns, each approximately a meter in diameter, forming nine rings.

★ **Earliest places of worship**
Many archaeologists are of the opinion that the decorated Upper Paleolithic caves of Europe (ca. 30,000–10,000 BC) were used as places of worship or religious ritual.

★ **Earliest alphabet**
The earliest known example of alphabetic writing is that found on clay tablets showing the 32 cuneiform (wedge-shaped) letters of the Ugaritic alphabet, a now-extinct Semitic language of Syria. The tablets were found in 1929 at Ugarit (now Ras Shamra), Syria and were dated to around 1450 BC.

★ **Earliest castle**
The 20-story Gomdan or Gumdan Castle, in the old city of Sana'a, Yemen, dates from before AD 200 and is now a UNESCO World Heritage site.

★ **Earliest parliament**
The earliest known legislative assembly, or ukkim, was a bicameral (two-chamber) gathering in Erech, Iraq, in ca. 2800 BC.

The oldest recorded legislative body is the Icelandic Althing founded in AD 930.

The earliest known use of the term 'parliament' came in an official royal document dating from December 19 1241, in which the term referred to a summons to King Henry III's Council in England.

★ **Oldest stained glass**
Pieces of stained glass dating back to before AD 850 (some possibly even back to the 7th century) were excavated by Rosemary Cramp (UK) at Monkwearmouth and Jarrow (both UK), set into a window of that date in St. Paul's Church, Jarrow, County Durham, UK.

★ **Earliest canal**
Early in 1968, archaeologists found relics of canals dating back to ca. 4000 BC near Mandali, Iraq.

★ **Earliest zoo**
The earliest known collection of animals was established at modern-day Puzurish, Iraq, by Shulgi, a 3rd-dynasty ruler of Ur from 2097 to 2094 BC.

★ **Earliest domestication of dogs**
Archaeologists believe that the Paleolithic humans in east Asia domesticated dogs (Canis familiaris) approximately 15,000 years ago by successfully breeding aggression out of wolves (C. lupus).

★ **Earliest domestication of horses**
Evidence from Ukraine indicates that the domestication of horses so that they could be ridden may have happened some time before 4000 BC.

★ **Oldest remains of modern humans**
The oldest remains of modern humans discovered so far date back 160,000 years. They consist of two complete crania, belonging to one adult and one child, and fragments from another adult skull. The remains were discovered in Ethiopia by a team of scientists led by Tim White of the University of California at Berkeley, USA.

Largest geoglyphs ⌃

The so-called Nazca lines are a group of gigantic figures (geoglyphs) engraved on the desert ground of Nazca, Peru, representing

plants, animals (monkey, above), insects, and a variety of geometric shapes. Most can only be appreciated from the air. The designs occupy a 190-mile² (500-km²) area of land and they average 600 ft (180 m) in length, although one perfectly formed arrow exceeds 1,600 ft (490 m).

Oldest ice body ⌄

In September 1991, the preserved remains of a Neolithic man were discovered, 5,300 years after he had

died, by two hikers on a melting glacier in the Tyrolean Alps on the Italian-Austrian border. Analysis of 'Ötzi' (below), as the mummy was named, and his belongings have given a new insight into the technology and culture of central Europe some 5,000 years ago.

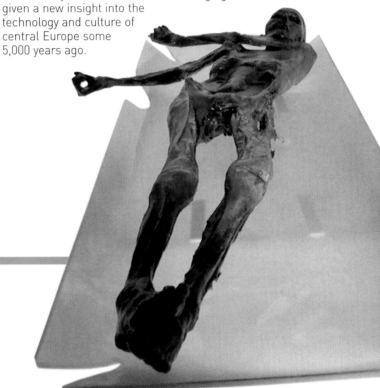

★ Oldest hominid footprints

A hominid is any primate of the family Hominidae, which includes modern man (*Homo sapiens*) and his ancestors. The oldest known human-like footprints were discovered in Laetoli, northern Tanzania, in 1978. They belong to two or three hominids striding upright on the ashy plains of the area some 3.6 million years ago. The trackway consists of some 70 footprints in two parallel trails about 100 ft (30 m) long.

★ Oldest mummy

Mummification dates from 2600 BC, or the 4th dynasty of the Egyptian pharaohs. The oldest complete mummy is of Wati, a court musician of ca. 2400 BC from the tomb of Nefer in Saqqâra, Egypt, found in 1944.

★ Oldest coin

The earliest coins recorded were made during the reign of King Gyges of Lydia, Turkey, in ca. 630 BC, and consisted of electrum, a naturally occurring amalgam of gold and silver.

★ Earliest measures

The *beqa* of the Amratian period of Egyptian civilization, ca. 3800 BC, found at Naqada, Egypt, are cylindrical weights with rounded ends. They weigh from 6.66 to 7.45 oz (188.7 to 211.2 g).

★ Oldest industry

Flint knapping, which involves the production of chopping tools and hand axes, dates back 2.5 million years in Ethiopia. The earliest evidence of trading in exotic stone and amber dates from ca. 28,000 BC in Europe.

★ Oldest batteries

Around a dozen clay jars, measuring about 5 in (13 cm) long and dating back about 2,000 years, are believed to be the world's oldest electrical cells, or batteries. Some reports claim that they were discovered in the basement of the Baghdad Museum, Iraq, by German archaeologist Wilhelm König in 1938. The jars contain a copper cylinder and an iron rod, along with signs of acidic corrosion. Modern

replicas of these objects have been shown to function as rudimentary electrical cells, and it is possible that they were used for electroplating.

★ Oldest Greek vessel excavated

The 'Kyrenia Ship' was built in the early 4th century BC and sank some 80 years later less than a mile off Kyrenia (northern Cyprus), carrying 400 amphorae (clay vessels) of Rhodian wine and volcanic grain from the island of Kos. The vessel, a 49-ft-long (15-m) open boat, was found in 1967 by a Cypriot diver. It is considered to be the finest preserved ship of the late classical period of Greek civilization, the time of Alexander the Great.

★ Earliest use of the wheel

The earliest documented use of the wheel for transport dates back 5,500 years to Mesopotamia (modern Iraq). Previous to this time, humans had moved heavy objects from one place to another by rolling them over logs.

★ Largest Bronze Age copper mine

The Great Orme Mines, Llandudno, UK, contain at least 5 miles (8 km) of accessible tunnels. They were mined for copper from around 1800 BC until the end of the Bronze Age (c. 750 BC). Mining occurred again from 1692 until 1881. The first chambers of the original mines were discovered in 1976.

Internet
Science & technology

Fastest-growing Internet service provider ⌄

Since its launch by NTT DoCoMo in February 1999, i-Mode has gained more than 40 million subscribers. i-Mode is a Japanese service specifically aimed at cell phone users.

⌃ Earliest e-mail

In 1971, Ray Tomlinson (USA, above) sent the first e-mail as an experiment to see if he could get two computers to exchange a message. It was Ray who decided to use the @ symbol to separate the recipient's name from their location. The first e-mail message was: 'QWERTYUIOP', the letters on the top line of a keyboard.

★ First hypertext browser
In October 1990, Tim Berners-Lee (UK) started work on a global hypertext browser. The result – the World Wide Web – was made available on the Internet in the summer of 1991. Berners-Lee had originally proposed a global hypertext project to let people combine their knowledge in a web of hypertext documents in 1989.

★ Largest Internet search engine
Google, with around 4.28 billion pages, has the largest continually refreshed index of webpages out of all the world's search engines. The company was founded by Larry Page and Sergey Brin (both USA). Google handles 200 million search queries every day – 2,000 a second during peak hours – and has an index of 3 trillion words.

★ Highest-capacity intercontinental Internet route
In 2003, the Internet routes between Europe and the USA/Canada had a bandwidth capacity of 386,221 megabits per second (Mbps). (This is the equivalent of between five and ten full-length DVD movies per second.) The lowest capacity was between Africa and USA/Canada, with a bandwidth capacity of 1,351.5 Mbps.

★ Largest Internet joke vote
Laughlab, an Internet experiment into humor, was conducted by psychologist Richard Wiseman, University of Hertfordshire, Hatfield, UK, and the British Association for the Advancement of Science. The experiment ran from September 2001 to October 2002, during which more than 40,000 jokes were submitted from the worldwide public, and around 2 million votes were cast on which one was the funniest.
If you'd like to find out what the winning joke was, and also see some of the runners-up, then visit our website: www.guinnessworldrecords.com/joke.

★ Most expensive Internet domain name
The Internet domain name business.com was sold by entrepreneur Marc Ostrofsky (USA) on December 1 1999 for $7.5 million.

★ Most searched-for plant and animal on the Internet
According to Google, the most searched-for plant on the Internet is the rose.
The most searched-for animal is the domestic cat, according to the same search engine.

★ Largest single e-commerce transaction
American Internet tycoon Mark Cuban (USA) bought a Gulfstream V business jet over the Internet in October 1999. The jet changed hands for $40 million.

★ Longest live event streamed over the Internet
Beginning on October 21 2001, the Canadian Musicians for Liberty Organization held the longest live event ever streamed over the Internet. Around 1,000 musicians, comprising various bands and solo artists, took turns playing live music to a small local audience as well as directly to the Internet (in both video and sound). The concert continued for 181 hours, with breaks of only a few minutes while the acts swapped over. The event was held to raise money for the Canadian Red Cross USA Relief Fund and took place at Touchdowns Bar and Grill, Mississauga, Ontario, Canada.

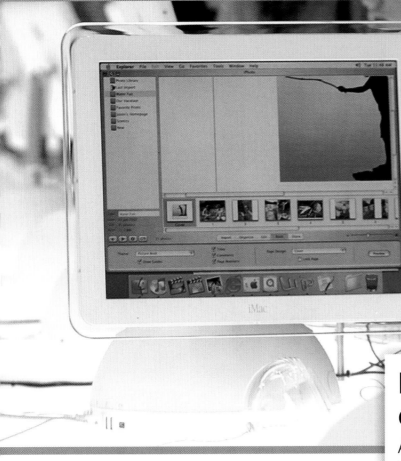

Most globally connected ⌃ city on the Internet

According to TeleGeography, London, UK, had an international Internet bandwidth of 550 gigabytes per second (Gbps) of Internet traffic in 2003. By contrast, New York City, USA, had an internet bandwidth of 339 Gbps in 2003.

★ Largest exclusive concert on the Internet

A record 9,804 people logged on to a concert by Queen drummer Roger Taylor (UK) and five band members for 45 minutes, at the Cyberbarn, Thursley, Surrey, UK, on September 24 1998. The concert was exclusive because it was held in Taylor's barn and the only audience was via the Internet.

★ Internet2 land speed record

Internet2 is a consortium of 206 universities working to develop the next generation of the Internet. On April 14 2004, an international team of scientists achieved a result of 69,073 terabit-meters per second, by transferring 838.86 gigabytes of data across 10,155 miles (16,343 kilometers) of network in 1588 seconds. This data rate was reached using Internet protocol version 4 (IPv4) and is roughly equivalent to 10,000 typical home broadband internetconnections. The start and end points were Luleå, Sweden, and San Jose, California, USA.

★ Largest Internet café

The cybercafé easyEverything in Times Square, New York, USA, opened on November 28 2000 with 760 computer terminals. It now has 648 terminals.

★ Country with the most Internet users

According to the International Telecommunication Union, in 2002 the USA had over 159 million Internet users out of a world total of 623.48 million online users.

★ Most Internet users by continent

According to the International Telecommunication Union, of the 623.48 million people online worldwide in 2002, 211.36 million were located in Asia.

★ Largest networked chess computer

On January 30 2004, Grand Master Peter Heine Nielsen (Denmark) played a game of chess against ChessBrain, the world's largest networked

chess computer. ChessBrain consisted of 2,070 computers located in 56 countries, which simultaneously combined their processing power.

The match, which took place in Copenhagen, Denmark, ended in a draw after 34 moves.

★ Oldest electronic spam

The oldest unsolicited mass e-mail was sent at 12:33 pm EDT on May 3 1978 by Gary Thuerk (USA), who was working for Digital Equipment Corp. (USA). It was sent to 397 e-mail accounts on the Advanced Research Projects Agency Network (ARPAnet) of the US Defense Dept., inviting account holders to a demonstration of the DECSYSTEM-2020, 2020T, 2060, and 2060T computers. ARPAnet is regarded as the predecessor to the Internet.

★ Oldest Internet bench

On August 6 2001, the world's first park bench with free access to the Internet was opened in Bury St. Edmunds, Suffolk, UK. The standard park bench was converted by msn.co.uk to allow four people to connect their laptops simultaneously, in an attempt to change the way people use the Internet.

★ Largest free web-based e-mail provider

Microsoft's Hotmail had over 170 million active accounts as of February 2004. Every day Hotmail adds 100,000 new users. It is available in 230 countries and has 12 million unique log-ins per month.

Hotmail was launched in 1996 and its name is derived from the HTML programming language.

Largest television ⩘ telephone vote

The record for the largest TV phone vote belongs to *American Idol 2* (FOX, USA) on May 21 2003, when 24 million viewers called in to the final of the show to vote for the winner of the pop contest (10 finalists, above) in Los Angeles, California, USA.

⭐ **Earliest telephone call**
The telephone was invented by Alexander Graham Bell (UK), who devised a way of converting human voices into electrical impulses, then back to voices. He filed his patent for the telephone on February 14 1876 at the New York Patent office, New York, USA. The first intelligible call occurred in March 1876 in Boston, Massachusetts, USA, when Bell phoned his assistant in a nearby room and said, 'Mr Watson – come here – I want to see you'.

⭐ **First pole-to-pole telephone call**
On April 28 1999, at 10:30 am (GMT), the first phone call took place between people at the North and South Poles. It was carried out by NASA employees Mike Comberiate and Andre Fortin (both USA). It became a conference call coordinated from NASA's Marshall Space Flight Center, and lasted 45 minutes. Taking part in the call were George Morrow, Tom Carlson, Joel Michalski, Mike Comberiate, Claire Parkinson, Vince Hurley, and Ron Ruhlman (all USA).

⭐ **Most international telephone calls by country**
According to TeleGeography, of the 155 billion minutes of international phone calls made in 2002, 40.3 billion minutes were made from the USA.

⭐ **Busiest international telephone route**
According to TeleGeography, the busiest international telephone route is between the USA and Canada. In 2002, there were some 10.9 billion minutes of two-way traffic between the two countries.

⭐ **Largest fleet of ocean sensors**
ARGO is a global network of free-floating ocean sensors designed to monitor global ocean-current patterns. The sensors drift at depths of up to 6,560 ft (2,000 m) then rise in order to transmit data via satellites. By January 8 2004, there were 996 active floats, with a total of 3,000 planned by 2006.

⭐ **Largest carrier of international phone calls**
According to TeleGeography, in 2002 the largest carrier of international telephone calls, in terms of outgoing traffic, was AT&T Corp. (USA), with 12,796.5 million minutes of communications.

⭐ **Longest telephone cable**
The world's longest submarine telephone cable is FLAG (Fibre-optic Link Around the Globe), which runs for 16,800 miles (27,000 km) from Japan to the UK. It links three continents (Europe, Africa, and Asia) and 11 countries, and can support 600,000 simultaneous telephone calls.

⭐ **Largest working telephone**
The world's largest operational telephone was exhibited on September 16 1988 at a festival to celebrate the 80th birthday of Centraal Beheer, an insurance company based in Apeldoorn, The Netherlands. It was 8 ft 1 in (2.47 m) high and 19 ft 11 in (6.06 m) long, and weighed 7,700 lb (3.5 tonnes). The handset, which was 23 ft 5 in (7.14 m) long, had to be lifted by crane for a call to be made.

⭐ **Largest telephone conference call**
On September 29 2003, US Presidential Democrat candidate Howard Dean (USA) conducted a telephone conference call from Los Angeles, California, USA, with his supporters. The greatest number of people simultaneously connected for at least 10 seconds was 3,466.

Earliest cellular telephone ⌃

The idea for a portable phone was conceived at Lucent Technologies' Bell Labs, New Jersey, USA, in 1947. The first actual portable phone handset was invented by Martin Cooper (USA, above) of Motorola, who made the first call on April 3 1973 to his rival, Joel Engel, research head at Bell Labs. The first commercial cell phone network was launched in Japan in 1979.

Largest switchboard ⌃

The switchboard at the Pentagon, Arlington, Virginia, USA, has 34,500 lines handling nearly 1 million calls a day through 100,000 miles (161,000 km) of telephone cable (Pentagon switchboard of 1950, above). Its busiest ever day was June 6 1994 – the 50th anniversary of D-day – when there were 1,502,415 calls.

★ Most cell phones per capita
According to statisticians NationMaster.com, Taiwan had 106.45 cell phones per 100 people in 2002.

★ Fastest text message sent around the world
On February 20 2002, at the 3GSM World Congress in Cannes, France, Logica sent a text message around the world by forwarding it to cell phones in six countries in six continents, and finally back to the original phone in Cannes. The message was received back in France only 3 min 17.53 sec after the original sender began typing in the message.

★ Largest animal sound archive
The world's largest animal sound archive, the British Library Sound Archive, London, UK, was established in 1969 and currently holds more than 130,000 wildlife recordings of sound-producing animals from all geographical areas. The sounds are used in numerous industries such as zoology, conservation, and television production – and some have even been sold as cell phone ringtones!

★ Fastest time to type a cell text message
James Trusler (UK) typed a set text of 160 characters on his cell phone in a time of 1 min 7 sec on the live TV show *The Panel*, Ten Network, Sydney, NSW, Australia, on September 24 2003.

★ Earliest instant telecommunication
The telegraph system, invented by Samuel Morse (USA), was the first form of instant communication that was applied commercially. The first link, from Washington, D.C. to Baltimore, Maryland, USA, was completed by May 1844. Morse sent the first message and soon the arrangements of dots and dashes was called Morse code.

★ Loudest signaling device
The Chrysler air raid sirens are the loudest sirens ever, capable of producing 138 decibels at a distance of 100 ft (30 m) – so loud that a normal person would be deafened within 200 ft (60 m) of one during operation.

★ Largest live satellite radio broadcast
On February 13 2002, Ana Ann's (UK) debut single 'Ride' was uplinked from the offices of Worldspace, London, UK, to Worldspace's AfriStar satellite and then beamed down to western Europe, the whole of Africa, and the Middle East.

★ Oldest commercial satellite station
Goonhilly Satellite Earth Station on the Lizard Peninsula, Cornwall, UK, has 59 antennae of various sizes in operation. 'Arthur' (Goonhilly One) began operation on July 11 1962 and continues to carry telephony and data traffic around the world. It received the first live transatlantic television signals from the Telstar satellite.

★ Earliest communications satellite
Echo 1 (sometimes called Echo 1A) was launched on July 10 1962 from Cape Canaveral, Florida, USA. It was a 98-ft-diameter (30-m) balloon with a reflective aluminum coating, allowing radio and television signals to be passively reflected back to Earth. It ceased operations on May 24 1968.

★ Largest civil communications satellite
The Astra 1-K was built by Alcatel Space (France). It had a mass of 11,570 lb (5,250 kg) and, fully deployed, would have been 121 ft (37 m) in length and 21 ft 7 in (6.6 m) in height. Upon its launch on November 26 2002, its Russian Proton booster failed, leaving the satellite stranded in low Earth orbit. It was safely de-orbited on December 10 2002 over the Pacific Ocean.

Space exploration
Science & technology

'There are things that are known and things that are unknown; in between is exploration' – **Anonymous**

The 'space race'

The first edition of *Guinness World Records* (formerly *The Guinness Book of Records*) was published six years before the first manned spaceflight by Yuri Gagarin (USSR) in 1961. In a special address to the US Congress in the same year, President John F. Kennedy (USA) announced the ambitious goal of landing an American on the Moon and returning him safely to Earth before the end of the 1960s. This sparked the 'space race' between the USA and the USSR that dominated the latter half of the 20th century, such that by the end of 2004 – a mere 101 years since the first flight by Orville Wright (USA) – man has stood on the surface of the Moon and sent probes to other planets and there is now a permanent space station orbiting Earth.

Early landmarks

The first man-made object to orbit the Earth was *Sputnik 1*, launched by the USSR on October 4 1957. It remained in orbit until January 4 1958. This was followed by *Sputnik 2* on November 3 1957, which remained in orbit until April 13 1958.

Sputnik 2 had a passenger – a dog named Laika. America's first foray into space was on January 31 1958, when *Explorer 1*, the first US satellite, lifted off from Cape Canaveral, Florida, USA. The year 1958 was also the year of the foundation of the National Aeronautics and Space Administration (NASA), which has controlled the American space program ever since.

Lunar success

Since the 1950s, advances in science and technology have enabled man to continue to push back the boundaries of space exploration. Some eight years after Yuri Gagarin's (USSR) first spaceflight, Neil Armstrong (USA) took that 'giant leap for mankind' in 1969 when he stepped onto the Moon.

1961
First manned spaceflight

The earliest manned spaceflight was by Cosmonaut Yuri Alekseyevich Gagarin (USSR) in *Vostok 1* on April 12 1961. *Vostok 1* was launched from the Baikonur Cosmodrome, Kazakhstan, USSR, at 9:07 am and landed near Smelovka, USSR, 115 minutes later. Gagarin ejected from *Vostok 1* 108 minutes into the flight as planned, and landed three minutes after his spacecraft by parachute. The maximum altitude during *Vostok 1*'s 25,394-mile (40,868-km) flight was listed at 203 miles (327 km), with a maximum speed of 17,560 mph (28,260 km/h).

1963
First woman in space

Valentina Tereshkova (USSR) was launched into space in *Vostok 6* on June 19 1963. At 26, she is the youngest woman ever to undertake such a mission.

1965
First space walk

Alexei Arkhipovich Leonov (USSR) was the first person to engage in EVA, or extra-vehicular activity, commonly known as a 'space walk', which he accomplished from *Voskhod 2* on March 18 1965.

1968
First manned lunar mission

On December 21 1968, *Apollo 8* was launched into space. The crew – Frank Borman, Jim Lovell, and Bill Anders (all USA) – were the first men to orbit the Moon. They achieved 10 orbits during their six-day mission.

Did you know...?

- 12 men in total have walked on the Moon.
- 16 nations are participating in the construction of the International Space Station.
- The greatest distance from Earth achieved by humans was when the crew of *Apollo 13* (Jim Lovell, Fred Haise, and John Swigert, all USA) were 158 miles (254 km) from the lunar surface, on the far side of the Moon, and 248,655 miles (400,171 km) above the Earth's surface, at 8:21 EDT on April 15 1970.

More recently, the development of the reusable space shuttle has made possible the construction and development of the International Space Station (ISS) that is now orbiting Earth – a project that has brought together many spacefaring nations. This has allowed scientists to carry out important onboard scientific experiments that benefit mankind. The picture bottom right shows John Herrington (USA) installing new equipment to the ISS's Canadarm2 on a scheduled space walk. China's first space-flight, in October 2003, was another important landmark in the history of space exploration: China is only the third nation to send a human into orbit.

Next stop Mars?
The exploration of our solar system is an ongoing project: in January 2004, following NASA's successful Mars Exploration Rover mission – which has brought the possibility of sending a human mission to Mars one step closer – President Bush (USA) called on NASA to 'prepare for new journeys to the worlds beyond our own'.

2002
Most spaceflights by an individual
To date, two astronauts have traveled into space a total of seven times: Jerry Ross (USA, below) flew his seventh mission (STS 110) on board the space shuttle *Atlantis* from April 8 to 19 2002. Franklin Chang-Dìaz (USA) flew his seventh mission on board the space shuttle *Endeavour* from June 5 to 19 2002.

2003
Longest maiden flight
Of the three nations to launch humans into space to date, the longest maiden flight is by the Chinese. On October 15 2003, Chinese 'taikonaut' Yang Liwei was sent into orbit on board the *Shenzou 5* spacecraft on a mission that lasted 21 hr 23 min from launch to touchdown.

1972
Longest manned Moon mission
From December 7 to 19 1972, the crew of *Apollo 17* stayed on the lunar surface for a record 74 hr 59 min 40 sec. During their stay Eugene Cernan and Harrison 'Jack' Schmitt (who became the twelfth man on the Moon) collected a record 243 lb 6 oz (110.4 kg) of rock and soil during their three EVAs totaling 22 hr 5 mins.

1969
First men on the Moon
Neil Armstrong (USA), commander of the *Apollo 11* mission, became the first man to set foot on the Moon, on the Sea of Tranquility, at 22:56.15 EDT on July 20 1969. He was followed out of the lunar module *Eagle* by Edwin 'Buzz' Aldrin Jr. (USA, above) while the command module *Columbia*, piloted by Michael Collins (USA), orbited above, before later re-docking.

Innovations from space technology

- Weather prediction
- Satellite navigation & communication
- TV satellite dishes
- Bar coding
- Medical imaging
- CAT scans
- High-density batteries
- Flat screen TVs
- Joysticks
- Water purification systems
- Cordless tools
- Pacemakers
- Heart monitors
- Ultrasound scanners
- Digital imaging
- Virtual reality programs
- Thermal clothing
- Radiation-blocking sunglasses
- Fire-fighting equipment
- Smoke detectors
- Shock-absorbing sneakers
- Invisible braces for teeth

Most reused spacecraft ⌄

NASA's space shuttle *Discovery* (below) was last launched on August 10 2001

at 4:10 pm CDT. Its mission (STS-105) was to deliver the *Leonardo* cargo module to the International Space Station and to deliver a new crew to the station. This was the 30th mission for *Discovery*, which has been in operation since August 30 1984.

★ Most accurate measure of the age of the universe

The Wilkinson Microwave Anisotropy Probe (WMAP) was designed to measure the cosmic microwave background of the universe – the heat echo of the Big Bang. The first results from WMAP, released on February 11 2003, reveal minute temperature differences in the early universe. This has allowed scientists to estimate the age of the universe at 13.7 billion years old, with a margin of error of just 1%.

★ Most people in space at the same time

The greatest number of people in space at any one time is 13. Seven Americans were aboard the space shuttle STS 67 *Endeavour*, three CIS cosmonauts were aboard the *Mir* space station, and two cosmonauts and a US astronaut were aboard *Soyuz TM21* on March 14 1995.

★ Most time spent in space

Russian cosmonaut Sergei Avdeyev logged a total of 747 days 14 hr 22 min on three spaceflights to the *Mir* space station from July 1992 to July 1999.

★ Longest manned spaceflight

Russian doctor Valeriy Poliyakov was launched to the *Mir* space station aboard *Soyuz TM18* on January 8 1994 and landed back on Earth in *Soyuz TM20* on March 22 1995, after a spaceflight lasting 437 days 17 hr 58 min 16 sec.

★ Longest spaceflight by a woman

Shannon Lucid (USA) was launched to the *Mir* space station aboard the US space shuttle STS 76 *Atlantis* on March 22 1996, and landed aboard STS 79 *Atlantis* on September 26 that year. Her spaceflight, which lasted 188 days 4 hr 14 sec, is the longest spaceflight by a woman. Her stay onboard the space station is also the longest by any US astronaut. Upon returning to Earth, she was awarded the Congressional Space Medal of Honor by President Clinton (USA).

★ Furthest distance traveled on another world

From January 16 to June 23 1973, the unmanned Soviet *Lunokhod 2* rover traveled a distance of 23 miles (37 km) on the surface of the Moon, further than any other manned or unmanned lunar or planetary rover.

★ Furthest distance traveled on Mars in one day

On sol 70 (corresponding to April 5 2004) of NASA's Mars Exploration rover mission, the robotic rover *Opportunity* traveled a total distance of 328 ft (100 m) across Meridiani Planum on Mars. As a comparison, Mars Pathfinder's *Sojourner* rover traveled 334 ft (102 m) during its entire mission in 1997.

★ Greatest spacecraft collision

On June 25 1997, an unmanned Russian *Progress* supply vehicle weighing 15,000 lb (7 tonnes) collided with the Russian *Mir* space station. Cosmonauts Vasily Tsibliev and Alexander Lazutkin (both Russia) onboard *Mir* had to work quickly to seal a breach in the hull of *Mir*'s *Spektr* module, while US astronaut Michael Foale prepared *Mir*'s *Soyuz* capsule for a possible evacuation. Although the loss of life was avoided, the station was left dangerously low on power and oxygen and temporarily tumbling out of control.

Oldest astronaut

John Glenn Jr. (USA, above) was 77 years 103 days old when he was launched into space as part of the crew of STS-95 *Discovery* on October 29 1998. The mission lasted 11 days, landing on November 7 1998.

Heaviest man-made object to reenter Earth's atmosphere

The Russian space station *Mir* (right) was de-orbited during a successful controlled reentry of Earth's atmosphere on March 23 2001. After 15 years in space, the 286,500-lb (130-tonne) outpost broke into incandescent pieces and splashed down in the ocean east of New Zealand. »

★ Longest space walk

Astronauts Jim Voss and Susan Helms (both USA) spent 8 hr 56 min outside in space on March 11 2001. Their job was to make room on the International Space Station for the Italian cargo module *Leonardo*, which was carried into space by the space shuttle *Discovery*. *Leonardo*'s payload included around 11,000 lb (5 tonnes) of supplies and equipment for the station.

★ Most durable space station

Mir, the central core module of the *Mir* space station (USSR/Russia), was launched into orbit on February 20 1986. Over the following 10 years, five modules and a docking port for US space shuttles were added to the complex. On March 23 2001, the space station was de-orbited and destroyed in a controlled reentry over the Pacific Ocean. More than a hundred people visited the *Mir* space station in its 15-year operational history.

★ Longest orbital survey of an outer planet

NASA's *Galileo* spacecraft was launched on October 18 1989. It reached the planet Jupiter on December 7 1995, where it slowed down and entered the orbit of the largest planet in the Solar System. *Galileo*'s survey of Jupiter and its moons represents the first time a man-made probe has orbited a world in the outer Solar System. With its onboard power and communications beginning to fail, *Galileo* burned up in the atmosphere of Jupiter on September 21 2003. This was a deliberate destruction of the spacecraft, which ensured there was no chance of it inadvertently colliding with Europa (one of Jupiter's 'moons') and contaminating it in the future.

★ Fastest atmospheric entry

On December 7 1995, a small probe released by the *Galileo* spacecraft began a fiery descent into the atmosphere of the giant planet Jupiter.

During this, the most difficult atmospheric entry ever, the *Galileo* probe reached a speed of 106,000 mph (170,000 km/h).

★ Largest planetary rover

Of the three robotic rovers sent to other planets, NASA's twin Mars Exploration rovers *Spirit* and *Opportunity* are the largest. Each has a mass of almost 396 lb (180 kg) and stands 4 ft 9 in (1.44 m) high.

★ Clearest image of a comet

On January 2 2004, NASA's *Stardust* spacecraft encountered comet *Wild 2* in order to collect samples of cometary dust for return to Earth. From the closest approach distance of about 146 miles (236 km), the spacecraft was able to obtain images of the icy nucleus at a resolution of just 50 ft (15 m) per pixel.

★ Most powerful gamma-ray telescope

Launched in 1991, the Compton Gamma-Ray Observatory is the most powerful gamma-ray

telescope to date. After nine years of observations, it re-entered the Earth's atmosphere and burned up on June 4 2000.

★ Most distant image of Earth

On February 4 1990, NASA's *Voyager 1* spacecraft turned its camera back toward the Sun and the planets. After 12.5 years in space, traveling away from Earth, *Voyager 1*'s camera took a picture of our home planet from a distance of almost 4 billion miles (6.5 billion km).

★ Longest extraterrestrial balloon flight

The twin Soviet spacecraft *Vega 1* and *Vega 2* were launched on December 15 and December 20 1984 respectively. Both probes encountered Venus in June 1985, and dropped packages into the Venusian atmosphere. Each package split into a lander and a balloon. The *Vega 2* balloon sent data about the Venusian atmosphere for 46.5 hours, before contact was lost.

Highest resolution digital camera ≪

The world's highest resolution digital camera is MegaCam, with a resolution of 320 million pixels. It is an astronomical camera used on the 11-ft 9.6-in (3.6-m) Canada–France–Hawaii telescope in the summit of Mauna Kea, Hawaii, USA (left). The camera was integrated with the telescope on June 28 2002.

★ Most detailed human dissection

The Visible Human Project is led by Dr. Victor Spitzer (USA) of the University of Colorado. The aim of the project is to create a virtual anatomy 'textbook'. Ultimately this digitized virtual body will be part of a medical simulator on which doctors and medical students will learn surgical techniques, in the manner of a pilot learning to fly by using an aeroplane simulator. To create these virtual humans, Dr. Spitzer and his team had to perform the most detailed human dissection.

The 'Visible Man' is a real cadaver that was sliced into 1,878 sections. The thickness of each cut was 1 mm (1,000 microns). The 'Visible Woman' cadaver was sliced into 5,189 slices, 0.33 mm (330 microns) thick. Each layer of the sliced cadaver was photographed with a digital camera and stored in a computer. Eventually, the recreation of the sliced images will form a minutely detailed 3-D virtual human body.

★ Furthest distance between patient and surgeon

On September 7 2001, Madeleine Schaal (France) had her gallbladder removed by a robot in an operating room at Strasbourg, France. Her surgeons, Jacques Marescaux and Michel Gagner (both France), remotely operated the ZEUS robotic surgical arms on a secure fiber-optic line from New York, USA, a total distance of 3,866 miles (6,222 km) away.

★ Highest capacity multimedia jukebox

The highest capacity multimedia jukebox available to date is the AV380, with 80 gigabytes of storage space on its internal hard drive. Created by Archos (France), the AV380 can store and play MP3 music tracks as well as MPEG4 video files. It was launched in August 2003.

★ Longest television display

A screen measuring 230 ft 10.8 in (70.4 m) long by 26 ft 2.4 in (8 m) high was built by Mitsubishi Electric (HK) and Mitsubishi Corporation (Japan).

Its installation at the Hong Kong Jockey Club, Shatin Horse Race Course, Hong Kong, China, was completed on May 25 2003.

★ Smallest color television screen

MicroEmissive Displays Ltd, Edinburgh, UK, has developed a tiny color television/video screen that measures just 0.15 x 0.11 in (3.84 x 2.88 mm). The ME1602, which can be linked to video cameras, DVD players, and VCRs, has a resolution of 160 x 120 pixels. It works using organic light-emitting diode technology.

★ Largest computer touch screen

Mega-mate, the largest computer touch screen in the world, was developed and built by Displaymate Touchscreens Ltd. (UK). Measuring 3.28 x 9.84 ft (1 x 3 m), with an area of 32.29 ft² (3 m²), it was specially commissioned by BRC Imagination Arts for Volkswagen's corporate identity center in Dresden, Germany, and delivered in November 2001.

★ Lightest document scanner

The Docupen is the lightest A4 document scanner, weighing a mere 1.75 oz (49.6 g). It was released by Planon System Solutions, Inc., Mississauga, Canada, in 2003.

★ Oldest computer mouse

The computer mouse was invented in 1964 by Douglas Engelbart (USA), who was awarded a US patent for it in 1970. It was described in the patent as an 'X-Y position indicator for a display system' and was nicknamed a mouse because of the resemblance of the wire to a tail.

★ Highest-jumping robot

Sandia National Laboratories (USA) has developed experimental 'hopper' robots that use combustion-driven pistons to jump to heights of 30 ft (9 m). The small robots have potential applications in planetary exploration, where several hoppers could be released by a lander to survey the surrounding landscape.

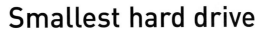

Smallest hard drive

The disk of the smallest hard drive measures

just 0.85 in (2.16 cm) across (below). It was created by Toshiba (Japan) and announced at the international Consumer Electronics Show in Las Vegas, Nevada, USA, in January 2004.

The smallest commercially available hard drives contain a disk just 1 in (2.5 cm) across. Of the models available in February 2004, the highest capacity is 2.2 gigabytes and is manufactured by GS Magicstor, Inc. (China).

Fastest running 〈〈 humanoid robot

QRIO, which stands for 'Quest for Curiosity', is Sony Corporation's latest advanced humanoid autonomous robot (above). It is the world's first bipedal robot capable of running (i.e. capable of moving while both legs are off the ground at the same time). QRIO is capable of running at 9 in/sec (23 cm/sec). The robot measures 23 in (58 cm) high and was revealed in September 2003.

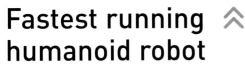

★ First business computer
LEO I (Lyons Electronic Office) was the first ever business computer. It began operations in November 1951 at the Lyons headquarters, London, UK. The first of its many business applications was the valuation of the weekly output of bread and cakes from Lyons' bakeries. LEO I was supplemented by the more advanced LEO II in May 1957, but continued operations into the 1960s.

★ First stored-program computer
The world's first stored-program computer was the Manchester University Mark I, which incorporated the Williams storage cathode ray tube (patented December 11 1946). It ran its first program, written by Tom Kilburn (UK), for 52 minutes on June 21 1948.

★ Earliest microprocessor
The first microprocessor was the 4004 chip, designed and built by Intel (USA). The first one was completed in January 1971. The size of a thumbnail, this first single-processor CPU had the same power as ENIAC (electronic numerical integrator and computer), the room-sized first electronic computer. The 4004 chip had 2,300 transistors and could perform around 100,000 instructions per second.

★ Most sophisticated battlefield simulator
The most sophisticated battlefield computer simulator is the Combined Arms Tactical Trainer. Situated at Warminster, UK, and Sennelager, Germany, it is capable of training more than 850 military personnel at once in an integrated, realistic combat scenario involving

vehicles, aircraft, soldiers, and commanders. Simulated combat arenas of more than 3,800 miles² (10,000 km²) are used. It was constructed for the UK's Ministry of Defence by Lockheed Martin (USA), and became operational on September 1 2002.

★ Fastest computer
The NEC Earth Simulator at the Yokohama Institute for Earth Sciences, Japan, is capable of 35.6 trillion calculations per second – roughly five times the speed of the previous record holder. Built by HNSX Supercomputers, a division of NEC, the computer is designed to simulate Earth's complex climate in order to predict climate change and global warming, which will have severe consequences for Japan.

★ First computer virus
The first computer program to replicate itself surreptitiously (i.e. a virus) was demonstrated by Fred Cohen, a student at the Massachusetts Institute of Technology, USA, on November 11 1983.

★ Most powerful quantum computer
Whereas normal computers use a string of zeroes and ones (bits) to represent data, experimental quantum computers use qubits, which can be a zero, one, or simultaneously both. On December 20 2001, IBM's Almaden Research Center, San Jose, California, USA, announced that they had used a seven-qubit quantum computer to calculate the factors of the number 15.

The computer used a billion billion molecules that have seven nuclear spins for the calculation. Consisting of the nuclei of five atoms of fluorine and two of carbon, these molecules are able to interact with each other as qubits.

⌄ Oldest dated cannon

The Dardanelles Gun (below), cast in Turkey in 1464 for

Sultan Mehmet II, is made from bronze, weighs 37,000 lb (16.8 tonnes), and measures 17 ft (5.2 m) long. It had a range of 5,250 ft (1,600 m) when firing a 23.5-in-diameter (600-mm), 670-lb (304-kg) projectile. The date is engraved on the cannon, which is displayed at the Royal Armouries, Fort Nelson, Hampshire, UK.

Largest suit of ⌄ animal armor

A suit of armor designed for an adult Asian elephant (right) was made in the late 16th or early 17th century in northern India during the Mughul Empire. It weighs 260 lb (118 kg) and, although part of the suit is missing, it is estimated that when complete with its original 8,439 individual metal plates, it would have weighed 350 lb (159 kg). The suit is currently on display at the Royal Armouries Museum in Leeds, UK. It is thought to be the only one of its kind in existence.

★ Largest gun

In the siege of Sevastopol, USSR (now Ukraine), in July 1942, the Germans used a gun with an 31.4-in (80-cm) caliber and a 94-ft 5-in-long (28.87-m) barrel. Built by Krupp (Germany), its remains were discovered near Metzenhof, Germany, in August 1945. When fully assembled, the gun measured 141 ft (42.9 m) in length and weighed 2,963,000 lb (1,344 tonnes).

★ Largest cannonball

The largest cannonball has a diameter of 36 in (91 cm) and weighs over 2,204 lb (1 tonne) when filled with its charge of 400 lb (180 kg) of gunpowder. It belongs to the Mallet mortar gun, which was designed by Robert Mallet (Ireland) and completed in March 1857. It is currently on display at the

Royal Armouries, Fort Nelson, Hampshire, UK. Mallet's mortar required 35 kg (77 lb) of powder to fire such a projectile to reach its range of 2.4 km (1.5 miles) and to bury the charge to a depth of 9.1 m (30 ft) in soft earth, something that would cause the effect of a small earthquake and ultimately lead to the collapse of structures.

★ Tallest suit of armor

The tallest suit of armor currently on display measures 6 ft 8 in (2.06 m) high. It was traditionally said to have been worn by England's John of Gaunt, Duke of Lancaster in the 14th century, but is actually German in origin and dated to around 1535. It is on display in The White Tower at the Tower of London, London, UK.

★ Earliest tank

The No.1 Lincoln built by William Foster & Co. Ltd. (UK), and modified to become Little Willie, first ran on September 6 1915. Tanks first saw action with the Heavy Section,

Machine Gun Corps (later the Tank Corps) at the Battle of Flers-Courcelette, France, on September 15 1916. The Mark I 'Male' tank, armed with a pair of 6-pounder guns and four machine guns, weighed 62,610 lb (28.4 tonnes) and was powered by a 105-hp (78-kW) motor, giving a top road speed of 3–4 mph (4.8–6.4 km/h).

★ Fastest tank

A production standard S 2000 Scorpion Peacekeeper tank (complete with appliqué hull armor, ballistic skirts, K10000 replaceable rubber pad track, and powered by an RS 2133 high-speed diesel engine) developed by Repaircraft plc (UK) achieved a speed of 51.10 mph (82.23 km/h) at the QinetiQ vehicle test track, Chertsey, UK, on March 26 2002. The speed is an average of two consecutive runs in opposite directions.

★ Heaviest tank

The heaviest tank ever was the German Panzerkampfwagen Maus II, which, at 423,280 lb

(192 tonnes), weighed as much as 130 modern sedans. By 1945, it had only reached the experimental stage and was abandoned. The heaviest operational tank used by any army was the 165,780-lb (75.2-tonne) 13-man French Char de Rupture 2C bis of 1922. It carried a 6.1-in (15.5-cm) howitzer and was powered by two 250-hp (186-kW) engines giving a maximum speed of 7.5 mph (12 km/h).

★ Most heavily armed tank

The Russian T-64, T-72, T-80, and T-90 tanks are all equipped with a 4.9-in (12.5-cm) gun-missile system. The American Sheridan light tank mounts a 6-in (15.2-cm) weapon that is a gun and a missile launcher combined, but this is not a long-barreled, high-velocity gun of the conventional type. The British Armoured Vehicle Royal Engineers (AVRE) Centurion had a 6.5-in (16.5-cm) low-velocity demolition gun.

Most accurate bomb ⌄

The US-built Joint Direct Attack Munition (JDAM, below), in

operation since 1997, is accurate to approximately 6 ft 6 in (2 m). JDAM is a steerable tail-kit attached to existing 'dumb bombs'. After release, the JDAM's location is continually checked by fixes from satellites.

⭐ **Most intelligent handgun**
The O'Dwyer Variable Lethality Law Enforcement (VLe) prototype pistol, made by Metal Storm Limited (Australia), has no moving parts: instead, projectiles are fired electronically by a built-in computer processor. The gun can only be fired by someone wearing an authorized transponder ring. The VLe has no magazine – the bullets are stacked behind one another in the barrel, and the handgrip – where the magazine would be on a conventional pistol – contains the electronic control systems. Capable of firing up to three shots in quick succession (within 1/500th of a second), the computer-controlled firing also allows the pistol to fire at a rate equivalent to 60,000 rounds per minute.

⭐ **Earliest use of infrared equipment in battle**
Infrared technology was first used in battle during World War II. Electric sniperscopes mounted on top of rifles converted the infrared light from enemy soldiers into visible light, enabling the shooter to fire accurately in darkness.

⭐ **Earliest successful test of a high-powered microwave weapon**
A successful test for a high-powered microwave (HPM) weapon on electronic equipment occurred in April 1999 under the observation of the Joint Command and Control Warfare Center of San Antonio, Texas, USA. HPMs are designed to bring maximum disruption to any military or civilian power system by discharging a powerful energy pulse that destroys any electronics within its 980-ft (300-m) range.

⭐ **Country with the most land mines or unexploded ordnance deployed**
The Egyptian Government has estimated that 19.7 million mines or unexploded ordnance (UXO) existed in Egypt as of November 2002. Most of the mines in Egypt were planted during World War II. According to the International Campaign to Ban Landmines there are between 85 and 125 million mines buried in countries around the world. In addition, over 200 million are stockpiled.

⭐ **Most widely used firearm**
The most widely used firearm is the Automatic Kalashnikov 1947 (AK-47). During the Cold War, the former USSR supplied AK-47s to anti-Western insurgents, and the rifle therefore became a symbol of left-wing revolution. Between 50 and 80 million copies and variations of the AK-47 have been produced globally.

⭐ **Earliest use of smallpox as a biological weapon**
During the French and Indian Wars of 1754–1767, British soldiers fighting in North America at that time distributed blankets contaminated with smallpox among the American Indians. Epidemics followed, killing more than 50% of the affected tribes.

⭐ **Largest radar installation**
The largest of the three radar installations in the US Ballistic Missile Early Warning System (BMEWS) is near Thule, Kalaallit Nunaat, Greenland, 931 miles (1,498 km) from the North Pole. Completed in 1960, it cost $500 million.

⭐ **Earliest use of a graphite bomb**
A graphite bomb (G-bomb) was first used in 1991 when Allied forces used it to disable 85% of Iraq's power supplies during the Gulf War. G-bombs work by exploding a cloud of thousands of ultrafine carbon-fiber wires over electrical installations, short-circuiting electrical systems.

⭐ **Largest non-nuclear conventional weapon in existence**
The Massive Ordnance Air Blast (MOAB), a precision-guided weapon, weighs 21,500 lb (9,752 kg). It was first tested by the US Air Force at the Eglin Air Force Armament Center, Florida, USA, on March 11 2003.

Air & sea warfare
Science & technology

Largest battleships in active service since the end of World War II

The battleships USS *Iowa* (above), *New Jersey*, *Missouri*, and *Wisconsin* are each 887 ft (270 m) long and have full-load displacements in excess of 90 million lb (41,000 tonnes). All were commissioned during World War II and were in active service at various times until the early 1990s. Each ship is armed with nine 16-in (40.64-cm) guns capable of firing 2,700-lb (1,225-kg) projectiles a distance of 23 miles (39 km), and, when operational, had a crew complement of around 1,900.

★ Fastest warship
The 78-ft (23.7-m-long), 220,000-lb (100-tonne) US Navy test surface-effect ship *SES-100B* attained a world record 91.9 knots (170 km/h or 105 mph) on January 25 1980 at the Chesapeake Bay Test Range, Maryland, USA. Similar to hovercraft, surface-effect ships travel on a cushion of air, but also have two sharp rigid hulls that remain in the water. Large fans under the ship create air pressure that is then trapped between the hulls, raising the ship.

★ Largest modern naval battle
The largest purely naval battle of modern times was the World War I Battle of Jutland on May 31 1916, in which 151 British Royal Navy warships faced 101 German warships. The Royal Navy lost 14 ships and 6,097 men, and the German fleet 11 ships and 2,545 men.

★ Largest amphibious ship
The US Navy's Wasp-class vessels have a full-load displacement of 80.5 million lb (36,500 tonnes) and a length of 844 ft (257 m). Capable of carrying aircraft, large numbers of troops, and various landing vessels, their primary role is to land troops on enemy shores. The ships also have 600-bed hospitals (the largest on any ship except for dedicated hospital ships). There are seven Wasp-class ships currently in service.

★ Largest warships
The warships with the largest full-load displacement are the Nimitz-class US Navy aircraft carriers USS *Nimitz*, *Dwight D. Eisenhower*, *Carl Vinson*, *Theodore Roosevelt*, *Abraham Lincoln*, *George Washington*, *John C. Stennis*, *Harry S. Truman*, and *Ronald Reagan*, the last five of which displace approximately 217 million lb (98,550 tonnes). They are 1,092 ft (333 m) long, have an 4.49-acre (1.82-hectare) flight deck, and are driven by four nuclear-powered 260,000-shp (194,000-kW) geared steam turbines. They can reach speeds in excess of 30 knots (56 km/h or 34.5 mph).

★ Largest stealth ship
The largest ship incorporating stealth technology is the Swedish Visby-class corvette, which is approximately 236 ft (72 m) long and has a displacement of 1.32 million lb (600 tonnes). Developed by the Kockums shipyard (Sweden), the carbon-fiber vessel is lighter than a conventional ship of its size, and features the large flat surfaces used in aircraft to provide low radar visibility. The Visby prototype made its maiden voyage in December 2001.

★ Longest military runway
The runway at Edwards Air Force Base on the west side of Rogers dry lake-bed at Muroc, California, USA, is 7.41 miles (11.92 km) in length.

★ Largest air force ever
The United States Army Air Corps (now the US Air Force) had 79,908 aircraft in July 1944 and 2,411,294 personnel in March 1944.

★ Fastest combat jet
The fastest combat jet is the Russian Mikoyan MiG-25 fighter (NATO code name 'Foxbat'). The 'Foxbat-B' has been tracked by radar at about Mach 3.2 (3.2 times the speed of sound – 3,395 km/h, or 2,110 mph). The MiG-25 was designed as a high-altitude interceptor and it can take off and climb to an altitude of 114,000 ft (35,000 m) in a little over four minutes.

Earliest ⌄ stealth ship

The US Navy *Sea Shadow* (below) was completed in the mid-1980s but only revealed to the public in 1993.

The bizarre looking twin-hulled ship is 164 ft (49.98 m) long, 68 ft (20.7 m) across, and has a full-load displacement of 1.25 million lb (569 tonnes). Built by Lockheed Martin, it has a crew of 10 and a top speed of 11.5 mph (18.5 km/h).

Navy with the ⌃ most aircraft

The US Navy has over 4,000 aircraft in service. It operates about

20 different types of fixed-wing aircraft, including carrier-based F-14 Tomcat, and F/A-18 Hornet (above) fighters, and various reconnaissance, transport, anti-submarine, and airborne command-post aircraft. It also operates six different types of helicopters and the unique new V-22 'Osprey' tilt rotor aircraft.

★ Most widely deployed military unmanned aircraft

By early 2004, the 'Predator' unmanned aerial vehicle (UAV) manufactured by General Atomics Aeronautical Systems (USA) had logged more than 65,000 flight hours, of which more than half were in combat areas such as Kosovo, Iraq, and Afghanistan. The 100th example of the aircraft, which has a wingspan of 48.7 ft (14.84 m) and a flight endurance time of over 40 hours, was delivered to the US military in February 2004.

★ Longest range air attacks

Seven B-52G 'Stratofortress' bombers left Barksdale Air Force Base, Louisiana, USA, on January 16 1991 to deliver air-launched cruise missiles against targets in Iraq after the start of the first Gulf War. Each flew 14,000 miles (22,500 km), refueling four times in flight, with the round-trip mission lasting some 35 hours.

★ Heaviest bomber in service

The Russian Tupolev Tu-160 'Blackjack' bomber has a maximum take-off weight of 606,270 lb (275 tonnes) and a maximum speed of about Mach 2.05 (roughly 2,200 km/h or 1,350 mph). Although a Boeing 747 has a higher maximum takeoff weight of 877,200 lb (397 tonnes), the 'Blackjack' is considerably smaller and, crucially, flies more than 2.5 times as fast.

★ Fastest operational bomber

The US variable-geometry or 'swing-wing' General Dynamics FB-111A has a maximum speed of Mach 2.5. The Russian swing-wing Tupolev Tu-22M, which is known to NATO as 'Backfire', has an estimated over-target speed of Mach 2 but could be as fast as Mach 2.5. Mach 2.5 is roughly equivalent to 1,650 mph (2,655 km/h).

★ Largest ever bomber wingspan

The American 10-engined Convair B 36J 'Peacemaker' had a 230-ft (70.1-m) wingspan. The aircraft, which had a maximum take-off weight of 410,000 lb (185 tonnes), was replaced in the 1950s by the Boeing B-52. The 'Peacemaker' had a top speed of 435 mph (700 km/h).

★ Most produced fighter of World War II

Over 36,000 Ilyushin Il-2 'Sturmovik' ground-attack aircraft are said to have been produced in Russia before, during, and immediately after World War II, making it the most produced aircraft of that conflict and one of the most numerous combat aircraft ever.

★ Fastest World War II propeller fighter

The German Dornier DO-335 was unique in having a tractive (pulling) propeller in its nose

and a propulsive (pushing) motor behind its cockpit. It had a maximum sustained speed of 413 mph (665 km/h), increasing to 477 mph (765 km/h) with emergency boost. Two models existed – A-1 and A-6 – the latter a two-seater night fighter. Only 28 were completed before the end of World War II.

★ Top scoring air ace in World War II

The highest officially attributed figure of aircraft shot down by any airman was 352 by Major Erich Hartmann (Germany). In one sortie on the Russian front on November 6 1943 he shot down a record 13 planes in 17 minutes. His last mission was on May 8 1945, when he shot down a YAK-7 fighter and later landed his plane to surrender to the British forces. He was handed over to the Russians who tried him for war crimes. He was sent to a work camp for 10 years.

Art & media

Contents

Largest cardboard-box sculpture ⌃

A cardboard-box sculpture of a red Ford Gran Torino car (above) that measured 88.1 ft (26.86 m) long, 23 ft (7.02 m) high, and 7.4 ft (2.26 m) wide was created to promote Empire Interactive's PS2 game of the 1970s TV show *Starsky & Hutch*. Completed on June 20 2003, it was unveiled in Spitalfields Market, London, UK, by designers from Wreck Age Productions (UK). The sculpture was made by 34 people in just over four days using 4,855 boxes and 286 rolls of tape.

★ Largest apple mosaic
An apple mosaic unveiled on September 29 2001 at Kivik, Österleden, Sweden, consisted of 25,000 apples. Entitled *Applecheek*, it measured 1,119 ft² (104 m²) and was designed by Emma Karp Laggar and Jan Laggar (both Sweden). Each apple was nailed to a board by a team of eight people to form an abstract image of Earth. Approximately 5,000 lb (2.26 tonnes) of 12 different apple varieties were used.

★ Largest photograph mosaic
Unveiled in Novena Square, Singapore, on July 12 2003, the world's largest photo mosaic, entitled *Smile Singapore!*, measured 20 ft 6 in x 50 ft (6.24 x 15.24 m) and contained 16,800 individual photographs to create a giant map of Singapore. The mosaic was organized by the Heartware

Network, and each photo represented a minimum $10 donation to charity.

★ Largest ball mosaic
A mosaic containing 11,430 toy balls forming the image of a boy measured 37 x 15 ft (11.2 x 4.5 m) and had a 100-ft (30.48-m) circumference. It was created by Danny O'Connor (USA) and was installed from June 2001 to April 2002 in the Massachusetts Museum of Contemporary Art in North Adams, Massachusetts, USA.

★ Largest balloon mosaic
A mosaic depicting the Chicago skyline was made from 70,884 balloons and measured 58 x 86 ft (17.6 x 26.21 m). It was created by delegates to the International Balloon Arts Convention on March 8 1999 in the lobby of the Hyatt Regency O'Hare, Rosemont, Illinois, USA.

★ Largest paper flower mosaic
The largest mosaic made of paper flowers measured 2,496 ft² (231.8 m²) and was assembled at East Point City, Tseung Kwan O, Hong Kong, China, on October 28 2001.

★ Largest flower mural
A flower mural that incorporated 770,000 fresh dahlias measured 20,117 ft² (1,868.94 m²) when it was created on August 7 2001. It was made by 1,250 people who represented 16 neighborhoods from the Dahlia Record Committee in Lemelerveld, The Netherlands. The flowers were glued on 900 individual panels, which were then all placed next to each other in a large square to make one continuous image.

★ Largest model made from canned food
On December 24 1998, a 8-ft 6-in-tall (2.58-m) Christmas tree made from 9,773 cans of food was displayed at the Hanford Mall,

Hanford, California, USA. The tree had an overall volume of 179.3 ft³ (5.07 m³).

★ Oldest paintings
The world's oldest reliably dated paintings were found on the walls of the Chauvet cave in southern France in 1994. The paintings range from 23,000 to 32,000 years old.

★ Largest painting
A painting of the sea that measured 92,419 ft² (8,586 m²) was completed by ID Culture at The Arena, Amsterdam, The Netherlands, to mark the venue's opening on August 14 1996. The size of the painting is equivalent to nearly four football fields.

★ Largest finger painting
A finger painting measuring 5,100 ft² (473.8 m²) was completed on July 22 2003. Its creation was led by artists Jignesh Patel and Munir Rehman (both India) on behalf of the people of Surrey Central, British Columbia, Canada.

Largest nude  photo shoot

On June 8 2003, 7,000 volunteers (above) collectively posed in the nude on a street in Barcelona (Spain) for photographer Spencer Tunick (USA).

Largest inflatable sculpture

An inflatable sculpture entitled *Blockhead* (right) is 114 ft 9.6 in (35 m) tall and was created by artist Paul McCarthy (USA) for display in front of the Tate Modern gallery, London, UK, from May 19 until October 2003. *Blockhead* is loosely based on the character Pinocchio.

★ **Largest handprint painting**
A 2,251.8-ft² (209.2-m²) handprint painting was created on November 15 2002 by 2,541 students organized by the Star Givers of Jeddah, Saudi Arabia. The image, created in honor of Queen Elizabeth II's Golden Jubilee, depicted the monarch's state coach pulled by horses and accompanied by yeoman wardens.

★ **Longest painting**
The longest acrylic painting on one continuous canvas measured 6,600 ft (2,011.68 m) on January 14 2002 at Celestial Court, Toronto, Ontario, Canada, and was created by artist Danny Fong (Canada). The painting, entitled *Thousand Horses*, depicts more than 1,500 horses in different seasons, weather, and backgrounds.

★ **Largest outdoor mural**
The Pueblo Levee Project in Pueblo, Colorado, USA, has produced the largest mural in the world at 178,200 ft² (16,554.8 m²). The connected murals are almost 2 miles (3.21 km) long and 58 ft (17.67 m) tall.

★ **Longest drawing**
A drawing that measured 9,251 ft (2,820 m) was created by approximately 2,000 children in Batenburg Square, Sofia, Bulgaria, on June 1 2003 as part of Children's Day. The theme of the artwork was 'My World'.

★ **Largest painting by numbers**
The largest painting by numbers measures 4,068 ft² (378 m²) and was created at the Island Festival, Dockyard Island, Budapest, Hungary, on July 28 2003.

★ **Artwork with the most artists**
The 48-ft-long (14.63-m), 8-ft-high (2.43-m) painting *A Little Dab of Texas*, designed by Jim Campbell (USA), was painted by 25,297 people. It was completed on June 14 1998 after 3 years 7 months. The finished painting was unveiled on September 5 1998 and exhibited in Washington, D.C., USA, later that year.

★ **Largest pencil drawing by one artist**
The largest pencil drawing by one artist, entitled *One World, One Song*, has an overall surface area of 2,002 ft² (185.99 m²) and was completed by art teacher T.J. Johnson (USA) on August 2 2002.

★ **Largest photographic exhibition**
A total of 16,609 photographs were displayed by Kodak Greece in the grounds of their head office in Athens on June 17 2003. The photos had been sent in by Greeks around the world, who had been asked to submit a smiling photo to welcome the return of the Olympic Games in 2004.

★ **Largest matchstick model**
Joseph Sciberras (Malta) constructed an exact scaled-down replica of St. Publius Parish Church, Floriana, Malta. It consisted of over three million matchsticks and measured 6 ft 7 in x 6 ft 7 in x 4 ft 11 in (2 x 2 x 1.5 m).

★ **Largest single gallery space**
The Guggenheim Museum in Bilbao, Spain, which opened on October 18 1997, has 450 ft (137.16 m) of gallery space.

★ **Most valuable piece of Art Nouveau**
A standard lamp in the form of three lotus blossoms by the Daum Brothers and Louis Majorelle (all France) sold for $1.78 million at Sotheby's, New York, USA, on December 2 1989.

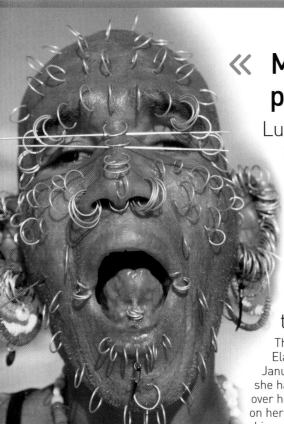

« Most pierced man

Luis Antonio Agüero (Cuba, left) sports 230 piercings on his body and head. His face alone carries more than 175 rings.

The most pierced woman is Elaine Davidson (UK). From January 1997 to May 2003 she had 1,500 piercings made over her body. Of these, 192 are on her ears, forehead, eyebrows, chin, nose, and tongue.

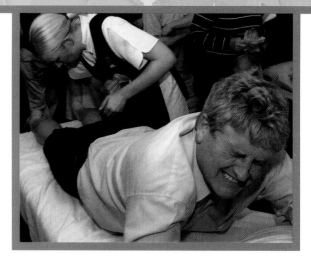

Most legs waxed ⌃ in an hour

Beautician Laura Mitchell (UK, above) hot-waxed 22 pairs of legs (16 men, 6 women) in one hour at the Globe Inn pub, Aberdeen, UK, on May 2 2002. The legs were fully stripped from the knee to the ankle, on the front, back, and sides.

★ Largest Hawaiian shirt
In March 1999, Hilo Hattie (USA), a retailer of Hawaiian fashions from Honolulu, Hawaii, USA, created an aloha shirt with a chest measurement of 14 ft (4.26 m), a waist measurement of 11 ft 6 in (3.5 m), and a neck measurement of 5 ft 0.5 in (1.53 m).

★ Largest sweater
An ecru-colored cable-stitch sweater made by the company Malhas Carjor of Palmeira, Portugal, on December 15 1998 had a chest measurement of 7 ft 2 in (2.2 m), a body length of 7 ft 11 in (2.43 m), and a sleeve length of 6 ft (1.85 m). Made from 70% acrylic and 30% wool, it was a scaled-up version of their Trintona design.

★ Largest pair of socks
A pair of nylon socks measuring 45 in (1.14 m) from top to toe and 10 in (25 cm) wide was constructed by Michael Roy Layne (USA) in October 1986 and hung outside City Hall, Boston, USA, to celebrate the Red Sox winning the American League Championship and playing in the World Series.

★ Longest scarf knitted by an individual
Ray Ettinger (USA) knitted a continuous scarf that measured 3,523 ft (1,073.8 m) long and 7 in (17.7 cm) wide on May 8 2001.

★ Longest zipper
The world's longest zipper was laid around the center of Sneek, The Netherlands, on September 5 1989. The brass zipper, made by Yoshida Ltd. (Netherlands), is 9,353 ft 8 in (2,851 m) long and consists of 2,565,900 metal teeth.

★ Largest underpants
The world's largest pair of cotton underwear measured 31 ft 4 in (9.54 m) wide and 16 ft (4.9 m) tall. It was created by the Exeter Council for Voluntary Service and unveiled on June 7 2003 at the Exeter County Rugby Ground, Devon, UK.

★ Most scissors used for cutting hair
Bruce Choy (USA) successfully styled a head of hair using eight pairs of scissors in one hand, controlling each pair independently. The record was set at his salon, Flyingshears, in San Francisco, California, USA, on March 11 2002.

★ Largest sandal
The largest sandal in the world measures 12 ft 10.8 in (3.93 m) long, 4 ft 9.6 in (1.46 m) wide, and 6 ft 3 in (1.9 m) high, and was constructed by Pearl Shoes in front of the Milli Shoes showroom, Lahore, Pakistan, in April 2002.

★ Most valuable piece of jewelry
The most valuable piece of jewelry is a pair of 58.6-karat and 61-karat diamond drop earrings bought and sold anonymously for $7.2 million at Sotheby's, Geneva, Switzerland, on November 14 1980 as part of the Magnificent Jewels auction.

★ Most valuable jacket
A jacket that once belonged to rock legend Jimi Hendrix (USA) sold to the Hard Rock Cafe chain for £35,000 ($49,185) at a sale organized by Sotheby's in the London branch of the Hard Rock Cafe (UK) on September 19 2000.

★ Most body piercings by surgical needles
Brent Moffat (Canada) inserted 700 18-gauge (0.47-in-long or 1.2-cm) surgical needles into his body in 7 hr 19 min at Metamorphosis Custom Piercing and Tattoo, Winnipeg, Manitoba, Canada, on January 15 2003.

★ Most body piercings in one session
Kam Ma (UK) received a total of 600 new piercings to his body without the aid of an anesthetic. All piercings were executed by Charlie Wilson (UK) in one continuous session that lasted from 9:15 am to 5:47 pm at Sunderland Body Art, Sunderland, Tyne and Wear, UK, on May 26 2002.

Largest handbag ⌃

In April 2003, a handbag measuring 12 ft 1 in tall, 11 ft 7 in wide, and 5 ft 3 in deep (3.7 x 3.54 x 1.6 m) made by the leather accessories company Santa Marinella (Brazil) was unveiled in the Shopping Center, Iquatemi, Brazil. It is an exact replica of the original and made from synthetic leather (stamped lined PVC) with natural cow leather trim. The giant handbag (above) was used to store canned goods for charity.

Smallest waist on a living person ⌃

Cathie Jung (USA, above), who stands 5 ft 8 in (1.72 m) tall, has a tiny 15-in (38.1-cm) waist. Cathie and husband Bob, an orthopedic surgeon, worked together to develop her tiny waist as part of their enthusiasm for Victorian dress. The 38-year-old mother of three started wearing a six-inch-wide training belt to gradually reduce her waist. Cathie does not eat a special diet or exercise to maintain her waist.

★ Most rhinestones on body
Body artist Maria Rosa Pons Abad (Spain) adorned a model's body with 30,361 rhinestones on the set of *El Show de los Récords*, Madrid, Spain, on November 22 2001.

★ Most tattooed man
Both Tom Leppard (UK) and Lucky Rich (UK) have approximately 99.9% of their bodies covered in tattoos. Tom, who resides on the Isle of Skye, Scotland, UK, has opted for a leopard print design, with all the skin between the dark spots tattooed saffron yellow. Lucky Rich has had his existing tattoos blacked over, with a white design tattooed on top.

★ Most tattooed woman
The world's most decorated woman is strip artiste Krystyne Kolorful (Canada). Tattoos cover 95% of her body and took 10 years to complete.

★ Fastest 'sheep to suit'
The fastest time to manufacture a three-piece woolen suit, from shearing the sheep to sewing the finished article, is 1 hr 2 min 36 sec, achieved by members of FH Monchengladbach, Germany, on January 28 1999. The record was broadcast on *Guinness – Die Show Der Rekorde* on January 30 1999.

★ Largest traveling wardrobe
For her 14-month debut on London's West End stage in *Mame*, Ginger Rogers (USA) arrived in England in 1969 with 118 pieces of luggage. Wisely, she came by ship.

★ Highest annual earnings by a supermodel
According to *Forbes* magazine, Gisele Bundchen (Brazil) took in $12.8 million from June 2002 to June 2003, thanks to deals with Victoria's Secret, Christian Dior, and Dolce & Gabbana.

★ Longest distance covered on a catwalk by a male model
From September 19 to 21 1983, Eddie Warke walked a total distance of 83.1 miles (133.7 km) on a catwalk at Parkes Hotel, Dublin, Republic of Ireland.

★ Most designers represented at one fashion show
A total of 89 different fashion designers from around the world were represented at Paris Fashion Week, France, in 1999. The event as a whole, which averaged 11 catwalk shows per day, outstrips all other international fashion showings and attracts the biggest following.

★ Highest hairstyle
Ladies' hairstyles literally reached their high point in the 1770s. Queen Marie Antoinette's (France) hair was the tallest documented hairstyle. It stood at 36 in (91.44 cm) high in 1775, and was decorated with a mass of ribbons and feathers that made it even higher.

★ Fastest haircut
Trevor Mitchell (UK) cut a full head of hair in 1 min 13 sec on November 26 1999 at the Southampton City Guildhall, UK, as part of BBC TV South's 'Children in Need' appeal. The event was seen live on BBC TV.

★ Most valuable item of head wear
The Alaskan State Museum bought a native North American Tlingit Kiksadi ceremonial frog helmet dating from ca. 1600 for $66,000 at an auction in New York City, USA, in November 1981.

Highest box office gross on an opening day «

The Matrix Reloaded (USA, 2003) took a record $42.5 million

on its opening day in the USA on May 15 2003 from a total of 3,603 theaters. Keanu Reeves (USA, left) stars as Neo in the *Matrix* trilogy.

★ Fastest $100 million box office gross

Two films have surpassed the $100-million mark in three days. The first was *Spider-Man* (USA, 2002), which opened on May 3 2002 at 3,615 theaters, followed by *The Matrix Reloaded* (USA, 2003), which opened on May 5 2003 at 3,603 theaters.

★ Fastest $200 million box office gross

From its May 3 2002 opening, *Spider-Man* (USA, 2002) passed the $200-million mark in ten days, taking $223.04 million by May 12 and beating the previous record of 13 days set by *Star Wars: Episode 1 – The Phantom Menace* (USA, 1999).

★ Largest box office loss

MGM's *Cutthroat Island* (USA, 1995), starring Geena Davis and directed by her then-husband Renny Harlin (both USA), cost over $100 million to produce, promote, and distribute, and reportedly earned back just $11 million – 11% of the cost.

★ Highest box office gross

James Cameron's (USA) *Titanic* (USA, 1997) was the first film to take $1 billion at the international box office, and had a total box office gross of $1.835 billion.

★ Highest box office gross (inflation adjusted)

Rising theater ticket prices mean the all-time top-grossing movies are nearly all recent releases. Although *Gone With The Wind* (USA, 1939) took $393.4 million at the international box office, in an inflation-adjusted list it comes top with a total gross of $3,785 billion. In the USA alone, *Gone With The Wind* had 283.1 million admissions compared with 130.9 million for *Titanic*.

★ Most expensive film made

Paramount's *Titanic* (USA, 1997), which overran its budget during production, cost just over $200 million to make. Originally given a $125-million budget, it was due to have been released in July 1997, but postproduction problems set the date back to December 1997, a delay that added to the cost.

★ Largest pre-production budget for a film

The war epic *Pearl Harbor* (USA, 2001), which began shooting on April 3 2000, had a pre-production budget of $145 million. The eventual total cost was $152.75 million.

★ Least expensive feature film made

The total cost of production for the film *Die Alive* (Canada, 2000), produced and directed by Jean-François Leduc (Canada), was CAN$563.62 ($378.82). It premiered on July 26 2001 at the Fantasi Film Festival, Montrèal, Canada.

★ Most prolific film producer

Since 1963, D. Rama Naidu (India) has produced a total of 110 films during his career in Indian cinema.

★ Living actor with most screen credits

Actor Christopher Lee (UK) has the most screen credits of any actor alive today, with 211. He has performed in English, French, Canadian, German, Russian, Norwegian, Swedish, Italian, Pakistani, Spanish, Japanese, American, Australian, and New Zealand productions, from *Corridor of Mirrors* (UK, 1947) to *Graduation Day* (USA, 2003).

★ Actress with most leading film roles in a career

Kinuyo Tanaka (Japan) made her debut role in *Genroku Onna* (Japan, 1924) and performed in a total of 241 films including her final role in *Daichi no Komoriuta* (Japan, 1974).

★ Actor with most leading film roles in a career

John Wayne (USA, born Marion Michael Morrison) appeared in 153 movies from *The Drop Kick* (USA, 1927) to *The Shootist* (USA, 1976). In all but 11 of these he played the lead.

Family with most stars on the Hollywood Walk of Fame ⌃

When Drew Barrymore (USA, above) received her star on the Hollywood Walk of Fame on February 4 2004, she became the seventh member of her family to be so honored.

Stars had previously been awarded to her father John D. Barrymore, her great-uncle Lionel Barrymore, her great-aunt Ethel Barrymore, her grandparents John Barrymore and Dolores Costello, and her great-grandfather Maurice Costello.

Fastest $1 billion box office gross

The Lord of the Rings: The Return of the King (NZ/USA 2003), the final installment of the trilogy, took $1 billion

at the international box office in just nine weeks four days from its release on December 17 2003. It marks only the second film in history to break the billion-dollar barrier, the first being *Titanic* (USA, 1997), which took the same amount in 11 weeks. The film, starring Orlando Bloom (UK, right) as Legolas, had accumulated a worldwide total of $1,005,380,412 in ticket sales by February 23 2004.

»

★ Most film roles in a career
Tom London (USA) made the first of his 2,000-plus screen performances in *The Great Train Robbery* (USA, 1903) as the locomotive driver (his job in real life). By 1919, he had starring roles at Universal. His last role was in *The Lone Texan* (USA, 1959).

★ Most Hollywood film performances in the same role
William Boyd (USA) played the cowboy Hopalong Cassidy in Paramount's 66 *Hopalong* full-length features beginning with *Hopalong Cassidy* (USA, 1935) and ending with *Strange Gamble* (USA, 1948).

★ Most stars on the Hollywood Walk of Fame
Gene Autry (USA), the actor, composer, and songwriter, has five stars on the Hollywood Walk of Fame strip – numbers 6,384, 6,520, 6,644, 6,667, and 7,000 Hollywood Boulevard – awarded for Recording, Motion Pictures, Television, Radio, and Theater.

★ Youngest No.1 box office star
Shirley Temple (USA, b. April 23 1928) was seven years old when she became No.1 at the box office in 1935, holding the title until 1938.

★ Oldest No.1 box office star
Marie Dressler (Canada, 1868–1934) was 64 when she became the No.1 box office star in 1933. Born Leila von Koerber in 1869, she began her film career in 1914 and won the Best Actress Oscar for playing the part of Min Divot in *Min and Bill* (USA, 1930).

★ Highest annual earnings by an actor
The world's top-earning actor is currently Will Smith (USA), who earned an estimated $60 million in 2002, according to the 2003 *Forbes* Celebrity 100 list.

★ Highest annual earnings by an actress
The world's top-earning actress is currently Jennifer Aniston (USA), who earned an estimated $35 million in 2002, according to the 2003 *Forbes* Celebrity 100 list.

★ Actor in most films grossing over $100 million at the box office
Harrison Ford (USA) has starred in a total of 15 movies that have grossed over $100 million at the international box office. The highest grossing was *Star Wars* (1997) with $798 million. Ford also holds the record for highest box office gross for an actor: his 27 films to date have grossed $3,369,662,963.

★ Actress in most films grossing over $100 million at the box office
By February 2004, the actress Julia Roberts (USA) had starred in 11 movies that have grossed at least $100 million at the international box office. Her top-grossing film was *Pretty Woman* (USA, 1990), which took a total of $463.4 million. Roberts' movies have grossed a record for an actress of $2,516,318,527.

★ Highest-paid actor per film
Bruce Willis (USA) received a total of $100 million for playing the part of Dr. Malcolm Crowe in the $55-million film *The Sixth Sense* (USA, 1999) through a combination of his salary and a percentage of the film's receipts.

★ Highest annual earnings by a film producer
Producer-director Steven Spielberg (USA) topped the 2003 *Forbes* Celebrity 100 list, having earned an estimated $200 million during 2002.

⟱ Earliest feature-length talkie

Alan Crossland's (USA) *The Jazz Singer* (USA, 1927) premiered on Broadway on October 6 1927. Warner Bros. intended the sound to be confined to music and songs, but Al Jolson (near left with May McAvoy, both USA) ad-libbed some speech, which led to 354 words being spoken in all: 340 by Jolson; 13 by Eugenie Besserer (USA), who played his mother; and one ('Stop!') by Warner Oland (Sweden), who played his father.

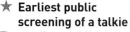

Largest annual ⟰ film output

India produces more feature-length films than any other country. A record 948 films were produced in 1990, and in 1994, 754 films were produced in a record 16 languages at India's three major centers of production – Mumbai (Bombay), Calcutta, and Madras.

★ Earliest public screening of a talkie

The earliest public presentation of sound on film was *The Arsonist* (Germany/USA, 1922), a short drama made using the Tri-Ergon process and shown at the Alhambra theater, Berlin, Germany, on September 17 1922. It starred Erwin Baron (USA), who played seven of the nine parts.

★ Oldest theater chain

The Wehrenberg Theatres chain first set up in 1906 with the opening of the Cherokee Theatre in St. Louis, Missouri, USA, by former blacksmith Fred Wehrenberg (USA). Still run by the Wehrenberg family today, it currently operates 15 theaters in the states of Missouri and Illinois.

★ Largest theater chain

Regal Entertainment Group, which includes Regal Cinemas, United Artists Theaters, and Edwards Theaters, operates 562 theaters with 6,119 screens (including two Imax screens) in 39 states of the USA.

★ First circular theater

The world's first circular theater is located in the European Park of the Moving Image at Futuroscope near Poitiers, France. It consists of nine projectors and nine screens covering a total surface area of 2,928 ft² (272 m²). The process enables the projection of nine electronically synchronized films offering a 360° field of vision.

★ Largest drive-in theater by screens

The Thunderbird Drive-in (also known as the Swap Shop Drive-in), Fort Lauderdale, Florida, USA, which opened with a single screen on November 22 1963, now has 13 screens of varying sizes, the largest (screen 9) being the original.

★ Largest drive-in theater screen ever

The Algiers Drive-in, Detroit, Michigan, USA, had a screen that measured 216 ft (65.8 m) wide and covered 4,800 ft² (445.9 m²). It first opened on August 15 1956 to show the western *The Searchers* (USA, 1956). The drive-in originally had a capacity of 1,200, which increased to 1,500 in 1977, but in 1985 the site was sold and is now a shopping center.

★ Smallest drive-in theater

Both the Harmony Drive-in of Harmony, Pennsylvania, USA, and the Highway 78 Drive-in of Bamberg, South Carolina, USA, could hold no more than 50 cars.

★ Largest permanent theater screen

The Panasonic IMAX Theatre at Darling Harbour, Sydney, Australia, holds the largest fixed projection screen in the world, measuring 117 x 97 ft (35.72 x 29.57 m). It opened in September 1996 and can seat 540 people.

★ Smallest purpose-built theater in operation

Cinema dei Piccoli was built by Alfredo Annibali (Italy) in 1934 in the park of Villa Borghese, Rome, Italy, and today covers an area of 769.83 ft² (71.52 m²). Originally called the Topolino Cinema (after the Italian name for Mickey Mouse), the theater used a Pathé-Baby 9.5-mm projector and bed sheets for the screen, and played 78 rpm records for background music. Restored in 1991, the cinema has 63 seats, a 16-ft 4.8-in x 8-ft 2.4-in (5 x 2.5-m) screen, stereo sound, and air-conditioning.

★ Smallest theater by seat capacity

Converted from an old workshop, the smallest theater in the world to operate as a regular commercial venture is The Screen Room on Broad Street, Nottingham, UK, which has 21 seats. The theater, owned by Steven Metcalf (UK), opened on September 27 2002 with the film *Lost in La Mancha* (USA/UK, 2002).

Widest film release in a single country ⌃

X2 (USA, 2003) was given the widest film release of any film in history when it opened in the USA at 3,741 theaters on May 2 2003. Showing on 7,316 screens, it took $85.6 million during the opening weekend, an average of $22,871 per theater. Famke Jannsen (Netherlands) and Halle Berry (USA, both above) were two of the movie's stars.

★ **Largest audience to attend a film premiere**
A total of 23,930 people attended the premiere of *Brewster McCloud* (USA, 1970) at the Houston Astrodome, Texas, USA, on December 5 1970. Paying from $2.50 to $50 (then per seat, the audience watched the film from a special 70-mm print made for the premiere at a cost of $12,000, which was projected onto a 156 x 60-ft (47.54 x 18.28-m) screen.

★ **Longest red carpet at a film premiere**
For the premiere of *Pirates of the Caribbean: Curse of the Black Pearl* (USA, 2003), held at Disneyland, Anaheim, California, USA, on June 28 2003, a red carpet stretched 900 ft (274 m) from Disneyland's entrance along Main Street USA to the Rivers of America in Frontierland.

★ **Longest nonstop theater show**
A total of 136 feature films were shown consecutively during a 250-hour marathon at the 100 Years of Cinema Festival, Montreal, Canada, from June 11 to 22 1992.

★ **Movie watching marathon**
An audience of 11 people – Erik Acosta, Dina Agrapides, Eric Bailey, Kim Binal, Wayne Diana, Mark Huang, Cheryl Jones, Daniel Koenig, Ron Mathewson, Allan Press, and Nathan Snook – watched 34 films for 66 hr 30 min at an event organized by online DVD rental company Netflix.com at the Times Square Studios, New York City, USA, from December 5 to 8 2003.

★ **Longest film documentary**
Grandmother Martha (1996), a documentary about the life of ex-actress and entertainer Martha Stelloo (Netherlands), runs for 24 hr 12 min. The film was written, produced, and directed by Sydney Ling (Netherlands).

★ **Widest theater screen**
A temporary screen was used at the 1937 Paris Exposition to show Henri Chrétien's (France) hypergonar films, which were the precursor of cinerama. The concave screen had a width of 297 ft (90.5 m) and was 33 ft (9.9 m) high.

★ **Country with the most theaters per capita**
Belarus has more theaters per capita than any other country in the world, with one theater for every 2,734 inhabitants. In all, the country has 3,780 theaters for its population of 10,335,382.

★ **Highest annual theater attendance**
The largest theater audience ever in one year was 4.49 billion admissions, achieved in the USA in 1929.

★ **Highest annual theater attendance per capita**
With a population of 279,384 and a total of 1,531,000 admissions at 46 theaters in 2003, Iceland has a greater theater attendance per capita than any other country. This figure translates as 5,480 visits per 1,000 people per year.

★ **Lowest annual theater attendance per capita**
Malaysia has a population of 22,662,365 and had a total of 336,000 theater admissions in 2003. This figure translates as 14.83 visits per 1,000 people per year.

★ **Longest first run of a film in one theater**
Romance in Lushan (China, 1980) first opened at the Jiangxi Movie Circulation and Screening Company, Lushan, China, on July 12 1980 and has been shown four times a day since then. As of December 8 2001, the film had been seen by 1,336,638 patrons.

« Most Oscars won by a film

At the 2004 American Academy Awards ceremony held on

February 29 2004, the third installment of the *The Lord of the Rings* trilogy, *The Return of the King* (NZ/USA, 2003), won all 11 of its nominations. The film, directed by Peter Jackson, walked away with Best Picture, Best Director, Art Direction, Costume Design, Visual Effects, Sound, Editing, Makeup, Screenplay Based on Material Previously Produced or Published, Original Score, and Original Song. Pictured from left to right are Frances Walsh, Peter Jackson, and Philippa Boyens (all New Zealand) picking up their Oscars for Best Screenplay.

The Return of the King shares this record of 11 Oscar wins with two other films. The first to achieve the record was *Ben-Hur* (USA, 1959), which won 11 Oscars from 12 nominations on April 4 1960, followed by *Titanic* (USA, 1997) from 14 nominations on March 23 1998.

★ Longest Oscar-winning career

Katharine Hepburn (USA) had the distinction of having the longest Oscar award-winning career, spanning 48 years 13 days from her first Oscar for *Morning Glory* (USA, 1932) on March 16 1934 to her last for *On Golden Pond* (USA, 1981) on March 29 1982.

★ Most Oscars for acting won by a film

Both *A Streetcar Named Desire* (USA, 1951) and *Network* (USA, 1976) won three acting Oscars, in 1952 and 1977 respectively. No film has yet won all four acting Oscars.

★ Most Best Actor wins

Seven actors have won Best Actor awards twice: Spencer Tracy (USA) for *Captains Courageous* (USA, 1937) and *Boys Town* (USA 1938); Fredric March (USA) for *Dr. Jekyll and Mr. Hyde* (USA, 1932) and *The Best Years of Our Lives* (USA, 1946); Gary Cooper (USA) for *Sergeant York* (USA, 1941) and *High Noon* (USA, 1952); Marlon Brando (USA) for *On the Waterfront* (USA, 1954) and *The Godfather* (USA, 1972); Jack Nicholson (USA) for *One Flew Over the Cuckoo's Nest* (USA, 1975) and *As Good As It Gets* (USA, 1997); Dustin Hoffman (USA) for *Kramer vs. Kramer* (USA, 1979) and *Rain Man* (USA, 1988); and Tom Hanks (USA) for *Philadelphia* (USA, 1993) and *Forrest Gump* (USA, 1994).

★ Most Best Actor nominations for the same film

On March 5 1936, Clark Gable (USA), Charles Laughton (UK), and Franchot Tone (USA) were all nominated for Best Actor for their performances in *Mutiny on the Bounty* (USA, 1935). The winner was the fourth nominee, Victor McLaglen (UK), for *The Informer* (USA, 1935).

★ Most Best Actress nominations in the same year

At the 1929/30 Academy Awards held on November 5 1930, of the five actresses nominated for Best Actress in a Leading Role, two were nominated twice: Greta Garbo (Sweden) for *Anna Christie* (USA, 1930) and *Romance* (USA, 1930) and Norma Shearer (Canada) for *Their Own Desire* (USA, 1929) and *The Divorcee* (USA, 1930).

★ Oldest Best Actor winner

Henry Fonda (USA, 1905–82) won the Best Actor Oscar on March 29 1982 for his performance as Norman Thayer Jr. in *On Golden Pond* (USA, 1981) aged 75 years 317 days.

★ Oldest Best Actress winner

Jessica Tandy (UK, 1909–94) won the Best Actress Oscar for *Driving Miss Daisy* (USA, 1989) on March 29 1990 at the age of 80 years 295 days.

★ Oldest Best Supporting Actor winner

The oldest recipient of the Best Supporting Actor award is George Burns (USA, 1896–1996) for his role as Al Lewis in *The Sunshine Boys* (USA, 1975) on March 29 1976, when he was aged 80 years 68 days.

★ Most Best Director wins

John Ford (USA) won an Oscar for Best Director on four occasions: for *The Informer* (USA, 1936), *The Grapes of Wrath* (USA, 1940), *How Green Was My Valley* (USA, 1941), and *The Quiet Man* (USA, 1952).

★ Oldest actress nominated for an Oscar

Eva LeGallienne (UK, 1899–1991) was aged 82 years 80 days when she was nominated for the Best Supporting Actress Oscar for her role as Grandma Pearl in *Resurrection* (USA, 1980) for the ceremony held on March 31 1981.

★ Oldest actor nominated for an Oscar

Richard Farnsworth (USA, 1920–2000) was aged 79 years 207 days when the Academy nominated him Best Actor for his role as Alvin Straight in *The Straight Story* (USA, 1999) at the ceremony held on March 26 2000.

GWR TALKS TO
Keisha Castle-Hughes

Keisha Castle-Hughes (New Zealand) was 13 years 309 days old when she was nominated for Best Actress on January 27 2004 for her role of Paikea 'Pai' Apirana in *Whale Rider* (NZ/Germany, 2002). She is the youngest person to receive a Best Actress nomination.

How did you get into acting – was it something you always wanted to do?
Yes. However, I didn't think it would happen quite so soon! I hadn't done anything prior to this, not even a school play! A casting director, Diana Rowan, came to my school and asked me to come to a series of workshops and auditions. It went from there.

What aspects of your acting experience have you enjoyed?
We were about halfway through shooting when it suddenly dawned on me that I was really going to be in a film – that I was actually living my dream! The director, Niki Caro, was great to work with. She helped me so much, especially to understand Pai.

I've also traveled extensively for publicity and promotion – to Canada, the USA, Australia, the UK and Japan, and I'll also visit Greece, Spain and China.

What's your favorite movie to watch?
Typically teen – I love *Bring it On*.

Who are your favorite movie stars?
Julia Roberts and Johnny Depp.

What's it like being famous suddenly?
I haven't let this experience change my life too much. I just like to do normal kid stuff. I hang out with my friends. We talk about fashion, boys, music, clothes, and just general 'girl stuff'. School is also very important to me. It's always good to get back into it, but I find I really need to be focused.

Do you get recognized when you are out?
I do. I remember thinking about that before the film came out, wondering what it would be like with people staring at you. It's like I thought it would be – weird!

How does it feel to have a Guinness World Record?
Incredible! Especially since this was my first acting job!

What advice would you give to anyone who wants to go into acting?
If it's what you want to do, go for it! Be sure you have a clear goal in mind and be prepared to work hard. There's a lot of work involved right thoughout the whole acting experience.

★ Oldest recipient of an Oscar by a performer
Groucho Marx (USA, 1890–1977) received an Honorary Award in recognition of his brilliant creativity and for the unequaled achievements of the Marx Brothers in the art of motion picture comedy, on April 2 1974 aged 83 years 182 days.

★ Youngest Oscar winner
The youngest Oscar winner is Tatum O'Neal (USA, b. November 5 1963), who was 10 years 148 days old when she received the Best Supporting Actress award for *Paper Moon* (USA, 1973) on April 2 1974.

Shirley Temple was awarded an Honorary Oscar at the age of 6 years 310 days for her achievements in 1934.

★ Most wins for acting and writing
Emma Thompson (UK) won Best Actress in 1993 for her role in *Howards End* (UK/Japan, 1992) and was awarded Best Screenplay Based on Material from Another Medium for *Sense and Sensibility* (USA/UK, 1995) in 1996, making her the first person ever to win Oscars for both acting and writing.

★ Most Oscar-winning generations
The only family to contain three generations of Oscar winners are the Hustons (all USA). Walter Huston (1884–1950) won Best Supporting Actor for *The Treasure of the Sierra Madre* (USA, 1948). His son John (1906–87) won Best Director for the same film and John's daughter Angelica (b. July 8 1951) won Best Supporting Actress for *Prizzi's Honor* (USA, 1985).

★ Most ceremonies presented
Bob Hope (USA) served as master of ceremonies on Oscar night a total of 16 times (alone and in conjunction with others), participating in a record 27 Academy Awards presentations.

★ Longest speech
After receiving the Best Actress award for her title role in *Mrs. Miniver* (USA, 1942) at the 1942 Academy Awards held on March 4 1943, Greer Garson (UK) made a speech that lasted 5 min 30 sec.

★ Most people thanked by an Oscar winner
On March 13 1947, Olivia de Havilland (UK/USA; b. Japan) won Best Actress as Josephine Norris in *To Each His Own* (USA, 1946). In her speech she thanked 27 people by name.

★ Longest ceremony
The 71st Academy Awards ceremony, hosted by Whoopi Goldberg (USA) and broadcast by the ABC network, lasted 4 hr 2 min on March 21 1999.

Most Oscar nominations

Title	Name	Nominated	Won
Actor	Jack Nicholson (USA)	12	2
Actress	Meryl Streep (USA)	13	2
Director	William Wyler (USA)	12	3
Consecutively	Walt Disney (USA)	9	1
Ever	Walt Disney (USA)	64	26
Best Foreign Language Film	France	34	12
Foreign Language Film	*Crouching Tiger, Hidden Dragon* (Taipei, 2000)	10	4
Living person	John Williams (USA)	40	5
Before winning	Randy Newman (USA)	16	1
Without winning	Roland Anderson (USA)	15	0
Without winning (actor)	Richard Burton (UK)	7	0
	*Peter O'Toole (UK)	7	0
Without winning (film)	*The Turning Point* (USA, 1977)	11	0
	The Color Purple (USA, 1986)	11	0
One role	Barry Fitzgerald (Ireland)	2	1

* In 2003 he was finally acknowledged with an Honorary Award.

Movie production
Art & media

★ GWR TALKS TO
Vic Armstrong

In a career spanning five decades, Vic Armstrong (UK) has been a stuntman and stunt coordinator in more than 250 films, including the Indiana Jones trilogy. He has also doubled for every actor to have played the title role in the James Bond series. He currently holds the record for the most prolific movie stuntman.

Have you ever been badly injured?
I've had my share of injuries – it goes with the territory, as they say. I've broken a leg, shoulder, ribs, nose, arm, collarbone, etc., but even Michael Schumacher crashes his Formula One car occasionally and he is the best in the world at what he does.

Most edited single ⌃⌃ sequence in a movie

For the chariot race scene in *Ben-Hur* (USA, 1925, above), editor Lloyd Nosler (USA) had to compress 200,000 ft (60,960 m) of film into a sparse 750 ft (228.6 m). With a ratio of 267:1, it is the most edited scene in cinema history.

How old were you when you started your career?
I got into stunt work when I was 17 years old by lending a stuntman a horse for the movie *Arabesque* (USA, 1966) with Gregory Peck (USA) and Sophia Loren (Italy). I was then asked to go and ride the horse as there was a big sequence involving lots of big jumps and from that day on all I did was stunt work.

Which film did you enjoy working on the most?
My favorite would have to be *Raiders of the Lost Ark* (USA,1980) – I'm second from left, above – but I also have a soft spot for all the James Bond films I've worked on.

What's the scariest stunt you've been involved with?
All stunts are scary, but one of the scariest was a 100-ft (30-m) fall I did on *The Final Conflict* (UK/USA, 1981).

What advice would you give?
You need to achieve a skill that will make you better than the average person. Mine was riding horses, which came from my days as an amateur steeplechase rider. Then you have to stay cool, calm, and collected and analyze each situation to make sure it's safe and within your capabilities.

How do you feel about your Guinness World Record?
I'm very proud: it's a great accolade for me and rates right alongside my Oscar and my BAFTA. I used to read the book when I was a lad: I *never* thought I'd get into it.

What's your favorite Guinness World Record?
I'd go for Tony McCoy (UK), who rode the most steeplechase winners ever. As I started off in life dreaming of doing this, I can really relate to his amazing achievement.

★ **Largest film studio**
The largest film studio complex is at Universal City, Los Angeles, California, USA. The site, called the Back Lot, opened in 1915 and comprises 561 buildings and 34 soundstages totaling 420 acres (170 hectares). Recent films made there by Universal Pictures include *Hulk* (USA, 2003) and *Thunderbirds* (USA, 2004).

★ **Largest indoor film set**
The UFO landing site built for the climax of Steven Spielberg's *Close Encounters of the Third Kind* (USA, 1977) measured 90 x 450 x 250 ft (27 x 137 x 76 m). Constructed in a 10 million-ft^3 (283,000-m^3) dirigible hangar at Mobile, Alabama, USA, the building had six times the capacity of the largest soundstage in Hollywood.

★ **Largest production crew for a feature film**
The largest number of craftspeople and technicians employed on a dramatic feature was 532 for the World War I flying story *Sky Bandits*

(UK title *Gunbus*; UK, 1986), directed by Zoran Perisic (Yugoslavia) with a cast that included Nicholas Lyndhurst and Adrian Dunbar (both UK).

★ **Largest annual film output by a Hollywood studio**
The highest output of any Hollywood studio was 101 features made by Paramount in 1921. The highest of the sound era was 68, jointly held by Paramount in 1936 and Warner Bros. in 1937.

★ **Largest land-based prop**
The 60-ft-long (18-m), 40-ft-high (12-m) wooden horse of Troy used in Robert Wise's *Helen of Troy* (USA/Italy, 1954) weighed 179,191 lb (81,280 kg). It took 30 trees and over 1,000 lb (453 kg) of nails to build it.

★ **Most retakes for one scene with dialogue**
It was claimed that Stanley Kubrick (USA) demanded 127 retakes for a scene with Shelley Duval (USA) in *The Shining* (USA, 1980).

Largest frame format used in film »

Imax (right) uses 70-mm film, three times larger than the standard 35-mm film usually used.

With a dimension of 1.96 x 2.74 in (5 x 7 cm), the film has 15 perforations per frame as opposed to the standard five.

★ **Longest take in a commercially made film**
In *A Free Soul* (USA, 1931), there is a 14-minute uninterrupted monologue by Lionel Barrymore (USA). Since a reel of camera film only lasts ten minutes, the take was achieved by using more than one camera.

Alfred Hitchcock's (UK) *Rope* (USA, 1948) was shot in eight ten-minute takes (apart from one cut to the housekeeper in the first reel). The effect was of one continuous shot, since the action of the story occupied the same time period – 80 minutes – as the length of film.

★ **Longest film shot on a single camera**
Russkij Kovcheg (*Russian Ark*; Russia, 2002), directed by Aleksandr Sokurov (Russia), was the first uncompressed high-definition film. It was shot on a single camera for 90 minutes on December 23 2001. The final film was shown without any cuts or edits on May 22 2002 at the Cannes Film Festival,

France, with a running time of 96 minutes (including title sequence and credits).

★ **Longest monologue in a dramatic film**
In *L'Aigle à Deux Têtes* (*The Eagle has Two Heads*, France, 1948) written and directed by Jean Cocteau (France), a 20-minute speech was made by the character Natasha, played by Edwige Feuillère (France).

★ **Most extensive screen test**
To find the actress to play Scarlett O'Hara in *Gone with the Wind* (USA, 1939), MGM shot 149,000 ft (45,415 m) of black-and-white test film and another 13,000 ft (3,962 m) of color with 60 actresses, none of whom got the part.

★ **Most extensive digital character on film**
Created by WETA Digital, the computer-generated character Gollum in *The Lord of the Rings: The Two Towers* (NZ/USA, 2002) had 250 facial expressions and 300 moving muscles. Gollum's body

movements were based on those of actor Andy Serkis (UK), who filmed every scene in which Gollum appears wearing a unitard body stocking to facilitate the later addition of computer-generated images (CGIs).

★ **Longest video documentary about an individual**
A documentary on Elvis Presley (USA) called *The Definitive Elvis Collection* produced by Passport International Productions (USA) is 13 hr 52 min long (including titles). It features over 200 interviews with Elvis's friends, family, fans, and co-stars. Production began in January 2000 and it was released on DVD/VHS on July 16 2002.

★ **Longest running film series**
Over 46 years, 103 features were made about the 19th-century martial arts hero Huang Fei-Hong, starting with *The True Story of Huang Fei-Hong* (Hong Kong, 1949)

and continuing to the latest production, *Once Upon a Time in China 5* (Hong Kong, 1995).

★ **Longest film ever made**
The Cure for Insomnia (USA, 1987), directed by John Henry Timmis IV, is 85 hours long. It premiered in its entirety at the School of the Art Institute of Chicago, Illinois, USA, from January 31 to February 3 1987.

★ **Most valuable film costume**
A blue and white gingham dress worn by Judy Garland (USA) as Dorothy in the MGM film *The Wizard of Oz* (USA, 1939) was sold at Christie's, London, UK, on December 9 1999 for £199,500 (then $324,068).

★ **Shortest stuntman**
Measured on October 20 2003, stuntman Kiran Shah (UK) stands 4 ft 1.7 in (1.263 m) tall. He has performed stunts in 31 movies including being perspective stunt-double for Elijah Wood (USA) in *The Lord of the Rings* trilogy (NZ/USA, 2001–2003).

Animation
Art & media

Longest stop-motion » feature film

Chicken Run (UK, 2000), directed by Peter Lord and Nick Park

(both UK), was released with a running time of 82 minutes and has 118,080 shots filmed using the 'stop-motion' special-effects technique. (A normal live-action feature has between 500 and 1,000 shots.)

Chicken Run also holds the record for the most plasticine used in a feature film. Animators used 5,240 lb (2,380 kg) of plasticine during filming.

★ **Largest budget for an animation**
Walt Disney's *Tarzan* (USA, 1999), first released on June 17 1999, was made with a budget of $150 million. It was the first film to use the 'deep canvas' technique, which allows 2-D hand-drawn characters to exist in a 3-D environment.

★ **Most successful virtual band**
The most successful virtual band is the Gorillaz (UK), with global album sales of 3 million for their eponymous debut, including 1.3 million in the USA and certified sales of 600,000 in the UK. The release peaked at No. 3 on the UK album chart, went top 20 in the USA, and was No.1 on the Eurochart. The animated fourpiece were nominated for six BRIT awards and one Grammy in 2001.

★ **Highest box office gross for an animation**
Walt Disney's *The Lion King* (USA, 1994) took $777.9 million at the box office. The film

starred the voices of Rowan Atkinson (UK) as Zazu the hornbill, Jeremy Irons (UK) as Simba's uncle Scar, and Whoopi Goldberg (USA) as Shenzi the hyena.

★ **Highest box office gross for an animation (inflation adjusted)**
Walt Disney's first full-length feature film, *Snow White and the Seven Dwarfs* (USA, 1937), took $184.9 million at the box office worldwide – equivalent to $1,633,582,523 today.

★ **Fastest $100 million box office gross for an animation**
Finding Nemo (USA, 2003), the computer-animated film from Walt Disney and Pixar Animation Studios, cost $94 million to make and reached the $100 million mark

at the US box office in eight days from its release on May 30 2003 at 3,374 theaters.

★ **Most expensive computer-animated film**
Monsters, Inc. (USA, 2001), from Walt Disney and Pixar Animation Studios, had a budget of $115 million.

★ **Earliest animal cartoon**
Old Doc Yak, a tailcoated billy goat in striped pants, was brought to the screen by *Chicago Tribune* cartoonist Sidney Smith (USA) in a Selig Polyscope series started in July 1913. It was Smith's much-loved animal cartoon characters who gave animated films a distinct appeal of their own as suitable entertainment for children.

★ **First feature color cartoon**
The earliest full-length color cartoon talkie was Argentina's *Peludópolis*, made in 1931 by Quirino Cristiani (Argentina).

★ **Earliest color cartoon series**
The Red Head Comedies (USA, 1923), each a satire of an historical event by the Lee-Bradford Corporation, was the very first cartoon series.

★ **First full-length cartoon**
The earliest full-length feature cartoon was *El Apóstol* (Argentina, 1917), written and directed by Federico Valle (Argentina), with a running time of 70 minutes. Compiled from 58,000 drawings, it took 12 months to finish.

★ **Earliest cartoon talkie release**
Dave and Max Fleischer's (both Austria) *Come Take a Trip in my Airship* (USA, 1924) opened with the animated figure of a woman in a white dress chattering as the lead-in to the song.

★ **First all-talking cartoon**
On September 1 1928, Paul Terry's (USA) *Dinner Time* (USA, 1928) was premiered at the Mark Strand Theatre, New York, USA.

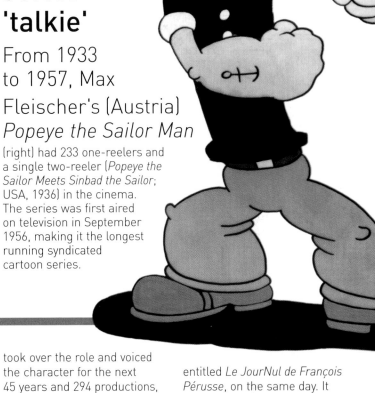

Longest ›› cartoon series 'talkie'

From 1933 to 1957, Max Fleischer's (Austria) *Popeye the Sailor Man* (right) had 233 one-reelers and a single two-reeler (*Popeye the Sailor Meets Sinbad the Sailor*; USA, 1936) in the cinema. The series was first aired on television in September 1956, making it the longest running syndicated cartoon series.

Highest box office ⌃ gross for an animation on an opening weekend

Finding Nemo (USA, 2003, above) directed by Andrew Stanton and Lee Unkrich (both USA) opened in the USA on May 30 2003 to take $70,251,710 at the box office from 3,374 theaters. The tale of a father fish trying to find his son features the voices of Albert Brooks, Ellen DeGeneres, and Willem Dafoe (all USA).

★ Cartoon character most often portrayed on screen

Zorro, created by Johnston McCulley (USA), has been portrayed in a record 69 films. He was also the first comic-strip character to be the subject of a major feature film, *The Mark of Zorro* (USA, 1920).

★ Most valuable cartoon poster

A film poster for a Walt Disney film short, *Alice's Day At Sea* (USA, 1924), depicting Alice astride a fish above the waves, was sold at Christie's, London, UK, in April 1994 for £23,100 (then $34,072).

★ Earliest cartoon merchandise

Pat Sullivan's (USA) Felix the Cat, who appeared in 1919 as the animal that 'kept on walking,' was not only the first cartoon character

to attain the celebrity of a human star, but was, in 1924, also the first to be an image on packaging. Felix was then merchandized as a phenomenally successful cuddly toy two years later.

★ Most characters voiced by one artist in a TV cartoon series

Kara Tritton (UK) voiced 198 cartoon characters for 75 episodes over six series of *Blues Clues* (Nick Jr., UK). Kara gave voices to furniture (Postbox, Paper Recycling Bin), food (Mr. Salt and Mrs. Pepper), animals (Owl, Hippo), ghosts, planets, and people.

★ Longest working career for a cartoon voice-over

For the first few weeks, the original film series *Popeye* was voiced by William Costello (USA). Then in 1934, for the film *Let You and Him Fight*, Jack Mercer (USA)

took over the role and voiced the character for the next 45 years and 294 productions, including the TV cartoons.

★ Most valuable color animation cell

One of the 150,000 color cells (a clear plastic sheet onto which animation drawings are traced and then hand painted) from Walt Disney's *Snow White and the Seven Dwarfs* (USA, 1937) was sold by art dealer Guthrie Courvoisier (USA) in 1991 for $222,525.

★ Most valuable black-and-white animation cell

On May 16 1989, a black-and-white drawing from Walt Disney's *The Orphan's Benefit* (USA, 1934), depicting Donald Duck being punched by an orphan, raised $286,000 at Christie's, New York, USA.

★ Fastest script-to-screen animation production

KliK Animation in Montreal, Canada, produced and aired a topical one-minute animation,

entitled *Le JourNul de François Pérusse*, on the same day. It premiered on February 8 1999 after the 6 pm news on the Canadian TVA network.

★ Longest full-length film made without a camera

Frame by frame, artist José Antonio Sistiaga (Spain) painted his 75-minute animated one-man production, *Scope, Color, Muda* (Spain, 1970) directly on to the film stock. It took him 17 months from 1968 to 1970 to complete.

★ Most Emmy awards won for an animated TV series

By September 2003, *The Simpsons* (FOX, USA) had won a total of 20 Emmy awards: eight for Outstanding Animated Program (one hour or less) in 1990, 1991, 1995, 1997, 1998, 2000, 2001, and 2003; 10 for Outstanding Voice-Over Performance in 1992 (six), 1993, 1998, 2001, and 2003; and two for Outstanding Music and Lyrics in 1997 and 1998.

Oldest magic society

Houdini (Hungary/USA, above) was one of the most famous illusionists in history. Nicknamed the King of Handcuffs, he was especially well known as an escape artist. Apart from inventing and performing illusions, he owned a share in the famous Martinka's magic shop in New York City, USA, and he was president of the Society of American Magicians from 1917 until his death in 1926. This is the oldest magic society in the world and was founded in Martinka's on May 10 1902 with only 24 members.

Highest annual earnings by a magician

David Copperfield (USA, above) had the highest annual earnings of any magician in 2002 with $55 million according to the 2003 *Forbes* Celebrity 100 list. The star of TV shows for both ABC and CBS, Copperfield has performed illusions such as making a jet plane disappear and walking through the Great Wall of China.

★ Highest viewing figures for a TV magic show
Magician Doug Henning (Canada) attracted more than 50 million viewers for the first of his eight *World of Magic* one-hour television specials. The show, directed by Walter C. Miller (USA), was first transmitted live on NBC in the USA on December 26 1975, guest starring Gene Kelly (USA). Henning performed spellbinding illusions including a re-creation of Harry Houdini's famous water torture cell, as well as close-up magic.

★ Longest running TV magic show
Dick 'Mr. Magic' Williams (USA) hosted 1,200 programs of WMC-TV's *Magicland*, a weekly half-hour magic show that was on air for 23 years from January 1966 to January 1989.

★ Largest illusion ever staged
The largest illusion ever staged was presented by David Copperfield (USA), who created the illusion of vanishing the Statue of Liberty in New York, USA, on his fifth television special, *The Magic of David Copperfield*, aired on CBS in 1983. The illusion was invented by Jim Steinmeyer and constructed by John Gaughan (both USA).

★ Most copied stage illusion
Invented by Robert Harbin (South Africa) in 1965, the Zig Zag Girl is the most popularly performed stage illusion in the world. A girl, standing in an upright cabinet, is apparently cut into three pieces and has the middle of her body pulled to one side. It was copied so quickly that Harbin published a highly priced book in 1970 (limited to 500 copies) that allowed each purchaser to build one version of the prop. It is estimated that at least 15,000 Zig Zag illusions have been built to date, meaning that 14,500 are unauthorized copies.

★ Most escapes from handcuffs
Nick Janson (UK) has escaped from handcuffs locked on him by more than 1,760 different police officers around the world since 1954.

★ Lowest Death Dive escape
In 1997, Australian Robert Gallup was leg-manacled, handcuffed, chained, put into a secured mailbag, and then locked in a cage with a 8-ft^2 (0.74-m^2) floor area before being thrown out of a C-123 transport plane at 18,000 ft (5,485 m) above the Mojave Desert, California, USA. With less than a minute before impact and traveling at 150 mph (240 km/h), he escaped from the sack and cage to reach his parachute secured on the outside of the cage and deployed it with enough altitude to land safely.

★ Fastest transformation illusion
Internationally renowned illusionists The Pendragons (both USA) present Houdini's metamorphosis illusion at a speed that would have fooled its inventor. Jonathan Pendragon is locked in a trunk on top of which his wife Charlotte stands. She conceals herself behind a curtain which drops after just 0.25 seconds to reveal her transformation into her husband. She, of course, is now locked in the trunk.

★ Largest magic society
Founded in 1968 in New York, USA, The International Magicians' Society boasts 37,000 members worldwide, including, among others, David Copperfield (USA).

Most expensive magic show ever staged »

Siegfried and Roy at the Mirage, Las Vegas, Nevada, USA, starring the German illusionists Siegfried Fischbacher (near right) and Roy Horn (far right), cost over $28 million to stage when it opened on February 1 1990. The show, which featured dozens of wild animals, including an elephant and a giant fire-breathing mechanical dragon, and a cast of 60, closed after its 5,750th performance on October 3 2003 after Roy was seriously injured by a white tiger called Montacore.

★ **Earliest presentation of 'sawing' a woman in half**
The first illusionist to seemingly saw a woman in half was its inventor Percy Selbit (UK, b. Percy Tibbles) on January 17 1921 at the Finsbury Park Empire, London, UK.

★ **Most living creatures produced during a magic performance**
Penn & Teller (USA) produced more than 80,000 bees during their television special *Don't Try This At Home* filmed in 1990. In their British TV version of the routine, the bees were replaced with a safer alternative – bluebottle flies.

★ **Longest running theater of magic**
John Nevil Maskelyne and George Cooke (both UK) founded, produced, and starred in the Maskelyne & Cooke magic theater at the Egyptian Hall, Piccadilly, London, UK, from May 26 1873 to December 10 1904. Maskelyne and business partner David Devant (UK) moved the business to St. George's

Hall, Langham Place, London, UK, on January 2 1905 where the daily shows were regularly continued by three generations of the Maskelyne family until October 14 1933 – a span of more than 60 years.

★ **Longest magic show**
Dr. A. Alexander (India) performed his magic show for 24 hours on February 27–28 2004 at Renew 2000 Community Centre, St. Antony's Church Complex, Palakkarai, Tiruchirappalli, India, making it the longest by an individual before a paying audience.

★ **Most magical effects in a stage play**
Directed and adapted by Ken Hill (UK), *The Invisible Man*, which opened in the West End at the Vaudeville Theatre, London, UK, on February 20 1993, featured a total of 53 different magic effects and illusions.

★ **Youngest magician**
The Yamagami Brothers (both Japan, Yoshinosuke b. August 11 1994 and

Akinoshin b. December 1 1995) are the youngest professional illusion artists. Their debut appearance was on April 17 2001 when they were aged 6 years 229 days and 5 years 128 days respectively.

★ **Most non-magicians taught to present a trick in a single location**
Magician Luis de Matos (Portugal) taught 52,000 people a simple method to apparently vanish 52,001 silk handkerchiefs simultaneously at the Estádio do Dragão soccer stadium, Porto, Portugal. The effect (not the lesson) was shown live on RTP television on November 16 2003.

★ **Oldest magic shop**
The world's oldest family-run magic business is Davenports, founded in 1898 by Lewis Davenport (UK) who opened his shop on London's Ryles Road in 1903 and another on Mile End Road in 1908. The business was inherited by his son George in 1926 and is now

run by his granddaughter Betty, who took over in 1961. The shop moved to its current location in The Strand in 1984.

★ **Largest magic convention**
The Blackpool Magicians' Club convention is held annually at the Opera House and Winter Gardens, Blackpool, Lancashire, UK, on the last weekend in February. First held in 1952, it attracts over 3,000 people from around the world.

★ **Oldest weekly magic magazine**
Abracadabra, first edited by Goodliffe (UK), was first published on February 2 1946 in Birmingham, UK. Currently edited by Donald Bevan (UK), issue 3,029 was published on February 19 2004.

★ **Highest selling magic magazine**
First published in September 1991, *MAGIC: The Magazine for Magicians* is published monthly by Stagewrite Publishing, Inc., Las Vegas, USA, with an international circulation of 9,691.

Greatest comic-reading nation ⌃

In Japan, manga comics (above) represent 40% of all printed material sold. Thirteen weekly magazines by the largest publishers, together with 10 biweeklies and about 20 monthlies, represent the core of this industry. Throughout the 1990s, yearly sales of manga reached an average of 600 billion yen ($5.5 billion), with roughly 60% spent on magazines and 40% on paperbacks. At any given time, at least 10 of these magazines reach sales of 1 million or more copies per issue. People of all ages read manga yet currently much of the market is targeted at adults.

Largest first-edition print run ⌃

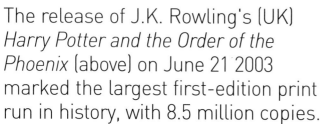

The release of J.K. Rowling's (UK) *Harry Potter and the Order of the Phoenix* (above) on June 21 2003 marked the largest first-edition print run in history, with 8.5 million copies.

★ All-time best-selling book
Excluding noncopyright works such as the Bible and the Koran, the world's all-time best-selling book is *Guinness World Records* (formerly *The Guinness Book of Records*). Since it was first published in October 1955, global sales in some 37 languages have exceeded 100 million (by October 2003).

★ Fastest selling fiction book
Released on July 8 2000, the 3.8 million initial print run of *Harry Potter and the Goblet of Fire*, J.K. Rowling's (UK) fourth Harry Potter book, is the fastest selling book in history. The book broke all sales records with an

estimated 3 million copies sold after just 48 hours. (There are currently 27.6 million copies of the first three Harry Potter books in print.)

★ Longest running comic
Since its first edition was published on December 4 1937, *The Dandy* has been published continuously by DC Thomson & Co. of Dundee, UK. The weekly comic's best known character is Desperate Dan, an unshaven cowboy from a town called Cactusville, whose favorite food is cow pie.

★ Best-selling cookbook
Betty Crocker's Quick and Easy Cookbook is the best-selling cookbook of all time with

50 million copies sold since 1950. Betty Crocker of General Mills is one of the most successful corporate trademarks of all time – the name appears on more than 130 General Mills products, sales of which amount to over $500 million a year.

★ Longest novel
Published in 2003, *Knickers* by Simon Roberts (UK) contains a total of 14,156,074 characters (each letter counts as one character and spaces are also counted as one character each).

★ Longest poem ever published
The lengthiest poem ever published is the Kirghiz folk epic *Manas*, which appeared in printed form in 1958 but which has never been translated into English. According to the *Dictionary of Oriental Literatures*, this three-part epic runs to about 500,000 lines. Translated excerpts appear in *The Elek Book of Oriental Verse*.

★ Most widely read catalog
The IKEA catalog of Swedish flat-packed furniture is the world's most widely read catalog, with 130 million copies printed every year. It is translated into 28 languages and distributed across 36 countries.

★ Longest kept diary
Ernest Loftus (Zimbabwe) kept a daily diary for over 91 years. He began writing on May 4 1896 at the age of 12 and continued until his death on July 7 1987, aged 103 years 178 days.

★ Largest published crossword
In July 1982, Robert Turcot (Canada) compiled a crossword comprising 82,951 squares. It contained 12,489 clues across and 13,125 down, and covered 38.21 ft² (3.55 m²). The first ever crossword was created by journalist Arthur Wynne (UK) and published on December 21 1913 in the Sunday newspaper *New York World* (USA). It had the shape of a diamond and contained no internal black squares.

Fastest selling ⌃ nonfiction book

Living History, former first lady Hillary Rodham Clinton's (USA) memoir of her life with

US President Bill Clinton (USA) and his relationship with the intern Monica Lewinsky (USA), is the fastest selling nonfiction book in history, shifting 200,000 copies on its first day of sales in the USA in June 2003.

Largest published book ⌄

The world's largest published book, entitled *Bhutan*, weighs 133 lb (60.3 kg), contains 114 full-color pages, and measures 5 ft high and 7 ft wide (1.52 m x 2.13 m) when opened. It was devised by teams from MIT (Massachusetts Institute of Technology), Acme Bookbinding, and the Friendly Planet, and unveiled on December 15 2003 in New York, USA.

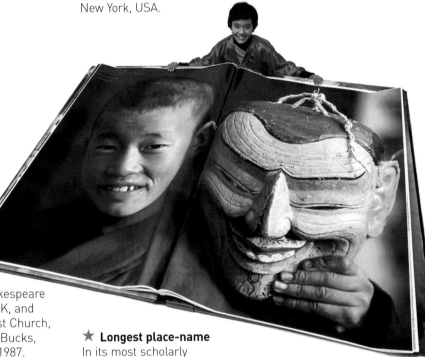

★ Heaviest ever newspaper
The most massive single issue of a newspaper was the Sunday *New York Times* of September 14 1987, which weighed more than 12 lb (5.4 kg) and contained 1,612 pages.

★ Earliest newspaper to achieve a circulation of a million
The earliest newspaper to achieve a circulation of 1 million copies was *Le Petit Journal*, published in Paris, France. It reached this figure in 1886.

★ Biggest sign language mass participation
A total of 1,920 children signed simultaneously to perform a song on 'World Children's Day at McDonald's 2003.' This event took place in Olympian City, Hong Kong, China, on October 5 2003.

★ Longest reading-aloud marathon by an individual
Adrian Hilton (UK) recited the complete works of Shakespeare in a 'Bardathon' lasting 110 hr 46 min on the site of the Globe Theatre at the Shakespeare Festival, London, UK, and the Gold Hill Baptist Church, Chalfont St. Peter, Bucks, UK, on July 16–21 1987.

★ Greatest living linguist
The greatest living linguist is Gregg M. Cox (USA), who can read and write in 64 languages (speaking 14 fluently) and 11 different dialects.

★ Most common language
The most common first language is Chinese, spoken by more than 1.1 billion people. The 'common speech' (Pûtônghuà) is the standard form of Chinese, with a pronunciation based on that of Beijing.

The most widespread as well as the second most spoken language is English, with a conservative estimate of 800 million speakers. Of these, some 310 million are native speakers, mainly in the USA (about 270 million) and the UK (60 million). The third most spoken language is Spanish.

★ Longest place-name
In its most scholarly transliteration, Krungthep Mahanakhon, the 167-letter official name for Bangkok, the capital of Thailand, has 175 letters. The official short version (without capital letters, which are not used in Thai) consists of 111 letters (6 words): *krungthephphramahanakhon bowonratanakosin mahintharayuthaya mahadilokphiphobnovpharad radchataniburirom udomsantisug.*

★ Most complex languages
The Amele language of Papua New Guinea has the most verb forms, with over 69,000 finite forms and 860 infinitive forms of the verb. Haida, the North American Indian language, has the most prefixes (70), and Tabasaran, a language of southeast Dagestan, uses the most noun cases (48). The Eskimo language used by the Inuit has 63 forms of the present tense, and simple nouns have as many as 252 inflections.

★ Language with most consonants
The language with the largest number of distinct consonantal sounds was that of the Ubykhs in the Caucasus, with 81. Ubykh speakers migrated from the Caucasus to Turkey in the 19th century, and the last fully competent speaker, Tevfik Esenc, died in Istanbul in October 1992.

★ Largest postcard
In August 1994, two huge postcards measuring 310 ft² (28.8 m²) were sent by the Canadian National Defence Headquarters to the Canadian headquarters of peacekeeping units, serving in Bosnia and Herzegovina and in Rwanda.

Highest paid « TV actress per episode

As of April 2004, the highest paid TV actresses per episode were Jennifer Aniston (left), Lisa Kudrow, and Courteney Cox Arquette (all USA), who played the female leads in *Friends* (NBC, USA) since 1994 and earned approximately $1 million each per episode in the show's final series. Helen Hunt (USA) also reportedly earned $1 million per episode of *Mad About You* (NBC, USA) in the 1990s.

Highest paid ⌃ TV actor per episode

The world's highest paid TV actor per episode is Ray Romano (USA, above), who earned $1.8 million per episode of *Everybody Loves Raymond* (CBS, USA) for the eighth series in 2004/05.

★ **Longest running TV variety show**
Sábado Gigante (Univision Television Network, USA) has been broadcast every Saturday evening since August 8 1962. The Spanish-language show was created and has been continually hosted by Mario Kreutzberger (Chile), or 'Don Francisco' as he is more popularly known. Each three-hour episode is filmed in front of a live audience.

★ **Largest TV contract**
In May 2003, Oprah Winfrey (USA) signed a contract worth $279 million with the American TV station ABC to host *The Oprah Winfrey Show* for an extra two years until 2008. The show is among the highest rated daytime shows, with an average US weekly audience of 26 million.

★ **Longest working career as a TV chef**
Eva Vicenta Uranga Roig Vda. de Zarate (Mexico), or 'Mrs. Zarate' as she is better known, hosted her first cookery show, *Cocina Al Minuto* (Televisora Tapatia, Mexico), on December 1 1960. She currently hosts the same show under the name of *Hasta La Cocina* for Televisa Guadalajara Co. in Guadalajara, Jalisco, Mexico. Mrs. Zarate has spent 6,610 hours cooking for TV shows. She was born on July 13 1920, making her one of the oldest TV hosts in the world.

★ **Longest running TV quiz show**
It's Academic (NBC, USA) has been on air weekly since October 7 1961. The show, which features high-school teams competing against each other, was created by Sophie Altman (USA) and entered its 43rd season in fall 2003.

★ **Longest TV quiz program**
The longest TV quiz programme began at 8:15 pm on August 29 2003, finishing 52 hr 45 min later at 1 am on September 1 2003. The show was broadcast on 9Live (Germany) and cohosted by Thomas Schürmann, Anna Heesch, Alida-Nadine Kurras, Robin Bade, and Jörg Draeger (all Germany) from the studio in Ismaning, Germany. Callers phoned in to answer a quiz question and hopefully win a cash prize, which increased with each wrong answer. On this occasion, 2,346 callers phoned in to try to win €1 million ($1.2 million), answering approximately 1,500 questions.

★ **Longest running TV show**
Meet the Press (NBC, USA) was first transmitted on November 6 1947 and has been aired subsequently each week since September 12 1948.

★ **Longest time in the same role in a TV series**
Helen Wagner (USA) has played the character of Nancy Hughes McClosky in *As The World Turns* (CBS, USA) since it premiered on April 2 1956. The 12,000th episode was broadcast on May 6 2003.

★ **Longest working career of a TV director on the same program**
The weekly sports show *Estadio Uno*, produced by SIFAR SA, Uruguay, and currently broadcast on Channel 5 of Sistema Nacional de Televisión, has been directed continuously by Julio Sánchez Padilla (Uruguay) since it was first aired on July 5 1970.

★ **Most expensive TV program**
The world's most expensive TV program, in terms of cost per episode, is *ER* (NBC, USA). At its peak, in January 1998, the makers, Warner Bros. (USA), agreed to a three-year deal with NBC for 22 one-hour episodes to be made at a cost of $13.1 million each.

Highest paid TV drama ⌄ actor per episode

Noah Wyle (USA, below) earned approximately $400,000 per episode of *ER* (NBC, USA) for the 2003/04 series. Wyle plays the character of the head doctor, Dr. John Carter.

Most durable TV host ⌃

Patrick Moore (UK, above) holds records for both the world's most durable TV host and the longest running TV show with the same host, for his monthly program *The Sky at Night* (BBC, UK), which he has hosted without a break since April 24 1957. Episode number 614 was aired on February 2 2004.

★ **Most prolific TV scriptwriter**
Since 1942, the output of Ted (later Lord) Willis is estimated to have been 20 million words. From 1949 until his death in 1992, he wrote 41 TV series, including the first seven years and 2.25 million words of *Dixon of Dock Green*, which ran on BBC Television, UK, from 1955 until 1976. He also wrote 37 stage plays and 39 feature films.

★ **Most successful TV soap opera**
Dallas (CBS, USA) began in 1978 as a miniseries. By 1980, it had been watched by about 83 million people in the USA, giving it a share of 76% of the television audience – a record at the time. It had also been seen in more than 90 countries, often in locally dubbed versions. After 11 years and 353 episodes, the last episode was broadcast in the USA on May 3 1991.

★ **Longest TV talk show marathon**
The record for the longest TV talk show marathon is 30 hours and is held by both Zoltán Kováry

(Hungary) and Vador Lladó (Spain). Kováry continually interviewed guests and hosted from 4 pm on February 13 2003 until 10 pm on February 14 2003 at the Fix.tv studios, Budapest, Hungary; Lladó of Flaix TV did the same from May 3 to 4 2002 in Barcelona, Spain.

★ **Longest running sports TV program**
Scotsport (Scottish TV, UK) first aired on September 18 1957 at 10:30 pm and is still running. The weekly show is hosted by Jim Delahunt (UK).

★ **Highest fee per minute for an actor in a TV advertisement**
Nicole Kidman (Australia) reportedly earned $3.71 million for acting in a four-minute commercial for Chanel No. 5 in December 2003. This figure represents $928,800 per minute.

★ **Most Emmy Awards for the same show ever**
Sesame Street (PBS, USA) has won 91 Emmy Awards. The program premiered on TV

in 1969, and features puppet characters the Muppets, designed by Jim Henson (USA).

★ **Most prolific TV, film, and theater stuntman**
Since 1968, Roy Alon (UK) has been credited for working on 893 TV, film, and theater productions as either a stunt coordinator, performer or 2nd Unit Director as of February 20 2004. This total includes 11 theater productions, 36 commercials, 144 feature films (including all the Superman movies and most of the Bond series), and 701 TV shows.

★ **Longest running children's magazine program**
Blue Peter (BBC, UK) was first transmitted from London's Lime Grove Studios on October 16

1958, and celebrated 45 years on air in October 2003. So far it has had 29 hosts.

★ **Longest running pop show**
The first edition of *Top of the Pops* (BBC, UK) was presented by DJ Jimmy Savile (UK) on January 1 1964. The show celebrated its 2,000th edition on September 13 2002 and its 40th year on air in January 2004.

★ **Most TV variety shows hosted by same host**
The most live variety TV shows hosted by the same host is 5,000 as of April 5 2002. Fuji Television Network, Inc.'s *Waratte Iitomo!* has been hosted by Kazuyoshi Morita (Japan), aka Tamori, since its first episode on October 4 1982.

Largest TV audience ⌃ for a space event

The first moonwalk by the *Apollo 11* astronauts was watched on TV by an estimated 600 million people, a fifth of the world's population at the time. The astronauts, Neil Armstrong, Edwin 'Buzz' Aldrin, and Michael Collins (all USA, above), were the stars of a parade through New York City, USA, to celebrate their achievement on August 14 1969.

Most valuable ⌃ TV costume

The Superman suit from the 1955 series *The Adventures of Superman* (above) sold for a record $129,800 (£81,307) at the Profiles in History auction, Los Angeles, California, USA, on July 31 2003. The suit was worn by George Reeves (USA) in the title role.

★ Most watched TV network
The state-owned station China Central Television (CCTV) is transmitted to 90% of all viewers in China. It is estimated that more than 1.1 billion people have access to television in China.

★ Earliest television sponsor
On June 19 1946, Gillette sponsored the broadcast of a boxing match between Joe Louis and Billy Conn (both USA) in New York City, USA.

★ Earliest color TV transmission
On July 3 1928, John Logie Baird (UK) showed television images of red and blue scarves, a UK policeman's helmet, a man poking his tongue out, the glowing end of a cigarette and a bunch of roses during a demonstration at his studios in Covent Garden, London, UK.

★ Earliest underwater TV
The first public demonstration of underwater TV occurred on August 26 1952 at the 19th National Radio and Television Exhibition, London, UK. Marconi Siebe Gorman showed model divers working on a sunken ship on monitor sets. The cameras used to film the divers weighed 1,984 lb (900 kg), cost $6,400 (£3,500) and could transmit from depths of 1,492 ft (455 m).

★ Deepest live-TV broadcast by a presenter
Alastair Fothergill (UK) carried out an underwater broadcast at a depth of 1.5 miles (2.4 km) on *Abyss Live* (BBC, UK). The broadcast was televised on September 29 2002 from inside a MIR submersible, along the Mid-Atlantic Ridge off the east coast of the USA.

★ Earliest public TV commercial
On June 27 1941, the first open public TV commercial ever was broadcast on NBC's WNBT station in New York, USA, for a Bulova watch.

★ Most awards won by a TV commercial
The Levi 'Drugstore' 501 jeans television commercial won 33 awards in 1995. These included a Lion D'Or for director Michel Gondry (France) and a Grand Clio Award for the commercial.

★ Longest running TV commercial
The Discount Tire Company's 'Thank you' advert, produced by Swartwout Productions (USA), first aired in 1975. The same commercial has been aired continuously every year in parts of the USA.

★ Longest running TV chat show
The Tonight Show (NBC, USA) first aired on September 27 1954 hosted by Steve Allen (USA). *The Tonight Show With Jay Leno* has been hosted by Jay Leno (USA) since 1992, when he took over from Johnny Carson (USA). Carson began hosting the show in 1962 and moved it to its present location in Hollywood, California, USA.

★ Longest running TV drama
Procter & Gamble Productions' *Guiding Light* (CBS, USA) was first aired on CBS on June 30 1952, and is still shown each week day. It was originally broadcast as a radio serial on WLW Radio in 1937, then made the transition to TV in 1952.

★ Longest running TV forum
Question Time (BBC, UK) was first broadcast on 25 September 1979 and still runs weekly in the UK. The programme allows a TV studio audience and viewers at home to question a panel of top decision-makers about current policies and topics.

Largest music TV network ⌃

MTV began broadcasting on August 1 1981 and is currently transmitted to approximately 340 million households in 140 countries. This means it can be seen by one in three of the world's total TV audience. Britney Spears, Madonna and Christina Aguilera (all USA, above left to right,) are shown here performing at the 20th Annual MTV Video Music Awards in August 2003.

★ GWR TALKS TO
Matt Groening

The Simpsons (FOX, USA), which is now watched in more than 70 countries, had its 326th episode on February 22 2004. It is the longest running prime-time animated series and had won 20 Emmy Awards as of September 2003, a record for an animated TV series. GWR talks to the creator of this much-loved TV phenomenon, cartoonist Matt Groening (USA).

Congratulations! What's it like to be an official Guinness World Record holder?
It really is an unexpected thrill. I don't care about awards, but to be in the *Guinness World Records* book is really great. It's something I'd never expected, you know, and I'm glad it's a record to be proud of. There are certain records you don't want to have... I'm glad I've not been sitting in baked beans!

The show also has a record for its many guest stars. Why are celebs so keen to appear?
Firstly, it's the easiest gig in showbusiness! You can show up in curlers and barefoot, speak into the microphone and be on your merry way. You can literally phone it in – we've done phone hook-ups with some big stars. But it's more fun when we convince the stars to come in. When Mick Jagger was at the FOX studios, people on the show were very excited. That's why

we do it – to entertain ourselves! We've had Michael Jackson as a 300-lb white guy who thought he was Michael Jackson; we've had Elizabeth Taylor doing the voice of Maggie; Paul McCartney, George Harrison and Ringo Starr.

But of all the people, I think *The Simpsons*' writing team was most excited to have Adam West, the original TV Batman!

What advice do you have for kids who want to work in TV?
My advice to kids who want to work in TV is don't spend all your time watching TV! One of the things about working in TV is that it's like a voracious beast... you need to keep filling it with content. So cram your brain full of culture, history, science and politics, and you'll do very well in TV.

Do you have a favorite episode?
Ah, I like a lot of the very early episodes, particularly ones with Lisa. When Lisa first meets Bleeding Gums Murphy, her saxophone mentor, I was

amazed that the show could actually be moving, given how garish the characters were drawn.

You'll need to last 30 years to beat the record for the longest running comedy show on TV. Do you think you can do it?
Aaah, I hope so! I don't see any end in sight. It doesn't get easier to come up with new stories, but we continue to surprise ourselves. And that's basically our goal – to keep things surprising. It gets harder as the decades roll by. Everybody who likes the show compares the latest episode to their favorite, and it's hard to measure up to the past sometimes. But we're trying!

MATT GROENING

Music & entertainment

Contents

Most weeks at No.1 and No. 2 on US singles chart

For eight weeks, from December 20 2003 to February 7 2004, Hip-Hop act OutKast (USA, below) had singles at No.1 and No. 2 on the US singles chart with 'Hey Ya!' and 'The Way You Move' respectively.

Biggest jump to No.1 on US singles chart

Kelly Clarkson (USA, above), winner of *American Idol*, broke a record set in 1964 by The Beatles (UK) when her first single, 'A Moment Like This,' jumped from No. 53 to No.1 in October 2002. Its first-week sales of 236,000 were bigger than those for the rest of the Hot 100 combined.

★ GWR TALKS TO
Sir Paul McCartney

Sir Paul McCartney (UK, above) currently holds 22 Guinness World Records – more than any other person. He holds 16 records as a member of The Beatles (UK), the biggest selling group of all time. He also holds world records in his own right, including the earliest live debut performance of a classical work on the Internet (the 75-minute *Standing Stone* broadcast on November 19 1997), and the record for the largest paying audience for a rock stadium concert, which he achieved on April 21 1990 when more than 184,000 fans attended his concert at the Maracanã Stadium, Rio de Janeiro, Brazil.

Were you a fan of *Guinness World Records* as a child?
Yes, as kids my friends and I were fans, we had many favorites – tallest, smallest, etc., and we used to dip into it for amazing facts. I never thought I'd get a world record myself!

How did you celebrate your first No.1?
That was 'From Me to You,' which hit the top of the UK chart back in 1963. It was a long time coming, so we partied a lot.

Did The Beatles expect to set so many records?
We certainly didn't realize we were going to get into the record book, though we wanted to, like everyone else. It's an honor for a kid who sat in the pub and hoped to be the tiddlywinks champion of the world to get to our level of success.

Why do you think that sales of The Beatles' albums continue to rise?
A lot of the sales are to young people, which is funny because we all assumed it would be a lot of older people like ourselves on a nostalgia trip. Without being too immodest, I think that the writing was very good and it still holds up.

Are there any other world records that you'd like to have a go at?
I'm working on tallest man! My main ambition is just to enjoy life.

What advice would you give to anyone wanting to go into the music industry?
Work hard, be true to yourself and love what you do.

★ **Biggest selling single in the world since UK charts began**
The biggest selling single sales since UK charts began on November 14 1952 is Elton John's (UK) 'Candle In The Wind 1997'/'Something About The Way You Look Tonight,' with worldwide sales of 33 million. By October 20 1997, it had also reached No.1 in 22 countries. All Elton John's artist royalties and PolyGram's profits were donated to the Diana, Princess of Wales Memorial Fund.

★ **Biggest selling single by a group**
'Rock Around The Clock' sold an unaudited 25 million copies. Written by James E. Myers (USA), aka Jimmy DeKnight, and Max C. Freedman (USA), it was recorded on April 12 1954 by Bill Haley and His Comets (USA).

★ **Most UK singles to debut at No.1**
Westlife (Ireland) had 12 singles debut at No.1 in the UK chart from May 1 1999 to November 22 2003.

Best UK solo album chart start ⌃

Robbie Williams (UK, above) had five successive No.1s on the UK album chart. The albums, released from September 1997 to November 2002, are: *Life Thru A Lens* (1997), *I've Been Expecting You* (1998), *Sing When You're Winning* (2000), *Swing When You're Winning* (2001), and *Escapology* (2002). From January 1 2000 to December 31 2003, he sold 5,608,000 albums in the UK – more than any other UK album act. Robbie has also won a record 14 British Record Industry Trust (BRIT) awards.

★ **Most consecutive No.1 singles**

From July 28 1997 to January 21 2004, 19 consecutive singles by The KinKi Kids (Japan) debuted at No.1 on the Japanese chart.

★ **Biggest jump to No.1 on UK singles chart**

Irish boy band Westlife's single 'Unbreakable' made an unprecedented leap from No.195 to No.1 on the UK Top 200 in November 2002.

★ **Biggest first UK chart week for a single**

Will Young's (UK) debut single 'Anything Is Possible'/ 'Evergreen' sold 1,108,269 copies in its first 'chart week' – i.e. its total sales from February 25 to March 2 2002 – including 385,000 on its first day of release. It went on to sell an unprecedented 2 million copies in the UK in 15 weeks.

★ **Biggest selling UK single by a female group**

'Wannabe' by The Spice Girls (UK), released in July 1996, spent seven weeks at No.1 in the UK,

selling 1.2 million copies. The single hit No.1 in a further 31 countries.

★ **Most hit singles on UK chart**

As of April 2004, Elvis Presley (USA) had scored 135 hit singles on the UK chart.

★ **Longest time spent on UK singles chart**

The longest time that a single has spent on the UK chart is 124 weeks for 'My Way' by Frank Sinatra (USA), which entered and reentered the chart ten times from April 1969 to April 1994.

★ **Biggest selling album ever**

Thriller by Michael Jackson (USA) has registered global sales of over 47 million copies to date since 1982.

★ **Biggest selling album on UK chart**

Over 4.5 million copies of The Beatles' (UK) *Sgt Pepper's Lonely Hearts Club Band* are reported to have been sold in the UK since its release in June 1967.

★ **Most albums on US chart simultaneously**

Three bands – The Beatles (UK), The Monkees (USA), and U2 (Ireland) – have all had seven albums on the US Top 200 simultaneously.

★ **Best-selling debut album in the USA**

Boston by Boston (USA), released in 1976, has sold over 16 million copies.

★ **Most No.1 albums on US chart by a group**

The Beatles had 19 US No.1 albums – more than double the number by Elvis Presley (USA) and The Rolling Stones (UK), both of whom have had nine No.1 albums. In all, The Beatles' albums have spent 133 weeks at the top spot.

★ **Biggest all-time sales by a group**

The all-time sales for The Beatles have been estimated by EMI at more than 1 billion discs and tapes.

★ **Biggest selling teenage artist**

Before she turned 20 years old on December 2 2001, Britney Spears (USA) had global sales of 37 million records.

★ **Most vocal edits on a single recording**

Brian Transeau (USA) incorporated a total of 6,178 vocal edits in the production of his track 'Simply Being Loved (Somnambulist),' which was released in August 2003. The single spent 11 weeks on the US charts.

Rock & country

Music & entertainment

Biggest selling ⌃ country album by a group

Since its release in 1998, *Wide Open Spaces* by the Dixie Chicks (USA, above) has sold 10 million copies.

★ Largest paying rock band concert attendance

The Molson Canadian Rocks for Toronto concert, which was held on July 30 2003 at Downsview Park in Toronto, Ontario, Canada, attracted a paying audience of 489,176. The SARS benefit gig raised $7,590,507 from ticket sales.

★ Largest free rock concert attendance

Rod Stewart's (UK) free concert at Copacabana Beach, Rio de Janeiro, Brazil, on New Year's Eve 1994, reportedly attracted an audience of 3.5 million.

★ Largest simultaneous charity rock concert

Live Aid was organized by Bob Geldof (Ireland) and included two concerts, simultaneously held in London, UK, and Philadelphia,

Pennsylvania, USA, on July 13 1985. More than 60 of rock music's biggest acts played for free to an estimated 1.5 billion TV viewers watching throughout the world, raising money for African famine relief. Geldof, then lead singer of the Boomtown Rats, was inspired to organize Live Aid after watching a BBC documentary on starvation in Ethiopia.

★ Largest rock star benefit concert

A concert held at Wembley Stadium, London, UK, on April 20 1992 in memory of rock star Freddie Mercury (UK), who died of AIDS, raised $35 million for AIDS charities. It was attended by about 75,000 people and is estimated to have been seen by almost 1 billion people in over 70 countries.

★ Most concerts performed in 50 days

During a tour of the USA, the rock band Jackyl (USA) played 101 concerts in 50 days, from September 12 to October 31 1998. Jackyl appeared in a total of 59 cities in 26 states.

★ Biggest rock earnings from one venue

The biggest gross from concerts played at a single venue is $38,684,050 by Bruce Springsteen (USA) from a series of 10 shows that he performed at Giants Stadium, New Jersey, USA, from July 15 to August 21 2003. The concerts were seen by a total of 566,560 people.

★ Highest grossing country music tour

Garth Brooks' (USA) three-year 'Sevens' tour, which commenced in March 1997, grossed a total of $105 million. He performed 350 shows in 100 cities with an average attendance of 55,000 people per show.

★ Most successful male country artist

Garth Brooks (USA) is the most successful country recording artist of all time, with album sales of more than 100 million since 1989. He has also sold more albums than any other solo artist in the USA.

★ Most successful female country artist

Reba McEntire (USA) is the biggest selling female country vocalist in the USA, with eight multiplatinum albums, 16 platinum albums, and 23 gold albums by February 2004, from a career spanning more than 25 years. She has sold 48 million albums in total.

★ Most successful country duo

Six albums by Brooks & Dunn (Kix Brooks and Ronnie Dunn, both USA) have sold more than 1 million copies and 17 of their singles have got to No.1 on the country chart, including 'Boot Scootin' Boogie' (1992), 'Little Miss Honky Tonk' (1995), and 'Husbands and Wives' (1998).

Shortest UK >> Top 10 single

The shortest single to chart on the UK Top 10 is Liam Lynch's (USA, right) 'United States of Whatever,' which was 1 min 26 sec long and entered the chart on December 7 2002, peaking at No.10.

Youngest ⌃ platinum album act

Billy Gilman (b. May 24 1988, USA, above) was 12 years 68 days old when his debut album *One Voice* was awarded a platinum certificate for achieving 1 million sales in the USA. The album was released on June 20 2000 and was certified platinum 12 weeks later in August 2000.

★ **Longest stay at No.1 by US rock single**
Canadian band Nickelback's single 'Too Bad' held the top spot on the US Mainstream Rock chart for a record-breaking 20 weeks from January to May 2002.

★ **Most simultaneous album entries in a week on US charts**
Seven different albums by US rock group Pearl Jam entered the US Top 200 chart on March 17 2001. These were part of a series of 23 albums recorded live at different venues around the USA. This feat broke the group's own record of five entries from a series of 25 simultaneously released live albums from concerts held during their successful European tour in 2000.

★ **Biggest selling album in the USA by a female solo artist**
Since its release on November 4 1997, Canadian country singer Shania Twain's album *Come On Over* has sold a total of 19 million copies in the USA and 30 million copies worldwide.

★ **Most weeks on US charts for an album by a female artist**
Patsy Cline's (USA) *12 Greatest Hits* was still on the US Country catalog album chart in February 2001, 722 weeks after first entering it. The album spent 251 weeks (almost five years) at No.1 in total.

★ **Most weeks on US Adult Contemporary chart**
Australian duo Savage Garden's single 'I Knew I Loved You' had spent a record 124 weeks on the US Adult Contemporary chart when it exited in February 2002, beating the record of 123 weeks set by another of their recordings, 'Truly Madly Deeply.'

★ **Most platinum RIAA albums by a country music artist**
Since 1981, George Strait (USA) has earned 26 Recording Industry Association of America (RIAA) platinum album awards (for sales of over 1 million copies in the USA) – with 12 of these albums selling more than 2 million copies. His total sales are over 62 million.

★ **Slowest climbing act on US charts**
Rock group Creed's (USA) track 'Higher' was on the US Hot 100 for a record 36 weeks before it finally climbed into the Top 10 in July 2000.

★ **Longest stay on the UK album chart**
Fleetwood Mac's (UK/USA) *Rumours* album, released on February 26 1977, spent 477 weeks on the UK album chart. It included four singles chart entries, though none of them reached the Top 20.

★ **Youngest female to top UK album charts**
Canadian singer/songwriter Avril Lavigne topped the UK album chart on January 11 2003 aged 18 years 106 days. The album, *Let Go*, made No.1 in its 18th week on the chart.

★ **Longest gap between US chart album hits**
There was a gap of 28 years between Santana's No.1 US album *Santana III* of November 1971 and their next No.1 *Supernatural* of October 1999. The latter gave the group phenomenal worldwide success, selling 21 million copies.

★ **Shortest music video**
In 1994, US metal band Brutal Truth produced a video 2.18 seconds in length to accompany their track 'Collateral Damage.' The video features a sequence of flash frames depicting popular conservative American cultural icons of the late 20th century.

★ **Loudest drummer**
A peak reading of 109.1 decibels was recorded during a show by The Jerome Experience (France) at the Celtic Warriors 10th Birthday Bash at Woodgreen Animal Shelter, Cambridgeshire, UK, on April 12 2003. The Jerome Experience is a one-man show featuring drummer Jérôme Dehèdin (France).

R&B & jazz
Music & entertainment

Most simultaneous R&B hits

Rapper 50 Cent (aka Curtis Jackson, USA, right) had nine simultaneous entries on the *Billboard* Top R&B/ Hip-Hop Singles & Tracks chart on May 10 2003.

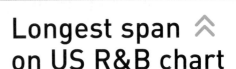

Longest span ⌃ on US R&B chart

Ray Charles (USA, above) has appeared on the US R&B singles chart for seven decades. He first charted as leader of The Maxine Trio with 'Confession Blues' in April 1949. His latest entry was in July 2002 with 'Mother,' a span of 53 years.

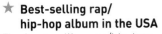

⭐ **Best-selling rap/ hip-hop album in the USA**
The best-selling rap/hip-hop album ever in the USA is *CrazySexyCool* by TLC (USA), which has achieved sales of 11 million, surpassing MC Hammer's (USA) *Please Hammer Don't Hurt 'Em* (which has sold 10 million units).

⭐ **Rap artist with the most US No.1 albums**
When *The Black Album* topped the US album charts in November 2003, Jay-Z (aka Shawn Carter, USA) became the only rap act to have scored six No.1 albums.

⭐ **Fastest selling female debut album**
Ashanti's (aka Ashanti S. Douglas, USA) eponymous debut album sold 503,000 copies in its first week on release in the USA in April 2002. In the same week, she became the first female performer to simultaneously hold the top two places on the Hot 100 singles chart with 'Foolish' and 'What's Luv?' (with Fat Joe).

⭐ **Biggest UK first-week hip-hop album sales**
Eminem's (aka Marshall Mathers III, USA) album *The Eminem Show* sold 315,000 copies in its first week on sale in the UK in June 2002. This gave him his second UK No.1 album, a feat that no other rap artist has achieved.

⭐ **Most successful remix album**
In February 2002, Jennifer Lopez's (USA) album *J To Tha Lo!: The Remixes* became the first remix album to top the US charts, with sales of over 1 million, including 156,000 in its first week.

⭐ **Best chart start**
Rap artist DMX (aka Earl Simmons, USA) is the only artist whose first five albums have entered the US chart at No.1. The records are *It's Dark And Hell Is Hot* (1998), *Flesh Of My Flesh Blood Of My Blood* (1999), *... And Then There Was X* (2000), *The Great Depression*, (2001) and *Grand Champ* (2003).

⭐ **Most consecutive weeks at No.1 on US singles chart**
'One Sweet Day' by Mariah Carey and Boyz II Men (both USA) topped the US chart for 16 consecutive weeks in 1995.

⭐ **Oldest MOBO winner**
The oldest Music of Black Origin (MOBO) award winner is B.B. King (USA), who was 73 years old in 1998 when he picked up the Award for Lifetime Achievement.

⭐ **Longest stay on US Rap singles chart**
'Hot Boyz' by Missy 'Misdemeanor' Elliott (aka Melissa Elliott), featuring Nas, Eve, and Q-Tip (all USA), spent a record 18 weeks at the top of the US Rap chart in 1999–2000.

⭐ **Longest US singles chart span**
Louis Armstrong (USA) first appeared on a *Billboard* chart on April 6 1946. His most recent entry to the listings

came in 1988, 17 years after his death, with 'What A Wonderful World' from the sound track to the film *Good Morning, Vietnam* (USA, 1987). Armstrong also had over 50 hits before the 'official' chart started in 1940, his first being 'Muskrat Ramble' in 1926, thus taking his span of hits to more than 61 years.

⭐ **Most consecutive weeks at No.1 by the same producer**
Hip-hop producer Irv Gotti (USA) produced the No.1 single on the US Hot 100 pop chart for a record 19 successive weeks from February 23 to June 22 2002. Chief executive officer of Murder Inc. Records, Gotti has worked with artists such as Ja Rule, Jay-Z, Ashanti, DMX, and Fat Joe.

⭐ **Youngest solo rap artist at No.1 on US Rap and R&B charts**
In July 2000, Lil' Bow Wow (aka Shad Lamar Moss, USA) went to No.1 on the US R&B and Rap charts with 'Bounce With Me' (featuring Xscape), aged only 13 years 4 months.

Most weeks at No.1 ⌃ on US singles chart by a girl band

The single 'Independent Woman,' released by Destiny's Child (USA, above) on November 20 2000, subsequently spent a record 11 weeks at the top of the US singles chart.

★ **Youngest solo artist at No.1 on US album chart**
Stevie Wonder (aka Steveland Morris, b. May 21 1950, USA) was 13 years 3 months old when his album *Little Stevie Wonder – The 12 Year Old Genius* topped the US charts in 1963.

★ **Youngest R&B chart entrant**
Hailie Jade Mathers (b. December 25 1995, USA) became the youngest performer, aged 6 years 210 days, to be credited with an R&B hit when 'My Dad's Gone Crazy' charted in August 2002. She performed on the track with her father, Eminem (USA).

★ **Biggest selling rap artist**
Rap legend 2Pac (aka Tupac Shakur, USA) has certified US album sales of 36 million, and has now had more hits after his death (at the age of 25 in September 1996) than he did while he was alive. The posthumous hits include three US No.1 albums, *The Don*

Killuminati (1997), *Until The End Of Time* (2001), and *Better Dayz* (2002), and an additional 16 US R&B chart singles.

★ **Fastest rap MC**
Rebel XD (aka Seandale Price, USA) beat his own record and rapped 683 syllables in 54.501 seconds on the set of *Guinness World Records: Primetime* in Los Angeles, California, USA, on June 24 1998.

★ **Fastest selling rap artist**
Eminem's (USA) album *The Marshall Mathers LP* sold 1.76 million copies in its first week in the USA in May 2000.

★ **Highest annual earnings by a rap act**
Eminem (USA) and rapper and producer Dr. Dre (aka Andre Young, USA) earned $35 million in 2002, according to the 2003 *Forbes* Celebrity 100 list.

★ **Largest rap group**
With 124 members, hip-hop outfit Minority Militia (USA) is the world's largest rap group.

Each member either raps, sings, plays an instrument, or produces on their 2001 album *The People's Army*, released on Low Town Records.

★ **Longest working career by a recording artist**
Jazz singer Adelaide Hall (USA) is the most durable recording artist, having released material over eight consecutive decades. Her first record, 'Creole Love Call,' was recorded with Duke Ellington on October 26 1927, and her last was made on June 16 1991 at the Cole Porter Centennial Gala in London, UK.

★ **Most Grammy awards won by a female artist**
Aretha Franklin (USA) has won 15 Grammys. She received her first in 1967 for Best Female R&B Vocal Performance with the song 'Respect.'

★ **Most Grammy awards won by a solo performer**
Stevie Wonder (USA) has won 19 Grammy awards. Since 1973, he has won Best Male R&B Vocal Performance six times.

★ **Hit act with the most grandchildren**
When soul singer Solomon Burke (USA) entered the US album chart in August 2002 with the Grammy-nominated *Don't Give Up On Me*, he had 65 grandchildren and 10 great-grandchildren.

★ **Earliest jazz record made**
The first jazz record included 'Indiana' and 'The Darktown Strutters' Ball' and was released on May 31 1917. It was recorded for the Columbia label in New York City, USA, in January 1917 by the Original Dixieland Jazz Band, led by Dominic 'Nick' James La Rocca (USA).

Largest animal orchestra

The animal orchestra with the most members is the 12-piece Thai Elephant Orchestra (above), ⌃⌃
which gives concerts at the Thai Elephant Conservation Centre, Lampang, Thailand. The orchestra was founded by Richard Lair and David Soldier (both USA) in 2000, with the aim of conserving the Asiatic elephant species.

★ **Most prolific composer**
Georg Philipp Telemann (Germany) wrote 12 complete sets of services – one cantata every Sunday – for a year, 78 services for special occasions, 40 operas, 600 to 700 orchestral suites, 44 passions, plus concertos, and other chamber music.

★ **Longest working operatic career**
Danshi Toyotake (Japan) sang Musume Gidayu (traditional Japanese narrative) for 91 years from the age of seven. Her professional career spanned 81 years.

★ **Longest opera**
Die Meistersinger von Nürnberg by Richard Wagner (Germany) is the longest of commonly performed operas. A normal uncut version, as performed by the Sadler's Wells company (UK) from August 24 to September 19 1968, entailed 5 hr 15 min of music.

★ **Largest orchestra**
A total of 6,452 musicians from the Vancouver Symphony Orchestra and music students from all over British Columbia, Canada, played 'Ten Minutes of Nine' – an arrangement by Frederick Schipizky of the 'Ode To Joy' from Beethoven's Ninth Symphony – for 9 min 44 sec at B.C. Place Stadium, Vancouver, Canada, on May 5 2000. It was conducted by Bramwell Tovey (UK).

★ **Largest cello ensemble**
A total of 1,013 cellists played in the 'Concert of 1,000 Cellists' held in Kobe, Japan, on November 29 1998, conducted by Kazuaki Momiyama (Japan). Nine pieces of music were performed, the longest of which was Bach's Suite in D Major at 8 min 26 sec.

★ **Largest simultaneous percussion performance**
A percussive rhythm was played for over six minutes by 10,102 people at an event held at the Hong Kong Coliseum, Hong Kong, China, on July 2 2002.

★ **Largest full drum-kit ensemble**
The largest complete drum-kit ensemble consisted of 264 participants who gathered to play at Tacoma Narrows Airport, Gig Harbor, Washington, USA, on March 29 2003 under the direction of Gerard Schwarz (USA), conductor of the Seattle Symphony Orchestra.

★ **Largest drum ensemble**
The largest drum ensemble consisted of 3,140 participants who gathered to play at the opening ceremony of the Hong Kong Drum Festival at Victoria Park, Hong Kong, China, on July 13 2003.

★ **Largest didgeridoo ensemble**
On April 19 2003, 210 musicians assembled to play didgeridoos for 20 minutes at the Helitherme Bad Waltersdorf, Austria.

★ **Largest harmonica ensemble**
Organized by CentrumKultury Zamek, 851 harmonica players gathered at the 10th Poznan Blues Festival, Poznan, Poland, to perform 'When the Saints Go Marching In' on September 13 2003.

★ **Most durable living organist**
Stanley Hayes (UK) has been the organist at St. David's Church, Thelbridge, Devon, UK, since 1926, when he was 13. He continues in the post, providing a regular voluntary service for Sunday worship, weddings, funerals, and baptisms.

Best-selling world music album ⌃

The 1998 Grammy award-winning album *Buena Vista Social Club* (1997) has sold over 4 million copies – 1.5 million of which were sold in the USA. The album brought together some of Cuba's best musicians, including Omara Portuondo and Teresita Garcia Caturla (both above), Ibrahim Ferrer, and Compay Segundo, as well as inspiring Wim Wender's cinema documentary *Buena Vista Social Club* (Germany, 1999).

Youngest ≫ person at No.1 in the classical charts

In November 1998, Charlotte Church (UK, right) entered the UK classical album charts with her debut album *Voice of an Angel* at the age of 12 years 9 months. The album was certified double platinum in the UK within four weeks of its release.

★ Longest working career of a conductor
Torstein Grythe (Norway) has conducted the Silver Boys Choir of Oslo, Norway, for 63 years since 1940 and still continues to do so at the age of 85.

★ Longest concert by a group
From September 21 to 23 2002, the group John Jerome Sangamam (India) played for 40 hours at St. Montford Indoor Stadium, Mylapore, Chennai, India. The 20-strong band performed over 500 different numbers, all in Tamil.

★ Longest international career of a sitarist
Indian classical sitarist Ravi Shankar's first sitar performance was in Allahabad, India, in 1939, and his first international sitar concert was in New York, USA, in 1956. However, Shankar's first international stage appearances in Europe and the USA took place earlier, as a dancer and musical accompanist in his brother

Uday Shankar's troupe in 1932, when he was aged 12. He continues to tour today, with dates in North America in 2004.

★ Best-selling Raï artist
Algerian Raï singer Khaled has sold over three million albums worldwide, including *Khaled*, which featured his first international hit 'Didi.' Other albums include *N'ssi N'ssi*, *Sahra*, and *Kenza*. The live album *1, 2, 3 Soleils* sold one million copies worldwide. Khaled is also the best-selling artist singing in Arabic.

★ Biggest selling bhangra solo artist
Malkit Singh (India) has sold an average of 260,000 copies of each of his albums, totaling sales of over 4.9 million records in his 20-year career. He also holds the record for the most recordings by a bhangra artist.

★ Longest running bhangra band
Bhujhangy, a bhangra band based in Birmingham (UK), has been performing and

recording bhangra albums since 1967. Balbir Singh (UK), who sings with his brother, Dalbir Singh (UK), is the only member of the band's original lineup.

★ Best-selling reggae album
Legend (1984), by the late Bob Marley (Jamaica), is the biggest selling reggae album of all time. In the UK, where it topped the chart, it has had certified sales of 1.8 million, and although it did not reach the Top 40 in the USA, it sold more than 10 million copies there.

★ Biggest selling album by a Latin artist
Mexican-born Carlos Santana's *Supernatural* album, released in June 1999, has sold 14 million copies in the USA and 21 million worldwide.

★ Biggest selling female Latin artist
Cuban-born singer Gloria Estefan has had total album sales estimated at over 35 million.

★ Most albums on Latin chart simultaneously
Shortly after her death on July 16 2003, the legendary 'Queen of Salsa' Celia Cruz (Cuba) had eight albums in the Top 10 of *Billboard*'s Tropical Latin album chart.

★ Biggest selling male Latin artist
Spanish vocalist Julio Iglesias is the most successful Latin music artist in the world, with reported global sales of more than 200 million albums.

★ Top selling album act in Japan
Utada Hikaru (Japan) is the only Japanese act to sell over two million copies each of three consecutive albums. Her 1999 debut album *First Love* was the biggest ever seller in Japan, shifting over 10 million copies; her second, *Distance*, sold over 5.5 million; and her third, *Deep River* (2002), sold 1.6 million on its first day and 2.3 million in the first five days.

Performance arts
Music & entertainment

« Heaviest building relocation on wheels

Built in 1910, the 5,816,000-lb (2,638-tonne) Shubert Theater (left) in Minneapolis, Minnesota, USA, was moved in one piece from Block E to a new site three blocks away on Hennepin Avenue over 12 days by Artspace Projects from February 9 to 21 1999.

★ Furthest building relocation

The linked five-story Gem Theater (built 1927) and Century Club building (built 1903) in Detroit, Michigan, USA, which weighed 5,500,000 lb (2,495 tonnes), was moved a distance of 1,850 ft (563 m) on 72 dollies, each with eight rubber tires, in 25 days from October 16 1997.

★ Largest purpose-built theater

The most capacious purpose-built theater is the Perth Entertainment Centre, Western Australia. It has 8,500 seats and a main stage area that measures 70 x 45 ft (21.3 x 13.7 m). It was opened on December 26 1974.

★ Largest theater stage

The world's largest stage is at the Hilton Theater at the Reno Hilton, Reno, Nevada, USA. It measures 175 x 241 ft (53.3 x 73.4 m). The stage has three main lifts, each capable of raising 143,961 lb (65.3 tonnes) and two turntables each with a circumference of 62 ft 6 in (19.1 m).

★ Most expensive stage prop

For the musical stage version of *Chitty Chitty Bang Bang*, which opened at the London Palladium, London, UK, on April 16 2002, the magical flying car of the title cost an estimated $1.07 million to make. The complete set, including the flying car, was designed by the award-winning set designer Anthony Ward (UK).

★ Most theatrical members of a family to appear on stage

A total of 24 direct members of the Hurst family, headed by Mike and Marjorie (both UK), performed at the Kenton Theatre, Henley-on-Thames, Oxfordshire, UK, in a production of *Puss In Boots* on December 19 and 20 2003. The performers, whose ages ranged from 1 to 63, included the Hursts' six children Timothy, Alexis, Muffin, Bryony, Jonas, and Adam, and their spouses Lynsey, Nathan, Ben, and Ruth, plus their grandchildren Ben, Ellie, Aisling, Cassian, Liberty, Flavia, Emerald, Tabitha, Antigone, Polyanna, Madeleine, and Amelie (all UK).

★ Longest working career of a theater director on the same production

Enrique Pineda (Mexico) directed the monologue *La Virgen Loca* (*The Crazy Virgin*), performed by Hosmé Israel (Mexico), from its premiere on August 24 1974 at the Teatro Rafael Solania, University of Veracruz, Mexico, until it closed on November 30 2003, a total of 29 years 98 days.

★ Longest working career of a theater producer on the same production

Mildred Ilse (USA), producer of *The Drunkard* (once the world's longest running play), was with the production for its entire run of 26 years 103 days from July 6 1933 to October 17 1959, a total of 9,477 performances, in Los Angeles, California, USA.

★ Longest working career in the same role

Terence Ranasinghe and his wife Malini (both Sri Lanka) have played the major roles in E.R. Sarachchandra's (Sri Lanka) *Sinhabahu* in over 5,000 theater performances from 1961 until 1991 – a total of 30 years.

★ Most ardent theatergoer

Howard Hughes, Prof. Emeritus of Texas Wesleyan College, Fort Worth, Texas, USA, attended a record 6,136 theater shows in the period 1956–87.

Longest theatrical run ⌃

The longest continuous run of any show in the world is *The Mousetrap* by Dame Agatha Christie (UK).

By February 29 2004, it had had 21,263 performances at St. Martin's Theatre, London, UK (above). The play celebrated its 50th anniversary in 2002.

Largest ≫ stage lift system

The stage of the Bellagio Theater, Las Vegas, Nevada, USA, measures 3,650 ft^2 (339 m^2) and is divided into four sections, supported by four hydraulic lifting systems. Each system raises one of the four sections synchronously (or not) through a pool containing 1.5 million gallons (5.6 million liters) of water. The lift system was specially manufactured for Cirque du Soleil's (Canada) 'O,' performed in, above, and under water (two members, right).

★ First professional stage actress

Margaret Hughes (UK, 1643–1719) appeared as Desdemona in Thomas Killigrew's version of *Othello, The Moor of Venice* on December 3 1660, at a converted tennis court called the Vere Street Theatre, London, UK.

★ Highest box office gross for a theater production

Since first opening at Her Majesty's Theatre, London, UK, on October 9 1986, Andrew Lloyd Webber's musical *The Phantom of the Opera* has played in 18 countries and taken over $3.2 billion at the box office.

★ Most scripted roles in different locations in one night

On February 24 2004, as part of Visit London's 'One Amazing Week,' Jerry Hall (USA) took on recognized scripted roles to appear at six different London West End theater productions during the course of a single night. Replacing a cast member each time, from her first appearance on stage at 7:30 pm to her last entrance at 10:09 pm, she was Monsieur André in *The Phantom of the Opera* at Her Majesty's Theatre; one of four prostitutes in *Les Misérables* at the Palace Theatre; Mr. Myers in *Fame* at the Aldwych Theatre; Brenda in *Blood Brothers* at the Phoenix Theatre; one of the six 'Swings' in *Anything Goes* at the Theatre Royal; and finally one of the 24 members of the ensemble in *Chitty Chitty Bang Bang* at the London Palladium.

★ Most costume changes demanded by a lead theatrical role

Michael Jibson (UK) achieved 29 complete costume changes during each performance as Joe Casey in the West End musical *Our House*, directed by Matthew Warchus (UK) at the Cambridge Theatre, London, UK, from October 28 2002 to August 16 2003. The quick-change costumes and illusion effects were designed by Paul Kieve (UK), allowing the fastest change to take just four seconds on stage. Assisted in the wings by principal dresser Murray Lane (UK), Warchus made additional partial changes during the 2-hr 10-min show.

★ Longest play

The Warp, a ten-part play cycle by Neil Oram performed at the Institute of Contemporary Arts, London, UK, on January 18–20 1979 and directed by Ken Campbell, lasted 18 hr 5 min. Russell Denton (UK) was on stage for all but five minutes.

★ Longest running musical

The off-Broadway musical *The Fantasticks* by Tom Jones and Harvey Schmidt (both USA) opened at the Sullivan Street Playhouse, New York, USA, on May 3 1960 and closed on January 13 2002, after 17,162 performances.

★ Longest one-man show to run in London's West End

An Evening with Tommy Steele opened at the Prince of Wales Theatre, London, UK, on October 11 1979 and closed on November 29 1980 – a total of 414 days.

★ Largest amateur puppet show

Working 463 puppets, a total of 402 puppeteers from Cockington Primary School (UK) performed the puppet show *Hurucan and the Feathered Snake* at the Riviera International Centre, Torquay, Devon, UK, on July 16 2003.

★ Longest theatrical run for a revue

The greatest number of performances of any theatrical presentation is 47,250 (to April 1986) for *The Golden Horseshoe Revue*, a variety show staged at Disneyland Park, Anaheim, California, USA, from July 16 1955 to October 12 1986. It was seen by 16 million people.

★ Longest running annual theater revue

The longest running annual revues were *The Ziegfeld Follies* (USA, 1907–57), which went through 25 editions.

Sport

Contents

Football
Sport

Longest touchdown in a Super Bowl

The longest touchdown in Super Bowl history is 85 yards, scored by Muhsin Muhammad (USA, near left), playing for the Carolina Panthers in Super Bowl XXXVIII, on February 1 2004

Most yards gained rushing in an NFL game

Jamal Lewis (USA, below) rushed for 295 yards playing for the Baltimore Ravens against the Cleveland Browns on September 14 2003, scoring two touchdowns.

★ **Most passes completed in a Super Bowl game**
Quarterback Tom Brady (USA) of the New England Patriots threw 32 completed passes in Super Bowl XXXVIII on February 1 2004 in Houston, Texas, USA.

★ **Most passes received in a Super Bowl career**
Jerry Rice (USA) received 33 passes during his four Super Bowl appearances in 1989–90, 1995, and 2003, playing for the San Francisco 49ers and the Oakland Raiders.

★ **Most field goals by an individual in a Super Bowl game**
The most field goals scored by an individual in a Super Bowl game is four, kicked by Don Chandler (Green Bay Packers) in 1968 and Ray Wersching (San Francisco 49ers) in 1982.

★ **Most team interceptions in a Super Bowl**
In Super Bowl XXXVII, played in San Diego, California, USA, on January 26 2003, the Tampa Bay Buccaneers made a record five interceptions, returning them for 172 yards and three touchdowns.

★ **Highest aggregate score in the Super Bowl**
The greatest aggregate score of 75 points was achieved in 1995 when the San Francisco 49ers beat the San Diego Chargers 49–26.

★ **Coach with most wins**
The most games won as head coach is 347 by Don Shula (USA) of the Baltimore Colts (1963–69) and Miami Dolphins (1970–95).

★ **Longest field goal**
The longest successful field goal in a National Football League (NFL) game is 63 yards by Tom Dempsey (USA) playing for the New Orleans Saints against the Detroit Lions on November 8 1970; and by Jason Elam (USA) playing for the Denver Broncos against the Jacksonville Jaguars on October 25 1998. Dempsey was born with no right hand, and no toes on his right foot (which was his kicking foot). He wore a modified shoe.

★ **Most NFL titles**
The Green Bay Packers have won a record 12 NFL titles, in 1929–31, 1936, 1939, 1944, 1961–62, 1965–67, 1996.

★ **Most points scored in a season**
The most points scored in a season is 176, by Paul Hornung (USA) for the Green Bay Packers in 1960.

★ **Most NFL games played**
George Blanda (USA) played in a record 340 games in a record 26 seasons in the NFL (Chicago Bears 1949–58, Baltimore Colts 1950, Houston Oilers 1960–66, and Oakland Raiders 1967–75).

★ **Highest score in an NFL regular season game**
The highest team score is 72 by the Washington Redskins against the New York Giants (41) at Washington on November 27 1966. The aggregate score of 113 is also a record.

★ **Most combined yards gained in an NFL season**
Lionel James (USA) gained 2,535 combined net yards in the 1985 NFL season playing for the San Diego Chargers.

★ **Most combined yards gained in an NFL career**
The most combined net yards gained in an NFL career is 21,803 by Walter Payton (USA), playing for the Chicago Bears from 1975 to 1987.

★ **Most touchdowns in an NFL game**
Ernie Nevers (USA) scored six touchdowns playing for the Chicago Cardinals against the Chicago Bears on November 28 1929, equaled by William Jones (USA) playing for the Cleveland Browns against the Chicago Bears on November 25 1951, and Gale Sayers (USA) playing for the Chicago Bears against the San Francisco 49ers on December 12 1965.

Most passes << received in an NFL season

Marvin Harrison (USA, left) received a record 143 passes in the 2002 NFL season playing for the Indianapolis Colts.

★ **Highest combined kick return yardage in an NFL season**
Michael Lewis (USA) of the New Orleans Saints set an NFL combined punt/kickoff return record with 2,432 yards in the 2002 season.

★ **Most passes received in an NFL career**
The most pass receptions in an NFL career is 1,519 by Jerry Rice (USA), playing for the San Francisco 49ers and the Oakland Raiders during 1985–2003.

★ **Most passes received in an NFL game**
Tom Fears (USA) caught 18 passes in an NFL game against the Green Bay Packers on December 3 1950, playing for the Los Angeles Rams.

★ **Most passes completed in an NFL game**
Drew Bledsoe (USA), playing for the New England Patriots, completed 45 passes in an NFL game against the Minnesota Vikings on November 13 1994.

★ **Most passes completed in an NFL regular season**
The most passes completed in an NFL regular season is 418 by quarterback Rich Gannon (USA) for the Oakland Raiders in the 2002 season.

★ **Most passes completed in an NFL career**
Dan Marino (USA) completed a total of 4,967 passes from 1983 until his retirement in 2000, playing for the Miami Dolphins. He holds many other records, including most yards gained passing in both a career (61,631) and a season (5,084 in 1984).

★ **Most field goals by an individual in an NFL game**
Jim Bakken (USA) scored seven field goals in an NFL game against the Pittsburgh Steelers on September 24 1967, playing for the St. Louis Cardinals.

★ **Most field goals by an individual in an NFL season**
Olindo Mare (USA) kicked 39 field goals in the 1999 NFL season, playing for the Miami Dolphins.

★ **Most field goals by an individual in an NFL career**
Gary Anderson (USA) kicked 465 field goals over his NFL career playing for the Pittsburgh Steelers (1982–94), Philadelphia Eagles 1995–96), San Francisco 49ers, (1997) and Minnesota Vikings (1999–2001).

★ **Most yards gained passing in an NFL career**
Dan Marino (USA) gained 61,361 yards passing during his NFL career from 1983 to 1999, playing for the Miami Dolphins. In 1998, Marino received the Man of the Year award from the NFL in recognition of his support of various children's charities.

★ **Most yards gained rushing in an NFL career**
Emmitt Smith (USA) of the Dallas Cowboys gained 17,418 yards rushing over his NFL career spanning 1990 to 2003.

★ **Most sacks made in an NFL career**
Bruce Smith (USA) has made 199 sacks in the course of his NFL career, playing for the Buffalo Bills (1985–2000) and the Washington Redskins (2000–03).

★ **Most NFL career interceptions**
Paul Krause (USA), a free safety from the University of Iowa, is the leading pass interceptor of all time with 81 steals during a 16-season career, playing for Washington Redskins (1964–67) and Minnesota Vikings (1968–79).

★ **Most interceptions in an NFL season**
The most interceptions made in an NFL season is 14 by Dick 'Night Train' Lane (USA) playing for the Los Angeles Rams in 1952, the first fully professional season. He returned them for 298 yards and two touchdowns.

★ **Most games officiated**
Raymond Longden (USA) has officiated at well over 2,000 football games, more than any other referee. He has officiated in more than 50 games a season since 1947.

Baseball
Sport

Highest »
paid player

The richest contract, based on the average annual salary for the duration of the contract, is $25.2 million by Alex Rodriguez (USA, left) of the Texas Rangers ($252 million over 10 years), signed in December 2000. Rodriguez moved to the New York Yankees before the start of the 2004 season, in a complicated deal that sees the Rangers cover the player's wages, paying $67 million of the $179 million left on his contract, and with the Yankees paying him $112 million over the next seven years.

★ **Most games played**
Pete Rose (USA) played in a record 3,562 games with a record 14,053 at bats for the Cincinnati Reds (1963–78 and 1984–86), Philadelphia Phillies (1979–83), and Montreal Expos (1984).

★ **Most consecutive games**
Calvin Edwin Ripken Jr. (USA) played a record 2,632 consecutive games for the Baltimore Orioles from May 30 1982 to September 19 1998.

★ **Most sacrifice bunts in a career**
The most sacrifice bunts made in professional baseball is 514 by Masahiro Kawai (Japan) during a career spanning 20 years from 1984 to 2003, playing for the Yomiuri Giants in Japan.

★ **Longest major league game**
The Chicago White Sox and the Milwaukee Brewers played a game lasting 8 hr 6 min on May 9 1984. The White Sox eventually won the game 7–6 in the 25th inning.

★ **Most strikeouts in a major league career**
Nolan Ryan (USA) threw 5,714 strikeouts over his career from 1966 to 1993, playing for the New York Mets, the California Angels, the Houston Astros, and the Texas Rangers.

★ **Most strikeouts in one major league game**
Roger Clemens (USA) threw 20 strikeouts in one game (9 innings) playing for the Boston Red Sox against the Seattle Mariners on April 29 1986 and against the Detroit Tigers on September 18 1996. The record was equaled by Kerry Wood (USA), playing for the Chicago Cubs against the Houston Astros on May 6 1998.

★ **Most runs in a major league career**
The most runs scored in a major league career is 2,295 by Rickey Henley Henderson (USA) up to 2003. Henderson began the first of his 25 seasons to date on June 24 1979 with the Oakland Athletics, and then went on to play for nine franchises before finishing the 2003 season with the Los Angeles Dodgers.

★ **Most doubles in a major league career**
Tris Speaker (USA) hit a record 792 doubles during his career, playing for the Boston Red Sox, the Cleveland Indians, the Washington Senators, and the Philadelphia Athletics from 1907 to 1928.

★ **Most triples in a major league career**
The most triples hit in a major league career is 309 by Sam Crawford (USA), playing for Cincinnati Reds and the Detroit Tigers from 1899 to 1917.

★ **Most no-hit games pitched in a major league career**
The most no-hitters pitched in a career is seven by Nolan Ryan (USA) from 1973 to 1991.

★ **Most major league games pitched**
By the end of the 2003 season, Jesse Orosco (USA) had pitched a total of 1,251 games for the New York Mets, Los Angeles Dodgers, Cleveland Indians, Milwaukee Brewers, Baltimore Orioles, St. Louis Cardinals, Minnesota Twins, New York Yankees, and San Diego Padres.

★ **Most stolen bases in a major league career**
Rickey Henley Henderson (USA) stole 1,406 bases during his career, from 1979 to 2003, playing for the Oakland Athletics, New York Yankees, Toronto Blue Jays, San Diego Padres, Anaheim Angels, Seattle Mariners, New York Mets, Boston Red Sox, and Los Angeles Dodgers.

★ **Highest batting average in a major league career**
The highest career batting average is .367 by Tyrus Raymond 'Ty' Cobb (USA), playing for the Detroit Tigers and Philadelphia Athletics from 1905 to 1928.

Oldest major >> league player

Leroy Robert 'Satchel' Paige (USA, right) began playing for the Cleveland Indians in 1948, aged 41. He pitched for the Kansas City Athletics at 59 years 80 days on September 25 1965.

Most home runs ⌃ in a season

Barry Bonds (USA, above) of the San Francisco Giants hit 73 home runs in the 2001 season.

★ **Most runs batted in in a major league career**
The most runs batted in in a career is 2,297 by Henry Hank Aaron (USA) from 1954 to 1976.

★ **Most runs in a major league season**
William Robert Hamilton (USA) scored a record 196 runs playing for the Philadelphia Phillies in 1894.

★ **Most consecutive major league games batted in safely**
Joseph Paul DiMaggio (USA), playing for the New York Yankees, safely batted in 56 consecutive games from May 15 to July 16 1941.

★ **Most consecutive hits in major league**
On June 19–21 1938, Michael Franklin 'Pinky' Higgins (USA) had 12 consecutive hits playing for the Boston Red Sox. Walter 'Moose' Dropo (USA) equaled this on July 14–15 1952, playing for the Detroit Tigers.

★ **Highest percentage home runs in a career**
During his career (1914–35), George Herman 'Babe' Ruth (USA) hit 714 homers from 8,399 times at bat, the highest home run percentage of 8.5% in major league history.

★ **Most home runs in a single game**
The most home runs in a major league game is four, first achieved by Robert Lincoln 'Bobby' Lowe (USA) for the Boston Beaneaters against the Cincinnati Reds on May 30 1894. The feat has been achieved many times since then.

★ **Most Cy Young Award wins**
The Cy Young Award, given annually since 1956 to the most outstanding pitcher in the major leagues, has gone to Roger Clemens (USA) a record six times. During this time, he played for the Boston Red Sox (1986, 1987, 1991), Toronto Blue Jays (1997–98), and New York Yankees (2001).

★ **Most wins of the Most Valuable World Series Player award**
The only men to have won the MVP twice are: Sanford 'Sandy' Koufax (USA), playing for the Los Angeles Dodgers (1963, 1965); Robert 'Bob' Gibson (USA), playing for the St. Louis Cardinals (1964, 1967); and Reginald Martinez 'Reggie' Jackson (USA), playing for the Oakland Athletics (1973) and New York Yankees (1977).

★ **Oldest World Series player**
Jack Quinn (USA) of the Philadelphia Athletics was 47 years 91 days old when he played on October 4 1930.

★ **Most durable announcer**
Ernest Harwell (USA) had a 55-year career that began in 1948 with the Brooklyn

Dodgers, followed by the New York Giants (1951–53), Baltimore Orioles (1954–59), and Detroit Tigers (1960–2002). In the course of his career, Harwell announced more than 8,300 major league baseball games.

★ **Largest replica bat**
The world's biggest ever replica baseball bat is 120 ft (36.5 m) in length and weighs 68,000 lb (30,844 kg) and was made by bat manufacturer Hillerich Bradsby (USA). The bat is modeled on the 'R43' bat made for Babe Ruth in 1927 by the same manufacturer.

★ **Fastest hit in Finnish baseball**
Sami Ahola (Finland) hit a ball at a speed of 108.1 mph (174 km/h) at the Lahti Indoor Arena, Finland, on February 20 2002.

Basketball
Sport

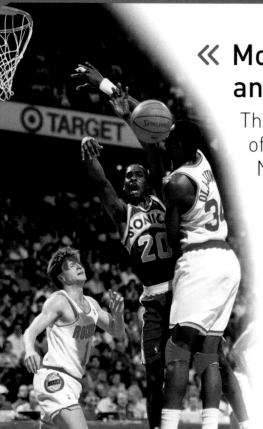

« Most blocks in an NBA career

The greatest number of blocks in a National Basketball Association (NBA) career is 3,830 in 1,238 games by Hakeem Olajuwon (USA, near left), playing for the Houston Rockets (1984–2001) and the Toronto Raptors (2001–02).

Most NBA ⌃ Championship titles

The Boston Celtics have won a total of 16 NBA Championship titles, in 1957, 1959–66, 1968–69, 1974, 1976, 1981, 1984, and 1986. In their last three championship-winning years, their team included record-breaker Robert Parish (USA, above).

★ Highest aggregate score in an NBA game

The highest aggregate score in an NBA game is 370, which occurred when the Detroit Pistons beat the Denver Nuggets 186-184 at Denver, Colorado, USA, on December 13 1983. The game went into overtime after a 145–145 tie.

★ Most consecutive NBA wins

The Los Angeles Lakers won 33 games in succession from November 5 1971 to January 7 1972.

★ Most wins in an NBA season

In the 1995/96 season, the Chicago Bulls won a total of 72 games.

★ Most losses in an NBA season

The highest number of losses incurred in a season was by the Philadelphia 76ers, who were defeated 73 times and won just nine games during an 82-game season.

This run of bad luck included a 20-game losing streak in the 1972/73 season.

★ Most points in an NBA season

Wilt Chamberlain (USA) scored 4,029 points while playing for the Philadelphia Warriors in the 1961/62 season.

During this season, Chamberlain also set the record for the highest scoring average in a season, with 50.4 points per game, and scored 1,597 field goals, the most in a season.

★ Most points scored by an individual in an NBA game

Wilt Chamberlain (USA) scored 100 points for the Philadelphia 76ers against the New York Knicks on March 2 1962.

★ Most three-point field goals in an NBA season

Dennis Scott (USA) scored 267 three-point field goals for the Orlando Magic in 1996/97.

★ Most three-point field goals in an NBA career

Reggie Miller (USA) scored 2,426 three-point field goals for the Indiana Pacers from 1987 to 2004.

★ Most consecutive NBA games played

A.C. Green (USA) played 1,177 consecutive games for the Los Angeles Lakers, Phoenix Suns, Dallas Mavericks, and Miami Heat from November 19 1986 to March 20 2001.

★ Most games played in an NBA career

Robert Parish (USA) played 1,611 regular-season games during his NBA career from 1976 to 1997. He achieved this record over 21 seasons playing for four teams: the Golden State Warriors

(1976–80), the Boston Celtics (1980–94), the Charlotte Hornets (1994–96), and the Chicago Bulls (1996–97).

★ Most free throws in an NBA career

The greatest number of free throws made in a career is 9,715 in 1,458 games by Karl Malone (USA) playing for the Utah Jazz (1985–2003) and the Los Angeles Lakers (2003–04).

★ Most rebounds in an NBA career

Wilt Chamberlain (USA) had 23,924 rebounds in 1,045 games. During his NBA career he played for the Philadelphia Warriors (1959–62), the San Francisco Warriors (1962–65), the Philadelphia 76ers (1964–68), and the Los Angeles Lakers (1968–73).

Highest point- ⌄ scoring average in an NBA career

The highest point-scoring average for players who have exceeded 10,000 points is 30.1 by Michael Jordan (USA, below), who scored a total of 32,292 points in 1,072 games playing for the Chicago Bulls (1984–98) and the Washington Wizards (2001–03).

★ Most points scored in an NBA career

The greatest number of points scored in an NBA career is 38,387 (at an average of 24.6 points per game) by Kareem Abdul-Jabbar (b. Ferdinand Lewis Alcindor, USA) from 1969 to 1989. This total includes 15,837 field goals that were scored in regular season games and 5,762 points – including 2,356 field goals – that were scored in play-off games.

★ Most NBA play-off appearances in a career

During his playing career, Kareem Abdul-Jabbar (USA) took part in 237 play-off games. He played for the Milwaukee Bucks from 1969 to 1975 and the Los Angeles Lakers from 1975 to 1989.

★ Most fouls in an NBA career

Kareem Abdul-Jabbar committed a total of 4,657 fouls in 1,560 games during a playing career that lasted from 1969 to 1989.

★ Most steals and assists in an NBA career

John Stockton (USA) made 3,265 steals in 1,504 games, playing for the Utah Jazz from 1984 to 2003.

Stockton made a total of 15,806 assists in 1,504 games playing for the Utah Jazz from 1984 to 2003, another world record.

★ Tallest player

Suleiman Ali Nashnush (Libya) was reputed to be 8 ft 0.25 in (2.45 m) when he played for his national team in 1962.

★ Longest time to spin a basketball on one finger

Zhao Guang (China) spun a regulation basketball on one finger while maintaining the spin for 3 hr 59 min on January 29 2003 in Shenyang, China.

★ Longest basketball marathon

A match lasting 26 hr 42 min was played at Warwick Academy, at the Bermuda College Gym, Paget, Bermuda, on March 15–16 2003. The Blue and White teams played a total of 27 games against each other.

★ Most basketballs dribbled simultaneously by one person

Joseph Odhiambo (USA) dribbled six basketballs simultaneously on August 15 2000 at his home in Mesa, Arizona, USA. This beat his previous record of dribbling five basketballs at once.

★ Most consecutive shots with head

Eyal Horn (Israel) made a total of 19 consecutive layups, controlling and shooting the ball using only his head, on the set of *Guinness Rekord TV*, Stockholm, Sweden, on November 29 2001.

★ Most consecutive free throws

Ted St. Martin (USA) made 5,221 consecutive free throws at Jacksonville, Florida, USA, on April 28 1996.

★ Most free throws in one minute

David Bergström (Sweden) made 48 free throws in one minute at Fyrishov, Uppsala, Sweden, on October 2 2001. The attempt was filmed by *Guinness Rekord TV*, Sweden.

★ Most three-pointers in one minute

Lea Hakala (Finland) made 19 successful three-point shots in a minute on the set of *Guinness World Records*, Helsinki, Finland, on October 22 2001.

★ Greatest distance to dribble a basketball in 24 hours

Suresh Joachim (Australia) dribbled a basketball a distance of 97.37 miles (156.71 km) at Vulkanhallen, Oslo, Norway, on March 30–31 2001.

★ Longest goal thrown in an exhibition match

Iain McKinney (UK) scored a basketball goal from a distance of 90 ft 6 in (27.6 m) playing for the Sheffield Sharks at Ponds Forge, Sheffield, South Yorkshire, UK, on April 8 1996.

Ice hockey
Sport

Most NHL career wins ⌃ by a goaltender

Having begun his career with the Montreal Canadiens in 1985, goalie Patrick Roy (Canada, above) of the Colorado Avalanche had 516 wins up to the end of the 2002 regular season. With 22 shutouts, Roy also holds the record for the most shutouts by a goaltender in NHL play-off history.

★ **Most wins in a National Hockey League (NHL) season**
The Detroit Red Wings achieved 62 wins during the 1995/96 NHL season.

★ **Longest NHL winning streak**
The longest run of winning games – both at home and away – in NHL history is 17 by the Pittsburgh Penguins from March 9 to April 10 1993.

★ **Fewest defeats in an NHL season**
In the 1976/77 season, the Montreal Canadiens lost just eight games, the fewest ever in a season of 70 or more games, from 80 played (60 wins, 12 ties, and a record 132 points).

★ **Most losses in an NHL season**
The San Jose Sharks had 71 losses during the 1992/93 season, including a record 32 games lost at home.

★ **Most points scored in an NHL career**
Wayne Gretzky (Canada) scored 2,857 points for the Edmonton Oilers, Los Angeles Kings, St. Louis Blues, and New York Rangers from 1979 to 1999. The points total includes 894 goals and 1,963 assists, achieved in 1,487 games.

★ **Most goals scored in an NHL season**
Wayne Gretzky (Canada) scored 92 goals for the Edmonton Oilers during the 1981/82 season.

★ **Most goals scored by a team in an NHL season**
The Edmonton Oilers scored 446 goals in the 1983/84 season.

★ **Most goals scored by an individual in an NHL game**
Joe Malone (Canada) scored seven goals for the Québec Bulldogs in their game against the Toronto St. Patricks in Québec City, Québec, Canada, on January 31 1920.

★ **Longest NHL suspension for an infraction during a game**
Marty McSorley (USA) of the Boston Bruins incurred a 23-game suspension in February 2000 for hitting Vancouver Canucks' Donald Brashear (Canada) on the head with his stick in a game in Vancouver, British Columbia, Canada, on February 21 2000.

★ **Most penalty minutes in an NHL career**
In the 17 seasons from 1971 to 1988, Dave 'Tiger' Williams (Canada) had 3,966 penalty minutes – the most in NHL history – playing for the Toronto Maple Leafs, Vancouver Canucks, Detroit Red Wings, Los Angeles Kings, and the now-defunct Hartford Whalers.

★ **Most penalties against an individual in an NHL game**
Chris Nilan (USA) had a record 10 penalties called against him when playing for the Boston Bruins against the Hartford Whalers on March 31 1991.

★ **Most penalties in an NHL game**
The most penalties awarded in any NHL game is 85, when the Edmonton Oilers played the Los Angeles Kings in Los Angeles, California, USA, on February 28 1990.

★ **Most NHL goaltending appearances**
The most NHL goaltending appearances is 971 by Terry Sawchuk (Canada) for the Detroit Red Wings, Boston Bruins, Toronto Maple Leafs, Los Angeles Kings, and New York Rangers from 1949 to 1970.

Most women's ice hockey Olympic wins

Women's ice hockey has been contested twice at the Winter Olympics, in 1998 and 2002. The USA beat Canada in the final in 1998, and Canada (above) got revenge by beating the USA in the 2002 final.

Most hat tricks in an NHL career »

The most hat tricks scored in an NHL career is 50 by Wayne Gretzky (Canada, right), for the Edmonton Oilers, Los Angeles Kings, St. Louis Blues, and New York Rangers from 1979 to 1999.

★ Most goaltending shutouts in an NHL career
The most goaltending shutouts in an NHL career is 103 by Terry Sawchuk (Canada) for the Detroit Red Wings, Boston Bruins, Toronto Maple Leafs, Los Angeles Kings, and New York Rangers from 1949–70.

★ Most NHL All-Star selections
Gordie Howe (Canada) was selected 21 times for the NHL All-Star game while playing for the Detroit Red Wings from 1946 to 1979. He played in the first team 12 times and in the second team nine times.

★ Quickest goal scored in an NHL match
The quickest goals in an NHL match were scored five seconds after the opening whistle. This record is held by Doug Smail (Canada) for the Winnipeg Jets against the St. Louis Blues in Winnipeg, Manitoba, Canada, on December 20 1981; by Bryan John Trottier (Canada) for the New York Islanders against the Boston Bruins in

Boston, USA, on March 22 1984; and by Alexander Mogilny (Russia) for the Buffalo Sabers against the Toronto Maple Leafs in Toronto, Ontario, Canada, on December 21 1991.

★ Most ties in an NHL season
The Philadelphia Flyers played 24 tied games over a 76-game season in 1969/70.

★ Most men's ice hockey Olympic wins
Ice hockey was first contested at the Winter Olympics in 1920. The most wins is eight by the USSR – in 1956, 1964, 1968, 1972, 1976, 1984, 1988, and in 1992 – as the CIS, when all players were Russian.

★ Most points scored by an individual in a professional ice hockey game
A record 10 points in a game has been scored twice by two professional players: Jim Harrison (Canada) with three goals and seven assists for the Alberta (later Edmonton) Oilers in a World Hockey Association (WHA) match in Edmonton,

Canada, on January 30 1973; and Darryl Sittler (Canada) with six goals and four assists for the Toronto Maple Leafs against the Boston Bruins in an NHL match in Toronto, Ontario, Canada, on February 7 1976.

★ Most Stanley Cup wins by a team
The Montreal Canadiens have won the Stanley Cup 24 times (1916, 1924, 1930–31, 1944, 1946, 1953, 1956–60, 1965–66, 1968–69, 1971, 1973, 1976–79, 1986, and 1993) from a record 32 finals.

★ Most individual Stanley Cup wins
Henri Richard (Canada) had 11 individual Stanley Cup wins for the Montreal Canadiens from 1956 to 1975.

★ Most points scored in a Stanley Cup series
Wayne Gretzky (Canada) scored a record 47 points for the Edmonton Oilers in the 1985 Stanley Cup. The points scored included 17 goals and 30 assists, which are in themselves records.

★ Most games played in a professional ice hockey career
Gordon Howe (Canada) played 2,421 games in his professional ice hockey career from 1946 to 1979.

★ Largest ice hockey stick
An ice hockey stick made by the Millwork Home Centre in Oshawa, Ontario, Canada, measured 44 ft 3.6 in (13.5 m) from the heel of the blade to the top of the shaft on October 25 2003.

★ Most durable ice hockey player
The most durable ice hockey player is James Bernard Hawkins (USA), who began playing in organized hockey leagues in 1932 and played for a total of 71 years.

★ Ice hockey marathon
The longest duration for a game of ice hockey is 130 hr 7 min, played at the Moosomin Communiplex, Moosomin, Saskatchewan, Canada, on October 13–18 2003.

Fastest goal »
in a World Cup
soccer match

The quickest goal in a World Cup finals match, as recognized by the Fédération Internationale de Football Association (FIFA), was timed at 11 seconds. It was scored by Hakan Sukur of Turkey (far right) against the Republic of Korea at Daegu, Korea, on June 29 2002.

★ **Fastest World Cup red card**
Ion Vladoiu (Romania) was sent off after only three minutes in a World Cup finals match against Switzerland on June 22 1994 at the Pontiac Silverdome, Detroit, Michigan, USA.

★ **Most World Cup finals goals**
Gerd Müller scored 14 goals in World Cup finals tournaments for West Germany. This total includes 10 goals in 1970 in Mexico and four in West Germany in 1974, when the host nation went on to lift the trophy.

★ **Most goals in a single World Cup finals**
The most goals scored by an individual player in a World Cup finals tournament is 13 by Just Fontaine (France) in 1958 in Sweden.

★ **Most women's World Cup wins**
A women's World Cup competition was initiated in 1991 and is held quadrennially.

The tournament has been held on four occasions so far. The USA won two of these (1991 and 1999), while the winners in 1995 were Norway, with Germany winning in 2003.

★ **Most World Cup clean sheets**
Goalkeeper Peter Shilton (UK) played in 10 World Cup finals matches for England without conceding a single goal over three tournaments and a total of 17 games between 1982 and 1990.

★ **Most countries in FIFA World Cup qualifiers**
A total of 198 federations registered to play in the FIFA qualifiers for the 2002 World Cup, which were held jointly in South Korea and Japan. The soccer federations of Afghanistan, Burundi, New Guinea, Niger, and North Korea were the exceptions.

★ **Most World Cup wins**
FIFA instituted the first World Cup on July 13 1930 in Montevideo, Uruguay. The tournament is held every four years and has been won five times by Brazil, in 1958, 1962, 1970, 1994, and 2002.

★ **Highest score in an international match**
Australia defeated American Samoa 31–0 in a World Cup qualifying match at Coffs Harbour, New South Wales, Australia, on April 11 2001.

★ **Youngest scorer in a World Cup finals**
Edson Arantes do Nascimento, better known as Pelé, was aged 17 years 239 days when he scored for Brazil against Wales, in Gothenburg, Sweden, on June 19 1958.

★ **Youngest player in a World Cup finals**
The youngest person ever to play in a finals match is Norman Whiteside (UK), who played for Northern Ireland against Yugoslavia aged 17 years 41 days in Zaragoza, Spain, on June 17 1982.

★ **Oldest player in World Cup finals**
Albert Roger Milla (b. May 20 1952) played for Cameroon against Russia at Stanford, Palo Alto, California, USA, on June 28 1994 at the age of 42 years 39 days.
   During the course of this match, Milla also scored, making him the oldest person ever to score in the World Cup finals.

Most Africa Cup of ⌃ Nations wins

The record for the most wins of the Africa Cup of Nations is four, jointly

held by Ghana, who won in 1963, 1965, 1978, and 1982; Egypt, who won in 1957, 1959, 1986, and 1998; and Cameroon (above), who won in 1984, 1988, 2000, and 2002.

Fastest » international hat trick

Japanese international Masashi 'Gon' Nakayama (right)

scored a hat trick in 3 min 15 sec against Brunei during an Asian Cup qualifying match on February 16 2000. Nakayama netted on 1 minute, 2 minutes, and 3 min 15 sec, bettering the 62-year-old record set by George William Hall (UK), who scored three in 3 min 30 sec for England against Ireland at Old Trafford, Manchester, UK, on November 16 1938.

★ **Most goals scored by a goalkeeper in one game**
Paraguayan goalkeeper José Luis Chilavert scored a hat trick of penalties for Vélez Sarsfield in their 6–1 defeat of Ferro Carril Oeste on November 28 1999 in the Argentine professional league.

Chilavert specializes in penalties and free kicks. He is the only keeper to have scored in a World Cup qualifying game (against Argentina in Buenos Aires, 1997) and the only one to have taken a direct free kick in a World Cup (France, 1998).

He also holds the record for the most goals scored by a goalkeeper, with a total of 56 official league and international goals from July 1992 to October 2001. Chilavert currently plays for his country and for the French club Strasbourg.

★ **Most goals scored in an international by an individual**
During the record-breaking 31–0 defeat by Australia of American Samoa,

Archie Thompson (Australia) scored an international record 13 goals.

★ **Oldest regular player**
Enrique Alcocer (Mexico, b. August 28 1924) is currently the world's oldest regular soccer player. He plays for the Reforma Athletic Club in Mexico City, Mexico. Alcocer began playing regularly in 1936 for the Grosso Junior and High School in Mexico City, and subsequently played professionally for the Marte Football Club in 1944 in Mexico's first division before joining his current club in 1952.

★ **Largest tournament by players**
The Chappies Little League Cup competition was held in South Africa from March to September 2003, and was contested by 6,023 teams which included a total of 138,529 players. The tournament is the South African national schools' under-12 competition.

★ **Most durable referee**
Jozsef Magyar (Hungary) regularly refereed competitive soccer for 50 years. He gained his refereeing qualification in 1953 and officiated his last match on March 9 2003 in Sitke, Hungary, aged 80.

★ **Most women's international caps**
The greatest number of international appearances by a woman for a national team is 270 by Kristine Lilly (USA), who represented the USA from 1987 to 2004.

★ **Most men's international caps**
The most international appearances for a national team is 171 by Claudio Suarez for Mexico from 1992 to 2003.

★ **Most South American Championships**
Argentina won the South American Championship (known as the Copa América since 1975) a record 15 times from 1910 to 1993.

★ **Most expensive goalkeeper**
In July 2001, Gianluigi Buffon (Italy) transferred between Italian Serie A clubs Parma and Juventus for a record fee of $46.8 million.

★ **Highest score in a women's international**
The record score line of 21–0 has been achieved on four separate occasions: by Japan against Guam at Guangzhou, China, on December 5 1997; by Canada against Puerto Rico at Centennial Park, Toronto, Canada, on August 28 1998; and by Australia against American Samoa and by New Zealand against Samoa – both of these matches taking place at Mt. Smart Stadium, Auckland, New Zealand, on October 9 1998.

Soccer 2
Sport

Most English League Cup wins «

Liverpool (team members Michael Owen, far left, and Steven Gerrard, left; both UK) has won the English League Cup seven times, in 1981–84, 1995, 2001, and 2003.

★ **Largest attendance**
The greatest recorded crowd at any soccer match was 199,854 for the Brazil against Uruguay World Cup match in the Maracanã Municipal Stadium, Rio de Janeiro, Brazil, on July 16 1950.

★ **Largest soccer complex**
The National Sports Center at Blaines, Minnesota, USA, has 57 playing fields, 55 of which are playable at any one time.

★ **Furthest distance traveled between competitors in the same league**
The furthest distance traveled between two clubs in the top division of a professional national league is 2,979 miles (4,794 km) between the home stadiums of the US Major League Soccer teams Los Angeles Galaxy and New England Revolution.

★ **Most goals in a Champions League season**
The most goals scored in a UEFA Champions League season is 12 by Ruud van Nistelrooy (Netherlands) for Manchester United in the 2002/03 season.

★ **Fastest Champions League goal**
The fastest goal in a Champions League match was scored by Gilberto Silva (Brazil) in 20.07 seconds playing for Arsenal against PSV Eindhoven in Eindhoven, The Netherlands, on September 25 2002. Arsenal went on to win the game 4–0.

★ **Most Champions League goals**
The most goals in UEFA Champions League matches is 44 by Raúl González Blanco (Spain) playing for Real Madrid from 1992 until present.

★ **Highest score in a national cup final**
In 1935, Lausanne-Sports beat Nordstern Basel 10–0 in the Swiss Cup final. Two years later, they suffered defeat by the same score at the hands of Grasshopper Club (Zurich) in the 1937 Swiss Cup final.

★ **Most consecutive Champions League match victories**
The longest winning streak in the UEFA Champions League is 11 games by FC Barcelona in the 2002/03 season.

★ **Most Cup Winners' Cups**
The Cup Winners' Cup, contested until 1999 by the winners of the national cups in Europe, was won a record four times by FC Barcelona (1979, 1982, 1989, and 1997).

★ **Most assists in a Major League Soccer season**
Carlos Valderrama (Colombia) made 26 assists in a Major League Soccer season, playing for the Tampa Bay Mutiny in 2000.

★ **Longest clean sheet in goalkeeping**
Abel Resino (Spain) of Atlético de Madrid succeeded in preventing goals being scored past him in top-class competition for 1,275 min (just over 14 matches) during the 1990/91 La Liga season.

The record in international matches is 1,142 min (nearly 13 matches) by Dino Zoff (Italy) from September 1972 to June 1974.

★ **Most domestic league titles**
The most domestic league titles won by a soccer club is 50, by Rangers FC (UK) in the Scottish Division 1 and Premier Division Championships, from 1891 to 2003.

★ **Fastest time to score a hat trick**
Tommy Ross (UK) scored three goals in 90 seconds for Ross County against Nairn County at Dingwall, Ross-shire, UK, on November 28 1964.

★ **Most Futsal World Cup titles**
Since it was first held in 1989, the most wins at the Futsal (indoor soccer) World Cup is three by Brazil (1989, 1992, and 1996). The fourth tournament, held in 2000 in Guatemala, was won by Spain, who beat Brazil 4–3 in the final.

Most expensive soccer player »

The highest transfer fee for a player is

13 billion Spanish pesetas ($66 million) for Zinédine Zidane (France, right) for his transfer from Juventus to Real Madrid on July 9 2001.

Most career goals ⌃

Edson Arantes do Nascimento (Brazil, above), better known as Pelé, scored a total of 1,279 goals from September 7 1956 to October 1 1977 in 1,363 games. Pelé's best year was 1959, in which he scored 126 goals. The milésimo (1,000th) came from a penalty for his club Santos at the Maracanã Stadium, Rio de Janeiro, Brazil, on November 19 1969 in his 909th first-class match. He later added two more goals in special appearances.

★ Unbeaten premiership season
In the premiership season of 2003/04, Arsenal FC were unbeaten in 38 games, winning 26, drawing 12, and losing none. In the process they scored 73 goals and conceded 26, failing to score on only four occasions.

★ Most premiership goals
Alan Shearer (UK) scored 243 goals in the English Premiership. Shearer began his career with Southampton, before moving to Blackburn Rovers and finally to Newcastle United in July 1996 for a record fee of £15.6 million ($22.4 million).

★ Longest penalty shoot-out
In the Derby Community League (UK) under-10s cup match between Mickleover Lightning Blue Sox and Chellaston Boys 'B' on January 17 1998, a total of 66 penalties were taken to decide the match, which had finished 1–1. The Blue Sox eventually won the marathon shoot-out 2–1, with 35 penalties being saved, the rest going wide of the target.

★ Most consecutive passes
The most consecutive soccer passes is 557 and was set by members of the McDonald's Youth Football Scheme, Tsing Yi, Hong Kong, China, on May 4 2002.

★ Most goals scored direct from corners
The most goals scored in a match by an individual direct from corners is three by Steve Cromey (UK) for Ashgreen United against Dunlop FC on February 24 2002 at Bedworth, Warwickshire, UK, and by Daniel White (UK) for Street and Glastonbury under-11s against Westfield Boys on April 7 2002.

★ Most touches of a soccer ball in 30 seconds
The most touches of a soccer ball in 30 seconds, while keeping the ball in the air, is 141 by Ferdie Adoboe (USA) in New York, USA, on August 27 2003.
The women's record is 137 touches by Tasha-Nicole Terani (USA) in New York, USA, on August 27 2003.

★ Fastest ball control marathon distance
Jan Skorkovsky (Czechoslovakia) kept a soccer ball up while running a distance of 26.219 miles (42.195 km) in the Prague City Marathon in 7 hr 18 min 55 sec on July 8 1990.

★ Longest ball control with feet, legs, and head
Martinho Eduardo Orige (Brazil) juggled a regulation-size soccer ball for 19 hr 30 min nonstop with feet, legs, and head without the ball ever touching the ground at Padre Ezio Julli Gym in Araranguá, Brazil, on August 2–3 2003.

★ Longest ball control while lying down
Tomas Lundman (Sweden) managed to keep a regulation-size soccer ball up in the air using his feet while lying on his back for 7 min 36 sec at Angebo Svågagården Hudiksvall, Sweden, on September 20 2003.

★ Most soccer management rejection letters
The most rejection letters received for soccer management jobs is 29 by Richard Dixon (UK). Dixon applies only for jobs that are available and has received official letters from clubs such as Tottenham Hotspur, Manchester United, Atlético de Madrid, and the English and Cypriot national teams. The hobby began in 2000 when physical education teacher Dixon contracted infectious mononucleosis and applied for the Millwall job.

Rugby
Sport

Most Super League titles

The most Super League titles won by a team is four by St. Helens (above) in 1996, 1999, 2000, and 2002. The Super League is the UK's premier Rugby League competition, instituted in 1996.

★ **Most points by an individual player in a Rugby Union international**
In the World Cup qualifying match between Hong Kong and Singapore at Kuala Lumpur, Malaysia, on October 27 1994, Hong Kong's Ashley Billington scored 50 points (10 tries).

★ **Most penalties by an individual player in a Rugby Union international**
The record is shared by two players: Keiji Hirose kicked nine successful penalties for Japan against Tonga (44–17) in Tokyo, Japan, on May 9 1999; and Andrew Mehrtens also kicked nine for New Zealand against Australia (34–15) at Auckland, New Zealand, on July 24 1999.

★ **Most points in a Rugby Union international career**
Neil Jenkins (UK) scored 1,049 points in 87 matches (1,008 points in 83 matches for Wales, 41 points in four matches for the British Lions) from 1991 to March 2001.

★ **Fastest Rugby Union World Cup try**
Elton Flatley (Australia) scored a try just 18 seconds after kick-off when playing for Australia against Romania on October 18 2003 at the Suncorp Stadium, Brisbane, Queensland, Australia.

★ **Largest rugby tour**
From April 11 to 14 2003, 264 players and coaches from Ealing Rugby Club (UK) played matches on tour in Ireland.

★ **Most women's Rugby Union World Cup titles**
The women's World Cup has been contested four times (1991, 1994, 1998, and 2002). New Zealand has won the title twice, in 1998 and 2002, while the USA and England have one win apiece.

★ **Most wins in the Hong Kong Sevens**
First held in 1976, this is the world's most prestigious international tournament for seven-a-side Rugby Union. Fiji has won a record nine times, in 1977–78, 1980, 1984, 1990–92, and 1998–99. For 1997 the contest was replaced by the World Cup Sevens, which Fiji also won.

★ **Highest attendance at a Rugby Union match**
The largest paying attendance for a Rugby Union international is 109,874 for New Zealand's 39–35 victory over Australia at Stadium Australia, Sydney, Australia, on July 15 2000.

★ **Highest attendance at a Rugby League match**
A total of 104,583 spectators saw a Rugby League double header at Stadium Australia, Sydney, Australia, on March 7 1999. The Newcastle Knights beat the Manly Sea Eagles 41–18, and the Parramatta Eels beat the St George Illawarra Dragons 20–10.

★ **Most Rugby League World Cup wins**
The Rugby League World Cup competition was first held in 1954. Australia have most wins, with eight, in 1957, 1968, 1970, 1977, 1988, 1992, 1995, and 2000, as well as a win in the International Championship of 1975.

★ **Most Rugby League Challenge Cup wins**
The Rugby League Challenge Cup (inaugurated in the 1896/97 season) has been won a record 17 times by Wigan (in 1924, 1929, 1948, 1951, 1958–59, 1965, 1985, 1988–95, and 2002).

★ **Most National Rugby League (NRL) titles**
The Brisbane Broncos have won two NRL titles, in 1998 and 2000. The NRL is Australia's premier Rugby League competition. Instituted in 1998, it replaced the Australian Rugby League (1995–97), which in turn replaced the New South Wales Rugby League (1908–94).

Biggest Rugby Union World Cup match win ⌄

The largest winning margin recorded in Rugby Union World Cup matches is 142 points, when host nation Australia beat Namibia 142–0 in Adelaide, Australia, on October 25 2003. Matt Giteau (Australia) is pictured below scoring one of his tries.

Most Rugby Union ⌃ World Cup wins

The William Webb Ellis Trophy (above) is awarded to the winners of the Rugby Union World Cup (instituted in 1987). The most wins is two by Australia, in 1991 and 1999.

★ Most tries scored in an amateur Rugby League season
Richard Lopag (UK) scored 169 tries for the Deighton Juniors Under-13 side, West Yorkshire, UK, in the 2001/02 season.

★ Most hat tricks in a Rugby League season
Richard Lopag (UK) of Deighton Juniors Under-13s, Huddersfield, West Yorkshire, UK, scored 43 hat tricks during the 2001/02 season.

★ Fastest Rugby League hat trick
Chris Thorman (UK) scored a hat trick of tries within 6 min 54 sec of the start of a match, for Huddersfield Giants against Doncaster Dragons in the semifinal of the Buddies National League Cup at Doncaster, South Yorkshire, UK, on May 19 2002.

★ Most rugby tackles in one hour
Cranleigh RFC Under-11s made 1,644 rugby tackles in one hour on April 21 2002 at Cranleigh Rugby Club, Surrey, UK.

★ GWR TALKS TO
Jason Leonard OBE

Jason Leonard (UK, below right pictured with his International Rugby Players Association Asprey Special Merit Award, presented in 2002) played in 114 international Rugby Union matches for England from 1990 to 2004. The England prop became the most capped player of all time when he came on for Phil Vickery (UK) in the fourth minute of England's World Cup semifinal victory over France at the Telstra Stadium, Sydney, Australia, on November 16 2003. England won the match 24–7 with Leonard having been on the pitch for one minute.

Who inspires you?
Muhammad Ali, the Greatest.

Did you always want to be a rugby player?
At school, I wanted to be a soccer player – I was a pretty good defender – but then I discovered rugby, and that was that!

If you hadn't pursued a career in rugby what do you think you would have done?
When I left school, I worked in the building trade, so I'd probably have carried on with that.

Did you think your international career would go on this long?
When I started playing for England, back in 1990, 30 caps was considered a great career, so I'm amazed I managed to carry on playing for 14 years! I've recently decided to bow out of competitive rugby, but I've enjoyed every minute and achieved more than I could have ever dreamed of when I started, so I've no regrets.

What is your greatest achievement in rugby?
Winning the World Cup with England in Australia in 2003.

What advice would you give to young sportsmen and -women?
Enjoy it, and always give 100%.

Which is your favorite Guinness World Record?
Mine!

Cricket
Sport

Most test match «
appearances
Steve Waugh (Australia, left) played in 168 test matches from 1984 to 2004.

He scored 10,927 runs and took 92 wickets and 112 catches.

★ **Highest test team score**
Sri Lanka scored 952 for 6 against India at Colombo, Sri Lanka, on August 4–6 1997.

★ **Most runs in test cricket**
Allan Border (Australia) scored a total of 11,174 runs in 156 tests (an average of 50.56) from 1978 to 1994.

★ **Highest test batting average**
Don Bradman (Australia) retired with a batting average of 99.94 after playing for Australia in a total of 52 tests. He scored 6,996 runs in 80 innings from 1928 to 1948.

★ **Highest partnership in a test match**
The highest partnership is 576 for the second wicket by Sanath Jayasuriya at 340 and Roshan Mahanama (both Sri Lanka) at 225 for Sri Lanka against India at Colombo, Sri Lanka, on August 4–6 1997.

★ **Most test match wickets**
Muttiah Muralitharan (Sri Lanka) is the leading test match wicket-taker with 521 (average 22.76 runs per wicket) in 89 matches, from August 1992 to May 2004.

★ **Most catches by a wicket keeper in test cricket**
Ian Healy (Australia) made a total of 366 catches (in 119 tests) playing for Australia from 1988 to 1999.

★ **Most catches by a fielder in test cricket**
Mark Waugh (Australia) made 181 catches in 128 tests for Australia from 1990 to 2003.

★ **Most 'ducks' in test cricket**
The player who has the dubious honor of registering the most 'ducks' (a score of nothing) in test cricket is Courtney Walsh (Jamaica) with 43 in 185 innings for the West Indies from November 1984 to April 2001.

★ **Most sixes in a test match innings**
Wasim Akram (Pakistan) hit 12 sixes in his 257 not out for Pakistan against Zimbabwe at Sheikhupura, Pakistan, on October 18–20 1996.

★ **Most extras conceded in a test match**
The West Indies conceded 71 extras in Pakistan's first innings at Georgetown, Guyana, on April 3–4 1988. The figure consisted of 21 byes, eight leg byes, four wides, and 38 no-balls.

★ **Most test centuries**
Sunil Gavaskar (India) scored a total of 34 centuries (in 214 innings) playing for India from 1971 to 1987.

★ **Longest test match**
The longest-lasting recorded cricket match was the 'timeless' test between England and South Africa at Durban, South Africa, from March 3 to 14 1939. Neither side was able to secure victory and the match was abandoned after 10 days (the eighth day was rained out)

because the ship taking the England team home was due to leave. The total playing time was 43 hr 16 min and a record test match aggregate of 1,981 runs was scored.

★ **Most consecutive test wins**
Australia recorded a run of 16 successive test victories when they beat India by 10 wickets at Mumbai (Bombay), India, in March 2001.

★ **Youngest test player**
The youngest test player ever is Hasan Raza (Pakistan, b. March 11 1982), who made his debut aged 14 years 227 days against Zimbabwe at Faisalabad, Pakistan, on October 24 1996.

★ **Most catches by a fielder in a World Cup match**
The greatest number of catches in a cricket World Cup match is four by Mohammad Kaif (India) against Sri Lanka in Johannesburg, South Africa, on March 10 2003.

Highest « test innings

Brian Lara (Trinidad, left) scored 400 not out for West Indies v. England at Antigua Recreation Ground, St. John's, Antigua, on April 10–12 2004. The innings included four sixes and 43 fours, in a team total of 751–5. Lara became the only player to have set this record twice, having previously scored 375 against the same opposition on the same ground in April 1994.

Fastest bowling ⌃

The highest electronically measured speed for a ball bowled by any bowler is 100.23 mph (161.3 km/h) by Shoaib Akhtar (Pakistan, above) against England on February 22 2003 in a World Cup match at Newlands, Cape Town, South Africa.

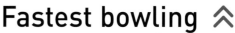

★ Most catches by a fielder in a World Cup career
Ricky Ponting (Australia) made 18 catches in 28 matches from 1996 to 2003.

★ Most catches by a fielder in a cricket World Cup tournament
Ricky Ponting (Australia) took 11 catches in the World Cup tournament in South Africa in 2003.

★ Highest team score in World Cup cricket
The highest team score in a World Cup match is 398 for 5 by Sri Lanka against Kenya at Kandy, Sri Lanka, on March 6 1996.

The lowest team score is 36 by Canada against Sri Lanka at Boland Park, Paarl, South Africa, on February 19 2003.

★ Most centuries in first-class cricket
Jack Hobbs (UK) scored 197 centuries out of a total of 1,315 innings while playing for Surrey and England from 1905 to 1934.

★ Highest individual innings score
Brian Charles Lara (Trinidad) scored 501 not out in 7 hr 54 min playing for Warwickshire against Durham at Edgbaston, UK, from June 3 to 6 1994.

During his innings he also broke two other cricketing records: the most runs in a day (390 on June 6) and the most runs from strokes worth four or more (308, comprising 62 fours and 10 sixes).

★ Highest individual score in one-day internationals
Saeed Anwar (Pakistan) scored 194 while playing for Pakistan against India at Madras (Chennai), India, on May 21 1997.

★ Most runs off a ball
Garry Chapman (Australia), partnered by Chris Veal (Australia), scored 17 (all run, with no overthrows) off a single delivery while playing for Banyule against Macleod at Windsor Reserve, Victoria, Australia, on October 13 1990. Chapman had pulled the ball to mid-wicket, where it disappeared into 10-in-high (25-cm) grass.

★ Most runs off one over
The first batsman ever to score 36 runs off a six-ball over was Garfield St. Aubrun Sobers (Barbados) off Malcolm Andrew Nash (UK) for Nottinghamshire against Glamorgan at Swansea on August 31 1968.

Ravishankar Jayadritha Shastri (India) achieved the same feat for Bombay against Baroda in Mumbai (Bombay), India, on January 10 1985 off the bowling of Tilak Raj Sharma (India).

★ Longest cricket marathon
Cricket Club des Ormes (France) played a cricket marathon of 26 hr 13 min at Dol de Bretagne, France, on June 21–22 2003. Two teams of 12 played six matches in all, with the Young Guns team winning five matches to the Veterans' one.

★ Oldest umpire
After playing professionally for Staffordshire, UK, as a younger man, Joe Filliston (UK) applied to become an umpire at the age of 82. The Marylebone Cricket Club invited him to umpire for the Lord's Taverners on many occasions and he was still umpiring at the age of 100.

★ Youngest cricketer to hit six sixes in an over
The youngest cricketer to hit six consecutive sixes in the same over is Anthony McMahon (UK), who achieved the feat at the age of 13 years 261 days, on May 24 2003, while playing for Chester-le-Street against Eppleton at Eppleton Cricket Club, Durham, UK.

Highest beach volleyball ⤼ career earnings (AVP tour)

Karch Kiraly (USA, below) has won a record $2,929,158 in official Association of Volleyball Professionals (AVP) Tour earnings through to the end of the 2002 season.

Most men's handball ⤼ World Championships won

Two countries have won the men's world title four times. Sweden (1999 team members, above) won in 1954, 1958, 1990, and 1999, and Romania in 1961, 1964, 1970, and 1974.

★ **Most men's volleyball World Championships**
The USSR has won six titles (in 1949, 1952, 1960, 1962, 1978, and 1982).

★ **Most women's volleyball World Championships**
World Championships were instituted in 1952 for women, and the USSR has won a record five titles (in 1952, 1956, 1960, 1970, and 1990).

★ **Most beach volleyball titles (AVP tour)**
Karch Kiraly (USA) has won a record 143 AVP tour titles through the end of the 2003 season.

★ **Most Olympic medals for men's volleyball**
The record for men is three, held jointly by Yuriy Mikhailovich Poyarkov (USSR), who won gold medals in 1964

and 1968 and a bronze in 1972; Katsutoshi Nekoda (Japan), who won gold in 1972, silver in 1968, and bronze in 1964; and Steve Timmons (USA), who won gold in 1984 and 1988, and bronze in 1992.

★ **Longest volleyball marathon**
The longest game of volleyball played was one of 24 hr 10 min at the Vocational School Center, Torgau, Germany, on September 30–October 1 2002.

★ **Handball target shooting**
Jonas Källman (Sweden) hit eight handball targets in 30 seconds on the set of *Guinness Rekord TV*, Stockholm, Sweden, on November 27 2001.

★ **Most women's World Championships handball titles won**
Three women's titles (all indoor unless stated) have been won by Romania in 1956, 1960, (both outdoor) and 1962; the GDR in 1971, 1975, and 1978; and the USSR in 1982, 1986, and 1990.

★ **Highest score in an international handball match**
In August 1981, the USSR beat Afghanistan 86–2 in the 'Friendly Army Tournament' at Miskolc, Hungary.

★ **Longest handball marathon**
The longest game of handball was 70 hours, set by 12 players from the HV Mighty/Stevo team in Geesteren, Tubbergen, The Netherlands, on August 30–September 2 2001.

★ **Most women's lacrosse World Championships**
The first World Cup was held in 1982, replacing the World Championships, which had been held three times since 1969. The USA has won a record six times (in 1974, 1982, 1989, 1993, 1997, and 2001).

★ **Most men's lacrosse World Championships**
The USA has won eight of the nine World Championships (in 1967, 1974, 1982, 1986, 1990, 1994, 1998, and 2002).

Canada won the other world title in 1978, beating the USA 17–16 after extra time – in what was the first drawn international match.

★ **Highest score in men's lacrosse**
The highest score in a World Cup match is Scotland's 34–3 win over Germany in Manchester, UK, on July 25 1994. In the World Cup premier division, the record score is the USA's 33–2 win over Japan in Manchester on July 21 1994.

★ **Highest score in women's lacrosse**
The highest score by an international team was by Great Britain and Ireland with their 40–0 defeat of Long Island during their 1967 tour of the USA.

★ **Longest lacrosse throw**
The longest recorded lacrosse throw is 488 ft 6 in (148.91 m), by Barnet Quinn (Canada) on September 10 1892.

Most Champions' trophies in women's hockey »

The women's Champions' trophy, first held in 1987, has been won a record six times by Australia,

They won in 1991, 1993, 1995, 1997, 1999, and 2003. Pictured are Wendy Alcorn (far right), playing for Australia against China (Zhaoxa Chen, near right).

★ **Most korfball World Championships**
The Netherlands has won the World Championships (instituted 1978) a record six times, in 1978, 1984, 1987, 1995, 1999, and 2003.

★ **Highest score in a korfball World Championship final**
The highest team score in the final of the World Championships is 23 by The Netherlands against Belgium (11) in 1999.

★ **Longest korfball marathon**
Members of the korfball club de Vinken in Vinkeveen, The Netherlands, played a game of korfball lasting 26 hr 2 min on May 23–24 2001.

★ **Biggest winning margin in a korfball World Championship final**
In the final of the Centennial Championship, held in Rotterdam, The Netherlands, on November 9 2003, there was a winning margin of 13 points, between The Netherlands (22) and Belgium (9).

★ **Most World Games titles won for korfball**
Korfball was first held as part of the World Games in 1985 and the most titles won is five (every occasion the event has been held) by The Netherlands, in 1985, 1989, 1993, 1997, and 2001. In winning these five titles, The Netherlands has never lost a match.

★ **Highest score in international women's hockey**
The England women's hockey team beat France 23–0 in Merton, Greater London, UK, on February 3 1923.

★ **Highest score in international men's hockey**
The highest international score was when India defeated the USA 24–1 in Los Angeles, California, USA, in the 1932 Olympic Games.

★ **Most women's hockey World Cups won**
The Fédération Internationale de Hockey (FIH) World Cup for women was first held in 1974.

The most wins is five by The Netherlands (in 1974, 1978, 1983, 1986, and 1990).

★ **Most men's hockey World Cup titles**
The FIH World Cup for men was first held in 1971. The most wins is four by Pakistan (in 1971, 1978, 1982, and 1994).

★ **Most Champions' trophies in men's hockey**
This competition was first held in 1978 and has been contested annually since 1980 by the top six men's teams in the world. The most wins is eight by Germany (1986–88 as West Germany, 1991–92, 1995, 1997, and 2001).

★ **Most goals scored in an international hockey career**
David Ashman (UK) has scored a record 2,326 goals having played for Hampshire, Southampton, Southampton Kestrals, and Hamble Old Boys (for whom he has scored 2,165 goals, a record for one club), in 1958–99.

★ **Most goals scored in an international hockey career**
The greatest number of goals scored in international hockey is 267 by Paul Litjens (Netherlands) in 177 games.

★ **Highest attendance for a hockey match**
The match between England and the USA at Wembley, London, UK, on March 11 1978 was attended by 65,165 people.

★ **Most hockey Olympics umpired**
Graham Dennis Nash (UK) umpired in five successive Olympics (1976–92) and retired after the Barcelona Games, having officiated in a record 144 international matches.

★ **Largest hockey stick**
A hockey stick made by the Jubilee Committee of AMHC Upward, Arnhem, The Netherlands, measured 39 ft 7 in (12.07 m) long and weighed 1,278 lb (580 kg) on September 11 1999.

Most goals « in an Australian football career

Tony Lockett (Australia, left) scored 1,357 goals during his Australian Football League (AFL) career playing for St. Kilda and the Sydney Swans from 1983 to 1999.

Most yards passing in ⌃ a Canadian football career

Damon Allen (Canada, above) threw for a record 61,802 yards during his CFL career for Edmonton Eskimos, Ottawa Roughriders, Hamilton Tiger-Cats, Memphis Mad Dogs, British Columbia Lions, and Toronto Argonauts from 1985 to 2003.

★ **Most AFL Premiership titles**
Two clubs have won the AFL Premiership 16 times: Carlton, from 1906 to 1995, and Essendon, from 1897 to 2000.

★ **Highest AFL team score**
The AFL record for one team is 239 (37–17) by Geelong against Brisbane on May 3 1992.

★ **Highest aggregate score in an AFL match**
The highest aggregate record score is 345 points when St. Kilda beat Melbourne 204–141 on May 6 1978.

★ **Most goals kicked in an AFL Grand Final**
Two players have kicked nine goals in an AFL Grand Final: Gordon Coventry (Australia) for Collingwood against Richmond in the 1928 AFL Grand Final and Gary Ablett (Australia) for Geelong against Hawthorn in the 1989 AFL Grand Final.

★ **Most goals scored in a debut**
The greatest number of goals scored in an Australian Rules football debut is 12, by John Coleman (Australia) playing for Essendon against Hawthorn in Round One of the 1949 season.

★ **Most goals by an individual in an AFL season**
The AFL season's record is 150 and has been reached by two players: Bob Pratt (South Melbourne) in 1934 and Peter Hudson (Hawthorn) in 1971.

★ **Most games played in an AFL career**
Michael Tuck (Australia) played 426 AFL games in his career from 1972 to 1991.

★ **Longest winning streak**
Geelong won 23 consecutive games in the AFL Premiership in the 1952/53 season.

★ **Longest losing streak**
University lost 51 consecutive games in the AFL Premiership from 1912 to 1914.

★ **Largest disciplinary fines for a single AFL match**
The highest disciplinary fines imposed as a result of a single AFL match is AUS$67,500 ($49,773). The fines were incurred during a match between Western Bulldogs and St. Kilda on May 4 2003. Nine players from each team were fined and one player was banned for three matches.

★ **Most consecutive CFL games played**
Bob Cameron (Canada) played 353 consecutive Canadian Football League (CFL) games for the Winnipeg Blue Bombers from 1980 to 2000.

★ **Most CFL games played in a career**
Lui Passaglia (Canada) played in 408 CFL games for the British Columbia Lions (aka the BC Lions) from 1976 to 2000. He also scored a CFL career record 3,991 points for the BC Lions from 1976 to 2000.

★ **Most points in a CFL game**
Bob McNamara (Canada) scored 36 points for the Winnipeg Blue Bombers against the BC Lions on October 13 1956.

★ **Most points in a CFL season**
Lance Chomyc (Canada) scored a season record 236 points for the Toronto Argonauts in 1991.

★ **Longest field goal in a CFL game**
The longest field goal in a regular game was 62 yards. It was kicked by Paul McCallum (Canada) for the Saskatchewan Roughriders against the Edmonton Eskimos on October 27 2001.

★ **Most Grey Cup wins**
The Toronto Argonauts have won the Grey Cup a record 14 times from 1914 to 1997.

Most yards ≫ receiving in a CFL career

Allen Pitts (Canada, right) gained a total of 14,891 yards receiving for the Calgary Stampeders during his CFL career from 1990 to 2000.

★ **Most receptions in a CFL season**
Derrell Mitchell (Canada) made a record 160 pass receptions for the Toronto Argonauts in 1998.

★ **Most pass receptions in a CFL career**
The greatest number of passes caught over the course of a CFL career is 972, by Darren Flutie (Canada) playing for the BC Lions, Edmonton Eskimos, and Hamilton Tiger-Cats from 1991 to 2002.

★ **Longest rush in a CFL game**
Two players have gained 109 yards running from the line of scrimmage: George Dixon (Canada) for the Montreal Alouettes against the Ottawa Roughriders on September 2 1963; and Willie Fleming (USA) for the BC Lions against the Edmonton Eskimos on October 17 1964.

★ **Longest punt in a CFL game**
Zenon Andrusyshun (Canada) kicked a punt a distance of 108 yards for the Toronto Argonauts against the Edmonton Eskimos on October 23 1977.

★ **Most punt return touchdowns in a CFL career**
Henry Williams (Canada) returned a total of 26 punts for touchdowns during his CFL career for the Edmonton Eskimos from 1986 to 1999.

★ **Most touchdowns scored in a CFL season**
Milt Stegall (Canada) scored a record 23 touchdowns for the Winnipeg Blue Bombers in 2002.

★ **Most touchdowns scored in a CFL career**
George Reed (Canada) scored a total of 137 touchdowns for the Saskatchewan Roughriders during his CFL career from 1963 to 1975.

★ **Most yards rushing in a CFL career**
George Reed (Canada) rushed for a career-record 16,116 yards for the Saskatchewan Roughriders from 1963 to 1975.

★ **Most kicks blocked in a CFL career**
The greatest number of kicks blocked over the course of a CFL career is 10 by Gerald Vaughn (Canada) while playing for three teams – the Calgary Stampeders, the Winnipeg Blue Bombers, and the Hamilton Tiger-Cats – from 1993 to 2002.

★ **Longest pass completion in Canadian football**
The longest pass completion in the CFL covered a distance of 109 yards and has been achieved by three different sets of players: Sam Etcheverry to Hal Patterson (both Canada) for the Montreal Alouettes against the Hamilton Tiger-Cats on September 22 1956; Jerry Keeling to Terry Evanshen (both Canada) for the Calgary Stampeders against the Winnipeg Blue Bombers on September 27 1966; and Damon Allen to Albert Jackson (both Canada) for the BC Lions against the Montreal Alouettes on August 21 2002.

★ **Most Shinty Challenge Cup team wins**
From 1907 to 1986, Newtonmore won the Camanachd Association Challenge Cup (instituted in 1896 and also known as the Scottish Cup) 28 times. Shinty is a game similar to Ireland's hurling and is played almost exclusively in Scotland.

★ **Most Shinty Challenge Cup winners' medals won by an individual**
David Ritchie and Hugh Chisholm (both UK) of Newtonmore have won 12 Challenge Cup winners' medals each.

★ **Highest score in a Shinty cup final**
Kingussie beat Newtonmore 12–1 at Fort William, Highland, UK, in 1997.

★ **Highest individual score in a Shinty cup final**
John Macmillan Mactaggart (UK) scored 10 hails, or goals, for Mid-Argyll in a Camanachd Cup match in 1938.

Tennis
Sport

Fastest ≫ tennis serve

The fastest tennis service by a man (measured with modern equipment) is 150 mph (241.4 km/h) by Andy Roddick (USA, right) during a Davis Cup match against Stefan Koubek (Austria) at the Mohegan Sun Arena, Uncasville, Connecticut, USA, on February 6 2004.

★ **Fastest serve by a woman**
Venus Williams (USA) served at 127.4 mph (205 km/h) during the European Indoor Championships in Zurich, Switzerland, on October 16 1998.

★ **Youngest female world No.1**
Martina Hingis (Switzerland, b. September 30 1980 in the former Czechoslovakia) was 16 years 182 days when she became world No.1 on March 31 1997. She is also the youngest female Wimbledon champion: she was 15 years 282 days when she won the ladies doubles in 1996 with partner Helena Sukova (Czechoslovakia).

★ **Youngest male world No.1**
Marat Mikhailovich Safin (Russia, b. January 27 1980) was 20 years 234 days when he achieved the world No.1 ranking by winning the President's Cup tournament in Tashkent, Uzbekistan, on September 17 2000.

★ **Youngest Davis Cup player**
The youngest player to compete in the Davis Cup is Kenny Banzer (Liechtenstein) at the age of 14 years 5 days on February 16 2000 against Algeria.

★ **Most consecutive Davis Cup wins**
The USA won a record seven consecutive Davis Cup tournaments in 1920–26. Their reign was brought to an end by France in 1927, who went on to keep the title for six years, the second longest winning streak, before losing to Great Britain in 1933.

★ **Most Davis Cup wins**
The most wins in the Davis Cup, the men's international team championship, has been 31 by the USA from 1900 to 1995.

★ **Oldest Davis Cup player**
The oldest player to compete in the Davis Cup is Yaka-Garonfin Koptigan (Togo, b. December 23

1941) aged 59 years 147 days on May 27 2001.

★ **Most Wimbledon men's singles titles**
Pete Sampras (USA) won seven Wimbledon men's singles tennis titles in 1993–95 and 1997–2000.

★ **Most Wimbledon singles titles won by a woman**
The most Wimbledon singles tennis titles won by a woman is nine by Martina Navratilova (USA) in 1978–79, 1982–87, and 1990.

★ **Best wild card performance at Wimbledon**
The best ever performance by a wild card entrant at the Wimbledon Championships was that of Goran Ivanisevic (Croatia) in 2001. Invited to play in the competition by the All England Club, Ivanisevic, ranked 125th in the world, won the men's singles title by beating Pat Rafter (Australia) 6–3, 3–6, 6–3, 2–6, 9–7 in the final. The Croatian's popular win came in his fourth final

appearance, and he also served a record 213 aces throughout the tournament, including 27 in the final.

★ **Longest Wimbledon career**
The longest Wimbledon tennis career is 55 years and is held by Jean Borotra (France), who competed in the men's singles competition 35 times from 1922 to 1964. He then went on to compete in the men's veteran doubles and the mixed doubles events from 1965 to 1977, retiring when he was 78.

★ **Oldest US Open champion**
Margaret du Pont (USA, b. March 4 1918) won the mixed doubles at the age of 42 years 166 days in 1960.

★ **Youngest US Open champion**
Vincent Richards (USA, b. March 20 1903) was 15 years 139 days when he won the men's doubles with Bill Tilden (USA) in 1918.

Oldest Wimbledon champion

The oldest main draw Wimbledon tennis champion >> is Martina Navratilova (USA, right). She was 46 years 261 days when she won the mixed doubles with Leander Paes (India) on July 6 2003.

Most French Open ⌃ singles tennis titles won by a man

Björn Borg (Sweden, above) won six French Open singles titles in 1974–75 and 1978–81.

★ **Youngest female to win the US Open singles championship**
Tracey Austin (USA, b. December 12 1962) was 16 years 271 days when she won the women's singles in 1979.

★ **Youngest male to win the US Open singles championship**
Pete Sampras (USA, b. August 12 1971) was 19 years 28 days when he won the US Open on September 9 1990.

★ **Most US Open singles titles won by a woman**
Molla Mallory (née Bjurstedt, Norway) won eight US Open singles tennis titles in 1915–18, 1920–22, and 1926.

★ **Most US Open singles titles won by a man**
The most US Open singles tennis titles won by a man is seven and is shared by Bill Tilden (USA) in 1920–25 and 1929, Richard Sears (USA) in 1881–87, and William Larned (USA) in 1901, 1902, and 1907–11.

★ **Most French Open singles titles won by a woman**
Chris Evert (USA) won seven French Open singles tennis titles in 1974, 1975, 1979, 1980, 1983, 1985, and 1986.

★ **Most Australian Open singles titles won by a man**
Roy Emerson (Australia) won a record six Australian Open singles tennis titles in 1961 and 1963–67.

★ **Most men's wheelchair tennis World Team Cups**
The World Team Cup for wheelchair tennis has been contested annually since 1985. The USA has won the men's competition a record nine times (1985–91, 1995, and 1997).

★ **Most Grand Slam tournament singles titles won**
Margaret Court (Australia) won 24 Grand Slam tournament singles from 1960 to 1973.

★ **Oldest tennis player**
The oldest tennis player is José Guadalupe Leal Lemus (Mexico, b. December 13 1902), who began playing tennis in 1925 and has been playing regularly ever since, a total of 79 years. Now aged 101, he currently plays every Wednesday at the Club Campestre Morelia, Morelia, Mexico, with a group of doctors 20–25 years his junior.

★ **Longest singles marathon**
The longest competitive singles match lasted 25 hr 25 min and was played between Christian Albrecht Barschel and Hauke Daene (both Germany) on September 12–13 2003 at Mölln Tennis Club, Mölln, Germany.

★ **Longest doubles marathon**
The longest competitive doubles tennis match lasted 48 hr 6 min and was played between Jaroslaw Kadzielewski and Rafal Siupka, and Mateusz Zatorski and Kamil Milian (all Poland) on August 30 to September 1 2002 at Giliwice Sports Hall, Poland.

★ **Longest doubles marathon by one pair**
The longest competitive doubles tennis match, by one pair playing against all comers, lasted 26 hours and was played by Mike Geraghty and Francis Power (both Ireland) on June 20–21 2003 at Galway Lawn Tennis Club, Galway, Ireland.

Most Uber Cup wins

China holds the record for the most wins at

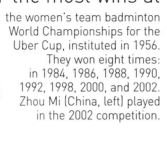

the women's team badminton World Championships for the Uber Cup, instituted in 1956. They won eight times: in 1984, 1986, 1988, 1990, 1992, 1998, 2000, and 2002. Zhou Mi (China, left) played in the 2002 competition.

Most men's table tennis World Championship wins

Viktor Barna (Hungary, above) won a record five men's singles table tennis World Championships (1930, 1932–35).

★ **Most badminton World Championships titles**
A record five titles have been won by Park Joo-bong (South Korea), for the men's doubles in 1985 and 1991 and mixed doubles in 1985, 1989, and 1991.

★ **Most mixed team badminton World Championship wins**
The most wins at the mixed team badminton World Championships for the Sudirman Cup (instituted in 1989) is four by China, in 1995, 1997, 1999, 2001.

★ **Most badminton World Cup women's singles wins**
Susi Susanti (Indonesia) won five World Cup women's singles tournaments in 1989, 1993–94, and 1996–97.

★ **Most badminton Thomas Cup wins**
The most wins at the men's world team badminton championships for the Thomas Cup (instituted in 1948) is 13 by Indonesia (1958, 1961, 1964, 1970, 1973, 1976, 1979, 1984, 1994, 1996, 1998, 2000, and 2002).

★ **Most badminton World Championship singles titles**
Four Chinese players have each won two individual world titles. Yang Yang won the men's singles in 1987 and 1989, and the women's singles have been won by Li Lingwei in 1983 and 1989; by Han Aiping in 1985 and 1987; and by Ye Zhaoying in 1995 and 1997.

★ **Longest badminton match in competition**
In the final of the men's singles at the 1997 World Championships at Glasgow, UK, on June 1, Peter Rasmussen (Denmark) beat Sun Jun (China) 16–17, 18–13, 15–10 in a match that lasted 2 hr 4 min.

★ **Shortest badminton match**
Ra Kyung-min (South Korea) beat Julia Mann (England) 11–2, 11–1 in 6 minutes during the Uber Cup in Hong Kong on May 19 1996.

★ **Oldest badminton player**
Henry Paynter (Canada, b. February 24 1907) is an active member of the Kelowna Badminton Club, British Columbia, Canada, and was still playing regularly in March 2004, aged 97.

★ **Highest speed of a shuttlecock off a badminton racket**
In tests at Warwickshire Racquets and Health Club, UK, on November 5 1996, Simon Archer (UK) hit a shuttlecock at a measured speed of 162 mph (260 km/h).

★ **Longest table tennis singles marathon**
The longest marathon singles match was 132 hr 31 min by Danny Price and Randy Nunes (both USA) at Cherry Hill, New Jersey, USA, on August 20–26 1978.

★ **Longest table tennis doubles marathon**
On April 9–13 1979, Lance, Phil, and Mark Warren and Bill Weir (all USA) played doubles table tennis for 101 hr 1 min 11 sec in Sacramento, California, USA,

★ **Most women's table tennis World Championships**
Angelica Rozeanu (Romania) won a record six consecutive women's singles table tennis World Championship titles from 1950 to 1955.

★ **Longest table tennis rally**
John Duffy and Kevin Schick (both New Zealand) achieved a table tennis rally lasting 5 hr 2 min 18.5 sec at Whangarei, New Zealand, on November 5 1977.

★ **Most combined team wins at the racquetball World Championships**
The World Championships were instituted in 1981, have been held biennially since 1984, and are based on the US version of the game. The USA has won a record ten combined team titles, in 1981, 1984, 1986 (tie with Canada), 1988, 1990, 1992, 1994, 1996, 1998, and 2002.

Most men's world team squash titles ⌃⌃

Australia have won eight men's world team titles, in 1967, 1969, 1971, 1973, 1989, 1991, 2001, and 2003. David Palmer (Australia, above) was one of the players in the 2001 World Championship team.

★ **Most women's racquetball World Championship wins**
The most women's racquetball World Championships won by an individual is three by Michelle Gould (USA) in 1992, 1994, and 1996.

★ **Most women's team wins at the racquetball World Championships**
The USA has won nine women's team titles, in 1986, 1988, 1990, 1992, 1994, 1996, 1998, 2000, and 2002.

★ **Most wheelchair racquetball World Championships**
Chip Parmelly (USA) won a record three wheelchair racquetball World Championships, in 1990, 1992, and 1994.

★ **Most men's Real Tennis World Championships**
The first recorded Real Tennis world champion was Clerg (France) in ca. 1740. Jacques Edmond Barre (France) held the title for a record 33 years from 1829 to 1962. Pierre Etchebaster (France) holds the record for the greatest number of successful defenses of the title with eight during his career (1928–52).

★ **Most women's Real Tennis World Championships**
Instituted in 1985, the women's World Championships has been won six times by Penny Lumley (née Fellows, UK) in 1989, 1991, 1995, 1997, 1999, and 2003.

★ **Oldest Real Tennis court**
The oldest of the surviving active Real Tennis courts in Great Britain is that at Falkland Palace, Fife, built by King James V of Scotland in 1539.

★ **Most squash World Open Championship titles**
Jansher Khan (Pakistan) won a record eight World Open titles, in 1987, 1989, 1990, and 1992–96.

★ **Most squash club championships**
The most club championships won by an individual at the same club is 21 (including a record 17 consecutively) by Carole Cameron (UK) at the Thurso and District Squash Club, Thurso, Caithness, UK, in 1982–85 and 1987–2003.

★ **Most squash World Championships**
Jahangir Khan (Pakistan) won six World Open titles, in 1981–85 and 1988. He has also won the International Squash Rackets Federation world individual title three times, in 1979, 1983, and 1985.

★ **Most women's squash World Championship wins**
The women's title has been won seven times by Australia, in 1981, 1983, 1992, 1994, 1996, 1998, and 2002.

★ **Most women's world team titles for squash**
Sarah Fitzgerald (Australia) has won five women's World Open titles, in 1996–98 and 2001–02.

★ **Longest squash match**
The longest recorded competitive match was one of 2 hr 45 min when Jahangir Khan (Pakistan) beat Gamal Awad (Egypt) 9–10, 9–5, 9–7, 9–2, the first game lasting a record 1 hr 11 min, in the final of the Patrick International Festival in Chichester, West Sussex, UK, on March 30 1983.

★ **Highest speed of a squash ball**
In tests at Wimbledon Squash and Badminton Club in January 1988, Roy Buckland hit a squash ball by an overhead service at a measured speed of 144.6 mph (232.7 km/h) over the distance to the front wall. This is equivalent to an initial speed at the racket of 150.8 mph (242.6 km/h).

Athletics 1
Sport

Most men's gold >> medals in the athletics World Championships

The World Championships were inaugurated in 1983, when they were held in Helsinki, Finland. The greatest number of World Championship men's gold medals won by an individual is nine, by Michael Johnson (USA, right), who won the 200 m in 1991 and 1995, the 400 m in 1993, 1995, 1997, and 1999, and the 4 x 400-m relay in 1993, 1995, and 1999.

Fastest 10,000 m ^

Haile Gebrselassie (Ethiopia, above) ran 26:22.75 for the men's 10,000-m event at Hengelo, The Netherlands, on June 1 1998. He also holds the record for the fastest 5,000 m (12:39.36).

Men's indoor world records

Event	Record	Name & nationality	Venue	Date
TRACK				
50 m	5.56	Donovan Bailey (Canada)	Reno, USA	February 9 1996
		Maurice Greene (USA)	Los Angeles, USA	February 3 1999
60 m	6.39	Maurice Greene (USA)	Madrid, Spain	February 3 1998
		Maurice Greene (USA)	Atlanta, USA	March 3 2001
200 m	19.92	Frank Fredericks (Namibia)	Liévin, France	February 18 1996
400 m	44.63	Michael Johnson (USA)	Atlanta, USA	March 4 1995
800 m	1:42.67	Wilson Kipketer (Denmark)	Paris, France	March 9 1997
1,000 m	2:14.36	Wilson Kipketer (Denmark)	Birmingham, UK	February 20 2000
1,500 m	3:31.18	Hicham El Guerrouj (Morocco)	Stuttgart, Germany	February 2 1997
1 mile	3:48.45	Hicham El Guerrouj (Morocco)	Ghent, Belgium	February 12 1997
3,000 m	7:24.90	Daniel Komen (Kenya)	Budapest, Hungary	February 6 1998
5,000 m	12:49.60*	Kenenisa Bekele (Ethiopia)	Birmingham, UK	February 20 2004
50-m hurdles	6.25	Mark McCoy (Canada)	Kobe, Japan	March 5 1986
60-m hurdles	7.30	Colin Jackson (GB)	Sindelfingen, Germany	March 6 1994
4 x 200-m relay	1:22.11	Great Britain (Linford Christie, Darren Braithwaite, Ade Mafe, John Regis)	Glasgow, UK	March 3 1991
4 x 400-m relay	3:02.83	USA (Andre Morris, Dameon Johnson, Deon Minor, Milton Campbell)	Maebashi, Japan	March 7 1999
5,000-m walk	18:07.08	Mikhail Shchennikov (Russia)	Moscow, Russia	February 14 1995
FIELD				
High jump	7 ft 11.6 in (2.43 m)	Javier Sotomayor (Cuba)	Budapest, Hungary	March 4 1989
Pole vault	20 ft 2 in (6.15 m)	Sergei Bubka (Ukraine)	Donetsk, Ukraine	February 21 1993
Long jump	28 ft 9.96 in (8.79 m)	Carl Lewis (USA)	New York City, USA	January 27 1984
Triple jump	58 ft 5 in (17.83 m)	Aliecer Urrutia (Cuba)	Sindelfingen, Germany	March 1 1997
Shot put	74 ft 4 in (22.66 m)	Randy Barnes (USA)	Los Angeles, USA	January 20 1989
Heptathlon	6,476 points	Dan O'Brien (USA) Events: 60-m 6.67 sec; long jump 25 ft 6.2 in (7.84 m); shot put 52 ft 6.6 in (16.02 m); high jump 6 ft 11.76 in (2.13 m); 60 m hurdles 7.85 sec; pole vault 17 ft 0.7 in (5.20 m); 1,000 m 2:57.96	Toronto, Canada	March 13–14 1993

* From January 1 1987, the International Athletics Association Federation (IAAF) recognized world indoor records. Prior to that, the best performances had been noted as world bests. After this date, performances needed to better the world best performances to be officially accepted by the IAAF as records.

★ Most women's gold medals in the athletics World Championships

Gail Devers (USA) won five World Championship gold medals: for the 100 m in 1993, the 100-m hurdles in 1993, 1995, and 1999, and for the 4 x 100-m in 1997.

★ Most men's successive World Championship athletics wins in a single event

Sergei Bubka (Ukraine) won six athletics World Championships in the pole vault event from 1983 to 1997.

★ Most women's athletics World Championship medals

Merlene Ottey (Jamaica) won 14 athletics World Championship medals from 1983 to 1997: gold for 200 m in 1993 and 1995 and 4 x 100-m in 1991; silver for 100 m in 1993 and 1995, 200 m in 1983, and 4 x 100-m in 1991; and bronze for 100 m in 1987 and 1991, 200 m in 1987, 1991, and 1997, and 4 x 100-m in 1983 and 1993.

Most men's athletics ∧ Olympic medals

Paavo Nurmi (Finland, above right) won 12 Olympic medals (nine gold and three silver) in the Games of 1920, 1924, and 1928.

Men's outdoor world records

Event	Record	Name & nationality	Venue	Date
TRACK				
100 m	9.78	Tim Montgomery (USA)	Paris, France	September 14 2002
200 m	19.32	Michael Johnson (USA)	Atlanta, USA	August 1 1996
400 m	43.18	Michael Johnson (USA)	Seville, Spain,	August 26 1999
800 m	1:41.11	Wilson Kipketer (Denmark)	Cologne, Germany	August 24 1997
1,000 m	2:11.96	Noah Ngeny (Kenya)	Rieti, Italy	September 5 1999
1,500 m	3:26.00	Hicham El Guerrouj (Morocco)	Rome, Italy	July 14 1998
1 mile	3:43.13	Hicham El Guerrouj (Morocco)	Rome, Italy	July 7 1999
2,000 m	4:44.79	Hicham El Guerrouj (Morocco)	Berlin, Germany	September 7 1999
3,000 m	7:20.67	Daniel Komen (Kenya)	Rieti, Italy	September 1 1996
5,000 m	12:39.36	Haile Gebrselassie (Ethiopia)	Helsinki, Finland	June 13 1998
10,000 m	26:22.75	Haile Gebrselassie (Ethiopia)	Hengelo, The Netherlands	June 1 1998
20,000 m	56:55.60	Arturo Barrios (Mexico, now USA)	La Flèche, France	March 30 1991
25,000 m	1:13:55.80	Toshihiko Seko (Japan)	Christchurch, New Zealand	March 22 1981
30,000 m	1:29:18.80	Toshihiko Seko (Japan)	Christchurch, New Zealand	March 22 1981
1 hour	21,101 m	Arturo Barrios (Mexico, now USA)	La Flèche, France	March 30 1991
110-m hurdles	12.91	Colin Jackson (GB)	Stuttgart, Germany	August 20 1993
400-m hurdles	46.78	Kevin Young (USA)	Barcelona, Spain	August 6 1992
3,000-m steeplechase	7:55.28	Brahim Boulami (Morocco)	Brussels, Belgium	August 24 2001
4 x 100-m relay	37.40	USA (Michael Marsh, Leroy Burrell, Dennis Mitchell, Carl Lewis)	Barcelona, Spain	August 8 1992
		USA (John Drummond, Andre Cason, Dennis Mitchell, Leroy Burrell)	Stuttgart, Germany	August 21 1993
4 x 200-m relay	1:18.68	USA (Michael Marsh, Leroy Burrell, Floyd Heard, Carl Lewis)	Santa Monica Track Club, Walnut, USA	April 17 1994
4 x 400-m relay	2:54.20	USA (Jerome Young, Antonio Pettigrew, Tyree Washington, Michael Johnson)	New York City, USA	July 23 1998
4 x 800-m relay	7:03.89	Great Britain (Peter Elliott, Garry Cook, Steve Cram, Sebastian Coe)	London, UK	August 30 1982
4 x 1,500-m relay	14:38.80	West Germany (Thomas Wessinghage, Harald Hudak, Michael Lederer, Karl Fleschen)	Cologne, Germany	August 17 1977
FIELD				
High jump	8 ft 0.25 in (2.45 m)	Javier Sotomayor (Cuba)	Salamanca, Spain	July 27 1993
Pole vault	20 ft 1.68 in (6.14 m)	Sergei Bubka (Ukraine)	Sestriere, Italy	July 31 1994
Long jump	29 ft 4.32 in (8.95 m)	Mike Powell (USA)	Tokyo, Japan	August 30 1991
Triple jump	60 ft (18.29 m)	Jonathan Edwards (GB)	Gothenburg, Sweden	August 7 1995
Shot put	75 ft 10.2 in (23.12 m)	Randy Barnes (USA)	Los Angeles, USA	May 20 1990
Discus	243 ft (74.08 m)	Jürgen Schult (GDR)	Neubrandenburg, Germany	June 6 1986
Hammer	284 ft 7 in (86.74 m)	Yuriy Sedykh (USSR)	Stuttgart, Germany	August 30 1986
Javelin	323 ft 1 in (98.48 m)	Jan Zelezny (Czech Republic)	Jena, Germany	May 25 1996
Decathlon Day 1: Day 2:	9,026 points	Roman Sebrle (Czech Republic) Events: 100 m 10.64 sec; long jump 26 ft 7.25 in (8.11 m); shot put 15.33 m (50 ft 3.7 in); high jump 6 ft 11.4 in (2.12 m); 110-m hurdles 13.92 sec; discus 157 ft 2.5 in (47.92 m); pole vault 15 ft 9 in (4.80 m); javelin 230 ft 2 in (70.16 m); 1,500 m 4:21.98	Götzis, Austria	May 26–27 2001

★ Most men's athletics World Championship medals

Carl Lewis (USA) won a total of 10 World Championship medals. He won eight gold medals – for the 100 m, long jump, and 4 x 100-m relay in 1983; the 100 m, long jump, and 4 x 100-m relay in 1987; and the 100 m and 4 x 100-m relay in 1991 – as well as silver for the long jump in 1991 and bronze for the 200 m in 1993.

★ Most men's athletics Olympic gold medals

Raymond Clarence Ewry (USA) won 10 Olympic gold medals, in the standing high, long, and triple jumps in 1900, 1904, 1906, and 1908.

★ Most women's athletics Olympic gold medals

The most gold medals won by a woman is four, shared by: Francina 'Fanny' Elsje Blankers-Koen (Netherlands) for the 100 m, 200 m, 80-m hurdles, and the 4 x 100-m relay, in 1948; Elizabeth 'Betty' Cuthbert (Australia) for the 100 m, 200 m, and 4 x 100-m relay in 1956 and the 400 m in 1964; Bärbel Wöckel (GDR) in the 200 m and 4 x 100-m relay in 1976 and 1980; and Evelyn Ashford (USA) in the 100 m in 1984 and the 4 x 100-m relay in 1984, 1988, and 1992.

★ Most athletics Olympic gold medals in one Games

Paavo Nurmi (Finland) won five gold medals in 1924: in the men's 1,500 m, 5,000 m, 10,000-m cross-country, and the 3,000-m team and cross-country team events.

The most medals won in individual events is four by Alvin Christian Kraenzlein (USA), who won the men's 60 m, 110-m hurdles, 200-m hurdles, and long jump in 1900.

★ Most women's athletics Olympic medals

Three women athletes share this record: Shirley Barbara de la Hunty (Australia) won seven medals – three gold, one silver, and three bronze – in the 1948, 1952, and 1956 Games.

A reread of the photo finish indicates that she finished third, not fourth, in the 1948 200-m event, thus unofficially increasing her medal haul to eight. Irena Szewinska (Poland) won a total of seven medals – three gold, two silver, and two bronze – in 1964, 1968, 1972, and 1976, and is the only woman athlete to win a medal in four successive Games. Merlene Ottey (Jamaica) has also won seven medals – two silver and five bronze – in 1980, 1984, 1992, and 1996.

The men's 100 m is a classic record that holds a unique place in sport, with the record holder arguably able to claim the title of world's fastest man. The history of this event encompasses many of the greatest names in athletics.

10.2 seconds

In the first edition of *Guinness World Records* (formerly *The Guinness Book of Records*) in 1955, the record for the men's 100 m was 10.2 seconds and was jointly held by six athletes: Jesse Owens (USA, who ran this time in 1936), Harold Davis (USA, 1941), Lloyd LaBeach (USA, 1948), Norwood 'Barney' Ewell (USA, 1948), McDonald Bailey (Trinidad, 1951), and Heinz Fütterer (West Germany, 1954).

Unlike today, many records set before January 1977 were hand-timed using stopwatches that were accurate to the nearest tenth of a second. This meant that an athlete needed to break the record by a clear tenth of a second to set a new record, increasing the odds of joint record holders. Today, automatic electronic timers accurately register up to one hundredth of a second, meaning that it is possible to ratify records with smaller margins than ever before.

In 1956, two further names were added to the 10.2-second record: Americans Bobby Morrow and Ira Murchison both ran times of 10.2 seconds that year. The 10.2-second barrier was finally breached in August 1956 by Willie Williams (USA), and his time of 10.1 seconds was equaled by four other athletes before the 10-second time was eventually set by Armin Hary (West Germany) in 1960.

Under 10 seconds

Electronic timing was introduced at the Mexico Olympics in 1968. The first athlete to have his electronically timed run recognized by the International Amateur Athletics Federation (IAAF) as a record was Jim Hines (USA), who ran 9.95 seconds for Olympic gold. The IAAF recognized Hines' 9.95 time, but continued to recognize the other 11 athletes who shared or equaled the existing record of 9.9 seconds, until Carl Lewis (USA) ran the 100 m in an amazing time of 9.86 seconds in 1991.

A record-breaking decade

The 1980s saw extraordinary 100-m runs. Calvin Smith (USA) ran 9.93 seconds in 1983 and Carl Lewis equaled this time in 1987 before running a new time of 9.92 at the Seoul Olympics in 1988. Lewis actually finished in the silver medal position behind Ben Johnson (Canada) in the Olympic final, but Johnson failed the mandatory drug test, and his 9.79 time was disqualified, allowing Lewis to take gold. During the race, Lewis looked over at Johnson three times, which cost him a precious hundredth of a second.

Rivalry

The next six years marked a great rivalry between Carl Lewis and Leroy Burrell (USA), and further hundredths of a second were shaved off the record. Burrell set a new time for the 100 m on June 14 1991 in New York with 9.90 seconds, but Lewis snatched it back later that year with a new record of 9.86. This race at the World Championships in Tokyo was rated as one of the greatest 100 m of all time, with six athletes beating 10 seconds, and the top two (Lewis and Burrell) beating the listed world record. Burrell broke the record again in 1994 running a time of 9.85, but lost it to Donovan Bailey (Canada) in July 1996 with a time of 9.84. Bailey won this race with an incredible final burst of speed; he was only in fifth place at 50 m, but had moved up to first place by the 90-m mark.

Maurice Greene (USA) dominated the 100 m for the following three years, culminating with his 9.79-second run in June 1999.

Fastest man on Earth

Maurice Green's record was finally broken by Tim Montgomery (USA) on September 14 2002 in Paris at the IAAF Grand Prix final. Montgomery flew out of the starting blocks, winning in 9.78 seconds (0.42 seconds faster than the record set by Jesse Owens in 1936), and running at an average speed of 22.9 mph (36.8 km/h).

1936
Jesse Owens 10.2 seconds

1960
Armin Hary 10 seconds

1968
Jim Hines 9.95 seconds

1983
Calvin Smith 9.93 seconds

Men's 100-m record breakers

Time	Athlete	Date	Venue
10.2	Jesse Owens (USA)	June 20 1936	Chicago
10.1	Willie Williams (USA)	August 3 1956	Berlin
10.0	Armin Hary (West Germany)	June 21 1960	Zurich
9.9	Jim Hines (USA)	June 20 1968	Sacramento
9.95	Jim Hines (USA)	October 14 1968	Mexico City
9.93	Calvin Smith (USA)	July 3 1983	Colorado
9.92	Carl Lewis (USA)	September 24 1988	Seoul
9.90	Leroy Burrell (USA)	June 14 1991	New York
9.86	Carl Lewis (USA)	August 25 1991	Tokyo
9.85	Leroy Burrell (USA)	July 6 1994	Lausanne
9.84	Donovan Bailey (Canada)	July 27 1996	Atlanta
9.79	Maurice Greene (USA)	June 16 1999	Athens
9.78	Tim Montgomery (USA)	September 14 2002	Paris

★ GWR TALKS TO
Tim Montgomery

When did you realize that you wanted to pursue a career in athletics?
As a very young child, I knew that I was athletic and pretty fast, but I didn't look at it as the profession for me until later on in my life. I remember when I had to cut the grass and I would run around our huge yard and overexert myself until I would just pass out! I guess I was about 14 when people began to recognize that I had great potential to be a top-class athlete.

Who encouraged you?
My mother was always a great source of motivation and support. She encouraged me to dream big and reach for anything I desired. I also received encouragement from coaches, teachers, and many other people.

What's your typical training day?
Very strenuous. We practice six days a week for several hours a day. Every day varies. One day we may be doing intervals and blocks/starts and the next day we have running drills followed by weight training.

Do you have to follow a special diet?
Not really. I train really hard so I don't have to diet. But you have to be sensible and eat healthily or else it could jeopardize your training. I will say, however, that I'm a big fan of pizza!

What do you consider to be your greatest achievement?
The world record is very important to me. I can't describe what it feels like to know that you've beaten everyone in the world and that you can be considered the best on the entire planet! Another favorite moment was when I set the world junior record in 1994.

Is it true that you once competed in borrowed shoes and still won?
Yes! My luggage got lost and I had to borrow Marion Jones's shoes. That definitely has to be the most hilarious and odd thing that has ever happened to me.

What does being a record holder mean to you?
To know that you hold one of the most coveted titles in the sport makes you feel like you can touch the sky. It has been a confirmation that if you work hard and be persistent and keep the faith you can overcome even the greatest obstacles.

Who was your idol when you were growing up?
Muhammad Ali. I loved everything about him: his gracefulness in the ring, his attitude, his athletic ability... everything!

What are your future goals?
I'd love to break my own record! On a personal level, I'd like to start up and run the Tim Montgomery Foundation to help young people reach their goals and overcome adversity and other challenges in life.

What advice would you give to youngsters who want to pursue a career in athletics?
If you believe in yourself, what other people think won't matter. If you want to play a sport or break a record, there is nothing stopping you except you.

What gives you your drive?
God, my family, and myself. With those three things, I can and will reach all my goals.

1991
Carl Lewis 9.86 seconds

1996
Donovan Bailey 9.84 seconds

1999
Maurice Greene 9.79 seconds

⌃ 2002
Tim Montgomery 9.78 seconds

Women's outdoor world records

Event	Record	Name & nationality	Venue	Date
TRACK				
100 m	10.49	Florence Griffith-Joyner (USA)	Indianapolis, USA	July 16 1998
200 m	21.34	Florence Griffith-Joyner (USA)	Seoul, South Korea	September 29 1988
400 m	47.60	Marita Koch (GDR)	Canberra, Australia	October 6 1985
800 m	1:53.28	Jarmila Kratochvílová (Czechoslovakia)	Munich, Germany	July 26 1983
1,000 m	2:28.98	Svetlana Masterkova (Russia)	Brussels, Belgium	August 23 1996
1,500 m	3:50.46	Qu Yunxia (China)	Beijing, China	September 11 1993
1 mile	4:12.56	Svetlana Masterkova (Russia)	Zurich, Switzerland	August 14 1996
2,000 m	5:25.36	Sonia O'Sullivan (Ireland)	Edinburgh, UK	July 8 1994
3,000 m	8:06.11	Wang Junxia (China)	Beijing, China	September 13 1993
5,000 m	14:28.09	Jiang Bo (China)	Beijing, China	October 23 1997
10,000 m	29:31.78	Wang Junxia (China)	Beijing, China	September 8 1993
20,000 m	1:05:26.60	Tegla Loroupe (Kenya)	Borgholzhausen, Germany	September 3 2000
25,000 m	1:27:05.90	Tegla Loroupe (Kenya)	Megerkirchen, Germany	September 21 2002
30,000 m	1:45:50.00	Tegla Loroupe (Kenya)	Warstein, Germany	June 6 2003
1 hour	18,340 m	Tegla Loroupe (Kenya)	Borgholzhausen, Germany	August 7 1998
100-m hurdles	12.21	Yordanka Donkova (Bulgaria)	Stara Zagora, Bulgaria	August 20 1988
400-m hurdles	52.34	Yuliya Pechonkina (Russia)	Tula, Russia	August 8 2003
3,000-m steeplechase	9:08.33	Gulnara Samitova (Russia)	Tula, Russia	August 10 2003
4 x 100-m relay	41.37	GDR (Silke Gladisch, Sabine Rieger, Ingrid Auerswald, Marlies Göhr)	Canberra, Australia	October 6 1985
4 x 200-m relay	1:27.46	USA 'Blue' (LaTasha Jenkins, Latasha Colander Richardson, Nanceen Perry, Marion Jones)	Philadelphia, USA	April 29 2000
4 x 400-m relay	3:15.17	USSR (Tatyana Ledovskaya, Olga Nazarova, Maria Pinigina, Olga Bryzgina)	Seoul, South Korea	October 1 1988
4 x 800-m relay	7:50.17	USSR (Nadezhda Olizarenko, Lyubov Gurina, Lyudmila Borisova, Irina Podyalovskaya)	Moscow, Russia	August 5 1984
FIELD				
High jump	6 ft 10.25 in (2.09 m)	Stefka Kostadinova (Bulgaria)	Rome, Italy	August 30 1987
Pole vault	15 ft 9.75 in (4.82 m)	Yelena Isinbayeva (Russia)	Gateshead, UK	July 13 2003
Long jump	24 ft 8.25 in (7.52 m)	Galina Chistyakova (USSR)	St. Petersburg, Russia	June 1 1988
Triple jump	50 ft 10.25 in (15.50 m)	Inessa Kravets (Ukraine)	Gothenburg, Sweden	August 10 1995
Shot put	74 ft 3 in (22.63 m)	Natalya Lisovskaya (USSR)	Moscow, Russia	June 7 1987
Discus	252 ft (76.80 m)	Gabriele Reinsch (GDR)	Neubrandenburg, Germany	July 9 1988
Javelin	234 ft 8 in (71.54 m)	Osleidys Menédez (Cuba)	Réthymno, Greece	July 1 2001
Heptathlon	7,291 points	Jacqueline Joyner-Kersee (USA)	Seoul, South Korea	September 23–24 1988

Events: 100-m hurdles 12.69 sec; high jump 6 ft 1.25 in (1.86 m); shot put 51 ft 10 in (15.80 m); 200 m 22.56 sec; long jump 23 ft 10.25 in (7.27 m); javelin 149 ft 10 in (45.66 m); 800 m 2:8.51

Most successive wins by a woman in the athletics World Championships

Astrid Kumbernuss (Germany, right) won three successive shot put events from 1995 to 1999.

★ **Fastest 100 x 1-mile relay**

The record for 100 miles (160 km) by 100 runners is 7 hr 35 min 55.4 sec by the Canadian Milers Athletic Club at York University, Toronto, Ontario, Canada, on December 20 1998.

The equivalent women's record was set by the Canadian Women's Milers Club who completed a 100 x 1-mile relay in a time of 9 hr 23 min 39 sec on December 27 1999.

★ **Most athletics world records set on one day**

Jesse Owens (USA) set six world records in 45 minutes at Ann Arbor, Michigan, USA, on May 25 1935 with a 9.4-sec 100 yd at 3:15 pm, a 26-ft 8.25-in-long (8.13-m) jump at 3:25 pm, a 20.3-sec 220 yd (and 200 m) at 3:45 pm, and a 22.6-sec 220-yd low hurdles at 4 pm (which also included a record for the 200-m hurdles).

★ **Longest winning sequence in a track event**

Ed Moses (USA) dominated the men's 400-m hurdling event for almost 10 years. His record of 122 consecutive wins began on September 2 1977 and ended when he was beaten by Danny Harris (USA) in Madrid, Spain, on June 4 1987.

★ **Longest winning sequence in a field event**

Iolanda Balas (Romania) won 150 consecutive competitions in the high jump from 1956 to 1967.

★ **Greatest standing long jump**

The farthest long jump from a standing position is 12 ft 2 in (3.71 m) by Arne Tvervaag (Norway) in 1968.

The women's best is 9 ft 7 in (2.92 m) by Annelin Mannes (Norway) at Flisa, Norway, on March 7 1981.

★ **Greatest standing high jump**

The greatest high jump from a standing position is 6 ft 2.75 in (1.90 m) by Rune Almen (Sweden) at Karlstad, Sweden, on May 3 1980.

The women's best is 4 ft 11.75 in (1.52 m) achieved by Grete Bjordalsbakka (Norway) in 1984.

★ **Fastest 1,000-mile relay by a team of 10**

Willie Mtolo, Graham Meyer, Jan van Rooyen, Dimitri Grishine, Daniel Radebe, Pio Mpolokeng, Oliver Kandiero, Frans Moyo, Simon Mele, and Philip Molefi (all South Africa) ran a 1,000-mile (1,600-km) relay from Cape Town to Johannesburg, South Africa, in 99 hr 3 min 27 sec from August 14 to 18 2002.

★ **Fastest men's 100 x 1,000-m relay**

A team from the Centro Universitario Sportivo, Bari, Italy, completed a 100 x 1,000-m relay in 5 hr 13 min 21.9 sec on March 14 1999.

★ **Most participants in a relay race**

A total of 7,175 runners (287 teams of 25) participated in the Batavierenrace from Nijmegen to Enschede, The Netherlands, on April 24 1999.

Fastest women's indoor 800 m ⌃

Jolanda Ceplak (Slovenia, above) set a new record for the women's

indoor 800-m event on March 3 2002 in Vienna, Austria, with a time of 1 min 55.82 sec.

Women's indoor world records

Event	Record	Name & nationality	Venue	Date
TRACK				
50 m	5.96	Irina Privalova (Russia)	Madrid, Spain	February 9 1995
60 m	6.92	Irina Privalova (Russia)	Madrid, Spain	February 11 1993 February 9 1995
200 m	21.87	Merlene Ottey (Jamaica)	Liévin, France	February 13 1993
400 m	49.59	Jarmila Kratochvílová (Czechoslovakia)	Milan, Italy	March 7 1982
800 m	1:55.82	Jolanda Ceplak (Slovenia)	Vienna, Austria	March 3 2002
1,000 m	2:30.94	Maria Mutola (Mozambique)	Stockholm, Sweden	February 25 1999
1,500 m	3:59.98	Regina Jacobs (USA)	Boston, USA	February 2 2003
1 mile	4:17.14	Doina Melinte (Romania)	East Rutherford, USA	February 9 1990
3,000 m	8:29.15	Berhane Adere (Ethiopia)	Stuttgart, Garmany	February 3 2002
5,000 m	14:39.29	Berhane Adere (Ethiopia)	Stuttgart, Germany	January 31 2004
50-m hurdles	6.58	Cornelia Oschkenat (GDR)	Berlin, Germany	February 20 1988
60-m hurdles	7.69	Lyudmila Engquist (Russia)	Chelyabinsk, Russia	February 4 1993
4 x 200-m relay	1:32.55	SC Eintracht Hamm (Helga Arendt, Silke-Beate Knoll, Mechthild Kluth, Gisela Kinzel, all West Germany)	Dortmund, Germany	February 19 1988
		LG Olympia Dortmund Karlsruhe (Esther Möller, Gabi Rockmeier, Birgit Rockmeier, Andrea Philipp, all Germany)	Germany	February 21 1999
4 x 400-m relay	3:24.25	Russia (Tatyana Chebykina, Svetlana Goncharenko, Olga Kotlyarova, Natalya Nazarova)	Maebashi, Japan	March 7 1999
3,000-m walk	11:40.33	Claudia Iovan (Romania)	Bucharest, Romania	January 30 1999
FIELD				
High jump	6 ft 9.5 in (2.07 m)	Heike Henkel (Germany)	Karlsruhe, Germany	February 9 1992
Pole vault	15 ft 11 in (4.85 m)	Svetlana Feofanova (Russia)	Athens, Greece	February 22 2004
Long jump	24 ft 2.25 in (7.37 m)	Heike Drechsler (GDR)	Vienna, Austria	February 13 1988
Triple jump	49 ft 9 in (15.16 m)	Ashia Hansen (GB)	Valencia, Spain	February 28 1998
Shot put	73 ft 10 in (22.50 m)	Helena Fibingerová (Czechoslovakia)	Jablonec, Czechoslovakia	February 19 1977
Pentathlon	4,991 points	Irina Belova (Russia) Events: 60-m hurdles 8.22 sec; high jump 6 ft 4 in (1.93 m); shot put 43 ft 5.75 in (13.25 m); long jump 21 ft 10.75 in (6.67 m); 800 m 2:10.26.	Berlin, Germany	February 14–15 1992

★ **Most athletics Indoor World Championship medals**

Merlene Ottey (Jamaica) won six Indoor World Championship medals in individual events: three gold (60 m in 1995 and 200 m in 1989 and 1991), two silver (60 m in 1991 and 200 m in 1987), and one bronze (60 m in 1989).

The men's record is five medals and is held jointly by Ivan Pedroso (Cuba), for the long jump (gold in 1993, 1995, 1997, 1999, and 2001) and Javier Sotomayor (Cuba) for the high jump (gold in 1989, 1993, 1995, and 1999 and bronze in 1991).

★ **Greatest average mileage run daily**

During the year from August 1 1996 to July 31 1997, Tirtha Kumar Phani (India) ran every day, running 14,021.7 miles (22,565.76 km) in total. This equates to an average of 38.41 miles (61.824 km) per day.

Highest altitude marathon

The biennial Everest marathon, « which was first run on November 27 1987, begins at Gorak Shep at an altitude of 17,100 ft (5,212 m), and ends at Namche Bazar at 11,300 ft (3,444 m). The men's record is 3 hr 56 min 10 sec by Hari Roka (Nepal), set in 1999, and the women's record is 5 hr 16 min 3 sec, set by Anne Stentiford (UK) in 1997.

Men's ultra-long distance world records

Event	Record	Name, nationality & venue	Date
100 km	6:10:20	Don Ritchie (GB), London, UK	October 28 1978
100 miles	11:30:51	Don Ritchie (GB), London, UK	October 15 1977
1,000 km	5 days 16:17:00	Yiannis Kouros (Greece), Colac, Australia	November 26– December 1 1984
1,000 miles	11 days 13:54:58	Piotr Silikin (Lithuania), Nanango, Australia	March 11–23 1998
24 hours	188.589 miles (303.506 km)	Yiannis Kouros (Australia), Adelaide, Australia	October 4–5 1997
6 days	635.083 miles (1,022.068 km)	Yiannis Kouros (Greece), New York, USA	July 2–8 1984

Women's ultra-long distance world records

Event	Record	Name, nationality & venue	Date
100 km	7:23:28	Valentina Liakhova (Russia), Nantes, France	September 28 1996
100 miles	14:29:44	Ann Trason (USA), Santa Rosa, USA	March 18–19 1989
1,000 km	8 days 00:27:06	Eleanor Robinson (GB), Nanango, Australia	March 11–18 1998
1,000 miles	13 days 01:54:02	Eleanor Robinson (GB), Nanango, Australia	March 11–24 1998
24 hours	149.234 miles (240.169 km)	Eleanor Adams (GB), Melbourne, Australia	August 19–20 1989

★ Most individual medals won at half marathon World Championships
The most individual medals won at the IAAF Half Marathon World Championships is eight by Lidia Simon-Slavuteanu (Romania). From 1996 to 2000, she won three team gold, one team silver, one individual silver, and three individual bronze. The men's record is five medals by Hendrick Ramaala (South Africa) – two team gold, one team silver, and two individual silver from 1997 to 1999.

★ Most team wins in the half marathon World Championships
The most team wins at the IAAF Half Marathon World Championships is seven for men by Kenya (1992–95, 1997, 2000, 2002), and six for women by Romania (1993–97, 2000).

★ Largest half marathon
The world's largest half marathon is The BUPA Great North Run between Newcastle-upon-Tyne and South Shields, Tyne and Wear, UK. For the 2000 event held on October 22, there were 36,822 finishers out of 50,173 entries.

★ Fastest half marathon speed march
William MacLennan (UK) completed a half marathon wearing full military combat gear and carrying a 40-lb (18-kg) backpack, in 1 hr 43 min 42 sec at the Redcar Half Marathon, North Yorkshire, UK, on March 25 2001.

★ Most marathons run in a calendar year
The most marathons completed in one year is 100 by Angela Gargano (Italy). Starting with the Dubai Marathon on January 11 2002, she went on to run 99 more, the last of which was the Maratona di San Silvestro, Italy, on December 31 2002.

★ Fastest aggregate time to run a marathon on each continent
From February 13 to May 23 1999, Tim Rogers (UK) ran a marathon on each of the seven continents in an aggregate time of 34 hr 23 min 8 sec. The attempt took 99 days to complete, which is also a record for the shortest duration.

The women's world record is 37 hr 20 sec by Kimi Puntillo (USA), who ran them all from November 3 1996 to October 4 1998. The attempt took 700 days to complete – a record in itself.

Fastest 25-km ⩗ and 30-km road races

Naoko Takahashi (Japan, above) ran the 25-km women's road race in

Berlin, Germany, in 1 hr 22 min 31 sec on September 30 2001. At the same event, she also set the record for the 30-km race, finishing in a time of 1 hr 39 min 2 sec.

Most individual cross-country wins »

The greatest number of men's individual cross-country victories in the World Championships is five by Paul Tergat (right) in 1995–99 and John Ngugi (both Kenya) in 1986–89 and 1992.

Men's road race

Event	Record	Name, nationality & venue	Date
10 km	27:02	Haile Gebrselassie (Ethiopia), Doha, Qatar	December 11 2002
15 km	41:29	Felix Limo (Kenya), Nijmegen, The Netherlands	November 11 2001
20 km	56:18	Paul Tergat (Kenya), Milan, Italy	April 4 1998
Half marathon	59:17	Paul Tergat (Kenya), Milan, Italy	April 4 1998
25 km	1:13:14	Rodgers Rop (Kenya), Berlin, Germany	May 6 2001
30 km	1:28:36	Takayuki Matsumiya (Japan), Kumamoto, Japan	February 16 2003
Marathon (26 miles 385 yards)	*2:04:55	Paul Tergat (Kenya), Berlin, Germany	September 28 2003
100 km	6:13:33	Takahiro Sunanda (Japan), Yubetsu, Japan	June 21 1998

* The marathon record printed in the first edition of *Guinness World Records* in 1955 was 2:17:39.4

Women's road race

Event	Record	Name, nationality & venue	Date
10 km	30:21	Paula Radcliffe (GB), San Juan, Puerto Rico	February 23 2003
15 km	46:57	Elana Meyer (RSA), Cape Town, South Africa	November 2 1991
20 km	1:03:26	Paula Radcliffe (GB), Bristol, UK	October 6 2001
Half marathon	1:06:44	Elana Meyer (RSA), Tokyo, Japan	January 15 1999
25 km	1:22:31	Naoko Takahashi (Japan), Berlin, Germany	September 30 2001
30 km	1:39:02	Naoko Takahashi (Japan), Berlin, Germany	September 30 2001
Marathon	2:15:25	Paula Radcliffe (UK), London, UK	April 13 2003
100 km	6:33:11	Tomoe Abe (Japan), Yufutsu, Japan	June 25 2000

★ **Fastest time to complete three marathons in three days**
The fastest combined time for three marathons in three days is 8 hr 22 min 31 sec by Raymond Hubbard (UK). The races were held from April 16 to 18 1988: Belfast 2 hr 45 min 55 sec; London 2 hr 48 min 45 sec; and Boston 2 hr 47 min 51 sec.

★ **Fastest speed march marathon by an individual**
Chris Chandler (UK) set an individual record in the RAF Swinderby Marathon at Swinderby, Lincolnshire, UK, on September 25 1992, when he completed the marathon carrying a pack weighing 40 lb (18 kg). His time was 3 hr 56 min 10 sec.

★ **Fastest marathon speed march without rifles**
The fastest time for a team of eight to 10 to complete a marathon while carrying 40-lb (18-kg) backpacks is 4 hr 19 min 7 sec by eight members of 29 Commando Regiment

Royal Artillery at the Luton Marathon, Bedfordshire, UK, on November 29 1998.

★ **Fastest marathon speed march team with rifles**
A team of nine representing II Squadron RAF Regiment from RAF Hullavington, Wiltshire, UK, completed the London Marathon in 4 hr 33 min 58 sec on April 21 1991. Each carried a pack weighing at least 40 lb (18 kg), including a rifle.

Fastest men's 20-km road walk «

Jefferson Pérez, (Ecuador, left) set a new record of 1 hr 17 min 21 sec for the men's 20-km road walk in Paris St.-Denis, France, on August 23 2003.

Men's walking world records

Event	Record	Name & nationality	Venue	Date
TRACK				
20 km	1:17:25.6	Bernardo Segura (Mexico)	Fana, Norway	May 7 1994
30 km	2:01:44.1	Maurizio Damilano (Italy)	Cuneo, Italy	October 4 1992
50 km	3:40:57.9	Thierry Toutain (France)	Héricourt, France	September 29 1997
2 hrs	29,572 m	Maurizio Damilano (Italy)	Cuneo, Italy	October 4 1992
ROAD				
20 km	1:17:21.0	Jefferson Pérez (Ecuador)	Paris St.-Denis, France	August 23 2003
50 km	3:36:03.0	Robert Korzeniowski (Poland)	Paris St.-Denis, France	August 27 2003

Women's walking world records

Event	Record	Name & nationality	Venue	Date
TRACK				
10 km	41:56.23	Nadezhda Ryashkina (USSR)	Seattle, USA	July 24 1990
20 km	1:26:52.30	Olimpiada Ivanova (Russia)	Brisbane, Australia	September 6 2001
ROAD				
20 km	1:26:22.0	Yang Wang (China)	Guangzhou, China	November 19 2001
	equal	Yelena Nikolayeva (Russia)	Cheboksary, Russia	May 18 2003

★ Longest running race ever

The longest running race ever staged was the 1929 transcontinental race from New York City, to Los Angeles, California, USA, a distance of 3,635 miles (5,850 km). Johnny Salo (Finland) won in 79 days, running from March 31 to June 17. His elapsed time of 525 hr 57 min 20 sec at an average speed of 6.91 mph (11.12 km/h) left him only 2 min 47 sec ahead of Englishman Pietro 'Peter' Gavuzzi.

★ Oldest marathon

The Boston Marathon was first held on April 19 1897, when it was run over 24 miles 1,232 yd (39 km). John A. Kelley (USA) finished the Boston Marathon 61 times from 1928 to 1992, winning in 1935 and 1945.

★ Most marathons completed

Horst Preisler (Germany) ran 949 races of 26 miles 385 yd or longer from 1974 to March 25 2000.

★ Most consecutive weekends of marathon running

Richard Worley (USA) ran either a marathon or an ultramarathon (a race longer than marathon distance) for 159 consecutive weekends. The first was the Walt Disney World Marathon in Orlando, Florida, USA, on January 5 1997, and the last was the Houston Methodist Marathon in Houston, Texas, USA, on January 16 2000. In the course of the records, Richard ran a marathon in all 50 US states in one year, for three consecutive years.

★ Fastest baby-carriage-pushing half marathon

Martin de Scally (South Africa) completed the Vaal Half Marathon in Vereeniging, South Africa, in a time of 1 hr 21 min 1 sec on March 2 2003 while pushing a baby carriage.

The women's equivalent record is 1 hr 30 min 51 sec by Nancy Schubring (USA) at the Mike May Races Half Marathon, Vassar, Michigan, USA, on September 15 2001.

★ Fastest baby-carriage-pushing marathon

The fastest time to run a marathon while pushing a baby carriage is 3 hr 54 min 36 sec, by Han Frenken (Netherlands) at the Leidsche Rijn Marathon, Utrecht, The Netherlands, on April 21 2003.

★ Fastest skipping marathon

The fastest time to complete a marathon while skipping rather than running is 5 hr 55 min 13 sec by Ashrita Furman (USA) at the Comox Valley Roads Marathon, Vancouver Island, British Columbia, Canada, on August 31 2003.

★ Fastest half marathon in a two-person pantomime costume

On October 6 2002, Paul Donaghy and Steve Langley (both UK) completed the Great North Run, Newcastle, Tyne and Wear, UK, in a time of 2 hr 9 min 13 sec wearing a pantomime camel costume.

Oldest female ⌄ marathon finisher

Jenny Wood-Allen (UK, below, b. 1911) ran the London Marathon on April 14 2002 aged 90 years 145 days, in 11 hr 34 min.

Treadmill world records

Event	Record	Name & nationality	Venue	Date
TEAM				
1,000,000 m (Team of 12)	82 hr 46 sec	HMP Downview UK	Sutton, UK	August 14–17 2000
12 hours (women)	161.3 km (100.2 miles)	Australia	Prahran, Australia	September 5 2003
12 hours (men)	178.6 km (110.9 miles)	Australia	Prahran, Australia	September 5 2003
INDIVIDUAL				
24 hours (female)	151.48 km (94.12 miles)	Georgina McConnell (Australia)	Wests Illawerra, Unanderra, Australia	November 25 2003
24 hours (male)	222.41 km (138.2 miles)	Tony Mangan (Ireland)	Dublin, Ireland	October 25 2003
48 hours	372.08 km (231.2 miles)	Tony Mangan (Ireland)	Dublin, Ireland	October 26 2003
1 week	283.2 miles (455.83 km)	David Taylor (Australia)	Wests Illawerra, Unanderra, Australia	November 30 2003
100 km	9 hr 5 min 37 sec	Richard Donovan (Ireland)	Galway, Ireland	July 31 2003
100 miles	16 hr 23 min 16 sec	Andrew Rivett (UK)	Alverthorpe, UK	April 6 2003

Walking backwards world records

Event	Record	Name & nationality	Venue	Date
100 m	13.60	Ferdie Ato Adoboe (Ghana)	Northampton, USA	July 25 1991
200 m	32.78	Timothy Bud Badyna (USA)	Santa Clarita, USA	January 17 2001
1 km	3:36.07	Thomas Dold (Germany)	Messkirch, Germany	July 13 2003
1 mile	6:00:2.35	D. Joseph James (India)	Coimbatore, India	August 10 2002
10 km	45:00:31.0	Vangal A. Mathiyazhagan (India)	Coimbatore, India	May 30 1999
Marathon	3:53:17.0	Timothy Bud Badyna (USA)	Toledo, USA	April 24 1994
24 hours	95.40 miles (153.52 km)	Anthony Thornton (USA)	Minneapolis, USA	December 31 1988 – January 1 1989

★ **Fastest 10-km road race in a two-person pantomime costume**
Wearing a pantomime camel costume, Simon Wiles and Les Morton (both UK) set a time of 44 min 2 sec for the Percy Pud 10-km race in Loxley, Sheffield, South Yorkshire, UK, on December 2 2001.

★ **Fastest three-legged marathon**
Identical twins Nick and Alastair Benbow (both UK) set a three-legged running record in the London Marathon with a time of 3 hr 40 min 16 sec on April 26 1998. They were tied together at the wrist and shared a pair of three-legged running trousers. They also hold the equivalent half-marathon record: they ran the London Half Marathon in 1 hr 37 min 53 sec on March 2 2003.

★ **Most siblings to complete a marathon**
The eight Hughes brothers – Richard, Harry, Declan, Owen, Seamus, Patrick, Cathal, and Vincent (all Ireland) – competed in and completed the Dublin Marathon on October 29 1984.

★ **Oldest male marathon finisher**
On October 10 1976, 98-year-old Dimitrion Yordanidis (Greece) ran a marathon in 7 hr 33 min in Athens, Greece.

★ **Fastest 24-hour running relay by a team of 10**
The greatest distance covered in 24 hours by a team of 10 is 302.281 miles (487.343 km) by Puma Tyneside RC at Monkton Stadium, Jarrow, Tyne and Wear, UK, from September 10 to 11 1994.

★ **Fastest 100-mile relay by a team of 10**
Ten cadets from the 2331 (St. Ives) Squadron Air Training Corps completed 100 miles in relay in 10 hr 21 min 35 sec at the St. Ivo Outdoor Centre, St. Ives, Cambridgeshire, UK, on September 21 2003. The team members were Sgt. M. Trace, CWO C. Trace, Sgt. D. Dew, Cpl. L. McGregor, CWO J. Martin, Sgt. B. Blewett, Comm. T. Philpot, Cpl. J. Young, CWO A. Owen, and Cpl. R. Jepp.

★ **Fastest backward run from Los Angeles to New York**
Arvind Pandya (India) ran backward across the USA from Los Angeles, California, to New York City in 107 days from August 18 to December 3 1984. Arvind runs backward in marathons and races all over the world to raise funds for various public causes. He has raised money for good causes in Africa, India, and Europe.

Combat
Sport

Most heavyweight boxing world title recaptures ⌃

Three boxers have regained the heavyweight championship of the world twice. Muhammad Ali (USA, above right) first won the title on February 25 1964, defeating Sonny Liston (USA). Having been stripped of the title by the world boxing authorities on April 28 1967, he beat George Foreman (USA) on October 30 1974. He then won the WBA title from Leon Spinks (USA) on September 15 1978 after losing to him on February 15 1978.

Evander Holyfield (USA) won the title in October 1990 by defeating James Douglas (USA). He regained the WBA and IBF versions when he beat Riddick Bowe (USA) in November 1993 and regained the WBA version again, on November 9 1996, when he defeated Mike Tyson.

Lennox Lewis (UK) was awarded the WBC title in January 1993 after the then champion Riddick Bowe (USA) refused to fight him. He then won the WBC title on February 7 1995, beating Oliver McCall (USA), and regained the WBC, IBF, and IBO titles when he defeated Hasim Rahman (USA) on November 17 2001.

★ Most undefeated boxing matches

Edward Henry Greb (USA) was unbeaten in a sequence of 178 bouts in 1916–23 (including 117 'no decisions,' of which five were unofficial losses). Of boxers with complete records, Packey McFarland (USA) had 97 fights (five draws) in 1905–15 without a defeat. Pedro Carrasco (Spain) won 83 consecutive fights from April 22 1964 to September 3 1970, drew once, and had a further nine wins before his loss to Armando Ramos (USA) in a World Boxing Council (WBC) lightweight contest on February 18 1972.

★ Longest reign as world heavyweight boxing champion

Joe Louis (USA) was champion for 11 years 252 days, from June 22 1937 – when he knocked out James Joseph Braddock (USA) in the eighth round in Chicago, Illinois, USA – until announcing his retirement on March 1 1949. During his reign, Louis made a record 25 defenses of his title.

★ Shortest reign as world boxing champion

Tony Canzoneri (USA) was world light-welterweight champion for 33 days, from May 21 to June 23 1933, the shortest period for a boxer to have won and lost a world title in the ring.

★ Most heavyweight titles won by a former middleweight

This remarkable feat has been achieved only twice in 106 years. The first time was by Robert James 'Bob' Fitzsimmons (UK) when he knocked out James J. Corbett (USA) in Carson City, Nevada, USA, on March 17 1897. Roy Jones Jr. (USA) matched this when he beat John Ruiz (USA) for the World Boxing Association (WBA) title by unanimous decision on March 2 2003 in Las Vegas, Nevada, USA.

★ Heaviest heavyweight boxing world champion

Primo Carnera (Italy), the 'Ambling Alp' who won the title from Jack Sharkey (USA) in New York City, USA, on June 29 1933, scaled 260 lb (118 kg) for this fight but his peak weight was 269 lb (122 kg).

★ Longest boxing fight

The world title fight (under Queensberry rules) between the lightweights Joe Gans (USA) and Oscar Matthew 'Battling' Nelson (Denmark), the 'Durable Dane,' in Goldfield, Nevada, USA, on September 3 1906 was terminated in the 42nd round when Gans was declared the winner on a foul.

★ Youngest national heavyweight champion

Bill Sutherley (UK) won the Scottish Amateur Boxing Association (ABA) heavyweight title on February 23 1961, at the age of only 18 years and 11 days.

★ Youngest boxing world champion

Wilfred Benitez (Puerto Rico) was 17 years 176 days when he won the WBA light-welterweight title in San Juan, Puerto Rico, on March 6 1976.

Most World ⟨⟨ Championship wrestling titles

Aleksandr Karelin (Russia, above left) won a record 12 world titles in the Greco-Roman under-130-kg class from 1988 to 1999.

Largest ⟩⟩ Sumo yokozuna wrestler

Hawaiian-born Chad Rowan, alias Akebono (right), became the first foreign rikishi to be promoted to the top rank of yokozuna in January 1993. At 6 ft 8 in (2.04 m) and 501 lb (227 kg), he is the tallest and the heaviest yokozuna in sumo history.

★ Youngest world heavyweight boxing champion

Mike Tyson (USA) was 20 years 144 days when he beat Trevor Berbick (USA) to win the WBC belt in Las Vegas, Nevada, USA, on November 22 1986. He added the WBA version when he beat James 'Bonecrusher' Smith on March 7 1987 at the age of 20 years 249 days. He became undisputed champion on August 2 1987 when he beat Tony Tucker (USA) for the International Boxing Federation (IBF) title.

★ Most knockouts in a boxing career

The greatest number of finishes classed as 'knockouts' in a career is 145 (129 in professional bouts) by Archie Moore (USA, b. Archibald Lee Wright).

★ Undefeated heavyweight boxing world champion

Rocky Marciano (USA, b. Rocco Francis Marchegiano) is the only world champion at any weight to have won every fight of his entire completed professional career, from March 17 1947 to September 21 1955 (he announced his retirement on April 27 1956); 43 of his 49 fights were by knockouts or stoppages.

★ Longest boxing career

Bob Fitzsimmons (UK) had a career lasting more than 31 years (1883–1914). On December 20 1905, aged 42 years 208 days, he had his last world title bout. Jack Johnson (USA) also had a career of over 31 years, 1897–1928.

★ Most jujitsu team World Championships

The World Council of Jiu-Jitsu Organizations has staged World Championships biennially since 1984. Canada has won the team competition on five occasions (1984, 1986, 1988, 1992, and 1994).

★ Most team kata titles at a karate World Championship

A kata team event was introduced at the 1986 karate World Championships. Of the nine championships held biennially since, in both the men's and women's disciplines, Japan has failed to win on only four occasions out of 16 competitions in both classes.

★ Most countries represented at a karate World Championship

At the 16th staging of the biennial karate World Championships, held in 2002 in Madrid, Spain, 84 countries were represented.

★ Most competitors at a karate World Championship

In 1988, a total of 1,157 competitors took part in the karate World Championships at the ninth staging of the biennial tournament in Cairo, Egypt.

★ Fastest 100-man kumite ('sparring') karate

On March 22 1995, Francisco Alves Filho (Brazil) defeated 100 consecutive opponents in full-contact knockdown fighting in 3 hr 8 min. He won 26 fights by Ippon (full points), 50 by decision, and drew 24. He did not lose a single fight.

★ Most judo throws in one hour

The most judo throws completed in one hour by a pair is 3,786 by Dale Moore and Nigel Townsend (both UK) at Esporta Health Club, Chiswick Park, Greater London, UK, on February 23 2002.

★ Most judo throws in 10 hours

Csaba Mezei and Zoltán Farkas (both Hungary) of the Szany judo sport team completed 57,603 judo throws in a 10-hour period at the Szany Sports Hall, Szany, Hungary, on May 1 2003.

★ Most bout successes in annual sumo tournaments

Yokozuna Mitsugu Akimoto, aka Chiyonofuji (Japan), set a record for domination of one of the six annual tournaments by winning the Kyushu Basho for eight successive years (1981–88). He also holds the record for the most career wins (1,045) and Makunouchi (top division) wins (807).

Women's ⟱ +75-kg total

Ding Meiyuan (China, below) achieved a record total lift of 300 kg in Sydney, Australia, on September 22 2000. She also set the +75-kg snatch record with a lift of 137.5 kg in Vancouver, Canada, on November 21 2003.

Most Olympic ≪ weight lifting gold medals

Three competitors have won a record total of three Olympic weight lifting gold medals: Naim Suleymanoglü (Turkey) at the Olympic Games in 1988, 1992, and 1996; Pyrros Dimas (Greece, left) in 1992, 1996, and 2000; and Akakios Kakiasvili (Greece) in 1992, 1996, and 2000.

In 1992, Kakiasvili was known as Kakhi Kakhiachbili and he represented the EUN/CIS, also known as the Unified Team of the former Soviet Republics.

★ Most Olympic weight lifting medals
Norbert Schemansky (USA) won four Olympic weight lifting medals from 1948 to 1964.

★ Youngest weight lifting record breaker
Naim Suleymanoglü (Turkey, b. January 23 1967) was 16 years 62 days old when he set the world records for clean and jerk, at 160 kg, and combined total, at 285 kg, at Allentown, New Jersey, USA, on March 26 1983.

★ Most accumulative weight bench-pressed in one hour
Eamonn Keane (Ireland) lifted a total weight of 305,300 lb (138,480 kg) in one hour at World Gym, Marina del Ray, California, USA, on July 22 2003.

★ Greatest multiple of body weight lifted by a man
Lamar Gant (USA) was the first man to deadlift nearly five times his own body weight. He lifted 661 lb (299.5 kg), when he weighed 131 lb (59.5 kg), in 1985.

Men's weight lifting world records

Body weight	Event	Weight, name, & nationality		Venue	Date
56 kg	Clean & jerk	168 kg	Halil Mutlu (Turkey)	Trencín, Slovakia	April 24 2001
	Snatch	138.5 kg	Halil Mutlu (Turkey)	Antalya, Turkey	November 4 2001
	Total	305.0 kg	Halil Mutlu (Turkey)	Sydney, Australia	September 16 2000
62 kg	Clean & jerk	182.5 kg	Maosheng Le (China)	Busan, Korea	October 2 2002
	Snatch	153 kg	Zhiyong Shi (China)	Izmir, Turkey	June 28 2002
	Total	325 kg	World Standard		
69 kg	Clean & jerk	197.5 kg	Guozheng Zhang (China)	Qinhuangdao, China	September 11 2003
	Snatch	165 kg	Georgi Markov (Bulgaria)	Sydney, Australia	September 20 2000
	Total	357.5 kg	Galabin Boevski (Bulgaria)	Athens, Greece	November 24 1999
77 kg	Clean & jerk	210 kg	Oleg Perepetchenov (Russia)	Trencín, Slovakia	April 27 2001
	Snatch	173 kg	Sergey Filimonov (Kazakhstan)	Busan, Korea	October 4 2002
	Total	377.5 kg	Plamen Zhelyazkov (Bulgaria)	Doha, Qatar	March 27 2002
85 kg	Clean & jerk	218 kg	Zhang Yong (China)	Tel Aviv, Israel	April 25 1998
	Snatch	182.5 kg	Andrei Ribakov (Bulgaria)	Havirov, Czech Republic	June 2 2002
	Total	395 kg	World Standard		
94 kg	Clean & jerk	232.5 kg	Szymon Kolecki (Poland)	Sofia, Bulgaria	April 29 2000
	Snatch	188 kg	Akakios Kakiashvilis (Greece)	Athens, Greece	November 27 1999
	Total	417.5 kg	World Standard		
105 kg	Clean & jerk	242.5 kg	World Standard		
	Snatch	198.5 kg	Marcin Dolega (Poland)	Havirov, Czech Republic	June 4 2002
	Total	440 kg	World Standard		
+105 kg	Clean & jerk	263 kg	Hossein Rezazadeh (Iran)	Warsaw, Poland	November 26 2002
	Snatch	213.0 kg	Hossein Rezazadeh (Iran)	Qinhuangdao, China	September 14 2003
	Total	472.5 kg	Hossein Rezazadeh (Iran)	Sydney, Australia	September 26 2000

From January 1 1998, the International Weightlifting Federation (IWF) introduced modified body weight categories, thereby making the then world records redundant. This is the new listing with the world standards for the new body weight categories. Results achieved at IWF-approved competitions exceeding the world standards by 0.5 kg for snatch or clean and jerk, or by 2.5 kg for the total, will be recognized as world records.

★ Greatest multiple of body weight lifted by a woman using one arm
Cammie Lynn Lusko (USA) became the first woman to lift more than her body weight with one arm. She lifted a total weight of 131 lb (59.5 kg) when she had a bodyweight of 128 lb 7 oz (58.3 kg), at Milwaukee, Wisconsin, USA, on May 21 1983.

★ Most push-ups in one minute
Jack Zatorski (USA) performed 133 push-ups in one minute at Fort Lauderdale, Florida, USA, on March 1 2003.

Men's 56-kg >> clean and jerk

Halil Mutlu (Turkey, right) lifted a record 168 kg

at Trencin, Slovakia, on April 24 2001. He also set the record for men's snatch, with a lift of 138.5 kg in Antalya, Turkey, on November 4 2001, and for the total, with a lift of 305 kg in Sydney, New South Wales, Australia, on September 16 2000.

★ **Most push-ups in one minute using the back of the hands**

Steve Bugdale (UK) completed 89 push-ups in one minute at Plymstock Health and Fitness Club, Plymouth, Devon, UK, on May 12 2003.

★ **Most push-ups in one hour using the back of the hand of one arm**

Bruce Swatton (UK) completed 441 one-arm push-ups in one hour at Plymstock Health and Fitness Club, Plymouth, Devon, UK, on May 12 2003.

★ **Most sit-ups in one minute using an abdominal frame**

B.M. Gopikrishnan (India) carried out 138 sit-ups in one minute using an abdominal frame at Somers Town Community Sports Centre, London, UK, on December 9 2003.

Gopikrishnan also holds the record for most sit-ups in one hour using an abdominal frame. He completed 8,367 sit-ups at Gundeldinger Hall, Basel, Switzerland, on December 20 2003.

Women's weight lifting world records

Body weight	Event	Weight, name, & nationality		Venue	Date
48 kg	Clean & jerk	116.5 kg	Zhuo Li (China)	Qinhuangdao, China	September 10 2003
	Snatch	93.5 kg	Zhuo Li (China)	Qinhuangdao, China	September 10 2003
	Total	207.5 kg	Mingjuan Wang (China)	Warsaw, Poland	November 19 2002
53 kg	Clean & jerk	127.5 kg	Xueju Li (China)	Busan, South Korea	November 20 2002
	Snatch	102.5 kg	Ri Song Hui (North Korea)	Warsaw, Poland	October 1 2002
	Total	225 kg	Yang Xia (China)	Sydney, Australia	September 18 2000
58 kg	Clean & jerk	133 kg	Caiyan Sun (China)	Izmir, Turkey	June 28 2002
	Snatch	110 kg	Li Wang (China)	Bali, Indonesia	August 10 2003
	Total	240 kg	Li Wang (China)	Bali, Indonesia	August 10 2003
63 kg	Clean & jerk	138 kg	Natalia Skakun (Ukraine)	Vancouver, Canada	November 18 2003
	Snatch	113.5 kg	Anna Batsiushka (Belarus)	Vancouver, Canada	November 18 2003
	Total	247.5 kg	Xia Liu (China)	Qinhuangdao, China	September 12 2003
69 kg	Clean & jerk	150 kg	Chunhong Liu (China)	Vancouver, Canada	November 19 2003
	Snatch	120 kg	Chunhong Liu (China)	Vancouver, Canada	November 19 2003
	Total	270 kg	Chunhong Liu (China)	Vancouver, Canada	November 19 2003
75 kg	Clean & jerk	152.5 kg	Ruiping Sun (China)	Busan, South Korea	October 7 2002
	Snatch	118.5 kg	Ruiping Sun (China)	Busan, South Korea	October 7 2002
	Total	270 kg	Ruiping Sun (China)	Busan, South Korea	October 7 2000
+75 kg	Clean & jerk	168.5 kg	Dan Sun (China)	Hyderabad, India	October 31 2003
	Snatch	137.5 kg	Ding Meiyuan (China)	Vancouver, Canada	November 21 2003
	Total	300 kg	Ding Meiyuan (China)	Sydney, Australia	September 22 2000

★ **Greatest height attained on a climbing machine in one hour**

Paddy Doyle (UK) climbed to a height of 3,144 ft (958.29 m) on a 'VersaClimber' machine in one hour, while carrying a 40-lb (18.1-kg) pack, on the TV show *This Morning*, Carlton TV Studios, London, UK, on October 17 2002.

★ **Fastest time to climb the height of Everest on a machine**

Kelvin Turner (UK) climbed the equivalent of the height of Mount Everest (29,035 ft or 8,850 m) in a time of 2 hr 57 min 56.5 sec on February 19 2003 at the LivingWell Health Club, Redland, Bristol, UK.

★ **Most skips by an individual in 24 hours**

Jim Payne (Ireland) skipped 141,221 jumps of a rope in 24 hours at City Square Shopping Centre, Waterford, Ireland, on March 26–27 2004. The attempt was carried out to raise funds for Our Lady's Hospital for Sick Children in Crumlin, Ireland.

Most men's Alpine skiing Olympic medals ⌄

The most Olympic Games medals won by a man is seven by Kjetil André Aamodt (Norway, below) who, in addition to his record three gold medals, has won two silver (for the downhill and combined events in 1994), and two bronze (for the giant slalom in 1992 and the supergiant slalom in 1994).

Most women's ⌃ Alpine skiing Olympic gold medals

Four women have won three Olympic gold medals: Vreni Schneider (Switzerland, above) (giant slalom in 1988, slalom in 1988 and 1994); Katja Seizinger (Germany) (downhill in 1994 and 1998, combined in 1998); Deborah Compagnoni (Italy) (supergiant slalom in 1992, giant slalom in 1994 and 1998); and Janica Kostelic (Croatia) (combined, giant slalom, and slalom in 2002).

★ **Highest speed in an Olympic downhill race**
On February 13 1998, Jean-Luc Crétier (France) attained an average speed of 66.81 mph (107.53 km/h) in the Olympic downhill race at Nagano, Japan.

★ **Fastest World Cup downhill speed**
Armin Assinger (Austria) reached a speed of 69.8 mph (112.4 km/h) at Sierra Nevada, Spain, on March 15 1993.

★ **Most World Cup downhill wins**
Franz Klammer (Austria) won 25 downhill races from 1974 to 1984.

★ **Longest downhill ski run**
The Weissfluhjoch-Küblis Parsenn course, near Davos, Switzerland, measures 7.6 miles (12.23 km).

★ **Most men's Alpine skiing Olympic gold medals**
The most Alpine skiing Olympic gold medals won by a male is three. The record is shared by Anton 'Toni' Sailer (Austria) for downhill, slalom, and giant slalom in 1956; Jean-Claude Killy (France) for downhill, slalom, and giant slalom in 1968; Alberto Tomba (Italy) for slalom and giant slalom in 1988 and giant slalom in 1992; and Kjetil André Aamodt (Norway), for supergiant slalom in 1992 and 2002 and the combined event in 2002.

★ **Most women's Alpine skiing Olympic medals**
Two women have won five skiing medals in the Olympic Games. In addition to her record three gold medals, Vreni Schneider (Switzerland) won silver in the combined event and bronze in the giant slalom in 1994. Katja Seizinger (Germany) won bronze in the 1992 and 1998 supergiant slalom in addition to her three gold successes.

★ **Most men's Alpine skiing World Championship titles**
The Alpine skiing World Championships debuted at Murren, Switzerland, in 1931. Anton 'Toni' Sailer (Austria) has won a record seven titles: all four titles in 1956 (giant slalom, slalom, downhill, and non-Olympic Alpine combination) and the downhill, giant slalom, and combined in 1958.

★ **Most women's Alpine skiing World Championship titles**
Christl Cranz (Germany) has won the most Alpine skiing World Championship titles, with seven individual – four slalom (in 1934 and from 1937 to 1939) and three downhill (in 1935, 1937, and 1939) – and five combined (in 1934 and 1935, and 1937 to 1939). She also won the gold medal for the combined in the 1936 Olympic Games.

★ **Highest speed by a skier**
Philippe Goitschel (France) reached a speed of 155.77 mph (250.7 km/h) at Les Arcs, France, on April 23 2002.

★ **Highest speed by a female skier**
Karine Dubouchet (France) reached a speed of 150.53 mph (242.26 km/h) at Les Arcs, France, in May 1999.

★ **Most World Cup race wins**
The most individual event wins is 86 (46 giant slalom, 40 slalom, from a total of 287 races) by Ingemar Stenmark (Sweden) from 1974 to 1989, including a men's record 13 in one season in 1978/79, of which 10 were part of a record 14 successive giant slalom wins from March 18 1978 (Ingemar's 22nd birthday) to January 21 1980.

★ **Most women's World Cup race wins**
Annemarie Moser (née Proll, Austria) won 62 individual event wins from 1970 to 1979, including a record 11 consecutive downhill wins from December 1972 to January 1974. She has also claimed the World Cup Overall Champion title (downhill and slalom events combined) a record six times since the tour began in 1967.

★ **Most men's freestyle World Cup titles**
Eric Laboureix (France) won five men's freestyle World Cup titles, from 1986 to 1988 and in 1990 and 1991.

Most 'vertical feet' skied by a man « in 24 hours

On April 29 1998, Chris Kent, Edi Podivinsky (left), Luke Sauder (all Canada), and Dominique Perret (Switzerland) skied 353,600 ft (107,777 m) in 14 hr 30 min on a slope at Blue River, British Columbia, Canada. They completed the run 73 times and were lifted back to the summit each time by helicopter. Podivinsky is shown here in action at the World Cup in Wengen, Switzerland, in 2000.

★ Most women's freestyle World Cup titles
Connie Kissling (Switzerland) won 10 World Cup freestyle titles from 1983 to 1992.

★ Most freestyle skiing World Championship titles
The first World Championships were held at Tignes, France, in 1986, when titles were awarded in ballet, moguls, aerials, and combined events. Edgar Grospiron (France) has won a record three World Championship titles: moguls in 1989 and 1991, and aerials in 1995. He also won an Olympic title in 1992.

The greatest number of world titles won by a woman is also three by Candice Gilg (France), who won the moguls in 1993, 1995, and 1997.

★ Most somersaults and twists in a freestyle aerial jump
The greatest number of twists and somersaults achieved in a freestyle jump was set by Matt Chojnacki (USA), who completed a quadruple-twisting quadruple back flip at Winter Park Resort, Colorado, USA, on April 4 2001.

★ Most Nations Cup wins
The Nations Cup is awarded according to the combined results of individual performances by men and women in the World Cup. The Cup has been won 22 times by Austria, in 1969, 1973–80, 1982, and 1990–2001.

★ Farthest vertical distance skied in 12 hours
The greatest vertical distance skied in a 12-hour period by an individual, skiing both the downhill and the uphill sections, is 33,070 ft (10,080 m) by Manfred Tod (Austria) at Mariazeller Burgeralpe, Austria, on February 24 2003.

★ Most 'vertical feet' skied by a woman in 24 hours
Jennifer Hughes (USA) skied 305,525 vertical feet (93,124 m) at Atlin, British Columbia, Canada, on April 20 1998. She was accompanied by snowboarder Tammy McMinn (USA) during her record attempt and the two women were lifted from the bottom of the run to the top by helicopter.

★ Longest competitive ski jump by a man
Andreas Goldberger (Austria) made a ski jump of 738 ft (225 m) at Planica, Slovenia, on March 18 2000.

★ Longest ski jump by a woman
Eva Ganster (Austria) achieved a distance of 367 ft (112 m) in the ski jump at Bischofshofen, Austria, on January 7 1994.

★ Most ski flips in 10 minutes
Tommy Waltner (USA) completed 23 front inverted aerial jumps within 10 minutes on April 25 2000. The event took place on Aspen Mountain, Colorado, USA, in order to raise money for Waltner's 'Loops for Lupus' campaign.

★ Largest flare run
The largest flare run ever consisted of 1,321 skiers and snowboarders who followed a course of 4.3 miles (7 km) between Piz Martegnas and Savognin, Switzerland, on January 1 2000 while carrying flares.

★ Longest ski lift
The Grindelwald–Männlichen gondola ski lift in Switzerland is 3.88 miles (6,239 m) long.

★ Most men's medals in Olympic biathlon
Ricco Gross (Germany) won seven Olympic biathlon medals: three golds (4 x 7.5 km in 1992, 1994, and 1998), three silvers (10 km in 1992 and 1994, and 4 x 7.5 km in 2002) and a bronze (for the pursuit in 2002).

★ Most women's medals in Olympic biathlon
Uschi Disl (Germany) won a total of eight Olympic biathlon medals: two golds (4 x 7.5 km in 1998 and 2002), four silvers (3 x 7.5 km in 1992, 4 x 7.5 km in 1994, and 7.5 km in 1998 and 2002), and two bronzes (15 km in 1994 and 1998).

Winter sports 2

Most men's snowboarding World Cup titles

Mathieu Bozzetto (France, right) has won six titles: the overall in 1999 and 2000 and the slalom/ parallel slalom in 1999–2002.

Highest average speed in major 50-km Nordic skiing

The record time for a 50-km race in a major championship is 1 hr 54 min 46 sec by Aleksey Prokurorov (Russia, above) at Thunder Bay, Canada, on March 19 1994, at an average speed of 16.24 mph (26.14 km/h).

★ Highest snowboarding speed
Darren Powell (Australia) reached a speed of 125.459 mph (201.907 km/h) at Les Arcs, France, on May 2 1999.

★ Fastest snowboard on a bobsled run
Reto Lamm (Switzerland) surfed down a bobsled run on his snowboard at 49.7 mph (80 km/h) at Königssee, Germany, in November 1998 for *Guinness – Die Show der Rekorde*.

★ Most snowboarding World Cup titles
The greatest number of titles won is 16 by Karine Ruby (France). She won overall titles in 1996–98 and 2001–02; the slalom/parallel slalom in 1996–98 and 2002; the giant slalom in 1995–98 and 2001; and the snowboard cross in 1997 and 2001.

The first snowboarding World Cup series began in 1995, with World Championships inaugurated the following year.

★ Most snowboarding championship titles
The greatest number of snowboarding titles won (including Olympic titles) is three, by Karine Ruby. She won the giant slalom in 1996, the Olympic title in 1998 (the first year that snowboarding became an Olympic sport), and the snowboard cross in 1997.

★ Most X-Games snowboarding medals
Shaun Palmer (USA) has won a record three gold medals at the Winter ESPN X-Games for the Boarder X discipline (1997–99) since the inaugural X-Games in 1997. Across all the disciplines, he has won a total of six gold medals at the X-Games.

The most X-Games snowboarding medals won by a woman is six, by Barrett Christy (USA).

★ Oldest sled dog racing trail
The oldest established sled dog trail is the 1,049-mile (1,688-km) Iditarod Trail, which runs from Anchorage to Nome, Alaska, USA. The trail has existed since 1910 and has been the course of an annual race since 1967.

★ Longest trail in dogsled racing
The longest race is run on the 1,243-mile (2,000-km) Berengia Trail from Esso to Markovo, Russia, which started as a 155-mile (250-km) route in April 1990. Now established as an annual event, the fastest time to complete the trail was achieved in 1991 by Pavel Lazarev (USSR) in 10 days 18 hr 17 min 56 sec. His time was equivalent to an average speed of 5 mph (8 km/h).

★ Most ski orienteering World Championship team wins
Sweden has won the men's relay title six times, in 1977, 1980, 1982, 1984, 1990, and 1996.

Finland has won the women's relay eight times, in 1975, 1977, 1980, 1988, 1990, 1998, 2000, and 2004.

Vidar Benjaminsen (Norway) has won a record 15 medals, including four gold, two individual, and two relay.

★ Most individual ski orienteering World Championships
Ragnhild Bratberg (Norway) has won four individual titles: the classic in 1986 and 1990 and the sprint in 1988 and 1990.

The men's record is also four by Nicolo Corradini (Italy), who won the classic in 1994 and 1996 and the sprint in 1994 and 2000.

★ Most Nordic skiing Olympic gold medals
Bjørn Dæhlie (Norway) won eight Olympic gold medals for Nordic skiing (on the flat), for the 15 km, 50 km, and 4 x 10 km in 1992; the 10 km and 15 km in 1994; and the 10 km, 50 km, and 4 x 10 km in 1998.

The most Olympic gold medals won by a woman is six by Lyubov Yegorova (Russia), for the 10 km, 15 km, and 4 x 5 km in 1992, and the 5 km, 10 km, and 4 x 5 km in 1994.

Most « snowboarding Olympic medals

Since the introduction of snowboarding to the Winter Olympics in 1998, the most medals won is two by Ross Powers (USA, left), who won gold for the half pipe in 2002 and bronze for the same event in 1998; and Karine Ruby (France), who won gold for parallel giant slalom in 1998 and silver for the same event in 2002.

★ Most World Nordic Championship title wins

The first World Nordic Championships were those of the 1924 Winter Olympics in Chamonix, France. The most titles won by a woman is 17 by Yelena Välbe (Russia). Her total consists of 10 individual and seven relay wins from 1989 to 1998. With an additional seven medals, her total of 24 is also a record.

The most titles (including those for the Olympics) won by a man is 17 by Bjørn Dæhlie (Norway) – 12 individual and five relay from 1991 to 1998. Dæhlie won a record 29 medals from 1991 to 1999.

★ Most Olympic Nordic skiing medals

The greatest number of medals won by a man in Nordic skiing is 12 by Bjørn Dæhlie (Norway), who in addition to his record eight gold medals, also won four silver from 1992 to 1998.

The record for women is 10 by Raisa Smetanina (USSR/CIS), who won four gold (the 5 km in 1980, the 10 km in 1976, and the

Snowshoe race					
Event	**Time**	**Name & nationality**	**Venue**		**Date**
Men					
100 m	13.23	Keith Sendziak (USA)	Gabriels, New York, USA		February 27 1999
200 m	28.73	Birger Ohlsson (Sweden)	Gabriels, New York, USA		February 27 1999
400 m	1:03.24	Birger Ohlsson (Sweden)	Gabriels, New York, USA		February 27 1999
1,500-m run	5:20.47	Matthew Dougherty (USA)	Saranac Lake, New York, USA		February 23 2002
1,500-m walk	8:37.00	Michel Lavoie (Canada)	St. Luc, Québec, Canada		February 17 1996
Women					
100 m	14.98	Mary Shanly (USA)	St. Luc, Québec, Canada		February 17 1996
200 m	34.31	Mary Shanly (USA)	St. Luc, Québec, Canada		February 17 1996
400 m	1:24.43	Ann Herbowy (USA)	Gabriels, New York, USA		February 27 1999
1,500-m run	6:51.67	Rebecca Harman (USA)	Saranac Lake, New York, USA		February 23 2002
1,500-m walk	10:46.00	Lynn Dextradeur (Canada)	Hull, Québec, Canada		Unknown 1989

4 x 5 km in 1976 and 1992), five silver (the 10 km in 1984 and 1988, the 5 km in 1976, the 20 km in 1984, and the 4 x 5 km in 1980), and one bronze (the 20 km in 1988).

★ Greatest Nordic skiing distance in 24 hours

Seppo-Juhani Savolainen (Finland) covered 258.2 miles (415.5 km) at Saariselk, Finland, on April 8–9 1988.

Kamila Horakova (Czech Republic) achieved a women's record distance of 206.91 miles

(333 km) in the event from April 12 to 13 2000 at the Canmore Nordic Centre, Alberta, Canada.

★ Most Nordic ski-jumping World Championships

Birger Ruud (Norway) won five ski-jumping titles in 1931–32 and 1935–37.

Ruud is the only person to have won Olympic events in each of the dissimilar Alpine and Nordic disciplines. In 1936, he won the ski-jumping and the Alpine downhill (which

was not then a separate event, but only a segment of the combined event).

★ Most Nordic combined skiing Olympic gold medals

The most gold medals won at the Olympic Games is three by Ulrich Wehling (GDR), for the individual in 1972, 1976, and 1980; and Sampaa Lajunen (Finland), for the individual, sprint, and relay in 2002. Lajunen also won silver at individual and relay in 1998, for a record total of five medals.

Most Olympic Games ⌄ curling wins

Curling became an Olympic sport in 1998. It has only been part of the Olympics twice altogether and to date four countries have won one title each. In 1998, Switzerland won the men's title and Canada won the women's. In the 2002 Games, Norway's men's team (Lars Vaagberg, below) and Great Britain's women's team were the winners.

Fastest lugeing speed ⌃

Tony Benshoof (USA, above) reached a speed of 86.6 mph (139.39 km/h) on the track built for the 2002 Olympics at Park City, Utah, USA, on October 16 2001. The speed was reached during training for the 2001 Luge World Cup Series.

★ **Fastest game of curling**
Eight curlers from the Burlington Golf and Country Club curled an eight-end game in 47 min 24 sec, with time penalties of 5 min 30 sec, at Burlington, Ontario, Canada, on April 4 1986. The time is taken from when the first rock crosses the near hog-line until the last rock comes to a stop.

★ **Longest curling stone throw**
Eddie Kulbacki (Canada) threw a curling stone a distance of 576 ft 4 in (175.66 m) at Park Lake, Neepawa, Manitoba, Canada, on January 29 1989. The attempt took place on a specially prepared sheet of curling ice on frozen Park Lake a record 1,200 ft (365.76 m) long.

★ **Most World Championship and Olympic Games luge wins by a man**
The most single-seater World Championship and Olympic titles (instituted in 1953) won is six by Georg Hackl (GDR/ Germany) in 1989, 1990, 1992, 1994, 1997, and 1998. Jan Behrendt and Stefan Krausse (both GDR/Germany) have won a record six two-seater titles, in 1989, 1991–93, 1995, and 1998.

★ **Most Olympic gold luge medals by a woman**
Steffi Walter (née Martin, GDR) won two gold medals for lugeing, with victories at the women's single-seater luge event in 1984 and 1988.

★ **Most luge World Championship titles by a woman**
Margit Schumann (GDR) won four luge World Championships, in 1973–75 and 1977.

★ **Youngest Olympic bobsled champion**
William Guy Fiske (USA) was 16 years 260 days old when he won the gold medal with the five-man bobsled team during the 1928 Winter Olympics held at St Moritz, Switzerland.

★ **Oldest Olympic bobsled champion**
Jay O'Brien (USA) was 47 years 357 days old when he won the gold medal with the four-man bobsled team during the 1932 Winter Olympics held at Lake Placid, New York, USA.

★ **Most individual Olympic bobsled medals**
Bogdan Musiol (GDR) won a record seven individual Olympic bobsled medals (one gold, five silver, one bronze) from 1980 to 1992.

★ **Most Olympic gold bobsled medals won by an individual**
Meinhard Nehmer and Bernhard Germeshausen (both GDR) have each won three gold bobsled medals, in the 1976 two-man and the 1976 and 1980 four-man events.

★ **Most individual World Championship bobsled titles**
The greatest number of bobsled World Championship titles won by an individual is 11 by Eugenio Monti (Italy) from 1957 to 1968. He accomplished this feat by winning eight two-man titles and three four-man titles.

★ **Most bobsled World Championships by a women's team**
A women's bobsled World Championships was introduced in 2000 and the sport made its debut at the 2002 Winter Olympic Games. Since 2000, Germany has won the title a record three times, in 2000, 2003, and 2004.

★ **Most medals won at the women's bobsled World Championships**
Since the introduction of the bobsled to the World Championships in 2000, the greatest number of medals won by an individual is four by Susi-Lisa Erdmann (Germany). She won gold in 2004 (with Kristina Bader) and in 2003 (with Annegret Dietrich), and bronze in 2001 (with Tanja Hees) and in 2002 (with Nicole Herschmann).

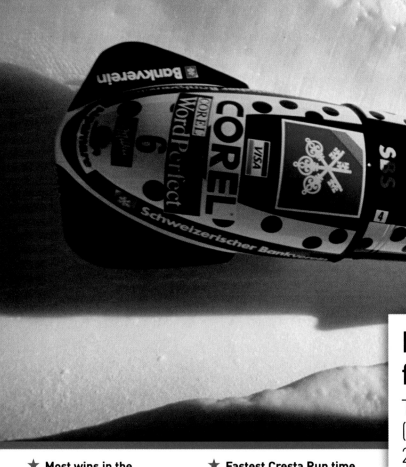

Most wins in the ⌃ four-man bobsled

The world four-man bobsled title (instituted in 1924) has been won 20 times by Switzerland (above), in 1924, 1936, 1939, 1947, 1954–57, 1971–73, 1975, 1982–83, 1986–90, and 1993. This total includes a record five Olympic victories, in 1924, 1936, 1956, 1972, and 1988.

★ Most wins in the two-man bobsled World Championships and Olympic Games

Switzerland has won the two-man bobsled title 17 times, in 1935, 1947–50, 1953, 1955, 1977–80, 1982–83, 1987, 1990, 1992, and 1994. It has also had a record four Olympic wins, in 1948, 1980, 1992, and 1994.

★ Fastest Cresta Run completion time

The Cresta Run, which dates from 1884, is 3,977 ft (1,212 m) long and has a drop of 514 ft (157 m). On February 13 1999, James Sunley (UK) made the run in 50.09 seconds at an average speed of 54.13 mph (87.11 km/h).

★ Most Cresta Run wins

The greatest number of wins in the Cresta Run Curzon Cup competition (instituted in 1910) is eight by 1948 Olympic champion Nino Bibbia (Italy) in 1950, 1957–58, 1960, 1962–64, and 1969; and by Franco Gansser (Switzerland) in 1981, 1983–86, 1988–89, and 1991.

★ Fastest Cresta Run time from Junction

On January 17 1999, Johannes Badrutt (Switzerland) made a time of 41.02 seconds and covered a distance of 2,921 ft (890 m) on the Cresta Run starting at Junction, the second point of the run from which competitors can officially start.

★ Most Olympic gold figure skating medals by a man

Gillis Grafstrom (Sweden) won three gold medals in 1920, 1924, and 1928, and a silver in 1932.

★ Most Olympic gold figure skating medals by a woman

Sonja Henie (Norway) won three gold medals at the 1928, 1932, and 1936 Winter Olympics.

★ Most Olympic gold figure skating medals as a pair

Irina Rodnina (USSR) won three pairs figure skating Olympic gold medals, with two different partners. In 1972, she won the gold with Alexei Ulanov, and in 1976 and 1980 she won the gold with Alexandr Zaitsev (both USSR).

★ Most figure skating Grand Slams by a man

The most figure skating Grand Slams – which consist of the European, World, and Olympic titles – won by a man is two by Karl Schäfer (Austria) in 1932 and 1936.

★ Most figure skating Grand Slams by a woman

Two women have won two figure skating Grand Slams: Sonja Henie (Norway) in 1932 and 1936, and Katarina Witt (West Germany) in 1984 and 1988.

★ Most figure skating pairs World Championship titles

Irina Rodnina won 10 World Championship pairs titles (instituted in 1908) – four with Aleksey Nikolayevich Ulanov in 1969–72 and six with her husband Aleksandr Gennadyevich Zaitsev (all USSR) in 1973–78.

The most ice dance titles (instituted in 1952) won is six by Lyudmila Alekseyevna Pakhomova and her husband Aleksandr Georgiyevich Gorshkov (both USSR) in 1970–74 and 1976. The pair also won the first ever Olympic ice dance title in 1976.

★ Most continuous upright spins by an ice-skater

The most continuous upright spins on ice skates on one foot is 115 by Lucinda Ruh (Switzerland) at Chelsea Piers Sky Rink, New York City, USA, on April 3 2003.

★ Longest jump flip by a figure skater

Robin John Cousins (UK) achieved 19 ft 1 in (5.81 m) in an axel jump and 18 ft (5.48 m) with a back flip at Richmond Ice Rink, Surrey, UK, on November 16 1983.

Fastest 500 m speed skating »

Hiroyasu Shimizu (Japan, right) achieved a record time of 34.32 seconds in the men's 500 m speed skating competition in Salt Lake City, Utah, USA, on March 10 2001.

★ **Greatest ice-skating distance in 24 hours**
Martinus Kuiper (Netherlands) skated a total distance of 339.67 miles (546.65 km) in Alkmaar, The Netherlands, on December 12–13 1988.

★ **Most speed skating sprint World Championship wins**
Igor Zhelezovskiy (USSR/Belarus) has won a record total of six men's sprint titles. His victories came in 1985–86, 1989, and 1991–93.

★ **Most men's speed skating Olympic gold medals**
The greatest number of Olympic gold medals won by a man is five. The record is shared by two speed skaters: Clas Thunberg (Finland) in 1924 and 1928 (including one tied); and Eric Arthur Heiden (USA) who, uniquely, won all his gold medals at one Games at Lake Placid, New York, USA, in 1980. In the process, he broke a world speed record.

★ **Most women's speed skating Olympic gold medals**
The most Olympic speed skating gold medals won by a woman is six by Lidiya Pavlovna Skoblikova (USSR), who won two golds in 1960 and four in 1964.

★ **Most men's World Championship speed skating titles**
The most World Championship speed skating titles won by a man is five. The record is shared between two speed skaters. Oscar Mathisen (Norway) won titles in 1908–9 and 1912–14, while Clas Thunberg (Finland) won in 1923, 1925, 1928–29, and 1931.

★ **Most women's speed skating World Championship titles**
The most titles won by a woman is eight by Gunda Niemann-Stirnemann (Germany) in 1991–93 and 1995–99.

★ **Most speed skating Single Distance World Championship titles**
The Single Distance World Championships were instituted in 1996. Since that time, Gunda Niemann-Stirnemann (Germany) has won 11 titles: the 1,500 m in 1997, the 3,000 m in 1996–99 and 2001, and the 5,000 m in 1997–2001.
  The greatest number of titles won by a man is seven by Gianni Romme (Netherlands). He won the 5,000 m in 1998–2000 and the 10,000 m in 1996–98 and 2000.

Men's speed skating world records

Event	Time	Name & nationality	Venue	Date
500 m	34.32	Hiroyasu Shimizu (Japan)	Salt Lake City, USA	March 10 2001
1,000 m	1:07.18	Gerard van Velde (Netherlands)	Salt Lake City, USA	February 16 2002
1,500 m	1:43.95	Derek Parra (USA)	Salt Lake City, USA	February 19 2002
3,000 m	3:42.75	Gianni Romme (Netherlands)	Calgary, Canada	August 11 2000
5,000 m	6:14.66	Jochem Uytdehaage (Netherlands)	Salt Lake City, USA	February 9 2002
10,000 m	12:58.92	Jochem Uytdehaage (Netherlands)	Salt Lake City, USA	February 22 2002
Short track				
500 m	41.184*	Jean-Francois Monette (Canada)	Calgary, Canada	October 18 2003
1,000 m	1:24.674*	Jiajun Li (China)	Bormio, Italy	February 2 2004
1,500 m	2:10.639*	Hyun-Soo Ahn (Korea)	Marquette, USA	October 24 2003
3,000 m	4:32.646*	Hyun-Soo Ahn (Korea)	Beijing, China	December 7 2003
5,000-m relay	6:43.730	Canada (Eric Bédard, Marc Gagnon, Jean-Francois Monette, Mathieu Turcotte)	Calgary, Canada	October 14 2001
* Subject to ratification by the International Skating Union (ISU) Council				

Fastest women's 1,500 m speed skating

Anni Friesinger (Germany, below foreground) achieved a time of 1 min 54.02 sec in Salt Lake City, Utah, USA, on February 20 2002.

Longest ice-skating race

The *Elfstedentocht* ('Tour of the 11 Towns' above), which started in the 17th century, covers 124.27 miles (200 km). It was held in The Netherlands in 1909–63, 1985–86, and 1997. As the weather does not permit an annual race in The Netherlands, *Elfstedentocht*s also take place at alternative venues. The record men's time is 5 hr 40 min 37 sec by Dries van Wijhe (Netherlands); the women's record is 5 hr 48 min 8 sec by Alida Pasveer (Netherlands), both at Lake Weissensee, Austria, on February 11 1989.

★ **Lowest men's speed skating World Championship score**
The lowest, and therefore best, score achieved for the men's World Championship speed skating title is 152.651 points by Rintje Ritsma (Netherlands) in Hamar, Norway, on February 6–7 1999.

★ **Lowest women's speed skating World Championship score**
The lowest score for a woman is 161.479 points, achieved by Gunda Niemann-Stirnemann (Germany) in Hamar, Norway, on February 6–7 1999.

★ **Most men's short-track speed skating Olympic medals**
Marc Gagnon (Canada) has won a total of five Olympic medals for short-track speed skating. His record tally includes three gold medals (for the 500 m in 2002 and the relay in 1998 and 2002) and two bronze medals (for the 1,000 m in 1994 and the 1,500 m in 2002).

★ **Most women's short-track speed skating Olympic medals**
Two women have won five medals. Chun Lee-kyung (South Korea) won four gold medals (the 1,000 m in 1994 and 1998, and the relay in 1994 and 1998) and one bronze (the 500 m in 1998). Yang Yang (China) won four silver medals (the 500 m in 1998, the 1,000 m in 1998, and the relay in 1998 and 2002) and one bronze (the 1,000 m in 2002).

★ **Most wins in men's short-track speed skating World Championships**
The most successful skater in these championships, which were instituted in 1978, has been Marc Gagnon (Canada). He was men's overall champion in 1993–94, 1996, and 1998.

★ **Most wins in women's short-track speed skating World Championships**
In the women's competition, the most successful skaters have been Sylvie Daigle (Canada), with victories in 1983 and 1988–90, and Yang Yang (China), who was champion in 1998–2001.

Women's speed skating world records

Event	Time	Name & nationality	Venue	Date
500 m	37.22	Catriona LeMay Doan (Canada)	Calgary, Canada	December 9 2001
1,000 m	1:13.83	Christine Witty (USA)	Salt Lake City, USA	February 17 2002
1,500 m	1:54.02	Anni Friesinger (Germany)	Salt Lake City, USA	February 20 2002
3,000 m	3:57.70	Claudia Pechstein (Germany)	Salt Lake City, USA	February 10 2002
5,000 m	6:46.91	Claudia Pechstein (Germany)	Salt Lake City, USA	February 23 2002
Short track				
500 m	43.671	Evgenia Radanova (Bulgaria)	Calgary, Canada	October 19 2001
1,000 m	1:30.483	Chun-Sa Byun (Korea)	Budapest, Hungary	February 3 2002
1,500 m	2:18.861*	Eun-Ju Jung (Korea)	Beijing, China	January 11 2004
3,000 m	5:01.976	Choi Eun-kyung (South Korea)	Calgary, Canada	October 22 2000
3,000-m relay	4:12.793	South Korea (Park Hye-won, Joo Min-jin, Choi Min-kyung, Choi Eun-kyung)	Salt Lake City, USA	February 20 2002
*Subject to ratification by the ISU Council				

Golf
Sport

Youngest golfer to play ⌃ in the Ryder Cup

Sergio Garcia (Spain, above) competed for Europe in the Ryder Cup in 1999 aged 19 years 8 months and 15 days.

Highest career earnings on the US LPGA Tour ⌃

Annika Sorenstam (Sweden, above) earned $13,199,874 on the US Ladies Professional Golf Association (LPGA) Tour from 1993 to the end of 2003. She also holds the record for the highest season's earnings on the US LPGA Tour, earning $2,863,904.

★ **Most British Open titles**
Harry Vardon (UK) won six British Open titles, in 1896, 1898, 1899, 1903, 1911, and 1914.

★ **Most US Open titles**
Four golfers have won the US Open four times: Willie Anderson (UK) in 1901 and 1903–05; Bobby Jones Jr. (USA) in 1923, 1926, 1929, and 1930; Ben Hogan (USA) in 1948, 1950, 1951, and 1953; and Jack Nicklaus (USA) in 1962, 1967, 1972, and 1980.

★ **Most Solheim Cup wins**
The Solheim Cup, the women's equivalent of the Ryder Cup, was first held in 1990 and is contested biennially between the top professional players of Europe and the USA. The

USA has won five times: 1990, 1994, 1996, 1998, and 2002. Europe won three times, in 1992, 2000, and 2003.

★ **Most successful Ryder Cup captain**
The most successful Ryder Cup captain is Walter Hagen (USA) with four wins. Hagen captained the US team to victory in 1927, 1931, 1935, and 1937. He was one of the most colorful sports personalities of his time, and is credited with doing more than any other golfer to influence the perception of his profession.

★ **Lowest score over 18 holes by a woman**
The lowest recorded score on an 18-hole course over 5,600 yd (5,120 m) for a woman is 59

by Annika Sorenstam (Sweden) in the 2001 Standard Register PING tournament at Moon Valley Country Club, Phoenix, Arizona, USA, on March 16 2001.

★ **Biggest margin of victory in a golf tournament**
The biggest margin of victory in a major golf tournament was achieved by Tiger Woods (USA), who won the 2000 US Open by 15 shots. He finished with a round of 67 to add to rounds of 65, 69, and 71 for a 12-under-par total of 272.

★ **Lowest individual score at the World Cup**
The lowest individual total score for the four rounds of the World Cup is 263 by Tiger Woods (USA) at Kuala Lumpur, Malaysia, from November 18 to 21 1999.

★ **Most US PGA Driving Distance titles**
Driving distance is the average number of yards per measured drive and is measured on two holes per round. Care is taken to select two holes

that face in opposite directions to counteract the effects of wind, and drives are measured to the point at which they come to rest, regardless of whether they are on the fairway or not. John Daly (USA) won 11 US PGA Driving Distance titles from 1991 to 1993 and from 1995 to 2002. His longest average drive was 306.8 yd (280.44 m) in 2002.

★ **Most consecutive holes-in-one**
There are at least 20 cases of holes-in-one (or 'aces') being achieved in two consecutive holes, of which the greatest was Norman L. Manley's (USA) unique 'double albatross' on the par-4 330-yd (301-m) seventh hole and par-4 290-yd (265-m) eighth hole on the Del Valle Country Club course, Saugus, California, USA, on September 2 1964.
An albatross occurs when a player completes a hole three under par, and is therefore a hole-in-one only when hit on a par-4 hole.

Highest career earnings on the US PGA circuit »

Tiger Woods (USA, right) won $41,508,265 from August 1996 to March 2004 on the US Professional Golfers' Association (PGA) circuit. He also holds the record for the highest season's earnings on the US PGA Tour, earning $9,188,321.

★ **Most holes-in-one by husband and wife at same hole**
John and Jenny Dixon (both UK) scored consecutive holes-in-one during a four-ball competition on the third hole at Knaresborough Golf Club, Knaresborough, North Yorkshire, UK, on August 22 1996. This was equaled by Elmer and Marilyn James (both USA) on the 16th at Halifax Plantation Golf Club, Ormond, Florida, USA, on April 19 1998.

★ **Most holes played in 24 hours**
Ian Colston (Australia) played 22 rounds and five holes (401 holes) at Bendigo Golf Club, Victoria, Australia, (par 73 – 6,061 yd or 5,542 m) on November 27–28 1971.

★ **Most holes played in 24 hours using a golf cart**
On August 6–7 1990, David Cavalier (USA) played 846 holes at Arrowhead Country Club, North Canton, Ohio, USA, on a nine-hole course 3,013 yd (2,755 m) in length.

★ **Most holes played in a year**
Leo Fritz (USA) played a record 10,550 holes in 1998.

★ **Most walking golfers on a single course in 24 hours**
The greatest number of walking golfers to complete a full round on the same course on the same day is 491 on the Torrance course at St. Andrews Bay Golf Resort and Spa, St. Andrews, Fife, UK, on June 8 2003.

★ **Largest bunker**
The world's biggest bunker (or 'trap') is Hell's Half Acre on the 585-yd (535-m) seventh hole of the Pine Valley course, Clementon, New Jersey, USA, built in 1912 and generally regarded as the world's most testing course. The hazard starts 280 yd (265 m) from the tee and extends another 150 yd (137 m) to the next section of fairway.

★ **Longest tournament putt**
The longest recorded holed putt in a major tournament is 110 ft (33.5 m) by Jack Nicklaus (USA) in the 1964 Tournament of

Champions, and Nick Price (Zimbabwe) in the 1992 US PGA.
Bob Cook (USA) sank a putt measured at 140 ft 2.75 in (42.74 m) on the 18th hole at St. Andrews in the International Fourball Pro Am Tournament on October 1 1976.

★ **Longest nontournament putt**
On November 6 2001, Fergus Muir (UK) sank a putt measuring 375 ft (114.3 m) on the Eden Course at St. Andrews Links, Fife, UK.

★ **Longest golf carry with one hand**
Petri Takkunen (Finland) drove a golf ball 236.22 yd (216 m) using only one hand at Ruukkigolf, Pohja, Finland, on June 16 2003.

★ **Greatest distance between two rounds of golf played on the same day**
The greatest distance between two rounds of golf played on the same day is 7,496 miles (12,063 km) by Larry Olmsted (USA), who played two full

18-hole rounds at New South Wales Golf Club, Sydney, Australia, and then Pelican Hill Golf Club, Newport Beach, California, USA, on February 18 2004.

★ **Fastest round of golf by an individual**
With great variations in the lengths of golf courses, speed records are of little comparative value, even for rounds under par. The fastest round played when the golf ball comes to rest before each new stroke is 27 min 9 sec by James Carvill (UK) at Warrenpoint Golf Course, County Down, UK, who completed 18 holes over 6,154 yd (5,628 m) on June 18 1987.

★ **Fastest round of golf by a team**
The WBAP News/Talk 820 (USA) team of golfers completed 18 holes in 8 min 47 sec at Bridlewood Golf Club, Flower Mound, Texas, USA, on August 12 2003. A total of 95 golfers took part on an 18-hole course measuring 6,021 yd (5,505 m) in length.

Water sports 1

Most water polo ∧ World Championships

Water polo was first held at the World Swimming Championships in 1973. The most wins is two by Italy (1978 and 1994; above, back), the USSR (1975 and 1982), Yugoslavia (1986 and 1991), and Spain (1998 and 2001).

Largest « 'paddle-in' wave surfed

A wave measuring 50 ft (15.2 m) in height from trough to crest was ridden by Taylor Knox (USA, left) at a break known as Killers at Todos Santos Island off Ensenada, Mexico, on February 22 1998. Knox caught the wave by using an arm-powered paddle-in rather than being towed.

★ Most water polo Olympic medals

Five players share the record of three gold medals: George Wilkinson in 1900, 1908, and 1912; Paulo 'Paul' Radmilovic and Charles Sidney Smith in 1908, 1912, and 1920 (all GB); and Desz Gyarmati and György Kárpáti (both Hungary) in 1952, 1956, and 1964.

Paul Radmilovic also won a gold for the 4 x 200-m freestyle relay swimming in 1908.

★ Most water polo goals in an international game

The greatest number of goals scored by an individual in a water polo international is 13 by Debbie Handley for Australia (16) against Canada (10) at the World Championship in Guayaquil, Ecuador, in 1982.

★ Longest water polo marathon

A match lasting 24 hours was played by Rapido 82 Haarlem at the De Planeet pool, Haarlem, The Netherlands, from April 30 to May 1 1999.

★ Longest water-skiing marathon

Ralph Hildebrand and Dave Phillips (both Canada) water-skied simultaneously for 56 hr 35 min 3 sec around Indian Arm, Rocky Point, British Columbia, Canada. They completed their feat on June 12 1994 after covering a distance of 1,337.46 miles (2,152.3 km) at an average speed of 30 mph (48 km/h). While skiing at night, they used infrared binoculars and spotlights.

★ Most barefoot water-skiing World Championships

The record is held jointly by Kim Lampard (Australia), for wins in 1980, 1982, 1985, and 1986, and Jennifer Calleri (USA), who won in 1990, 1992, 1994, and 1996.

The most titles won by a man is three by Brett Wing (Australia), in 1978, 1980, and 1982, and Ron Scarpa (USA), in 1992, 1996, and 1998.

The team title has been won six times by the USA, in 1988, 1990, 1992, 1994, 1996, and 1998.

★ Largest wave surfed (unlimited)

The largest wave successfully surfed had a face 70 ft (21.3 m) in height. It was ridden by Pete Cabrinha (USA) at a break known as Jaws (Peahi) on the North Shore of Maui, Hawaii, USA, on January 10 2004. He was towed into the wave using a wave runner.

★ Most amateur surfing World Championships

Surfing's World Amateur Championships were inaugurated in May 1964 in Sydney, Australia. The greatest number of titles won is three by Michael Novakov (Australia), who won the knee-board event in 1982, 1984, and 1986.

★ Longest surfboard ride on a river bore

The longest recorded rides on a river bore have been set on the Severn bore, UK. The Official British Surfing Association distance record for riding a surfboard is 5.7 miles (9.1 km) by David Lawson (UK) from Windmill Hill to Maisemore Weir (both Gloucestershire, UK) on August 29 1996.

★ Longest continuous journey by a kite surfer

Fabrice Collard, Kent Marincovik, and Neil Hutchinson (all USA) traveled a distance of 88 nautical miles (101.3 miles or 163 km) between Key West, Florida, USA, and Varadero, Cuba, on boards pulled by kites on December 21 2001.

Their journey, during which they were not permitted to touch any other vessel, lasted 8 hr 38 min at an average speed of 12 knots (14 mph or 22 km/h).

★ Most windsurfing World Championships

From 1979 to 1983, Stephan van den Berg (Netherlands) won five windsurfing world titles.

★ Longest windsurfing marathon

Sergiy Naidych (Ukraine) windsurfed for 71 hr 30 min at Radyschev Lake, Simerferopol, Crimea, Ukraine, from June 6 to 9 2003.

Most men's »
professional surfing
World Championships

The most Association of Surfing Professionals (ASP) Tour World Championship titles won by a man is six by Kelly Slater (USA, right), in 1992 and 1994–98.

The equivalent women's title has been won six times by Layne Beachley (Australia) from 1998 to 2003.

★ Longest windsurfing journey

Steve Fisher (USA) crossed the Pacific from California to Hawaii on *Da Slipper II*, a highly modified 17-ft 8-in-long (5.4-m) Windsurfer. The 2,269-nautical mile (2,612-mile or 4,203-km) journey took a total of 47 days and Steve arrived on a beach on Maui, Hawaii, on September 3 1997.

★ Fastest time to windsurf across the Atlantic

Sergio Ferrero (Italy) windsurfed across the Atlantic from the Canary Islands to Barbados, a distance of approximately 2,600 nautical miles (3,100 miles or 5,000 km) in 24 days from June 6 to 30 1982.

★ Most consecutive days spent surfing

Dale Webster (USA) has surfed every day since September 2 1975, passing his 10,407th consecutive day of surfing on February 29 2004. He set himself the condition that a 'surf' should consist of catching at least three waves to shore.

Water-skiing – Men's world records

Event	Score	Name/Nationality	Venue	Date
Slalom	1 buoy/9.75-m line	Jeff Rogers (USA) Andy Mapple (GB) Jamie Beauchesne (USA)	Charleston, South Carolina, USA Miami, Florida, USA Charleston, South Carolina, USA	August 31 1997 October 4 1998 July 6 2003
Tricks	12,320 points	Nicolas Le Forestier (France)	Chaugey, France	July 13 2003
Ski fly	298 ft 10 in (91.1 m)	Jaret Llewellyn (Canada)	Orlando, Florida, USA	May 4 2000
Jump	235 ft 9.6 in (71.9 m)	Jimmy Siemers (USA)	Lago Santa Fe, Texas, USA	August 10 2003
Overall	2,818.8 points	Jaret Llewellyn (Canada)	Seffner, Florida, USA	September 29 2002

Water-skiing – Women's world records

Event	Score	Name/Nationality	Venue	Date
Slalom	1 buoy/10.25-m line	Kristi Overton Johnson (USA)	West Palm Beach, Florida, USA	September 14 1996
Tricks	8,630 points	Tawn Larsen Hahn (USA)	Wilmington, Illinois, USA	July 11 1999
Ski fly	227 ft 7 in (69.4 m)	Elena Milakova (Russia)	Pine Mountain, Georgia, USA	May 26 2002
Jump	186 ft (56.6 m)	Elena Milakova (Russia)	Rio Linda, California, USA	July 27 2002
Overall	2,854.01 points	Elena Milakova (Russia)	Hazelwood Ski World, Lincolnshire, UK	July 29 2001

Barefoot water-skiing – Men's world records

Event	Score	Name/Nationality	Venue	Date
Jump	89 ft 9.6 in (27.4 m)	David Small (GB)	Mulwala Water Ski Park, New South Wales, Australia	February 8 2004
Slalom	20.5 crossings of the wake in 15 sec	Brian Fuchs (USA)	Liverpool, New South Wales, Australia	April 1994
Tricks	9,550 points	David Small (GB)	Mulwala Water Ski Park, New South Wales, Australia	February 5 2004

Barefoot water-skiing – Women's world records

Event	Score	Name/Nationality	Venue	Date
Jump	67 ft 6.9 in (20.6 m)	Nadine de Villiers (RSA)	Roodeplaat Dam, South Africa	March 4 2000
Slalom	17.0 crossings of the wake in 15 sec	Nadine de Villiers (RSA)	Wolwekrans, South Africa	January 5 2001
Tricks	4,400 points	Nadine de Villiers (RSA)	Wolwekrans, South Africa	January 5 2001

Water sports 2

Eskimo rolls

Event	Record	Name & nationality	Venue	Date
Fastest 1,000 (no paddle)	31 min 55 sec	Colin Hill (UK)	Durham, UK	March 12 1987
Fastest 1,000 (paddle)	34 min 43 sec	Ray Hudspith (UK)	Newcastle Upon Tyne, UK	March 20 1987
Fastest 100 (no paddle)	2 min 39 sec	Colin Hill (UK)	London, UK	February 22 1987
Fastest 100 (paddle)	3 min 7 sec	Ray Hudspith (UK)	Tyne and Wear, UK	March 3 1991
Fastest 100 (female, paddle)	3 min 42 sec	Helen Barnes (UK)	London, UK	August 2 2000
Most consecutive	1,796	Randy Fine (USA)	Florida, USA	June 8 1991
Tandem (paddle) (one minute)	23	Emmanuel Baclet & Yann Hascoet (France)	Benodet, France	July 29 2003

Rowing world records

Event	Time	Name & nationality	Regatta	Date
Men				
Single sculls	6:36.33	Marcel Hacker (Germany)	Seville, Spain	2002
Double sculls	6:04.37	Luka Spik, Iztok Cop (Slovenia)	St. Catharines, Canada	1999
Quadruple sculls	5:37.68	Italy	Indianapolis, USA	1994
Coxless pairs	6:14.27	Matthew Pinsent, James Cracknell (GB)	Seville, Spain	2002
Coxless fours	5:41.35	Germany	Seville, Spain	2002
*Coxed pairs	6:42.16	Igor Boraska, Tihomir Frankovic, Milan Razov (Croatia)	Indianapolis, USA	1994
*Coxed fours	5:58.96	Germany	Vienna, Austria	1991
Coxed eights	5:22.80	The Netherlands	St. Catharines, Canada	1999
Women				
Single sculls	7:07.71	Roumiana Neykova (Bulgaria)	Seville, Spain	2002
Double sculls	6:38.78	Georgina Evers-Swindell, Caroline Evers-Swindell (New Zealand)	Seville, Spain	2002
Quadruple sculls	6:10.80	Germany	Duisburg, Germany	1996
Coxless pairs	6:53.80	Georgeta Andrunache, Viorica Susanu (Romania)	Seville, Spain	2002
*Coxless fours	6:25.47	Canada	Vienna, Austria	1991
Coxed eights	5:57.02	Romania	Lucerne, Switzerland	1999
Men's lightweight				
*Single sculls	6:47.97	Karsten Nielsen (Denmark)	St. Catharines, Canada	1999
Double sculls	6:10.80	Elia Luini, Leonardo Pettinari (Italy)	Seville, Spain	2002
*Quadruple sculls	5:45.18	Italy	Montreal, Canada	1992
*Coxless pairs	6:29.97	Christian Yantani Garces, Miguel Cerda Silva (Chile)	Seville, Spain	2002
Coxless fours	5:45.60	Denmark	Lucerne, Switzerland	1999
*Coxed eights	5:30.24	Germany	Montreal, Canada	1992
Women's lightweight				
*Single sculls	7:15.88	Marit van Eupen (Netherlands)	Lucerne, Switzerland	1999
Double sculls	6:50.63	Berit Christoffersen, Lene Andersson (Denmark)	Copenhagen, Denmark	1995
*Quadruple sculls	6:29.55	Australia	Seville, Spain	2002
*Coxless pairs	7:18.32	Eliza Blair, Justine Joyce (Australia)	Aiguebelette, France	1997

* denotes non-Olympic boat classes

Fastest single sculls ⤊

Roumiana Neykova (Bulgaria, above) set a record of 7 min 7.71 sec for the single sculls in Seville, Spain, in 2002.

★ **Most men's World & Olympic canoeing titles**
The men's record is 13 by Gert Fredriksson (Sweden), 1948–60, Rüdiger Helm (GDR), 1976–83, and Ivan Patzaichin (Romania), 1968–84.

★ **Most canoeing gold medals won at a single Olympic Games**
The most gold medals at one Games is three by Vladimir Parfenovich (USSR) in 1980 and Ian Ferguson (New Zealand) in 1984.

★ **Most consecutive kayak cartwheels**
Koya Morita (Japan) set a record of 264 consecutive cartwheels in a kayak on the Tama River, Ome-shi, Japan, on August 17 2003. One kayak cartwheel is a full 360° rotation – vertically rather than horizontally.

★ **Greatest distance by canoe in 24 hours**
Ian Adamson (USA) paddled 203.3 miles (327.1 km) in a canoe on the Colorado River from Gore Canyon, Colorado, to Potash, Utah, USA, from June 7 to 8 1997.

The record for the same time canoeing on the ocean is held by Randy Fine (USA), who paddled 120.6 miles (194.1 km) along the Florida coast on June 26–27 1986.

★ **Fastest 75-ft descent by canoe**
Shaun Baker (UK) descended a vertical height of 75 ft (22.86 m) in 19.9 seconds in a canoe on a river in Snowdonia, UK, on August 26 2000.

★ **Most women's Olympic & World canoeing titles**
Birgit Fischer (GDR/Germany) won seven Olympic gold medals from 1980 to 2000. She also won three silver medals for a record total of 10 medals. In addition, she won 29 world titles from 1979 to 1998, for a record 34 titles overall.

Apnea – free-diving world records

	Depth	Name & nationality	Venue	Date
Constant weight				
Men	311 ft (95 m)	Herbert Nitsch (Austria)	Dellach, Millstatter See, Austria	September 4 2003
Women	229 ft (70 m)	Tanya Streeter (UK)	Guadeloupe, France	May 11 2001
Constant weight without fins				
Men	200 ft (61 m)	Stig Åvall Severinsen (Denmark)	Puerto de la Cruz, Venezuela	September 28 2003
Women	141 ft (43 m)	Mandy-Rae Cruickshank (Canada)	Vancouver, Canada	September 1 2003
Variable weight				
Men	393 ft (120 m)	Patrick Musimu (Belgium)	Playa del Carmen, Mexico	November 12 2002
Women	400 ft (122 m)	Tanya Streeter (UK)	Turks and Caicos	July 21 2003
No limits				
Men	531 ft (162 m)	Loic Leferme (France)	Nice, France	October 20 2002
Women	525 ft (160 m)	Tanya Streeter (USA)	Turks and Caicos	August 17 2002.
Free immersion				
Men	331 ft (101 m)	Carlos Coste (Venezuela)	Puerto de la Cruz, Venezuela	October 4 2003
Women	232 ft (71 m)	Annabel Briseno (USA)	Kona, Hawaii, USA	November 15 2003
Dynamic apnea with fins				
Men	656 ft (200 m)	Peter Pedersen (Denmark)	Randers, Denmark	July 18 2003
Women	492 ft (150 m) (25 m pool)	Nathalie Desreac (France)	Réunion Island, France	November 14 1998
	492 ft (150 m) (50 m pool)	Natalia Molchanova (Russia)	Limassol, Cyprus	May 26 2003
Dynamic apnea without fins				
Men	544 ft (166 m)	Stig Åvall Severinsen (Denmark)	Aarhus, Denmark	July 19 2003
Women	328 ft (100 m)	Renate De Bruyn (Netherlands)	Eindhoven, The Netherlands	October 10 2003
Static apnea				
Men	8 min 24 sec	Stephane Mifsud (France)	Rouen, France	November 8 2003
Women	6 min 21 sec	Annabel Briseno (USA)	Kona, Hawaii, USA	November 13 2003

GWR TALKS TO
Tanya Streeter

Free diver Tanya Streeter (UK, right) currently holds three free-diving world records: the no-limits free dive (525 ft or 160 m), free diving with a constant weight (229 ft or 70 m), and the variable weight free-diving record of 400 ft (122 m), which she set on the Atlantic islands of Turks and Caicos on July 21 2003. Free diving involves staying underwater for as long as possible on just one breath. Some free-diving records require diving to incredible depths.

How and when did you first become interested in free diving?
I grew up on a Caribbean island and I was a good snorkeler. Technically, snorkeling is free diving; any time you take a breath and go underwater you're free diving. I started free diving when I was 25. I was inspired by people around me who knew more about the sport than I did.

What's your training regime?
A huge part of this sport is about fitness and being in peak physical condition. Much of my training is endurance based: I do a lot of spinning (static bicycling), and lots of aerobic training to get my cardiovascular system working efficiently. Then there's the conditioning work, getting my body used to not breathing, and operating without breathing during the course of the dive; this work is often pool based. Finally, free diving is largely dependent on mental strength, so I need to train myself mentally, which is probably the hardest part.

Is it fair to say that free diving is an extreme sport?
No, absolutely not. People think that because we can hold our breaths for so long, or dive so deep, we must in some way be superhuman, or are attempting to do very extreme things, when really what we're attempting to do is on the extreme edge of human potential. Most people will have tried to swim as far as they can underwater on one breath: when you compare their 40 seconds with our six minutes, what free divers do seems impossible.

Free diving is also a very controlled environment isn't it?
It is. We have to consider every element of the dive. People breathe instinctively; once you take away that option, it makes you think about absolutely everything you're going to need to do to be able to breathe again. It's highly, highly controlled.

What do you consider your greatest achievement so far?
I don't think that my achievement in my sport has actually been at the forefront for me; it's the fact that I have the opportunity to inspire people. I get lots of e-mails from people who have read about me and were inspired, and I get much more emotional satisfaction from that than I ever have done from a world record. I train very hard and I face every human fear that everyone else faces when embracing challenges. But it's the personal experience and the journey to those goals that stay with you. Never giving up on a goal has taught me the most.

What advice would you give someone wanting to free dive?
Safety. You must never do any breath-hold activity alone, even if it's just holding your breath in a pool. You must get some instruction, because it's more complicated than it seems. Many free divers like myself are happy to give advice, but this sport should only be done with at least one companion, never alone.

Swimming
Sport

Women's swimming (short course)

Event	Time	Name & nationality	Venue	Date
50-m freestyle	23.59	Therese Alshammar (Sweden)	Athens, Greece	March 18 2000
100-m freestyle	52.17	Therese Alshammar (Sweden)	Athens, Greece	March 17 2000
200-m freestyle	1:54.04	Lindsay Benko (USA)	Moscow, Russia	April 7 2002
400-m freestyle	3:59.53	Lindsay Benko (USA)	Berlin, Germany	January 26 2003
800-m freestyle	8:13.35	Sachiko Yamada (Japan)	Nishinomya-shi, Japan	January 24 2004
1,500-m freestyle	15:43.31	Petra Schneider (GDR)	Gainesville, USA	January 10 1982
4 x 50-m freestyle	1:37.52	The Netherlands (Hinkelien Schreuder, Annabel Kosten, Chantal Groot, Marleen Veldhuis)	Dublin, Ireland	December 12 2003
4 x 100-m freestyle	3:34.55	China (Le Jingyi, Na Chao, Shan Ying, Nian Yin)	Gothenburg, Sweden	April 19 1997
4 x 200-m freestyle	7:46.30	China (Xu Yanvei, Zhu Yingven, Tang Jingzhi, Yang Yu)	Moscow, Russia	April 3 2002
50-m butterfly	25.36	Anna-Karin Kammerling (Sweden)	Stockholm, Sweden	January 25 2001
100-m butterfly	0:56.34	Natalie Coughlin (USA)	New York, USA	November 22 2002
200-m butterfly	2:04.04	Yu Yang (China)	Berlin, Germany	January 18 2004
50-m backstroke	26.83	Hui Li (China)	Shanghai, China	December 2 2001
100-m backstroke	0:56.71	Natalie Coughlin (USA)	New York, USA	November 23 2002
200-m backstroke	2:03.62	Natalie Coughlin (USA)	New York, USA	November 27 2001
50-m breaststroke	29.96	Emma Igelström (Sweden)	Moscow, Russia	April 4 2002
100-m breaststroke	1:05.09	Leisel Jones (Australia)	Melbourne, Australia	November 28 2003
200-m breaststroke	2:17.75	Leisel Jones (Australia)	Melbourne, Australia	November 29 2003
100-m medley	58.80	Natalie Coughlin (USA)	New York, USA	November 23 2003
200-m medley	2:07.79	Allison Wagner (USA)	Palma de Mallorca, Spain	December 5 1993
400-m medley	4:27.83	Yana Klochkova (Ukraine)	Paris, France	January 19 2002
4 x 50-m medley	1:48.31	Sweden (Therese Alshammar, Emma Igelström, Anna-Karin Kammerling, Johanna Sjöberg)	Valencia, Spain	December 16 2000
4 x 100-m medley	3:55.78	Sweden (Therese Alshammar, Emma Igelström, Anna-Karin Kammerling, Johanna Sjöberg)	Moscow, Russia	April 5 2002

Men's 200-m ⬆ short course backstroke

Aaron Peirsol (USA, above) completed the men's 200-m short course backstroke in a record time of 1 min 51.17 sec in Moscow, Russia, on April 7 2002. He also holds the record for the long course race over the same distance, with a time of 1 min 55.15 sec, recorded in Minneapolis, USA, on March 20 2002.

★ **Most Olympic diving medals**
The most medals won by a diver is five. Klaus Dibiasi (Italy) won three gold and two silver (1964–76), and Greg Louganis (USA) won four golds and one silver (1976, 1984, and 1988). Dibiasi is the only diver to win the same event (high board) at three successive Games (1968–76). Two divers have won high board and springboard doubles at two Games: Patricia Joan McCormick (née Keller, USA) in 1952 and 1956, and Louganis in 1984 and 1988.

Men's swimming (short course)

Event	Time	Name & nationality	Venue	Date
50-m freestyle	21.13	Mark Foster (GB)	Paris, France	January 28 2001
100-m freestyle	46.74	Aleksandr Popov (Russia)	Gelsenkirchen, Germany	March 19 1994
200-m freestyle	1:41.10	Ian Thorpe (Australia)	Berlin, Germany	February 6 2000
400-m freestyle	3:34.58	Grant Hackett (Australia)	Sydney, Australia	July 18 2002
800-m freestyle	7:25.28	Grant Hackett (Australia)	Perth, Australia	August 3 2001
1,500-m freestyle	14:10.10	Grant Hackett (Australia)	Perth, Australia	August 7 2001
4 x 50-m freestyle	1:25.55	The Netherlands (Mark Veens, Johan Kenkhuis, Gijs Damen, Pieter van de Hoogenband)	Dublin, Ireland	December 14 2003
4 x 100-m freestyle	3:09.57	Sweden (Johan Nyström, Lars Frolander, Mattias Ohlin, Stefan Nystrand)	Athens, Greece	March 16 2000
4 x 200-m freestyle	6:56.41	Australia (William Kirby, Ian Thorpe, Michael Klim, Grant Hackett)	Perth, Australia	August 7 2001
50-m butterfly	22.74	Geoff Huegill (Australia)	Berlin, Germany	
100-m butterfly	50.02	Cavic Milorad (Serbia and Montenegro)	Dublin, Ireland	December 12 2003
200-m butterfly	1:50.73	Frank Esposito (France)	Antibes, France	December 8 2002
50-m backstroke	23.31	Matthew Welsh (Australia)	Melbourne, Australia	September 2 2002
100-m backstroke	50.58	Thomas Rupprath (Germany)	Melbourne, Australia	December 8 2002
200-m backstroke	1:51.17	Aaron Peirsol (USA)	Moscow, Russia	April 7 2002
50-m breaststroke	26.20	Oleg Lissogor (Ukraine)	Berlin, Germany	January 26 2002
100-m breaststroke	57.47	Ed Moses (USA)	Stockholm, Sweden	January 23 2002
200-m breaststroke	2:02.92	Ed Moses (USA)	Berlin, Germany	January 17 2004
100-m medley	52.63	Peter Mankoc (Slovenia)	Antwerp, Belgium	December 15 2001
200-m medley	1:54.65	Jani Sievinen (Finland)	Kuopio, Finland	April 21 1994
400-m medley	4:02.72	Brian Johns (Canada)	Victoria, Canada	February 21 2003
4 x 50-m medley	1:34.46	Germany (Thomas Rupprath, Mark Warnecke, Fabian Friedrich, Carstein Dehmlow)	Dublin, Ireland	December 11 2003
4 x 100-m medley	3:28.12	Australia (Matthew Welsh, Jim Pipes, Geoff Huegill, Ashley Callus)	Melbourne, Australia	September 4 2002

Women's swimming (long course)

Event	Time	Name & nationality	Venue	Date
50-m freestyle	24.13	Inge de Bruijn (Netherlands)	Sydney, Australia	September 22 2000
100-m freestyle	53.77	Inge de Bruijn (Netherlands)	Sydney, Australia	September 20 2000
200-m freestyle	1:56.64	Franziska van Almsick (Germany)	Berlin, Germany	August 3 2002
400-m freestyle	4:03.85	Janet Evans (USA)	Seoul, South Korea	September 22 1988
800-m freestyle	8:16.22	Janet Evans (USA)	Tokyo, Japan	August 20 1989
1,500-m freestyle	15:52.10	Janet Evans (USA)	Orlando, USA	March 26 1988
4 x 100-m freestyle relay	3:36.60	Germany (Franziska van Almsick, Petra Dallmann, Sandra Volker, Kathrin Meibner)	Berlin, Germany	July 29 2002
4 x 200-m freestyle relay	7:55.47	GDR (Manuela Stellmach, Astrid Strauss, Anke Möhring, Heike Friedrich)	Strasbourg, France	August 18 1987
50-m butterfly	25.57	Anna-Karin Kammerling (Sweden)	Berlin, Germany	July 31 2000
100-m butterfly	56.61	Inge de Bruijn (Netherlands)	Sydney, Australia	September 17 2000
200-m butterfly	2:05.78	Otylia Jedrejczak (Poland)	Berlin, Germany	August 2 2002
50-m backstroke	28.25	Sandra Voelker (Germany)	Berlin, Germany	June 17 2000
100-m backstroke	59.58	Natalie Coughlin (USA)	Fort Lauderdale, USA	August 13 2002
200-m backstroke	2:06.62	Krisztina Egerszegi (Hungary)	Athens, Greece	August 25 1991
50-m breaststroke	30.57	Zoe Baker (UK)	Manchester, UK	July 30 2002
100-m breaststroke	1:06.52	Penny Heyns (South Africa)	Sydney, Australia	August 23 1999
200-m breaststroke	2:22.99	Hui Qi (China)	Hangzhou, China	April 13 2001
200-m medley	2:09.72	Wu Yanyan (China)	Shanghai, China	October 17 1997
400-m medley	4:33.59	Yana Klochkova (Ukraine)	Sydney, Australia	September 16 2000
4 x 100-m medley relay	3:58.30	USA (Megan Quann, Jenny Thompson, B.J. Bedford, Dara Torres)	Sydney, Australia	September 23 2000

Men's swimming (long course)

Event	Time	Name & nationality	Venue	Date
50-m freestyle	21.64	Alexander Popov (Russia)	Moscow, Russia	June 16 2000
100-m freestyle	47.84	Pieter van den Hoogenband (Netherlands)	Sydney, Australia	September 19 2000
200-m freestyle	1:44.06	Ian Thorpe (Australia)	Fukuoka, Japan	July 25 2001
400-m freestyle	3:40.17	Ian Thorpe (Australia)	Fukuoka, Japan	July 22 2001
800-m freestyle	7:39.16	Ian Thorpe (Australia)	Fukuoka, Japan	July 24 2001
1,500-m freestyle	14:34.56	Grant Hackett (Australia)	Fukuoka, Japan	July 29 2001
4 x 100-m freestyle relay	3:13.67	Australia (Michael Klim, Chris Fydler, Ashley Callus, Ian Thorpe)	Sydney, Australia	September 16 2000
4 x 200-m freestyle relay	7:04.66	Australia (Grant Hackett, Michael Klim, William Kirby, Ian Thorpe)	Fukuoka, Japan	July 27 2001
50-m butterfly	23.44	Geoff Huegill (Australia)	Fukuoka, Japan	July 27 2001
100-m butterfly	51.81	Michael Klim (Australia)	Canberra, Australia	December 12 1999
200-m butterfly	1:54.58	Michael Phelps (USA)	Fukuoka, Japan	July 24 2001
50-m backstroke	24.99	Lenny Krayzelburg (USA)	Sydney, Australia	August 28 1999
100-m backstroke	53.60	Lenny Krayzelburg (USA)	Sydney, Australia	August 24 1999
200-m backstroke	1:55.15	Aaron Peirsol (USA)	Minneapolis, USA	March 20 2002
50-m breaststroke	27.18	Oleg Lisogor (Ukraine)	Berlin, Germany	August 2 2002
100-m breaststroke	59.94	Roman Sloudnov (Russia)	Fukuoka, Japan	July 23 2001
200-m breaststroke	2:10.16	Mike Barrowman (USA)	Barcelona, Spain	July 29 1992
200-m medley	1:55.94	Michael Phelps (USA)	Maryland, USA	August 9 2003
400-m medley	4:09.09	Michael Phelps (USA)	Barcelona, Spain	July 27 2003
4 x 100-m medley relay	3:33.48	USA (Aaron Peirsol, Brendon Hanson, Michael Phelps, Jason Lezak)	Yokohama, Japan	August 29 2002

Most women's Olympic medals ⌃

Three women have won eight medals. Dawn Fraser (Australia, above right) won four golds and four silvers (1956–64); Kornelia Ender (GDR) won four golds and four silvers (1972–76); and Shirley Babashoff (USA) won two golds and six silvers (1972–76).

★ **Most diving World Championships**

Greg Louganis (USA) won five world titles – high board in 1978, and high board and springboard in 1982 and 1986 – and four Olympic gold medals in 1984 and 1988. Philip George Boggs (USA) also won three golds in one event, for springboard in 1973, 1975, and 1978.

★ **Most men's Olympic swimming medals**

Mark Spitz (USA) won nine gold medals: the 100-m and 200-m freestyle (1972), the 100-m and 200-m butterfly (1972), 4 x 100-m freestyle (1968 and 1972), the 4 x 200-m freestyle (1968 and 1972), and the 4 x 100-m medley (1972). All but one of these (the 4 x 200-m freestyle of 1968) were also new world records. He also won a silver (100-m butterfly) and a bronze (100-m freestyle) in 1968, giving him a record 11 medals in all.

★ **Most individual Olympic swimming gold medals**

Krisztina Egerszegi (Hungary) won five gold medals: 100-m backstroke (1992), 200-m backstroke (1988, 1992, and 1996) and 400-m medley (1992).

Five men have four Olympic golds: Charles Meldrum Daniels (USA) for the 100-m freestyle (1906 and 1908), 220-yd freestyle (1904), and 440-yd freestyle (1904); Roland Matthes (GDR) for the 100-m and 200-m backstroke (1968 and 1972); Mark Spitz (USA) for the 100-m and 200-m freestyle, and the 100-m and 200-m butterfly (1972); Tamás Daryni (Hungary) for the 200-m and 400-m medley (1988 and 1992); and Aleksandr Popov (Russia) for the 50-m and 100-m freestyle (1992 and 1996).

★ **Farthest distance swum**

Martin Strel (Slovenia) swam the Mississippi River, USA, from its source in northern Minnesota to the Gulf of Mexico, from July 4 to September 9 2002. He swam a total of 2,360 miles (3,797 km) in 68 days.

Most show jumping World Cup wins »

The show jumping World Cup (instituted 1979) has been won three times by Hugo Simon (Austria) in 1979, 1996, and 1997; and Rodrigo Pessoa (Brazil, right) in 1998–2000. Pessoa's wins were all on the same horse, Gandini Baloubet du Rouet (right).

Most horse racing ⌃ career wins by a jockey

Laffit Pincay Jr. (USA, above far right) rode a total of 9,531 winners from May 16 1964 to March 1 2003.

Pincay announced his retirement aged 56 at the end of April 2003, nearly two months after breaking his neck in a fall at Santa Anita, California, USA.

★ **Most men's show jumping World Championships**
The most show jumping World Championships won by a man is two, by Hans Günter Winkler (Germany) in 1954 and 1955 and Raimondo d'Inzeo (Italy) in 1956 and 1960.

★ **Most women's show jumping World Championships**
Janou Tissot (France) won two World Championship titles on Rocket in 1970 and 1974.

★ **Most show jumping World Championship team titles**
The most show jumping team World Championship titles is two and the record is shared by France in 1982 and 1990, Germany in 1994 and 1998, and the USA in 1986 and 2002.

★ **Most Badminton wins**
The Badminton Three-Day Event (instituted 1949) has been won six times by Lucinda Green (UK) in 1973 (on Be Fair), 1976 (Wide Awake), 1977 (George), 1979 (Killaire), 1983 (Regal Realm), and 1984 (Beagle Bay).

★ **Jockey with most St. Leger wins**
From 1821 to 1846, jockey Bill Scott (UK) won the St. Leger (instituted 1776), the world's oldest classic race, nine times.

★ **Fastest time to run the St. Leger**
In 1926, Coronach ran the St. Leger in a time of 3 min 1.6 sec. This was equaled by Windsor Lad in 1934.

★ **Fastest time to run the Epsom Derby**
In 1995, Lammtarra ran the Epsom Derby in 2 min 32.3 sec.

★ **Fastest time to run the Kentucky Derby**
Secretariat, ridden by Ron Turcotte (Canada), ran a record time of 1 min 59.4 sec on May 5 1973 at Churchill Downs, Kentucky, USA.

★ **Greatest total prize money for a day's racing**
The Dubai World Cup race meeting at Nad Al Sheba, Dubai, United Arab Emirates, held annually in March, has total prize money of $15.25 million. Since 2002, the seven-race meeting has included the world's richest race, the Dubai World Cup.

★ **Highest amount won in a single race**
The highest amount won in one horse race is $3.6 million for the Dubai World Cup by: Dubai Millennium, 2000; Captain Steve, 2001; Street Cry, 2002; Moon Ballard, 2003; and Pleasantly Perfect, 2004.

★ **Oldest horse to win a race**
Al Jabal, a purebred Arabian horse, ridden by Brian Boulton and owned by Andrea Boulton (both UK), was aged 19 years when he won the Three Horseshoes Handicap Stakes on June 9 2002 at Barbury Castle, Wiltshire, UK.

★ **Most polo World Championships**
Argentina has won three polo World Championships: in 1987 in Argentina, 1992 in Chile, and 1998 in the USA.

★ **Most goals in polo World Championships**
Argentina has scored 35 goals during final matches of the polo World Championships.

★ **Highest rodeo earnings**
Ty Murray (USA) holds three records for rodeo earnings: he has record career earnings of $2,931,227 won from 1989 to 2002; he won the most prize money in a single season with $377,358 earned in 1998; and he won the most money at a single rodeo with a win of $124,821 at the National Finals Rodeo in Las Vegas, Nevada, USA, in 1993.

★ **Highest bull riding score**
Wade Leslie (USA) scored 100 points out of a possible 100 on Wolfman Skoal at Central Point, Oregon, USA, in 1991.

★ **Highest bareback riding score**
Wes Stevenson (USA) scored 94 out of a possible 100 on Kesler Rodeo's Cover Girl in Dallas, Texas, USA, in 2002.

Highest saddle bronc score ⌃

The highest scored saddle bronc ride is 95 out of a possible 100 by Glen O'Neill (Australia, above) on Franklin's Airwolf at Innisfail, Alberta, Canada, in 1996; and also by Doug Vold (USA) on Transport at Meadow Lake, Saskatchewan, Canada, in 1979.

★ GWR TALKS TO
Tony McCoy

Jockey Tony McCoy (UK, above) holds the record for the most steeplechase wins in a career, with 2,078 winners ridden from 1992 to May 2004. He has also won more steeplechase races in a season than any other jockey, with 289 in 2001/2002.

What first got you interested in horses and how old were you when you started riding?
My dad had horses and I thought that I'd like to ride them – I was fortunate enough to have my own ponies. I also liked watching it on TV. I first sat on a horse when I was about seven or eight but I started racing at the age of 16 – the age you have to be to compete legally.

What do you do to keep fit for your sport?
With riding every day I don't really have to do anything to keep fit. If you do a certain activity a lot, that keeps you fit for that activity. If I was having time off I'd use my gym.

What's your favorite memory from your career so far?
That would be a few years ago when I broke Sir Gordon Richards' 55-year record for the most wins in a season – he was champion flat jockey 26 times.

Is your record for steeplechase wins in a career as special?
Yes, it's a different type of record. Every record you hold is special, but with this one, so many great jockeys before me set it, like John Francome, Peter Scudamore, Richard Dunwoody; and being able to say that I've brought home more winners than them means a lot as they were the people I looked up to when I was younger.

So are they also your idols?
They are definitely, very much so, and I'm very lucky now as they're my friends as well, even though when I was young and growing up I looked up to them a lot.

What's your favorite racecourse?
For me personally, Cheltenham because it's just got a brilliant atmosphere. Liverpool's not too bad either.

What's the most races you've ridden in one day?
The most in one day is 11. The most wins in one day is five.

What keeps you going? What's your motivation?
I love doing it and the day I don't enjoy doing it I won't do it. Anyone that's lucky enough to earn their living from their sport would tell you how lucky they are.

If you had to name one major goal that you haven't achieved so far, what would it be?
I have to win the Grand National. It's not really happening at the moment. It's one of the biggest courses and one of the biggest sporting events in the world.

You're an inspiration to those wishing to get involved in the sport. Is that important to you?
If you can help young children or get them involved in any sport it's great, and if they have as much luck as I have had, then they're going to be very lucky people.

Greatest « paragliding altitude gain

Robbie Whittal (UK, left) achieved a record height gain of 14,849 ft (4,526 m) at Brandvlei, South Africa, on January 6 1993. As a comparison, Boeing 747s normally cruise at 32,808 ft (10,000 m).

The greatest height gained with a paraglider by a female is 14,189 ft (4,325 m) by Kat Thurston (UK) over Kuruman, South Africa, on January 1 1996.

Most parachutists to ⌃ jump from a balloon

Thirty members of Paraclub Flevo (above), Lelystad, The Netherlands, jumped from a balloon over Markelo, The Netherlands, on May 10 2003.

★ **Longest free-fall parachute jump**
Eugene Andreev (USSR) holds the official Fédération Aéronautique Internationale (FAI) record for the longest free-fall parachute jump after falling for 80,380 ft (24,500 m) from an altitude of 83,523 ft (25,458 m) near the city of Saratov, Russia, on November 1 1962.

★ **Largest FAI-approved free-fall parachute formation**
A free-fall formation consisting of 357 sky divers from more than 40 countries was formed over Takhli, Thailand, on February 6 2004. The event was organized by World Team '04 and formed part of the Thailand Royal Sky Celebration, which was supported by the Royal Thai Air Force and took place in honor of the Thai royal family.

★ **Most parachute descents**
On July 13 2003, Don Kellner (USA) made his 34,000th free-fall sky dive in accordance with the US Parachute Association basic safety requirements. He made his first jump on June 14 1961.

Cheryl Stearns (USA) holds the corresponding women's record, with a total of 15,560 descents as of August 2003.

★ **Most people to tandem parachute in 24 hours**
The greatest number of tandem parachute jumps performed from the same airfield in a 24-hour period is 41, achieved at The Big Jump 2001 event at Hinton Airfield, Banbury, Oxfordshire, UK, on September 16 2001.

★ **Largest canopy formation**
The largest canopy formation consisted of 70 parachutes and was formed by an American-led international team over Lake Wales, Florida, USA, on November 29 2003. The formation involved 15 'layers' of parachutes stacked on top of one another, with each parachutist in contact with the canopy of the person below them.

★ **Highest static-line parachute jump with a round canopy**
Graham Spicer and Martin Cruickshank (both UK) completed a static-line parachute jump using round canopies from an altitude of 30,300 ft (9,235 m) over Yolo County, California, USA, on September 19 2002. Both men are members of the Association of British Military Parachutists.

★ **Longest flight by powered parachute (absolute)**
The official FAI record for the longest distance flown in a single hop by powered parachute is 400 miles (644 km), by Juan Ramon Morillas Salmeron (Spain), from Almonte, Huelva, Spain, to Minuesa, Teruel, Spain, on June 21 1998.

★ **Fastest speed in a paraglider over a 25-km triangular course**
The fastest speed achieved over a 15.53-mile (25-km) triangular course for an official FAI world record is 17.55 mph (28.26 km/h) by Patrick Berod (France) at Albertville, France, on June 27 1995.

The fastest speed achieved by a woman is 14.13 mph (22.75 km/h) by Fiona Macaskill (UK) at Plaine Joux, France, on April 24 2003.

★ **Greatest distance in a paraglider**
On June 21 2002, William Gadd (Canada) traveled a distance of 423.4 km (263.08 miles) by paraglider, from Zapata, Texas, to south of Ozona, Texas, USA.

The greatest distance flown by a woman in a paraglider is 177.1 miles (285 km) by Kat Thurston (UK) from Kuruman, South Africa, on December 25 1995.

★ **Greatest distance in a tandem paraglider**
Richard Westgate and Jim Coutts (both UK) flew a tandem paraglider for a total distance of 136.95 miles (220.4 km) without landing from Quixada, Brazil, to Bom Principio, Brazil, on November 30 2000.

Greatest absolute altitude ⌃ in a glider

Robert Harris (USA) achieved a height of 49,009 ft (14,938 m) in a glider over California City, USA, on February 17 1986.

The women's single-seater glider world record for absolute altitude was set by Sabrina Jackintell (USA), who achieved a height of 41,460 ft (12,637 m) over Black Forest Gliderport, Colorado Springs, USA, on February 14 1979.

★ Greatest height gain in a tandem paraglider

The height gain record for a tandem paraglider is 14,370 ft (4,380 m), achieved by Richard and Guy Westgate (both UK) at Kuruman, South Africa, on January 1 1996.

★ Most men's hang gliding World Championships

World championships for hang gliding were first held in 1976. The most individual wins is three by Tomas Suchanek (Czech Republic) in 1991, 1993, and 1995, and Manfred Ruhmer (Austria) in 1999, 2001, and 2003.

The women's hang gliding World Championships were first held in 1987. The most individual wins is three by Kari Castle (USA) in 1996, 2000, and 2002.

★ Greatest distance flown in a hang glider

The greatest distance flown when setting an official FAI hang gliding record is 435.33 miles (700.6 km) by Manfred Ruhmer (Austria) from Zapata, Texas, to Lamesa, Texas, USA, on July 17 2001.

★ Greatest straight distance in a hang glider by a woman

The FAI straight-line distance record by a woman in a hang glider is 250.7 miles (403.5 km), achieved by Kari Castle (USA) at Zapata, Texas, USA, on July 28 2001.

★ Greatest return distance in a hang glider

Rohan Holtkamp (Australia) achieved a record out-and-return distance of 205.4 miles (330.6 km) at Eucla, Australia, on February 12 1998.

The farthest out-and-return distance traveled by a woman with a hang glider is 89.38 miles (143.85 km), achieved by Tascha McLellan (New Zealand) at Forbes, Australia, on January 3 1999.

★ Greatest distance in triangular hang gliding

Tomas Suchanek (Czech Republic) achieved a record triangular-course distance of 221.9 miles (357.12 km) at Riverside, New South Wales, Australia, on December 16 2000.

The equivalent women's record is 103.9 miles (167.2 km), achieved by Nichola Hamilton (UK) on January 2 1997 at Croydon Hay, New South Wales, Australia.

★ Greatest height gain in a hang glider

Larry Tudor (USA) achieved a height of 14,250 ft (4,343 m) over Owens Valley, California, USA, on August 4 1985.

Judy Leden (UK) achieved the equivalent women's record with a height of 13,025 ft (3,970 m) on December 1 1992 at Kuruman, South Africa.

★ Most consecutive loops in a hang glider

Chad Elchin performed 95 consecutive loops at the Highland Aerosports flight park at Ridgely, Maryland, USA, on July 16 2001. Elchin was towed to 15,900 ft (4,846 m) and looped his Aeros Stealth Combat nonstop down to 700 ft (213 m), at speeds ranging from 17 to 80 mph (28–128 km/h).

★ Fastest speed in a glider

The highest average speed reached in a glider when setting an official FAI world record is 153.78 mph (247.49 km/h) by James and Thomas Payne (both USA) when setting the out-and-return course of 500 km (310 miles) speed record at California City, USA, on March 3 1999.

★ Greatest altitude gain in a glider

The greatest height gain in a glider is 42,303 ft (12,894 m) by Paul F. Bikle (USA) over Lancaster, California, USA, on February 25 1961.

The equivalent record for women is a height of 33,504 ft (10,212 m), achieved by Yvonne Loader (New Zealand) at Omarama, New Zealand, on January 12 1988.

Target sports
Sport

Highest women's team FITA outdoor recurve score ⌄

In 1992, the South Korea women's team (Kim Soo-nyung [below], Cho Youn-jeong, and Lee Eun-kyung) scored 4,094 points out of a possible 4,320 in the single FITA round, women's team category in Barcelona, Spain. The international governing body of archery, the Fédération Internationale de Tir à l'Arc (FITA), was founded in 1931. FITA regulates archery around the world through more than 125 member associations.

Most MacRobertson ⌃ Shield wins

The MacRobertson Shield (instituted 1925) has been won a record 12 times

by the Great Britain croquet team (GB team member David Foulser, above): 1925, 1937, 1956, 1963, 1969, 1974, 1982, 1990, 1993, 1996, 2000, and 2003.

Archery indoor records

Event	Pts	Name & nationality	Venue	Date
18 m				
Men	597	Michele Frangilli (Italy)	Nîmes, France	January 2001
Women	591	Lina Herasymenko (Ukraine)	Istanbul, Turkey	March 1997
25 m				
Men	598	Michele Frangilli (Italy)	Gallarate, Italy	November 2001
Women	592	Petra Ericsson (Sweden)	Oulu, Finland	March 1991

Archery men (single FITA rounds)

Event	Pts	Name & nationality	Venue	Date
FITA	1,379	Oh Kyo-moon (South Korea)	Wonju, South Korea	Nov 2000
90 m	337	Jang Yong-ho (South Korea)	New York, USA	July 2003
70 m	347	Choi Young-kwang (South Korea)	Hongseong, South Korea	Aug 2002
50 m	351	Kim Kyung-ho (South Korea)	Wonju, South Korea	Sept 1997
30 m	360/17	Kye Dong-hyun (South Korea)	Cheongju, South Korea	Sept 2002
Team	4,074	South Korea (Jang Yong-ho, Choi Young-kwang, Im Bong-hyun)	New York, USA	July 2003

Archery women (single FITA rounds)

Event	Pts	Name & nationality	Venue	Date
FITA	1,388	Park Seong-hyun (South Korea)	Yechoen, South Korea	March 2003
70 m	348	Lee Hee-jeong (South Korea)	Cheongju, South Korea	Oct 2001
60 m	350	Kim Jo-soon (South Korea)	Wonju, South Korea	Sept 1998
50 m	350	Park Seong-hyun (South Korea)	Yechoen, South Korea	March 2003
30 m	360/14	Lee Hyun-jeong (South Korea)	Cheongju, South Korea	Oct 2001
Team	4,094	South Korea (Kim Soo-nyung, Lee Eun-kyung, Cho Yuon-jeong)	Barcelona, Spain	Aug 1992

★ Highest archery score in 24 hours

The highest point score in 24 hours shooting FITA 18 rounds is 26,064 by Michael Howson and Stephen Howard (both UK) at Oakbank Sports College, Keighley, West Yorkshire, UK, on November 11–12 2000.

★ Longest rifle shooting marathon

Five members of the St. Sebastianus Schützenbruderchaft Ettringen 1901 eV shooting club shot for 26 hours at Ettringen, Germany, on September 20–21 2003. The five members were: Karl Westhoften, Rainer Lanz, Dieter Franken, Christian Lanz, and Manfred Savelsberg (all Germany), who shot from three positions – prone, standing, and kneeling – and followed all International Shooting Sport Federation (ISSF) regulations.

★ Highest skeet shooting score by a woman

Svetlana Demina (Russia) set a world record on June 1 1999 with her score of 99 (75 + 24) in the women's skeet-shooting event held in Kumamoto City, Japan.

★ Highest men's trapshooting score

Marcello Tittarelli (Italy) shot an incredible 150 out of 150 (125 + 25) in the men's trapshooting 125 targets on June 11 1996 at the World Cup in Suhl, Germany. In the trap events, named after the device that launches clay targets into the air, a bank of three traps is set at varying heights and angles within a trench in front of each shooter. The shooter does not know which of the three traps will release next. As each target is released, the shooter is allowed two shots.

★ Highest men's rifle shooting score (50 m, three positions)

With an overall score of 1,287.9, Rajmond Debevec (Slovenia) set a world record for the men's rifle 50 m (3 x 40 shots) in Munich, Germany, on August 29 1992.

Youngest professional ⌃ snooker World Champion

Stephen Hendry (above, UK, b. January 13 1969) became the youngest professional snooker World Champion at 21 years 106 days on April 29 1990.

★ **Most croquet World Championship wins by an individual**

The first croquet World Championships were held at the Hurlingham Club, London, UK, in 1989 and have been held annually since. The most wins is four by Robert Fulford (UK) in 1990, 1992, 1994, and 1997.

★ **Most national croquet titles won by an individual**

Bob Jackson (New Zealand) won the New Zealand croquet Open Championship Singles title 14 times – 1975, 1978, 1982–84, 1989, 1991–92, 1995, 1997–99, and 2002–03.

★ **Longest indoor 'bowls' marathon**

Six members of Arnos Bowling Club, Southgate, UK, played indoor bowls for a record 36 hours on April 20–21 2002.

★ **Highest bowling pin-fall in one lane over 24 hours**

The highest pin-fall achieved bowling on one lane in 24 hours is 36,781 by

12 bowlers at Go Bowling, Dunstable, Bedfordshire, UK, from August 21 to 22 2003.

★ **Longest bowling marathon**

The longest bowling marathon is 52 hr 15 min by Fred Miller (UK) at the AMF Bowling Centre in Wigan, Lancashire, UK, from February 28 to March 2 2003.

★ **Most darts World Championship titles**

The most darts World Championship titles won is 11 by Phil Taylor (GB). He won the World Darts Organization (WDO) championship in 1990 and 1992, and the Professional Darts Corporation (PDC) championship in 1995–2002 and 2004.

★ **Fastest snooker 147 break**

The fastest snooker 147 break in a professional tournament is 5 min 20 sec by Ronnie O'Sullivan (UK) during the 1997 World Championships held at Sheffield, South Yorkshire, UK, on April 21 1997. The only way to get a 147 clearance is to

'pot' the black ball after every red, then clear the colored balls in order: yellow, green, brown, blue, pink, and black.

★ **Highest break in snooker**

Wally West (UK) recorded a break of 151 in a snooker match at the Hounslow Lucania, London, UK, in October 1976. The break involved a free ball, which created an 'extra' red, when all 15 reds were still on the table. In these very exceptional circumstances, the maximum break is 155.

★ **Longest billiards marathon**

Pierre De Coster (Belgium) played billiards against all comers for 181 hr 8 min at SK Kampenhout clubhouse, Kampenhout, Belgium, from

June 3 to 10 2003. De Coster played a total of 820 games, winning 518.

★ **Longest pool marathon by a team**

A four-man team played pool for 120 hours at the Heritage Inn, Brooks, Alberta, Canada, from January 15 to 20 2003. The team members were Jack Nemeth, Doug Webster, Harlan Ivarson, and Doug Prenevost (all Canada).

★ **Longest pool marathon by an individual**

Raf Goossens (Belgium) played pool against all comers for 75 hr 19 min 17 sec at Café St.-Jozef, Kampenhout, Belgium, from February 19 to 22 2003.

Motor sports 1
Sport

Largest NASCAR ⩓ Speedway

Talladega Superspeedway (above) in Alabama, USA, is the largest National Association for Stock Car Auto Racing (NASCAR) Speedway. The tri-oval-shaped track is 2.66 miles (4.28 km) long, has a banking angle of 33°, and can accommodate more than 143,000 seated guests and thousands more in the 215-acre (87-hectare) infield.

The track was known as Alabama International Motor Speedway when it opened in 1969 and was built at a cost of more than $4 million.

★ **Most wins in a NASCAR season**
Richard Petty (USA) won 27 races in 1967. During the same season, Petty also set the mark for the most consecutive wins, with 10.

Petty holds a number of other NASCAR records. He won a record 200 races during his NASCAR career, which lasted from 1958 to 1992, and achieved an unrivaled 126 pole positions during this time, winning 61 races from the front of the grid.

Petty also started 1,184 races during his career, more than any other NASCAR driver.

★ **Most NASCAR titles**
Since the NASCAR Championship was first held in 1949, two drivers have won it a total of seven times: Richard Petty (USA) in 1964, 1967, 1971–72, 1974–75, and 1979; and Dale Earnhardt (USA) in 1980, 1986–87, 1990–91, and 1993–94.

★ **Most consecutive NASCAR Championships**
Eight drivers have won back-to-back NASCAR Championships, but only one, Cale Yarborough (USA), has won three Championships consecutively, from 1976 to 1978.

★ **Most Formula One Grand Prix wins by a driver**
Michael Schumacher (Germany) won a total of 70 Formula One Grand Prix races from 1991 to 2003.

Schumacher holds the record for the most points scored in a Formula One career, with 1,038 points from 1991 to 2003.

He also holds the record for the greatest number of points scored by a driver in a Formula One season, after scoring 144 points in 2002.

During the same season, Schumacher also won an unrivaled 11 Formula One Grand Prix.

★ **Most consecutive wins of the same Grand Prix**
Ayrton Senna (Brazil) took first place in the Monaco Grand Prix a total of five times in a row from 1989 to 1993.

Senna's exceptional career was tragically cut short when he was killed on May 1 1994 while competing in the San Marino Grand Prix.

★ **Most consecutive Formula One pole positions**
Alain Prost (France) had seven consecutive Formula One pole positions in the 1993 season driving for the Williams-Renault team. Prost was also world champion that year.

★ **Most Formula One pole positions in season**
The greatest number of Formula One pole positions in a season by one driver is 14 by Nigel Mansell (UK). Driving for the Williams-Renault team in 1992, Mansell won the World Championship before switching over to Indy cars the following year, winning the 1993 Indy car series at his first attempt.

★ **Most Formula One pole positions in a career**
The greatest number of Formula One pole positions is 65 by Ayrton Senna (Brazil) from 161 races (including 41 wins), from 1985 to 1994, for the Toleman, Lotus, McLaren, and Williams teams.

Most World Drivers' Championship wins ⌄

Inaugurated in 1950, the World Drivers' Championship has been won a record six times by Michael Schumacher (Germany, below) in 1994–95 and 2000–03.

Most wins by an ⌃ individual at the Le Mans 24-hour race

Jacky Ickx (Belgium, above left) won the Le Mans 24-hour race six times, in 1969, 1975–77, and 1981–82.

★ Most Formula One fastest laps in a season
The greatest number of fastest laps recorded by one driver in a Formula One season is nine by Mika Hakkinen (Finland) in 2000 while driving for the McLaren-Mercedes team.

Hakkinen finished the World Drivers' Championship second that year with 89 points. Michael Schumacher (Germany) won the Championship with a total of 108 points.

★ Oldest Grand Prix driver
The oldest ever Grand Prix driver was Louis Alexandre Chiron (Monaco, 1899–1979), who finished sixth in the Monaco Grand Prix on May 22 1955 at the age of 55 years 292 days.

★ Youngest Grand Prix driver
The youngest driver ever to qualify for a Grand Prix was Michael Christopher Thackwell (New Zealand, b. March 30 1961). He took part in the Canadian Grand Prix on September 28 1980 at the age of 19 years 182 days.

★ Oldest Formula One world champion
Juan Manuel Fangio (Argentina, b. June 24 1911) won his last World Championship on August 4 1957 at the age of 46 years 41 days.

★ Youngest Formula One world champion
The youngest ever Formula One world champion was Emerson Fittipaldi (Brazil, b. December 12 1946), who won his first World Championship on September 10 1972 aged 25 years 273 days.

★ Youngest driver to claim a Formula One World Championship point
When he finished in sixth place in the Brazilian Grand Prix on March 26 2000, Jenson Button (UK, b. January 19 1980) was only 20 years 67 days old.

Button originally finished in seventh position, out of the points, but after McLaren driver David Coulthard (UK) was disqualified from his second-place finish, Button was promoted to a points-scoring position.

★ Most Formula One Grand Prix retirements
The greatest number of race retirements in Formula One is 135 by Andrea de Cesaris (Italy), during a career that spanned 14 years from 1980 to 1994.

De Cesaris also has the dubious honor of holding the record for most Grand Prix races (208) without a victory.

★ Most Grand Prix wins by a constructor
As of the end of the 2003 season, Ferrari (Italy) had won 166 Formula One Grand Prix races.

★ Most Formula One Constructors' World Championship titles
Ferrari has won 13 Formula One Constructors' World Championship titles, in 1961, 1964, 1975–77, 1979, 1982–83, and 1999–2003.

★ Most points by a constructor in a Formula One season
In the 2002 Formula One season, the Ferrari team amassed 221 World Championship points. The team's drivers that year were Michael Schumacher (Germany) and Reubens Barichello (Brazil).

The Ferrari team won 15 races out of 17 and wrapped up both the drivers' and the constructors' titles in record time.

★ Most wins by a constructor in a Formula One season
The greatest number of wins by a constructor in a Formula One season is 15. This feat has been achieved by two teams: McLaren in 1988 and Ferrari in 2002.

★ Most team wins at the Le Mans 24-hour race
Porsche has won the Le Mans 24-hour race on 16 occasions, in 1970–71, 1976–77, 1979, 1981–87, 1993, and 1996–98.

Most superbike World Championship ⟪ pole positions

Troy Corser (Australia, left) achieved 28 pole positions in the superbike World Championships from 1995 to 2001.

Most motorcycle World Championship 250-cc titles ⌃⌃

Two riders have won the 250-cc World Championship four times: Max Biaggi (Italy, leading above) from 1994 to 1997 and Phil Read (UK) in 1964, 1965, 1968, and 1971.

★ **Longest motorcycle race circuit**
The 'Mountain' circuit on the Isle of Man, over which the principal TT (Tourist Trophy) races have been run since 1911 (with minor amendments in 1920), has 264 curves and corners and measures 37.73 miles (60.72 km).

★ **Most superbikes World Championship race wins by a manufacturer**
Ducati (Italy) won 219 superbikes World Championship races from 1988 to 2004.

★ **Most superbikes World Championship titles won by a manufacturer**
Ducati (Italy) has won 12 superbikes World Championships manufacturers' titles, in 1991–96 and 1998–2003.

★ **Most superbikes World Championship pole positions by a manufacturer**
In the superbikes World Championships from 1988 to 2004, Ducati (Italy) achieved a record 118 pole positions.

★ **Most superbikes World Championship titles**
Carl Fogarty (UK) won four superbikes World Championship titles, in 1994, 1995, 1998, and 1999.

★ **Most superbikes World Championship race wins**
Carl Fogarty (UK) won a record 59 races in superbikes World Championships from 1992 to 1999.

★ **Most sidecar World Championship titles**
The most sidecar World Championship titles won by the same pair is five, by Klaus Enders and Ralph Engelhardt (both Germany) riding a BMW machine in 1967, 1969, and 1972–74.

★ **Most 500-cc motocross World Championship titles**
Two riders have both won five 500-cc motocross World Championships: Roger de Coster (Belgium) in 1971–73 and 1975–76, and Joel Smets (Belgium) in 1995, 1997–98, 2000, and 2003.

★ **Most 250-cc motocross World Championship titles**
Joël Robert (Belgium) won six 250-cc motocross World Championships, in 1964 and 1968–72. From April 25 1964 to June 18 1972, he won a record 50 250-cc Grand Prix.

★ **Most 125-cc motocross World Championship titles**
The 125-cc class of the motocross World Championship has been won three times by three riders: Gaston Rahier (Belgium) in 1975–77, Harry Everts (Belgium) in 1979–81, and Alessio Chiodi (Italy) in 1997–99.

★ **Most motorcycle World Championship 500-cc titles**
The most motorcycling World Championship 500-cc titles won is eight by Giacomo Agostini (Italy) from 1966 to 1972 and in 1975.

★ **Most motorcycle World Championship 350-cc titles**
Giacomo Agostini (Italy) won seven motorcycling World Championship 350-cc titles from 1968 to 1974.

★ **Most motorcycle World Championship 125-cc titles**
Angel Roldán Nieto (Spain) won seven motorcycling World Championship 125-cc titles, in 1971, 1972, 1979, and 1981–84.

★ **Most motorcycle World Championship 80-cc titles**
Jorge Martinez (Spain) won three motorcycling World Championship 80-cc titles from 1986 to 1988. This class ran for only six years from 1984 to 1989.

★ **Most motorcycle World Championship 50-cc titles**
Angel Roldán Nieto (Spain) won six motorcycling World Championship 50-cc titles in 1969, 1970, 1972, and 1975–77.

★ **Lowest elapsed time for a National Hot Rod Association (NHRA) drag racing Pro Stock motorbike**
Angelle Savoie (USA) covered 440 yd in 7.049 seconds on her Suzuki Pro Stock motorbike in Matthews, Louisiana, USA, in May 2002.

Most rally World Championship race wins ⌃⌃

Two drivers have each won 25 World Championship races: Colin McRae (UK) in 1993–2002 and Carlos Sainz (Spain, driving above) in 1990–2003.

★ **Fastest speed for an NHRA Pro Stock motorbike**
Matt Hines (USA) achieved 194.10 mph (312.37 km/h) on a Suzuki in Englishtown, New Jersey, USA, in May 2001 – the highest terminal velocity for a gasoline-driven piston-engined motorcycle (Pro Stock) .

★ **Lowest elapsed time for an NHRA Pro Stock car**
Greg Anderson (USA) covered 440 yd in 6.670 seconds driving a Pontiac Grand Am in Concord, North Carolina, USA, on May 18 2003.

★ **Fastest speed in an NHRA Pro Stock car**
Set by Greg Anderson (USA) in Concord, North Carolina, USA, on May 18 2003, the highest terminal velocity for a Pro Stock car is 207.18 mph (333.42 km/h).

★ **Lowest elapsed time for an NHRA Top Fuel drag racer**
Anthony Schumacher (USA) covered 440 yd in 4.441 seconds in a McKinney dragster at Long Grove, Illinois, USA, on October 4 2003. Top Fuel cars run on 90% nitromethane and 10% methanol, also known as racing alcohol. As a result, the engine is about 2.4 times as powerful as a similar displacement engine running gasoline and produces at least 8,000 horsepower.

★ **Fastest speed for an NHRA Top Fuel drag racer**
The highest terminal velocity at the end of a 440-yd run is 333.25 mph (536.31 km/h) by Douglas Kalitta (USA) at Ypsilanti, Michigan, USA, on November 9 2003 in a McKinney dragster.

★ **Lowest elapsed time in an NHRA funny car**
John Force (USA) covered 440 yd in 4.721 seconds in a Ford Mustang in Yorba Linda, California, USA, on June 1 2003. Funny cars are rear-wheel-driven dragsters with a massive front-mounted engine and huge, distinctive rear wheels.

★ **Fastest speed in an NHRA funny car**
Gary Scelzi (USA) reached 329.18 mph (529.76 km/h) from a standing start over 440 yd in a Dodge Stratus in Fresno, California, USA, on September 28 2003.

★ **Most rally World Championship race wins in a season**
Didier Auriol (France) won a record six rally World Championship races in 1992.

★ **Youngest rally World Championship driver**
The youngest driver to compete in a Fédération Internationale de l'Automobile (FIA) World Championship rally is Jari-Matti Latvala (Finland), who was 18 years 61 days when he drove in the 50th Acropolis Rally, Athens, Greece, on June 6–8 2003.

★ **Most rally World Championship race wins by a manufacturer**
Lancia (Italy) won 73 rally World Championship races from 1972 to 2004.

★ **Most rally World Championship wins by a manufacturer**
Lancia (Italy) won 11 rally World Championship titles from 1972 to 1992.

★ **Most Dakar Rally wins**
Ari Vatanen (Finland) has won the Dakar Rally a record four times, first in 1987 and then on three more occasions from 1989 to 1991.

★ **Most Dakar Rally bike category wins**
Stéphane Peterhansel (France) had a record six wins in the bike category of the Dakar Rally in 1991–93, 1995, and 1997–98.

Bicycling
Sport

Most Tour de France wins

Lance Armstrong (USA, right) **»** has won the Tour de France a record five times from 1999 to 2003. He

shares this record with Jacques Anquetil (France) in 1957, 1961–64; Eddy Merckx (Belgium) in 1969–72 and 1974; Bernard Hinault (France) in 1978–79, 1981–82, and 1985; and Miguel Indurain (Spain) in 1991–95.

★ Fastest women's 200 m, unpaced, flying start
The fastest unpaced 200 m bicycled from a flying start is 10.831 seconds by Olga Slyusareva (Russia) in Moscow, Russia, on April 25 1993.

★ Fastest men's 200 m, unpaced, flying start
Curtis Harnett (Canada) bicycled a distance of 200 m in 9.865 seconds from an unpaced flying start in Bogota, Colombia, on September 28 1995.

★ Fastest women's 500 m, unpaced, flying start
The fastest unpaced 500 m bicycled from a flying start is 29.655 seconds, by Erika Salumäe (USSR, now Estonia), in Moscow, USSR, on August 6 1987.

★ Fastest men's 500 m, unpaced, flying start
Arnaud Duble (France) finished the men's 500 m unpaced in 25.850 seconds from a flying start in La Paz, Bolivia, on October 10 2001.

★ Fastest women's 500 m, unpaced, standing start
The fastest unpaced 500 m bicycled from a standing start is 34.000 seconds, by Yong Hua Jiang (China), in Kunming, China, on August 10 2002.

★ Fastest men's 1 km, unpaced, standing start
The world record time for the 1-km bike race is 58.875 seconds by Arnaud Tournant (France) in La Paz, Bolivia, on October 10 2001.

★ Fastest women's 3 km, unpaced, standing start
The world record for the 3-km Women's Individual Cycling Pursuit race is 3 min 30.816 sec, set by Leontien Zijlaard-van Moorsel (Netherlands) at the 2000 Olympic Games held in Sydney, Australia, on September 17 2000.

★ Fastest men's team 4 km, unpaced, standing start
The Australian team consisting of Peter Dawson, Graham Brown, Mark Renshaw, and Luke Roberts bicycled 4 km in 3 min 59.583 sec. The time was set at the Commonwealth Games in Manchester, UK, on August 1 2002.

★ Fastest men's 4 km, unpaced, standing start
Chris Boardman (UK) bicycled a distance of 4 km in 4 min 11.114 sec in Manchester, UK, on August 29 1996.

★ Greatest distance bicycled in 24 hours
The 24-hour record behind pace is 1,216.8 miles (1,958.196 km) by Michael Secrest (USA) at Phoenix International Raceway, Arizona, USA, on April 26–27 1990. Solo and unpaced, Secrest achieved a distance of 532.74 miles (857.36 km) over the same time at the Olympic Velodrome, California State University, Carson, USA, on October 23–24 1997.

★ Farthest bicycling in an hour, unpaced, standing start
The official Union Cycliste Internationale (UCI) one-hour record of 30.72 miles (49.441 km) was set in Manchester, UK, on October 27 2000 by Chris Boardman (UK).

★ Greatest distance bicycled in one hour by a woman, unpaced, standing start
The official UCI one-hour record by a woman is 28.02 miles (45.094 km) by Jeanie Longo (France) in Mexico City, Mexico, on December 7 2000.

★ Longest one-day bicycle race
The longest one-day 'massed start' road race is the Bordeaux–Paris event in France, which is 342–385 miles (551–620 km) long, depending on the route.

★ Fastest bicycling end-to-end
Andy Wilkinson (UK) bicycled from Land's End, Cornwall, to John O'Groats, Highland, UK, in 1 day 21 hr 2 min 18 sec from September 29 to October 1 1990.
   The holder of the women's record is Pauline Strong (UK). She finished the distance in 2 days 6 hr 49 min 45 sec from July 28 to 30 1990.

Biggest winning ⌃ margin in a Tour de France

The greatest time gap between the winner and the runner-up

at the finish of a Tour de France is 28 min 27 sec, between Fausto Coppi (Italy, above left) and Stan Ockers (Belgium) in 1952.

Most downhill ⌃ mountain-biking World Championships won by a woman

Anne-Caroline Chausson (France, above) has won 10

downhill World Championships – three in the junior championship from 1993 to 1995 and seven in the senior class from 1996 to 2002.

★ **Fastest trans-Europe two-person relay cycle**
Kevin Moreland and Guy Lawton (both UK), supported by the Twisting Compass Team, bicycled in relay from Tarifa, Spain, to North Cape, Norway, in a time of 9 days 20 hr 43 min from July 6 to 16 2002.

★ **Youngest Tour de France winner**
Henri Cornet (France) was aged 19 years 350 days when he won the Tour de France in 1904. Cornet actually finished the race in fifth position, but was awarded the victory after the first four riders were all disqualified.

★ **Oldest Tour de France winner**
Firmin Lambot (Belgium) was 36 years 4 months when he won the Tour de France in 1922.

★ **Closest Tour de France race**
The closest Tour de France race ever was in 1989 when, after 2,030 miles (3,267 km) over 23 days (July 1–23), Greg LeMond (USA) completed

the Tour in 87 hr 38 min 35 sec, beating Laurent Fignon (France) to the finish in Paris by 8 seconds.

★ **Most Tour de France stage wins**
Eddie Merckx (Belgium) has 34 Tour de France stage wins. Merckx also shares the record for the most overall Tour victories with five won in 1969–72 and in 1974.

★ **Fastest average speed in the Tour de France**
During the 1999 Tour, Lance Armstrong (USA) cycled at an average speed of 25.026 mph (40.276 km/h).

★ **Most Tour of Spain wins**
The most wins in the Tour of Spain bicycling race is three by Tony Rominger (Switzerland) from 1992 to 1994.

★ **Most Tour of Italy wins**
The most Tour of Italy wins is five and is shared by Alfredo Binda (Italy) in 1925, 1927–29, and 1933; Fausto Coppi (Italy) in 1940, 1947, 1949, and

1952–53; and Eddy Merckx (Belgium) in 1968, 1970, and 1972–74.

★ **Fastest trans-Australia bicycling**
Tomio Uranyu (Japan) bicycled from Perth, Western Australia, to Sydney, New South Wales, in 9 days 23 hr 25 min from March 28 to April 7 1992.
The women's record is held by Helen Shelley (Australia), who bicycled the distance in 13 days 2 hr 55 min from April 24 to May 7 1999.

★ **Fastest bicyclist on snow**
The fastest ever speed attained bicycling downhill on snow or ice is 132 mph (212.139 km/h),

by downhill mountain bike racer Christian Taillefer (France) on a Peugeot bicycle at the speed ski slope in Vars, France, in March 1998.

★ **Most downhill mountain-biking World Championship wins**
Nicolas Vouilloz (France) had a record 10 World Championship wins – three in the junior championships from 1992 to 1994 and seven in the senior class in 1995–99 and 2001–02.

★ **Most downhill mountain-biking World Cup event wins**
Nicolas Vouilloz (France) won 16 World Cups from 1992 to 2001.

Wheel skills
Sport

Highest air on a skateboard ⌄

Professional skateboarder Danny Way (USA, below) performed a 18-ft 3-in (5.56-m) method air off the top of a 20-ft (6-m) quarter pipe at Point X Camp near Aguanga, California, USA, on April 17 2002. The height was measured from the top of the ramp.

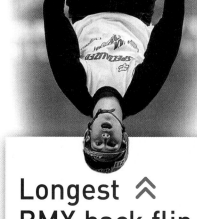

Longest ⌃ BMX back flip

On February 9 2002, Allan Cooke

(USA, above) performed a 54-ft (16.45-m) back flip on his BMX between two specially constructed ramps at Point X Camp near Aguanga, California, USA.

★ Longest skateboard journey
The longest recorded journeys by skateboard were completed by Jack Smith (USA) in July 1976 and again in July 1984, when he covered just under 3,000 miles (4,830 km) between Lebanon, Oregon, and Williamsburg, Virginia, USA.

★ Highest skateboarding ollie
On February 6 2000, Danny Wainwright (UK) popped the highest ollie at 44.5 in (113 cm) off flat ground to win the Reese Forbes Ollie Challenge at the ASR Show, Long Beach, California, USA.

★ Highest skateboard drop into a quarter pipe
Adil Dyani (Norway) dropped into a 18-ft-high (5.5-m) quarter-pipe ramp from a height of 30 ft (9.15 m) on a skateboard in Oslo, Norway, on October 4 2003. The drop was effectively made from 12 ft (3.65 m) above the ramp lip.

★ Highest skateboarding jump
Trevor Baxter (UK) cleared a bar set at 5 ft 5 in (1.65 m) by jumping off a moving skateboard and landing on it after it had passed under the bar, in Grenoble, France, on September 14 1982.

★ Fastest speed on a skateboard
Gary Hardwick (USA) reached 62.55 mph (100.66 km/h) in a standing position in Fountain Hills, Arizona, USA, on September 26 1998.

★ Fastest speed on a street luge
The highest speed set for riding a skateboard in a prone position is 78.37 mph (126.12 km/h) by Roger Hickey (USA) on a course near Los Angeles, California, USA, on March 15 1990.

★ Longest 50-50 rail grind on a skateboard
The longest skateboard rail grind is 33 ft 10 in (10.31 m) by Chad Fernandez (USA) on the *Today* show in New York City, USA, on August 25 2003.

★ Most continuous skateboard revolutions
Richard Carrasco (USA) completed a total of 142 continuous 360° revolutions on a skateboard on August 11 2000 in Santa Ana, California, USA.

★ Longest ramp jump on a skateboard
Danny Way (USA) performed a 65-ft (19.8-m) skateboard jump between two ramps at Point X Camp near Aguanga, California, USA, on April 16 2002.

★ Highest BMX vertical air
Mat Hoffman (USA) achieved a 26-ft 6-in (8.07-m) air from a 24-ft-tall (7.3-m) quarter-pipe ramp on March 20 2001, in Oklahoma City, USA. Hoffman was towed by a motorcycle in the run-up to the jump to reach the required speed.

★ Highest bunny hop
Bruno Arnold (France) achieved the highest ever bunny hop on a mountain bike, clearing a 3-ft 10.2-in-high (1.17-m) horizontal bar without using a ramp on the set of *L'Été de tous les Records*, Le Touquet, France, on July 24 2003.

★ Highest vertical drop on a bicycle
Walter Belli (Italy) and David Cachón Labrador (Spain) both rode their BMX bicycles off a 13-ft 1-in-high (4-m) platform and continued to bicycle upon landing without their feet touching the ground on the set of *El Show de los Récords*, Madrid, Spain, on December 5 2001. In accordance with the record rules, they were not allowed a run-up before dropping off the platform.

Highest Moto X ⌃ Step Up jump

The greatest height achieved in the XGames Moto Cross Step Up event is 35 ft (10.67 m) by Tommy Clowers (USA, above) on August 18 2000. The feat is a motorcycle high-jump, in which riders must try to clear a bar placed at the top of a steep take-off ramp. This record is the equivalent of jumping onto the roof of a two-story building. In the photo above, Clowers is performing a trick called a mulisha air.

★ Highest ramp jump on a BMX bike

Timo Pritzel (Germany) and Jesús Fuentes (Spain) cleared a bar 16 ft 9.5 in (5.12 m) above floor level using BMX bicycles on the set of *El Show de los Récords*, Madrid, Spain, on September 21 2001.

★ Longest power-assisted ramp jump by bicycle

Professional stunt rider Colin Winkelmann (USA) jumped his BMX bicycle 116 ft 11 in (35.63 m) after being towed to a speed of approximately 60 mph (100 km/h) behind a motorcycle at Agoura Hills, California, USA, on December 20 2000 for the *Guinness World Records: Primetime* TV show.

★ Longest standing jump on a mountain bike

Marc Caisso (France) achieved a standing-bike-jump distance of 9 ft 6 in (2.9 m) on his mountain bike at the studios of *L'Émission des Records*, Paris, France, on October 26 2000.

★ Longest endo with feet off the pedals

Martti Kuoppa (Finland) was able to maintain a wheelie on the front wheel of his BMX for 23.25 seconds, while covering a distance of 328 ft (100 m) and without his feet touching the bike's pedals, on June 26 2001 in Helsinki, Finland.

★ Most BMX gyrator spins in one minute

The record for the greatest number of gyrator spins in one minute is 29 by Sam Foakes (UK) for BBC1's *Blue Peter* in London, UK, on March 11 2002.

★ Farthest distance on a unicycle in one hour

Dieter Dölling (Germany) covered 6.617 miles (10.65 km) in one hour around an indoor track on July 11 1998.

★ Fastest 100 m on a unicycle

Peter Rosendahl (USA) covered 328 ft (100 m) in 12.11 seconds, at a speed of 18.47 mph (29.72 km/h), from a standing start in Las Vegas, Nevada, USA, on March 25 1994.

★ Most skipping revolutions in one minute on a unicycle

Amy Shields (USA) performed 209 skips (or rope revolutions) on a unicycle in one minute in St. Paul, Minnesota, USA, on February 23 2002.

★ Highest in-line skate ramp jump

José Félix Hormaetxe Henry (Spain) cleared a bar set at 14 ft 9 in (4.5 m) on in-line skates at the studios of *El Show de los Récords*, Madrid, Spain, on December 14 2001.

★ Farthest distance on in-line skates in one hour

Massimilliano Sorrentino (Italy) covered 23.254 miles (37.425 km) on in-line skates in one hour in Rieti, Italy, on July 27 2003.

★ Longest and fastest journey on in-line skates

Russell 'Rusty' Moncrief (USA) crossed the USA on in-line skates in 69 days 8 hr 45 min from January 5 to March 15 2002. He started out from Crescent Beach, near Jacksonville, Florida, and completed his journey at Soltana Beach, near San Diego, California, after covering 2,595 miles (4,175 km).

★ Greatest distance on in-line skates in 24 hours

Kimberly Ames (USA) covered 283.07 miles (455.55 km) in 24 hours on in-line skates in Portland, Oregon, USA, on October 2 1994.

Most consecutive ⌄ bog snorkeling World Championships

Steve Griffiths (UK, below) is the only person to have won the bog snorkeling World Championships three times, consecutively, from 1985 to 1987. This annual event takes place in the dense Waen Rhydd peat bog on the southern outskirts of Llanwrtyd Wells, Powys, UK.

Most toe wrestling ⌃ World Championships

Alan Nash (UK) has won five toe wrestling World Championships, in 1994, 1996–97, 2000, and 2002. The women's category has been won four times by Karen Davies (UK) from 1999 to 2002. The Championships are held annually on the first Saturday in June at Ye Olde Royal Oak, Wetton, Staffordshire, UK. Contestants must push an opponent's foot to the other side of a specially constructed ring called a 'toerack' using only their toes.

★ Most entrants at a bog snorkeling World Championships

Entrants in the bog snorkeling World Championships have to complete two lengths of a 60-yd (54.8-m) trench cut through a peat bog as quickly as possible, wearing snorkels and flippers. On August 25 2003, 96 people entered the competition at Waen Rhydd peat bog, Llanwrtyd Wells, Powys, UK. Fifteen-year-old Philip John (UK) won in a record time of 1 min 35 sec.

★ Farthest distance to throw a rolling pin

Lori La Deane Adams (USA) threw a rolling pin weighing 2 lb (970 g) a distance of 175 ft 5 in (53.47 m) at the Iowa State Fair, Iowa, USA, on August 21 1979.

★ Farthest haggis hurl

Alan Pettigrew (UK) threw a haggis (of minimum weight 1 lb 8 oz or 680 g) a distance of 180 ft 10 in (55.11 m) at Inchmurrin, Argyll, UK, on May 24 1984.

★ Fastest 40-m walk on water

The fastest time to walk 131 ft (40 m) on water using self-propelled buoyancy shoes was 1 min 10.8 sec. It was achieved by the team Gemini Dawn on April 11 2003 at the Royal Commonwealth Pool, Edinburgh, UK. The event was part of the 2003 Edinburgh Science Festival.

★ Most sheep shorn manually in eight hours

The record for the most sheep shorn manually with scissors and hand blade in eight hours is 50. János Marton (Hungary) achieved the feat, without any breaks, on April 26 2003 at Hódmezővásárhely Animal Husbandry Show, Hódmezővásárhely, Hungary.

★ Farthest dyno climbing by a man

In dyno climbing, participants launch themselves from one set of handholds to a higher set with no intermediate holds. Matt Heason (UK) achieved a distance of 8.53 ft (2.6 m) in the Bendcrete Dyno Competition held at the Edge Climbing Centre, Sheffield, South Yorkshire, UK, on April 20 2002.

★ Farthest dyno climbing by a woman

The farthest distance achieved by a woman is 6.233 ft (1.9 m) by Katherine Schirrmacher (UK) at the Bendcrete Dyno Competition held at the Edge Climbing Centre, Sheffield, South Yorkshire, UK, on April 20 2002.

★ Longest soccer field

The annual Shrovetide Football Match has been played for more than 300 years. It is a game short on rules and long on physical contact between the two teams from Ashbourne, Derbyshire, UK: the Up'ards (those born north of the River Henmore) and the Down'ards (those born south of the river). The goals are the waterwheels at Clifton (target for the Down'ards) and Stursdton (target for the Up'ards) 3 miles (4.8 km) apart. The most goals in modern times was three in a day, but one a day is average.

★ Greatest competitive distance flown in a career by a pigeon

Brazilian Beauty, a blue check hen owned by Robert Koch (South Africa), flew 25,507 miles (41,050 km) during a competitive career that lasted from 1990 to 1997.

★ Longest shaft achieved by a man in kiiking

The aim of kiiking, a sport native to Scandinavian and Baltic countries, is to complete a 360° revolution on a swing. Success is measured by the length of the shafts of the swing – the longer the shafts the better. The longest shaft used to successfully complete a rotation is 23 ft (7.01 m) by Andrus Aasamäe (Estonia) at Rakveres, Estonia, on July 16 2000.

★ Longest shaft achieved by a woman in kiiking

The longest shaft used to successfully complete a rotation in kiiking by a woman is 19 ft 2.7 in (5.86 m) by Kätlin Kink (Estonia) at Pärnus, Estonia, on September 2 2001.

World Championships ⌃ with the heaviest participants

The World Elephant Polo Association (WEPA) was founded in 1982 and has hosted a championship tournament (above) every year since. Elephant polo is played by riders on elephants, four to a team. The invitational tournament is held every December on a grass airfield in Megauly, on the edge of the Royal Chitwan National Park in Nepal.

★ **Most pea-shooting World Championships**
Mike Fordham (UK) won a total of seven pea-shooting World Championships, in 1977–78, 1981, 1983–85, and 1992.

★ **Most coal-bag carrying titles by a man**
Terry Lyons (UK) holds the record for the most titles at the annual Coal Carrying Championship race at Gawthorpe, West Yorkshire, UK, held on Easter Monday every year. Lyons carried a 110-lb (50-kg) bag of coal over the 3,322-ft (1,012.5-m) course and won the race every year from 1977 to 1985 inclusively, with the sole exception of 1980, when the race was won by Colin Claypole (UK).

★ **Fastest individual coal-bag carrying by a man**
On April 1 1991, David Jones (UK) carried a 110-lb (50-kg) bag over the course of the annual Coal Carrying Championship race at Gawthorpe, West Yorkshire, UK, in 4 min 6 sec.

★ **Fastest individual coal-bag carrying by a woman**
Ruth Clegg (UK) holds the women's record for the annual Coal Carrying Championship race at Gawthorpe, West Yorkshire, UK, carrying a 44-lb (20-kg) bag over the course in 5 min 4 sec on April 6 2002.

★ **Most horseshoe pitching World Championship wins by a man**
Ted Allen (USA) won a total of 10 horseshoe pitching World Championships from 1933 to 1959. Since their inception, the Championships have been played at irregular intervals, but have been held every year since 1946.

★ **Most horseshoe pitching World Championships wins by a woman**
Vicki Chappelle Winston (USA) won an unrivaled 10 horseshoe pitching World Championships in the women's category. She won the first of her titles in 1956, and the last in 1981. Her other championship wins were in 1958–59, 1961, 1963, 1966–67, 1969, and 1975.

★ **Most ringers in a horseshoe pitching World Championship game**
The term 'ringer' describes a horseshoe that comes to rest encircling the stake. The most ringers scored by an individual in a horseshoe pitching World Championship games is 175 by Glen Henton (USA) in 1965.

★ **Longest horseshoe pitching winning streak**
The longest winning streak in the horseshoe pitching World Championships is 69 games by Fernando Isais (USA) from 1950 to 1952.

★ **Largest Wellington boot race**
The most participants to take part in and finish a race while wearing Wellington boots is 981. The race was held at Waimea College, Nelson, New Zealand, on September 3 2003.

★ **Most extreme ironing World Championships**
On September 20–21 2002, the inaugural extreme ironing World Championships, organized by the German Extreme Ironing Section (GEIS), was held in Munich, Germany. It was won by Inga Kosak (Germany) with a score of 522. Participants are scored on style and textile, and against the clock, over five disciplines: Forest, Water, Rocky, Urban, and Freestyle.

Index

Acknowledgments

Special thanks go to the following people for their work during the production of this year's edition:

Jim Booth, Nicky Boxall, James Bradley, Caroline Butler, Scott Christie, Ann Collins, Chris Darley, Sam Fay, Marco Frigatti, Lisa Gibbs, Sophie Gimber, Simon Gold, James Herbert, Mary Hill, Laura Hughes, Caius Julyan, Peter Laker, Joyce Lee, Scott Lindsay, Anthony Liu, Andi Mercer, Shazia Mirza, Rob Molloy, Alistair Richards, David Roberts, Nicola Savage, Malcolm Smith, Ryan Tunstall, Kate White, Sophie Whiting.

The team also wishes to thank the following individuals and organizations:

Academy of Motion Picture Arts and Sciences, Ernest Adams, AIDA (Association Internationale pour le Développement del'Apnée), Dr Leslie Aiello, Airports Council International, Amnesty International, Dr Martyn Amos, Jorgen Vaaben Andersen, Anritsu, Antietam Recreation Centre, Vic Armstrong, Gee Armytage, Sir David Attenborough, Australia Zoo, Ron Baalke, Capt Mike Baker, Bank of England, Ken Bannister, Mike Bannister, Dr Peter Barham, Peter Baroody, Brenda Barton (World Food Program), BBC, Guenter Bechly, Bryan Berg, Gabe Bevilacqua, Jackie Bibby, Aase Bjerner, Richard Boatfield, Ian Bottomley (Royal Armouries, Leeds), Dr Richard Bourgerie, BP, Britannica Book of the Year, British Academy of Film & Television Arts, British Airways, British Antarctic Survey, British Board of Film Classification, British Flydog Association, British Geological Survey, British Llamaand Alpaca Association, British Museum, British National Space Centre, Prof John Brown, BT, Dr Robert Angus Buchanan, Prof Michael Burrows, CAIDA, Caltech, Cambridge University, Cancer Research UK, Dr Robert Carney, Casella CEL inc., John Cassidy, Keisha Castle-Hughes, CERN, Dr Franklin Chang-Diaz, Dr Hubert Chanson, Prof Phil Charles, Janina Chilcot, Chinese Embassy (London), Christie's, CIA World Factbook, Admiral Roy Clare, Isabelle Clark, Richard Clark, Stephen Clarke, Bridget Clifford (Royal Armouries Library, Tower of London), CMR/TNS Media Intelligence, Competitive Media Reporting/TNS Media Intelligence, ConocoPhillips, Dr Mike Coughlan, Dr Paul Craddock, Sarah Crane (Bernard Matthews plc), Dr Phillip Cribb, Crufts, Prof Mike Cruise, Cushman, Wakefield Healey & Baker, Dr Pam Dalton, Danmarks Kaninavlerforening (DK), Prof Kris Davidson, Dr Ashley Davies, Jim DeBosh, Deutschland GmbH for RTL, Dr David Dilcher, Discovery News,

Martin Dodge, Gary Duval, Edinburgh Science Festival, EETimes, Dr Farouk El-Baz, Dr Cynan Ellis-Evans, Mark Elmore, Elysium, Dr John Emsley, Encyclopaedia Britannica, Louis Epstein, ESA, eTForecasts, Exeter University, FAI (Fédération Aeronautique Internationale), Dr Xiaohui Fan, David Feldman, FIA (Fédération Internationale de l'Automobile), Sir Ranulph Fiennes, FIM (Fédération Internationale de Motocyclisme), FINA (Fédération Internationale de Natation Amateur), Max Finberg, Sarah Finney, Firefly Encyclopedia of Birds, FIRS (Fédération Internationale de Roller Skating), FIS (Fédération Internationale de Ski), FISA (Fédération Internationale des Sociétés d'Aviron), FITA (Fédération Internationale de Tir a l'Arc), Forbes, Brian Ford, Ford Press Office, Foreign &Commonwealth Office, Freemont Street Experience, Jono Friedman, Keith Friedman, Arran Frood, Ashrita Furman, Tim Furniss, Drew Gardner, Bill Gates, Martin Gedny, Geological Society of London, Dr Richard Ghail, Lois Gibson, Andy Gillard (Scootering magazine), Globastat, Carlos Gómez, Antonio González, Kim Goodman, Stephanie Gordon, Steve Gould, Visual Impact, Chris Gravett, Woburn Abbey, GRF, Matt Groening, Cornelius Growweblaar, Prof John Guest, Guinness World Records: Die Grössten Weltrekorde – Endemol, Guinness World Records: Fifty Years, Fifty Records – Granada for ITV, Dr Jim Gunson, Stuart Haggard, Nicholas Hall (Royal Armouries, Fort Nelson), Mary Hanson, Andy Harris, Ziggy Harrison-Tikisci, Colin Hart, Harvard-Smithsonian Center for Astrophysics, Roger Hawkins, Peter Haynes, Ron Hildebrant, Peter Hillary, Sir Edmund Hillary, Dr Paul Hillyard, Neil Holloway, Adam Honeywill, Hoovers, Dr David Horne, Graham Hudson, Paul Hughes, IAAF (International Association of Athletics Federation), IHPVA (International Human Powered Vehicle Association), IMDB, Imperial College London, Institute of Nanotechnology, Intel, International Energy Agency, International Tea Committee Ltd ISAF (International Sailing Federation), IWF (International Weightlifting Federation), IWSF (International Water Ski Federation), Jetstream Servers, Prof Steve Jones, Cathie Jung, Sandra & Myles Kannemeyer, Emily Kao, Robin Karpan (Alton Museum of History of Art), Dr Nichol Keith, Keo Films, Michael Kettman, Paul Kieve, Prof Joseph Kirschvink, Naomi Kitchener, Ron Klemenic, Jay Koch, Sir John Kreb, Arthur M Kyengo, L'Été De Tous Les Records – R et G Productions for France 3, Lancaster University, Steve Landis, Dr Rolf Landua, Dr Roger Launius, Bernard Lavery, Peter Lavinger, Andy Lee, Alain Leger, Jason Leonard, Dr Melinda Lewis, Martin Lindsey,

Martin Lockheed,Los Alamos National Laboratories, Dr Robert Loss, Louisiana State University, Dané Ludik, Dr Karl Lyons, The Magnificent Seven, Simone Mangaroo, Prof Giles Marion, Brian Marsden, Dr Jim Marshall, Jenny Marshall, Jessie Masson, Dave McAleer, Sir Paul McCartney, Tony McCoy, Grant McLachlan, Dr Alan McNaught, Medlowlands Stadium, The Met Office, Mi2g, Microsoft Corporation, Lucy Millington, Alice Mills, Chris Mills, Rosie Mills, Dr Edgar Mitchell, Hia Mofmann, Monell Chemical Senses Center, Tim Montgomery, Dr Sir Patrick Moore, Prof Jon Morse, Mosaique crew, Pam & Gary Mount, Munich Re, Sal Murillo, Munt Martin, NASA, National Academy of Sciences, National Federation of Master Window & General Cleaners, National Geographic, National Hamster Council, National Maritime Museum, National Physical Laboratory, National Science Foundation, Natural History Museum, Randy Nelson, NetNames, FFG Neustrashimy, Dr Ted Nield, A C Nielsen, NOAA, Richard Noble, Henry Northcroft, Barry Norman (WKVL Amusement Research Library), Andrew Nottage, Oracle, Oxford University, PADI (Professional Association of Diving Instructors), PAF, Morag & Stephen Paskins, John Payne, Jack Pearce, Giles Porter (Visual Impact), PPARC, Carla Prashad (Ascent Media Group), Productschap voor Gedistilleerde Dranken, Publishers Weekly, Salvador Pujol Miralles, Qinetiq, Lee Redmond, John Reed (WSSRC – sailing governing body), Prof Sir Martin Rees, William, Benjamin & Jeremy Rees, Victoria Reeves, Regional Planetary Image Facility (University College London), Iain Reid, Ian Ridpath, Graeme Rimer (Royal Armouries), Dan Roddick, Dr Mervyn Rose, Ros Rossington, Andrew Rotz, Mary Rotz, Royal Astronomical Society, Royal Botanical Gardens, Kew, Royal Horticultural Society, The Royal Institution, Royal Philips Electronics, Royal Society of Chemistry, Russia Monitor, Rutherford Appleton Laboratory, Ryan Sampson, Jeff Saward (Caerdroia – The Journal of Mazes and Labyrinths), Science Museum (London), Search Engine Watch, Istvan Sebestyen, Dr Paul Selden, Prof Dick Selley, SETI Institute, Bill Sharp, Dr Craig Sharp, Brunel University, Dr Seth Shostak, Dr Martin Siegert, Siemens, Frank Simon, The Smithsonian Institution, Peter Smithurst (Royal Armouries, Fort Nelson), Sotheby's, Lara Speicher, Graham Spicer, SpinaHering Marcelo (World Food Program), Statistics Iceland, Tanya Streeter, Peter Strongwater, Strongwater Studios, Danny Sullivan, Greg Swift, The Tate Modern, Debbie Tawse, Charlie Taylor, Heather Tinsley, Turhune Orchards,

UIM (Union Internationale Motonautique), UK Planetary Forum, Prof Martin Uman, UN Factbook, United Nations Centre for International Crime Prevention, University of Bath, University of Birmingham, University of Boston, University of Colorado, University of Dundee, University of Florida, University of Greenwich, University of Hertfordshire, University of Oklahoma, University of Southampton, US Drug Enforcement Agency, Melga van der Herwe, Juhani Virola, Geoff Wald, Dr David Wark, Prof Kevin Warwick, Dr David Webb, Mark Wells (Controller, Entertainment, Granada), Kelly Wessel (WFDF –World Flying Disc Federation), Wildlife Campus (South Africa), Prof Andrew Willmott, Punch Wilson, Richard Winter, Prof Richard Wiseman, Greg Wood, The World Bank Group, World Footbag Association, World Health Organization, World Meteorological Organization, World Sailing Speed Record Council, World Tourism Organization, World Wildlife Fund, Malaysia, Prof Joshua Wurman, www.EverestNews.com, www.globastat.com, www.landspeed.com, www.nationmaster.com, www.nua.com, Dr David Wynn-Williams, Robert Young.

Additionally to the many (too many to list individually) websites, periodicals and newspapers around the world for their help.

Picture credits

4   (see pp 80, 73, 131, 144, 190, 180, 103, 239)
6   Getty Images (2), Rex Features (2), Betty Halvagi, Drew Gardner/Guinness World Records
8   Getty Images, Corbis
9   Getty Images, Rex Features
10 Topham Pictures, C/o RTL/Gregorowius, Primetime, Drew Gardner/Guinness World Records
12 (see pp 27, 22, 28, 37, 38)
14 Rex Features, Corbis
15 Corbis, Drew Gardner/ Guinness World Records.
16 Corbis (3)
17 Corbis (2), Associated Press, Guinness World Records
18 Science Photo Library (2)
19 Science Photo Library
20 Drew Gardner/Guinness World Records
21 Rex Features (2)
22 Rex Features, Corbis
23 Rex Features
24 Drew Gardner/ Guinness World Records, NewsPix
25 Rex Features, c/o Susan Jones
26 Drew Gardner/Guinness World Records
27 Drew Gardner/Guinness World Records (3)
28 c/o Banana George
29 c/o Lee Stewart, Getty Images
30 c/o NYAA Youth Achievement Award Council
31 c/o Renshi Manoj Gupta Liu Dawei, Xiahua News Agency
32 © Richard Creed
33 c/o Ian Kershaw, c/o Royal Marine Reserves
34 c/o David Huxley, c/o Chad Netherland
35 Drew Gardner/Guinness World Records
36 c/o Sanjeev Babu
37 c/o Cunning Stunts, Drew Gardner/Guinness World Records
38 Rex Features
39 Rex Features (2)
40 Associated Press, P A Photos
41 Reuters
42 c/o Chris & Erin Ratay, Rex Features, Getty Images
43 Drew Gardner/Guinness World Records
44 see (pp 73, 75, 51, 71)
46 © Lynette Cook
47 Science Photo Library (2)
48 NASA/JPL (2)
49 NASA/JPL/Malin Space Science Systems NASA/JPL
50 Science Photo Library, Reven Wurman, Science Photo Library
51 Science Photo Library
52 Alamy, Corbis
53 National Geographic Image Collection

54 © Simon Freshfield, Associated Press (3), Corbis
55 Getty Images, Associated Press, Corbis
56 Science Photo Library
57 NASA / Visible Earth, Corbis
58 Associated Press
59 Corbis
60 NHPA
61 Alamy (2), Rex Features
62 Corbis (2)
63 RSPB Images
64 Nature Picture Library, Alamy
65 Alamy
66 Corbis, Alamy
67 Corbis, Ardea
68 Corbis
69 c/o Yoichiro Kawamura, NHPA, Corbis
70 Rex Features, Alamy
71 Corbis
72 c/o Charles Dodman, c/o Linda Skeels-Hopson
73 © Lori Cope/Country World Newspaper, c/o Janice Wolf
74 Corbis (2), Rex Features
75 Nature Picture Library
76 c/o Aharon Shemoel
77 Rex Features (2)
78 (see pp 80, 85, 83, 91, 87)
80 Corbis (2)
81 Getty Images
82 P A Photos, Getty Images
83 Rex Features
84 Still Pictures, Rex Features
85 Associated Press
86 Associated Press
87 Getty Images, Rex Features
88 Rex Features, National Geographic, Image Collection
89 Alamy, Tiffany Gibson
90 Getty Images (2)
91 Getty Images (2)
92 Corbis (2)
93 Corbis
94 Getty Images, Alamy
95 Corbis
96 Corbis (2)
97 Getty Images
98 Drew Gardner/Guinness World Records
99 Rex Features (2)
100 (see pp 103,102,107,110)
102 c/o Duncan Toys Company, Rex Features
103 Corbis
104 c/o Game Show Network, c/o John J Bain
105 c/o Calgary Zoo, c/o Giancarlo Francenella
106 Drew Gardner/Guinness World Records, c/o Lucky Meisenheimer
107 Drew Gardner/Guinness World Records
108 Christie's Images, Rex Features
109 Christie's Images
110 Drew Gardner/Guinness World Records, c/o Del Lawson

111 c/o Newmarket Recreation
112 c/o The Odeon Leicester Square, c/o Hyatt Regency Hotel Vancouver
113 © North News and Pictures, Newcastle Upon Tyne, Rex Features
114 c/o Windsor Certified Farmers Market
115 c/o Nestle Italy, c/o Mohegan Sun Hotel
116 (see pp 131,120,126,141,143)
118 Corbis, Getty Images
119 Alamy
120 © Cliff Tan Anlong, Catholic High School, Singapore (all illus), Corbis (2), Alamy
121 © Torsten Jacobi, Alamy
122 Corbis
123 Corbis, Getty Images
124 Garden Picture Library c/o Stewarts GardenLands
125 Corbis
126 Corbis
127 Rex Features, c/o Cedar Point Amusement Park
128 c/o Northlandz
129 Getty Images, National Railway Museum/Science & Society Picture Library
130 Dempsey's World Record Associates, Corbis
131 c/o Dodge
132 Rex Features, from the Collections of The Henry Ford, Corbis (2) Getty Images/Hulton Archive
133 Rex Features (2), Corbis (2)
134 © John Cassidy, c/o Brad Graham
135 c/o Tom Wiberg, c/o Triumph
136 c/o Stone Manganese, Marine Ltd., Getty Images/Hulton Archive
137 Corbis
138 Getty Images/ Hulton Archive
139 Corbis (2)
140 Getty Images (2)
141 Corbis (2)
142 NASA/KSC
143 Corbis, Drew Gardner/ Guinness World Records
144 Getty Images
145 (see pp 148, 150, 159), c/o U.S. Navy
146 Science Photo Library
147 c/o Argonne National Laboratory, CCLRC Rutherford, Appleton Laboratory
148 Corbis, Science Photo Library
149 Science Photo Library
150 Alamy
151 Corbis, Rex Features
152 Alamy, © Jason Grow
153 Getty Images
154 Getty Images
155 Corbis (2)
156 Novosti, Getty Images/ Hulton Archive, Corbis, Associated Press

157 NASA (3), NASA/KSC, Getty Images
158 NASA/KSC
159 NASA/JSC, NASA
160 Corbis
161 Getty Images, c/o Toshiba
162 © The Board of Trustees of the Armouries (2)
163 Getty Images
164 c/o U.S. Navy
165 c/o U.S. Navy (2)
166 (see pp 180,170,178,182,186)
168 Rex Features
169 Getty Images, Rex Features
170 Corbis, c/o Laura Mitchell
171 c/o Santa Marinella, Drew Gardner/Guinness World Records
172 The Matrix Reloaded © 2003 WV Films LLC
173 Rex Features, The Lord of the Rings: The Return of the King © MMIII NLP All rights reserved Photo by Pierre Vinet Photo appears courtesy of New Line Productions, Inc.
174 Corbis (2)
175 X2 © 2003 Twentieth Century Fox All Rights Reserved
176 Getty Images
177 Getty Images
178 © Roy Alon Stunts, Corbis
179 P A Photos
180 Rex Features
181 © Disney Enterprises, Inc./ Pixar Animation Studios Ronald Grant Archive
182 Getty Images, Associated Press
183 Rex Features
184 Associated Press, Corbis
185 Rex Features, National Geographic Image Collection
186 Getty Images (2)
187 Rex Features, Getty Images
188 Getty Images, Corbis
189 Getty Images (see p 189 for The Simpsons)
190 London Features International
191 Getty Images, (see pp 195, 199, 201)
192 Rex Features, Getty Images (2)
193 Getty Images
194 Rex Features
195 Getty Images (2)
196 Rex Features, Getty Images
197 Rex Features
198 Rex Features
199 Rex Features, London Features International
200 c/o Artspace Projects, Inc.
201 Rex Features (2)
202 see (pp 251,204,215,242,267)
204 Getty Images (2)
205 Getty Images
206 Getty Images
207 Getty Images (2)
208 Getty Images (2)

209 Getty Images
210 Getty Images
211 Getty Images (2)
212 Getty Images
213 Getty Images (2)
214 Getty Images
215 Getty Images (2)
216 Getty Images
217 Getty Images (3)
218 Getty Images
219 Getty Images (2)
220 Getty Images, Associated Press
221 Getty Images
222 NewsPix, Associated Press
223 Reuters
224 Getty Images
225 Getty Images (2)
226 Getty Images, Getty Images/Hulton Archive, Hulton Archive
227 NewsPix
228 Getty Images (2)
229 Getty Images
230 Getty Images (2), Associated Press, Getty Images
231 Getty Images, Corbis, Getty Images (2)
232 Getty Images
233 Getty Images
234 Getty Images
235 Associated Press, Getty Images
236 Getty Images
237 P A Photos
238 Getty Images
239 Getty Images, Rex Features
240 Corbis, Getty Images
241 Getty Images
242 Getty Images, Corbis
243 Getty Images
244 Getty Images (2)
245 Getty Images
246 Getty Images (2)
247 Getty Images
248 Corbis
249 Reuters (2)
250 Getty Images (2)
251 Getty Images
252 Getty Images (2)
253 Getty Images
254 Getty Images
255 Associated Press
256 Getty Images
257 Getty Images
258 Reuters, Corbis
259 Reuters, Getty Images
260 Airsport Photo Library, c/o Paraclub Flevo
261 Airsport Photo Library
262 Empics, Leo Nikora
263 Getty Images
264 Getty Images
265 Getty Images (2)
266 Getty Images (2)
267 Getty Images
268 Corbis
269 Corbis, Getty Images
270 Getty Images, Corbis
271 Buzz Pictures
272 Rex Features (2)
273 Getty Images

Be a record breaker!

If you think you've got what it takes to be a Guinness World Record holder, then we want to hear from you!

1. Decide which record you want to break

If you think you have what it takes to join our exclusive record-breaking club, then read on. There are thousands of records to choose from. You could gather a large group of people to break a mass participation record, or perhaps you have an unusual collection. You might even suggest something new. If this is the case, what we are looking for is a challenge that is inspiring, interesting, requires skill, and is likely to attract subsequent challenges from people all around the world.

2. Make an application

You need to contact us BEFORE you make your attempt – do not send us any evidence or documentation before we have assessed your proposal. Every Guinness World Record is governed by a unique set of rules that MUST be followed. You need to apply for these rules before you can make an attempt. If you have a new record idea, you need to find out if we have accepted your proposal before you attempt the record. If we like your idea, we will draw up rules specifically for your attempt in order to set a standard for all subsequent challenges. The easiest and fastest way to make an application is via our website. Click on the link that says 'Make a Record Attempt,' which will take you to an online application form. You'll be asked to choose a password, which we will send you with a membership number to allow you access to our new tracking system. Through this you can monitor the progress of your claim and ask any questions about your record attempt. If you don't have Internet access, you can contact us by mail. Ensure that you have provided adequate contact details. Please be aware that proposals received this way take much longer to process than those received via the website.

Our website:
www.guinnessworldrecords.com

Write to us:
Guinness World Records
338 Euston Road
London NW1 3BD
UK

Call us: +44 (0) 870 241 6632
Fax us: +44 (0) 20 7891 4501

3. Wait until you hear from us

Once your application has been processed, your proposal will be passed on to one of our specialist researchers. If the application is successful, we will contact you with the corresponding rules and regulations that must be strictly adhered to for the attempt to be considered. We'll also send you some general guidelines that explain the evidence you need to provide to have your record attempt verified. If we reject your proposal we will explain why and, if appropriate, suggest an alternative idea.

4. Organizing the record attempt

We can provide you with advice and guidance regarding record-related questions. As long as there is no violation of the guidelines, your record attempt can be organized in any way you choose. Guinness World Record adjudicators are able to attend events but we will charge a fee for this. Please remember that all record attempts are undertaken at the sole risk of the competitor and Guinness World Records cannot be held responsible for any liability arising out of any record attempt.

5. Have your attempt verified

Once you've completed your attempt, you must send us a package containing all the verification documents we have requested (i.e. photographs, videos, witness statements, and, where required, other more specialized items that will depend on your specific record attempt). All evidence must be sent to our mailing address, clearly marked with your membership number and claim identification number (which will have been provided in prior correspondence). If your claim passes all inspections, including a final scrutiny from the Keeper of the Records, you will be declared a Guinness World Record holder! Please bear in mind that with over 60,000 claims coming in every year, it can take some time to process every claim – so please be patient!

6. Recognition of your attempt

All Guinness World Record holders receive a complimentary certificate to commemorate their achievement. We cannot guarantee that any specific record will appear in our book, as the record selection changes annually. But as long as you hold onto your current world record, there is always the chance that your record could appear in a future edition.

Good luck!